BUSINESS Policy
4th edition
A Canadian Casebook

MARY M. CROSSAN

JOSEPH N. FRY

J. PETER KILLING

RODERICK E. WHITE

The University of Western Ontario

Prentice Hall Inc.,
Scarborough, Ontario

Canadian Cataloguing in Publication Data

Main entry under title:

Business policy: a Canadian casebook

4th ed.
ISBN 0-13-569732-8

1. Corporate planning - Canada - Case studies. 2. Corporate planning - Case studies. 3. Industrial management - Canada - Case studies. 4. Industrial management - Case studies. I. Crossan, Mary M.

HF5351.F79 1997   658.4'01'0971   C96-930617-2

Prentice-Hall, Inc., Upper Saddle River, New Jersey
Prentice-Hall International (UK) Limited, London
Prentice-Hall of Australia, Pty. Limited, Sydney
Prentice-Hall Hispanoamericana, S.A., Mexico City
Prentice-Hall of India Private Limited, New Delhi
Prentice-Hall of Japan, Inc., Tokyo
Simon & Schuster Asia Private Limited, Singapore
Editora Prentice-Hall do Brasil, Ltda., Rio de Janeiro

ISBN 0-13-569732-8

Acquisitions Editor: Patrick Ferrier
Developmental Editor: Lesley Mann
Copy Editor: Jean Ferrier
Production Editor: Lisa Berland
Production Coordinator: Julie Preston
Permissions/Photo Research: Marijke Leupen
Cover Design: Julia Hall
Page Layout: Phyllis Seto

All cases in this book were prepared as a basis for class discussion rather than to illustrate either effective or ineffective handling of an administrative situation.

We welcome readers' comments, which can be sent by e-mail to collegeinfo_pubcanada@prenhall.com

1 2 3 4 5   HP   01 00 99 98 97

Printed and bound in the United States.

CONTENTS

PART THREE Strategy—Resource/Capabilities 107

PART FOUR   Strategy—Organization

PART FIVE   Strategy—Management Preferences

Ken Shelstad is the president of a growing and prosperous company. He is involved in every aspect of the business, works long hours, and appears to thrive on pressure and action. He says, however, that he is getting concerned about the stress on himself and his organization, and that it may be time for a change. What should be done?

Aer Lingus, the Irish National Airline, has been remarkably successful in diversifying from its reliance on the airline industry. This case is about the pursuit of a new initiative in robotics which has led to a potential acquisition of a promising Canadian software company. The owner would remain as general manager and 25% shareholder of the firm, but concerns are growing over how well he will take direction from Aer Lingus.

Diane McGarry, Chairman, CEO and President of Xerox Canada has been meeting with her leadership team since eight o'clock in the morning to craft the organization's new vision statement. Three and a half hours into the meeting the team hits a road block. With 30 minutes left in the session, McGarry must decide whether and how to proceed.

Foreign sourcing often means reliance on suppliers whose labour practices are not consistent with North American standards. Should individuals and companies turn a blind eye or take action in these circumstances? Fifth Column takes this issue to a very personal level to sharpen the issues and put tangible meaning into the debate.

PART SIX   Business Scope and Competitive Advantage

Cooper has a "once in a lifetime" opportunity to acquire the skate and hockey equipment assets of CCM Limited. Under the pressure of CCM's imminent liquidation, Cooper management must decide whether to bid for the assets and, if so, how much to offer.

PART EIGHT Competing in Foreign Markets

PART NINE   Managing Strategic Change

PART TEN Strategic Analysis and Personal Action

PART ELEVEN Comprehensive

PREFACE

This fourth edition of *Business Policy: A Canadian Casebook* introduces 21 new cases to augment some of the old favourites. Several new sections have been added to underscore the global nature of Canadian business. The new section "Competing in the North American Market" reflects the reality of NAFTA, in which Canadian companies are seeking to expand into the United States and Mexico. In the Damark Packaging case, the company is presented with a large product order from a Mexican distributor. The case captures the issues of a small Canadian company deciding whether to apply its resources against opportunities in the U.S., Mexico or Europe. The Labatt–FEMSA case provides an opportunity to analyze Labatt's potential joint venture with the Mexican FEMSA brewery. On a different note, the GE Energy Management case provides the opportunity to assess how managers in Canadian subsidiaries manage under a global corporate umbrella. The Bank of Montreal case examines the possibilities for a large Canadian enterprise to participate in the U.S. market. The "Competing in Foreign Markets" section introduces four cases as vehicles to examine some of the classic business policy issues in the context of foreign markets, including Dialogue: A Russian Joint Venture, Kentucky Fried Chicken in China, Canadian Aviation Electronics in Korea, and Escorts in India.

Consistent with the request by our readers both to broaden the service orientation of the cases and to augment the strategic change section, we have added 15 new cases that are not manufacturing oriented, and three new strategic change cases. We have also tried to strike a balance between cases that capture the issues of small- to medium-sized companies and those of larger firms. Many of the new cases are supplemented with video clips from the classroom. In cases like Sabena Belgian World Airlines, the cases can be more appropriately called a video-case, given the interactive nature of the case series and video. Sabena, along with the Nestlé-Rowntree Series, are award-winning cases in the Strategic Management category of the European case competition. To obtain these videos, contact Case and Publication Services at the Richard Ivey School of Business, University of Western Ontario, London, Ontario N6A 3K7; telephone (519)661-3208; E-mail to: CPS@Ivey.uwo.ca

Finally, the new section "Strategic Analysis and Personal Action" introduces two new cases, Taco Bell and Sabena, which capture the emergent nature of strategy through a series of cases that require students to respond in the moment to a variety of situations. The cases demonstrate the perspective of strategy as a "pattern" of decisions, and ground the notion of strategy in personal action.

As always, the underlying theme of the cases is that of a general manager facing issues of strategy formulation and implementation, strategic change and personal action. The cases are complex and intended for students with a basic command of the functional areas of business. All have been classroom tested at Western, and many are used at other schools.

A complete set of teaching notes is available to adopters of this book. The notes provide a thorough analysis of each of the cases plus suggestions for case sequencing, assignments, teaching approach and supplementary readings and references.

The cases in this book were prepared with the generous cooperation and assistance of a large number of executives. One of the continuing delights of the casewriting process is the opportunity for us to meet and to learn from these individuals. We owe them a great, collective vote of thanks.

There has been a notable change in the roster of authors for this edition. Mary Crossan, who has taught Business Policy at Western for six years, has contributed a substantial number of cases and has taken over as lead author for this new edition. Mike Geringer, who had contributed to the previous edition, is now teaching at California Polytechnic State University. We thank him for his previous contributions to the casebook, and for the three cases that we have retained in this edition (IPL Inc., Polysar-TORNAC and Mr. Jax).

Casewriting is an expensive process. It would not be possible without continued support from the general coffers of the Fund for Excellence at the Richard Ivey School of Business. Some of the businesses that we were studying also helped us indirectly by contributing to the Fund and others, directly, by picking up expenses ranging from airline tickets to the proverbial free lunch. Thank you all. We would also like to thank the International Institute for Management Development (IMD) in Lausanne, Switzerland, and the Case Research Journal for permission to use their cases.

The encouragement that is essential in sustaining a case development program comes from a supportive administrative context at Western, and from the help of our immediate colleagues. Ken Hardy, the Associate Dean of Research, has been a consistent supporter, as have our Deans past and present: Bud Johnston, Al Mikalachki, Adrian Ryans, and Larry Tapp. We have been greatly assisted by our teaching colleagues who have contributed cases, as noted below, and who have been an essential part of the work of testing, refining and, indeed, figuring out how to teach the cases: Jay Anand (Escorts), Paul Beamish (KFC in China, Victoria Heavy Equipment), Terry Deutscher (ICI Colours), Alan Morrison now at Thunderbird, the American Graduate School of International Management (Diaper Wars, KFC), and Chris Bart at McMaster University (Fifth Column). We have also had the opportunity of working with a cooperative and skilled group of Ph.D. candidates and research assistants, whose names and individual contributions are acknowledged in the cases on which they worked. Finally, we would like to thank Tom Poynter, now a management consultant, who did most of the background work on the Victoria Heavy Equipment case.

We are indebted to our publisher, Prentice Hall Canada, and in particular to Pat Ferrier, Lisa Penttila, Lesley Mann, Lisa Berland, and Jean Ferrier for their help, respectively, in promoting, producing, and editing this book. At our School we are, in particular, obliged to Sue O'Driscoll for her diligent and industrious effort in bringing everything together.

Mary M. Crossan
Joseph N. Fry
J. Peter Killing
Roderick E. White

London, Ontario
1997

INTRODUCTION

All of the cases in this book deal with problems facing general managers. Although some are disguised, all are based on real situations and raise issues that are in some way related to a firm's strategy. We have presented the cases in a logical and orderly progression—from analysis (what are the key elements in this firm's situation?) through desired action (what should be done?) to detailed implementation (how should it be done?). However, we do not recommend that the casebook be used alone. It should be employed in conjunction with either a policy textbook or an organized set of readings that present the basic concepts of strategy formulation and implementation, and the management of strategic change.

Our preferred text is *Strategic Analysis and Action*, third edition,[1] and the Diamond-E model on which it is based. This model links the firm's strategy with its environment, its resources, the preferences of its managers, and its organization. We have used it for a number of years, and have found that it permits useful insights not only into the cases presented in this book but also into a wide variety of other general management situations.

The key to using the Diamond-E model is to begin by identifying the firm's existing or proposed strategy. In *Strategic Analysis and Action*, third edition, we suggest that a description of a firm's strategy should include its goals, product-market focus, competitive premise and business system focus. The Diamond-E model can then be used to assess methodically the new or existing strategy by means of the following questions:

1. Is the strategy internally consistent?

2. Is the strategy consistent with the environment?

3. Is the strategy consistent with present or obtainable resources?

4. Is the strategy consistent with the firm's organizational attributes?

5. Is the strategy consistent with the personal preferences and beliefs of top management?

We have grouped the cases according to the strategy relationships in the Diamond-E model that they emphasize. This is a rough cut as strategic issues do not come in neat packages, but it does provide for a flow of emphasis over the progression of a course. The first five sections of the casebook correspond to the Diamond-E framework. In Part Six, Business Scope and Competitive Advantage, all elements of the Diamond-E need to be considered to assess the desirability of changing the product market focus, business system, and potentially the competitive premise of the strategy, through vertical or horizontal integration. Parts Seven and Eight also provide the opportunity to examine all elements of the Diamond-E in the context of foreign markets, with Part Seven focusing on the North American market and Part Eight providing cases with exposure to Russia, China, Korea and India.

---

[1] J.N. Fry and J.P. Killing, *Strategic Analysis and Action*, third edition (Scarborough, Ontario: Prentice Hall Canada Inc., 1995).

The Diamond-E Framework

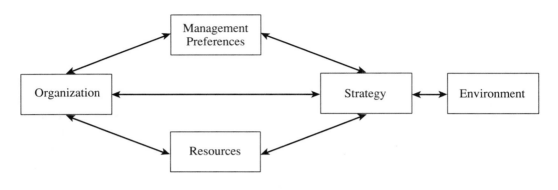

SOURCE: J.N. Fry and J.P. Killing, *Strategic Analysis and Action*, third edition (Scarborough, Ontario: Prentice Hall Canada Inc., 1995).

The five cases which comprise Part Nine, Managing Strategic Change, are the most difficult in the book. In these, the questions of *what* must be done and *how* it should be done need to be addressed simultaneously. The section in *Strategic Analysis and Action* dealing with this topic introduces three new variables for consideration: the *pace* at which the general manager should attempt to effect change, the *targets* to focus efforts on, and the *tactics* that should be employed. Each issue deserves close examination in these cases.

Part Ten, Strategic Analysis and Personal Action, presents two cases which accomplish three objectives: 1) to present strategic analysis from the perspective of a new manager rather than a CEO or senior manager; 2) to demonstrate the incremental and emergent nature of strategy as a "pattern" of decisions; and 3) to challenge students to understand and internalize the personal attributes required to think and act strategically.

The Nestlé-Rowntree Series in Part Eleven is a comprehensive case series. The (A) case provides a vehicle to do a thorough assessment of a global industry using George Yip's framework. The follow-on cases require the students to decide and act.

We hope that you find these cases enjoyable as well as instructive. We have lived with most of them for several years now, yet they still give us a great deal of satisfaction, provoke dialogue among us, and give us new insights.

INTRODUCTION TO STRATEGIC MANAGEMENT

PART 1

DESIGNER CLASSICS CARPET MANUFACTURING LTD.

Roderick E. White

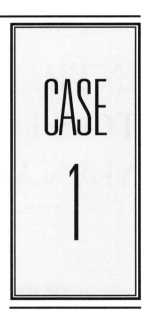

CASE 1

Jim Dunlop, a self-admitted entrepreneur and the principal owner of Designer Classics Carpet (DCC), had just received the financial results for 1986. Dunlop, age 39, had gotten into the custom wool carpet business four years earlier by acquiring the assets of Conestoga Carpet, a failed company located in Waterloo, Ontario. Using over $300 000 of his own capital, he had modernized and added some production equipment, moved the plant to a nearby location, added new products, and perhaps most importantly, expanded the firm's market scope greatly through his own efforts.

In mid-January 1987, as Dunlop reflected on the four-year financial summary (Exhibit 1), he was proud of the large increases in sales. However, this growth had resulted in scheduling problems and bottlenecks in the plant. Additional sales from the Waterloo plant would require alleviating these problems. Dunlop, always on the lookout for opportunities to expand and strengthen the business, had recently acquired a wool yarn spinning mill in Waterford, about 75 kilometres from Waterloo. This purchase would allow DCC to set specific standards for its yarn and secure a source of supply for this major raw material. Several other growth opportunities could be pursued. Preliminary negotiations were underway for the acquisition of Elite Carpet, a woven carpet manufacturer in Quebec with $5.1 million in sales and significant unused capacity. Dunlop was also considering the establishment of an importing/distribution company in Seattle, Washington,

Roderick E. White of the Western Business School prepared this case. Copyright © 1992, The University of Western Ontario. This material is not covered under authorization from CanCopy or any reproduction rights organization. Any form of reproduction, storage or transmittal of this material is prohibited without written permission from Western Business School, The University of Western Ontario, London, Canada N6A 3K7

to bring in custom wool carpets from Thailand. In addition, one of DCC's major dealers in the U.S. had expressed an interest in selling a minority interest to DCC.

Picking up on new initiatives would have to be done by Jim Dunlop. There was no one else available. Since he also had to deal with many of the day-to-day demands of the business, establishing priorities and timing were critical.

THE BUSINESS

All of DCC's current products were custom ordered for residential and commercial buyers. Each was unique in size, colour, pattern and texture. Sales were made through sales agents and dealers, with only a very few direct transactions with customers. In 1986, residential customers accounted for about 20% of annual sales. Of the remaining 80% for commercial applications, half were used as carpet murals for subdividing passenger aircraft, and the remainder were sold as floor covering in offices and hotels.

Products and Markets

Costing between $50 per square metre for broadloom and up to $500 per square metre for a hand tufted product, custom carpets appealed to small, specialized segments of the carpet market. The *custom* wool carpet market in North America was estimated to be approximately $300 million and growing at 15% annually (Table 1). In all except the aircraft segment, DCC's share was not large. Currently, commercial sales outside North America were small, less than 10% of the total; Canada accounted for about 20% of DCC's sales; and the U.S., about 70%.

TABLE 1   North American Custom Wool Carpet Market

Market Segment	Size	DCC's Share	Sales
Residential	18%	2.0%	20%
Commercial:			40%
Hotel	50%	1.5%	
Office	30%	2.0%	
Aircraft	2%	60%	40%
	$ 300m		

SOURCE: Estimates by Jim Dunlop and selected carpet dealers.

Residential Segment

Custom wool carpet appealed to upscale home-owners. The home-owner would either deal directly with a dealer having in-house design expertise, or through an interior decorator/designer who would ultimately source through a dealer. Many dealers served both the residential and commercial market. Some dealers competed with manufacturers for part of the value added by doing not only the design work but also their own in-house "cutting and pasting" of the carpet. However, this was the exception and most dealers preferred to have the carpet completed by the manufacturer. No really close substitutes existed for wool carpets. High-end synthetics did not have the same "feel" or snob appeal. Oriental rugs could be viewed as an alternative to the customer, but generally had somewhat different applications, and appealed to different customer tastes than custom wool area carpets.

Quality was important in all DCC's markets, as was on-time delivery performance. Order lead times for the residential segment were typically three to five months; rapid response to orders was not usually critical, since customers generally ordered well in advance. Customers did not tend to comparison shop for price.

This segment was believed to be growing at 10–15% percent annually.

Commercial Segment

This segment was composed of two different customer groups: office and hotel. Office applications were limited to lobbies, board rooms and executive suites. Recently the U.S. office market appeared to be growing, but the Canadian market was in decline. The other group, luxury hotels, used this product in high visibility areas like lobbies. *Woven* wool carpets were typically used in rooms. Luxury hotels were increasing their penetration of the North American market.

Delivery time was important, especially for most office applications, as was price. Some hotel chains had in-house designers, but many hotels and most office customers used an outside design house or carpet consultant to develop specifications and aid in product selection. Roughly 80% of the business was tendered directly to carpet manufacturers, and the remainder was placed through dealers.

Aircraft Segment

Carpet murals were used for decorative purposes on bulkhead walls in some commercial passenger and corporate aircraft. Currently carpet murals were not used by air carriers outside North America. Approximately 50% of the North American fleet had these murals. However, recent proposed changes in FAA regulations governing material content of aircraft cabin interiors had put this market in jeopardy. Although Dunlop believed the likelihood of a permanent ban on wool bulkhead murals was unlikely, sales could be disrupted during negotiations between the FAA and aircraft manufacturers.

Customers in this segment were somewhat price sensitive, but tended to buy on reputation for quality. Airlines working with a design house and/or the firm finishing the aircraft's interior would develop carpet specifications. Orders were placed by the finisher, either the aircraft manufacturer (e.g., Boeing) or a specialized interior finisher (e.g., Innotech Aviation), with an aircraft supply house or directly with the manufacturer. In the U.S., one supply house handled a large part of the aircraft interiors market, including floor and wall coverings, seats, etc. as well as bulkhead murals. DCC was this firm's exclusive supplier of carpet murals. Eighty-five percent of sales in this segment were made in the U.S.; and 15% in Canada primarily to Canadian Pacific Airlines.

DCC's Position

DCC faced three major competitors (Table 2). The remaining competition was fragmented, although some were significant in small niches (e.g., Carter and Carousel).

TABLE 2   Competitive Position

	Market Share— Excluding Aircraft	Market Share— Aircraft
Hong Kong Carpet	65%	—
Edward Fields	5	10%
V'Soske	4	9
Designer Classics	2	60
Carousel	0.5	14
Carter	0.5	8
Other	24	

SOURCE: Industry estimates.

Hong Kong Carpet (HKC) was a large, apparently well-financed corporation with manufacturing facilities scattered around the Far East. It produced under several different labels. HKC was believed to be the low-cost producer and typically offered the lowest price, but also had a reputation for somewhat lower quality and had 12- to 24-week delivery times. HKC had extensive dealer representation in North America and advertised exclusively to dealers.

Fields and V'Soske were similar in many respects. Both were high-priced and high-quality with long delivery times: about 21 weeks for Fields and, partly because of its Puerto Rican production facilities, 23 weeks for V'Soske. V'Soske utilized exclusive dealers and had strong representatives in most markets. Fields, headquartered in New York City, had company showrooms in major metropolitan centres. Like V'Soske, Fields branded its product and had high awareness.

DCC, by way of comparison, was medium to high quality and price. DCC had the ability to deliver a small sample of the desired colour, pattern and texture, within ten days to two weeks; compared to four weeks for most of the competition. The finished order would follow in about six weeks. According to Dunlop, DCC was able to offer faster sample turnaround because of their proximity to major customers and the capabilities of the sample making department. To the extent economically feasible, sample making had separate facilities. However, some equipment, tufting and dying, was shared with regular manufacturing and inevitable conflicts arose. While still good compared to other manufacturers, this turnaround time, because of capacity constraints and labour turnover, had been increasing. DCC did not have a strong brand identity, and in certain markets, the prior association with Conestoga was a hindrance. All four major manufacturers, including DCC, had in-house dye facilities.

THE COMPANY

DCC's product range was all wool and made to order. It included completely hand tufted carpets and murals, machine tufted and overtufted carpets (machine tufted but finished by hand), both for broadloom (wall-to-wall) and area applications. As shown in Table 3, gross profit margins differed amongst product categories.

TABLE 3 **DCC Cost and Gross Profit by Major Custom Tufted Product Group**
(percent of selling price)

	Hand Tufted	Hand + Machine			Machine Tufted	
	Area	*Broadloom*	*Area*	*Aircraft*	*Broadloom*	*Area*
Materials	34%	44%	30%	20%	49%	29%
Labour	52	34	43	31	22	37
Gross Profit	14	22	27	49	29	34

SOURCE: Sales records August through October 1986.

Marketing and Distribution

In total, DCC had about 200 customers. However, the top ten accounted for 61% of sales during 1986, and the top two for 53%. One of these was an aircraft supply house representing DCC's carpet murals, and the other was a residential and commercial dealer in the southwestern U.S. The old Conestoga Carpet had focused almost exclusively on the Toronto residential and commercial market. Over the last four years, Jim Dunlop, with his real flair for sales and marketing, had expanded distribution and sales into the U.S. market, and the airline carpet mural business in particular.

Designer Classics had two salespersons covering the U.S. They serviced the dealer network as well as direct sales to major hotel customers. The company had one European sales representative with responsibility for direct sales to hotel clients, and an agent network in six countries that sold to local dealers. Two sales agents, one in Europe and the other in the U.S., covered the aircraft market. The company's general sales manager, with an in-house staff of three, handled Canadian sales, both through the dealer network and direct to hotels and aircraft finishers. Jim Dunlop maintained contact with key customers, and was involved in developing most new dealer or agent relationships. His salesmanship and interpersonal abilities were important strengths in this area.

Once access to the customer was established, the selling task involved producing a suitable sample. The ability to match the colour, texture and pattern needs of the customer with this sample was critical to making the sale. Delivery of a finished product consistent with the sample was important to a firm's reputation. Accomplishing this required close coordination with the production department. The importance of delivery and price varied by segment.

Manufacturing

The production process was a custom job shop. Basic steps for a tufted carpet are outlined in Exhibit 2. The mix of skills varied; dyeing was a complicated operation—part art, part science, requiring a high level of skill and experience. Finishing was semi-skilled; an operator could be trained in one to two months. However, because this step was the last in the chain, mistakes were costly. Tufting skill requirements varied with the complexity of the pattern.

DCC had trouble retaining production employees. The Kitchener-Waterloo area was in the midst of an economic boom. Unemployment was 4%, and an Employment Canada official reported that unskilled labourers were changing jobs for as little as 10¢ to 15¢ per hour wage differentials. DCC currently paid $6.20 for unskilled labour (after a three-month probationary period). The factory workforce of 101 people, many of them recent immigrants to Canada, turned over by 34% in 1986.

The labour situation was further complicated by the company's recent unionization. The union and the company were negotiating their second contract, and management's goal was to achieve a "no wage increase" settlement. Historically, DCC had not laid off plant workers, even when sales volumes were low. Dunlop had taken the unionization as a personal affront, and was determined not to lend legitimacy by conceding a wage increase in the upcoming contract negotiations. He felt most employees did not want a union, and he was anxious to return his firm to non-union status.

Union problems aside, labour availability was limiting output in certain areas. In hand tufting, it was difficult to get reliable, low-cost labour. In addition to the availability of labour, variability in skill requirements on a job-by-job, pattern-by-pattern basis complicated breaking this bottleneck. Capital requirements for expanding hand tufting capacity were small. However, bottlenecks existed in other areas. There were quality and capacity problems in the dye shop. Waterloo had very hard water, which required softening before use in dyeing operations. The addition of storage tanks for softened water, an investment of about $12 000, would hopefully solve this problem, reducing delays and rework. The quality of wool yarn had also been affecting the dyeing process, causing delays and rework. It was hoped the acquisition of Waterford Spinning Mills would alleviate this problem.

In order to meet demand, DCC's key manufacturing operations were operating three shifts of eight hours each on weekdays, and two 12-hour shifts on weekends. The business was somewhat seasonal, increasing during the last quarter of the year. During the October to December 1986 period, over 70% of orders were late, averaging 15 days; 90% were labelled RUSH. In addition, quality as measured by remakes had been deteriorating (Exhibit 3). Adding more capacity would be expensive and, Dunlop suspected, unnecessary. He felt the real problem lay with manufacturing management:

> The growth in sales has overtaxed our current manufacturing management. We have gone from 14 to 130 employees over the last four years. The ability to manage a schedule in a complex job shop is now very important. It has been complicated by quality and availability problems for wool yarn.
>
> We need someone with experience managing a complicated job shop. The specifics of the carpet business can be picked up quickly.

And while Jim Dunlop understood the importance of manufacturing to his business, he had stated:

Manufacturing frustrates me, it's not something I'm personally really interested in or good at. I'm a marketer rather than an administrator.

Two months earlier Dunlop had created and staffed the position of manufacturing manager. This person was to help sort out the problems at the Waterloo plant and assume overall responsibilities for all of DCC's manufacturing plants, Waterford Spinning Mills, and the Elite plant, if purchased. The individual hired for this position had recently, by way of letter and without explanation, informed Dunlop of his immediate resignation. The position remained unfilled.

Suppliers

In addition to labour, the other key input into the product was wool yarn. Raw wool from Great Britain and New Zealand was most suitable for high-quality carpets. There were numerous suppliers of raw wool. DCC used a broker who bought their wool at auction; and while a "commodity," it varied dramatically in quality and required considerable buying expertise. Spinners were then contracted to process the wool into yarn. In North America, there were seven wool carpet yarn producers. The recently purchased Waterford Spinning Mills, with some equipment modifications and additions, could supply about 95% of DCC's wool yarn requirements and still have considerable additional capacity. The remaining 5% of DCC's requirements were yarn types Waterford could not make.

Waterford Spinning Mills (WSM) had been purchased because of quality and delivery problems with two yarn suppliers. The plant became available when Sunbeam, which had been spinning yarn for its electric blankets, decided to exit this part of the business. Sunbeam had another larger facility in the area, and in order to avoid any bad feelings from a plant, closure was prepared to "give the spinning equipment to DCC." Dunlop Holdings had purchased the old building and equipment for $110 000. However, conversion to spinning wool for carpets required purchasing some additional (used) equipment and building improvements at a cost of $65 000. The deal closed in July 1986, and the plant was producing (at a low level) by August. By year end things were running relatively smoothly, and capacity exceeded demand.

Dunlop knew of no other custom carpet manufacturer with their own spinning mill. WSM was already providing more consistent quality and delivery of this major raw material. This facilitated operations at Waterloo. Failure of an earlier supplier to meet delivery promises had resulted in disruptions to the manufacturing process, and on one occasion a plant shut down. DCC had been partially coping with this supply problem by holding large yarn inventories. When the WSM operation was coordinated with DCC's Waterloo plant, much of the inventory could be held as raw fleece at WSM.

Other materials, like poly backing, were easily available. Production equipment, while specialized, could be obtained from several suppliers.

Financial Capacity

DCC had substantial leverage (Exhibit 1). However, working capital could be financed by customer deposits, normally 50% of sales and government assisted financing for export sales.

After the sale of an earlier venture in the production of turkey breeding stock, Jim Dunlop had emerged with considerable personal wealth. He commented on his willingness to infuse additional capital into the business:

We've been the rounds with venture capitalists. They have a real get-rich-quick mentality and I do not foresee us using them.

Our financial policy is to leverage these operations as much as possible through the use of debt. However, if the right opportunity should come along, Dunlop Holdings[1] would be willing to back it financially. I do attempt to limit our exposure. I have not given personal guarantees for DCC's obligation. In addition, DCC only holds the operating assets. Real estate assets are held by a separate company owned by my wife, and DCC makes lease payments.

Management and Organization

Jim Dunlop and the four key managers described below made up the management group:

Name	Position	Time with DCC	Background
Jim Dunlop	Owner	4 years	International marketing
Larry Weiss	V.P. Finance	2 years	Chartered accountant
Chris Spence	Controller	3 years	Accounting at Electrohome
Wayne Pauli	Sales Manager	1 year	Large-scale manufacturing
—	Manufacturing Mgr		
Rick Hennige	Plant Manager	4 years	Conestoga Carpets

In the pursuit of opportunities, Dunlop spent almost half his time away from the office. As a result, the firm did not have a full-time, resident general manager. Jim Dunlop did most of the missionary marketing, but also felt it was important for him to be involved in key operational decisions. Even when he was away, Dunlop maintained daily contact with the office. However, problems between functions often remained unresolved and decisions unmade during his absence.

Employees received annual bonuses as part of their regular pay cheques. They were set at Jim Dunlop's discretion. All supervisors were required to make an annual performance appraisal of their subordinates.

Personally, Dunlop had some aggressive goals for the company:

Dunlop Holdings, of which DCC is a part, will continue to have rapid growth and some diversification. We plan to stay within architectural and design materials and services, but might add fabric, other kinds of flooring, like hardwood, things like that. Of course any decision will be made when the opportunity knocks.

I would like us, in the foreseeable future, to grow to $100 million in sales. We will probably, at some point, have to go public to finance this growth. You might say I want to build a little empire, a significant Canadian, even international, entity in this field.

Of course my role has to change as we grow. I've been very active in the business, heavily involved in marketing. I'll have to get more involved in general management.

---

[1] A family holding company which held DCC and several other ventures.

STRATEGIC INITIATIVES

Dunlop and DCC were confronting several important decisions. Perhaps the most significant was the acquisition of Elite Carpet in Quebec.

Elite was the only manufacturer of *woven* wool carpets remaining in Canada. The woven product was more equipment, less labour intensive, and more long-run oriented than custom tufted carpets. Woven carpets could have intricate but necessarily repetitive patterns. Unique patterning, overtufting, sculpting and custom borders were only possible with a custom tufted product.

Elite's product was currently sold only in Canada, primarily to hotels. Woven carpets tended to be used in corridors, restaurants and rooms, whereas tufted custom carpets were used in lobbies and suites. Elite's reputation and good sales representation in the Canadian market and the overlap in customer group with DCC, and the potential in the U.S. for Elite's product was what initially had attracted Dunlop's interest.

Dunlop had visited their facility in Ste. Therese, Quebec, in 1984 to explore the possibility of the two companies collaborating on contracts requiring both tufted and woven carpets, but nothing had come of this initial contact. In early 1986 Dunlop had again approached Elite, this time to suggest they manufacture a woven line for DCC to brand and distribute. The proposal had been rejected. However, when they learned of the WSM acquisition, Elite had enquired about sourcing yarn. Dunlop had invited the president of Elite to Waterloo in October. At this time Dunlop had proposed the purchase of an equity interest in Elite. Unexpectedly, Elite's president had asked if Dunlop would like to buy all of Elite.

Jim Dunlop was surprised by the proposal for an outright purchase, and visited Elite in late December 1986. Elite's management had not been prepared to provide detailed financial statements at this time. However, Dunlop had learned that since the firm had been sold by its original Scottish owners to the employees in 1978, Elite had declining sales and losses in six and small profits in only two of the subsequent years. For the 11-month fiscal year ended in October, Elite had sales of $5.1 million, gross profits of $1.1 million, and an operating loss of $138 000 with an estimated tax loss carried forward of $750 000. Total current assets were about $1.7 million; total current liabilities, $1.8 million. Fixed assets including the land and building were $1.1 million. Long-term debt was about $500 000 and equity about $600 000 (but this latter amount included a $1.12 million government "loan"). The current assets were made up of about $1 million in good quality accounts receivable and $700 000 in inventory. Dunlop judged the inventory level was too high, but based on a quick walk-through inspection, it appeared to be current. The building and production equipment appeared well maintained.

Dunlop also learned that Elite was under pressure from their banker to secure additional financing and turn around their sales and profit performance. Dunlop foresaw several areas for improvement. Elite currently purchased yarn from England and paid a 12% duty. There was no duty on fleece. WSM could provide yarn at less than the price Elite was paying their English supplier before duty and transportation costs. Yarn costs were about 35% of sales. Furthermore, WSM had more than sufficient yarn capacity to supply Elite's needs. By combining product lines, sales effort and expanding the sale of Elite's products beyond Canada, Dunlop felt sales could be increased considerably. The plant had estimated capacity to support over $25 million in sales. Some savings could also be realized by centralizing administration and bookkeeping.

While net book value for the company was negative, Dunlop felt he would have to offer something for its equity. He was informed that about 100 of the employees had each invested $3 000 when they had purchased the company in 1978. In addition, the bank would expect an equity infusion.

On another front, Dunlop had been having discussions with his major U.S. wholesaler/agent about an exchange of ownership. Dunlop explained:

> My major wholesaler in the U.S. accounts for about 35–40% of our sales. Because they're so important to DCC, we've been talking about an exchange of shares. Although we haven't gotten to specifics, they have very few hard assets, basically an office, a few sales people and a phone, we would probably give 4% of DCC for 25% of their operation. It's a small business and the owner takes a large salary, but I'm more interested in cementing the relationship than making a big return on my investment.

Dunlop also wanted to set up an importing company, probably in Seattle, Washington, in order to bring in hand tufted carpets from Thailand. DCC already did a small amount of importing of hand tufted carpets. Rather than lose a sale to a price sensitive customer who was willing to accept longer delivery terms, DCC sales representatives would offer the import option. The order would be placed through Dunco International, another company owned by Dunlop Holdings, with a supplier in Thailand.

Geographic growth was also being pursued. DCC had two European agents, and had just hired a full time representative based in England. Much of this offshore business was for major commercial development projects. For example, through a European dealer DCC had just been asked to bid on a major hotel/commercial complex in the Middle East. DCC's international competitiveness was influenced by strong local competition, the 14% tariff and currency fluctuations. This latter factor was currently in DCC's favour.

EXHIBIT 1   DCC Financial Summary ($000s)

	Designer Classics Carpet				WSM
	1983	*1984*	*1985*	*1986*	*1986*
Gross Sales	1 140	2 430	3 721	5 200	
Less deductions**		380	595	810	
Net Sales		2 050	3 126	4 390	
Cost of Goods Sold					
Labour	160	435	530	700	
Material	610	677	792	1 142	
Overhead —variable	206	331	507	680	
— fixed		219	408	500	
Gross Margin	164	388	889	1 368	
Selling Expense**	226	150	285	580	
Unusual item				75*	
Administrative Expense	159	346	497	650	
Income Before Tax	(209)	(108)	108	63	
Excluding unusual item				138	
Assets					
Accounts receivable			769	1 036	51
Inventories			412	707	18
Prepaid expenses			86	117	4
Total Current Assets			1 268	1 862	73
Machinery & Equipment (net)			349	363	183[†]
Trademarks				10	
Total Assets	591	1 380	1 617	2 234	256
Liabilities & Equity					
Bank loans			139	298	39
Accounts payable[††]			688	801	67
Payable to affiliates				49	
ODC export loans			157	423	
Shareholder loan			11	10	
l-t principal due			51	68	
Total Current Liabilities			1 046	1 648	106
Long-term Debt			310	235	139[††]
Equity & Retained Earnings			261	352	10
Total	591	1 380	1 617	2 234	256
Number of Employees	45	60	85	130	

* Unusual item: upfront payment to U.S. sales representative who delivered no sales.
** Commissions to agents, duties, freight, etc. included as selling expense in 1983 deducted from sales 1984 onward.
† Includes land (25), buildings (103) and equipment (58) less depreciation (3).
†† Includes Small Business Loan and loan from parent company (48).

EXHIBIT 2   DCC Tufted Carpet: Production Steps

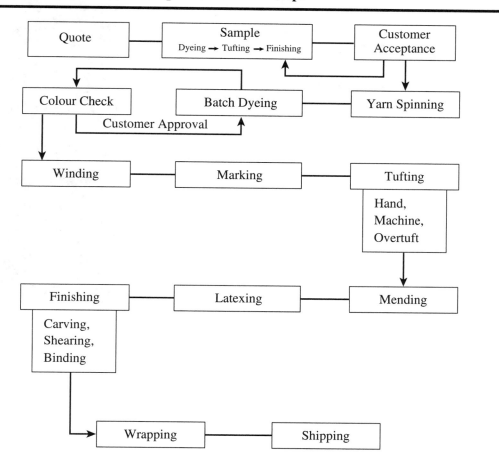

EXHIBIT 3   DCC Remake Charges as a Percentage of Sales

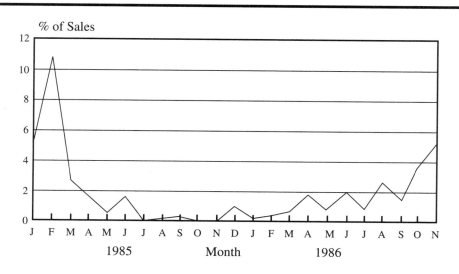

STRATEGY—ENVIRONMENT

PART 2

WELLINGTON INSURANCE (A)

Mary M. Crossan and Julian Birkinshaw

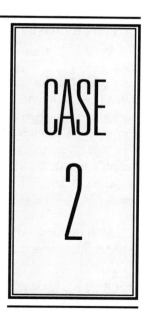

CASE

2

Murray Wallace, the newly appointed President and Chief Executive Officer (CEO) of Wellington Insurance, realized that he needed to take action swiftly. It was late January 1988, and Wallace had held the post of CEO for less than a month. In that time he had made a comprehensive assessment of Wellington's operations, and had concluded that the company was in a very poor state of health. A consultant's report described Wellington as "a company without hope." It was Wallace's job to prove the consultant wrong.

Wallace had been offered the job of CEO several months earlier by Trilon, the parent company of Wellington. Through his experience as a Wellington board member, and an initial assessment of Wellington's competitive position, he concluded that the best course of action was to sell Wellington. Trilon's board did not take his advice, having committed themselves to maintaining a portfolio of diversified financial services. They asked Wallace to take the job, beginning on January 1, 1988. Despite the need for a sustained long-term change at Wellington, quarterly reporting to Trilon also created a sense of urgency in Wallace's task.

There were multiple problems at Wellington, not least of which was the low morale of the employees. Wallace was aware that a number of change programs had been implemented over the years, with very little apparent success. As a result he realized that any initiatives he came up with would probably be seen as "just another change program." He began to consider what action he could take that would have a positive impact on the attitudes of the employees.

THE GENERAL INSURANCE INDUSTRY

The basic principle of insurance was to share the losses of few among many. It was originally conceived in the shipping industry, through the formation of syndicates of ship-owners who each contributed a "premium" to a common fund that would be used in the event of an accident. The last hundred years, however, had seen a rapid rise in individual prosperity, and in particular the ownership of cars and houses, such that most insurance became directed toward consumers. Commercial ventures made up the minority.

There were two principal types of insurance: Life insurance, which protected the policyholder's health and life; and General insurance, which protected the policyholder's possessions. A critical difference from the insurance companies' point of view was that life insurance usually included a guaranteed payout (on death) while general insurance made payments only to the minority who incurred material loss. Life insurance was the larger industry with 1987 Canadian revenues of $41 billion, compared to $17 billion for general insurance. The combined figures represented 0.6% of the Gross Domestic Product (GDP).

The primary function of the general insurance company was to calculate an appropriate premium for every risk, such as damage to the policyholder's automobile or theft from the home, so that the income received in premiums was larger than the outlay in claims (called underwriting). A secondary role was to invest the policyholders' premiums until claims were made. This provided a relatively predictable return to counterbalance the erratic returns from risk-sharing. A third aspect of the general insurance company's work was loss reduction and prevention: through its experience in dealing with a large number of claims, the insurance company was ideally placed to educate the consumer on how to avoid accidents, deter theft and reduce loss.

Performance measures for general insurance firms were designed to reflect the distinction between underwriting and investment. The key measures are presented in Table 1.

TABLE 1 Key Financial Ratios in General Insurance

Earned Loss Ratio	The percentage of total premiums paid out as claims. A figure of 70 indicated that for every $1 in policy premiums collected $0.70 was paid out in insurance claims.
Total Expense Ratio	Earned Loss Ratio
Combined Ratio	The earned loss ratio plus the total expense ratio. A figure of less than 100 indicated that the company had made a profit on its underwriting activities.

Investment income was usually quoted as a dollar sum rather than a percentage, and was added to the underwriting profit (loss) to arrive at the total profit. Thus a combined ratio of 108 on total premiums of $1 million represented an underwriting loss of $80 000. If the investment income for the year were $100 000 the company would still make a profit of $20 000.

Business Functions in General Insurance

A general insurance company was typically organized into three main functional areas: underwriting, claims, and marketing and sales.

UNDERWRITING Whenever a new customer required insurance, or its established customers' policies were up for renewal, the underwriters calculated an appropriate premium based on the previous history of the individual, age, sex and so on. For commercial customers (i.e., businesses) premiums were based on industry statistics and an assessment of the business facilities.

CLAIMS Whenever a claim was made, such as an automobile accident or a theft, the claims department worked with the customer and his or her broker to ensure satisfactory payment. Damage would be assessed by an appraiser, either over the telephone or in person. The adjustor would do the rest of the work: ensuring the policy was valid, arranging any legal documentation, and arranging payment.

MARKETING AND SALES This function was responsible for the product: the coverage offered, its price, the commission rate (to brokers), any special features, and the segment of the market it targeted. Marketing employees worked with brokers and with the general public to increase awareness of product features.

Every insurance company also had a number of other functions, including capital investment, actuarial work, legal work, and accounting, but these typically involved much smaller numbers of staff.

THE CANADIAN GENERAL INSURANCE INDUSTRY

The Canadian industry had 350 licensed companies in 1988. The top eight held less than 40% of the market, and no single company held more than 7%. In addition there were a number of mutual companies (in which the shareholders were policyholders), and four government-owned auto-insurance companies. Of the $17 billion 1987 revenues, $4 billion were attributable to the government-owned companies. Only 40% of the market was held by Canadian-controlled firms. The rest was held by multinational insurance companies such as Zurich and Royal Insurance. There were no significant multinational Canadian companies.

The industry was heavily regulated to ensure that companies had both the capital reserves and expertise to fulfil their obligations to policyholders. Entry requirements were, however, considered to be straightforward. Foreign acquisitions of Canadian companies were typically not restricted, except in Quebec where foreign ownership was limited to 25%.

Market Segments

The market for general insurance was divided into six sectors. Automobile insurance was by far the largest, accounting for $5.5 billion out of the private-sector total premiums of $11 billion,[1] and was generally the least profitable as well. Property insurance accounted for $3.8 billion of the total, with the remainder being taken up by the various specialty lines: liability, surety and fidelity, boiler and machinery, and marine and aircraft. Most insurance companies and brokers distinguished between "personal lines" and "commercial lines." Personal lines were just written in auto and property; commercial lines were written in all six areas. The major difference between the two was the high level of individual attention needed for commercial assessments. Typically, each business would be assessed through a personal visit by an underwriter, whereas individuals were assessed according to a prescribed formula.

The prevailing wisdom in the industry was to offer a broad range of products across most or all sectors. Automobile insurance, in particular, was offered by nearly all companies because of its predominance, and because there were opportunities to cross-sell into property. A number of companies had opted for a more focused strategy. Cigna specialized in commercial lines only, and Pilot had deliberately restricted its operations to Ontario, with a focus on personal automobile within that. Evidence suggested that a focused strategy could be effective if well executed, but was inherently more risky than the full-line alternative.

Product Characteristics

Most consumers viewed insurance as a commodity. In the automobile and property sectors every insurance company offered similar coverage, and claims were infrequent enough that speed of payment and service were hard to compare. Attempts had been made to differentiate products by branding or by special features, but these were quickly copied. Furthermore, there was no cost to the customer for transferring business to another company, and contracts were renewed annually or biannually. The consequence was that there was little company loyalty, and in periods of price fluctuations many customers changed company. A further concern to the industry was the inelasticity of demand. Insurance purchases were often legislated (e.g., liability insurance) and usually bought grudgingly. A lower price, for property insurance for example, did not encourage customers to buy more insurance. For any individual company, however, volume could be substantially affected by price because it was being achieved at the expense of competitors. A low price strategy, for example, would likely have the effect of increasing sales but with a corresponding drop in quality. Companies did not just want customers: they wanted customers who were unlikely to make claims. The opposing strategies of increasing sales and weeding out the high-risk businesses represented an ongoing dilemma for insurance companies.

There was some potential for differentiation in the niche lines such as surety and fidelity or boiler and machinery because there was a considerable amount of direct contact with the customer. High quality service was rewarded through word-of-mouth referrals so that reputation, rather than price alone, became a source of competitive advantage. These niches were too small to be the focus of the business, but represented a profitable sideline for any company that could secure a position.

---

[1] Note that the private sector revenues of $13 billion (1987) consisted of $11 billion premiums and $2 billion investment income.

Industry Characteristics

While the barriers to entry were moderate, the costs of exiting the insurance industry were substantial. Companies were liable for up to seven years for claims, and often the reserved sums of money were insufficient to pay for future costs. Thus, a company exiting the industry could expect several years of future expenses, with no revenues against which to offset them. The result was an industry with far too many players, all competing on price. Profitability was low, and the consolidation among players, long anticipated in the industry, had not happened. As one analyst commented: "If you can't make a decent return on revenues of $200 million, you think twice about expanding to $400 million." Evidence in the Canadian market suggested that significant economies of scale were attainable up to about $300 million revenues. Only two players were substantially larger than $300 million and both reputedly had organizational difficulties. However, it was not known whether these difficulties stemmed from the additional complexities of running a larger business, or whether they were attributable to a lack of strategic focus.

Size did, however, confer advantages of a different sort on the multinational insurance companies. By operating in multiple jurisdictions these companies had a certain amount of flexibility in deciding where they would realize profits. A poor performance in Canada, for example, could effectively be smoothed over as long as money was being made elsewhere. This cross-subsidization allowed the multinationals to take a very long-term perspective on their portfolio of operations. The multinationals were also better positioned to pick up the commercial business of multinational customers, such as liability insurance for international trade.

The general insurance industry had typically been very cyclical, with changes in income from year to year as high as 10% of sales. At its peak the industry had excess capital; therefore, insurance companies cut prices or extended coverage to gain market share. This resulted in lower premiums, a reduced capital base and a reduced profit margin. After a number of years of lean profits the major players would push up their prices again to reasonable levels, only to begin price-cutting again. In recent years the upturns had become shorter and the downturns more severe, with the effect that underwriting profits had become something of a rarity. Exhibit 1 shows average industry income for the period 1977–87.

The Broker System

The brokerage industry was highly fragmented with upwards of 3 000 competitors in Canada. They ranged in size from the two-person personal lines broker, with maybe 1 000 customers, up to the big multinational broker interested only in commercial lines for large corporations. A small minority of insurance companies, such as State Farm and Allstate, had tied brokers who were obliged to sell that company's products. All the rest were independent, and saw themselves as agents acting in the best interests of their clients. The depressed state of the insurance industry was hitting the tied broker companies particularly hard, as they were obliged to maintain their brokers regardless of volume. It was rumoured that Allstate's Canadian business was for sale.

Independent brokers typically dealt with several insurance companies and selected policies for their clients according to the client's specific needs. The decision was usually made on the basis of price, but brokers were free to recommend insurance companies with which they had a good relationship, or which provided exceptional service. They were also free to push their worst business (i.e., most risky) towards less-favoured companies. Broker commissions varied from 10% to 25% depending on the segment and on the precise arrangement with the insurance company.

Most independent brokers felt very strongly about retaining their independence. They saw objectivity and freedom of choice as their major services to the customer, and viewed with suspicion or outright rejection any attempt by insurance companies to tie them in to certain products. Nonetheless, insurance companies used a variety of tactics to gain preferential status with their brokers. Some worked on providing swift, efficient claims services; some competed on price or commission; others offered a "contingent profits" scheme whereby the broker received a share in the company's profits over a certain dollar amount. The dividing link between creating a strong relationship with brokers, and encroaching on their independence, was very fine.

The traditional way of doing business in general insurance was to manage the combined ratio, as investment returns were fairly standard across companies. Most companies achieved this through careful underwriting, maintenance of steady relations with brokers, and careful attention to costs in the management and administrative side of the business. One way of ensuring that costs were kept down was to operate with a "centralized" structure, whereby most functions stayed at head office and only those who had frequent contact with customers (e.g., appraisers) positioned themselves in the field. The disadvantage of this approach was that customer responsiveness suffered. Claims could not be assessed quickly, and brokers reported dissatisfaction in dealing with their insurers by phone rather than in person. Some companies had regional sales and marketing offices to alleviate this concern, but most viewed cost control as more important.

The low-cost strategy used by most competitors was responsible for the vicious price-cutting that had damaged the industry's profitability. Some observers thought that opportunities existed for innovative companies to differentiate themselves and break out of the price war, but this had not occurred. Insurance was a very "old fashioned" industry and competitors tended to preserve the status quo.

Trends in the Industry

The underwriting side of general insurance (as measured by the combined ratio figure) was an erratic but persistent money loser in the period 1978–88, and it was only the booming equities market that had sustained the industry. Ten percent annual increases in premiums had been necessary to counter the increasing number of claims and inflation, but now consumers were pressuring governments to legislate lower increases. Nowhere was this problem more acute than in Ontario, where the Liberal government had recently put a rates freeze on the automobile insurance market. Insurers were already losing money in this sector, and were pressuring the government to consider a "no-fault"[2] insurance package that would stabilize and reduce claims.

---

[2] No-fault insurance was intended to reduce the number of questionable damage claims by making each insurance company pay all the costs of its client, regardless of fault. It was expected to lower insurance costs at the expense of the legal profession.

The Canadian insurance industry was not expecting to be severely affected by the antici-pated Free Trade Agreement with the U.S. Insurance companies in the U.S. were generally much larger than their Canadian counterparts (up to $3 billion in revenues), but this was thought to give them very little advantage: because each state had its own set of regulations, the full scope of insurance activities was duplicated in each one. Furthermore, the Canadian mar-ket had been open to foreign competition for years, with American and European companies out-numbering Canadian in the top ranks. The trend in recent years, in fact, had been the exit of a number of American players, who saw the Canadian market as unattractive. They were in a posi-tion to use their continuing American revenues to offset the exit costs from Canada.

Further changes in the insurance industry were anticipated if recent policy proposals to break down the traditional barriers among financial institutions went through. The current laws required separate institutions for insurance companies, banks, trust companies and secu-rities firms (the "four financial pillars"). If these laws were relaxed, diversified financial insti-tutions were expected to form. The consequence for the general insurance industry was expected to be a shake-out in which the successful companies were bought up by the major banks, and the less-successful driven out of business. Change at the retail end was also ex-pected, as the broker industry would be duplicating the service of the traditional branch net-work. Analysts were unsure how this conflict of interests would be resolved. Some saw the insurance broker as a dying breed, unable to compete with the efficient coverage of a retail bank branch network. Others argued that brokers would always retain their competitive advan-tage over banks. As one broker commented: "You can call me at three in the morning when you've just been burgled, and I'll do my job. Try doing that with a bank."

WELLINGTON INSURANCE AND TRILON CORPORATION

Wellington Insurance had been in existence since 1840 under a number of different names. In 1982 it was purchased by Fireman's Fund Insurance Co., an American general insurance com-pany owned by American Express, and became known as "Fireman's Fund Insurance Com-pany of Canada." It wrote property and automobile insurance to individuals (about 300 000) and to small or medium-sized businesses (about 40 000). Operations spanned Canada, but about 50% of the company's business was in Ontario. In 1984 the Company's premium vol-ume was $166 million, or about 2% of the national market, making it the fourteenth largest general insurer in Canada.

In January of 1985, the company was bought by Trilon Corporation for $143 million and renamed Wellington Insurance. Trilon was part of Edward and Peter Bronfman's business em-pire. It had been set up as a management company to oversee the Bronfman's financial ser-vices interests. Trilon already had strong positions in life insurance (London Life), trust service (Royal TrustCo) and Real Estate broking (Royal LePage). The purchase of Fireman's Fund of Canada gave it access to the general insurance industry as well. Trilon's management recognized that these businesses, along with investment banking, were complementary to one another. Trilon expected to generate synergies through cross-selling, integrated broker net-works and a consistent approach to customer service. The possibility of future deregulation in the financial services industry was a further rationale for Trilon's acquisition strategy.

The Trilon Business Strategy

Under CEO George Collins (Wallace's predecessor), Wellington's objective had been to reach Trilon's target return on equity of 15%, a significant increase over the 1985 figure of 9.4%. There were two main thrusts to the strategy: overhead reduction, and broker partnerships.

The overhead reduction program was implemented through a massive re-centralization in November of 1985. Staff levels in each branch office were cut by 40–80%. In London, Ontario, for example the numbers were reduced from eight down to four. Those functions that could easily operate over the phone, such as underwriting, were centralized in Toronto, and all other functions began to report back to supervisors based in Toronto rather than spread through the regions.

Staffing costs were significantly reduced through this strategy, but parts of the business started to suffer. The first problem was a backlog in the claims area, as the reduced number of adjustors struggled to keep up with the new claims. This had the immediate effect of damaging customer service and also broker confidence. "There were people out there who never got their car looked at in two or three weeks," commented one employee, "And when they did it was with a different adjustor each time."

A further consequence of the understaffing was in underwriting: "We had such a backlog that there was no underwriting being done. Work was being processed, but we didn't know what we had on the books. There were many high-risk policies that got through." One employee estimated that a backlog of 40 000 pieces of paper had accumulated by 1987.

The second major thrust was a partnership strategy with brokers called "Partnership Pact." The logic was to create partnerships with a select number of brokers so that the interests of both could be better served. Wellington would buy a 25% stake in each broker's business, and the broker would give a minimum of 25% of his or her business to Wellington. Wellington was to receive preferred status in its chosen segments, and in return profits for that business would be split between the broker and Wellington. Long term it was hoped that the brokers would stock other Trilon products such as life insurance and investment plans.

The Partnership Pact strategy never got off the ground. It met with considerable resistance from the Canadian Federation of Insurance Agents and Brokers Associations Agents and Brokers Association (CFIABA). They valued their independent status, and thought that Wellington's proposal was a departure from "virtually all that Federation sees as being an independent agent."[3] The scheme was quickly dropped, but the relationship with brokers had been soured. Their loss of confidence in Wellington was manifested in a loss of business as Wellington's market share dropped from 2.1% to 1.5% in two years.

The State of the Insurance Industry in 1987

At the same time as Wellington's self-imposed problems, the entire general insurance industry was going through its worst downturn ever. Overcapacity in the industry, in terms of number of competitors, had led to severe price cutting, while claims continued to rise. In 1985 the industry had a combined loss on underwriting of $1.2 billion, a new record. Only strong invest-

---

[3] Conrad Speirs, President CFIABA, at the 1985 Independent Brokers Association of Ontario convention.

ment returns prevented a negative return on equity. At the same time, the Ontario Automobile Insurance industry was going through a crisis. All insurers were incurring heavy losses, but the government had frozen rate increases. Steps were being taken to bring in a no-fault scheme which would lower claims, but for the period since 1985, all auto insurers in Ontario had been badly hit. Wellington was amongst the worst hit, with 40% of its total business in the Ontario Auto segment. For the period 1985–87 it achieved combined ratios of 123.7%, 108.9% and 117.9% respectively. Exhibits 2, 3 and 4 summarize Wellington's performance for the period 1981–87.

THE APPOINTMENT OF MURRAY WALLACE

Toward the end of 1987 Trilon decided that changes were necessary at Wellington Insurance, and appointed Murray Wallace to take over as the new President and CEO on January 1, 1988. Wallace was a senior executive at Royal Trust, a sister company, but had considerable experience in the insurance industry through a period as the president of Saskatchewan's government insurance business. His mandate was to do whatever it took to turn the company around. Trilon had a target return on equity of 15% for all its operating companies. However, Wallace understood that financial targets were really only one measure of a successful turnaround. Equally important was a fundamental change in the way the company operated so that brokers regained their respect for Wellington and staff regained control of internal operations.

Assessment of Internal Operations

The Wellington that Murray Wallace took control of was a very traditional, bureaucratic organization (see Exhibit 5). It had six levels of management, most at the vice-president level. They were distributed through eight centres, but with the vast majority at head office in Toronto. The structure was primarily functional, so that staff belonged to claims, underwriting or sales and rarely communicated with each other. Each manager was responsible for a certain business portfolio, and had strict limits on his or her signing authority. Large claims, for example, had to be referred several steps up the ladder before they could be processed.

   The organization was complicated by the fact that each sales group (responsible for a certain region) also had functional staff, such as adjustors or claims managers. These people were accountable both to their region manager and also to the appropriate functional vice-president. They had to ensure that their actions met with the approval of both managers. As a result, processing was often very slow. Furthermore, each region was centralized, so that the few "field" offices such as London, Ontario, still had to refer back to head office for critical functions such as underwriting. London office staff commented that they would spend hours every day discussing claims or premiums by phone with their supervisors in Toronto. They thought that the dual reporting lines, and the lack of face-to-face contact with managers, were detracting from their ability to serve their customers.

   Staff morale was described by John Carpenter, the new Chief Operating Officer (COO), as "deplorable." The backlog in claims, the recent staffing cuts, and the rigid structure had all taken their toll on employee motivation, so that a feeling of demoralization had set in. Carpenter commented: "We had some good people, but they were constrained by the structure. There was no focus on the company." Another employee added that the commitment to the company was missing: "If anybody had got a job elsewhere at that point, he would have gone."

Other aspects of the organization also contributed to the malaise. Promotion was based largely on years in the company rather than on performance; salaries were adjusted on a seniority basis, so that there was no reward for creativity or initiative; and training programs were effectively non-existent. The hierarchical nature of the business was underlined by the physical layout of the building. Each executive had a mahogany-walled suite with a separate dining room, while the rest of the employees were segregated by functional area in an open-plan arrangement. Wallace realized that change at Wellington would hit senior management the hardest. They had the most to lose, and would certainly be expected to resist any move that threatened the security and comfort of their privileged position.

Another critical area of concern was information processing. "The systems to provide timely and reliable information were not in place," observed Carpenter. This had the effect that management did not know which segments or geographical regions were losing money, and also handicapped the claims and underwriting staff in their regular activities.

A final concern became apparent as Wallace began to explore Wellington's financial statements in more detail. In simple terms the company was under-reserved. The previous management had not set aside enough income to cover likely future claims, so that short-term earnings were inflated but long-term earnings damaged. Wallace realized that the shortfall in reserves, estimated at around $15 million, would have to be made up over the following seven-year period.

Wallace's Recommendations

The insurance industry, like much of the financial services sector, had resisted change for a long time. Wallace was convinced that the time was ripe for some new thinking. Product offerings were all very much the same between companies, but he was sure that Wellington could differentiate in one crucial way: customer responsiveness. "There is a real sense of 'this is the way things have always been done' in this industry. Brokers and customers don't know what it means to get good service. They have never dealt with a company that will bend over backwards to help them." Wallace believed that Wellington could avoid the worst effects of the cyclicity in the industry, and extract a premium price, if an effective customer-oriented operation were put in place. "Brokers should be recommending Wellington because it turns around claims in record time, not because it is the best price," said Wallace.

Wallace was also impressed by the focused strategies of companies like Pilot and Lloyd's non-marine. These companies had achieved strong results by specializing in certain product segments and geographical areas. Wellington had traditionally been a full-line competitor, but could feasibly reduce its volume to focus its scope of operations in this way. A third possible strategic direction that Wallace foresaw was to push for a short-term turnaround, and then sell the company. This would not be easy either, but represented a less drastic shift than the realignment demanded by a differentiation or focus strategy.

One of Wallace's first actions as CEO was to meet with Wellington brokers from across the country. Samples of their comments are listed in Exhibit 6. The process underlined Wallace's belief in a customer service-based strategy, and also drew his attention to the notion of a decentralized organization. Under this structure, all key functions would be grouped together in the field, in close proximity to brokers and customers. Rather than deferring to a central unit for underwriting and claims servicing, each unit would be self-contained and autonomous. Wallace's major concern about a decentralized structure was that no company was using that organizational form. The most successful companies in the industry, in fact, operated with well-managed centralized structures.

The biggest headache for Wallace was the apparent lack of concern for the company's problems among the staff. The company had been through so many changes of ownership that they saw Wallace's appointment as "just another change." Wellington's results were poor, but the company was still turning a small profit. As one manager commented: "Most employees had been doing the same thing for 15 years. They were not interested in any new ideas."

The picture was not all gloom, however. With Trilon as the parent company, Wellington had access to capital, experienced managers and a commitment to long-term profitability. Changes would not have to be compromised for short-term results. In addition, Wallace concluded that the company had some well-respected products, and a lot of good people. In an industry noted for its lack of innovation and dynamism, Wallace predicted that any company, Wellington included, could steal a march on its rivals with some creative management.

Thriving on Chaos

Wallace had developed a clear management philosophy through extensive reading and his own management experiences. His greatest influence was management guru Tom Peters, author of the bestselling *In Search of Excellence* and a number of other books. In particular, Peters' most recent book, *Thriving on Chaos*, detailed a number of strategies for change along the lines of customer responsiveness, empowerment and leadership. Table 2 lists some of the key prescriptions. Wallace found the ideas appealing, and in his previous job at Royal Trust he had begun to put some of them into practice. Wallace wondered if it would be possible to implement the *Thriving on Chaos* prescriptions at Wellington.

TABLE 2   *Thriving on Chaos* Prescriptions

Creating Total Customer Responsiveness	*Achieving Flexibility by Empowering People*	*A New View of Leadership at All Levels*
Specialize/create niches	Involve everyone in everything	Develop an inspiring vision
Provide top quality	Use self-managing teams	Manage by example
Provide superior service	Listen/celebrate/recognize	Practice visible management
Achieve extraordinary responsiveness	Spend time lavishly on recruiting	Defer to the front line
Become obsessed with listening	Train and retrain	Delegate
Make sales and service forces into heroes	Provide incentive pay for everyone	Pursue horizontal management
Launch a customer revolution	Simplify/reduce structure	Evaluate everyone on their love of change
	Reconceive the middle manager's role	Create a sense of urgency
	Eliminate bureaucratic rules	

EXHIBIT 1   **Canadian General Insurance Industry Aggregate Results 1977–87**

Year	Underwriting Income	Investment Income	Net Income	Average Combined Ratio
1977	$ 20m			
1978	69m			
1979	− 163m			
1980	− 513m			
1981	− 890m	$ 937m	$ 160m	111.4%
1982	− 562m	1 054m	456m	108.5
1983	− 328m	1 119m	741m	104.5
1984	− 916m	1 255m	362m	111.7
1985	−1 260m	1 350m	383m	114.0
1986	− 555m	1 509m	1 004m	105.2
1987	− 535m	1 706m	1 165m	104.8

SOURCE: *Canadian Underwriter* 1977–87.

EXHIBIT 2   **Wellington's Market Performance 1981–87**

Year	Ranking in Canada (market share based)	Market share % (on net premiums earned)
1981	15th	1.68%
1982	12th	2.42%
1983	14th	2.28%
1984	14th	2.13%
1985	18th	1.75%
1986	19th	1.52%
1987	19th	1.55%

SOURCE: *Canadian Underwriter* 1981–87.

EXHIBIT 3   **Wellington Key Financial Performance Data 1977–87**

Year	Sales (i.e., net premiums)	Costs (i.e., claims)	Earned Loss Ratio	Total Expense Ratio	Com-bined Ratio	Under-writing Income	Invest-ment Income	Net Income
1977	$123m	$ 73m	59.7%					
1978	124m	79m	63.7					
1979	125m	90m	71.8					
1980	127m	102m	79.0					
1981	131m	104m	79.3	38.9%	118.2%	–$24m	$24m	$ 0
1982	162m	120m	74.0	36.1	110.1	– 16m	27m	11m
1983	168m	126m	74.8	33.3	108.1	– 13m	34m	21m
1984	167m	143m	85.5	33.7	119.2	– 32m	26m	–6m
1985	157m	135m	85.7	38.0	123.7	– 37m	41m	4m
1986	163m	125m	77.0	31.9	108.9	– 15m	53m	38m
1987	172m	145m	84.0	33.8	117.9	– 31m	51m	20m

SOURCE: *Canadian Underwriter* 1977–87.

EXHIBIT 4   Wellington's Business Segmentented by Line and Province, 1987

(A): Segmented by product line

Line	Net Prem. Earned ($000)	Net Claims ($000)	Earned Loss Ratio
Property — personal	$ 45 012	$ 27 336	60.7%
Property — commercial	17 573	12 099	68.8
Property — total	62 585	39 435	63.0
Automobile — liability	50 120	59 234	118.2
Automobile — personal acdt.	7 658	5 976	78.0
Automobile — other	47 412	35 688	75.3
Automobile — total	105 190	100 898	95.9
Boiler and Machinery	3	17	566.7
Fidelity	173	−49	−28.3
Liability	3 416	4 078	117.8
Surety	164	168	102.4
Marine	846	523	61.8
Total for 1987	172 422	145 070	84.1

(B): Segmented by province

Province ($000)	Premiums Earned ($000)	Province	Premiums Earned
Newfoundland	$ 911	Manitoba	$ 2 451
PEI	1 271	Saskatchewan	59
Nova Scotia	14 128	Alberta	14 278
New Brunswick	1 752	British Columbia	18 790
Quebec	18 496	Yukon & NWT	37
Ontario	100 249	Total	172 422

SOURCE: *Canadian Underwriter*, May 1987.

EXHIBIT 5   Simplified Organization Chart, 1987

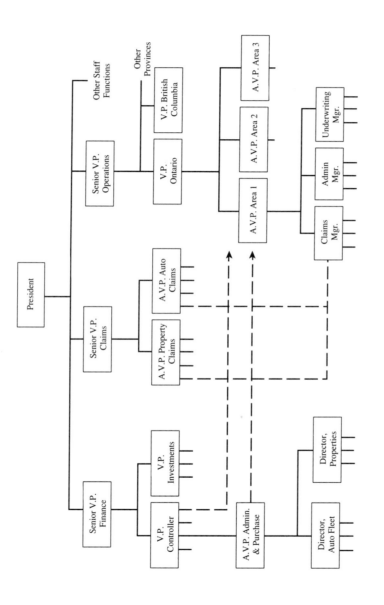

All area-based functional managers report to a Regional V.P. and a Functional Manager/V.P. Profit responsibility is held by both operations managers (for a geographic portfolio) and functional managers (e.g. for all auto claims)

SOURCE: Company interviews

EXHIBIT 6   Broker Comments

These comments were collected from brokers in January 1988, on a trans-Canada tour by Murray Wallace.

"First class products, good prices, but your service...."

"It sure would be nice to get our policies within a reasonable time."

"I wish you'd get the policy right the first time, most of the time anyway."

"I don't want to talk to a different person every time I call."

"I do expect a return phone call when I leave a message."

"It would be so much easier for me if you had an office right here in town."

"I want to deal with the person who makes decisions."

AIKENHEAD'S

Mary M. Crossan and
Catherine Paul-Chowdhury

CASE 3

Wen Stephen Bebis placed his business plan in front of Molson Companies Ltd. in 1991, the landscape of Canadian companies in the home improvement industry did not include any warehouse stores. His proposal for the first in a series of home improvement warehouses (HIW) would change the face of Canadian retailing.

WAREHOUSE CONCEPT

Having its origins in U.S. retailing, the warehouse concept was burgeoning, and impacting on almost every area of retailing. In the U.S., Wal-Mart, Kmart, Toys " Я " Us, Home Depot, Circuit City Stores, Office Depot, Target Stores, and Costco were among the giant power retailers who were expected to put 50% of retailers out of business by the year 2000.

Every mega-retailer had its own formula. Some focused solely on price, while others attempted to combine the traditional advantages of large volume discount stores, in terms of price and selection, with the customer service of its smaller competitors. Doing so meant gaining the maximum benefit out of every aspect of operations.

The mega stores sought more than volume discounts and low prices from their suppliers, although this was clearly one of their major strengths. For example, Wal-Mart and Kmart both

Mary M. Crossan and Catherine Paul-Chowdhury of the Western Business School prepared this case. Copyright © 1995, The University of Western Ontario. This material is not covered under authorization from CanCopy or any reproduction rights organization. Any form of reproduction, storage or transmittal of this material is prohibited without written permission from Western Business School, The University of Western Ontario, London, Canada N6A 3K7

abandoned the brand named "Totes" slippers in favour of a manufacturer who was able to knock-off the concept at a 25% discount. Their strengths, however, extended beyond the clout they wielded to obtain preferential pricing. They worked with their suppliers to develop products that customers wanted, often getting exclusives on some merchandise. One of the areas in which they had made their greatest gains was in inventory management which enabled them to substantially reduce costs. From electronic hook-ups with suppliers to mandatory bar-coding, the mega-retailers had been able to hold operating and selling expenses to as low as 15% of sales versus 28% for their counterparts. As a result they needed only operating margins in the low teens to cover their costs as opposed to traditional retailers who required margins around 30%.

In-store management of merchandise was also critical. Products that didn't move were quickly identified and replaced. While a number of the chains varied on the degree of in-store customer service, some of the more successful warehouses actually provided more in-store service than traditional retailers.

Marketing costs were significantly reduced, since most of the mega-retailers promised "everyday low prices," often with some associated guarantee of having the lowest prices. The focus was, therefore, placed on advertising the store concept, as opposed to a myriad of individual products.

AIKENHEAD'S CONCEPT

The Aikenhead's name had a rich history in the Toronto market. Founded in 1830 as Canada's first hardware chain, it grew into a major wholesaling operation with 19 retail stores when it was purchased by Molson's in 1971. The Molson companies, which also owned Beaver Lumber, were very interested in the warehouse concept since they had witnessed the impact of the concept in the U.S. market, on mid-level home centres, like Beaver. They believed that in order to protect and strengthen their market share in Canada, they would have to pursue warehouse retailing early in the game. The proposed Aikenhead's concept would be radically different from the original flagship store in downtown Toronto, which had recently undergone a name change to "Armoury Hardware" to reflect the difference in concept.

The proposed Aikenhead's concept was intended to mirror the very successful U.S. Home Depot chain which was founded in 1978. Home Depot was the largest home improvement retailer with sales of $5.1 billion from 178 outlets in 15 states. Given the higher margins and lower operating expenses of Home Depot, it was estimated that its EBIT of 6.4%, and its return on net assets of 27.5% in 1988 were double that of competitors who followed a traditional retail format. As stated in Aikenhead's business plan:

> The high sales volumes, better buying techniques, focused advertising, intense customer service, everyday low pricing and deep and wide assortments combine to make warehouse home centre retailing one of the fastest growing success stories in terms of sales, profit and investment.

Table 1 provides a comparison of the proposed Aikenhead's home improvement warehouse (HIW) concept and the typical home centre as identified in the Aikenhead's business plan. Table 2 provides a comparison of the sales and profitability of the two concepts. Examples of some of the special customer services to be offered by Aikenhead's, including computerized deck and kitchen designs, and free "how to" videos, can be found in Exhibit 1.

TABLE 1   Comparison Between HIW and Typical Home Centre

	HIW	*Typical Home Centre*
Size	100 000 sq. ft. 22–26' ceilings	40–60 000 sq. ft. 10–14' ceilings
Sku's	30–40 000 sku's	10–20 000 sku's
Asst/Mix	In depth assortment of all HI products including professional quality	Limited to the best sellers of each category
Fixtures	All pallet racking and cantilever	Gondola with some pallet racking and cantilever
Display Format	Bulk oriented Goods are cut cased and massively displayed	Most goods are hung on pegs, hooks or displayed neatly on shelves
Staffing	90% full time	Split to mostly part timers with full-time management
Service	Knowledgeable tradespeople committed to customer service Teach customers to do-it themselves Knowledgeable tradespeople on staff in all departments	Most employees are utilized to stock away merchandise Limited service
Supply & Logistics	Worldwide manufacturers Purchase direct from the manufacturers Large quantity, bulk buying, solid trucks, container loads, rail cars 2–4 week leadtime	Worldwide manufacturers Purchase through distributors, wholesalers and brokers Small quantities, common carriers, mixed trucks 7–10 day leadtime
Capital Requirements	$6–7 million/store (excluding real estate)	$3–4 million/store (excluding real estate)
Pricing	Everyday low pricing Always the best price on every item, everyday; pricing driven by the market Negotiate special buys from vendors on key products with savings passed onto the customer The price leader on key commodity items	Higher pricing with sales Selectively sharp on some items, others are based on the store margin budget Run sales on items and absorb profit loss Follows behind the warehouse stores or ignores them
Customer Mix	Do-it-yourselfers Buy-it yourselfers Professional business customer Customer profile is determined by store placement; insures store will be heavily oriented to the homeowner Over 50% of the customers are female	Not focused on any particular type of customer; some have strong contractor orientation Customer profile varies depending on store location; could be mostly contractors Mostly men with women a smaller minority

TABLE 2   Comparative Sales and Profitability

Performance	HIW	Typical Home Centre
Sales	$24.2 million	$10–12 million
Operating exp.	20.6%	25.9%
EBIT	6.4%	3.4%
RONA (before tax)	27.5%	12.9%

MARKET STUDIES

While the HIW concept had been extremely successful in the U.S., there was no Canadian precedent to test the viability of the concept in the new market. However, the Price Club and Toys "Я" Us had already successfully penetrated the Canadian market. To probe the level of receptivity of Canadians to the HIW concept, $1 million was spent on market studies in the Toronto area which is where the "roll-out" would begin.

Focus groups in the Toronto market indicated that consumers were not particularly loyal as shown by the following types of comments on their shopping habits:

I drove around until I found the best deal.

We shop through catalogues in advance.

I make up a list and look for sales over the next two to three weeks.

While customers perceived that the HIW concept might provide value in terms of convenient shopping, they indicated some scepticism about whether it would provide a high level of service, low prices, convenient location and a wide assortment of branded products. Further research showed that over 80% of shoppers in metropolitan markets were willing to drive 30 minutes to a store with competitive prices. Most consumers would be attracted to the store for its large selection of products and competitive prices.

As well, the research indicated that Canada's 14 largest urban areas, representing one third of its population, could support close to 40 stores with an estimated market size of $3.6 billion.

COMPETITION

Aikenhead's would be stepping into a market with well-established and successful competitors. In 1990, Canadian Tire dominated the industry with sales of $3.1 billion through 418 outlets. Beaver Lumber, which was also owned by Molson's, generated sales of $1.1 billion through 158 outlets. While Canadian Tire and Beaver Lumber characterized the retailing format of the larger retailers, there were chains of independent retailers such as Home Hardware that generated significant sales volumes. Through 985 outlets, Home Hardware generated sales of $850 million. A synopsis of Canadian Tire, Beaver Lumber and Home Hardware is provided in Exhibit 2.

In the Toronto market, with estimated sales for retail home improvement of $482 million, Canadian Tire was the dominant player with a market share of 37% from a base of 33 stores. Beaver Lumber had a 14% market share with 11 stores. Lansing Buildall, Lumber City and Pascal Hardware each had less than 10% of the market. Many smaller retailers such as Home Hardware or other independents made up the remainder of the market. While Bebis viewed every retailer or contractor who sold home improvement products as a competitor, he was confident that Aikenhead's concept would provide it with a superior competitive position in the Canadian context. His primary concern was to establish Aikenhead's before Home Depot entered the market. Molson's believed it would have a few years before Home Depot entered the Canadian market, since in early 1990, when Molson approached Home Depot to form a joint venture, Home Depot indicated they were more interested in pursuing growth opportunities in the U.S.

However, Aikenhead's expected to expand the market, not just to divide the pie a little differently. It viewed itself competing for the consumer's discretionary dollars, and not just for the existing amount spent on home improvement. By making home improvement projects easier and more affordable, it was felt that the entire market had much more room to grow.

In spite of the success U.S. retailers had enjoyed, and the potential that existed in the market according to the research conducted, Bebis was concerned about implementation. The most difficult aspect of the plan was its execution. One of the first things Bebis discovered about the Canadian market was the general lack of pride in the retail sector. He suggested that "in the U.S., individuals do an MBA to get into retail, while in Canada they do an MBA to get out of retail." Executing the Aikenhead's concept would require a revolution in the way retail was conducted; but, more importantly, what was needed was a revolution in the way people thought of retail.

PHILOSOPHY/EXECUTION

Execution would go far beyond the words on the page of the business plan which attempted to capture the Aikenhead's corporate philosophy:

> Aikenhead's believes that performing to a standard of excellence in everything we do will optimize the earnings potential of the enterprise.

> Fundamental to this standard of excellence are the following philosophical underpinnings:

>> Our customers will decide our destiny. We work as a team in which every transaction must convey integrity, value and satisfaction.

>> Our employees are our greatest resource. Each is an individual who must be treated with dignity and respect. This will be achieved through providing a work environment which embraces open communications, opportunity, equality and individual fulfilment.

At the outset, the plan tried to identify some of the behaviours that would support the philosophy of a high level of customer service, including getting a carriage for the customer, walking a customer to a product location rather than pointing, and helping the customer carry products to the checkout.

A critical part of the plan was to employ knowledgeable sales people, and to provide even further training on the culture of the company and the products offered. However, candidates would have to be more than just knowledgeable. Aikenhead's would be looking for individuals who were self-starters, had a high degree of energy, were social, confident, ambitious and could communicate well. Since the organizational structure would be very flat, it was important that all individuals be capable of making decisions. The 200 people to be recruited for the first store opening in March 1992 would swell to 1500, with nine stores, by 1994.

Aikenhead's would have no commissions, or associate (Aikenhead's referred to employees as associates) discounts, as it was felt that they got in the way of customer service and were costly to track. However, associates would be well compensated. Aikenhead's expected to be one of the highest paying retailers in Canada. As well, associates would be provided with the opportunity to earn a financial stake in the business, and bonuses based on store performance. Bebis stated this philosophy:

> In order to get high calibre people, we must: a) pay well; b) offer benefits which are equal to if not better than those offered elsewhere in the industry; c) treat the associates like human beings; d) offer them an environment in which they can grow as individuals; e) encourage them to use their creativity and intelligence; and f) listen to them.

Bebis stated that he would rather hire one associate at $10 per hour than two associates at $6 per hour. With motivated and knowledgeable associates, Bebis saw the benefits of a higher level of sales turnover, arising from the extra care and attention provided to customers and to merchandising products. Training would be used extensively to aid in the development of a new retail mindset. Many of the associates would be coming from traditional retail backgrounds in which the standard was that "there was never enough time to do something right the first time, but enough time to do it over." At Aikenhead's, associates would be encouraged to seek out labour saving devices to free up the time required to do things right in the first place. Information systems would play a major role in executing the strategy. Systems would be used to reduce costs and to enhance service throughout the organization.

Bebis envisioned that systems would tie Aikenhead's into its supplier network in order to garner efficiencies in ordering, shipping, receiving and billing. If Aikenhead's could reduce a supplier's operating expenses, it was expected that these savings would be passed on to Aikenhead's in the form of lower product costs. Aikenhead's expected to have a partnership relationship with its suppliers, that for many, would require dramatic changes to their business, including selling directly to Aikenhead's. Selling directly meant that manufacturers would have to learn how to service a retailer, while absorbing the additional costs of acting as a warehouse and distribution centre that delivers directly to individual stores. A synopsis of two major suppliers is provided in Exhibit 3.

As well, Aikenhead's would use the same information systems to reduce its own operating expenses and to enhance service. For example, systems designed to track products could be used to manage inventory levels, respond to customer inquiries, establish sales patterns to support decisions about product mix, staffing levels, and to provide information on performance levels.

The company would be organized along functional lines as outlined in Exhibit 4. Each of the vice-presidents had already been recruited. Their profiles are provided in Exhibit 5. Given the flat structure, and the close proximity of the Aikenhead's "home office" which would be adjacent to their first store, executives would be able to stay close to the customer and to remain aware of the cross-functional challenges in running the business.

LEADERSHIP

When Molson's decided to pursue the HIW business, they decided that they needed a CEO who was knowledgeable about warehouse retailing, was an entrepreneur, a self-starter and one who could "make it happen." They hired Bebis as their first employee. Bebis described his view of the business as follows:

> I always wanted to open and operate my own business as an entrepreneur but never had the money. The opportunity to come to Canada and to open the first full size warehouse store in the industry and to run the show from scratch using someone else's money was a dream come true. The reasons I chose Canada were that it was virgin territory for our concept; we would blaze new trails and this was very exciting. I was with Home Depot for six years. I was a small fish in a big pond. By coming to Canada, I was able to become the number one guy and to create a new company from the ground up. This opportunity only comes around once in a lifetime and I wanted to take advantage of it.

When Bebis joined Aikenhead's, Molson's had bought into the concept and had agreed to one store. At that time the name had not even been selected. Bebis described his introduction to the business:

> The one thing I remember fondly is showing up for work the first day and not having a phone or a pencil and certainly not an office. It truly was a greenfield start. I worked out of a hotel room and had to rent office space for myself and buy office furniture. Bob Wittman and I also designed the first store.

Bebis described his leadership role in implementing the concept:

> It was a matter of setting high goals, demanding excellence in the execution of achieving those goals and never wavering from our focus. I have an unwavering commitment to customer service. I am focused and never let up. I believe that constant hammering, constant retraining, constant reinforcement of our mission and why we are here are critical to our success. Being able to go through brick walls to make things happen is definitely one of my strong points.

Bebis knew that to execute the concept, leadership would be required at every level of the organization. Teeth were put into the concept of "empowerment" through the design of the systems and the structure of the organization. The flat organizational structure meant that associates would be required to make key decisions. Training provided them with the knowledge to make the decisions, and the tools were put in place to aid in the process. For example, information systems and in-store terminals enabled them to advise customers on the status of products. Furthermore, each of the 200 store associates would be authorized to contact suppliers as needed, in an industry in which supplier contact had previously only been made at the most senior levels of the organization. Résumés were already pouring in for the first store. While many people questioned opening the store during a recession, Bebis suggested that it was an ideal time to establish a new business. Deals could be made on real estate, suppliers were hungry for business, and Bebis had his pick of some of the best people in the industry. With construction at a stand still, there were hundreds of professional plumbers, electricians and carpenters who would jump at the chance to supplement their sporadic business with the opportunity for steady work. As Bebis submitted the business plan to Molson's, the question in his mind was not whether the Aikenhead's concept would work, but how big and how fast he should grow the business.

EXHIBIT 1   Special Customer Services

- Computerized Kitchen Design
- Computerized Deck Design
- Product Fairs
- Department Demos
- Multiple Credit Plans
- Lock Keying / Duplicate Keys
- Glass Cutting
- Lumber Cutting — Mini Blinds Cutting
- Delivery
- Special Orders — Kitchen, Bath, Millwork
- Free Project Advice
- Computerized Colour Matching / Mixing
- Short / No Wait Checkouts
- Cash Only Lines
- Scanning
- Free Use of How To Videos
- Use of Car Carrier Racks
- Free Use of Insulation Blower With Purchase
- Sprinkling System Design
- Assistance in Loading Cars
- Equipment Rentals, i.e., Post Hole Digger; Insulation Blower; File Cutter

EXHIBIT 2   Competitors

Beaver Lumber

Beaver Lumber was owned by The Molson Companies Limited, Aikenhead's parent. With 158 locations across Canada, Beaver Lumber was a retailer of building and lumber supplies. As well, it carried a full range of home improvement merchandise. The company served two distinct sets of customers: individuals and, in rural areas, contractors. It was billed as "Canada's largest do-it-yourself retailer." The chain had sales of $1 074 million in 1991, down from $1 129 million in 1990. Operating profit was $29.1 million in 1991, down from $44.8 million in 1990.

Beaver Lumber had a mixture of corporate-owned and franchised stores. Stores were free to purchase products either from a Beaver Lumber distribution centre or from other distributors. The corporation earned its return partly on the sale of goods through the distribution centre, but mainly from the 50–50 split of net income from the franchised stores. The typical Beaver Lumber store was 30 000 square feet in size, with approximately 50 employees. Over 50% of the stores were in secondary urban or rural markets.

Traditionally, the urban stores had performed poorly. They had higher prices and limited product breadth and depth compared to their competitors. Stores in the smaller centres, however, profited from extensive high-margin business with building contractors. Beaver Lumber differentiated itself from its competitors by offering credit to contractors. For this reason, the stores typically had unusually high levels of accounts receivable. Indeed, its was the infrastructure required to support these financing activities which contributed to Beaver Lumber's higher costs and prices.

Beaver Lumber introduced a number of strategic and operating initiatives in 1991. It began to move toward a more centralized organizational structure, in order to exercise greater control over inventories. The company announced plans to increase the number of products carried by its stores by up to 5 000 stocking units. It introduced six different standardized store layouts, and doubled the number of hours of training for store managers. The information system at Beaver Lumber had been in place for approximately 15 years.

Canadian Tire

Canada's largest hardgoods retailer, Canadian Tire had sales of $3.0 billion in 1991, down from approximately $3.1 billion the year before. Net earnings were $127 million, a 12% drop from 1990 levels. Sales of hardware represented 25% of Canadian Tire's revenues, while sales of automotive and sporting goods comprised the remaining 75%.

Canadian Tire had two operating divisions: the Merchandise Business Group, representing 80% of revenues, which supplied goods and services to the company's Associate stores, and the Diversified Business Group comprised mainly of the Petroleum Division and Canadian Tire Acceptance, the financial services division.

The company employed approximately 3 800 full-time and 1 500 part-time workers across the country, in addition to those hired by the firm's Associate Dealers. The Associate Dealer stores were not franchises. Instead, they functioned much like auto dealerships, with five-year contracts to purchase their products from Canadian Tire's Merchandise Business Group. The corporation wielded significant power in its relationship with the Associated Dealers. Margins had traditionally been evenly split between the Corporation and the Dealer, but in the mid-1980s Canadian Tire forced up its share by several percentage points. Canadian Tire earned its return from selling goods and services to its Associated Dealers, and required that dealers purchase all but the most specialized products from the corporation.

Canadian Tire had identified the trend toward an increasingly competitive marketplace. It saw its challenge as balancing short-term seasonality and business cycle fluctuations with longer-term changes in buying behaviour, demographics and technology. The company described their customers as demanding low-cost distribution of commodity products, as well as better quality, service and selection.

Canadian Tire considered its competitive advantages to be its entrepreneurial Associate Dealers, convenience of location (77% of the Canadian population lives within a 15-minute drive of a Canadian Tire store), and consumer awareness. Its interrelated business units allowed synergies in cross-merchandising, marketing and information management. Traditionally, information systems played a crucial role in the company's development and competitive positioning. It invested heavily in information technology, resulting in inventory control and management systems at both corporate and store levels which were far superior to those of competitors. Investment in IS was ongoing, with individual stores upgrading their systems every couple of years.

Canadian Tire stores varied widely in size, from 2 500 to 40 000 square feet. Approximately 25 000 products or product sizes were sold.

In summary, the distribution channels at both Beaver Lumber and Canadian Tire were as follows:

Home Hardware

Home Hardware, with 985 outlets, was Canada's largest dealer-owned chain. Approximately 80 of these stores were located in the Metro Toronto area. The dealers were independents who had organized themselves into a buying group. In 1990, Home Hardware generated $850 million in sales.

Home Hardware considered its competitive advantage to be convenient location. It believed that, while customers might be willing to drive across town for a lower price on big-ticket items, they would choose the closest store for smaller purchases.

Because Home Hardware dealers did not have the backing of a large corporation, they sometimes had difficulty securing bank financing. As a result, the stores tended to be understocked compared to their competitors. The outlets varied greatly in size, but tended to be smaller overall than their competitors.

EXHIBIT 3   Suppliers

Suppliers of products to the Canadian home improvement industry operated within similar distribution channels. Manufacturers sold to distributors, who in turn serviced retail outlets. Distributors were responsible for meeting the demands of the retailer which included on-time delivery, in-store merchandising and servicing, and "hands on" product knowledge and training. They were also responsible for dealing with special shipping instructions, EDI requirements, UPC packaging requirements and the handling of any problems with product quality.

Suppliers did, however, differ from each other along at least three dimensions. The first dimension was the degree of perceived elasticity of demand for their products. For example, Manco, a major manufacturer of a fairly standard product for the home improvement industry, believed that the overall demand for their products was relatively inelastic; a lower price would not result in an increase in demand. In general, it was felt that demand was reasonably fixed and a change in distribution would not impact purchase decisions to a great extent. On the other hand, Hardco, a major manufacturer of tools for the home improvement industry believed that the overall demand for its product was affected by the efforts on the part of retailers to market their product in ways that expanded the home improvement industry's share of customer's discretionary dollars.

The second way that suppliers differed was the degree to which they dominated distribution channels and shelf space. For example, given Manco's market dominance, it was extremely difficult for new competitors to enter the business. Customers did not demand a wide selection in the product category and therefore retailers were not willing to give a lot of shelf space to the product. Similarly, distributors carried only a few products, and therefore Manco dominated the channel.

Finally, suppliers differed in terms of their geographic market focus and the degree of integration of their operations. For example, Manco Canada was part of Manco worldwide which was amongst the largest manufacturers of the product line in the world. However, there was little integration between the Canadian company and its parent. This meant that the Canadian operation had not closely observed other parts of the organization which were responding to dramatic industry change. At Hardco, however, international operations were well-integrated. The Canadian operation had watched its U.S. counterpart deal with radical changes in the U.S. industry, and had been waiting for the same pressures to be exerted on the Canadian market.

EXHIBIT 4   Organizational Chart 1991

Home Improvement Warehouse—Corporate

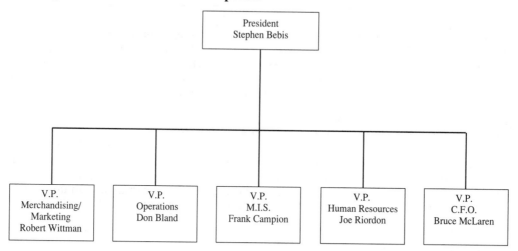

Store Operations Model

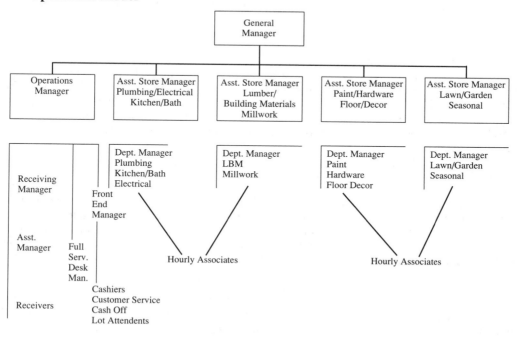

EXHIBIT 5   The Management Team

Stephen Bebis (President)

Steve is a superbly qualified retailing executive. His 20 years of experience have given him a clear understanding of the synergies required to keep all components of an enterprise functioning optimally for the achievement of superior results. His increasingly significant marketing and merchandising responsibilities with Sears Roebuck & Co., Grossman's and, most recently, Home Depot have provided him with the cross-category knowledge necessary to guarantee merchandising success and customer acceptance.

Robert J. Wittman (Vice-President, Merchandising and Marketing)

Bob has a wide range of business experience acquired through 25 years in retailing. He has served in various merchandising capacities with such organizations as Supermarkets General, Loblaws (Canada), Grossman's, Bradlees Department Stores, Somerville Lumber and Home Quarters Warehouse Inc. Bob is an intuitive marketer with a thorough understanding of the categories, assortments and presentations essential to the success of a warehouse home improvement store.

Donald C. Bland (Vice-President, Operations)

Don is a seasoned specialist with 25 years of experience. His progressively increased responsibilities in both merchandising and operations with such companies as Target Stores, Montgomery Ward, The J.L. Hudson Division of Dayton Hudson Corporation, Lechemere Inc. and Home Quarters Warehouse Inc. have provided him with top-flight retail executive credentials. His strategic as well as operational management competence will contribute a great deal to the success of this enterprise.

Frank D. Campion (Vice-President, Information Systems)

Frank is an Information Systems specialist whose experience in the United States Navy, Haines Furniture, Camellia Food Stores and Home Quarters Warehouse Inc. have given him the superb qualifications needed to provide this organization with state-of-the-art systems support. Frank understands the systems needs and the solutions essential to enhancing warehouse store operations through systems that optimize both customer and management information services.

Joseph P. Riordon (Vice-President, Human Resources)

Joe is the epitome of the consummate retailing Human Resources executive. His experience with the Allstate Insurance Company, Royal Trust, Boots Drugstores (Canada) Ltd. and F.W. Woolworth Company Ltd. have provided him with a broad operational and human resource base. He has a thorough understanding of all the component aspects of people management and will be a highly effective link in the cross-functional optimization of people in our company.

Bruce W. McLaren (Vice-President, Finance)

Bruce McLaren is a highly competent financial executive who has, during his career, designed and implemented virtually every type of financial system and/or process relating to the retail sector. His progressive experience with Thorne Riddell, Sears Canada and Kmart has provided Bruce with a profound understanding of the retail environment, and the role of the finance function in it, which will allow him to be a strong contributor to the organization's success.

SOURCE: Aikenhead's Business Plan.

THE DIAPER WAR: KIMBERLY-CLARK VERSUS PROCTER & GAMBLE

Allen J. Morrison and Kerry S. McLellan

CASE 4

On November 1, 1989, the management of Kimberly-Clark (K-C) watched with great interest and concern as Procter & Gamble (P&G) announced the appointment of a new CEO, Edwin Artzt. Artzt had considerable international experience in the disposable diapers industry and management at K-C wondered if his appointment would signal a new phase of competition within the industry.

Six months earlier, prior to Artzt's appointment, P&G had introduced gender-specific disposables with designer colours. While a significant product improvement, gender-specific disposables were not in the tradition of the technological competitive breakthroughs of the past. K-C had responded with test marketing of a similar product, but a national roll-out would still be several months away.

The decision to proceed with a national roll-out was tempered by concern that such a move would acknowledge P&G's leadership in the marketplace. Furthermore, K-C managers questioned whether a move into gender-specific disposables would distract the company from important research and development efforts aimed at the environmental concerns now confronting the industry. In considering options, K-C management was faced with significant financial constraints and they wondered if greater opportunities would be available outside the increasingly competitive North American industry. International opportunities in Europe and

Japan merited greater attention, particularly given recent moves by overseas competitors to enter the North American diaper industry. Also of interest to K-C management were the company's ongoing efforts to build a market position for its adult incontinence products. As K-C faced the 1990s, managers braced for heightened competition and wondered how and when to respond.

THE NORTH AMERICAN DIAPER INDUSTRY

The Development of Disposable Diapers

The disposable diaper, invented in postwar Sweden, was introduced to America by Johnson & Johnson in the late 1940s. Kendall and Parke Davis entered the market a decade later. At that time, marketing efforts were focused on travelling parents with infants. Research and development efforts tried to increase product effectiveness by improving the methods of matting the absorbent tissue.

These early diapers, used with fastening pins and plastic pants, were generally perceived as ineffective in keeping either babies or parents dry. With slow sales, prices for the product remained high (10¢ each for disposables versus 3¢–5¢ for cloth diaper services and 1¢–2¢ for home laundered diapers). As a result, most firms remained uninterested in making significant investments in this market segment.

Procter & Gamble's Entry: Pampers

There are several stories surrounding the motivation for P&G's initial interest in disposable diaper products. One version cited the frustration of a senior engineer with the state of disposable diaper technology in the 1950s. The engineer was a new grandfather who felt a strong motivation to develop a better product. The other popularized story involved the complaints of a nun in charge of the nursery at a Cincinnati Catholic Hospital. She complained to company personnel regarding the sanitary problems of cloth diapers. Her comments spurred action at the firm to develop a product that would meet the needs of her nursery.

While P&G's initial interest in disposable diapers was surrounded by stories of chance, the firm's commercialization of the product was clearly motivated by shrewd analysis. By the late 1950s, the firm was beginning to recognize elements of opportunity in this dismally viewed market sector. Although the industry was fragmented and the market undeveloped, the conditions fit well with P&G's strategy of trying to introduce products into markets where there was a reasonable expectation that a premium segment niche could be created by effective marketing and superior product characteristics. In 1957, cellulose fibre research began in earnest, spurred on by P&G's purchase of the Charmin Paper Company.

In 1961, P&G announced its entry into the disposable diapers industry with the introduction of Pampers; test marketing began a year later. Pampers provided a clear technological breakthrough from previous products as it was the first disposable diaper to use a plastic backsheet coupled with absorbent wadding and a porous rayon sheet facing the baby's skin. Despite these advantages, however, the product did not achieve P&G's sales targets, and thus

Pampers was not distributed nationally. This early market failure was blamed on the product's high price of 10¢ per diaper which was similar to that charged by other firms and reflected the underlying manufacturing cost structure of Pampers. The cost problem reflected P&G's production approach of purchasing partially completed components to be assembled later. This manufacturing process, while the norm in the industry, was both expensive and time-consuming.

Recognizing production inefficiencies, P&G concentrated research efforts on reducing the manufacturing costs of the disposable product. In 1964, the firm's engineers developed a continuous process technology that allowed the manufacture of diapers at speeds of 400 per minute. This process proved many times faster than the previous manufacturing method and allowed the use of minimally processed raw materials. This advance, as well as changes in purchasing, allowed P&G to cut costs significantly. As a result, Pampers was reintroduced into a second test market site at a price of 5.5¢ per diaper. The test was very successful and a national introduction followed in 1966. Full national distribution was achieved by 1969.

Kimberly-Clark's Entry: Kimbies

Diaper research at K-C also began in earnest in the mid-1960s, focusing primarily on new product technology. The firm used its experience with feminine napkins to develop a product that used fluff pulp in place of tissue. The pulp provided cheaper and better absorbency. These advantages, coupled with the introduction of adhesive tabs and an improved shape, were incorporated into a new product, called Kimbies, introduced by K-C in 1968. The use of fluff pulp as the primary absorbent material provided competitive cost savings. Kimbies was parity priced with Pampers but competitive cost savings were not passed through to consumers. Rather, K-C reinvested the excess profit into further product improvements. This strategy fit with industry market research that showed a strong relationship between improved product features and market and sales growth. The cost of product improvements could be passed on, as many consumers seemed to show a high degree of price indifference.

Other competitors active during the late 1960s included Scott Paper, Borden, and International Paper. All three were experimenting with a two-piece disposable diaper system in the mid-1960s. This system, which relied on technology developed in Europe, involved a disposable inner liner and a reusable plastic outer shell. The product also had a distinct advantage over Pampers in that the diapers used snaps instead of pins.

By 1970, a competitive pattern had begun to emerge in the industry. Rivalry was increasingly focused on product innovation. However, these improvements were not always translated into market share gains for reasons that appeared to be two-fold: poor marketing communication of product benefits, and the inability of some firms to reduce manufacturing costs to P&G's level. In spite of what some regarded as an inferior product, Pampers appeared unstoppable. By 1970, P&G peaked with an estimated market share of 92%. Observers began recognizing that technology alone was not enough and that many of the large industrial-focused paper companies might be in an untenable position in the industry.

Industry Shake-Out

There was a rapid shake-out of the disposable diaper industry in the early 1970s. The restructuring was hastened by a constant series of modifications undertaken by P&G to further strengthen its Pampers line. For example, the company converted from tissue to fluff pulp in 1972 and to adhesive tabs in 1973. As a result of the heightened competition, Borden exited the industry in 1970, Scott left the U.S. market in 1971, International Paper stopped U.S. production in 1972, and Johnson & Johnson's Chicopee discontinued its brand in 1972. Other competitors retreated slowly as continuous costly improvements upped the ante. P&G's dominant position was maintained until K-C's Kimbies began to gather steam in the 1972–74 period.

In 1971, Darwin Smith was appointed as the new president of K-C. Smith's objective was to reduce K-C's reliance on core newsprint and paper operations and to strengthen its position in consumer products. This transformation took several years to complete and involved the selling off of various mills and woodlands, and the strengthening of the company's market leading Kleenex and Kotex brands. This strategic refocusing produced a war-chest of $350 million that was to be used for further expansion into consumer products.

K-C's Kimbies was an early benefactor of this shift in strategy. Buoyed by increased marketing expenditures, Kimbies' market share peaked in 1974 at 20%. However, as the decade progressed, management did not pay enough attention to Kimbies' performance and sales began to decline.

In spite of the transformation in the industry, disposable diapers were only used regularly on about 35% of babies in 1976. Total market growth remained flat. To most parents, the benefits of disposables were still not large enough to support their added cost.

THE COMPETITION INCREASES

Procter & Gamble Introduces Luvs

In 1976, P&G announced the test marketing and selected regional introduction of a premium diaper product, Luvs. This diaper offered several improvements over Pampers, including a fitted, elasticized shape and a more effective absorbent structure. Luvs was priced 25–30% above Pampers. This introduction was intended to create a new premium market segment, moving Pampers into a middle segment. P&G continued regional market testing for more than two years but seemed indecisive on a national rollout decision. Many observers believed that this hesitation was related to test market results indicating a large negative impact on Pampers.

Kimberly-Clark Introduces Huggies

By 1978, K-C's corporate transformation was nearly complete and attention was refocused on the diaper sector. That year, K-C introduced Huggies to replace Kimbies. The product was superior to both Pampers and Luvs. It was better fitting, more absorbent, and offered an improved tape fastening system. In support of the new product, K-C hired top marketing talent and backed the introduction with large promotional and advertising investments.

At the time of Huggies' introduction, Luvs was still available only on a limited regional basis. P&G's indecision provided K-C with a tremendous opportunity to develop a product with characteristics superior to Luvs. Because of the introduction of Huggies, P&G was forced to complete the national rollout of Luvs. Luvs, suffering from inferior performance relative to that of Huggies, was unable to gain control of the premium segment. K-C continued to produce Kimbies for the market's middle segment, but concentrated resources on Huggies, allowing Kimbies to die a slow death. National distribution of Kimbies was discontinued in 1983.

Huggies' sales grew rapidly as consumers discovered the diaper's superior characteristics. Sales growth came not only through market share growth, but also as a result of the increased usage of disposable diapers. With Huggies, consumers could now see the benefit of switching from traditional cloth diapers to disposable products. Market penetration of disposables increased rapidly.

Procter & Gamble Responds

P&G initially did little to respond to K-C's new market entry. Part of the reason for the slow response was that K-C had introduced Huggies after upgrading its manufacturing processes and P&G had large investments in older diaper machines. P&G was clearly hesitant to make the huge investments necessary to match K-C production processes. This older technology limited P&G's ability to match K-C's product modifications and put the company at somewhat of a cost disadvantage. To avoid this expense, P&G aggressively promoted Pampers; however, sales continued to slump. Brand market share fluctuated widely during the 1981–89 period, with the early 1980s being the most difficult period for P&G (Exhibit 1).

By 1983, market research began to convince P&G management that the middle sector was disappearing. Consumers either wanted the best products for which they seemed willing to pay a premium price or they wanted low priced—typically private label—products, regardless of performance. Pampers appeared to be stuck in the middle.

It was not until late 1984, when Huggies had captured 30% of the market, that P&G upgraded its products with comparable features and fought to regain market share. There were two elements in the strategy. First, P&G decided to reposition Pampers as a premium product, comparable to Luvs. The repositioning was accomplished through improvements in Pampers' shape and fastening system, and a major improvement in absorbent structure. Also, to improve cost structure and offer the improved features, P&G made major investments in its production system. The competitive upgrade of P&G's diaper lines was very expensive, costing an estimated $500 million for a new plant and equipment. A further $225 million in additional advertising and promotion support was used to re-launch P&G's slumping brands.

The technological leap-frog competition was on. In the first half of 1986 alone, seven of P&G's 19 patent searches involved diaper product improvements (Exhibit 2). These searches were the subject of great interest to K-C researchers.

New Technology Results in Super-Thin Diapers

During 1986, the competition entered a new stage of intense technological rivalry with both P&G and K-C introducing super-thin, super-absorbent disposables. The new diapers contained polyacrylate, a powder crystal that absorbed 50 times its weight in liquid. By using polyacrylate, diapers could be manufactured that were 30% thinner. The two firms had to re-educate consumers into not associating absorbency with thickness. The campaign was a success and parents seemed to like the new diaper's sleek profile and improved performance. P&G and K-C were able to achieve transportation cost savings and retailers were pleased with improved shelf utilization.

P&G introduced the new technology into the U.S. early in 1986. K-C's introduction followed nine months later. P&G's competitive leadership in North America, however, did not come from development work in the U.S., but rather from access to technology developed in Japan, where the company had considerable operations. Because K-C lacked a significant presence in the Japanese market, the company had been forced to follow P&G's introduction in North America. Initially, P&G and K-C were dependent on Japanese suppliers for polyacrylate and neither was able to obtain the North American licence. After two years, however, Cellanese, a U.S. chemical firm, was given a licence to manufacture the product in North America.

The introduction of super-thin technology clearly hastened the demise of the mid-market segment. Super-thin technology was regarded as so unique that its use would automatically position a product at the high end of the market. The repositioning of Pampers in 1984 and the withdrawal of Kimbies in 1983 represented an effective abandonment of the mid-price segment of the market by the major industry players. During the later half of the 1980s, neither P&G nor K-C attempted to introduce products to fill the now largely unserved mid-price market segment. During the early 1980s, however, P&G and K-C had continued to test products aimed at the low-priced segment. K-C tested Snuggems, and P&G experimented with Simply Pampers. Neither product received national distribution, although regional testing continued until the later part of the 1980s. The inability of P&G and K-C to place products in the low-priced segment was primarily the result of the reluctance of mass merchandisers to give Snuggems or Simply Pampers adequate shelf space. The retailers were able to earn much higher margins from their private label brands, targeted at the same segment.

HEAD-TO-HEAD COMPETITION

By the Fall of 1989, the industry had effectively evolved into a duopoly dominated by K-C with a 32% market share, and P&G with a 49% market share. Both companies sold super-thin diapers exclusively. In 1989, total retail sales of disposable diapers exceeded $4.5 billion in the United States and $400 million in Canada. The disposable diaper market appeared saturated with little growth in total market size expected.

As a duopoly, competition between P&G and K-C was intense. Given the huge fixed costs involved in the production of disposable diapers, it was estimated that each percentage gained in market share resulted in $6–10 million in additional annual profit. As a result, competition extended beyond research and development to marketing and promotion, and to manufacturing.

Marketing and Promotion

The war between P&G and K-C started with ads in the magazines that appealed to expectant mothers. The fight entered a more open, intense phase when the companies fought to get their products into maternity wards and pediatricians' offices, where their use carried an implied endorsement by the medical community. Only a handful of promotional firms were allowed to distribute samples in hospitals and both K-C and P&G paid for their services.

Once the free samples had been used, mothers realized just how expensive disposables would be. In 1989, at a price of 18¢–36¢ each, depending on size, it would cost $1 400–1 700 to diaper one child for 2.5 years in brand name disposables. It was estimated that the cost of cloth diapers supplied by diaper services was comparable, but could be up to 20% lower depending on the type of service provided. Generic or private label disposables were about 30% cheaper than national brands, but most suffered from distressing performance problems. Cloth diapers washed at home would cost $600 or less.

Increasingly, however, price was being discounted as a purchasing criterion. With up to 75% of new mothers working outside the home, many families often valued time and convenience more than money. Similarly, as family size diminished, parents showed an increased willingness to spend money on outfitting babies. This trend meant that more and more families were prepared to pay for quality disposable diapers.

In North America, P&G and K-C were each estimated to spend a total of more than $110 million annually on diaper promotion. This promotion primarily involved commercials and coupons. Retailers often used diapers as loss leaders and the companies supported these activities through volume rebates based upon the number of tons of diapers sold. Couponing potentially saved a consumer 10–15%, but the unwritten rule was that neither firm would undercut the other.

In addition to traditional means of promotion, both firms had successfully tried other innovative measures. P&G had used Pamper Care Vans, staffed by nurses, visiting malls and fairs. The firm had also sponsored childbirth classes and infant communication literature. K-C had countered with a public relations and advertising campaign showing Huggies as the diaper used by baby Elizabeth in the movie *Baby Boom*. After the firms had found these innovative promotional methods effective, they began diverting increased resources to their use.

Both firms had a record of using extensive test marketing prior to national introduction. In the 1960s and 1970s, it took three to five years from test market to complete national distribution. P&G and K-C had cut this time down to months. Despite the pressures on rapid market launch, both firms had continued to conduct extensive test market research.

Manufacturing

The production of disposable diapers was capital intensive. The process was a continuous flow of assembly using large, complex, high speed machines. The machines were several hundred feet long with a cost range of $2–4 million, depending on speed and features. Usually several machines were grouped at each plant location. As a result of the high capital costs, capacity planning and utilization were essential to profitability. Both P&G and K-C attempted to operate their diaper machines 24 hours a day, seven days a week.

Additions to manufacturing capacity required a lead time of 12–18 months, slowing the national rollout of new products. In addition, most facilities needed several months to work the bugs out of new equipment. In the past, uncertain market share forecasts and fluctuations had led to capacity surpluses and product shortages for both firms. The competition between P&G and K-C had resulted in a history of wide swings in market share. Ironically, manufacturing costs for both firms would have benefited from reasonable industry stability.

Despite technological improvements, diapers were still a bulky product and transportation costs were estimated to comprise at least 7% of the retail value. To minimize transportation costs, both K-C and P&G had traditionally built regional plants. Transportation costs had been 50% higher prior to the introduction of super-thin, super-absorbent technology.

THE FUTURE BASIS OF COMPETITION

As the rivalry between P&G and K-C heated up, it was uncertain whether the principal focus of the competitive battle would remain fixed on technological innovation and strong promotional support. Some observers thought that consumers would likely pay for only so much technology. Yet the stakes were high and both companies were very intent on winning the battle. It was estimated that K-C and P&G both enjoyed net profit margins of 15% on diapers, as compared to less than 10% on most of their other consumer paper products. In determining the future basis of competition, both P&G and K-C had different resource bases and corporate interests. These are described in the following two sections.

Procter & Gamble Company

In 1989, P&G was a leading competitor in the U.S. household and personal care products industries with $13.3 billion in U.S. sales. For detailed financials, see Exhibit 3. P&G's products held dominant positions in North America in a variety of sectors including detergents (Tide, Cheer), bar soap (Ivory), toothpaste (Crest), shampoo (Head and Shoulders), coffee (Folgers), bakery mixes (Duncan Hines), shortening (Crisco), and peanut butter (Jiff). Disposable diapers were an important product group that comprised approximately 17% of the firm's total sales in North America.

Historically, most of P&G's annual growth had come from the expansion of existing brands where the company's marketing expertise was well known. In building these brands, P&G typically followed a strategy based on developing a superior consumer product, branding it, positioning it as a premium product, and then developing the brand through advertising and promotion. The strategy was consistent with the company's objectives of having top brands and highest market shares in its class. The company strongly believed that profitability would come from dominant market positions.

P&G's marketing strengths were supported by core competencies in research and development. With shorter product lifecycles for many non-food consumer products, R&D was becoming increasingly important to the company. Much of the company's R&D efforts were focused on upgrading existing products. However, in the late 1980s, the firm was devoting large amounts of R&D resources towards several new products, such as Olestra, a fat substitute. In 1989, total P&G research and development expenditures were $628 million, approximately $100 million of which diapers were estimated to have received. Some industry observers had suggested that the slowdown of innovations in the diaper wars may have been partially a result of P&G channelling R&D resources to new product areas.

In addition to being a dominant competitor in the U.S. household products and personal care products industries, P&G also had a strong position in several key international markets. In 1989, international sales surpassed $8.5 billion and income from international operations soared to $417 million, up almost 37% from the previous year. Sales growth in Europe and Japan was particularly impressive, with European sales up almost 15% and Japanese sales up more than 40% over 1988 figures. Performance in international markets was led by strong showings in diapers and detergents.

Kimberly-Clark

In 1989, K-C was a leading manufacturer and marketer of personal, health care and industrial products made primarily from natural and synthetic fibres. In 1989, the firm had revenues of $5.7 billion with a net income of $424 million. Detailed financials are found in Exhibits 4 and 5. Well-known products manufactured by K-C included Kleenex facial tissues, Kotex and New Freedom feminine care products, Hi-Dri household towels and Depend incontinence products. For product analysis, see Exhibit 6. Huggies disposable diapers were K-C's largest single product, contributing $1.4 billion to 1989 sales and an estimated 37% of net income.

K-C was organized into three divisions. By far the largest of these was the personal, health care and industrial products division. Personal products included disposable diapers, feminine care products, disposable hand towels and various incontinence products. Health care products included primarily surgical gowns, packs and wraps. Industrial products included cleaning wipers made of unwoven materials. Together, the division's products contributed 77% of K-C's 1989 sales and 78% of its net income.

K-C also manufactured newsprint and groundwood printing papers, premium business and correspondence papers, cigarette papers, tobacco products and specialty papers. These operations were part of the firm's second division that represented 19% of corporate sales and net income. The importance of the woodlands-related products to K-C had diminished throughout much of the 1970s and 1980s as the company shifted resources into consumer products. The two divisions were, however, closely linked to the degree that many of K-C's consumer products relied on cellulose fibres supplied by the company's woodlands operations. It was estimated that 65% of the wood pulp needs for consumer products were supplied in-house, a level considered high in the industry. It was thought that vertical control provided the advantage of flexibility and security under rapidly changing competitive conditions.

Observers noted that prices for newsprint and paper products had been highly cyclical during much of the 1980s. In 1989, there was an indication that prices were softening and would likely remain depressed as large amounts of capacity were expected to be added to the industry in the early 1990s.

The company's smallest division (4% of revenues and 3% of net income) operated a business aircraft maintenance and refurbishing subsidiary, and Midwest Express Airlines, a commercial airline based in Milwaukee, Wisconsin.

K-C's international operations provided 29% of company sales and 30% of the operating income in 1989. The company's major markets, on a consolidated basis, were Canada, the

United Kingdom, France, the Philippines and Brazil. K-C had several international equity investments; the largest, in Mexico, provided $36 million in net income. In 1989, K-C manufactured disposable diapers in nine countries and had sales in more than 100 countries. Outside North America and Europe, however, sales of disposable diapers were very low, largely because of undeveloped markets. Also, after K-C had abandoned the Japanese market, its potential for expansion into growing Asian markets was weakened.

INTERNATIONAL OPPORTUNITIES AND THREATS

After the introduction of super-thin technology from Japan, it became increasingly apparent that the competitive conditions in North America could not be viewed in isolation. By the late 1980s, competitive conditions in both Europe and Japan were having a significant influence on opportunities and threats facing North American competitors.

Japan

Historically, Japanese consumers had enjoyed better quality cloth diapers than consumers in other countries, thus slowing the acceptance of disposables. After World War II, the new Japanese government appointed a special commission to examine the national supply of diapers. The commission came up with a unique system involving a cloth diaper liner and a woven, absorbent cotton overpanty. This system received the approval of the Japanese Medical Society, significantly increasing its acceptance in traditional Japanese society. In recent years, however, the consumer benefits provided by disposables have become more apparent. Changing roles of women in Japanese society have also led to a rapid growth in the demand for disposable diapers.

P&G's competitive experiences in Japan's diaper industry were remarkably similar to its experiences in North America. In the early 1970s, P&G enjoyed a market share greater than 90% of the Japanese disposable market. However, as in North America, the product had performance problems and total market penetration was weak. P&G's biggest problem was complacency. In 1982, P&G was making its diapers with old-fashioned wood pulp. In the same year Japan's Uni-Charm Corp. (1989 Sales: $600 million) introduced a highly absorbent, granulated polymer to soak up wetness and hold it in the form of a gel, keeping babies dry longer. In 1984, KAO Corporation, a Japanese soapmaker (1989 Sales: $4 Billion) launched a similar brand of super-thin diapers under the brand name Merries. P&G did not begin selling its polymer-packed Pampers in Japan until January 1985. By that time P&G's share of the Japanese market had fallen below 7%. In 1985, Uni-Charm controlled almost half the market and KAO about 30%.

In recommitting to the Japanese market, P&G recognized that Japanese product technology was years ahead of U.S. levels. Being well positioned in Japan meant that P&G would have greater access to Japanese technology which could be exported back to the U.S to use in its battle with K-C. Because K-C had sold its interest in its Japanese equity company in 1987, it was not a major competitor in this market.

By 1989, the Japanese market had not yet reached the same level of maturity demonstrated in the U.S. While the market was worth over $1 billion in 1989, the penetration estimates varied from 35% to 50%. However, Japanese parents changed their babies twice as often as North American parents and therefore used many more diapers. Industry estimates indicated that the Japanese market, if developed to the same degree as the U.S. (85–90% penetration), would be almost as large as the U.S. This result was despite a population size of less than half. As a result, there was tremendous opportunity for growth in the Japanese market.

Faced with intense domestic competition, Japanese firms historically showed little interest in moving internationally. However, there was growing concern in North America that Japanese preoccupation with domestic competition might not last. When in 1988 KAO acquired Jergens Ltd., the U.S. producer of personal care products, several analysts speculated that this move was the beachhead for a major Japanese thrust into the North American market for personal products, including disposable diapers. There was also speculation in the press that Uni-Charm had begun negotiations with Weyerhauser to set up joint production-distribution operations in the U.S. Weyerhauser was a large, integrated U.S. forest products company that held a 50% share of the low-priced, private label market for disposable diapers. It was known that Weyerhauser had been considering a major move into the mid-priced segment for disposables.

Europe

The development of the disposable diapers industry in Europe was decidedly different from that in North America. Europeans began producing disposable diapers using a two-piece system in the early 1960s. Unlike the North American industry, however, the European industry did not experience a high degree of rationalization. There were two main reasons for this. First, Europe was composed of very different, often protected national markets. As a result, production, marketing, and distribution economies were limited. Second, no large European industry leaders emerged and foreign competitors from North America and Japan were preoccupied with domestic competitive battles. As a result, several strong country-specific firms emerged. Beginning in the mid-1980s, both P&G and K-C began to refocus attention on Europe, achieving some success. However, by 1989 the market was still fragmented with neither firm enjoying the dominant position experienced in their domestic market. The use of super-thin technology, pioneered in Japan and promoted in North America, was gradually becoming the industry norm in Europe.

Penetration of disposables diapers varied widely across Europe. In Scandinavia, the market had been saturated at least five to ten years prior to the North American market. Consumer demand appeared to be entering a new phase, becoming increasingly preoccupied with environmental concerns. Many consumers were experimenting with a variety of alternatives to disposables. Other countries were undergoing similar experiences. In France, 98 out of 100 diaper changes were done using disposables. However, in southern Europe, penetration levels were much lower and the market less sophisticated. Here, the percentage of women employed outside the home was lower, and many observers felt that these markets offered significant growth opportunities. The development of a unified internal market for Europe promised potential industry rationalization opportunities.

By 1989, P&G had established a strong presence in the fragmented European market with a major plant in Germany. At this time, K-C had not moved aggressively into this market. An issue faced by both companies was whether limited investment capital for expensive market development would be better spent at home or overseas; and if overseas, in which market?

Also of concern was the potential reaction of European firms, both overseas and in North America, to the perceived aggressiveness of U.S. firms.

ADDITIONAL ISSUES

The Environment

In 1989, almost 19 billion disposable diapers were sold in North America. This produced an estimated 4–5.5 billion pounds of discarded diapers. In some residential landfills, tests showed that disposable diapers constituted almost 5% of the total volume (industry studies showed a much lower estimate of 1–2%), leading to widespread criticism of the industry for the non-biodegradable nature of the plastics in the product. (It took an estimated 250 years for a plastic disposable diaper to biodegrade.) Environmental groups had highlighted concerns about potential health risks for sanitation workers and the threat to ground water. As the environmental movement gathered steam, many industry experts feared that unless more environmentally friendly disposable diapers were introduced, consumers would increasingly seek out alternative diapering systems.

Additional regulatory pressures were also appearing because of the perceived environmental problem. By 1989, legislation taxing, regulating or banning the sale of disposable diapers had been introduced in eleven U.S. states. It was expected that most other states would consider similar legislation during the early 1990s. However, the legislation had not yet impacted the diaper industry, as most punitive measures were not scheduled to come into effect until 1992–94.

There were signs that the seriousness of the environmental problem had not fully reached either P&G or K-C. For example, Sue Hale, associate director of P&G's public relations was quoted in 1989 as defending the firm's disposable diapers as being 60–70% biodegradable. Richard R. Nicolosi, vice-president in charge of P&G's worldwide diaper operations, was quoted as saying, "We don't think mothers are willing to give up one of the greatest new products of the postwar era."

Although K-C had a note in its 1989 annual report citing the potential seriousness of the threat, the company had been reticent about specific plans for dealing with the issue. According to Tina Barry, vice-president of corporate communications at K-C, "We're working with our suppliers to find a reliable plastic that is biodegradable. But we haven't come across any plastic material that breaks down and maintains product performance and reliability."

By 1989, no promising technologies had been introduced to address these rising environmental concerns. This situation was in contrast to the Japanese market where the market leaders had avoided or minimized the use of non-biodegradable plastics. It was also recognized that Japanese firms had considerable technological experience with biodegradable external retaining fabrics. Both P&G and K-C had yet to adopt such technology.

Both firms were trying to divert criticism by testing small-scale recycling projects. The diapers were washed and the components separated. Then the pulp was sanitized and sold to paper mills. The plastic was recovered for use in flower pots and garbage bags. However, the cost of recycling was much higher than the value of the components recovered. Added to this problem were the difficulties associated with collection of soiled diapers.

It was believed that unless environmentally friendly disposables were introduced, cloth diapers would be the main benefactor of the environmental movement. In the late 1980s, both Fisher-Price and Gerber had begun to re-examine this market and had introduced form-fitting, two-piece diaper systems. Claims that cloth diapers were environmentally friendly were countered by the industry with studies showing that the laundering of cloth diapers used six times the amount of water as was used in the manufacture of disposables and the laundering created ten times as much water pollution.

Product Diversification

As the North American disposable diaper market became saturated, both P&G and K-C sought other market opportunities that might utilize the technological expertise gained from their diaper rivalry. One avenue that seemed particularly attractive was increased development of incontinence products for adults. Incontinence products appeared to be an ideal product extension for the super-thin technology used in disposable diapers. With the improvement in incontinence product performance, sales and market penetration had exploded. Some estimated that sales in the U.S. would be as high as $1 billion in 1990, and that the potential size of this market could eventually exceed that of diapers. Of the 31 million North Americans over 65, it was estimated that about 10% had a problem with incontinence. An aging population would allow total market growth opportunities as well as growth through increased penetration.

The fight for the incontinence market was shaping up to be a replay of the disposable diaper war, with the same players. A difference in this competition was the contrasting strengths possessed by each firm in the distribution network. P&G dominated the institutional distribution channel while K-C was the leader in the commercial-retail channel. K-C had broken important new ground in this market and strengthened its distribution position by successfully developing a television advertising program that tastefully promoted the benefits of its incontinence products.

In May 1989, K-C also began the rollout of its new Huggies Pull-Up Training Pants. This product would extend the length of time children would use Huggies through months of toilet training. By November, national distribution had not yet been achieved but early market results in Western states were promising. Although P&G was watching the product carefully and had registered trademarks suitable for a similar line, the company had not yet responded with its own introduction.

Recent Events

On November 1, 1989, P&G announced the appointment of Edwin Artzt as the company's new CEO. Artzt, who was chosen for the position over an heir apparent, had directed P&G's international operations since 1984. In that capacity he had been responsible for the company's spectacular recovery in Japan, particularly in diapers, and its double digit growth in Asia and Europe.

K-C was particularly concerned about the possible impact that Artzt's appointment might have on its intense competition with P&G in the North American diaper industry. Managers at K-C wondered whether the appointment of Artzt signalled a shift in P&G's emphasis away from the U.S. market place. They also speculated whether his appointment was designed to strengthen P&G's access to new Japanese technology that could produce more environmentally friendly diapers. In response to these concerns, K-C managers wondered what sort of action to take, either internationally or in North America.

As a backdrop to the technological challenges that lay ahead, there had been ongoing litigation between P&G and K-C over the use of proprietary technologies. P&G had sued K-C for patent infringement on technology developed for elastic waistbands. K-C countersued, claiming P&G had unlawfully monopolized the market for disposable diapers and was in violation of antitrust laws. While industry observers did not expect significant damages to be awarded in either suit—indeed, neither firm had noted material reserves on its financial statements—both P&G and K-C remained very interested in and suspicious of the other's research activities.

With external pressures mounting, the nature of the competition in the North American disposable diaper industry showed signs of change in 1989. For the first time, neither of the two competitors had introduced major product improvements; instead, each made style changes. In the summer of 1989, P&G had introduced His and Hers diapers with designer colour patterns and special absorbent pads strategically placed for boy and girl babies. P&G had backed the introduction with a huge advertising and promotional campaign which made it difficult to gauge the true market share impacts of the new products. In response, K-C had introduced mild product line extensions and had developed a similar product which was in the test marketing phase. It was estimated that a similar national product introduction for K-C would cost $50–75 million.

In responding to mounting competitive pressures, both K-C and P&G recognized that balance between short-term and long-term perspectives was essential. The focus of this balance was, however, the basis of considerable uncertainty.

EXHIBIT 1   **Market Share Data** (% of U.S. retail shipments)

Brand	1980	1981	1982	1983	1984	1985	1986	1987	1988	1989
K-C Huggies	7.1	11.7	12.3	18.1	24.0	33.0	31.0	31.3	31.7	32.0
P&G Pampers	55.7	48.0	44.7	40.0	35.0	30.5	34.0	38.0	35.6	31.6
P&G Luvs	9.8	17.2	18.0	17.7	17.5	18.4	20.0	17.0	16.1	17.4
Other	27.4	23.1	25.0	24.2	23.5	18.1	15.0	13.7	17.6	19.0

SOURCE: Various publicly available documents on product shipments.

EXHIBIT 2   **Procter & Gamble U.S. Patent Searches** (first half 1986)

Patent	Title
4 562 930	Easy-Open Laminated Container with Optional Re-closing Means and Method of Making
* 4 563 185	Disposable Diaper Having Elasticized Waistband with Non-Linear Severed Edge
4 564 633	Compositions and Methods Useful for Producing Analgesia
4 566 884	Ether Polycarboxylates
4 568 556	Margarine Product and Process
4 571 391	Chromium Acetylacetonate as a Dietary Supplement and Pharmaceutical Agent
* 4 571 924	Method and Apparatus of Manufacturing Porous Pouches Containing Granular Product
* 4 573 966	Disposable Waste-Containment Garment
* 4 576 962	Prostaglandin Analogues
* 4 578 068	Absorbent Laminate Structure
* 4 578 071	Disposable Absorbent Article Having an Improved Liquid Migration Resistant Perimeter Construction
* 4 578 073	Composite Waste-Containment Garment Having Disposable Elasticized Insert
4 578 200	Fabric Softeners
4 582 216	Easy Open-Reclosable Container with Pouring Lip/Drain Surface
4 584 203	Dough Rolling Process for Laminated Cookies
4 589 676	Sanitary Napkin
4 590 006	Oral Compositions
4 591 533	Coffee Product and Process
4 594 184	Chlorine Bleach Compatible Liquid Detergent Compositions
4 596 714	Process for Making a Baked Filled Snack

* Patents related to Disposable Diaper Research.
SOURCE: First Boston Equity Research, August 1986.

EXHIBIT 3 **Proctor & Gamble Consolidated Statement of Earning**
(millions of dollars except per share amounts)

	Year Ended June 30		
	1989	*1988*	*1987*
Income			
Net sales	$21 398	$19 336	$17 000
Interest and other income	291	155	163
	21 689	19 491	17 163
Costs and Expenses			
Cost of products sold	13 371	11 880	10 411
Marketing, administrative and other expenses	5 988	5 660	4 977
Interest expense	391	321	53
Provision for restructuring	—	—	805
	19 750	17 861	16 546
Earnings Before Income Taxes	1 939	1 630	617
Income Taxes	733	610	290
Net Earnings	1 206	1 020	327

Segment Information (millions of dollars)

Geographic Areas		*U.S.*	*Inter-national*	*Corporate*	*Total*
Net Sales	1987	$11 805	$5 524	$ (329)	$17 000
	1988	12 423	7 294	(381)	19 336
	1989	13 312	8 529	(443)	21 398
Net Earnings*	1987	329	120	(122)	327
	1988	864	305	(149)	1 020
	1989	927	417	(138)	1 206

* Net earnings have been reduced by $357 million in the U.S. and $102 million in International by the provision for restructuring.

EXHIBIT 3   (continued)

Consolidated Balance Sheet (millions of dollars)

	June 30	
	1989	*1988*
Assets		
Current assets	6 578	5 593
Property Plant and Equipment	6 793	6 778
Goodwill and Other Intangible Assets	2 305	1 944
Other Assets	675	505
Total	$16 351	$14 820
Liabilities and Shareholders' Equity		
Current liabilities	4 656	4 224
Long-Term Debt	3 698	2 462
Other Liabilities	447	475
Deferred Income Taxes	1 335	1 322
Shareholders' Equity	6 215	6 337
Total	$16 351	$14 820

SOURCE: Procter & Gamble, *1989 Annual Report.*

EXHIBIT 4 — Kimberly-Clark Corporation and Subsidiaries Consolidated Income Statement

(millions of dollars except per share amounts)

	Year Ended December 31		
	1989	*1988*	*1987*
Net sales	$5 733.6	$5 393.5	$ 4 884.7
Cost of products sold	3 654.1	3 404.2	3 065.9
Distribution expenses	195.8	185.2	181.2
Gross profit	1 883.7	1 804.1	1 637.6
Advertising promotion and selling expense	813.4	784.1	674.9
Research expense	118.0	110.9	110.5
General expense	278.9	268.5	266.1
Operating profit	673.4	640.6	586.1
Interest income	19.3	11.2	7.2
Other income	24.2	24.2	26.2
Interest expense	(68.2)	(80.6)	(65.6)
Other expense	(17.9)	(11.5)	(19.8)
Income before income taxes	630.8	583.9	534.1
Provision for income taxes	242.4	229.8	230.5
Income before equity interests	388.4	354.1	303.6
Share of net income of equity companies	49.3	46.0	35.3
Minority owners' share of subsidiaries' net income	(13.9)	(21.5)	(13.7)
Net income	$ 423.8	$ 378.6	$ 325.0

EXHIBIT 4   (continued)

Consolidated Balance Sheet (millions of dollars)

	1989	1988
Assets		
Total current assets	$1 443.2	$1 278.3
Net fixed assets	3 040.9	2 575.3
Investments in equity companies	296.6	291.7
Deferred charges and other assets	142.3	121.8
	$4 923.0	$4 267.6
Liabilities		
Total current liabilities	$1 263.2	$ 925.7
Long-term debt	745.1	743.3
Other non-current liabilities	79.9	53.7
Deferred income taxes	643.5	585.0
Minority owners' interests in subsidiaries	105.5	94.3
Total stockholders' equity	2 085.8	1 865.5
	$4 923.0	$4 267.6

SOURCE: Kimberly-Clark, *1989 Annual Report.*

EXHIBIT 5 **Kimberly-Clark Corporation and Subsidiaries Analysis of 1989 Consolidated Operating Results** (millions of dollars)

Geographic Areas	1989	% Change vs. 1988	% of 1989 Consolidated
Sales			
North America	$4 664.0	+ 6.4%	81.3%
Outside North America	1 087.1	+ 6.0	19.0
Adjustments	(17.5)		(.3)
Consolidated	$5 733.6	+ 6.3%	100.0%
Net Income			
North America	$ 316.7	+ 12.1%	74.8%
Outside North America	107.1	+ 11.3	25.2
Consolidated	$ 423.8	+ 11.9%	100.0%

SOURCE: Kimberly-Clark, *1989 Annual Report.*

EXHIBIT 5   (continued)

Segment Breakdown 1981–89 (millions of dollars)

	1981	1982	1983	1984	1985	1986	1987	1988	1989
Net Sales									
Consumer Products Division	$2 103	$2 205	$2 464	$2 734	$3 172	$3 370	$3 809	$4 165	$4 481
Forestry Division	$ 781	742	795	845	856	876	1 001	1 121	1 096
Aviation Division	44	61	75	97	118	99	125	166	211
Subtotal	$2 928	$3 008	$3 334	$3 676	$4 146	$4 345	$4 935	$5 452	$5 788
(Interclass)	(42)	(62)	(60)	(60)	(73)	(42)	(50)	(59)	(54)
Total	$2 886	$2 946	$3 274	$3 616	$4 073	$4 303	$4 885	$5 393	$5 734
Operating Income									
Consumer Products Division	$ 171	$ 173	$ 221	$ 263	$ 361	$ 363	$ 434	$ 435	$ 535
Forestry Division	120	109	118	139	162	145	177	204	129
Aviation Division	3	7	8	11	2	9	13	23	26
Subtotal	$ 294	$ 289	$ 347	$ 413	$ 525	$ 516	$ 624	$ 662	$ 690
Corporate	(16)	(19)	(31)	(38)	(39)	(32)	(38)	(21)	(17)
Total	$ 278	$ 270	$ 316	$ 375	$ 486	$ 485	$ 586	$ 641	$ 673
Return on Average Assets									
Consumer Products Division	11.4%	10.5%	12.0%	12.7%	15.3%	14.0%	15.9%	14.2%	15.0%
Forestry Division	22.5	19.6	20.4	23.9	27.1	22.8	26.0	27.7	15.7
Aviation Division	5.0	10.8	12.3	15.0	2.8	12.3	17.0	17.4	6.5
Subtotal	14%	12.7%	13.9%	15.1%	17.4%	15.7%	17.9%	12.0%	11.9%
Unallocated/Interclass	N.M.	N.M.	N.M.	N.M.	N.M.	N.M.	N.M.	N.M.	N.M.
Total	11.7%	10.6%	11.3%	12.3%	14.6%	13.5%	15.5%	11.9%	11.7%

SOURCE: "Duff & Phelps Research Report," Kimberly-Clark, *Annual Report*, November 1988.

EXHIBIT 6   Kimberly-Clark Consumer, Health Care Industrial Products (millions of dollars)

Domestic Categories	1987 Est. Sales	1987 Est. Oper. Profit	1988 Est. Mkt. Share	Est. Rank of Brands	Major Competitors/Mkt. Share
Disposable Diapers	$1 220	$220	32%	2	Pampers 35% Luvs 16% (PG); Private Label 17%
Facial Tissue	450	52	45%	1	Puffs 17% (PG); Scotties 10% (Scott Paper)
Feminine Pads	270	21	26%	2	J&J 37%; Always 20% (PG); Maxithins 5%; Private Label 12%
Tampons	30	2	6%	4	Tambrands 58%; Playtex 26%; J&J 8%
Paper Household Towels	170	10	10%	4	Scott Paper 23%; PG 20%; James River 11%
Bathroom Tissue	35	0	N.M.	N.M.	PG 30%; Scott Paper 19%; James River 13%
Table Napkins	30	2	N.M.	N.M.	Scott Paper 23%; James River 8%
Consumer Incont. Products	60	3	49%	1	Attends 28% (PG); Serenity 8% (J&J); Private Label 15%
Inst./Ind. Tissue Products	170	5			
Inst. Healthcare	180	4			
Other Non-wovens	176	4			
Medical	30	2			
Total Domestic	2 821	325			
Canada	250	20			
Sub-Total North America	3 071	345			
Outside North America	738	89			
Total Consumer Division	3 809	434			

SOURCE: "Duff & Phelps Research Report," Kimberly-Clark, *Annual Report*, November 1988.

CANADIAN AIRLINES CORP.

Joseph N. Fry, Roderick E. White and Nick Bontis

CASE 5

In early 1995, the senior management of Canadian Airlines Corp. (CA) set a June 30 deadline for the completion of plans and negotiations aimed at improving the airline's cost position by some 14% per available seat mile, or approximately $325 million on an annualized basis. This initiative, they anticipated, would improve profitability and cashflow enough to allow the airline over time to renew its fleet and take advantage of new transborder and international markets. The alternative, in their view, was bleak. The company would have to downsize, which meant focusing operations on currently profitable international routes, exiting many markets and implementing major layoffs.

The cost savings were being pursued by an unprecedented joint management–labour group called the Strategic Planning Steering Committee (SPSC). The SPSC, which included representatives from five of six of CA's unions, had worked to achieve a mutual understanding of CA's performance and to clarify its basic strategic options. The SPSC had concluded that change was necessary—simply continuing on an "as is" basis left the airline exposed to the next industry downturn and insufficiently profitable in the good years to support the necessary fleet renewal program. On these grounds the SPSC had created alternative growth/cost-cut versus downsize scenarios, referred to respectively as Plan A and Plan B. They had then initiated projects and negotiations aimed at achieving the cost improvements deemed essential for the success of Plan A.

As June 30 approached it was becoming increasingly apparent that the SPSC, in spite of substantial progress in which improvements amounting to some $110 million (of the $325 million target) had been agreed, was not going to be able to complete in time all the necessary negotiations and arrangements. An immediate issue for senior management was whether to continue with Plan A negotiations, or to honour the self-imposed deadline and take steps to implement Plan B.

CA was no stranger to critical situations. Its development, from a profitable regional carrier in the mid-1980s to one of Canada's two national airlines in 1995, was marked by a series of difficult challenges. The airline industry had proven to be a tough environment in which to profit and survive. Management was abundantly aware of this, and understood that the history of the airline, and in parallel, that of the industry, was important in shaping perceptions of the current situation, and of the possibilities for dealing with it.

BEGINNINGS TO 1985: THE INDUSTRY UNDER REGULATION

The path of development of the airline industry had been dominated by two basic federal government policies—government ownership and regulation. Under the first, the government chose in 1937 to form Trans Canada Airlines, the predecessor of Air Canada (AC), as a crown corporation and as its chosen instrument for the development of a domestic and, subsequently, an international air transportation infrastructure. Under the second, the government chose to regulate the industry, establishing agencies, most latterly the Canada Transport Commission (CTC), with the authority to pursue "public convenience and necessity" in approving, for example, licences for new routes, exit from established routes, fares, schedules, and mergers and acquisitions.

Over the 50 plus years preceding the early 1980s the industry grew, under regulation, from a host of early operators into a loose, three-tiered structure of scheduled national, regional and commuter/short-haul carriers (see Exhibit 1). Charter, or non-scheduled service was a fourth segment.

THE NATIONAL CARRIERS By the early 1980s, there were two major Canadian-based carriers, AC and privately owned CP Air (Canadian Pacific Air Lines). Though both airlines operated domestic and international services, AC was, by a factor of three, the dominant carrier (see Table 1). Domestically, AC's trunk or long haul network covered Canada's major cities. This network was supported by AC's own regional service which was particularly strong in the East, and was bolstered in the West by cooperation with a regional carrier, PWA (Pacific Western Airlines). Relatively speaking, CP Air (Canadian Pacific Air Lines) had a thin national network, having been constrained by regulation to a secondary role behind AC. CP Air was quite strong regionally in the West but relied very heavily on interline arrangements with regional carriers for coverage and feed in the East.

The international services of the two airlines were split by government policy. International air traffic was controlled by a series of bilateral agreements between countries. In setting up these agreements and designating the Canadian carrier, the Canadian government had followed a policy referred to as "division of the skies." AC was made the primary and almost exclusive carrier on routes to Europe, the U.S. and the Caribbean while CP Air was favoured over the Pacific and to South America.

THE REGIONAL CARRIERS Prior to deregulation there were a number of "independent" regional airlines—Pacific Western Airlines (PWA), Nordair, Québecair and Eastern Provincial Airlines—flying jet aircraft on mid-length, domestic routes and feeding traffic to the transcontinental and international carriers. For the most part the regional airlines operated in cooperation with the national carriers, providing feed from, and distribution to, points that the latter were not vitally interested in. Where routes overlapped there was competition, but always within the moderating context of regulation. And, at the margin, the regionals were constrained from expansion into long-haul by their equipment, which was typically small jets such as Boeing 737s, and again, by regulation.

Among the regionals, PWA (see Table 1) was notable for the success of its operations in the West and North and for its apparent expansion ambitions as and when regulatory limits were relaxed. PWA owned a modern fleet of 737s and was pressing these into extensions of its regional service, including a Calgary to Toronto flight which was legitimized by a stop in Brandon, Manitoba. At the same time, PWA served in an important feeder role to AC for Western Canada. In anticipation of deregulation, AC had started looking for more secure feed and thus, closer ties with PWA. So in 1985 for example, AC and PWA purchased equal equity positions in Air Ontario (a short-haul carrier).

The market value of PWA common shares in 1985 equalled about $150 million versus a book value of $200 million and a liquidation value (before severance and other costs) of $420 million. The high liquidation value according to industry analysts was due to the market value of PWA's 737 aircraft being 100% higher than book value.

TABLE 1   Profiles of AC, PWA and CP Air

Measure	AC (1982)	AC (1985)	PWA (1982)	PWA (1985)	CP (1982)	CP (1985)
Revenue ($ million)	2 305.9	2 772.5	318.7	352.7	862.8	1 119.2
Operating Income	−25.8	1.5	25.3	6.2	−26.2	34.7
Net Income	−35.6	−14.8	6.3	13.4	−34.6	−23.5
RPM* (billions)	13.6	14.1	1.3	1.5	5.5	7.0
Number of Employees	23 300	22 100	3 046	2 873	7 994	8 578

Note: *Refer to Appendix A for definitions.
SOURCE: Company Reports.

THE COMMUTER/SHORT-HAUL CARRIERS By 1984 there were 700 smaller Canadian carriers that operated one or more propjet aircraft on short and often remote routes. It was uneconomical to fly larger jet aircraft on low traffic routes of less than 250 kilometres. These services seldom overlapped those of the nationals and regionals. In spite of their numbers the short-haul carriers accounted for only 8% of the passengers flown.

THE CHARTER CARRIERS Prior to deregulation charter service was entirely separate from regularly scheduled service. Charters began by carrying plane-loads of vacationers to international tourist destinations. By the 1980s a domestic charter business had developed. No mixing of charter and scheduled service was allowed and certain "fences" were imposed: membership in a group, minimum stays, no change in itinerary or cancellation, full prepayment, etc. In order to improve their equipment utilization, all of Canada's scheduled carriers operated charter services, but these were of minor importance to their total revenues—about 3% in the case of AC and CP Air, and 17% for PWA. Wardair was the foremost of the purely charter operators and had built up a solid business and a remarkable reputation for fine service.

Anticipating Deregulation

In the late 1970s and early 1980s dissatisfaction had built among consumer groups and industry participants. Regulation was variously thought to limit service, increase prices, and stifle innovation, and to be increasingly irrelevant to the purposes for which it was created, such as safety, reasonable cost, and national accessibility. National governments had a history of using their airline(s) to achieve social and technological objectives, and undeniably, the motives influencing government engagement in an airline overlapped into an expression of national pride. Governments had, among other things, restricted ownership, controlled prices, set operating and safety standards, and allocated routes and frequencies.

However, regulation had not guaranteed carriers' monopolies on all routes. If traffic between two cities could support an additional carrier, or the incumbent carrier was deemed not to be providing adequate service, than a competitor's licence application might be approved. However, the incumbent, as part of the approval process, had the opportunity to object. The nature of this competitive process was characterized by orderly arrangements of "give and take" between the CTC and the airlines as well as among the airlines themselves, where allied relationships were the norm (e.g., PWA as a regional feeder for AC).

The national carriers were not exactly prospering in this regulated context either. After taking a profit hit in the 1981 recession, neither AC nor CP Air was able to report more than marginal profits and losses as the economy improved through 1985. Critics of regulation also lashed out at AC, claiming that its status as a crown corporation had allowed it to become dominant, but not particularly driven by concerns for cost, service and profits.

As the disenchantment with a regulated industry grew, the federal government started to "liberalize" regulation and give notice of impending deregulation. By 1985, the honourable Don Mazankowski, the Minister of Transport at the time, introduced a paper entitled "Freedom to Move" which criticized the economic regulation of air transport and proposed future steps toward a deregulated regime.

With deregulation looming, AC seemed to be courting PWA in order to face CP Air head-on in Western Canada. At one point it was rumoured that AC and PWA were discussing an arrangement under which AC would fly all the trunk routes using wide-bodied aircraft and PWA would fly shorter hauls in narrow-bodied aircraft. Furthermore, there was talk of the pending privatization of AC, as federal officials and airline analysts realized that only a private AC—removed from the grasp of the government—would survive an industry shakedown expected from post-deregulation.

Lessons from the U.S. Deregulation Experience

The U.S. experience with deregulation was traumatic. Deregulation was introduced in late 1978 with no provisions for a transitional phase. Airlines were no longer required to apply for route licensing or fare changes. Any carrier was able to fly any route provided it was "fit, willing and able." Many carriers expanded rapidly by expanding their route structures, increasing flight frequencies, purchasing new equipment, and acquiring other carriers. The resulting overcapacity led to an almost continuous series of price wars. These, in turn made cost a critical variable for survival. But under regulation, costs had been of secondary importance and most carriers were poorly prepared for this dramatic change.

In the inevitable industry shakeout some long standing airlines were put out of business or onto the ropes (e.g., Branff, PanAm, Eastern), some new operators went in and out of business (People Express), and the remaining healthy carriers pressed to find elements of competitive advantage and security. The carriers that survived developed strategic tools such as frequent flyer plans (FFPs) and computerized reservation systems (CRSs)—see Appendix A for an elaboration of these and other industry terms. They also moved to establish hub and spoke networks and to attempt to dominate particular hubs. But the wars continued nonetheless in what observers called "the pursuit of Pyrrhic victories in market share."

1985–90: DEREGULATION AND RESTRUCTURING

As deregulation proceeded the Canadian airline industry started into a period of rapid consolidation. By 1990 there would be just two vertically integrated carrier groups, Air Canada and Canadian Airlines (see Exhibit 1 for a genealogy of major Canadian air carriers). The major events of the 1985–90 period were the emergence of CA, the privatization of AC, the absorption of the second and third level carriers into the major groups, and the emergence of a bitter rivalry between the AC and CA camps.

The Emergence of Canadian Airlines

CA emerged in the 1985–90 period as the consequence of an aggressive and unexpected acquisitions program by PWA of first CP Air and later Wardair.

THE CP AIR ACQUISITION With the door to unregulated expansion opening, CP Air moved in 1985–86 to acquire three eastern regional carriers—Eastern Provincial Airways (EPA), Nordair, and Québecair—and seemed to be rising to pose a serious challenge to AC's dominance in Eastern Canada. But CP Air's parent, the railway-based conglomerate CP Ltd., was ambiguous about airline expansion, and when a chance came in 1987 to sell CP Air, it did. The buyer, in a move that shocked the industry, was the much smaller PWA. The purchase price was $300 million, some of which was funded by a previously arranged major fleet refinancing on the part of PWA.

To help fund expansion, PWA had earlier entered into a major financing transaction involving the forward sale and sale-leaseback of 16 of its Boeing 737-200 aircraft. The market for new and used aircraft had been very buoyant through the 1980s. Aircraft in use were appreciating in value; positions for delivery of new aircraft were traded as a valuable commodity. Gains in the purchase and sale of aircraft had become a major element in airline profit and cash flow. For PWA, the fleet sale generated net cash infusions of $24 and $67 million for 1985 and 1986.

THE WARDAIR ACQUISITION By January 1988, Wardair was straining to stay in flight. Through its history it had been a successful charter operator, but with deregulation, it had launched an aggressive and, in retrospect, foolhardy campaign to become a major scheduled domestic carrier. Wardair triggered a fierce round of price wars which it had neither the financial capacity nor the operating abilities to sustain. So once again, in April 1989, CA surprised the airline industry by announcing the purchase of Wardair, including its brand new fleet of Airbus aircraft.

By late 1989, fuel prices began to rise quickly as a result of significant increases in the price of crude oil. Faced with these economic trends, CA made the decision to amalgamate its operations with Wardair as quickly as possible. A new fleet plan was announced. The plan included the sale of the Wardair Airbus A310 aircraft for a projected $900 million in proceeds. This money would be used to substantially reduce the company's debt and assist in the funding of replacement aircraft.

PWA had begun the period of deregulation as a regional carrier flying one type of aircraft (Boeing 737). Following the CP Air and Wardair acquisitions it was a major international and domestic carrier flying a mixed fleet of aircraft from Europe in the east to China in the west, from Resolute Bay in the North to Buenos Aires in the South. The new operating entity bore the name Canadian Airlines but in the beginning it was actually an amalgam of its six precursor companies—PWA, CP Air, EPA, Nordair, Québecair and Wardair. Operational and cultural integration was underway but still incomplete.

The new CA had emerged as AC's major competitor. All inter-relationships between PWA/CA and Air Canada were severed. Interline agreements were terminated and PWA's interest in Air Ontario was sold to AC. While still smaller than AC there was a feeling at CA that AC was vulnerable; they believed that years of regulation and government ownership had left AC with high costs and stodgy management.

The Privatization of Air Canada

With deregulation in the horizon, AC and others had argued that its status as a crown corporation would hold back its ability to compete effectively. The arguments prevailed and in 1988 AC announced a planned public offering of treasury common shares, proceeds to be used for the acquisition of aircraft and other operational needs. The initial offering yielded $234 million. Full privatization of the airline occurred in July 1989, when the Federal Government offered its remaining 57% interest for $474 million. The privatization of AC represented a recognition by the federal government that it did not require a state-owned airline to fulfil its public policy goals. AC was now free to pursue a purely commercial strategy.

The Decade Ends

The structure of the airline industry had changed dramatically during the 1980s. By the end of the decade two major integrated carriers had emerged. Each ranged from short-haul through regional, transcontinental and international service. While broadly similar there were important differences.

The outcome of the formation of CA was a faltering airline. AC posted better earnings in 1989 and 1990. The Wardair purchase had created financial pressures because the cashflow from the sale of Wardair's aircraft did not materialize as expected. Furthermore, CA's profits were under pressure from the price war, first initiated by Wardair but continued sporadically by AC and CA.

The restructuring of the industry had left the two carriers battling in a very competitive, deregulated environment. CA and AC, once allies, now faced off in a new era of competitive rivalry (see Table 2 for relative positions and Exhibit 3 for financial data).

1990–95: COMPETITIVE RIVALRY

The intense rivalry between CA and AC continued into the 1990s—price and capacity battles for market share were commonplace. Both airlines experienced substantial losses but CA, partly because it had entered the battle in a weakened state, verged on bankruptcy. Because of its dire circumstances CA reluctantly considered merger proposals from AC. But these discussions in no way diminished the continued rivalry in the marketplace.

TABLE 2   Relative Positions in 1990

Measure	Canadian Airlines	Air Canada
Cashflow from Operations	–$ 43 million	$ 41 million
Interest and Lease Coverage	0.60 X	1.01 X
Current Ratio	0.74 to 1	1.47 to 1
Debt to Equity	2.47 to 1	3.63 to 1
Total Fleet	88	115
Average Passenger Journey	2 479 km	1 405 km
Personnel Cost per ASK	2.3¢	3.0¢
Canadian Destinations	109 cities	74 cities
United States Destinations	7 cities	19 cities
International Destinations	24 cities	25 cities
Frequency: Toronto–Montréal	15 per day	20 per day
Frequency: Toronto–Vancouver	6 per day	6 per day
Frequency: Vancouver–Calgary	14 per day	7 per day

SOURCE: Company Reports.

Capacity Wars

AC and CA were unable, through the marketplace, to achieve capacity and fare levels that allowed either airline to be profitable. During this period AC aggressively added capacity even when confronted by declining load factors. In late 1992 CA had announced a 15% reduction in domestic capacity. AC did not follow suit. CA claimed that AC was flooding the market with excess capacity and driving down fares and load factors. It launched a $1 billion law suit against its rival for alleged damages. The capacity situation continued to be so problematic that Rhys Eyton, chairman of CA at the time, appealed to the federal Transport Minister to take action. Eyton said CA

> desperately wants to avoid 'reregulation' of the airline industry but it may be necessary on a temporary basis if AC refuses to cut its capacity, something CA has been willing to do.

He went on to say

> Canada's airline industry is being 'decimated' because of an estimated 20% overcapacity in the domestic industry (a figure also quoted by AC). We'll both be out of business if we allow this to go on.[1]

There was no direct response by the government to this appeal. As a result of the intense rivalry (and poor market conditions) CA lost over $500 million in 1992, effectively eliminating the company's accumulated equity. This opened the door to merger proposals from AC which CA's board could not ignore.

Merger Proposals

AC made various merger and purchase offers to CA beginning in 1992. In September 1992 the boards of the two companies reached an agreement to pursue a merger. The reaction by CA employees was immediate and vociferous, as suggested by the following report:

> "Better dead than red," said a pilot in the uniform of Canadian Airlines. With those four words he expressed the depth and emotion that surrounds the proposed merger of Canadian Airlines and Air Canada and illustrated just how difficult it will be to meld the blue and red cultures if the deal goes through. "We don't understand this hatred," an Air Canada pilot said. "It doesn't seem reasonable. As it is we work together now, sharing information, like what the ride is like." But whether it's reasonable or not, many Canadian Airlines employees dread the thought of working in an Air Canada environment, and their dread grows as merger of the two carriers comes closer to reality .... if the airlines are merged, at least 6 000 and possibly many more employees will lose their jobs. That has emotions running high at both airlines but especially at Canadian Airlines. Many employees believe that because theirs is the younger company, it will bear the brunt of the layoffs.[2]

AC dropped their merger proposal two months later stating that the consolidation would not produce a single, viable merged airline and would not be in the best interests of its shareholders. At the same time, the federal government reluctantly agreed to loan CA $50 million to aid in its restructuring plan—an amount much smaller than the company had requested. Soon after CA temporarily ceased payments to its creditors.

During the failed merger proposal from AC, CA had also been negotiating with AMR Corp., the parent company of American Airlines. In November 1992 they announced a comprehensive strategic alliance which included a $246 million equity infusion from AMR, a marketing arrangement whereby each airline would participate in the other's FFP and a "services agreement" between the airlines. But several hurdles remained before the alliance could be consummated.

---

[1] *Globe and Mail,* February 19, 1993.
[2] *Globe and Mail,* October 13, 1992.

The deal required a restructuring of CA's financial arrangements with shareholders, lenders and lessors. It involved a substantial debt to equity conversion. A continuation and expansion of the $200 million Employee Investment Plan was also needed. Substantially all of CA's employees were participating in a payroll reduction plan whereby employees received a portion of their wages, to a maximum of $200 million over a four-year period, in the form of rights to acquire common shares of the company. Last but not least, the completion of the services agreement involved the withdrawal by CA from its Gemini CRS and the transfer of those activities to AMR's Sabre system. In the financial press AMR Corp. pointed out that, among other things, its investment in CA was justified by the incremental contribution to its Sabre system.

Gemini was a joint venture between CA, AC and the Covia[3] group. In order to withdraw CA needed the approval of the other partners. This was something AC was not willing to provide. CA, in a precedent setting legal manoeuvre, appealed to the Competition Tribunal to set aside the Gemini partnership agreement.

In November 1993, CA was released by the Competition Tribunal from Gemini. AC promptly appealed this decision. AC then offered to purchase CA's international routes for $250 million in cash and the assumption of $800 million in obligations. CA's international routes—specifically the Pacific Rim destinations—were a sought after asset. Since AC was traditionally precluded by the government for these highly profitable routes, it felt that the only alternative was to purchase them outright. Not willing to give up its lucrative routes, but desperately short of cash, CA rejected the deal and pursued its partnership with AMR Corp.

In January 1994 AC changed its tactics and dropped its appeal of the Gemini decision, clearing the way for the CA–AMR alliance. The next day AC was awarded the right to fly to Osaka, Japan by the federal government. Speculation about a "deal" was later confirmed when a disgruntled Hollis Harris (Chairman, President and CEO of AC) declared:

> Some members of the cabinet looked at me right in the eye and said that if I would pull the appeal on the Gemini issue and let them go with American Airlines they promised I would have Osaka, Hong Kong, and the Peoples Republic of China negotiated. I said 'you've got a deal.'[4]

However, AC was not immediately given rights to Hong Kong or China as reportedly promised.

The Global Perspective

While AC and CA were locked in their intense rivalry the world of global air travel was changing. Total international traffic would grow at 5.6% a year, while world-wide domestic traffic would increase by 4.7% a year.[5] In particular, the Pacific Rim and Latin America were growing faster than any other region. Global networks were emerging to exploit this growth. It was predicted that eventually air travel would be dominated by less than a dozen global airline consortia. Four of the most imposing groups were: British Airways–US Air–Quantas; KLM–Northwest; Delta–Swissair–Singapore Airlines; and Lufthansa–United Airlines. Neither AC or CA was part of a significant global consortia although both had established links to carriers outside of Canada.

---

[3] Controlled by United Airlines.

[4] *Globe and Mail,* December 22, 1994.

[5] Boeing Commercial Airline Group, *Current Market Outlook,* May 1994.

During the early 1990s AC had pursued an ownership position with USAir. Its route structure had a good fit with AC's network. However, British Airways eventually secured an ownership position with USAir, further developing its global network while taking AC out of the equation.

AC was eager to find a large American partner. In April 1993, AC completed a $450 million investment in Houston-based Continental Airlines. Continental had just emerged from Chapter 11 bankruptcy protection (under which it had operated since December 1990). AC's equity interest was equal to 19.6%. Continental was three times AC's size based upon capacity (see Exhibit 2). But their route structures had few points of interconnection; only Houston and Newark.

With the Gemini dispute settled, CA established a strong alliance with American Airlines (AA). AA was the largest domestic U.S. carrier (see Exhibit 2). The link with CA made a strong North American alliance. In 1995, after the ratification of the Canada–U.S. "open skies" agreement, CA and AA integrated their transborder flight schedules and set up extensive code-sharing. However, AA was less dominant internationally. In particular, the Pacific Rim was a weak area. CA's Far East routes offered some help in addressing this shortcoming.

Canada–U.S. Open Skies Treaty

The weakest link in CA's route structure relative to AC, was in its limited number of destinations to the U.S. In 1990, CA had only one-third the number of U.S. destinations of AC. By 1995, the disparity was slightly diminished. But what CA really needed was a new air travel agreement between Canada and the U.S. Eventually they got it.

In February 1995 a new "open-skies" agreement was signed. It allowed Canadian carriers immediate access to United States destinations without restrictions on capacity, frequency or aircraft, with the exception of Chicago's O'Hare airport and New York's La Guardia airport, which both had restrictions on takeoff and landing slots. American carriers had similar rights, except their unlimited access to Toronto was postponed for three years, and to Montréal and Vancouver for two years. The deal did not provide for cabotage rights within each country's domestic market (see Appendix A for glossary of terms and Appendix C for further description on U.S. carriers).

Competitive Threat from the Charters

While the country's dominant scheduled carriers, CA and AC, jockeyed for position in the marketplace, other contenders emerged to occupy a significant and expanding position. The growth of domestic charter airlines over the past few years had been substantial. Domestic traffic on charter carriers had swelled from 19 700 passengers in 1989 to almost 789 000 in 1993.[6] Table 3 from Statistics Canada shows how the rising contenders have grown in importance.

---

[6] SOURCE: Statistics Canada.

TABLE 3 Charters Increase of Market Share on Key City Pairs

City Pair	1989	1993
Vancouver–Toronto	5.5%	31.4%
Montréal–Vancouver	3.0%	28.3%

A CA executive shed some further insight on the remarkable growth of the charters:

> Charters' ability to reallocate capacity to suit demand is one reason for their competitive edge. The key factor to their success, however, is their numerous cost advantages—lower ownership costs, lower administration costs, a simplified fleet and lower unit-labour costs [both wages and productivity], to name a few. All of this adds up to an average cost per ASM ranging from four and a half to seven cents, compared to ours at twelve and a half cents.

CA and AC still offered many advantages over chartered carriers, especially for business travellers, who desired frequency, consistency and service and wanted to associate themselves with the scheduled carriers' FFPs. Charters, on the other hand, had minimal service and did not own their own CRSs. Although charters had been limited by their "non-scheduled service" status under regulation, they had since been freed from that constraint. Nevertheless, they chose to keep many features of charter service after the policy change, and continued to provide the lowest priced service. The presence of low-cost domestic charter carriers made it difficult for AC and CA to raise fares and manage capacity.

With the new "open skies" agreement in place, it was possible for CA to increase its exposure to the U.S. Furthermore, CA was strategically better positioned for a future as an international carrier given its foothold on key international routes to the Pacific Rim and Latin America (two of the fastest growing regions in the world) and its alliance with American Airlines (one of the largest carriers in the world). Given its weak financial position, CA still continued to seek ways to increase its customer base and thus raise its load factors and yields (see Appendix A for these and other definitions and Appendix B for a review of industry revenue and cost structure).

PRESENT SITUATION

After several dismal years, both of Canada's airlines announced improving financial performance by early 1995. Each was attempting to reposition itself to build market position, respond to cost pressures, and rehabilitate their balance sheets.

Airline employees and analysts watched the recent developments south of the border closely. Wages for equity swaps, wage reductions and productivity concessions became the norm in the US industry. Wage for equity packages had been granted at United, Northwest, America West, TWA, and most recently, at Southwest which was already the lowest cost carrier in the U.S. Southwest's pilots agreed to a ten-year contract with no wage increases in years one through five. This effectively "lowered the limbo bar" for all other North American airlines as they went through their cost reduction dance.[7]

---

[7] Tony Hine, Scotia McLeod Inc. *Transportation and Environment Services Outlook,* Dec. 8, 1994.

AC had improved its financial performance in virtually every financial and operating category and markedly improved its operating statistics (see Exhibit 3). Compared with other major airlines, AC had the most modern and efficient fleet of airplanes in the world.[8] Notwithstanding this positive news, Hollis Harris warned:

> If AC is to survive as an independent entity, and not become a branch plant of a foreign airline, growth must be our destiny—not unbridled or unfocussed growth, but sustainable growth which enhances the security of all AC stakeholders. Despite AC's return to profitability last year [1994] at near record levels, I challenge the notion that we have accomplished our mission.[9]

Senior management at AC declared that the purpose for their $500 million equity issue in the spring of 1995 was: (1) to open new international routes to Hong Kong, Madrid and Israel, (2) to buy new aircraft, (3) to improve airport facilities, and (4) for general corporate purposes. CA was still smaller than its main adversary but somewhat leaner (lower unit costs, see Exhibit 4 for a comparative graph on revenue and cost management). Although CA and its employees had already suffered through numerous challenges and concessions in the last few years, senior management understood that the recent AMR Corp. capital infusion was for debt refinancing and not any new strategic developments. The airline also recognized that its domestic operations were still not as profitable as its international routes. In order of operating income per ASM, the regions of Japan and South East Asia made the most profit for CA, while flights to Continental Europe, Northern Canada, and within the Eastern Triangle (Toronto, Montréal, Ottawa) were still struggling.

Fundamental change was required if the company was going to survive in the future. Since the unionized employees had recently become partial owners, it was only logical that they should also help decide the fate of their airline (see Table 4 for a company profile). This resulted in the forming of a new joint labour–management committee to decide upon CA's new strategic options and direction.

TABLE 4   CA Employee Profile

Period	February 1988 *(Post PWA/CP Air Merger)*	December 1989 *(Post Wardair Acquisition)*	March 1995 *(Pre SPSC Target Date)*
Union members	10 525	12 375	12 060
Non-union employees	2 712	2 671	2 179
Total	13 237	15 046	14 239

Strategic Planning Steering Committee (SPSC)

Senior management realized that if any solutions were to be found by the SPSC, they would have to involve all of the key stakeholders of the airline, including the union members who had steadily been investing in the company since late 1992. The role of the SPSC was to join labour and management together to help reduce costs, improve productivity, expand customer

---

[8] Tony Hine, Scotia McLeod Inc. *Globe and Mail*, June 10, 1994.
[9] Air Canada 1994 *Annual Report*.

loyalty, and establish a viable future for the airline. This new joint endeavour began a process of fundamentally rewriting the rules of traditional labour–management relations. All unions participated with the exception of CUPE (the union representing the flight attendants), which had declined the invitation to get involved until their contract was renegotiated in December 1995. CUPE's absence, although noticeable, did not inhibit the SPSC's progress.

The process was totally "open book," with management and labour sharing all of the operational and financial information about the airline. The urgency of CA's financial requirements was driving the SPSC's agenda. Information sharing between unions and management did not have an impeccable history. Union members had often felt that management figures were not truly reflective of the operations. However, communications in this particular process showed much improvement because management's view of the dire financial situation was reiterated by two external parties. First, the pilot's union had an opportunity to audit the figures themselves and they agreed with management's view of the unstable financials. In addition, the Boston Consulting Group came in and reviewed the organization's position with the parties concerned and again reiterated CA's precarious situation. Exhibit 5 is a copy of the letter sent to all employees of CA identifying the target date of June 30, 1995, and detailing the two broad alternatives that the SPSC believed the airline faced, namely Plan A and Plan B.

Plan A: A Blueprint for Growth

Plan A entailed achieving and using a lower cost-base to increase market share in key domestic markets, especially transcontinental routes. The airline would pursue growth only on its more profitable international, transcontinental and transborder routes, while maintaining scope and improving the profitability of selected centres in its domestic system.

This plan would allow CA to achieve financial strength and generate enough cash to finance growth (to new Pacific-rim and U.S. destinations), revitalize the fleet (to meet Stage 3 noise requirements), ward off any competitors (to compete successfully with AC and the charters), and sustain any economic recession anticipated in the late 1990s. Plan A also offered the employment stability that could only be provided by working for a financially healthy company.

The SPSC believed that the long-term impact of Plan A would be to increase revenue and capacity dramatically. Schedules would be improved to offer greater frequency to the most popular destinations. Reducing costs per ASM would improve the competitive position of CA against AC and low-cost carriers, such as Canada 3000, Royal Air and Air Transat. Further, the SPSC also hoped that this particular plan would allow for broadened employee involvement in all aspects of the decision-making process for the future.

As a prototype for Plan A, the 1995 Summer Initiative Program was proposed on the basis that a growth strategy founded on higher productivity and greater revenues could succeed. The $27 million in performance improvements identified by the program would permit the addition of three widebody aircraft—and 12% capacity—to key domestic routes. As the early summer results accumulated, however, speculation mounted as to whether the $27 million in projected contribution would be fully realized since traffic gains had been hard to come by.

One difficulty with Plan A was that in order to get the required $325 million in savings for the airline, over $125 million in concessions from the union members would have to be realized. These concessions were to be primarily in the form of productivity improvements; significant wage cuts and layoffs were not part of the plan. Employees at CA had been quite cooperative in the past, but were pessimistic about the future given that they perceived the AMR deal had not saved them as was envisioned. The tumultuous past of CA had left many employees sceptical and had strained management–union relations. If Plan A were to work, a whole new corporate-wide attitude in strategic renewal would have to take place.

Plan B: A Pattern for Reduction

The objective of Plan B was to downsize and restructure the airline. The result would be an airline that was eventually a fraction of CA's current size. The plan required exiting all unprofitable routes and routes that were not essential to support the international network. The non-core routes would be transferred to Canadian Regional and those that could not be transferred would be abandoned. Commercial alliances would be established with regional carriers to maintain domestic feed and support for Canadian Airline's FFP. In addition, all transborder routes (U.S.–Canada) would be flown largely by AA under code sharing with CA.

The SPSC envisioned a code-sharing agreement with American Airlines in order to feed CA's international and remaining domestic network. By streamlining the domestic network, CA hoped that the domestic fleet could be simplified to one wide-body aircraft type in order to maximize fleet utilization. The rest of the non-core airline components would be sold-off to generate short-term cash flow.

Under this scenario, massive layoffs would affect all areas of operation. The majority of the 737 fleet would be eliminated and all heavy maintenance would be contracted out. The difficulty with Plan B was the risk of losing security on domestic feed for CA's international flights. Also, the selling-off of unwanted equipment and space might involve significant write-offs.

Besides the two publicized alternatives that had been voiced by the SPSC, there was always the possibility of following a hybrid plan. CA could very well start with Plan A and eventually resort back to Plan B. This was considered a "stall tactic." In other words, the airline would continue with business as usual—except for a 14% lower cost base—and move later (maybe in 12 months) to drastically restructure. Conversely, if CA were to follow Plan B and become a smaller and more efficient operator, it may eventually want to grow from that position and attempt to increase its feed by further developing and expanding its route structure.

White Water at Canadian Airlines

The future of CA would entail as much "turbulence" as had been traversed in the past. For CA, the stakes were high because the carrier had said that within five years it would be the leader in all the markets in which it served.[10]

CA's Board of Directors had targeted June 30, 1995, to reach a new agreement with its unions. This mammoth task involved an unprecedented team effort among management, consultants and unions. The education campaign associated with these negotiations had created confusing and largely negative press coverage which, in turn, hurt CA's stock price on the market.

In the minds of many of those associated with CA, especially the exasperated union members, were the thoughts, "Is this just another restructuring task disguised as a management gimmick, or could this truly be the end of my job as I know it?"

---

[10] PWA Corporation (Canadian Airlines) 1994 *Annual Report*.

Senior management was now preparing a recommendation for their Board on how to proceed in the immediate period ahead.

EXHIBIT 1 Genealogy of Major Canadian Air Carriers

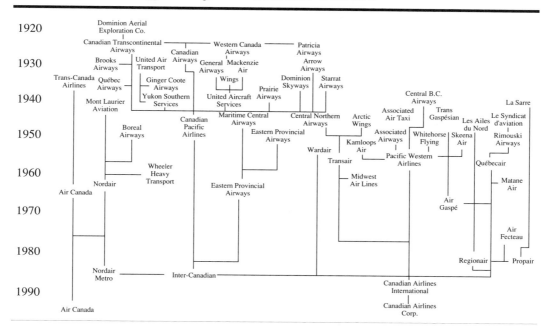

Industry Structure Before Deregulation (1983)—Three Tiered Levels

LEVEL I—national carriers   Air Canada, CP Air
LEVEL II—regional carriers   Eastern Provincial Airways, Nordair, Pacific Western
                                 Airlines, Québecair
LEVEL III—commuters   Air BC, Air Ontario, First Air, Northwest Territories
        and charters   Airways, Time Air, Air Maritime, Norcanair, Regionair,
                                 Austin Airways, Wardair

Industry Structure After Deregulation (1989)—An Emerging Duopoly

GROUP I	*GROUP II*
Air Canada	Canadian Airlines
Air Nova, Air Alliance, Air Ontario, Air Toronto, NWT Air, Air BC, First Air, City Express	Ontario Express, Air Atlantic, Wardair, Calm Air, Time Air, Nationair, Worldways, Crown Air

SOURCE: Casewriter's illustration and analysis (data taken from industry reports).

EXHIBIT 2 Comparative of Key Operating Statistics for Selected Airlines (Calendar Year 1993)

Rank	Airline	Revenue	Airline	Expenses	Airline	Income	Airline	Margin
1	AA	14 737	AA	14 173	AA	564	SI	14.7%
2	UA	14 354	UA	14 059	SI	548	KO	11.5%
3	LU	9 540	LU	9 786	KO	384	AA	3.8%
4	CO	5 775	CO	5 793	UA	295	AC	2.1%
5	AL	4 349	AL	4 406	AC	58	UA	2.1%
6	SI	3 737	SI	3 189	CO	−18	CO	−0.3%
7	KO	3 342	KO	2 958	CA	−48	AL	−1.3%
8	AC	2 699	AC	2 641	AL	−57	CA	−2.3%
9	CA	2 066	CA	2 114	LU	−246	LU	−2.6%

Rank	Airline	RPK	Airline	ASK	Airline	Load	Airline	Y/RPK
1	UA	162 527	AA	258 805	SI	71.5%	LU	18.1¢
2	AA	156 302	UA	242 052	CA	68.3%	AL	15.3¢
3	CO	68 114	CO	107 843	UA	67.1%	AC	13.2¢
4	LU	52 658	U	79 727	KO	67.1%	KO	13.1¢
5	SI	41 265	SI	57 738	LU	66.0%	CA	10.4¢
6	AL	28 377	AL	43 337	AL	65.5%	AA	9.4¢
7	KO	25 588	KO	38 125	AC	64.3%	SI	9.1¢
8	AC	20 491	AC	31 891	CO	63.2%	UA	8.8¢
9	CA	19 935	CA	29 171	AA	60.4%	CO	8.5¢

Rank	Airline	Y/ASK	Airline	C/RPK	Airline	C/ASK	Airline	π/ASK
1	LU	12.0¢	SI	7.7¢	CO	5.4¢	KO	1.01¢
2	AL	10.0¢	CO	8.5¢	AA	5.5¢	SI	0.95¢
3	KO	8.8¢	UA	8.7¢	SI	5.5¢	AA	0.22¢
4	AC	8.5¢	AA	9.1¢	UA	5.8¢	AC	0.18¢
5	CA	7.1¢	CA	10.6¢	CA	7.2¢	UA	0.12¢
6	SI	6.5¢	KO	11.6¢	KO	7.8¢	CO	−0.02¢
7	UA	5.9¢	AC	12.9¢	AC	8.3¢	AL	−0.13¢
8	AA	5.7¢	AL	15.5¢	AL	10.2¢	CA	−0.16¢
9	CO	5.4¢	LU	18.6¢	LU	12.3¢	LU	−0.31¢

Note: Currency figures in US$; statistics include both international and domestic travel.

AA	American Airlines	Revenue	Operating Revenue (US$ millions)	Load	Passenger load factor (%)
UA	United Airlines	Expenses	Operating Expenses (US$ millions)	Y/RPK	Revenue Yield per RPK (¢)
LU	Lufthansa	Income	Operating Income (US$ millions)	Y/ASK	Revenue Yield per ASK (¢)
CO	Continental Airlines	Margin	Income divided by Revenue (%)	C/RPK	Operating Expense per RPK (¢)
AL	Alitalia	RPK	Revenue passenger kilometres (millions)	C/ASK	Operating Expense per ASK (¢)
SI	Singapore Airlines	ASK	Available seat kilometres (millions)	π/ASK	Income divided by ASK (¢)
KO	Korean Air Lines				
AC	Air Canada				
CA	Canadian Airlines				

SOURCE: Casewriter's analysis (data taken from IATA World Air Transport Statistics).

EXHIBIT 3   Financial and Operating Results (1985 to 1994)

Canadian Airlines	*1994*	*1993*	*1992*	*1991*	*1990*	*1989*	*1988*	*1987*	*1986*	*1985*
Financial results										
Revenue	2 954	2 754	2 709	2 730	2 625	2 668	2 301	1 946	362	361
Expenses	2 883	2 819	2 818	2 843	2 636	2 678	2 223	1 782	336	354
Income	71	−65	−109	−112	−12	−10	78	164	25	6
Net Income	−38	−296	−547	−166	−19	−63	23	21	30	6
Total Assets	2 353	2 265	2 462	2 811	2 964	2 912	2 125	1 989	946	453
S/H's Equity	298	−267	25	570	605	622	495	472	321	290
Financial ratios										
Revenue Growth	7.3%	1.7%	−0.8%	4.0%	−1.6%	15.9%	18.2%	438%	0.3%	8.7%
Margin	2.4%	−2.4%	−4.0%	−4.1%	−0.4%	−0.4%	3.4%	8.4%	6.9%	1.7%
ROE	−123%	deficient	−184%	−28%	−3%	−2%	5%	5%	10%	2%
Operating statistics										
RPM	14.0	13.4	13.3	12.7	13.9	14.7	12.1	10.5	1.7	1.5
ASM	20.1	19.4	19.9	19.8	21.4	21.9	17.7	15.1	2.8	2.6
Load Factor (%)	69.3	69.2	66.9	64.1	64.8	67.3	68.8	69.6	59.9	58.3

Air Canada	*1994*	*1993*	*1992*	*1991*	*1990*	*1989*	*1988*	*1987*	*1986*	*1985*
Financial results										
Revenue	4 024	3 598	3 501	3 485	3 939	3 650	3 404	3 114	2 872	2 723
Expenses	3 780	3 521	3 646	3 649	3 950	3 547	3 296	3 011	2 759	2 721
Income	244	77	−145	−164	−11	103	108	103	113	2
Net Income	129	−326	−454	−218	−74	149	89	43	37	−15
Total Assets	4 997	5 039	4 810	4 921	4 579	4 121	3 437	3 084	2 923	2 545
S/H's Equity	365	230	316	770	988	1 062	913	590	548	513
Financial ratios										
Revenue Growth	11.8%	2.8%	0.5%	−11%	7.8%	7.2%	9.3%	8.4%	5.5%	9.0%
Operating Margin	6.1%	2.1%	−4.1%	−4.7%	1.3%	2.8%	3.2%	3.3%	3.9%	0.1%
ROE	47%	−238%	−86%	−25%	−7%	15 %	14%	8%	7%	−3%
Operating statistics										
RPM	14.9	13.8	14.4	13.7	16.6	16.3	15.6	14.4	14.4	14.1
ASM	23.7	21.2	21.6	20.0	23.2	23.3	21.8	20.2	21.3	21.7
Load Factor (%)	63.2	65.1	66.5	68.4	71.4	69.7	71.4	71.1	67.7	65.2

Note: Results in C$ million, Operating Statistics include Canadian Airlines International and Air Canada (not consolidated) RPMs and ASMs in billions.

SOURCE: Company Annual Reports.

EXHIBIT 4   **Canadian Airlines versus Air Canada (Revenue and Cost Management)**

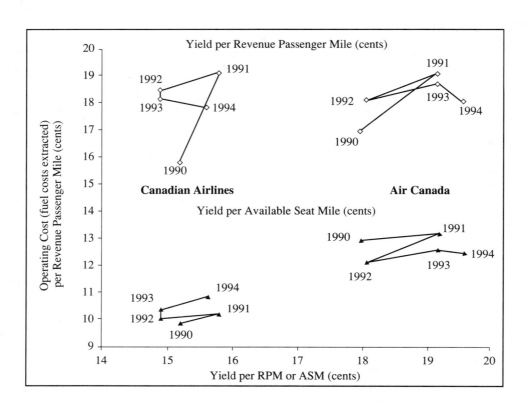

Selected Statistics Canadian Airlines	1994	1993	1992	1991	1990
Yield per RPM	15.6¢	14.9¢	14.9¢	15.8¢	15.2¢
Yield per ASM	10.8¢	10.3¢	10.0¢	10.1¢	9.8¢
Operating Cost (excl. fuel) per RPM	17.8¢	18.1¢	18.5¢	19.1¢	15.8¢
Fuel Cost per ASM	1.97¢	1.99¢	1.79¢	2.13¢	2.11¢

Air Canada					
Yield per RPM	19.6¢	19.2¢	18.1¢	19.2¢	18.0¢
Yield per ASM	12.4¢	12.5¢	12.0¢	13.1¢	12.8¢
Operating Cost (excl. fuel) per RPM	18.0¢	18.7¢	18.1¢	19.0¢	16.9¢
Fuel Cost per ASM	2.00¢	1.86¢	2.18¢	2.58¢	2.74¢

Note: Selected statistics include Canadian Airlines International and Air Canada (not consolidated).
SOURCE: Casewriter's illustration (data taken from company reports).

EXHIBIT 5   Copy of Letter Sent to All Employees of Canadian Airlines

May 15, 1995

Canadian

Dear Fellow Employee:

The Strategic Planning Steering Committee (SPSC) has had many successes to date. Achievements of this joint strategy process have been excellent. Joint labour and management teams met between January and March and identified $78 million in annualized cost savings and revenue enhancements which will now be built into our growth plan. These improvements will be in all areas of operation. Examples include fuel efficiencies, better weighing and measuring of cargo, and consistently collecting excess baggage charges.

Through a process of negotiations, joint teams of CALDA, CALPA, CAST, CAW and IAM representatives along with management, developed the Summer 1995 Initiative adding three new wide-body aircraft (two DC10s and a B767) to our summer fleet. These negotiations resulted in annualized savings of $27 million in work rules, scheduling and other productivity measures with no additional labour costs.

These successes to date, while substantial, are only the beginning of what we must achieve. We are now at a crossroad and it is time to choose; Plan A or Plan B.

Plan A: The Growth Plan

This plan will result in significant improvements to our profitability and consumer loyalty while building cash to buy new aircraft and renew our fleet. Plan A would allow us to take full advantage of new opportunities in the transborder and international markets. We would be able to add significantly more new aircraft and modernize or replace our B737 fleet to meet Stage 3 noise requirements. To achieve this growth, service new routes and rebuild our cash reserves, we must IMPROVE OUR COST POSITION BY 14% per available seat mile. Based on 1994 costs, this would total $325 million. Even with the savings identified to date, there is still some distance to go in closing the gap.

Performance Improvements	$ 78
1995 Summer Initiative	$ 27
Overhead (unrelated to Union)	$ 29
Amendments to Union Agreements	$125
Remaining gap yet to be allocated	$ 66
Total Required	$325

All of the unions and management in the SPSC process are working together to close the gap. We are stretching to save all monies possible from non-labour costs. Over the next two months, negotiations will also be proceeding using a mutual interest-based process that identifies how the long-term interests of workers are to be safeguarded, while at the same time improving the productivity of the airline.

Plan B: Downsizing

If we are unable to achieve the cost-savings required for growth, the company will be forced to address its unprofitable routes by downsizing and retrenching to its more profitable international flying. Plan B is being developed by the company as an alternative if Plan A fails. Under Plan B, Canadian would exit many cities, and massive layoffs would be anticipated.

The Choice

The SPSC clearly does not support Plan B but recognizes that the STATUS QUO IS UNACCEPTABLE. All of us will be faced with making a choice in the next **six weeks** between Plan A and Plan B. Plan A can mean increased security for our employees and the opportunities for personal and professional development that come with being part of a growing company. However, it will require sacrifices from each of us and these will be equitably distributed. Canadian's employees have proven we are willing to make sacrifices for a healthy and growing airline.

EXHIBIT 6 **Historical Stock Price Trend**

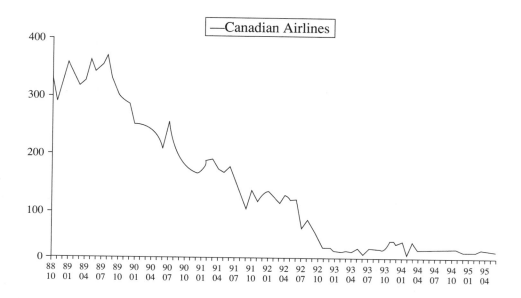

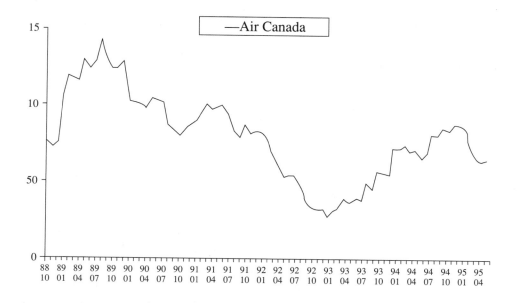

Note: Monthly close stock prices used for illustration.

SOURCE: Casewriter's illustration (data taken from Bloomberg).

APPENDIX A Glossary of Terms and Abbreviations

ASM	Available seat miles—the number of seats an airline provides times the number of miles they are flown; a measure of airline capacity.
Cabotage	The right of an airline to carry local traffic in a foreign market. As a general rule, cabotage is strictly prohibited. For example, Lufthansa is unable to board passengers originating in Atlanta for Dallas on its Frankfurt-Atlanta-Dallas service.
CRSs	Computerized Reservation Systems began with the American Airlines Sabre System. Originally used to track seat availability, it had expanded to include the booking of other travel services (e.g., car rental, hotels, etc.) and was critical to yield management and airline operations.
FFPs	Frequent flyer programs rewarded passengers with free trips and other benefits based on kilometres flown. First introduced by American Airlines, this marketing innovation favoured large carriers with extensive route systems on which customers could more readily accumulate mileage and select desirable reward destinations. Most larger airlines had initiated their own FFPs.
Load Factor	Revenue passenger miles divided by available seat miles; a measure of aircraft utilization.
RPM	Revenue passenger miles—the number of passengers times the number of miles they fly.
Six Freedoms	Each contracting state in a bilateral air agreement can grant to the other contracting state or states the following Six Freedoms in respect of scheduled international services:

1. The privilege to fly across the territory of another country without landing. For example, Olympic Airways flies from Montreal to Athens over Spain.
2. The privilege to land in another country for technical and other non-traffic purposes. For example, Aeroflot stops for a technical stop (take on fuel and food) in Gander, Newfoundland during its flight from Moscow to Havana.
3. The privilege to put down passengers, mail and cargo in another country. For example, Delta lets passengers off in Lisbon during its New York to Rome flight.

4. The privilege to take on/board passengers, mail and cargo in another country destined for Canada. For example, CA picks up passengers in Zurich and flies them into Calgary.

5. The privilege to take on passengers, mail and cargo in one foreign country for carriage to another foreign country. For example, CA on its Toronto to Frankfurt route can land in Ireland and pick up Irish passengers and carry them to Frankfurt and vice versa.

6. The privilege of carrying traffic between two foreign countries via one's own country. For example, an American passenger can board a CA flight in Los Angeles and go via Vancouver to Ho Chi Minh, Vietnam.

Unit Costs   Operating costs from scheduled operations divided by scheduled available seat miles.

Yield   The revenue per passenger mile an airline receives; it represents an aggregate of all the airfares and airline charges and is measured on a per mile basis.

APPENDIX B   Industry Revenue and Cost Structure

Four basic factors affect airline profitability: (1) the load factor; (2) the yield or ticket revenue; (3) the unit cost of operating the aircraft, and (4) other on-the-ground costs (i.e., ticketing, terminal operations, etc.). Profits can be enhanced by increasing yields and load factors or by lowering costs. Typically, an airline followed one of these three strategies: (1) a greater load factor for a constant revenue yield, (2) higher fares and hence greater revenue yield for a constant load factor, or (3) lower costs while maintaining yield and load factors.

PROFIT DYNAMIC

The operating profits from passenger traffic were determined by a simple relationship:

$$\text{operating profit} = \text{revenue} - \text{costs}$$

but revenue and aircraft costs can be re-stated in unit terms (per kilometre):

$$\text{operating profit} = ((\text{revenue} / \text{RPK} * \text{RPK}) - (\text{costs} / \text{ASK} * \text{ASK}))$$

Revenue / RPK is called yield, or unit revenue (how much the average passenger pays for one kilometre flown). Cost / ASK is called unit costs (the cost of flying an average airline seat (empty or full) one kilometre). So:

$$\text{operating profit} = (\text{yield} * \text{RPK}) - (\text{UC} * \text{ASK})$$

This can be re-stated as:

$$\text{operating profit} = ((\text{yield} * \text{RPK} / \text{ASK}) - \text{UC}) * \text{ASK}$$

Remember that RPK / ASK = Load Factor (LF), therefore:

$$\text{operating profit} = ((\text{yield} * \text{LF}) - \text{UC}) * \text{ASK}$$

Dividing both sides by ASK results in:

$$\text{operating profit} / \text{ASK} = \text{yield} * \text{LF} - \text{UC}$$

In simple terms, operating profit per available seat kilometre flown is equal to yield times load factor minus unit costs. While the basic formula is simple, the factors affecting revenue yields, load factors and units costs are more complex.

REVENUE STRUCTURE

Revenues were the result of the number of passengers flown times the fare, or price paid. About 90% of airline revenue was derived from passengers and 10% from cargo. The price passengers paid for an airline seat differed dramatically. Price varied by class of service, as well as within the same class. Airlines differentiated class of service by segmenting the aircraft cabin. Typically two classes of service were offered both domestically and internationally. AC and CA have economy and business class on all routes. Most American carriers call their products economy and first class.

First and business classes of service provided a separate cabin, larger seats, more personalized service, better food and other amenities. For these enhancements first-class fares were more than double full fare economy and business class carried a 15–30% premium.

Fares also differed dramatically in the economy cabin. Airlines created certain fences, or restrictions such as staying over a Saturday night, minimum stays, advanced booking and payment, penalties for cancellation and itinerary changes, etc. Passengers prepared to meet some or all of these restrictions could save up to 60% off full fare economy. In 1994 discounted fares accounted for 61% of domestic travel. Most of the fences were designed to prevent business travellers, who desired flexibility and convenience, from taking advantage of discounted fares. These fares (and the accompanying restrictions) accommodated the travel needs of the so-called VFR segment (vacationers, friends and relatives).

Share of passengers on any specific route (city pair) were disproportionate to frequency on that route (i.e., 60% of available departures often translated to 70% market share). This is because passengers tend to travel with the carrier that has the most frequent number of flights.

COST STRUCTURE

The airline industry was characterized by a high level of fixed costs. The major operating costs for airlines were wages and fuel. The proportion of operating costs varied substantially between the major carriers. Route structures contributed to some of the discrepancy. Shorter routes, and smaller and older aircraft tended to burn more fuel per available seat mile. However, once route structure and the aircraft type were selected, little could be done to affect fuel efficiency.

Fuel was significantly cheaper in western Canada and most expensive in Atlantic Canada (about a 50% premium), with central Canada costs falling midway between. As a result, because CA concentrated more of its activity in Alberta and British Columbia, it was able to fuel at an average rate cheaper than AC. However, any substantial regional advantage was mitigated by the need to fuel where you flew and by AC's ability to access that fuel as well. On-the-ground costs like airport gate fees, check-in, travel agent commissions, advertising, administration, etc. accounted for slightly less than half of total costs.

YIELD AND COST MANAGEMENT

Actually balancing an optimal pricing and cost strategy was complicated. Load factors could be improved by offering seasonal promotions and discounts, but cutting fares eroded revenue yield. Skillful balancing of this trade-off was vital to airline competitive advantage and profitability. Unit cost reductions were dependent upon increasing productivity of labour and equipment without diminishing passenger service and safety. A large proportion, 82% of airline operating costs were fixed or semi-variable; only 18% were truly variable—travel agency commissions, ticketing fees and meals. Semi-variable costs could be varied only by large and expensive "steps" over the medium- and long-term. The implications were that once an airline determined its route structure (the combination of destinations, frequencies and aircraft) fuel, crew and ground staff costs were largely fixed. Almost the same amount of fuel was used whether a plane flew empty or full; crew size was determined by the type of aircraft, not the passenger load.

The objective of yield management was to optimally balance load factor and yield to maximize operating profit. This task was entrusted to sophisticated computer software that was resident in each airline's CRS. All of the largest airlines had proprietary CRSs to coordinate booking and ticketing activity, yield and cost management, and accounting. Smaller airlines cooperated in joint systems, or licensed another airline's CRS. Sophisticated algorithms forecasted demand and attempted to optimize final load factor and yield.

Typically, Asian carriers had the lowest costs in the industry, followed in increasing order by the U.S., Canadian and European operators. An airline's comparative costs were heavily influenced by its unit and wage costs and by the productivity of its support operations. Exhibit 2 compares key operating statistics among several airlines. Airline executives learned to be cognizant of the sensitivity of these and other important variables. For example, management at CA studied the effects of certain important industry variables and their financial impact on operating income before tax.

Variable	*Financial Impact ($ millions)*
Increase of $1 per barrel of crude oil	$ − 11
Increase in passenger load factor by 1%	$ + 28
Domestic market growth of 1%	$ + 9
Domestic market share increase of 1%	$ + 20
A 1¢ increase in yield per RPK	$ + 185

APPENDIX C   Open Skies and U.S. Carriers

The advent of "open skies" would raise the prospects of increased competition between Canadian and U.S. airlines. In the short run, this competitive rivalry would be moderated by the current alliances in place (Canadian Airlines–American Airlines and Air Canada–Continental Airlines). However, in the long run, Canadian Airlines and Air Canada would feel strong pressure to establish links with one of the global airline consortiums. The following list describes the major U.S. carriers in the airline industry. The ultimate threat to Air Canada and Canadian Airlines will be when these carriers start demanding cabotage rights into Canada.

- American Airlines: largest carrier in the world (revenue and capacity)

    primary hubs include Dallas/Fort Worth and Chicago

    strong base of North Atlantic service

- United Airlines: largest carrier in the world (RPKs—revenue passenger kilometres)

    primary hubs include Chicago and Denver

    number one U.S. carrier in the Pacific market

- Delta Airlines: member of global consortium with Swissair and Singapore Airlines

    primary hubs include Atlanta and Cincinnati

    has conservative management with good operating record

- Northwest: member of global consortium with KLM

    primary hubs include Minneapolis/St. Paul and Detroit

    biggest U.S. challenger in the Pacific

- USAir: alliance with British Airways

    primary hubs include Pittsburgh and Washington

    focuses on domestic medium-haul traffic

- Southwest: considered the industry renegade

    lowest unit costs in the U.S. industry

    concentrates on specific city pairs

CANADA POST CORPORATION AND THE I-WAY

Mary M. Crossan, Bruce Lanning and Iris Berdrow Tiemessen

CASE 6

Since becoming a Crown Corporation in 1981, Canada Post Corporation (CPC) had transformed mail service in Canada from "simplistic" physical sorting to "intelligent" mechanized distribution. Massive infusions of technology had dramatically changed CPC's operations, personnel, corporate mission and self-perspective. In August 1994, Phil Lemay, the newly appointed senior vice-president of CPC's Electronic Products & Services, faced the challenge of assessing what impact the Information Superhighway (the I-way) would have on CPC's future.

Although commercialization of the I-way attracted increasing news media and business attention daily, no one could answer exactly what the I-way would become, who would have access to it, who would administer the network, and how it would change CPC and other information transfer businesses. It was a given that electronic mail (e-mail), which was not governed by CPC's monopoly over collection, sorting and distribution of lettermail, would have a negative impact on CPC's profitability. Accordingly, the Electronic Products & Services division was charged with developing CPC's electronic capabilities to counteract the threat and capitalize on the opportunities presented by the developing I-way.

THE CROWN CORPORATION

After becoming a Crown Corporation in 1981, CPC's first challenge was to convert itself from a government bureau into an effective operating company. This involved first building a management and organizational infrastructure to operate the business, then installing electronic systems to integrate operations and monitor performance. By 1987, the operating infrastructure was in place, allowing detailed daily scrutiny of performance against measurable standards.

Changes at CPC were not restricted to quality, on-time performance and accountability; fundamental product changes were made. Mail was no longer designated as first, second, third and fourth class, but in terms of the urgency surrounding its delivery. The new products—Lettermail, Special Letter, Priority Courier, Electronic Mail and Admail Plus—were priced on a time axis, not by size or weight alone. Faster delivery commitments by CPC extracted premium prices.

CPC's mail delivery system became a blended network of larger corporate-owned postal stations and smaller franchised outlets conveniently situated in retail stores. CPC no longer attempted to maintain and sort mail in smaller centres; it had consolidated "backroom" processing operations into large automated "plants." At the same time, it had converted a majority of its "front office" customer counters to franchises. This re-organization triggered a momentous change in CPC's self-perspective: no longer did it view itself as isolated mail-sorting facilities but, instead, as an integrated delivery network. To integrate its operations across this new network, CPC developed the Integrated Communications Network (ICN), a country-wide electronic network used to support the operation of CPC's business. Distant mail-processing machines communicated via ICN to compile data on processing of mail in local plants into a system-wide status report.

Complementing ICN were optical character readers (OCRs) which machine-read handwritten addresses; the Video Encoding System (VES) which displayed illegible addresses for human interpretation and coding, Letter Sorting Machines (LSMs) which eliminated multiple sorting and handling using postal codes to batch mail by final destination; and control systems such as the Air Routing Control System, the Surface Transportation Reporting System, and the Priority Courier Track & Trace System. The state-of-the-art National Control Centre (NCC) in Ottawa centralized management of the extended network of physical sites. The results of the previous day's operations were reviewed jointly by executives at the NCC and operations managers across Canada via a video-conference meeting. ICN was the foundation for these innovative systems.

Improvements in mail processing were developed by CPC in a mock-up of the postal system. The multi-million-dollar project called Paradigm enabled suppliers to identify areas in which they could add value to CPC's operations. In this way, CPC was able to experiment with new technology and eventually break away from its reliance on adapting innovations arising from the much larger U.S. Postal Service. Given the complexity of mail processing and the history of labour disputes in CPC, Paradigm also allowed management the opportunity to preview and refine contemplated changes, and then introduce successful modifications with confidence and reduced union resistance.

Because of the highly sophisticated systems and technologies that had been implemented, Canada Post Systems Management Ltd. (CPSML) was established as a separate consulting arm of CPC with the purpose of marketing CPC technology and expertise internationally. Innovations made by CPC such as the Priority Courier Track & Trace System, the NCC and CPC's ability as a project manager intrigued other postal administrations. CPSML had contracts to manage projects in 21 countries.

CPC's networked delivery system, value-added electronic products and associated networking competencies caused it to realign itself to focus on three major markets:

- Advertising: delivery of addressed and unaddressed advertising mail and publications;

- Physical Distribution: small package delivery, including Purolator Courier (see details of Purolator immediately below in CPC Operations); and

- Communications: delivery of information by physical and electronic media, predominantly lettermail.

The Advertising and Physical Distribution businesses continued to record small annual increases in sales revenue using CPC's collection, sorting and delivery expertise. CPC stimulated growth of Unaddressed Admail and Addressed Admail, its advertising products, through education and leadership within the advertising industry. Physical Distribution built upon its strength in the small package segment with plans to restructure the Priority Courier and Parcel products, incorporate Purolator, and increase international market share.

The future of the third division, Communications, was unclear. What information would be moved and how was unknown. The impact electronic transfer of information and communications on the I-way would have on lettermail was difficult to forecast. However, given that Communications generated 52% of CPC's annual revenue in 1993–94, the potential for the I-way to alter CPC operations was considerable. It was expected that, while physical electronic mail would experience rapid growth, lettermail volumes would remain constant, similar to the way ship traffic held constant with the introduction of air traffic, even though it had become a small percentage of overall overseas transport over time. The underlying assumption was that the electronic medium would grow with the overall communication market.

CPC'S CURRENT OPERATIONS

Since becoming a Crown Corporation, CPC had improved the quality of Canada's mail service and established the Canadian postal system as a leader in network technology. By 1993, mechanization of mail processing increased to 92% up from 20% in the early 1980s.

Recession in the Canadian economy in 1993–94 depressed activity of many commercial sectors and consequently, CPC's revenue. The result was a meagre operating profit of $26 million (0.6% operating margin) on turnover of $4 115 million. The final loss was $270 million following charges of $223 million for further reorganizations to enhance productivity and improve customer service. CPC ended 1993 with a retained earnings deficiency of $288 million.

Excluding additional revenue from the acquisition of Purolator, CPC revenue was flat at $340 million (8.8%) below plan. Meanwhile, costs of operations rose $262 million (6.8%) over 1992–93. Proforma statements for CPC are included in Exhibit 1.

By 1994 lettermail volume was showing minimal growth over the previous years. Strong growth was recorded in both physical distribution (16.6%—mostly as a result of the Purolator acquisition) and advertising (7.6%—as newspaper advertising dropped), continuing strong trends from previous years. Among advertising sub-segments, publications continued a five-year decline, decreasing by 10%. CPC's level of profitability was very sensitive to volume fluctuations; a 1% decline in volume would wipe out profits.

Millions of labour hours paid, including Purolator operations, were equal to 1992–93 such that efficiency of operations, reflected in greater volumes of mail handled per hour paid, improved by 4.5%. Productivity increases on mail processing operations amounted to 39% over the past 10 years. Wage rate increases, due to existing labour contracts, exceeded volume and inflation increases.

There were no work stoppages in 1993–94. In fact, other than a strike in 1991 amounting to 1% of annual hours of wages paid, disruptive labour stoppages had not occurred in five years. This was a sign of improved labour relations at CPC and stood in stark contrast to the labour relations of CPC in the 1980s and the former Post Office prior to 1981.

During 1993, CPC decided to outsource the integration, application development and support functions for its major internal systems. Three vendors were awarded three-year contracts totalling approximately $100 million, allowing CPC to sell approximately $142 million worth of computing and communications network and supporting assets to SHL Systemhouse of Montreal.

Outsourcing the computing and communications functions was the result of re-engineering activity within CPC. Its core competencies were focused on distribution activities; technology support processes and related infrastructure went to SHL, giving it the responsibility of meeting CPC's business requirements and maintaining CPC's technological sophistication at the state of the market.

In 1993, CPC acquired a 75% interest in PCL Courier Holdings Inc. for $55 million. PCL was the holding company for the Canadian operations of U.S.-based Purolator Courier. CPC acquired control in a bid to solidify its position in the Canadian courier and express package market as it competed with courier industry giants DHL Worldwide Express, Emery Worldwide, Federal Express and new services introduced by United Parcel Service (UPS). CPC viewed the purchase of Purolator as a strategic move ensuring expertise and funding to develop "competitive, technology-based, value-added services that customers demand." Purolator also operated differently than CPC, picking up most of its consignments and promising delivery the next morning, thereby expanding CPC's potential customer base. Purolator added sales of approximately $200 million to CPC's physical distribution division in 1993–94.

CPC's only shareholder continued to be Canada, represented by the government of the day. Consequently, CPC corporate policies were expected to change under the Liberal government elected in 1993. Policy was expected to change to emphasize employment; under the Conservatives, CPC's thrusts had been profitability, customer service and an improved human relations record.

THE INFORMATION SUPERHIGHWAY

The future I-way was touted as being "absolutely revolutionary" and "virtual anything" on one extreme, and condemned as being "pure hype" and "utter fiction" on the other. The advocates of the communication revolution envisioned individuals accessing information from I-way databases, not as drones simply downloading programming, but as participants interactively passing information, communicating with other individuals and corporations through high speed-high volume multimedia "pipelines." This would include the transferring and manipulating of information, playing video games, creating full-length cinema, and experiencing imaginative cybernetic worlds combining voice, video, graphics and images. Conversely, the nay-sayers saw the I-way as a glorified e-mail system, an expansion of existing commercial network services. In reality, nobody was able to confidently estimate the I-way's potential. Exhibit 2 provides assorted U.S. market data for industries that might conceivably be incorporated into the I-way mega-industry.

Mega-Industry

The I-way could be pictured as a mega-industry created by the technological convergence of once distinct industries. The boundaries of the mega-industry embraced *computing*—Apple, IBM, Intel, etc.; *content and entertainment*—Paramount, MGM, Columbia, etc.; and *distribution*—the Regional Bell Telephone companies, cable television (CATV) operators and broadcast networks. Each had an important role in making the I-way a reality: *computing* enabled the I-way, *content* created programming and information of interest and value, and *distribution* provided the infrastructure necessary to deliver *content*.

On one side of the triangle, software developers such as Microsoft Corp. and game makers Sega and Nintendo blended *computing* expertise with *content*. On the remaining sides, television broadcasting networks such as ABC, CBC, and Turner provided *content* and *distribution,* while AT&T dominated the bridge between *computing* and *distribution*. The Internet was pictured at the heart of the nascent multi-media industry. See Figure 1, The I-way Mega-Industry.

FIGURE 1   **The I-way Mega-Industry**

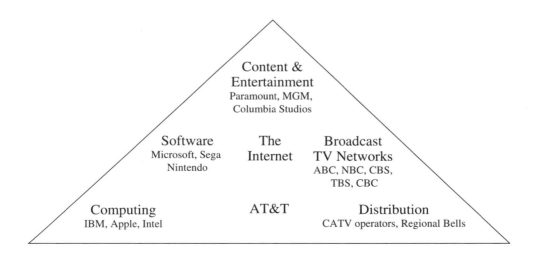

SOURCE: Adapted from *The Economist*, February 12, 1994.

Not portrayed in the two-dimensional figure above are vertical "food-chains" within each of the six industries. For instance in *computing*, Intel traditionally competed in the industrial market with its chip design and manufacturing function; Apple competed at the retail level for the end-user with personal computers; and IBM, which vertically and horizontally spanned the *computing* and software areas, competed at multiple levels—at the industrial level with chips and operating systems, at the corporate level with mainframes and customer service, and at the retail level with PCs and applications. Supplying each of these were a myriad of other industries and technologies.

Technological Developments

The information revolution was not a result of consumerism gone wild and demanding more quantity and more sophistication in viewing choice. In many ways, the consumer was not ready for the much-talked-about 500-channel universe, home shopping and mass customization of content. Technology made these advances possible. Four prime technological developments drove the I-way:

- data digitalisation and compression;
- falling prices of computer chips making interactive TV commercially viable;
- installation of fibre optic and coaxial cable networks enabling image transmission; and
- advances in application software enabling machine-human interaction.

As a result of these technological developments, it was speculated that the I-way would resemble a combination of high performance computer and high definition television. The "television" would supply the images and sound while the "highway" would consist of client-servers (powerful computers) transmitting data through "pipelines," "backbones" and "networks" of fibre optic (long distance telephone trunk lines) and coaxial cable (as used by CATV operators). Figure 2 demonstrates the main elements for the hypothesized network and combinations of key technologies. Satellite and cellular communications are omitted. They are appropriate in areas of low population density or inhospitable terrain making the extension of fibre/coaxial infrastructure unfeasible.

FIGURE 2   The Information Superhighway Network

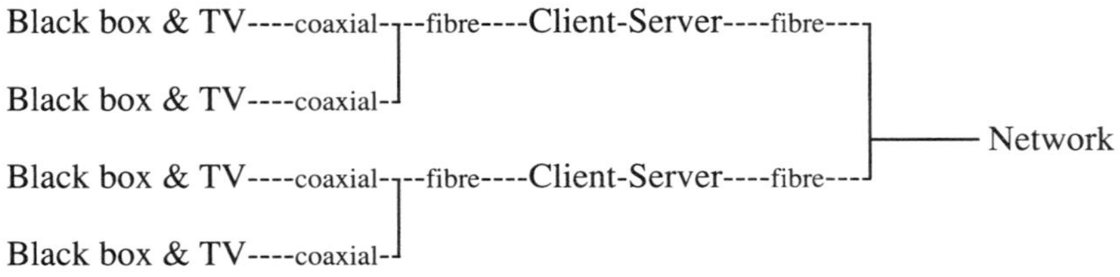

```
Black box & TV----coaxial-┐--fibre----Client-Server----fibre---┐
                          │                                    │
Black box & TV----coaxial-┘                                    │
                                                               ├──── Network
Black box & TV----coaxial-┐--fibre----Client-Server----fibre---┘
                          │
Black box & TV----coaxial-┘
```

SOURCE: *The Economist*, February 12, 1994.

This vision of the I-way was still unrefined. Uncertainty surrounded how commercialization would occur, what standards would prevail, whether CATV or telephone companies would dominate distribution and what degree of government involvement was desirable.

Government Reaction

If the predictions about the power and growth of the I-way were correct, national competitiveness and prosperity were at stake. The automobile had catapulted the United States into the fore in the mass production age and its proponents into industrial giants. The winners of this race would similarly propel their country(ies) into leadership of the information age where they would presumably enjoy a long period of prosperity with increased employment, gross domestic product and positive balance of payments.

Accordingly, national governments had commissioned studies to make recommendations on how to prepare for the I-way and how to incorporate it into national economies. Key concerns focused on privacy, copyright, universal access, and employment opportunities. High profile projects included Japan committing to spend US$200 billion to bring fibre to every home by 2010, and several U.S. government agencies with a budget of US$1.1 billion in 1994–95 for basic research on high performance computing and communication networks.

In Canada, the federal government had committed $26 million and was rumoured to be considering a further commitment of $2 billion. As part of the Canadian initiative, schools and regional governments in Ontario and New Brunswick were linked electronically in trial applications.

Industry Reaction

Between 1986 and 1993, acquisitions and mergers in the media and entertainment industries had created controversy by paying conspicuous premiums over book value for apparently limited synergy. However, by mid-1993, recognition of the convergence of content, distribution and computing validated some previous mergers and further broadened the scope of acquisition and merger combinations. A vision of the I-way mega-industry was forming and dictating the direction of merger activity.

For instance, programming and CATV operator Viacom was completing purchases of Paramount Communications and Blockbuster Entertainment in July 1994. Viacom wanted to control Paramount's valuable film library and a large network of retail outlets to manage distribution of that library in addition to its original CATV interest. (See Table 1).

Similarly, U.S. West and Time Warner merged in the belief that opportunity existed for telephone companies to distribute content on a pay-per-view basis. Trials were beginning in California. Table 2, Cross-Industry Mergers, illustrates industry convergence.

TABLE 1 The Ten Largest Media Acquisitions

Target	Acquirer	Effective Date	Value (US$ billions)

Warner Communications
  TV & motion picture production/distribution; publishing
	Time
	  publisher & cable TV
		Jan. 10, 1990	14.11

Paramount Communications
  motion picture production & distribution; cable TV; TV broadcasting; sports promotion
	Viacom
	  cable TV, subscription TV; motion picture production & distribution; satellite services (DBS); radio & TV broadcasting
		Partly completed	9.60

Blockbuster Entertainment
  video distribution & rentals
	Viacom
	  see above.
		July 1, 1994	8.40

MCA
  pre-recorded music; motion picture production & distribution; TV broadcasting
	Matsushita Electric
	  consumer electronics; computers; telecom & facsimile equipment; robotics
		Jan. 3, 1991	7.41

QVC
  home shopping network
	CBS
	  TV & radio broadcasting; TV film production/distribution
		Aug. 1, 1994	7.20

Columbia Pictures
  motion picture production & distribution; publishing— newspaper, magazines
	Sony
	  consumer electronics; pre-recorded music; motion picture production/ distribution; theatre; software/game
		Nov. 7, 1989	4.79

Viacom
  see above.
	National Amusements
	  theatres: radio & TV broadcasting: cable TV & subscription TV
		June 9, 1987	3.52

ABC
  TV broadcasting; TV film production
	Capital Cities
	  TV & radio broadcasting; TV film production
		Jan. 6, 1986	3.50

Liberty Media
  cable TV & subscription TV
	Tele-Communications (TCI)
	  cable TV; subscription TV
		pending	3.41

Triangle
  publications
	News Corp.
	  publishing—newspaper, magazines; radio & TV broadcasting; motion picture production & distribution
		Nov. 1, 1988	3.00

SOURCE: *Wall Street Journal*, July 1, 1994.

Table 3 illustrates the degree to which old industry boundaries were being eroded by one company, AT&T. Some of its investments were purportedly only to gain insight into the developing I-way and multimedia mega-industry. GO Corp., 3DO and Sierra Network were manufacturers of educational software and interactive games. Equity interest in these firms would presumably keep AT&T informed about developments in Content and Entertainment. Powerful parallel processing technology, personal communicators and "intelligent agents," even games, would help AT&T serve its customers better and help it to incorporate leading edge technology into its products and services. Refer to the NCR, Teradata, EO Inc., McCaw and General Magic acquisitions.

TABLE 2   Examples of Cross-Industry Mergers

Merger Partners	Value of Deal	Announced	Comments
U.S. West & Time Warner	US$ 2.5 billion	1993.05.17	
AT&T & McCaw Cellular	US$12.6 billion	1993.08.17	
Bell Atlantic & TCI (CATV)	US$21.4 billion	1993.10.13	terminated: 94.02.23
Viacom & Blockbuster	US$8.4 billion	1994.01.07	

SOURCE: *Forbes Magazine*, October 23, 1995, pp. 252–59.

TABLE 3   Erosion of Media and Information Industry Boundaries by AT&T

Date	Target	Technology	Value* or %
1988.07	joint venture w/ GTE	digital switching technology	US$112 million
1989.03	Paradyne	data communications equipment	100% of equity
1989.12	ISTEL	UK high tech telecommunications	US$285 million
1989.06	Italtel	Italian telcoms manufacturer	20% equity swap
1991.09	NCR	computers	US$7.5 bn-stock
1988-91	Sun Microsystems	investment unravels & is sold	(19% of Sun)
1991.09	EO Inc.	personal communicators, start-up	undisclosed %
1992.02	Teradata	parallel computing manufacturer	US$500 million
1992.10	GO Corp.	hand writing recognition startup	10% of equity
1992.12	General Magic	wireless communications software	undisclosed %
1993.01	3DO	interactive multimedia developer	5% of equity
1993.04	Shaye Communications	digital cordless phones	100%
1993.06	joint venture with SEGA	video play on telephone lines	50:50
1993.07	Sierra Network	on-line interactive network	20% of equity
1993.08	EO Inc.	above: increased ownership	51% of equity
1993.08	Knowledge Adventure	multimedia educational software	undisclosed %
1993.08	McCaw Cellular	U.S. nation-wide cellular service	US$12.6 bn-stock

*bn = billion

Source: "Robert Allen's Wireless Message," Industry Week (Vol. 242, No. 4), February 15, 1993, p. 17.
"Allen: Towards a Global Company," Fortune (Vol. 127, No. 10), May 17, 1993, p. 57. "The Tortoise and the Hare," Forbes (Vol. 151, No. 3), February 1, 1993, PP. 88–69, "Could AT & T Rule the World? Fortune (Vol. 127, No. 10), May 17, 1993, pp. 54–66. "AT &T and NCR: The Deal is Done," Telephony (Vol. 220, No. 19), May 13, 1991, pp. 16–18.

Moguls and Inventors, Deal-makers and Power-brokers

Powerful, influential and creative persons competed and cooperated to advance their visions of the I-way. Deal-makers such as Michael Ovitz, president of Hollywood talent agency Creative Artists Agency Inc. (CAA), discussed opportunities to make interactive commercials with Microsoft's Bill Gates. CAA would provide talent from its clientele which included Spielberg, Stallone, Cruise, Costner, Madonna and Jackson, while Microsoft would provide the gadgetry. The extent of Ovitz's and CAA's power was exemplified by their counselling Sony when it purchased Columbia Studios and Matsushita when it bought MCA, and by their seizure of the creative advertising for the Coca-Cola account from advertising giant McCann-Erickson Worldwide.

On the other hand, Paul Allen, the "other" founder/billionaire from Microsoft, was described as driven to make more money, not for its own sake, but to advance new concepts in multimedia software. The inventors such as Allen believed in limitless technological horizons.

Others, such as John Malone of Tele-Communications Inc. (TCI), a major U.S. CATV operator, were vocal and forceful in securing a position for themselves and their industry in the emerging mega-industry. After a proposed merger of TCI and Bell Atlantic had failed, Malone rallied three other CATV companies and amassed US$2 billion to form a consortium to challenge the Regional Bells. The CATV consortium planned to install their own fibre optic network in conjunction with their existing coaxial networks in order to provide "one-stop shopping" for high definition television, basic and wireless telephone, video-on-demand, and computer on-line services.

Personalities such as Michael Ovitz, Bill Gates, Paul Allen, John Malone and Bob Allen of AT&T were forging the development of the I-way. Some had stature as statesmen and diplomats able to overarch the industry; some were inventors and entrepreneurs with a smaller vision but willing to risk everything to bring their beliefs to fruition. Big opportunities and big egos were the rule.

VALUE-ADDED NETWORKS ON THE I-WAY: CPC'S THRUST

In 1985, CPC developed within Canada a hybrid postal product, Volume Electronic Mail (VEM), which relied on physical delivery to the final destination but incorporated electronic transfer in collection, sorting and distribution.

VEM service can be illustrated with the delivery routine for a company's monthly billing statements. The company would send CPC an electronic tape of its monthly billings, CPC would sort these data and batch them for distribution to the closest of seven regional VEM-printing sites, then transmit batches electronically to the appropriate site. Billings were printed on site, inserted in envelopes, and put into the local mail stream for delivery. Return envelopes and promotional material were prepared in bulk and distributed to VEM-printing sites in advance for inclusion with the statement. By 1994, planned enhancement of VEM included capturing returning cheques from the local mail stream, electronically scanning the cheques and transferring the proceeds to the creditor. For this customer, CPC was no longer just a technologically-advanced sorting and distribution operation; CPC would add value to the mail it handled through processing billing and collection of outstanding accounts.

By 1993, CPC's offerings had expanded to provide a variety of value-added services. These included Tracemail products which used bar-coding to track letters and parcels, and provided CPC with the capability to advise merchants and suppliers of the status of their consignments in CPC's delivery system. Another, Omnipost, allowed individuals to create letter-mail, fax or e-mail on their personal computers (PC) and transmit it to CPC for delivery to another PC, to a fax, or to a CPC print site for hard-copy hand delivery. Omnipost simply delivered "the mail" in the indicated form.

In March, 1993, Dr. Tucker, Lemay's predecessor at CPC, stated:

> The ability to send a message to anybody in physical or electronic form and get it back in physical or electronic form will be crucial for years to come. Canada Post will remain a key player in any complete distribution system because we still deliver the mail.

CPC's purpose was more than commercial in introducing Omnipost and other electronic products. The government of Canada had originated the former Post Office over 100 years ago with the express purpose of providing affordable and universal service to Canadians; the federal government and CPC continued to promote this mission. Hybrid electronic/physical products bridged the gap between technologically advanced large volume mailers and individual Canadians, ensuring cost-effective, universal access to the latest technology.

But CPC was not the only firm capable of adding value to information services as it did not hold a monopoly on the electronic transfer of information in Canada. Table 4 lists the key providers of value-added information services and their roles in information delivery. As various firms entered the market for value-added services, CPC needed to determine a strategy that would allow it to provide unique and substantive value to customers.

TABLE 4   Providers of Value-Added Information Services

Organization	Core Competency	Value-Added Network (VAN) Role
AT&T/Unitel	Voice/data communication	Network management and connectivity
BT North America	Voice/data communication	Network management and connectivity
Canada Post	Physical mail handling	Universal electronic/non-electronic linkage
Compuserve	Information services	Individual & small business coverage
Digital Equipment	Computer products	Computer & network management
GE Info Services	Information services	Individual & corporate coverage
IBM-IIN	Computer products	Computer & network management
Immedia Infomatic	Value-added network provider	Niche, focused on electronic commerce
MCI	Voice/data communication	Network management and connectivity
Prodigy	Information services	Individual & small business coverage
Royal Bank	Banking services	Business & financial services
Sprint	Voice/data communication	Network management and connectivity
WorldLinx/Mediatel	Voice/data communication	Network management and connectivity

SOURCE: *The Financial Post Magazine*, September 10, 1993.

A NEW POSTAL PARADIGM

By 1994, CPC had developed competencies that would be important for the physical and electronic communications businesses. For physical distribution, CPC had the most sophisticated delivery system in the nation; for electronic distribution, CPC had developed network management capabilities and had earned the reputation of being an "honest broker," retaining no memory of what was delivered to whom from whom. In fact, a recent market survey reported CPC's reputation for credibility and trustworthiness as exceeding the reputations of IBM, Bell Canada and the Government of Canada. As a consequence, CPC was often the carrier of choice in Canada.

CPC's services could be broken down by whether the sender or receiver was a corporate client or private citizen, and whether the medium of delivery was electronic or physical. However, to date there was no electronic-electronic routing, or physical-electronic routing. Electronic-physical routing accounted for $30 million of the total revenue generated. The percentage volume of mail for the overall business is depicted in Figure 3.

FIGURE 3   Corporate/Private, Sender/Receiver

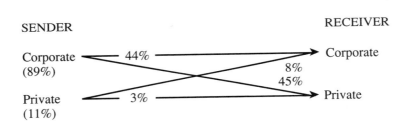

Moreover, CPC was the only organization that had access to every household and business in Canada, every business day—almost 12 million addresses. This unique distribution access was used by the Corporation as a resource to develop strategic alliances and exploit new market potentials. For example, CPC's involvement in Universal Bidirectional Interactive (UBI) was a result of its trusted position and universal access. UBI was a consortium of Le Groupe Videotron Ltée, Hydro-Quebec, the National Bank of Canada, Loto-Quebec, Videoway Communications Inc., the Hearst Corporation, and CPC. UBI would install terminals in 34 000 homes in Chicoutimi, Quebec, the Fall of 1995 to begin testing interactive technology enabling participants to pay their bills and receive personalized mail electronically.

CPC's interest in UBI was to manage the "directory" which provided the linchpin between points of communication, determining where, when and how individuals received communication. As an interface in what would be a very complex communication network involving different types of equipment and physical/electronic bridging, CPC would be in a position to orchestrate communication while offering a full range of physical and electronic delivery products.

RE-INVESTING IN CPC

Its reputation as an "honest broker" with "no memory" and as carrier of first choice, and its universal access to Canadians notwithstanding, CPC's ability to maintain its self-sufficiency depended upon earning a favourable return on assets amid increasing competition. With growth forecast at moderate levels, higher contributions needed to originate through cost efficiencies. Georges Clermont, president of CPC, commented that the greatest challenge facing Canada Post was enhancing its competitiveness to survive the onslaught of electronic competitors.

> Communicating through electronic means has already started, and it can overtake us very quickly if we're not careful. People go to new technologies or methods when the ones they are using become unreliable or too expensive. To protect our basic business, we must offer reliable and affordable services.

To that end, capital investment totalling $1.2 billion was planned for the next five years. Table 5 details the 1993–94 and 1994–95 capital budgets, $275 million (6.7% of revenue) and $200 million (4.3% of revenue) respectively. Business development, operational efficiencies and customer service were stressed in budgetary allocations with mail processing and distribution network equipment (OCRs, VES and LSMs) continuing to be updated internally, while community mail boxes and kiosks supported new delivery points.

TABLE 5   1993–94 and 1994–95 Capital Budget of Canada Post Corporation

Project	Budget	1994–95 Objectives	Main Focus
Business Development	1993–94: $29.9 million (11%) 1994–95: $16.1 million (8%t)	• protecting and increasing the market share & profitability of CPC's major products & services • continue developing hybrid electronic /print mail products	• revenue generation
Maintenance	1993–94: $66.9 million (24%) 1994–95: $75.3 million (38%)	• $60 million into community mail boxes and kiosks* maintenance • balance: maintaining processing & delivery equipment, capital improvements to maintain buildings & other assets, upgrading processing system's computer workstations & software	• customer service
Plant & Equipment Upgrade	1993–94: $98.8 million (36%) 1994–95: $90 million (45%)	• improved effectiveness and efficiency of processes in three areas: commercial operations, collection & delivery, processing & distribution	• cost reduction • customer service • customer information collection

TABLE 5 (continued)

Project	Budget	1994–95 Objectives	Main Focus
Systems & Other Improvements	1993–94: $79.4 million (29%) 1994–95: $18.6 million (9%)	• database and computer system development for monitoring performance, currently sales performance, marketing plans & product	• efficiency & effectiveness • management control
TOTAL: 1993–94 1994–95	$275 million $200 million	• 6.7% of actual revenue • 4.3% of budgeted revenue	

SOURCE: 1993–94 and 1994–95 Corporate Plan and Capital Budget of Canada Post Corporation.

THE DECISION

With this information as a beginning, Lemay evaluated the issues facing CPC. Most importantly, he recognized the need to further develop his assessment of what impact the I-way would have on CPC's future in electronic transfer of information before making recommendations on how CPC should position itself for the future.

EXHIBIT 1 Financial Statements and Pro Forma Statements 1990–98

Consolidated Statement of Income and Retained Earnings

	1990–91	1991–92	1992–93	*PROFORMA* 1993–94	1994–95	1995–96	1996–97	1997–98
Revenue from operations by market segment *(in millions of dollars)*								
Communications market	2 138	2 077	2 130	2 151	n.a.	n.a.	n.a.	n.a.
Advertising Market								
Addressed	268	312	341	343	n.a.	n.a.	n.a.	n.a.
Unaddressed	187	204	211	227	n.a.	n.a.	n.a.	n.a.
Publications	264	252	225	190	n.a.	n.a.	n.a.	n.a.
Sub-total	719	768	777	760	n.a.	n.a.	n.a.	n.a.
Package Distribution	620	673	694	871	n.a.	n.a.	n.a.	n.a.
Other revenue	262	286	308	333	n.a.	n.a.	n.a.	n.a.
Revenue from operations	3 739	3 804	3 909	4 115	4 695	4 992	5 097	5 330
Cost of operations	3 664	3 905	3 827	4 089	4 700	4 935	4 945	5 156
Income from operations	75	(101)	82	26	(5)	57	152	174
Income as a % of revenue	2.0%	—	2.1%	0.6%	—	1.1%	3.0%	3.3%
Other income (expense)	(61)	(27)	(56)	(296)	(41)	(47)	(44)	(38)
Income taxes					(1)	(1)	(49)	(59)
Net income (loss)	14	(128)	26	(270)	(47)	9	59	77
Return on Equity (%)	1.0%	—	1.9%	—	—	0.9%	5.3%	6.6%
Retained Earnings								
Equity restructuring					345			
Deficit	(30)	(44)	(18)	(288)	10	19	74	127

Consolidated Balance Sheet

Year ended *(in millions of dollars)*	*March 31* 1991	*March 31* 1992	*March 31* 1993	*March 26* 1994	*PROFORMA* 1995	1996	1997	1998
Current assets	547	299	291	373				
Fixed assets	1 947	1 847	1 884	1 842				
Other assets	168	286	319	398				
Current liabilities	740	682	686	899				
Net Assets	1 922	1 780	1 808	1 714	1 662	1 704	1 836	1 843
Long-term debt	135	135	135	279	275	275	275	195
Deferred liabilities & benefits	342	333	336	368	366	390	454	474
Equity of Canada	1 445	1 312	1 337	1 067	1 021	1 039	1 107	1 174

Consolidated Statement of Cash Flow

Year ended *(in millions of dollars)*	*March 31* 1992	*March 31* 1993	*March 26* 1994	*PROFORMA* 1995	1996	1997	1998
Cash provided by (used for)							
Operating activities	(37)	175	113	250	297	289	410
Financing activities	—	—	(6)	(4)	8	10	(70)
Dividends	(6)	—	—	—	—	(4)	(24)
Investment activities	(187)	(215)	(139)	(252)	(306)	(281)	(283)
Increase (decrease) in cash and short-term investments	(230)	(40)	(32)	(6)	(1)	14	33
Cash and short-term investments at beginning of year	333	103	63	31	25	24	38
Cash and short-term investments at end of year	103	63	31	25	24	38	71

SOURCE: Annual Statements, Corporate Plan and Capital Budgets of Canada Post Corporation

EXHIBIT 2   Estimated 1994 U.S. Domestic Expenditures for Selected products

Industry		US$ billions
Hardware		
TV, VCR, Camcorders		18.5
Computer Hardware		56.3
Radio & TV Communication		18.2
Telephone & Telegraph		17.5
Satellite & Ground		3.6
Total		114.1
Software		
Application tools	9.6	
Application solutions	14.0	
Systems software	12.6	
Packaged software (including Canada)		36.2
Networking		9.0
Total		45.2
Entertainment		
Motion Pictures—Box office		5.2
Pre-recorded music		11.8
Broadcast networks		30–35 range
Broadcast TV advertising		30.0
Program Sales		10.5
Home video & video rental/sales		13.5–19.3 range
Video games		5.0
CATV—basic service revenue		13.6
CATV—premium services, programming & advertising		15.6
Total		135.2
Services		
Data processing & network service		53.6
On-line information services		15.6
Local exchange	85.0	
Long distance (toll)	58.0	
Data communications, including Value-added networks (VANs)	30.0	
Satellite, paging & cellular	20.6	
Telephone services		193.6
Total		312.8
Retail Services		
Catalogue	70.0–80.0 range	
Electronic	4.0	
Mail order/home shopping		75.0

SOURCE: *The Economist*, February 12, 1994, S.S.1 and October 16, 1993, p. 21, and U.S. Department of Commerce & 1994 U.S Industrial Outlook, Chapters 24–31 (Estimated 1994 consumption).

STRATEGY— RESOURCE/ CAPABILITIES

PART

3

IPL INC.

J. Michael Geringer and Louis Hébert

In April 1988, Julien Métivier, CEO of IPL Inc., was reassessing his company's policy regarding involvement in custom molded plastic products. A leader in the Canadian injection molded plastics industry, IPL had traditionally relied on proprietary products rather than the manufacturing-on-order of custom products for other firms. However, since 1984, IPL had been supplying custom molded auto parts for the Ford Motor Company, and had recently been offered a contract to manufacture a large volume of additional parts for them. Despite its potential strategic benefits, several of IPL's managers were reluctant to accept the new contract because it threatened to dramatically increase the company's reliance on supplying custom molded products, particularly to a single large customer in a potentially unstable industry environment. Having only one month to respond to Ford's offer, Julien was concerned about how he should proceed.

THE CANADIAN PLASTIC PRODUCTS INDUSTRY

In 1986, the Canadian plastic products industry was composed of approximately 2 500 firms, representing more than 95 000 jobs. In about half of these firms, plastic processing represented the major or exclusive activity. The typical firm was small, with about 50 employees and sales under $4 million. The fragmented industry structure was due to the absence of significant entry barriers or governmental regulations during the industry's early years. A small investment in one or two used machines and some knowledge of mechanics was often a sufficient base for entry. Customers' emphasis on the cost of plastic products rather than on quality also helped constrain the development of larger firms, which could not be competitive with these low-cost competitors.

However, the proportion of firms with less than ten employees had been decreasing rapidly, dropping from 40% to 35% between 1983 and 1985. Several large corporations specializing in plastic processing and with sales above $100 million had subsequently emerged. This increasing concentration was closely related to consumers' growing emphasis on quality and performance of plastic products. In addition to traditional quality-oriented market niches such as electronics and aerospace, high-volume markets had begun demanding increased precision with regard to uniformity in the appearance, performance and physico-mechanic characteristics of the products.

In the early 1980s, Canadian plastics producers had average costs 5% to 15% greater than their U.S. counterparts. With a domestic plastics market approximately ten times that of Canada's, U.S. firms were often larger and more focused, and they could dedicate machines to the manufacture of a single product. As the number of products per machine increased, there tended to be an increase in tooling and maintenance costs, a decrease in machine utilization rates, and declining scale and experience curve benefits. Nevertheless, competitiveness of Canadian producers had been enhanced by favourable exchange rates, and a tariff of 13.5% on plastic goods from the U.S. versus 5.3% on goods shipped to the U.S.

Costs of plastic resins accounted for an average of 47% of manufacturers' sales in 1986, compared to 12%, 18%, 5% and 8% for labour, overhead, selling and administration, respectively. Most resins were commodity goods, supplied by a small number of large chemical companies. Production capacity constraints experienced by these North American suppliers had led to price increases up to 80% since 1987. In addition, transportation costs represented an important component of delivered costs, and shipment of products for more than 500 kilometres was often uneconomical.

Plastic products were generally classified as either custom molded or proprietary. Firms involved in custom molding were essentially subcontractors that used molds owned by customers for the molding-on-order of plastic products. Custom molders' superior pretax return on sales, estimated for 1985 at 9.3% versus 6.7% for producers of proprietary products, was due to the custom segment's higher risks and instability. In contrast, producers of proprietary products generally required greater financial capacity in order to cover the added costs of product development, mold-making, and sales and distribution. However, since they owned both the mold and the product, they were not dependent on the vagaries of subcontracting and were able to sell each product to more than one customer in order to amortize their investment in products and distribution channels. As a result, proprietary product producers tended to have a higher return on investment than did custom producers. Nevertheless, it was common for producers of proprietary products to also devote a portion of their activities to custom molding in order to increase utilization of production capacity.

In 1986, the packaging market was the largest outlet for plastic products, accounting for 39% of the resins consumed by the Canadian industry, compared to 27% and 11% for construction and automotive goods, respectively. In sales volume, the plastic packaging market was estimated at $1.13 billion in 1985, compared to $809 million in 1982. The remainder of the market for plastic products consisted principally of the furniture and furnishings industry with 6%, and electrical and electronics products, housewares, agriculture and toys, each with less than 5%.

THE PLASTIC AUTO PARTS INDUSTRY

Since 1975, the auto industry had been the fastest growing market for plastic products. Deliveries of plastic auto parts by Canadian producers reached $1.3 billion in 1985, compared to $928 million, $732 million, and $521 million in 1984, 1983 and 1982, respectively. The lower cost and lighter weight of plastic products, their ease of processing, technological advances, and efforts by resin suppliers to develop new automotive applications were the main factors promoting this evolution. Further growth was expected because, in 1986, plastics accounted for only 6% of the 56 million tons of materials used worldwide for the manufacture of autos.

North American auto-makers were the main consumers of auto parts, both plastic and non-plastic, delivered by Canadian producers. However, the major auto-makers varied in the extent to which they relied on external suppliers. Chrysler sourced about 70% of its parts and assemblies from external sources, compared to 50% for Ford and 30% for General Motors. The recent market success of foreign manufacturers, especially the Japanese, had resulted in trends toward lower costs, increased product quality, and a reduction in the number of suppliers. In addition, there was increased use of long-term supply contracts, often involving technological cooperation and joint development of parts and systems. However, in return for long-term contracts, suppliers often had to assume a larger part of the costs of tooling, R&D and warranties. Suppliers were also expected to reduce prices by 2–5% each year. Further rationalization of supplier networks was expected as auto-makers intensified their efforts to reduce the number of parts going into their vehicles, along with increased emphasis on purchase of sub-assemblies and finished components systems. Furthermore, just-in-time delivery systems were rapidly gaining acceptance. These systems demanded stringent quality controls, and imposed contract penalties of up to $1 000 a minute if supplier delivery problems caused the auto-maker's assembly line to be shut down. In response, many large suppliers of plastic parts and resins had invested in facilities close to the auto-makers' operations, and this trend threatened to raise a major barrier to the entry of new suppliers.

According to industry observers, Ford was at the forefront of trends toward rationalization of supplier networks and improvement of overall product quality. In 1986, Ford had expressed an intention to reduce its number of suppliers by 90% within five years and to develop lasting relationships with the remaining firms, especially those which obtained Q-1 or TQE (Total Quality Excellence) accreditations. These accreditations were awarded to suppliers which achieved Ford's requirements in quality control and management, as well as R&D and manufacturing capabilities. Such accreditation allowed a supplier's products to be integrated directly into Ford's assembly line without first undergoing quality control inspections.

The plastic auto parts industry was expected to become increasingly competitive as off-shore suppliers already involved with foreign auto-makers followed their customers into the North American market. Thus, the key challenges facing North American auto parts suppliers were the ability to achieve continued improvements in productivity and quality, and to survive the cyclical demand fluctuations characterizing the auto industry.

IPL'S BACKGROUND

Les Industries Provinciales Limitées was founded in 1939 by Emile Métivier in Saint-Damien, a small village about 80 kilometres southeast of Quebec City. Incorporated in 1945 under the IPL name, the firm was initially involved in the manufacture of wooden housewares like brushes, brooms and mops, and in the assembly of plastic toothbrushes. IPL began production of plastic goods after the 1953 acquisition of its supplier of toothbrush components. Over the years, IPL became involved in the manufacture and sale of a variety of plastic housewares and industrial pails, and abandoned production of wooden housewares.

Emile Métivier involved his four sons in IPL's operations during the company's early years. His eldest and youngest sons, Rémi and Julien, gained experience in the marketing and sales of industrial containers and housewares, respectively. Similarly, Clément managed the sawmill which the firm operated until 1961, and later worked on the development of a maple sap gathering system, while Benoît was involved in issues of production and machinery acquisition.

Upon Emile Métivier's death in 1971, his sons took over management of IPL, with Rémi, then 38, becoming CEO. By 1983, when Rémi became Chairman of the Board and Benoît replaced him as CEO, IPL's operational emphasis was on the development of proprietary lines of pails, containers, and material handling products. In 1985, IPL undertook an ambitious modernization program called "IPL 1990," whose objective was to enable IPL to be among the most technologically advanced firms in the North American plastic products industry. The five-year modernization program was financed in part through a 1985 public stock issue of one million shares at a price of $5.75 each, and resulted in IPL being listed on the Montreal Stock Exchange. In late 1986, Benoît left his position and terminated active participation in the firm's management or board activities, but remained a major shareholder and board member. His 48-year-old brother Julien, for many years IPL's only professionally trained manager, became CEO in February 1987.

IPL'S ORGANIZATION

In April 1988, IPL had a functional organization structure with three vice-presidents, a treasurer and five departmental managers reporting to the CEO (Exhibits 1 and 2). A fourth vice-president position, that of marketing, was abolished after the December 1987 departure of that person in response to growing divergences between him and other executives regarding IPL's future development. In addition, no children or close relatives of the Métivier brothers were involved in the firm's management. This situation was not expected to change in the near future.

The firm's operational and strategic management was under the direct responsibility of IPL's 11-person management committee, which usually met once a month. The vice-president of finance, as IPL's secretary, set the agenda for these meetings after consulting with the Committee's other members, but additional topics could be introduced at the end of the meetings. The same committee, without the vice-president of finance, met for several hours every Monday morning to deal with more day-to-day management issues. According to IPL's executives, this process permitted close control of the firm's production and marketing efforts. IPL also had a nine-member Board of Directors, which included two outside directors and the firm's largest shareholders (Exhibit 3). However, the Board's involvement in IPL's operations was limited to a quarterly review of the firm's performance and to formal ratification of the broad strategic orientations proposed by the management committee.

IPL's organization was characterized by a strong emphasis on informality, collegiality, and consensus decision making. The firm's executives believed these traits helped preserve IPL's family atmosphere and supported innovativeness, entrepreneurship, and teamwork. According to them, this atmosphere represented one of the major factors in the firm's success.

Strategy and Objectives

IPL specialized in the design, manufacture, printing and marketing of plastic products, mainly intended for industrial uses, and made of thermoplastic resins through injection molding. Except for a very limited amount of extrusion molding, the firm was not involved in any other molding process, like blow molding or thermoforming. Furthermore, IPL's policies had traditionally emphasized proprietary products rather than custom molding.

In addition to product mix, IPL distinguished itself from competitors through its emphasis on better quality and performance products, superior engineering and service, innovativeness and the capacity to meet customers' specific needs. According to François Béchard, IPL's success was based on "its ability to sell differentiated products at higher prices while cutting production costs through automation." IPL's executives also emphasized the importance of profitability rather than merely growth. As noted by Béchard, "we learned from the economic downturn in 1982 that it was prudent to maintain a working capital ratio of 2:1, and to keep our debt-to-equity ratio between 0.3 and 0.6. Although these objectives may slow down our growth somewhat, they allow us to keep our balance sheet very sound." IPL's objectives also included an annual growth in sales of 10%, a gross margin of 30%, a net profit after tax ratio of 6%, and the distribution of 25% of net profits in dividends (Exhibits 4 and 5 contain IPL's financial statements).

Products and Markets

With more than 600 products whose similarities were often limited to their manufacturing process, IPL viewed itself as a diversified producer of injection molded products (Exhibit 6). IPL's principal geographic markets stretched across Eastern Canada, from the Maritimes to Ontario, and into the northeastern U.S. In 1987, the Quebec market represented 47% of sales while the U.S., Ontario and Maritimes markets accounted for 25%, 19% and 9% of sales, respectively.

Pails and containers were IPL's largest and most profitable product line; they also accounted for almost all of the company's non-automotive sales outside Quebec. With capacities ranging from 1.4 to 130 litres, IPL offered a wider line of industrial and institutional pails and containers than any other Canadian producer. IPL also had the equipment and expertise for high quality printing of as many as five colours onto containers, a competence seldom found in the industrial container business but which was becoming an increasingly important criterion for selecting suppliers. Except for a handful of large food industry firms, IPL's customers were small- and medium-sized firms that were dissatisfied with the narrow choice of sizes offered by competitors. The customers were mostly in the food processing, chemical and construction industries, and used IPL's containers for a variety of goods, ranging from fruits and cement to chlorine for swimming pools.

In recent years, IPL continued to expand their product line. In 1985, a new line of pails and containers licensed for the Canadian market from the Danish firm Superfos, was marketed under the Flex-Off brand name. With 1987 sales of $2.5 million, these products appeared to have substantial growth potential. In 1987, IPL acquired the plastics division of Edmunston Paper Box Ltd. (EPB), located in Edmunston, New Brunswick, for $4 million. EPB's line of small-size, thin-wall containers for the food processing industry, including margarine, yogurt and ice-cream containers with capacities under five litres, complemented IPL's line of larger pails and containers. EPB's products were expected to achieve considerable sales growth, particularly in Quebec and Ontario, because of increased penetration provided by IPL's larger distribution network.

Due to the firm's capacity to meet specific customer needs, as well as the reliability and quality of its products, IPL's pails and containers were priced an average of 5% above competition. Historically, competition in the Canadian market had been moderate, mainly because it was divided among a small number of regional producers and no national company had yet emerged. With each producer dominating their own immediate market, as was the case for IPL in the Quebec market, there had been little incentive for firms to compete on price. However, this situation had begun to change in recent years, with a wave of acquisitions and the increasing presence of American competitors taking advantage of their larger scale of operations. Indeed, IPL was one of the few independent companies left in the Canadian industrial plastic containers business.

IPL's second largest product line was composed of two main types of material handling products. For the Government of Quebec, IPL manufactured rigid-wall, multi-cavity containers used in forest seedling production. With their supply contract ending in 1988, IPL was looking for new markets for this product. However, increasing concerns regarding the effectiveness of paper pots, the major substitute product, suggested that future market prospects for plastic seedling containers were substantial. On the other hand, IPL's carriers for soft drink bottles and milk containers had confronted increasing competition in recent years. Most users of these products had filled their "pipelines," and only replacement production would be needed in the future. In response, IPL was considering introducing related products into the Quebec market, such as European-designed beverage cases for the brewing industry, mobile bins for automated domestic garbage collection, and a line of material handling boxes.

Like most plastic processors, IPL devoted a portion of its operations to custom molding. Every year, IPL was involved in several small development projects for custom molded products intended for such industries as lobster fishing, furniture, or defense. Most of these projects resulted from unsolicited requests from companies looking for products meeting very particular requirements or applications. Currently, the major portion of these activities was related to automotive products molded for Ford.

IPL also manufactured a wide variety of plastic housewares like chopping boards, mixing bowls, wine racks, garbage cans, and chairs. The housewares line had been declining in relative importance, however, because it was perceived to be inconsistent with IPL's strategic focus. Opportunities in that segment were limited, especially since distribution channels were dominated by large housewares firms like Rubbermaid and Sterilite. IPL also produced a plastic-made system for gathering maple sap, the raw material for maple syrup. Quebec produced

70% of the world's maple syrup, a crop worth over $50 million annually to sap producers. IPL dominated the North American market for these systems and no significant competition was perceived to exist.

Marketing and Distribution

For sales and distribution of products to its 2 000 customers, IPL operated regional sales offices and warehouses in Montreal, Quebec, Toronto, Ontario, and Moncton, New Brunswick, as well as subsidiaries in Edmundston, New Brunswick, and Boston, Massachusetts. IPL's Canadian sales force, which included 12 salespeople and six manufacturers' representatives, had traditionally handled both the industrial containers and the material handling product lines. However, because of a commission system based on total sales volume, salespeople had tended to place greater emphasis on high turnover items such as pails. As a result, in 1988 IPL hired two representatives exclusively for material handling products. Eight additional representatives were responsible for sales of the maple sap gathering systems, while housewares were under the responsibility of two distributors and one salesperson. Furthermore, the company employed three Boston-based representatives to sell pails and containers in the U.S.

IPL's salespeople were under the direct supervision of the sales manager and they also interacted frequently with the product manager responsible for their product line. IPL's three product managers were responsible for the planning and development of their product lines and for customer service. They were essentially a communication and coordination link between the customers, the sales force and the firm's other departments.

In the case of auto parts, sales were made through a Detroit-based manufacturing agent who received a commission on sales. Direct responsibility for this business had traditionally been delegated to the former vice-president of marketing. However, since elimination of that position, the responsibility had been assumed by the vice-president of R&D.

Human Resources

As stated in IPL's corporate objectives, human resources were viewed as a major factor contributing to the firm's reputation for quality and innovativeness. Thus, the firm placed fundamental importance on both the quality and aspirations of its 500 employees, 80% of whom were unionized production workers affiliated with the Quebec Federation of Labour. IPL's commitment was evidenced by the $300 000 devoted annually to employee training, including the opportunity to take English lessons at company expense. IPL had also maintained overall employment levels, despite extensive modernization and automation of company facilities. The firm actively promoted participative management, including incentives for employee shareholding, and the creation of quality circles and other management–labour committees to ensure effective communication between management and the employees. Due to these efforts, implementation of IPL's modernization program had been accomplished without major resistance to change, and management viewed their relations with labour as excellent.

IPL was one of the few Canadian plastics firms to have established an in-house training centre to overcome chronic shortages of skilled labour in the plastics industry. As one IPL executive said, "This centre permits the training of excellent workers whose qualifications satisfy our needs. Yet, just as important, it also makes the workers more sensitive to IPL's culture and helps to preserve our firm's special, family-like work atmosphere." The firm's atmosphere could indeed be characterized as familial, with many employees being related among themselves or with executives. Traditional Quebec family names such as Chabot or Mercier were common throughout the firm. About 50% of the employees lived in Saint-Damien, with the remainder coming from nearby rural communities.

The firm also maintained strong community involvement. Besides being the largest single employer in an area dominated by small farms, forestry, fishing and hunting, IPL contributed as much as $150 000 annually for local charities, sports facilities and the Métivier arena. Moreover, the Métivier brothers had always tried to concentrate IPL's activities in Saint-Damien in recognition of the local population's continuing support.

Manufacturing and Technology

Industry specialists considered IPL's production facilities in Saint-Damien to be among the most modern in North America. For example, a leading plastics industry journal talked about "IPL's factory of the future" and asserted that "no other manufacturer in Canada has gone further into true CIM (Computer Integrated Manufacturing) than IPL."[1] Visitors were often astonished to find these ultra-modern facilities within a rural village of 2 300 inhabitants.

IPL's position as one of the industry's technological leaders was a direct result of the $24 million invested since 1985 as part of the "IPL 1990" program. Most of that investment had been used for the 1986 construction of new production facilities equipped with the most advanced technologies available, including computer numerical control injection molding machines, robots, automated guided vehicles for moving materials around the plant floor, CAD/CAM systems, and MRP II. This new plant had been built as an extension of IPL's existing facilities, resulting in some disturbance to the firm's operations during construction.

IPL's investment in technology allowed them to considerably reduce the gap between their production costs and those associated with large-scale production, while simultaneously maintaining manufacturing flexibility. Furthermore, IPL's facilities operated on a continuous, 24 hours a day, seven days a week basis, compared to the single shift, five days a week schedule typical in the industry. The company was thus able to achieve higher production volumes, which permitted more rapid amortization of equipment and enhanced the feasibility of continued investment in new technologies. The benefits from IPL's substantial investments in production facilities were readily apparent: in 1987, the first full year of operations within the new facilities, total productivity (the amount, in kilograms, of plastic molded per worker) had increased by 15%, inventories had been reduced by 33%, the average changeover time for a mold was cut from two to three hours to ten to fifteen minutes, the rejection rate for finished goods had fallen from 12% to 3%, and the product return rate had declined to almost zero. IPL's achievements in quality control were recognized in 1988 when the firm received the prestigious Mercure award for Total Quality from the Quebec Board of Trade. However, sales growth had been unable to keep up with IPL's rapid and substantial increases in productivity

---

[1] "Closing the Loop," *Canadian Plastics*, June 1988, p. 46, and "CIM Pays Off for Canadian custom molders," *Canadian Plastics*, May 1987, p. 24.

and production capacity. Consequently, the production capacity utilization rate had declined to 72% in early 1988.

IPL's investment in R&D, at 2% of sales, was more than twice the plastics industry average. The 15-person R&D department was responsible for continued automation of production, development of new products, and joint research with European companies, Ford, and universities and other research centres.

IPL'S INVOLVEMENT IN CUSTOM MOLDING

Due to the fluctuating nature of demand, as well as price sensitivity traditionally associated with custom molding, IPL had historically limited its involvement in this activity to 15% of total sales. However, this percentage had been raised to 25% when Benoît Métivier was CEO. The appearance of high-volume markets for custom molding, particularly in the auto industry, had encouraged this change. Collaboration with Ford represented a unique opportunity to enter a market offering rapid growth and profit potential, while capitalizing on IPL's skills in high-quality injection molding. Business with Ford was facilitated by the rapid accreditation of IPL's St. Damien plant as a Q-1 supplier in 1984, making them the first Canadian injection molder to receive that rating. Within the next year, IPL also expected the St. Damien facility to become the first plastics plant in Canada to receive Ford's TQE accreditation.

IPL's sales to Ford had risen from $300 000 in 1984 to $7 million in 1987, and they were expected to exceed $8 million in 1988. IPL had also become more than a mere custom molder for Ford. Initially, IPL had focused on production of non-visible internal parts, like bushings of car door opening mechanisms or internal dashboard parts. Ford considered these parts to be critical because they could involve, in the case of breakage or wear, repairs many times more expensive than their initial costs. Later, IPL began manufacturing visible parts, like external components of dashboards, in which product appearance was also of critical importance. In 1987, the firm became Ford's North American supplier for several visible parts, including air deflectors and steering wheel shrouds. Nevertheless, IPL had remained very selective about which parts it manufactured, and had limited its activities to a small number of high-volume parts.

FORD'S OFFER

For the last 18 months, IPL had been one of two North American firms developing visible, imitation leather parts for Ford's new world car planned to replace the Escort in 1990. Ford had recently offered IPL a five-year contract, beginning in spring 1989 and worth an estimated $10 million annually, for supply of these parts. As with other Ford contracts, the order volume was not guaranteed, but would depend on the sales volume of Ford's cars. All orders would be shipped F.O.B. to Ford's Detroit assembly plants from IPL's Saint-Damien facility. The contract's terms appeared to allow IPL a level of profitability equivalent to the industry's average, but included clauses permitting Ford to withdraw its business at any time and required price reductions of 5% annually, except for uncontrollable cost increases like resin prices. The contract would be in addition to existing business done with Ford, and could thus raise IPL's annual sales to that company to $18 million by 1990. Furthermore, the contract could be executed with IPL's current production capacity and with new equipment already on order. IPL had to respond to Ford's offer within the next month.

MANAGERS' ATTITUDES TOWARD THE AUTO PARTS BUSINESS

Involvement in the auto parts market had often been a source of disagreement among IPL's managers. In recent months, this issue had assumed renewed importance with the possibility of further growth of sales to Ford and, thus, of increasing IPL's reliance on custom molded products. Many IPL executives felt that the custom molding business was not sufficiently profitable, given the risks it usually involved. Initial indications were that the profitability of the recent Ford offer would be similar to or lower than IPL's earlier business, because of the required 5% annual reduction in prices. In addition, some concerns were voiced regarding IPL's increasing dependence on a single, much larger customer. IPL's managers clearly remembered the firm's previous experiences with custom molding. In the early 1970s, IPL had produced a large volume of custom molded products for another major transportation firm. However, IPL lost 25% of its sales volume overnight when that customer moved manufacturing in-house. These memories had been revived by rumours that auto-makers had recently placed orders for large injection molding machinery.

Julien Métivier felt that the automobile market could represent a lucrative opportunity if IPL was able to maintain a good margin on these products and to expand its customer base. However, he was not ruling out increased emphasis on IPL's other product lines, including rejuvenation of the housewares line with the introduction of new products related to gardening. IPL projected sales of up to $2 million in plant pots and plastic patio furniture within two years of the products' introduction.

Both Clément Métivier and Fernand Mercier, respectively IPL's Treasurer and V.P. of Administration, agreed with their CEO that IPL should expand its auto parts business, but only if expansion could be done in a controlled manner. However, they believed that it would soon become difficult to limit IPL's involvement in custom molding to 25% of sales. For them, as well as for several other managers, IPL appeared to have no choice but to eventually create an independent division to exclusively handle this business. However, it was still uncertain how this change could be implemented, due to production and marketing complexities associated with this move.

"IPL cannot afford *not* to be in the automobile parts market," asserted Jean-Marie Chabot, IPL's V.P. of R&D. According to him, all major advances in knowledge in the plastics industry came from work in the auto and aerospace industries. The auto parts market could thus be a priceless source of know-how if IPL was able to develop lasting relationships with auto-makers. He also felt that the auto firms' increasing emphasis on quality rather than just price was consistent with IPL's capabilities. Moreover, IPL was one of the few Canadian firms experienced in the use of the large machinery required for the molding of many automotive parts.

Without denying the benefits of cooperation with Ford in terms of sales and know-how, other executives were less supportive of an expansion of that business. They instead strongly favoured the development of proprietary products. Rémi Métivier, IPL's Chairman, felt that "IPL should at least stick to its 25% policy or further reduce its activities in custom molding and instead focus on the development of proprietary products, especially material handling products." IPL's sales forecasts for most material handling products were excellent. This was particularly the case for recycling boxes, already introduced in the market and whose sales were projected to reach $16 million within five years. IPL was also considering the development of mobile bins for domestic garbage collection, a product that within ten years could represent a potential $200 million market in Quebec alone. Nevertheless, extensive growth of these markets depended on municipal and provincial governments' willingness to adopt this technology of garbage collection on a large scale. Competition in the recycling box and mobile bins segments was also expected to be intense, as many companies had already entered or were expected to do so in the near future. In addition, with cooperation of a West German firm, IPL was developing beverage cases for the brewing industry to replace the traditional cardboard cases. However, IPL had been experiencing some difficulty selling the concept to the major breweries.

François Béchard, V.P. of Finance, also felt IPL should try to limit its vulnerability in the competitive auto parts business, consistent with the approach taken by large plastics firms like Rubbermaid, Scepter and Shaeffer. According to Béchard, IPL should instead take advantage of the proposed Canada-U.S. Free Trade Agreement, and work on increasing penetration of its proprietary products in the U.S. market, but this time with products adapted to the needs of American customers. In many instances, IPL's products had been judged too expensive, inadequate because of their metric sizes, or overengineered for the highly competitive and price sensitive U.S. market. Such problems helped explain why IPL's American subsidiary had been experiencing chronic deficits that reached $300 000 in 1987. As a result, IPL was currently considering investment of over $300 000 in molds for a five-gallon size pail. At a price of $4, management believed IPL could sell more than one million of these pails in Canada and an additional 750 000 south of the border. Because of lower prices in the U.S. market and competition of larger American firms already producing this type of container, margins in that market were expected to be less than half those of the Canadian market. However, IPL management believed this tradeoff was necessary in order to strengthen its U.S. market position.

Along the same lines, several managers suggested that IPL should have manufacturing facilities rather than merely a sales office in the Boston area. IPL was contemplating acquisition of a small U.S. manufacturer of high-quality industrial containers, or small-scale manufacturing of certain products in its U.S. facilities, in order to reduce tariff and transportation costs.

CONCLUSION

In light of the divergence in opinions among his managers, Julien Métivier knew it would be difficult to build a consensus around a particular alternative. However, within the next month, IPL had to respond to Ford's recent contract offer as well as deciding on several other projects the firm was considering. In making these decisions, Julien wanted to avoid major disagreements among IPL's executives and unnecessary threats to the company's successful strategy. He wondered what direction he should move the company and how he should proceed.

EXHIBIT 1 IPL Organization Chart

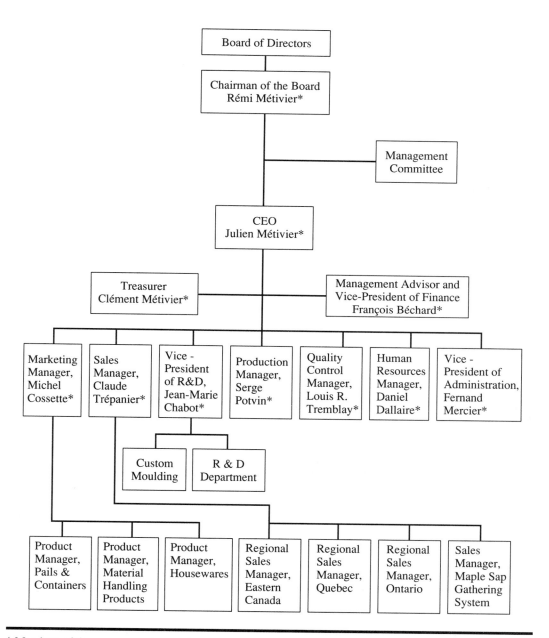

* Members of the management committee.

EXHIBIT 2   Personal Data on IPL's Key Managers as of April 1988

Name	Age	Position	Years with IPL	Background
Rémi Métivier*	54	Chairman of the Board	34	High school education; undergraduate courses in business (Laval University)
Julien Métivier*	50	Chief Executive Officer	28	Master in Commerce (Laval University)
Clément Métivier*	53	Treasurer	32	High school education; involved in costing system issues
Benoît Métivier	51	Director	31	High school education; resigned as CEO in 1986
François Béchard*	48	Vice-President of Finance and Secretary	20	MBA (Western); consultant; devoting 4 days/week to IPL from his Quebec City office
Fernand Mercier*	47	Vice-President of Administration	33	High school education
Jean-Marie Chabot*	43	Vice-President of R&D	20	B Engineering (Laval University)
Serge Potvin	34	Production Manager	9	B Engineering (Chicoutimi)
Claude Trépanier	52	Sales Manager	9	High school education; working with plastic companies such as Alibert and Vulcan for 20 years; left IPL between August 1987 and February 1988 to assume general management position at Anchor Plastics Inc.
Louis R. Tremblay	30	Quality Control Manager	6	B Engineering (Chicoutimi)
Daniel Dallaire	33	Human Resources	2	BBA (Sherbrooke); personnel agent and human resources manager with Securities Desjardins between 1981 and 1986
Michel Cossette	37	Marketing Manager	0.5	BSc (UQAM); different sales and marketing positions at IBM for 11 years and LGS Inc. for 3 years
Paul-Henri Fillion*	60	Director	1	President, Hoblab Inc.; ex-President of the Groupement Québécois d'Enterprises
Jean-Paul Lortie	60	Director	3	President and CEO, Sico Inc.

*Members of IPL's Board of Directors.

EXHIBIT 3   IPL Major Shareholders

Métivier brothers	76%
IPL vice-presidents	6
Other public shareholders[1]	18
Total[2]	100%

[1] About 60% of IPL's employees were shareholders.

[2] At the end of 1987, IPL announced its intention to repurchase 300 000 shares, or about 4.5% of the outstanding common shares. The main objective of this stock buy-back was to take advantage of the low price of IPL's stock. Following the decline of the stock indexes since October 1987, IPL's stock had dropped to $3, compared to an historic high of $12 in 1986. In April 1988, IPL stock was traded at $3.85.

EXHIBIT 4   IPL Consolidated Income Statement ($000)

	1987	*1986*	*1985*	*1984*	*1983*	*1982*	*1981*	*1980*
Sales	$48 409	$37 433	$36 719	$30 290	$25 318	$23 803	$23 882	$21 110
Cost of sales	34 808	27 762	25 788	21 646	17 524	17 184	17 593	14 731
Gross margin	13 601	9 671	10 931	8 644	7 794	6 619	6 289	6 379
Expenses								
Selling	5 528	4 595	4 265	3 202	2 790	2 981	3 068	2 594
Administrative	3 823	3 258	2 968	2 730	2 404	2 580	2 487	1 897
Financial	1 192	739	693	407	561	724	513	275
Total expenses	10 543	8 592	7 926	6 339	5 755	6 285	6 068	4 766
Operating profit	3 058	1 079	3 005	2 305	2 039	334	221	1 613
Gain (loss) on disposal of fixed assets	(41)	418	86					
Amortization of deferred grants	776	491	365					
Other revenue	278	518	258	314	510	132	129	207
Income before income taxes	4 071	2 506	3 714	2 619	2 549	466	350	1 820
Income taxes	1 581	1 014	1 243	977	913	131	218	762
Net income	$ 2 472	$ 1 492	$ 2 471	$ 1 642	$ 1 636	$ 335	$ 132	$ 1 058
Earnings per share	$ 0.37	$ 0.23	$ 0.45	$ 0.30	$ 0.30	$ 0.06	$ 0.02	$ 0.20
Stock price: High	9.50	12.00	7.625					
Low	3.00	6.00	5.75					

EXHIBIT 5 **IPL Consolidated Balance Sheet** ($000)

	1987	1986	1985	1984	1983
Assets					
Current assets					
Cash	$ 1 205	$ —	$ —	$ —	$ 183
Trade and other debtors	6 759	5 613	5 340	3 780	4 409
Inventories	6 489	5 366	4 532	4 629	3 381
Grant receivable	454	1 215	286	585	68
Income Taxes recoverable	400	1 562	—	—	—
Prepaid expenses	101	35	—	29	59
TOTAL CURRENT ASSETS	15 407	13 791	10 158	9 023	8 100
Long-term assets	24 575	20 264	11 357	7 095	5 997
Fixed assets	227	266	218	126	12
Balance of sale price of fixed assets	115	175	—	—	—
Deferred charges	1 049	1 052	684	209	131
TOTAL LONG-TERM ASSETS	26 966	21 757	12 259	7 430	6 130
TOTAL ASSETS	$41 662	$35 548	$22 417	$16 453	$14 240
Liabilities					
Current liabilities					
Bank loan and overdraft	—	700	1 182	162	—
Trade and accrued liabilities	4 492	3 864	3 749	2 706	2 501
Income taxes	—	—	186	91	533
Current portion, LT debt	1 605	1 300	400	1 254	912
TOTAL CURRENT LIABILITIES	6 097	5 864	5 577	4 213	3 946
Long-term liabilities					
Long-term debt	9 765	7 708	4 133	3 569	3 020
Deferred income taxes	3 377	2 626	1 883	1 649	1 545
Deferred grants	3 787	3 391	1 660	—	—
TOTAL LT LIABILITIES	16 929	13 725	7 676	5 218	4 565
Minority interest					
Equity					
Capital stock	6 828	6 254	323	82	18
Contributed surplus	—	—	—	294	294
Retained earnings	11 578	9 705	8 901	6 646	5 417
Total equity	18 406	15 959	9 224	7 022	5 729
TOTAL LIABILITIES AND EQUITY	$41 662	$35 548	$22 417	$16 453	$14 240

EXHIBIT 6   **IPL's Product Mix, 1987**

Product Lines	Products	Percent of Sales		Contribution Margin
Pails and containers	General-purpose pails Flex-Off pails and containers Margarine and fish containers Thin-wall containers	23% 5 10 4	} 42%	Above the firm's average
Material handling	Forest seedling containers Beverage cases	15 8	} 23%	Equivalent to firm's average
Custom molding	Auto parts (Ford) Other	16 9	} 25%	Below the firm's average
Housewares	Chopping boards, mixing bowls, wine racks, garbage cans, chairs, etc.	5		Equivalent to firm's average
Maple-sap gathering systems	—	5		Above the firm's average

HARLEQUIN ENTERPRISES LIMITED—1979

J. Peter Killing

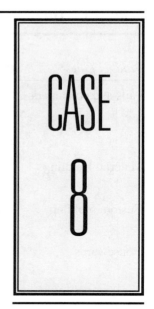

CASE

8

In 1979 Harlequin Enterprises was the largest publisher of romance novels in the world and was judged by many to be North America's most profitable publishing company. Harlequin's sales and profits had increased every year since 1970 and in 1979 were forecasted at $180 million and $20 million respectively. Harlequin romances were produced in nine languages and sold in more than 90 countries.

As the 1970s drew to a close, the pace of change at Harlequin seemed to be quickening. In 1978, for example, Harlequin had produced its first feature film, based on one of its romance novels, and opened its first retail store, designed to sell educational material produced by the company's "Scholar's Choice" division. In 1979 the company was launching its romance novels in Japan, Scandinavia, Mexico, Venezuela, and Greece, as well as adding new romance series in North America, Germany and Holland. As Larry Heisey, Harlequin's president, looked ahead, he stated:

> Strategies that served us well in the 1970s will be continued into the 1980s. We will work to develop our present resources, to make use of those growth channels that have been established, and to pursue the flexibility that will enable us to react to market opportunities. . . . We look to the 1980s as a time of great promise for this company.

J. Peter Killing of the Western Business School prepared this case. Copyright © 1983, The University of Western Ontario. This material is not covered under authorization from CanCopy or any reproduction rights organization. Any form of reproduction, storage or transmittal of this material is prohibited without written permission from Western Business School, The University of Western Ontario, London, Canada N6A 3K7

THE PUBLISHING INDUSTRY

Apart from educational material, publishing a book is typically a high-risk venture. Each book is a new product with all the risks attendant on any new product introduction. The risks vary with the author's reputation, the subject matter and the predictability of the market's response. Among the numerous decisions facing the publisher are selecting manuscripts out of the thousands submitted each year, deciding how many copies to print and deciding how to promote the book.

Insiders judged that the key to success in hardcover publishing was the creative genius needed to identify good young authors among the hundreds of would-be writers, and then publish and develop them throughout their careers. Sol Stein of Stein and Day Publishers commented that

> Most successful publishers are creative editors at heart, and contribute more than risk capital and marketing expertise to the books they publish. If a publisher does not add value to what he publishes, he's a printer, not a publisher.

Successful hardcover authors and their publishers could profit greatly from the sale of paperback publishing rights and film rights. In the 1970s, prices paid for paperback rights had skyrocketed, as softcover publishers bid astronomical amounts, frequently more than $1 million, for books they judged would sell the numbers necessary for paperback success.

These high prices raised the already high break-even volumes for paperback publishers. Publishers generally received about 50% of the retail price, of which about 13% (15¢ per book) would pay for printing costs, 10% for distribution, 10% for selling expenses, 5–7.5% for advertising and promotion, and the remainder would cover rights and overheads. If the publisher failed to sell enough books, the loss could be substantial. One result was that the mass paperback publishers in the United States earned only about 2% on sales of new releases, whereas Harlequin, using a distinctly different approach to the business, earned in the 15% range. Harlequin's financial results are summarized in Exhibit 1.

HARLEQUIN'S FORMULA: STANDARDIZATION

Harlequin's formula was fundamentally different from that of traditional publishers: content, length, artwork, size, basic formats and print were all standardized. Each book was not a new product, but rather an addition to a clearly defined product line. The consequences of this uniformity were significant. The reader was buying a Harlequin novel, and advertising promoted the Harlequin line, rather than a particular book or author. The standardized size made warehousing and distribution more efficient. A comparison of Harlequin's formula and the operations of traditional "one-off" publishers is presented in Table 1.

Because all its novels were aimed at the same target market—"any and all female readers over the age of 15"—Harlequin could afford to do a significant amount of market research, identifying its customers and their likes and dislikes. The average Harlequin reader was 35.5 years old, was married, had 2.5 children, was equally likely to be working or a housewife, and had probably finished high school. Harlequin described the relationship between its books and its readers as follows:

TABLE 1 **The Harlequin Formula**

	Harlequin	*One-Off Publisher*
Editorial	Emphasis on consistency with established guidelines	Requires separate judgement on potential consumer demand for each manuscript
Rights	Standardized process, usually for established amounts	Can be a complex process, involving subrights, hard/ soft cover deals and tying up authors for future books
Author Management	Less dependent of specific authors	Vulnerable to key authors changing publisher
Marketing	Builds the imprint/series	Builds each title/author
Selling	Emphasis on servicing, rack placement and maintaining distribution	Sell on strength of author, cover, critical reviews, special promotional tactics
Production	Consistent format, focus on efficiency	Emphasis on cover design, cost control secondary
Distribution/ order regulation/ information systems	Very sophisticated shipping and returns handling procedures	Traditionally has not received much attention and hence is not as sophisticated

SOURCE: Adapted from a Canada Consulting Group report.

The world of romantic fiction offers the reader delights of a kind which are absent from her everyday life. Identifying herself with the heroine, the romance reader can meet the strong, masterful hero of her dreams and be courted by him. Without stirring from her fireside, she can travel to other countries, learn about other ways of life, and meet new people. After the vicarious enjoyment provided by such literature, the reader can return to safe reality, where domineering males seldom have to be confronted and trips to exotic parts of the world never happen, so that illusion is always preserved. The romance provides compulsive reading and leaves a feeling of satisfaction and pleasure.

Harlequin's view that its novels could be sold "like other branded consumer products" perhaps explained why employees hired from mass-marketing companies such as Procter and Gamble had skills and aptitudes that led them to do well at Harlequin. The company's 1974 Annual Report documented it mass market focus, its use of sampling techniques, and its entry into television advertising, which in many cities increased sales by as much as 80%.

We are selling branded literature which can be promoted like other branded consumer products. Sampling techniques, the costs of which are prohibitive to the general publisher because of the variety of books published, are being used by Harlequin to expand its market. For example, several million books were distributed free to the trade in 1973 and 1974 for use in introducing our products to new consumers. Since September 1974, a television advertising campaign has been tested in ten cities in Canada and the United States. Expansion of this advertising will begin in 1975.

Responsibility for the development of Harlequin novels lay with the company's British editorial staff and stable of more than 100 writers, most of whom were also British. Harlequin had acquired this editorial expertise in 1971 when it purchased Mills and Boon, a long established British publisher of romance novels. The genius of the Mills and Boon editors, according to one observer, was that they were able to produce a consistency in the final product, even though many authors were contributing. Readers always knew what they were getting and were satisfied again and again. In addition to the work of its regular writers, Mills and Boon received approximately 5000 unsolicited manuscripts per year. Typically, about 50 of these were accepted.

Harlequin's editorial process did not generate or even encourage best-sellers. "Best-sellers would ruin our system," stated Bill Willson, Harlequin's vice-president of finance. "Our objective is steady growth in volume. We have no winners and no losers." All Harlequin books published in any month sold about the same number of copies. Unsold paperback books could be returned to the publisher for credit; a consequence of Harlequin's even and predictable sales was that its rate of return of unsold books was much lower than that of its competitors, 25–30% of sales versus 40–50%.

One industry analyst commented on Harlequin's approach to the industry as follows:

> You've got to realize that these guys at Harlequin revolutionized the North American book industry. They brought professional marketing and business techniques to an industry that seems to publish "for love rather than money." At retail, for instance, they ignored the bookstores. This was a good move because most people never enter bookstores. Instead they built Harlequin book racks and placed them in supermarkets, mass merchandisers and drug stores where women are. They made each of the books 192 pages by changing the type size. This allowed for standard packaging and six books would fit into each pocket on the rack. Once the books were accepted by the trade they went on a monthly standing order system like magazines. This allowed for uniform print runs, shipping containers, and so on. Everything was done for efficiency, prices were kept low and volumes skyrocketed.

Distribution

In late 1977, Harlequin established a national retail sales organization in Canada, ending a joint venture agreement with another publisher in which a single sales force had represented both companies. By early 1979 Harlequin executives declared themselves well satisfied with the new arrangement, which allowed the sales force to focus solely on Harlequin products.

In the U.S. Harlequin was represented by the Pocket Books Distribution Corporation, a wholly owned subsidiary of Simon and Schuster. Pocket Books' 120-person sales force was responsible for dealing with the 400 or so independent regional distributors who distributed Harlequin's books and the major chains who bought direct, and for ensuring that Harlequin books were properly displayed and managed at the retail level. In addition to handling the Harlequin romance series, the sales force carried Simon and Schuster's own pocket books which were "one-offs" issued monthly.

Harlequin did not print any of its own books. Harlequin novels that were sold in the U.S. were printed by a major American printer of mass market books and distributed through a distribution centre in Buffalo, New York. Harlequins sold in Canada were printed in Canada and distributed through the company's Stratford, Ontario, warehouse.

HARLEQUIN'S PRODUCTS AND MARKETS

The Romance Novel

The backbone of Harlequin's business was its two major series, Harlequin Presents and Harlequin Romances, which consistently produced over 90% of the company's sales and earnings. Originally Harlequin had published only the Romances line, consisting of very chaste conservative stories selected from the Mills and Boon line by the wife of one of Harlequin's founders. After a period of time, however, Mills and Boon executives suggested to Harlequin that they were not publishing Mills and Boon's most popular books. Arguing that the British and North American markets were not the same, Harlequin nevertheless tried a blind test— two of its choices and two of the slightly more "racy" Mills and Boon choices—on 500 of its North American customers. To the company's amazement the Mills and Boon selections were very popular and, bowing to its customers' wishes, Harlequin created the Presents line to offer Mills and Boon's less chaste romance stories. In early 1979 the still growing Presents line was increased from four titles per month to six in North America, and sales rose by 50%. At the same time the Romances line was cut back from eight titles per month to six, with the net result that in North America the two lines were selling very similar quantities of books.

Both the Presents and Romances lines were sold at retail and, since 1970, through Harlequin's "Reader Service" book club. This direct mail operation offered heavy Harlequin readers the possibility of purchasing every book the company published, delivered right to the front door. The book club was an important source of profit, as in the U.S. six books were sold through the book club for every ten sold at retail. Furthermore, a book sold through the book club yielded Harlequin the full cover price, whereas a book sold at retail netted the company approximately half the retail price, and required advertising, distribution costs, the acceptance of returns from retailers and so on. As one observer put it "No wonder the company is willing to pay the mailing costs for its book club members!"

Competition

No other publisher concentrated as heavily as Harlequin on the romance novel although, attracted by Harlequin's profit margins, most of the majors had made attempts to penetrate the market. Bantam Books, the largest, and generally considered the best-run conventional paperback publisher in North America, had tried to enter Harlequin's market in the early 1970s with a series titled Red Rose Romances. The line was a failure and had been phased out of existence by 1977. Four or five other major publishers had also attempted to penetrate the romantic novel market in the late 1960s and early 1970s. Consumers were offered Valentine Romances from Curtis Publishing, Rainbow Romances from New American Library, Hamilton House from Fawcett, and Candlelight Romances from Dell. The only one of these series selling in 1979 was Dell's, offering one or two new titles per month. Willson explained that the problem faced by all of these firms was their editorial content. The stories simply weren't good enough. Heisey agreed, adding:

> We are good managers and good marketers, I admit, and those things make us more profitable than we otherwise would be, but the essence of this firm is the editorial department and our group of more than 100 authors. It is these resources which make us unique, and it is precisely these resources which our competition cannot duplicate.

International Markets

Commencing in 1975, Harlequin began to establish foreign language ventures for its romance novels in countries around the world. Typically, a new venture would start with two or four titles per month, translated from the Romances or Presents lines, and then expand as the market allowed. In spite of predictions from many (male) publishers that the Harlequin line would not appeal to the women of their country, virtually all of the new ventures prospered. Entry costs were not high in most countries, and profits came quickly. Harlequin's major international moves are listed in Table 2.

TABLE 2   **International Expansion**

1975   Harlequin Holland established. Four titles per month. Extremely successful. Second line introduced in 1976. Further expansion in 1977 and 1978. Holland, together with Canada, has Harlequin's highest per capita (women over 15) market penetration rate.

1976   Harlequin paid $2.1 million for a 50% interest in the West German company that had been publishing Mills and Boon novels for several years. The company published five romance titles per month, plus a French detective series. In spite of new competition in the romance area in 1978, the company was performing well.

1977   Harlequin France established. In 1978 a four title per month series was launched, aimed at French, Belgian and Swiss markets. Line expanded in 1979. Company became profitable in 1979.

1978   Mills and Boon's Australian operation (established in 1973) took a major step forward with the introduction of TV advertising and a new line. A successful operation.

1979   New launches in Japan, Scandinavia, Greece, Mexico and Venezuela.

Harlequin's major new romance novel venture in 1979, representing an investment of $2 million, was its entry into the Japanese market. Despite skepticism from outsiders, initial market research had indicated that the appeal of Harlequin's product would be even stronger in Japan than North America. In early 1979 the company also entered its smallest foreign-language markets to date, those of the Scandinavian countries. A Harlequin executive explained the company's rationale:

> Harlequin's operation in Stockholm is the headquarters for publishing and marketing activities in the Swedish, Finnish and Norwegian languages. We will begin publishing romance fiction in Sweden and Finland in March, at the rate of four titles per month, and in Norway in April, at two titles per month. Denmark is currently being examined as a potential new market.

The four Scandinavian countries, with populations varying from 4.1 million to 8.3 million, will provide Harlequin with experience in the management of smaller markets. We also believe that, despite their size, they are potentially productive and represent a well-founded investment.

Literary Diversification

Harlequin's heavy dependence on the romance novel had been a source of concern to company executives for a number of years. In 1975 the company had attempted diversification with a line of science fiction novels for the North American market, known as the Laser series. In spite of an intense marketing effort the series was discontinued after 18 months and 58 titles. Heisey indicated that no one factor was responsible, suggesting that the problem was likely part editorial, part distribution, and part pricing (Appendix A).

Subsequent literary diversification attempts were more modest. In 1977, Mills and Boon created a series of romance stories in medical settings focusing on doctors and nurses, and these were introduced at the rate of two titles per month. In 1978 the Masquerade line of historical romances was also introduced at the rate of two titles per month. In Willson's view, these were "the same romance stories, but with long dresses." While both lines showed some initial promise, neither was expected to match the success of Harlequin Presents or Harlequin Romances.

In 1979 Harlequin took the somewhat bolder step of creating a new brand, Worldwide Library, which would act as an umbrella imprint for new products. The first of these was Mystique Books, introduced in March 1979. This romantic suspense series, adapted from a successful line of French novels, was introduced at the rate of four titles per month, with heavy television advertising. It did not carry the Harlequin name.

The importance that Harlequin placed on new series such as these was illustrated in the five-year plan of the North American book division, the company's most important business unit. This division's objective was a 30% annual increase in sales and profits throughout the early 1980s, to be achieved by increasing the U.S. penetration rate of the Presents and Romances lines closer to Canadian levels and at the same time, through the introduction of new "spin off" products, to reduce the overall dependence on those two lines to 65% of sales and profits by 1985. Harlequin's penetration rate in the U.S. (sales per woman over the age of 15) was approximately half that of the Canadian penetration rate.

Scholar's Choice

Scholar's Choice was created in the early 1970s when Harlequin acquired and merged two small Canadian companies involved in the production of educational material for schoolboards and teachers. Dissatisfied with what it described as "mixed results" from "less than buoyant Canadian institutional markets for educator supplies" during the mid-1970s, the company opened a retail store in Toronto in 1977. The success of this store led to a second Toronto store in 1978 and plans for seven more stores across Canada in 1979. All of these stores would sell educational material and would be wholly owned by the company.

Harlequin Films

Harlequin entered the movie-making business in 1977 with the $1.1 million film, "Leopard in the Snow." The movie featured no well-known actors, but it was based on a successful novel by one of Harlequin's established authors. The venture was a first step toward Harlequin's objective of "becoming to women what Walt Disney is to children." Willson elaborated on Harlequin's rationale:

> In the traditional film-making business there are a number of quite separate participants. The screenplay and actual creation of the movie is done by one group, financing by another group, distribution and marketing of the finished product by a variety of people. The people who actually create the product virtually lose control of it by the time it is marketed. Because so many conflicting groups are involved with different objectives and skills, the entire process is extremely inefficient.
>
> Harlequin could manage this process quite differently. We have the books for screenplays—over 2 000 on our backlist—and we have the finances to make the films. We know how to market and we have far more knowledge about our target market than most movie makers ever do. We could, once we gain confidence, use the distributors only to get the films into the theatres for a flat fee. We would do the promotion ourselves and take the financial risk.
>
> The other advantage to Harlequin is the same one that we have in the publishing business—consistency. For other producers, each film is a new product and new risk and the public has to be educated separately. We could advertise Harlequin films on a pretty intensive scale, and they could reinforce and be reinforced by the book sales. The potential may be tremendous.

The box office results of "Leopard in the Snow" were described by the company as "somewhat inconsistent" and further testing was to be done in 1979 to determine the feasibility of the concept.

Forward Integration

Harlequin's current three-year contract with Pocket Books was going to expire on December 31, 1979 and the company was considering ending the arrangement and establishing its own U.S. sales force. The following factors indicated that such a move might make sense:

1. *Cost.* Harlequin paid Pocket Books a set fee per book sold for the use of its U.S. sales force. As volumes continued to rise, so would Harlequin's total selling cost, even though Pocket Book's sales force costs were unlikely to increase. Harlequin executives estimated that they were already paying "well over half" the total cost of the Pocket Book sales force, even though the volumes of books it handled for Simon and Schuster and Harlequin were approximately equal. In fact, since Simon and Schuster's line consisted of "one-offs" which had to be "sold" to the distributors each month and the Harelquin line was all on automatic reorders, there was little doubt that Harlequin received less than half of the sales force's attention. The net result was that Harlequin felt it would get better service at lower cost from its own sales force.

2. *New Products.* As new products like the Mystique line were introduced to the U.S. market with increasing frequency, the attention given to each product line by the sales force would become extremely important. If such new lines were to be a success, Harlequin felt that it would need to be able to directly control the activities of its U.S. sales force.

3. *Returns*. One of the tasks of a Harlequin sales force was known as "order regulation." This job, which was to check with individual retailers to determine their return rate, was necessary because the independent distributors, set up to handle magazines, could not accurately monitor pocket book returns by customer. If the return rate was too high, books were being printed and distributed for no gain. If it was too low, retailers were stocking out and sales were being lost. Larry Heisey commented:

> I ran a check to see what kind of a job Pocket Books was doing for us on order regulation. We had about 400 distributors, each carrying Romances and Presents. That means we could have had up to 800 changes in order positions per month as wholesalers fine-tuned their demands to optimize our return rates. As I recall, there were only about 23 changes per month in the time period we checked. The Pocket Book's sales force simply wasn't managing the situation the way they should have been.

The only concern expressed at Harlequin about dropping Pocket Books was the possible reaction of Dick Snyder, the tough and aggressive president of Simon and Schuster. Snyder had become president of Simon and Schuster in 1975, the same year that the New York-based publisher was acquired by Gulf and Western, a large U.S. conglomerate. Snyder was interested in growth and profits, and was achieving results in both areas. *Newsweek* commented as follows:

> S&S has always been a best-seller house, but Snyder has turned it into the bastion of books-as-product—and the target of derision by other publishers who pride themselves on a commitment to good literature. He expects his editors to bring in twice as many titles per year as are required at other houses...
>
> The marketing staff is renowned for its aggressiveness—and high turnover rate. "Simon and Schuster runs a sales contest every year," former sales representative Jack O'Leary says only half jokingly. "The winners get to keep their jobs."

The Acquisition Program

In 1977, Heisey and Willson had estimated Harlequin's potential world market for romance novels (all non-communist countries) at $250 million, but as Harlequin's prices and volumes continued to rise, it became apparent that this estimate may have been too low. No matter how big the ultimate market, however, neither man felt that the company could penetrate this market any faster than it already was. They also emphasized that Harlequin's romantic fiction business could not profitably absorb all the cash it generated. As a result, Willson, with the approval of the Torstar Corporation (publisher of the *Toronto Star* newspaper) which had acquired 59% of Harlequin's shares in the late 1970s, hired several staff analysts and began a search for acquisitions. Early investigation revealed that the major U.S. paperback companies were not for sale, and the minor ones were not attractive.

Willson prepared a list to guide the search process (Exhibit 2), deciding that he was not interested in any company which would add less than 10% to Harlequin's profits. With more than $20 million in cash in 1977 and no debt to speak of, Willson had thought that $40 million would be a reasonable amount to spend on acquisitions; he visualized two major acquisitions, both in the U.S. One would be in the publishing business and the other in a related business.

By 1979, Willson and his group had made several acquisitions, but were still searching for one or two really sizeable takeover candidates. In mid-1977 they had purchased the Ideals Corporation of Milwaukee, a publisher of inspirational magazines and books, as well as greeting cards and a line of cookbooks, for $1.5 million. In 1978 Harlequin acquired a 78% interest in the Laufer Company of Hollywood, California, for $10.5 million, approximately $8 million of which represented goodwill. In the nine months ended December 31, 1977, Laufer earned US$814 000 on sales of $10 million. Laufer published eight monthly entertainment magazines including *Tiger Beat, Right On!* and *Rona Barrett's Hollywood*, for teenage and adult markets. The Laufer and Ideals businesses were subsequently combined to form the Harlequin Magazine Group. (An organization chart is presented in Exhibit 3.) During the first half of 1979 the magazine group acquired a 50% interest in *ARTnews* ("the most distinguished fine arts magazine in the United States"), a 60% interest in *Antiques World*, which was launched in 1979 as a sister publication to *ARTnews*, and a 57.5% interest in a new Toronto publication titled *Photo Life*.

THE FUTURE

As the financial results for the first six months of 1979 arrived, showing a 45% increase in sales (no doubt in part a result of the 20% and 30% price increases on the Presents and Romances lines in North America—bringing retail prices to $1.50 and $1.25 respectively) and a 23% gain in net income, Larry Heisey looked forward to the 1980s with keen anticipation.

> We believe the 1980s will be very important to Harlequin, even more so than the seventies. Our market research indicates substantial growth potential in the English-language markets. The rapid development of markets in Holland and French Canada to per capita levels nearly equivalent to those of English-speaking Canada, our most mature market, suggest the great potential of Mills & Boon romance fiction in other languages.
>
> The goals that we established for ourselves at the beginning of the seventies are being realized, generating an outstanding growth pattern. We have every reason to believe that this pattern will continue in the 1980s, for the company's financial resources are more than adequate to support an active expansion and diversification program.

EXHIBIT 1 Harlequin Summary of Financial Performance

	1978	1977	1976	1975	1974	1973	1972	1971	1970
OPERATING RESULTS ($000 000s)									
Net Revenues									
Publishing	n/a	n/a	44.1	35.1	24.8	16.4	11.0	4.0	3.0
Learning materials*	n/a	n/a	8.3	8.2	6.2	4.0	4.3	4.0	5.1
Total Net Revenues	$125.9	$80.9	$52.4	$43.2	$31.0	$20.4	$15.3	$ 8.0	$ 8.0
Net Earnings	$ 16.8	$12.5	$ 5.2	$ 4.4	$ 3.5	$ 3.0	$ 1.6	$ .5	$ .1
FINANCIAL POSITION ($000 000s)									
Cash and securities	22.5	24.0	9.3	4.2	3.5	3.2	1.1	1.2	
Total current assets	58.4	45.8	23.6	19.2	14.3	10.0	6.1	6.2	4.0
Current liabilities	25.2	21.2	10.5	8.4	7.0	5.0	3.4	4.0	2.1
Working capital	33.2	24.6	13.1	10.8	7.2	5.0	3.0	2.5	2.0
Net fixed assets	2.3	1.7	1.0	.9	.7	.5	.2	.2	.2
Other assets	14.1	6.4	5.8	3.7	3.7	3.7	4.0	4.0	2.2
Shareholders' equity	45.2	30.5	19.4	15.4	11.7	9.1	6.8	4.3	3.9
FINANCIAL RATIOS									
Net earnings on net revenues	13.3%	15.6%	10.2%	10.2%	11.4%	13.4%	10.3%	5.7%	1.4%
Net earnings on equity	37.1%	41.0%	27.5%	28.8%	30.2%	30.0%	23.2%	10.5%	2.8%
Working-capital ratio	2.3:1	2.2:1	2.3:1	2.3:1	2.0:1	2.0:1	1.8:1	1.7:1	1.7:1
Fully diluted earnings per share	$1.06	$.79	$.34	$.29	$.24	$.18	$.12	$.04	$.01
Dividends declared ($000 000s)	2.3	1.4	1.3	1.2	1.0	.4	.1	—	—
OTHER DATA									
Share price —low	7.75	3.83	2.75	1.33	.94	1.30	.44	.23	n/a
—high	16.00	9.00	3.79	3.25	1.72	1.83	1.67	.46	
Number of employees	980	881	584	332	313	240	201	157	188
Number of books sold (000 000s)	125	109	90	72	63	42	29	25	19

* Although exact figures were not available, learning materials were still a relatively low proportion of Harlequin sales in 1978.

EXHIBIT 2 Harlequin's Guide for Acquisitions

Potential Areas to Look for Acquisition in Publishing Business	*Areas to Consider for Acquisition in Related Industry*

1. Trade Books
  —paperback fiction and non-fiction
  —hardcover series and partworks
2. Reference Books
  —text books and learned journals
  —professional publishing: legal, medical, accounting
  —reference guides and handbooks
3. Magazines
  —consumer magazines
  —trade and business publications
4. Other publishing
  —greeting cards, stationery
  —sewing patterns
  —diaries and albums
  —music publishing
	1. Entertainment
	  —movies and television films
	  —records
	  —video tapes
	  —music
	2. Mass-marketed low-technology consumer products
	  —adult games
	  —children's games
	  —children's toys
	3. Handicraft and hobby products

EXHIBIT 3   Organization Chart Harlequin Enterprises Limited

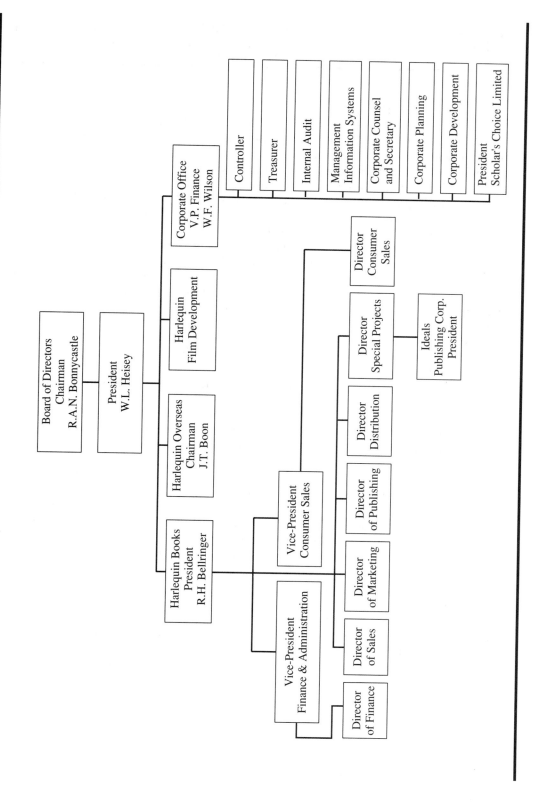

APPENDIX A   Why Harlequin Enterprises Fell Out of Love with Science Fiction by Brian M. Fraser

"It didn't work," says Harlequin Enterprises President W. Lawrence Heisey. "We didn't perceive that it would be profitable in the reasonably short-term future, so we decided to abandon it. Period."

Although noncommittal on the failure, Heisey said no one factor was responsible: "I think it was a lot of problems," he said. "it wasn't any one thing. I don't think the distribution was that bad; it probably begins with editorial and ends with pricing so it was a whole collection of problems. But it didn't work."

Hard-core SF enthusiasts were against the venture from the start, fearing science fiction would be watered down into pap for the masses. And, indeed, this was essentially true: the plots of the Laser books generally took standard ideas in the genre and sketched new adventure stores, but without much depth.

Like its romances, which are mainly sold in supermarkets and drug stores, Harlequin attempted to produce a uniform product in the science fiction category. It also hoped it would prove as addictive to young male readers as the light romances are for some housewives.

Harlequin put all its marketing expertise and resources behind the new SF paperbacks, beginning with six titles plus a free novel (*Seeds of Change* by Thomas F. Monteleone) as incentive to anyone who bought a Laser Book and returned a questionnaire. Like good marketers, they used these names to build a mailing list for promotional material.

An extensive publicity and advertising program was tied to the announcement. Major Canadian media carried articles, focusing on the worldwide financial success of the Harlequin Romances line.

To attract potential readers directly, full-page ads were placed in major science-fiction digest magazines, such as *Analog*, and in amateur fan magazines, such as *Locus*. And, with sage marketing skill, Harlequin also attempted to create a favourable selling environment through ads in *Publisher's Weekly* and the *West Coast Review of Books*, which are read by bookstore managers.

Harlequin even placed trial direct response ads in a girlie magazine, ran radio commercials in Toronto and U.S. test markets, and its ad agency, Compton Advertising of New York, tried out a television commercial.

These innovative merchandising techniques, not part of the repertoire of most Canadian publishers, have been used with some success on the romances.

"The failure can be attributed to a complete misunderstanding of the special appeal of science fiction and the nature of its addictive readers. Nobody in the know ever believed this venture would succeed," says veteran U.S. SF editor Donald Woolheim.

The inside-SF consensus is that Harlequin underestimated the intelligence of the science fiction reader who, unlike the devotees of Harlequin romances, looks for non-formula fiction, cerebral material with new and well-developed ideas.

It's conceivable that lack of adequate distribution may have been one of the prime reasons Harlequin pulled out. With the Romances line, Harlequin has been phenomenally successful in penetrating the grocery and drugstore markets, placing racks specifically for their interchangeable 12 titles a month. But no such breakthrough was evident with the Laser line.

SOURCE: Original article appeared in the *Financial Post*, December 17, 1977.

ARCHIMAX SYSTEMS LTD.

Joseph N. Fry and Stephen Jack

CASE 9

Early in June 1994, Charles Douglas, a recently graduated MBA, and an equally recent employee of Archimax Systems Ltd., met with R.J. Bates, the president of Archimax, to review plans for the company's exhibition booth at SIGGRAPH 94. Douglas was standing in for his boss, Gary Hopkins, who had just left for an extended holiday sailing in the Greek Islands, confident that the plans for the booth were set, and that Douglas would carry through with the implementation.

But Bates was not satisfied with the plans. He was concerned that the exhibit was not impressive enough and didn't fully reflect Archimax's accomplishments and technology. He instructed Douglas to make a number of significant changes in the content and mechanics of the presentation.

Douglas left the meeting with more than a few concerns. SIGGRAPH opened in just six weeks. He wasn't at all sure that the changes could be completed by then. Further, he had been cautioned in earlier conversations with Max Emery, the company controller, that cash was tight, and that holding the line on costs was important. Most recently, as Hopkins was preparing to leave on his holidays, Emery had warned, "no changes without agreement from Hopkins." But a quick guess indicated that the new requirements might add nearly $500 000 to the original estimates of slightly over $1 million for the exhibit. Finally, Douglas felt that he had been put in a situation in which his boss's boss had hijacked the project. The changes that Bates had in mind were in significant conflict with the approach Hopkins had been taking to the exhibit. What was he to make of this?

THE VIRTUAL REALITY INDUSTRY

The Technology

Archimax was a fledgling company in the emerging virtual reality industry. *Virtual reality* was the term given to the effects made possible by the convergence of two technologies, three-dimensional (3-D) computer imaging and robotics. By ingeniously merging the technologies, subjects in a virtual reality experience were given the illusion of an alternate reality, a world in which manufactured images and sensations were perceived as if they were reality itself. This effect was achieved by immersing the subject in an environment of created objects that looked and acted like real objects; (for example, a subject would feel a bump on visually "walking" into a wall image), and by adding other sensory input such as sound, temperature and smell. Flight training simulators were an early application of the possibilities of the concept of virtual reality. In current development projects, however, the ambitions of virtual reality were reaching well beyond the limited repertoires of simulators, to encompass a much wider range of user input and experience.

The creation of a virtual reality experience required the integration of a system of supporting equipment and related database, as illustrated in Exhibit 1. The main elements of hardware in a generic virtual reality system were: 1) an image generator, 2) a host computer, 3) an input device, and 4) an output device. The image generator processed input and database information to produce images—objects, colour, texture, motion, background, etc. Image generator manufacturers sold their product in units of capability called "channels," which were currently priced at $150 000 – $200 000 per channel. Image generators usually represented at least half of the cost of a virtual reality installation and were the key to the quality of the experience. Like most electronic equipment, image generator prices were falling, even as they increased in performance.

The host computer housed the custom database and software for the experience and operated to control the system by bringing together the stored data and input device feed to drive the image generator and associated output devices. The required host computer capabilities were on the order of a competent engineering workstation.

Input and output devices were directly dependent on the type of experience being created. The input devices for a car racing experience, for example, would include a gas pedal, brake, steering wheel and gear shift. The output devices for the same experience would include a head mounted or projection display system and a motion platform that would react to events as they occurred.

The database software was the raw material from which the virtual reality system produced the user's virtual world. The larger the database, the larger and the more detailed the world in which someone could participate—but also the more powerful and expensive the image generator and host computer/software would have to be. The minimum cost to create a database of usable size was about $175 000. Databases could be used in a number of sites and/or experiences if the targeted end results were similar.

THE VIRTUAL REALITY MARKET

The market for virtual reality applications was in its infancy and thus difficult to categorize and quantify. In general, virtual reality applications were positioned as an integral part of a broader, $6 billion, 3-D imaging market. Elements of virtual reality were found, for example, in such major 3-D imaging sub-markets as flight simulation, entertainment, computer assisted design, and Medical/Catscan. Among the 3-D sub-markets, however, the entertainment segment was widely regarded as the most attractive for the short-term development of virtual reality applications; with these applications leading, industry observers had forecast sales for virtual reality systems of about $1 billion in 1996.

The major prospective customer groups or channels in the entertainment business were: 1) mall developers and owners, 2) theme and amusement parks, 3) location-based entertainment centres such as casinos and retail stores, 4) edu-tainment centres such as museums and science centres, and 5) cross promotion prospects, such as beer and athletic shoe marketers. The appeal of virtual reality in these markets ranged from offering a quantum improvement over arcade games in malls and amusement parks, to providing a powerful custom designed package in the case of museums and product promoters, to the possibility of a proprietary range of experiences in a theme park. To this point, however, most customers had had minimal experience with virtual reality and were for the most part testing a promising, but unfamiliar and relatively expensive product. In many cases, and particularly with independent customers such as small amusement parks, prospective customers were seeking manufacturer support for their entry into virtual reality.

THE SUPPLY STRUCTURE

The supply structure of the virtual reality-entertainment market was split between specialized producers on the one hand and system integrators on the other. Within each of these categories there was a handful of sizeable companies and a multitude of smaller players. The specialized producers concentrated on one element of the system described in Exhibit 1, such as image generators, or database software. Among these specialized producers, Silicon Graphics Inc. (SGI) was by far the largest and best known company. SGI had been a pioneer in 3-D imaging and was best known for its engineering workstations for computer assisted design. SGI was a major supplier of image generators to companies assembling virtual reality entertainment experiences and was known to be working closely on product development with the video games giant, Sega. Other competent companies, such as Evans and Sutherland and Martin Marietta, sold image generators, and a wide and changing range of suppliers, most of which were small enterprises, worked on other systems and components such as database software development and robotics.

System integrators designed and assembled a total virtual reality product. The degree of vertical integration among the integrators was quite low, although some, such as Disney Imagineering, encompassed design and software, and others such as Evans and Sutherland, built their own image generators into their products. But even the large firms such as Sega relied heavily on the efforts of a range of independent suppliers.

Among the integrators, the larger firms such as Disney and Sega tended to concentrate on total experiences such as a full game park. Smaller integrators, such as Magic Edge and W Industries, focused on the development and sale of specific experiences. Some integrators had begun to develop the concept of indoor theme parks, called Location Based Entertainment Centres (LBEs). This new concept was a step forward in the value chain for the integrators as the LBEs would be stocked with the integrators' equipment. Some integrators planned to operate the locations and others planned to franchise. There were also independents seeking to design and operate/franchise LBEs. These companies had the theme and location but neither the equipment nor the software.

In spite of its promise, the market for virtual reality products had proven to be a difficult one. As one industry observer put it, "So far the only people who have made money in virtual reality are those who write about it—and SGI who sells to those who try." The shortage of proven products and markets meant that long-term financing was difficult to come by. The larger companies, of course, could rely on cash-flows from other product/markets, but many of the smaller companies were forced to operate on a shoestring and to devote a significant proportion of their energy to financial survival.

ARCHIMAX

Archimax was incorporated by R.J. Bates and Greg Raidler in Richmond, British Columbia, in 1989. Bates had just moved west after a successful marketing career which included experience in high tech and entertainment companies and in the operation of his own advertising and PR firm. From this experience he had become convinced that technical developments would make it possible to open new markets in entertainment, but he had been unable to persuade his employers of the potential of his vision. He had met Greg Raidler, an accomplished electronics engineer, at an industry association meeting and after a number of conversations the two decided to pursue a start-up from a new base.

For almost three years Bates worked from his home trying to raise money for a major development project and Raidler did contract work for various companies to keep the company afloat. The dream was to build a unique computer system, dubbed the C21, which would serve as an image generator and control system specifically for virtual reality applications in entertainment. Several small grants from the B.C. and federal governments had helped to keep the project alive, but the prospects of survival were pretty grim when Bates was introduced to Evan Lee.

Lee was a well-known personality in the west coast technical and financial communities. Earlier in his career he had built a very successful disk-drive company, only to see it crash as a result of over expansion and industry squeeze. Lee vowed at the time never to expand a project until the money was in the bank, and true to his word, he had used conservative strategies to rescue and rebuild two other computer industry start-ups. He was impressed by Bates and Raidler and ultimately a deal was struck under which he became a shareholder, and chairman, part time, of Archimax.

Lee's early moves were to raise some private funding for Archimax, and to arrange a public stock listing by way of a reverse takeover under which Archimax was acquired by a shell Vancouver Stock Exchange company. Most recently he had been instrumental in Archimax's acquisition of PS Technologies, an Austin, Texas, based developer of image generators.

THE ARCHIMAX STRATEGY

The focal point for Archimax's efforts remained with the development of virtual reality experiences for the entertainment market. A key element in this approach was the completion of the C21, which would give Archimax an industry leading position in low cost, high quality graphics. The C21 would be available for sale to equipment integrators but Archimax also intended to supplement the C21 through alliances to provide a complete product, for example, by working with design firms and software houses to provide a turnkey product and merchandising service to the theme parks and shopping malls.

C21 was an ambitious project. It was based on new technologies and design concepts which promised superior results and economies. As of June 1994, however, the C21 development program was behind schedule and over budget. Raidler was unperturbed by this, saying only that in a development project as complex as this, delays and unforeseen costs were bound to occur. He was confident that a working prototype would be completed by the end of 1994, with systems available for sale by mid 1995.

As a result of the delays with C21, the original Archimax was still very much a development company. Operations statements and balance sheets for the period ending April 30, 1994, and just prior to the PS Technologies acquisition, are presented in Exhibits 2 and 3. A rough statement of planned uses and sources of financing, including the PS Technologies acquisition, is outlined in Exhibit 4. Beyond this, Archimax's financial aims were to be self-financing from operations in two years.

The PS Technologies Acquisition

In Lee's view, the acquisition of PS Technologies fit into the overall Archimax strategy by providing some immediate credibility in image generation, a cash flow bridge, and a faster accumulation of the business base needed to secure a NASDAQ listing.

PS was an organization of about 40 people that operated as a division of Larson Electronics, a very large avionics and general electronics manufacturer based in Austin. PS had been losing money and had been through two years of uncertainty as its parent went through a process of refocusing on its core avionics products and customers. An assessment team from Archimax concluded that PS still had a nucleus of good technical people and some attractive projects underway, but that its sales force had been badly mauled in the ups and downs of the divestment process. Notably, PS had a fully developed product on the market, the PS 100 image generator and a $4 million agreement in principle to develop a custom product for Petco, a Taiwanese video game manufacturer. These products nicely fit into a capabilities/price range below the C21.

Lee was particularly intrigued by PS's inventory of fully and partly assembled PS100s, worth an estimated $2.8 million, albeit in a rapidly changing market. In late May of 1994 he made a deal for PS for $900 000 cash, Archimax shares valued at $1.8 million, and an assumption of $1.4 million of PS's liabilities. An immediate aim following this transaction was to generate cash as quickly as possible by selling off the PS100 inventory.

THE ARCHIMAX ORGANIZATION

The Archimax organization in Richmond consisted of fewer than 15 people and operated on a very informal basis. It was Douglas' view that management, from Bates on down, was stretched thin and was under tremendous pressure to balance their time between long-term needs and critical short-term demands.

At the time of the case Archimax was in the process of setting up PS Technologies to operate as an autonomous profit centre. It was thought that the freedom to operate, which had not been the Larson Electronics style, and the spur of tangible business goals would energize PS to work off its inventory and finalize a contract on the Petco development project. To Douglas, this was making a virtue of necessity—Archimax had minimal resources to commit to supervising and assisting PS management.

THE SIGGRAPH EXHIBIT

SIGGRAPH was the acronym for an industry association called the Special Interest Group on Graphics. To achieve its objectives of providing education and information on computer graphics, SIGGRAPH organized an annual convention that was the showcase for everything that was new to the graphics industry. The convention was known as an image show, where exhibitors demonstrated their best ideas, rather than a sales show aimed at specific product sale. Attendance had grown in the 15 years of SIGGRAPH's life to over 30 000 for the three-day show.

Early in the year, Lee and Bates had decided that Archimax needed exposure and that attendance at SIGGRAPH was an essential step. The task of carrying this through fell primarily to Gary Hopkins, vice-president for marketing and product development, and next to Bates and Raidler, the longest term member of the management team. In preliminary meetings it was decided that Archimax would commit to a 50' × 60' booth, which would rank it among the largest exhibits at the show. The prime concerns centred around the look of the booth and what the main focus would be. The problem was that the C21 was still in development and the PS100 was nothing new. Bates and Hopkins were concerned that too great a focus on a development project would create the impression of promoting "vapourware"—a term used in the industry for products that were announced even though they didn't exist. It was decided that Archimax would present a full virtual reality experience that demonstrated its design and integration capabilities, although, of necessity, outside suppliers would have to be used for the system components.

There was a further aim in developing the SIGGRAPH exhibit. The IAAPA (International Association of Amusement Parks of America) convention was scheduled three months after SIGGRAPH. IAPPA was a key sales show in the industry and would attract a very different audience of buyers and owners from amusement and theme parks. Archimax could use this same booth with some relatively inexpensive changes.

Work started on the design of the exhibit and sourcing of components. This was a major job that involved people from across the organization in very significant tasks. Hopkins worked full time and then some to get the concept and technical components agreed and to co-ordinate the effort of various internal and external participants. One major accomplishment was recruiting Apex Images, an emerging "hot" software developer, to collaborate in creating the exhibit database.

It was clear from the start that the exhibit would be an expensive proposition, but no specific numbers were available until Douglas put together a formal budget as one of his first tasks on joining Archimax. This budget, dated June 1 and calling for expenditures of $1 050 000, is outlined in Exhibit 5. Then, with the concepts, budget, and most arrangements seemingly settled, and Douglas working into the picture, a very tired Hopkins felt he could leave on a long-planned vacation. There had not been an opportunity in Bate's schedule for a final presentation and agreement, but Douglas could handle that within a week.

CONCLUSION

Following his meeting with Bates, Douglas sat back in his office and reviewed his situation. He recognized that he had been shaken by the events of the morning. He felt that his next actions would be critical to whatever role he was going to carve out for himself at Archimax. But what was that role? What would be the best course for himself and Archimax? And beneath this lay an even more fundamental concern. Did Archimax have a future in this emerging industry, or was it an illusion itself? He reflected on some advice given to him by a professor at the business school—that his challenge in this kind of company would be deciding on "how native you go."

EXHIBIT 1   **Virtual Reality Industry System**

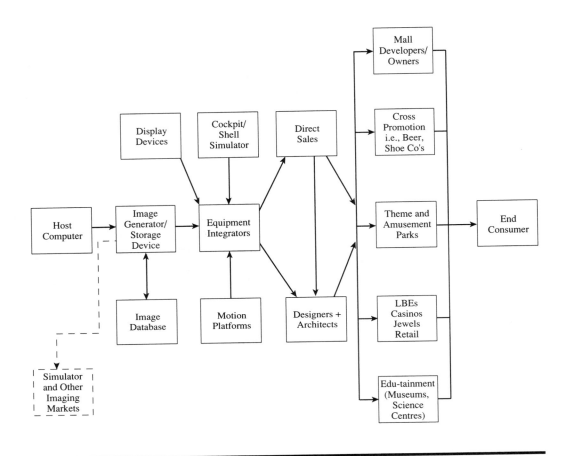

EXHIBIT 2 **Consolidated Balance Sheet April 30, 1994** (C$)

	April 30, 1994	*January 31, 1994*
ASSETS		
Current Assets		
Short-term Deposits	$ 523 900	$ 0
Grants Receivable	58 700	133 200
Subscription Receivable	0	882 000
Advances and Prepaid Expenses	37 300	31 300
Total Current Assets	$ 619 900	$ 1 046 500
Furniture and Equipment	92 600	52 700
Deferred Financing Costs	66 200	66 000
Total Assets	$ 778 700	$ 1 165 200
LIABILITIES AND SHAREHOLDERS' EQUITY		
Current Liabilities		
Bank Indebtedness	$ 94 900	$ 22 500
Accounts Payable	66 200	131 300
Total Current Liabilities	$ 161,100	$ 153 800
Debentures Payable	750,000	750 000
SHAREHOLDERS' EQUITY		
Capital Stock Issues and Outstanding:		
100 000 Class A Non-voting Preference Shares	100 000	100 000
4 750 000 Common Shares	1 286 100	396 600
Share Subscriptions	0	882 000
Deficit	(1 518 500)	(1 117 200)
Total Shareholders' Equity	($ 132 400)	$ 261 400
Total Liabilities and Shareholders' Equity	$ 778 700	$ 1 165 200

EXHIBIT 3 **Consolidated Statement of Operations Three Months Ended April 30, 1994** (C$)

Expenses	
General and Administrative	$ 105 700
Legal and Consulting	157 300
Research and Development	125 800
Research and Development	
—Government Assistance	(25 200)
Selling	10 200
Interest, Net	18 100
Depreciation and Amortization	9 400
Loss for the Period	($401 300)

EXHIBIT 4 Planned Sources and Uses of Cash

Item	
Monthly Cash Use by Archimax, Richmond	$ 60 000
Monthly Cash Use by Archimax-PS	375 000
SIGGRAPH Budget	1 050 000
IAAPA Budget	200 000
Debenture Payout (October)	750 000
PS Purchase	900 000
Total Uses	**$ 3 335 000**
Arranged Sources	
Private Investor (Late June)[1]	$ 750 000
New York Bridge Financing[1]	4 000 000
Public Offering of $15mm (November)[2]	15 000 000
Petco Development Money[3]	4 000 000
Total Sources	**$23 750 000**

[1] Conditional on applying for NASDAQ listing, which is dependant on an asset level that the PS purchase provided, stock trading at $2.50 per share. Money to be drawn down $2 million in August, $1 million in September, $1 million in October.

[2] Conditional on full NASDAQ listing. A full listing is dependent on a minimum of US$4 million in assets, US$2 million in net worth and a minimum of 300 shareholders.

[3] Part of PS purchase. Timing on funds was $1 million in June, the rest contingent on achieving development targets. The expected timing was $1 million in September, $1 million in November and $1 million in January.

EXHIBIT 5 Summary Of SIGGRAPH Budget June 1, 1994

Asset Purchase and Display Total	
Exhibition Booth	
Formula One Cars	
Software	
Projection Booth and Installation	
Projection Equipment	
Contingency—10%	
Sub-total—Asset Purchases	$ 875 000
Marketing Direct Cost	
SIGGRAPH Fee	
Promotional (Brochures, etc.)	
Total Direct Marketing Cost	130 000
Travel and Attendance	
19 people from Archimax, PS, and Apec	45 000
Grand Total	$ 1 050 000

POLYSAR LIMITED AND TORNAC RUBBER

J. Michael Geringer and William A. Pursell

CASE 10

As he strode his customary three kilometres to his Toronto office on November 8, 1988, Doug Henderson, the recently appointed group vice-president of Polysar Limited's Global Rubber business, knew that he would be facing a divided and emotionally charged rubber management team at the meeting he had scheduled for that day. The previous week he had presented the team members with a proposal outlining two alternative strategies for commercializing TORNAC, a hydrogenated nitrile rubber (H-NBR) which Polysar had developed for the emerging high-heat and oil-resistant segment of the rubber business. One of the proposed strategies was to continue the traditional Polysar approach of complete independence, and compete directly with the other two contenders in this segment: Bayer A.G. of Germany and Nippon Zeon of Japan. This option, supported by several of the team members, would require that Polysar assume all of the risk—but reap all of the potential rewards—associated with such independence. The alternative strategy, which also had several supporters on the team, was to forge a strategic alliance with Bayer, and thus share the risk and potential rewards arising from such an alliance. Doug was still uncertain about which alternative he should support, as well as how he should go about making and implementing such a decision without creating serious conflict, and possibly long-term divisions, among the team members. However, because of pressure from Bayer, and because the Polysar 1989 budget data had to be finalized imminently, he knew he would have to reach a decision on this issue within the next two weeks. He needed the rubber management team to explore each option thoroughly, and assist him in making the best decision.

THE SYNTHETIC RUBBER INDUSTRY

Synthetic rubber is a polymer synthesized from derivatives of oil and natural gas. Rubber polymers based on petroleum were first developed in the 1930s, and many different kinds of such polymers had been commercialized globally since that time. Wide-spread innovation in both processes and polymer products was normal for the industry. By 1988, nearly 70% of the rubber used globally was of the synthetic type.

Manufacturers of synthetic rubber polymers fell basically into three categories: oil and gas producers that had integrated forward through the intermediate raw materials into the final polymers; end-use polymer consumers (e.g., tire companies) who had integrated backwards into synthetic rubber to secure their supply source; and chemical companies which produced synthetic rubber polymers and the intermediate raw materials as a main-line business. Polysar fell into the third category, as did companies such as Dupont, Bayer, Enichem, and Nippon Zeon.

The capital costs associated with building synthetic rubber plants, providing facilities for the intermediate raw materials, and "cracking" oil and natural gas into usable petrochemical components, were large. A world-scale synthetic rubber plant normally cost in excess of $100 million, an intermediate raw material plant in the $200–300 million range, and a basic oil/gas "cracker" between $500–1 000 million.

The major producers of synthetic rubber polymers and their consumers were concentrated in the industrialized nations of the world, with the value of production in 1988 in the $15–20 billion range. The major end-uses for synthetic rubber arose from such industries as automotive, construction, general manufacturing, oil drilling and production, packaging and textiles.

Synthetic rubber polymers were produced globally in a wide variety of types. These ranged from so-called commodity or general purpose products (such as SBR rubber for tires), through products with some special performance feature, to highly sophisticated products with a combination of special features such as abrasion resistance, flexibility, oil resistance, high temperature resistance, impermeability to gases, design capability, and so on. With rapid advances in end-use and consumer technology, increasingly high standards of performance were being demanded, particularly in the high-end specialty performance segment. This accelerating trend toward replacing general purpose products with higher performance specialty products was expected to continue well into the future.

The Specialty Performance Segment

The synthetic rubber polymer business worldwide comprised approximately 80% general purpose products and 20% specialty products. The high-performance niche, represented by products such as Polysar's TORNAC Rubber, fell within the specialty category. Global volumes sharply contrasted between categories:

General purpose:	8 million tons
Specialty:	2 million tons
TORNAC type niche:	1–2 thousand tons

Prices also contrasted sharply depending upon product segment. General purpose products were normally sold for less than $1/lb, specialty products in the $1–$5/lb range, and the TORNAC Rubber niche in the $10–$15/lb range.

Within the specialty category, one of the major requirements was for synthetic rubber polymers with good heat, ozone (sunlight) and oil resistance. These properties were required for automotive, oil-well, aerospace and industrial component industries. The performance standards for these properties had risen steadily over the previous few decades, with technical requirements becoming increasingly difficult to meet. The main synthetic rubber which had historically been used for these special conditions was nitrile rubber (NBR). Product variations of NBR included many dozens of types for different end-uses and operating conditions. The major international producers of NBR in 1988 were as follows:

Company	Capacity (000 tons)	Plant Location
Nippon Zeon*	65	Japan, U.S., U.K.
Polysar	55	Canada, France
Bayer*	35	Germany
Enichem	35	Italy
Goodyear	34	France, U.S.
JSR	30	Japan
Uniroyal	20	U.S.

* Exhibits 1 and 2 have background information on Nippon Zeon and Bayer respectively.
SOURCE: International Institute of Synthetic Rubber Producers, 1988 statistical data.

The importance of nitrile rubber, and the companies' relative competitive positions globally, arose from the widely held assumption that the top 10% (the high-performance segment) of the NBR business was open to replacement by the superior heat, oil and abrasion resistant products represented by TORNAC rubber and its competitors: Bayer's THERBAN and Nippon Zeon's ZETPOL. Nitrile producers who did not possess a hydrogenated NBR product were vulnerable to the loss of the high growth, premium end of their specialty business, and the premium profit margins expected therefrom.[1]

Hydrogenated NBR Market (H-NBR)

H-NBR was a classic example of a product conceived, and developed in response to market pull from automotive and oil well industries. The increasing technical demands of these industries (spurred by such factors as smaller, hot-running car engines; pressure for fewer auto warranty claims in the face of Japanese competition; and the higher temperatures from deeper oil-well drilling) were not being satisfied by existing products. Regular nitrile rubber was being

---

[1] According to industry experts, average return on sales for the rubber industry as a whole was approximately 7–8%.

pushed beyond its performance limits, and more exotic products such as fluorelastomers lacked a proper balance of properties and required very high prices. What was needed was a product with a superior balance of oil, heat and ozone resistance, along with design capability, at an economic cost. H-NBR products were significantly better at satisfying these requirements than were regular NBR products.

In terms of market demand globally for H-NBR products, Polysar's market research study in 1986 (to support its production facility investment proposal early in 1987) included data in Table 1.

TABLE 1 H-NBR Market Forecast (tons)

	1986	*1991*		*1996*	
	Actual	*Base*	*Upside*	*Base*	*Upside*
U.S.	60	1 590	2 950	2 640	4 520
Europe	50	1 225	1 890	1 780	2 650
Japan	380	1 440	1 930	1 925	2 555
Other	—	—	300	—	700
Total	490	4 225	7 070	6 345	10 425

At that time, existing Bayer and Polysar facilities were pilot plants, as were 100 tons of the Nippon Zeon 600-ton capacity in Japan. In addition, Zeon had announced an expansion to 1 000 tons in 1987 as well as "evaluation of the feasibility of overseas production." Even with expansion by Nippon Zeon and possible commercialization of a new plant by Bayer in Germany, it was concluded by Polysar management in early 1987 that, based on the market research report, additional global production capacity would be required in the 1990s and, in particular, in the U.S. where the largest and fastest growing market was foreseen.

BACKGROUND ON POLYSAR

Polysar started out in 1943 as a Canadian producer of synthetic rubber to support the war effort; by 1988 it had become a major participant in the world's rubber, plastics and petrochemicals business. Its sales had grown to $2.5 billion, comprising 40% from synthetic rubber, 40% from petrochemicals, and 20% from plastics and diversified products. In synthetic rubber, Polysar was among the world's top three producers, and had been the global leader prior to closings of uneconomic facilities and the sale of non-strategic businesses in the 1987–88 period. Its range of rubber product types was still the broadest in the world, as was the geographic span of its production facilities.

Polysar's competitive strength had arisen from the scope of its international facilities and the comparable international experience of its people; from the technological orientation of its activities and the increasing breadth of its technology; and from its organizational emphasis on identifying and serving customer needs in the various geographic regions. It was particularly strong in the specialty rubber segment. In nitrile rubber, where H-NBR was expected to find its markets, Polysar held approximately 20% of both North American and European markets, and some 10% of the Japanese market.

Polysar's shareholder for most of the 1970s and 1980s had been Canada Development Corporation (CDC), but a fierce takeover battle in 1987, between Nova Corporation of Alberta and CDC, resulted in Polysar Ltd. becoming part of Nova in September 1988. Nova was a regionally oriented petrochemical, gas pipeline and energy company with operations located largely in Alberta. Historically, Nova's pipelines had transported more than 80% of marketed Canadian natural gas production. Its heavy involvement in this capital intensive industry was expected to continue, due to projections of strong growth of demand for gas in the U.S. and Canada through the mid-1990s. As shown in Exhibit 3, the Polysar acquisition substantially increased Nova's debt load, to a total of $4.3 billion. In addition, the Polysar rubber group had encountered difficult business conditions in 1988 and, by 1988's fourth quarter, was recording financial results some 20% below the level of operating income budgeted for that year.[2] According to Doug Henderson, however, "there was no particular financial pressure by Nova to consider an external TORNAC rubber alliance, although the senior management of Nova was kept constantly informed of the situation and the strategic alternatives being examined."

POLYSAR'S TORNAC RUBBER BUSINESS

As noted above, by the late 1970s and early 1980s, it had become clear to the management of Polysar's rubber division that the automotive industry's need for heat, oil and ozone resistant rubber polymers was not being met adequately by existing products. Not only were warranty claims from failed components becoming excessive, but North American cars were under increasing pressure from what were perceived to be higher quality Japanese vehicles.

Following extensive auto industry contacts, Polysar's R & D personnel had defined the required product parameters in 1981 to meet the above conditions. There followed a number of brain-storming sessions, involving R & D marketing and business managers, to examine the options for achieving such a product at economic cost, and to select a preferred route. More than 150 ideas were examined, and in early 1982, it had been decided to pursue a route of major chemical modification of nitrile rubber, a product in which Polysar was a world leader.

In making this decision, Polysar's management realized that Bayer in Germany had previously developed a nitrile-modified product in 1975, believed to have been R & D as opposed to market-driven. The process had been viewed by Polysar as inefficient and high cost, and Bayer was in fact trying to develop the European market from what was believed to be an uneconomic, semi-commercial 200-ton pilot plant facility. Polysar, therefore, decided in 1982 to develop its own product, based on R & D work it had already carried out on the "hydrogenation" of nitrile rubber.

It had been learned by Polysar that Dr. Gary Remple of the University of Waterloo was interested in, and involved with, "hydrogenation" of polymers to try to improve their performance. A contract was subsequently signed with Dr. Remple to develop a catalyst system to

---

[2] Nova Corporation's annual report noted that, for the last 6 months of 1988, the Rubber Division had assets of $1.4 billion, revenues of $417 million and operating income of $37 million.

meet the defined product requirements, working with Polysar's technology personnel. A new system was rapidly developed and patent applications were filed late in 1982.

Over the following three years, a number of steps had been taken to develop a satisfactory commercial product, including the installation of a "bench-scale" reactor initially, a "pilot plant" as an intermediate step, and the design and engineering for a full-scale production plant. As Dr. John Dunn, senior scientist at Polysar, said, "It was a high-risk situation—we had to choose the right product route; we had many millions of R & D and future facility investment dollars at stake; we had to get the technology right; we had to move fast and we needed to get lucky. With Gary Remple, we got lucky!"

Polysar's efforts with Dr. Remple were so successful that the new TORNAC rubber technology had been awarded a gold medal for invention in 1987 under the Canadian government's Business Excellence program. The final product was judged by Polysar's technical people to be markedly superior to the Bayer product on both cost and process technology.

Nippon Zeon also had developed its own approach to H-NBR in the early 1980s. A Japanese pilot plant with 100 ton/annum capacity had been built initially, followed by a commercial plant of 500 tons by 1985. Zeon had avoided contravening Bayer's patents by utilizing a different catalyst to accomplish the required chemical modification of nitrile rubber. Initially, the Zeon product had been thought by Polysar to be inferior to TORNAC, but ongoing development work by Zeon produced a fully competitive product by 1987.

POLYSAR'S RUBBER STRATEGY

In April 1987, a full-scale capital investment proposal by Polysar's management for a TORNAC H-NBR production facility in Orange, Texas, was approved by the Polysar board of directors. This site was selected primarily because, with potential customers expected to be aerospace, military, oil well and automotive related, strategic location within the U.S. was critical. In addition, much lower capital and plant installation costs prevailed in Texas relative to possible northern locations. Included in the management justification for the project were the following observations:

TORNAC's Fit With Strategic Plan

The mission of the Global Rubber Business is to be a leading global supplier of elastomers with emphasis on those market sectors offering superior quality of earnings. One of the five Corporate Strategic Directives to the Rubber Business dictates that the Rubber Business "shift technology emphasis with priority to new, high performance products and applications, including externally sourced innovation." The proposed entry into the TORNAC Rubber Business is the first major project which has been successfully advanced towards this goal. Moreover, TORNAC Rubbers are expected to complement and enhance Polysar's strategic global nitrile business in terms of long-term profitability and competitive advantage as a supplier of oil resistant elastomers.

It was apparent, therefore, that the TORNAC rubber thrust was not only an integral part of the 1987 global rubber business strategy, but was also part of a corporate strategy to move increasingly to higher value-added products. This was confirmed in the Polysar rubber business plan issued internally by rubber management in the last quarter of 1988 (Table 2).

TABLE 2   **Specialty Component of Rubber Business** (% by volume)

	Forecast 1977	*1988*	*1992*
Specialty	45	64	67
Commodity	55	36	33

The definition of specialty rubbers was given as:
- Unit margins exceeded 50% of net selling price.
- Based on proprietary process or product technology.
- Required high level of technical/marketing support.

TORNAC rubber was well within the definition of the type of business in which Polysar wanted to focus its resources.

Competitive Positioning

The April 1987, TORNAC rubber investment project for production facilities in Texas included the following observations by Polysar's rubber management:

> A very significant feature of the feedback on the H-NBR rubber market survey has been the prime importance of the U.S. area in demand forecasts. We believe that Nippon Zeon, the current leader for hydrogenated NBR, will be discouraged from a decision to invest in North American production (1) by a definitive announcement of Polysar's decision to build and operate a global scale TORNAC rubber plant in the U.S., and (2) by the recent announcement by Bayer to build and operate a THERBAN rubber plant in Germany. It is more likely that Nippon Zeon will further expand its ZETPOL Rubber plant in Japan as market demand warrants.
>
> Thus, it is our view that each of the three producers of H-NBR will dominate in a specific major geographic region and have influential positions in the others, (1) Nippon Zeon in the Asia Pacific region, (2) Bayer in Europe, and (3) Polysar in North and South America.
>
> Thus, there is every reason to believe that Polysar will gain ground rapidly with a North American TORNAC rubber facility and superior process technology.

These management observations were followed by their assumptions on market size and the share which could be anticipated by Polysar in a base case situation. Thus, they stated in the 1987 project justification:

> Assuming that the TORNAC rubber plant comes on stream in the fourth quarter of 1988, Polysar should be able to gain a significant market share globally by 1991 and develop a strong leadership position by 1996—including a dominant position in the U.S. (Table 3).

TABLE 3   **Polysar Market Share Projection: H-NBR** (%)

	U.S.	*Europe*	*Japan*	*Global*
1991	45	20	10	26
1996	65	35	18	43

It was clear, therefore, that the global leadership aspirations of the Polysar rubber management for this market niche depended upon strong demand growth in the U.S., in particular, and also in Europe, and on Polysar securing significant market shares in these two regions. Transportation costs were a negligible factor in inter-regional competition.

POLYSAR'S ORGANIZATION

Over several decades, it had been Polysar's experience that the most effective way to organize for major new projects or businesses was to establish a special team or group separate from the day-to-day organization. Such groups usually reported to a senior member of Polysar's management.

TORNAC rubber was no exception. An original product/process development team was established in 1983 reporting directly to the manager of technical development division. When the product was judged ready for commercialization in 1986, a separate business management organization was established under Keith Ascroft as TORNAC rubber business manager. He had line responsibility for a market development manager, a manufacturing manager, a technical/R&D manager and an engineering (plant construction) manager. Sales were channelled through the regular rubber sales organization.

What happened as a result of this type of organization was immense focus on and dedication to success on the part of the specially selected groups of people. Another result was the development of strong emotional attachments to such projects, and increasingly strong feelings of proprietorship as the business or project unfolded and started to grow. In 1988, the TORNAC rubber business group appeared to fit this pattern of dedication and ownership. They reported directly to Doug Henderson, the group vice-president, rubber.[3]

Financial Data

As part of the Polysar 1987 TORNAC rubber investment project, the following financial information was provided by Polysar's rubber management. In the five years prior to the facility investment proposal in early 1987, TORNAC rubber development costs (including a small pilot plant) were approximately $4 million, partially offset by a Canadian Government grant of $1 million. The investment project is shown in Table 4.

TABLE 4 **Polysar 1987 TORNAC Rubber Investment Project—Spending Profile** (US$ million)

	1986	*1987*	*1988*	*1991*	*Total*
Phase I (1 500 ton facility)	0.3	6.5	19.0	—	25.8
Phase II (3 000 ton facility)	—	—	—	5.2	5.2
					31.0

---

[3] See Exhibit 4, Polysar organization charts for 1985, 1987, 1988.

The anticipated discounted cash flow return (Base Case assumptions) on this investment was 22.8% for Phase I, and 26.5% for Phase I + II.[4] Polysar's hurdle rate in early 1987 was a minimum 20% discounted cash flow, with a 25% minimum rate for "high-risk" projects.

The 1987–88 Period

In the 18 months prior to the decision faced by Doug Henderson and his management in November 1988, several events had occurred which would have an impact on their deliberations.

Following Board approval in April 1987, the TORNAC rubber production facility investment in Orange, Texas, had gone ahead as planned under the direction of Keith Ascroft, the TORNAC rubber business manager. Towards the end of 1988, it was evident that the plant would come on stream at the turn of the year, as forecast, and its projected costs would be within the approval capital budget of U.S.$25.8 million.

Nippon Zeon not only had proceeded with the announced expansion of its Japanese H-NBR capacity in 1987 from 600 tons to 1 000 tons, but in fact had installed a total capacity of 1 800 tons by late 1988. A large proportion of Zeon's production had been directed toward auto industry applications such as engine drive belts, an $8–10 part whose failure could result in up to $1 000 in replacement costs. Moreover, in the third quarter of 1988, Zeon had announced its intention to construct a production plant in Clear Lake, Texas, with planned capacity of 1 500 tons. Bayer had announced a European production facility of 1 200 tons at the end of 1986, but by late 1988 had not yet proceeded with construction. It was believed by the Polysar management in 1988 that Bayer had neither the environmental clearance to build such a plant, nor a satisfactory production process for H-NBR at economic cost.

The overall global market growth for the Polysar 1989–93 operating plan, as projected at the end of 1988, was reasonably in line with the 1986 market research report on which the Polysar TORNAC rubber facility was based (Table 5).

TABLE 5   H-NBR Market Demand (tons)

	1986 Actual	1986 Market Research Base Case Forecast for 1990	1988 Revised Forecast for 1990
U.S.	60	1 410	200
Europe	50	400	500
Japan	380	900	2 000
Total	490	2 710	2 700

The key reason for the deviations between the 1986 and the 1988 geographic forecasts was the behaviour of the respective auto industries of the three geographic regions. The automotive engines developed by the Japanese companies, together with their incessant drive for quality, demanded the higher product performance offered by H-NBR, even at relatively high prices.

---

[4] For sensitivities around the Base Case and for projected cash flow and net income, see Exhibits 5 and 6.

The European auto manufacturers, spurred by Japanese competition and probably by Japanese-transplant production in Europe, also required higher performance products such as H-NBR. In North America, however, the automobile manufacturers had been extremely slow to adopt Japanese-type engine technology and did not appear to be ready to do the necessary development work, nor to pay higher short-term prices for longer-term quality assurance and reduced post-sale service levels on their automobiles.

The impact of these geographic disparities was immense on the actual and anticipated competitive and market share positions of the three competitors in the H-NBR business. Nippon Zeon was the big winner with essentially 100% of the Japanese market and a significant share of the other much smaller markets, with the help of its already proven commercial product. Bayer, from its semi-commercial pilot plant, benefited somewhat from European growth (although it was judged by Polysar management to be losing a great deal of money from its inefficient production process). Polysar, at the end of 1988, was faced with its own new plant of 1 500 tons in North America, an announced U.S. plant of Zeon of similar capacity, and a market in North America estimated at a mere 200 tons by 1990. Faced with such projections of overcapacity, discussion had begun regarding the attractiveness of exploring formation of an alliance in H-NBR with one of Polysar's competitors.

THE OPPOSING VIEWS

When he faced his management team that morning, Doug had determined that he would play the role of "devil's advocate" to both the "independence" and "alliance" sides of the question, although he was aware that he was in a difficult position to do so. As he stated to the team,

> As V.P.–Europe, I had been opposed to the original TORNAC rubber pilot plant investment decision in 1985, and the major production investment which was likely to follow. I had felt that it was too risky and speculative relative to other investment opportunities at that time. Since I just took over the global rubber group in the spring of this year, and have continued to express concern about future TORNAC rubber market forecasts, I know that my own impartiality is open to question by this management team. I am also aware that I have a reputation of being driven by shorter term results! I will try, nevertheless, to take a balanced position during the team's discussions.

As expected, the rubber management team had indeed become sharply divided on the strategic choice facing the TORNAC rubber business. Some members of the team felt that an alliance made good sense in terms of short-term financial benefit, especially since Polysar itself had just changed hands and was now part of Nova Corporation. It was expected that the servicing of Nova's high debt level, and its desire to expand its petrochemical and pipeline businesses (the latter business alone was anticipated to involve expenditures approaching $500 million annually during the early 1990s), would lead to pressure on its cash flow and create severe competition for scarce investment capital. They believed that the credibility of the rubber group as a whole would be in question for future investments if the TORNAC rubber project did not meet its short-term financial projections. This could represent a serious concern, since the rubber group was considering investment in several major projects during the next few years.

From a different perspective, the alliance choice was also supported by Dr. John Beaton, the rubber group's European vice-president, the geographic region where Bayer was particularly strong. He commented, "I support a TORNAC rubber alliance, not for short-term bottom line reasons, but because I believe that there could be real strategic benefits from working more closely with a company of Bayer's technological depth—and marrying this with Polysar's acknowledged skill in the marketplace." This kind of thinking also prevailed with Pierre Choquette, President, Polysar Polymers, to whom Doug Henderson reported. Although he did not participate in the rubber management team's H-NBR alliance debate, nor try to influence its outcome, Choquette's willingness to contemplate an alliance option was well-known. He had felt for some time that there could be real benefit from Bayer and Polysar working more closely together because the (polymer) customers of both companies were fairly similar, and they had common and aggressive competition from Japan. In contrast to this sentiment, Pierre's predecessor at Polysar (Bob Dudley, President, Polysar Ltd.), had been fundamentally opposed to any alliance which did not give majority ownership or control to Polysar.

The pro-alliance members of the team also felt that other advantages would accrue to Polysar from a Polysar/Bayer arrangement, e.g., joint production and R & D would help reduce potential experience curve benefits gained by Zeon, because it would lead to better products and lower costs faster than an independent approach; Polysar would gain an opportunity to participate in a joint European production facility expected to be needed in the late 1990s; joint use of the Texas facility would avoid the further supply/demand imbalance which would arise if Bayer proceeded with its announced European plant; and, finally, the two companies would be expected to work well together due to similar corporate cultures with strong technology emphasis. As a pro-alliance team member summed up: "In a sense, I see such a Polysar/ Bayer partnership on H-NBR to be a kind of insurance policy against a financial blood-bath which could arise if our forecast market and price numbers prove to be optimistic."

In sharp contrast, other team members were adamantly opposed to an alliance, stating that Polysar had a major competitive advantage over Bayer with a world-scale plant about to come on stream in the U.S. They felt that an alliance would sell Polysar's "birthright" on H-NBR technology and market positioning to a major global competitor, and that much greater benefits would accrue eventually to the TORNAC rubber business it remained as an independent competitor against Bayer and Nippon Zeon. Particularly strong in this view was Dr. Ron Britton, the rubber group's vice-president for North and South America, where Bayer's position was much weaker than in Europe. As Britton noted:

> I feel strongly that we would be giving away the opportunity of a lifetime in the specialty rubber area, without even giving it a chance. We have excellent technology, the only North American production facility about to come on stream, a European competitor whose uneconomic 200-ton pilot plant is sold out, and a U.S. market which looks extremely promising. With customer approvals already in hand from its European pilot plant, we will allow Bayer to move from its current weak position to one of strength in a major market with access to a local production facility. With all the promotion of TORNAC rubber which has been done in anticipation of the new Texas facility, the potential U.S. customers will be very confused indeed if we make an announcement of an alliance with one of our two competitors.

This view was supported vigorously by the TORNAC rubber technology management team. It was also echoed by the European sales director, who presided over perhaps the strongest of Polysar's regional marketing forces. He believed that Polysar's European Rubber sales force, which sold only rubber products, might have an advantage over Bayer in penetrating Tornac-type markets. This was because Bayer's sales force was responsible for a much broader line of polymer products, and thus might not be able to devote as much time to this particular product.

There was also a strong feeling by these same members of the team that, without a production-sharing deal with Polysar, Bayer would exit this segment of the specialty rubber business, leaving the world market to Polysar and Zeon alone. They were convinced that, with its existing high-pressure process technology, Bayer's production facility would be very high cost, would reflect two to three years' (10–15%) inflation in construction costs relative to the cost of building the earlier Polysar plant, and would have an intrinsic cost disadvantage of 25–30% by being built in Europe rather than the U.S. Gulf Coast.[5] They saw a total Bayer facility cost, with its particular process, being twice the level incurred by Polysar.

Supporting this anti-alliance view was the fact that Bayer had finally come to Polysar looking urgently for an arrangement which would give them economic supply within the anticipated major U.S. market. Moreover, the very fact that Zeon had recently announced the construction of a major U.S. H-NBR facility implied that they, in turn, saw a future U.S. market of significant size—in contrast to some views within Polysar that the U.S. market forecasts were wildly optimistic and uncertain. They justified their optimism by pointing to announcements by Japanese auto manufacturers of at least eight new assembly plants in North America, with a combined annual capacity of nearly two million vehicles by 1991. Also in support of this view was the belief that an alliance with Bayer would, after years of independent effort and progress by Polysar, cause a negative impact on morale and enthusiasm internally at Polysar, and damage the image and reputation of the company externally with customers. While Polysar had traditionally been recognized for their success in commercially adapting others' technologies, rather than for inventing technology themselves, Tornac represented an opportunity to help change this perspective both within and outside the company.

The advantages of an alliance for Bayer were, of course, seen clearly by all members of the rubber management team: the avoidance of a major, very high-risk, European facility investment by payment of an entry fee to the Polysar facility; production presence in the forecast major geographic growth market; access to an efficient production process and higher quality product technology for both U.S. and European customers; combined strength against a formidable Japanese competitor who had already established an initial specialty rubber production presence in Europe as well as the U.S.; and an opportunity to catch up in the marketplace and in technology with two competitors who had jumped well ahead of the product's original developer. As one team member said, "It would be a bit like letting the fox back into the chicken coop!"

John Mills, Global Marketing Manager–Specialty Rubbers, who was attending the management team meeting as an observer, noted: "It will not be an easy decision to make; in essence, the situation comes down to this—for Polysar, it appears that an alliance would mean short-term financial gain for long-term strategic pain; for Bayer, it would mean short-term financial pain for long-term strategic gain."

Difficult as it was, Doug Henderson knew that an immediate decision had to be made because, after lengthy exploratory discussions between Polysar and Bayer (initiated originally

---

[5] For the petrochemical industry, comparative all-in construction cost indices (called "Lang Factors") were available for different geographic regions of the world. For 1988–89 these indices were:

U.S. Gulf Coast:	100
Canada (Ontario):	110–115
Europe (Belgium, Germany):	125–130

by Polysar in 1986, but revived by Bayer in 1988), a fundamental decision point had been reached of a "go" or "no-go" nature.[6] Bayer executives had informed Doug that a decision must be made within the next two weeks. Moreover, Doug was about to submit his 1989 budget and five-year operating plan for final approval, and needed urgent resolution of this issue because of the potential major impact on the financial projections of the rubber group for the ensuing five years. Doug knew that, although the issues would be discussed at length among the rubber management team's members, ultimate responsibility for the alliance "go/no-go" decision would be his. He knew that a decision to pursue an independent approach for TOR-NAC would need to be carefully presented and supported in the budget. On the other hand, if he decided to pursue an alliance with Bayer, he would have to determine the minimum requirement for such a venture to be acceptable to his own management as well as his superiors. Moreover, he was aware that an alliance could take a number of different forms, and each of these would have to be explored from Polysar's viewpoint. While shared marketing of H-NBR might well be challenged for anti-trust reasons in the U.S. and Europe, Polysar's lawyers had assured him that no such worries would result from a joint production alliance. It was also necessary to examine such issues as degree of facility sharing, technology exchange, management fees, future facility expansion, future R & D innovations, possible European facilities, and initial and ongoing financial contributions. He decided to try to work these alliance choices through his rubber management team before reaching his final decision.

EXHIBIT 1 Nippon Zeon Profile

Nippon Zeon Co. Ltd. was established in Japan in 1950, and deals in the manufacture and sale of synthetic rubber and latices, as well as various plastics, chemicals and biochemicals. Nearly half of the company's net sales comes from synthetic rubbers and latices, a division that mainly produces oil resistant and general purpose rubber used in the automotive industry. The company's production is conducted at four plants in Japan, one in the United Kingdom, and three in the United States. Nippon Zeon has completed the purchase of three of B.F. Goodrich's businesses related to the production and sale of nitrile rubber (NBR), acrylic rubber, and epichlorohydrin rubber, respectively. In addition, a new plant in Houston, Texas, for the production of hydrogenated nitrile rubber (H-NBR) had been proposed, with completion scheduled for 1990.

---

[6] Informal contacts and Polysar's prior experience with Nippon Zeon resulted in essentially no support for the formation of an alliance with that firm for H-NBR products.

EXHIBIT 1   (continued)

Nippon Zeon Group Sales/Financial Data, 1989 (year ending March 31)

			US$ million
Net sales			830.3
Net income after tax			23.7
Total assets			1 080.9
Shareholders' equity			238.0
Number of employees			2 831.0
Sales breakdown	Synthetic Rubber	48%	
	Plastics	25%	
	Other	27%	

EXHIBIT 2   Bayer Profile

Bayer AG was established in 1863 in Germany to produce aniline dyestuffs. Today, the Bayer Group worldwide is comprised of some 460 affiliated companies manufacturing more than 10 000 different products with 170 000 employees.

In addition to being one of the largest and most diversified chemical manufacturers in the world, Bayer is ranked by sales as the third largest producer of photographic and imaging materials, and sixth largest in pharmaceuticals and other health-care products.

Bayer has a long history of technical innovation, ranging from the discovery of aspirin in the late 19th century and the world's first synthetic rubber, to polyurethane technology and some of today's most innovative chemical and health-related research. More than 12 000 employees are currently engaged in research and development worldwide, and Bayer holds 151 763 patents, a number virtually unequalled in the industries in which the company competes.

Bayer Group Sales, 1988

By Market			By Sector	
	US$	*%*		*%*
Europe	13.5	59	Polymers	17
N. America	4.6	20	Organic prods.	14
Latin America	1.4	6	Industrial prods.	21
Asia	2.4	11	Health care	18
Africa	1.0	4	Agrochemicals	13
			Imaging techs.	17
Total	22.9	100		100

EXHIBIT 3   Nova Corporation's Five-Year Financial Review

(millions of dollars,   except for common share amounts)

	1988	*1987*	*1986*[1]	*1985*	*1984*
Operating Results					
Revenue	$ 3 941	2 322	2 681	3 347	3 793
Operating income	978	528	573	674	677
Net income (loss)	424	179	100	(82)	203
Total Assets	$ 8 242	4 686	4 763	6 218	6 343
Capitalization					
Long-term debt	$ 4 304	2 434	2 461	2 704	2 901
Preferred shares[2]	216	329	827	862	780
Common equity[2]	1 974	1 303	649	563	743
Total capitalization	6 494	4 067	3 937	4 129	4 424
Cash Flow Data					
From operations	$ 863	478	547	609	658
Spending on plant property and equipment	439	200	326	387	624
Capital issued					
—long-term debt	1 646	218	100	124	411
—common and preferred equity	534[2]	31	982	125	24
Ratios					
Common shareholder					
Return on average common equity (%)	24.5	13.3	2.73	*	18.1
Capital					
Long-term debt to common equity	2.2:1	1.9:1	3.8:1	4.8:1	3.9:1
Interest coverage	2.9x	2.1x	2.1x	2.1x	1.7x

* Not comparable.

[1] Ownership in Husky Oil Ltd. was reduced to below 50%, and the investment was deconsolidated.

[2] Includes convertible debentures and warrants.

EXHIBIT 4   Polysar Organizations: 1985, 1987, 1988 Rubber Business Focus

A. 1985 TORNAC Rubber Pilot Plant Investment Decision

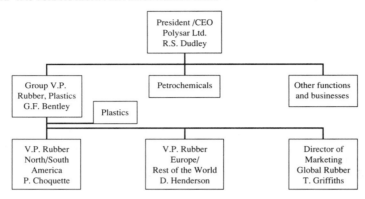

B. 1987 TORNAC Rubber Production Plant Investment Decision

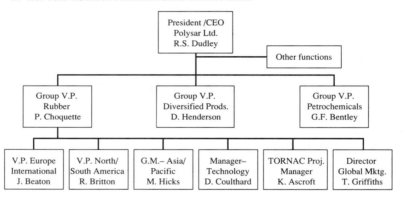

C. End 1988 Bayer H - NBR Alliance Issue

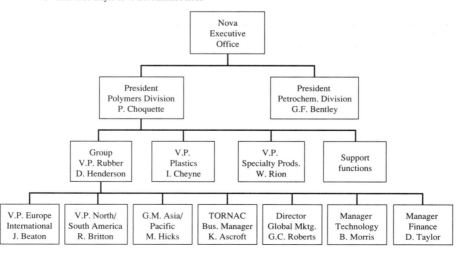

EXHIBIT 5   TORNAC Rubber Project Investment
Discounted Cash Flow Sensitivities
Base Case, 1991 (Phase I)

Sensitivities of different TORNAC rubber sales volumes, unit profit margins and capital investment costs, from those assumed for the 1991 Base Case, are shown below. These figures were contained in the 1987 Tornac rubber facilities investment proposal.

Differences from Base Case	Impact on Base Case DCF Outlook
If 1991 sales volume is:	
+30%	+3.4%
−10%	−1.4%
If 1991 unit profit margins are:	
+10%	+3.4%
−30%	−9.9%
If project capital investment costs are:	
+10%	−1.2%
−10%	+1.4%

EXHIBIT 6   **TORNAC Rubber Project Financial Projections, 1987–99**

The following graphs illustrate the anticipated cumulative cash-flow-after-tax and the net income-after-tax for the TORNAC rubber project to the end of its assumed life in 1999. These figures were contained in the 1987 Tornac rubber facilities investment proposal. Phase I (1 500 ton capacity) and Phase I + II (3 000 ton capacity) are displayed:

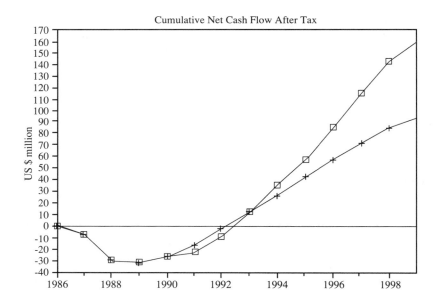

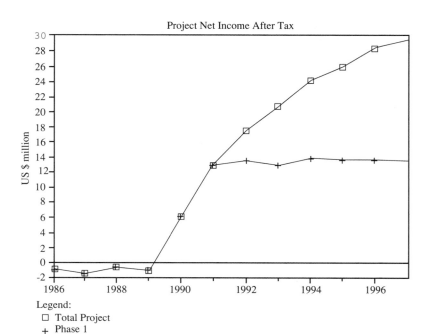

Legend:
☐ Total Project
+ Phase 1

STRATEGY—
ORGANIZATION

PART

4

CONTINENTAL REALTY

Joseph N. Fry and Randy A. Pepper

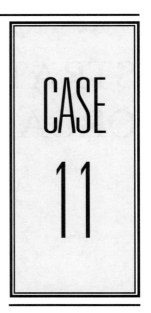

"This company has been immensely successful," said John Morrison, president of Continental Realty Ltd., as he looked west from his Vancouver office window, "and we intend to continue that way." His view of the skyline was punctuated by construction cranes rising above the foundations of new office towers. The west was booming and the company was growing apace. "The challenge," he said, "will be in finding the best people and keeping them with us."

BACKGROUND

Continental Realty was among the largest commercial and industrial real estate agencies in Canada. In its most recent fiscal year the company had acted in lease and sales transactions totalling more than $200 million. The first office and present headquarters of the company was in Vancouver. Branches operated in Calgary, Edmonton, Toronto, Houston and Phoenix. Continental currently employed over 40 agents; but its early days were very much the story of one man, Gordon Nelson, owner and chairman.

Nelson grew up in small-town Alberta, where he caught a sense of the coming promise of the west. He went east to obtain an Honours Business Administration degree from the University of Western Ontario, and then spent a year travelling and studying in Europe. On his return, he entered the real estate business. In three years he moved from Toronto to Winnipeg to Vancouver.

Nelson derived his approach to operating a real estate agency from his experience during these early years. His employers and colleagues were secretive—unwilling or unprepared to teach him the business. Information, even technical and background data, was treated as a resource to be rationed. Nelson persisted and eventually met a senior industry executive who was prepared to share his knowledge and who helped Nelson develop the technical expertise needed to move ahead in the business.

Nelson sold over $7 million worth of property in his first year with J.B. Hobbs & Co. in Vancouver. Shortly after, with two partners, he bought out the Hobbs agency and changed its name to Continental Realty.

Continental prospered, but the deal that established Nelson's reputation was Burrard Square. While examining an aerial photograph of Vancouver, Nelson became intrigued with a spread of property between the railway mainline and Burrard Inlet immediately west of the city's downtown core. The property, owned by Construction Aggregates Ltd., was the first fully assembled yet undeveloped parcel in the area. Through his investment contacts, Nelson determined that a British-financial firm, Tate Development Corp., was seeking attractive investment opportunities in North America. He evaluated Construction Aggregates' willingness to sell, convinced Tate of the property's investment potential, and the concept of Burrard Square was born. The steps from concept to reality were protracted, and marked by continuous negotiation as designs, approvals, financing and tenants were brought together. But five years later, in what was then a landmark deal for Vancouver, arrangements were completed and construction started on the multi-million dollar integrated apartment, commercial and retail complex.

After Burrard Square, Continental grew in volume and geographic coverage, and Nelson crystallized a strategy and set of operating policies that made the company unique in the industry.

THE BUSINESS

Continental confined its operations to the commercial and industrial realty markets, where it aimed to operate as one of the few true "agency" businesses, as compared to the hundreds of "brokerage" operations across the country. According to Bob McLaren, Continental's general manager, the distinction lay in the degree of professionalism in the operator's methods.

To draw a clear contrast, McLaren compared residential selling to Continental's approach. He explained, in his usual hyperbolic style:

> The residential business is largely a clearing-house operation. That's what the Multiple Listing Service (MLS) is all about. All the houses for sale are in a big pot with an index card and they are picked out of a hat and fed to the prospects. The residential realtor aims at completing a sales transaction. He derives his commission not from counselling his client but from moving the property.

It was not surprising, according to another industry source, that the popular image of a real estate broker was "a guy with a bright yellow jacket who leads housewives through endless kitchens and comments on the abundance of closet space."

Commercial and industrial negotiators, particularly Continental's, operated in a different world, with business clients and high-value properties. But the broker approach was also prevalent here. One of Canada's largest firms, a competitor of Continental, advertised a national computerized system that could quickly supply a list of potential properties to fit a client's space, location and cost requirements. To Continental, this shotgun approach served a client's interests poorly.

Continental negotiators operated on an exclusive basis, as the only agent attempting to sell or lease a client's property. Like a lawyer, a Continental negotiator would act for only one party in a transaction, the client, and in this relationship acted as much as an advisor as a salesperson. For example, he or she might advise a client not to accept an offer to purchase or lease if the agent established that it was not to the client's advantage. In this way, Continental sought to position itself as a true agency, more consistent with European than North American practice, under a single basic policy: "Treat the property as if it were your own."

If the cornerstone of Continental's agency concept was the exclusive concentration on client interest, the building blocks were formed from the creative pursuit of realty opportunities. The Burrard Square deal demonstrated this: through imagination, knowledge, and contacts, Nelson was well-positioned to conceive a project. Continental aimed to do more than represent other people's ideas or projects for clients, and in so doing add value to its agency role and, for that matter, to the economy as a whole.

In developing this approach, Continental pioneered a transformation in procedures for selling commercial and industrial real estate. For generations, the realty industry had been an old man's game, where commercial transactions took place among well-acquainted, senior colleagues. In such an environment, the building of social links was paramount in the operation of a successful realty business. Continental outflanked these industry norms by emphasizing technical and analytical skills. Gradually, the industry became a young person's field, where business relationships based on trust and skill became the basis of successful client–negotiator interaction.

Creating and negotiating a deal was the essence of the agency business. The following examples illustrate the frequently circuitous, sometimes protracted, and often frustrating aspects of a transaction.

A Land Assembly

A Canadian chartered bank approached Continental and R.E. Lang and Co., a significant Continental competitor, asking them to work together to assemble a major site in Edmonton's downtown core. Continental refused to collaborate, suggesting as an alternative that each agent propose six potential properties that the bank could then review. The bank agreed.

A senior Continental negotiator, through whom the initial contact had been made, took responsibility for the project. His activities included identifying potential rentable sites; judging the willingness of the site owners to sell and estimating prices; consulting with architects and planning consultants on the suitability of each site; checking out the necessary approvals and establishing a time frame for the regulatory process. He had to do all this discreetly and confidentially. Continental was first to propose sites to the bank and ultimately the bank chose a property on Continental's list.

The site selected was owned by an international utility company that had a policy of never selling its investment properties. The first step was to determine what amount to offer the company—an amount that would at least induce the utility to counter with an asking price. The situation was complicated by the bank's unwillingness to disclose its identity. This made the utility company even more nervous. It was not interested in selling to a speculator and giving that person the opportunity to flip the property at a later date.

After lengthy talks the utility sold, but on the condition that development would begin on the site within 18 months. The transaction had taken countless meetings over approximately six months. The Continental negotiator walked away with a handsome commission, however, and a good chance of becoming the leasing agent of the future bank tower.

Developing an Office Tower

Hugh Thorburn, a veteran Continental negotiator, first saw this potential opportunity while trying to lease space in a new office tower. Thorburn had attended a board meeting of the subsidiary of a large American mining firm to propose that an above-ground walkway be built between its building and an adjoining tower that he was trying to lease. At this meeting he learned that a committee was looking into the expansion of office space.

Conscious of its U.S. headquarters' attitudes, the subsidiary wanted to be very thorough in its examination of relocation space. It sent out an extremely detailed call for tender to 18 different office buildings in Vancouver. Meanwhile, Continental's general manager, Bob McLaren, who had been briefed by Thorburn on the mining company's search for space and who was the agent for a medium-sized Vancouver developer, decided that his client had the most suitable site for the mining company. The site was essentially raw land—a group of derelict buildings—but advantageously located for the mining firm. McLaren did not submit a proposal, but sent Thorburn a letter with a copy to the mining company outlining his client's plan to build on the site. The developer, inexperienced in the commercial market, was unwilling to begin construction unless the mining company was secured as lead tenant. Within two months McLaren obtained a letter of commitment from the mining subsidiary.

The mechanics of the process were as follows. As with most major development projects, McLaren's client had formed a team composed of an architect, a space planner, a contractor and a realty agent, to study the project's feasibility. Public relations and advertising people later helped to put presentations together. Proposal costs were shared between Continental Realty and the negotiator. In a deal such as this, McLaren was the "lister" of the property. His responsibilities included searching the property's title, preparing and distributing promotional material, advising the landowner on the project's marketability and negotiating with major tenants.

The amount of client/developer involvement usually depended on the client's size and experience in the negotiation process. In this deal, McLaren's nervous developer was constantly trying to involve himself in direct negotiations despite his inexperience in commercial dealing. It therefore became important for McLaren, a hard-nosed, number-oriented salesperson, to maintain firm control over his client. Meanwhile, the more affable Thorburn was continually assuring the mining company of the project's wisdom. As Thorburn observed, the different personalities of the two negotiators were very well suited to the job requirements.

"In a major leasing agreement," explained Thorburn, "the resolution of several common negotiating points determines the deal's success." Rent was not in dispute in this deal; however, the prospective tenant wanted to alter the building's design. The mining subsidiary was also determined to extend the lease period from 10 to 20 years, and to obtain a guaranteed lease rate should it require more space on additional floors. After all these points had been satisfactorily resolved, the mining company's Los Angeles head office decided that it wanted either 50% or 100% ownership of the building. McLaren's client agreed to a 50% equity participation by the mining firm. A further catch arose here, for Continental assessed the building's replacement value at $29.4 million, but the mining company's head office had authorized a capital expenditure of only $13 million. After several trips to the U.S. and hard negotiation, much of it aimed at avoiding having to resubmit a capital expenditure proposal and risk a turndown by the U.S. parent, the deal was concluded.

THE CONTINENTAL FORMULA

Providing genuine agency services had helped Continental grow, and charge full commission rates in the process. (The specific rates varied by the size, nature and location of the project, but were generally in the range of 3–5% of the dollar value of a transaction.) Gordon Nelson's ability to impose discipline on the activities of the high-flying, performance-oriented individuals who made up his negotiator team was a crucial ingredient in Continental's success. His company was known throughout the industry for its rigorous operating policies.

To remain with the firm, Continental negotiators (after a period of training) were required to generate a minimum of $90 000 in commissions annually. The average production in the past year for negotiators with greater than one year's experience was $234 000. Negotiator compensation was based on a sliding scale starting at 20% of commission generated, to 60% for commission earned over $100 000. The $15 000 salary was tied to the sliding scale, so that when a negotiator achieved the $90 000 minimum his total income would be $45 000. Negotiators were required to pay their own expenses, and they were not paid their share of commissions billed until Continental was in full receipt of the invoiced amounts.

Continental encouraged an open flow of information concerning client activity. Negotiators were required to submit a weekly applicant report, which identified their clients and outlined the probability of success of current deals. If clients were not so listed, they were regarded as fair game for other negotiators. This report allowed the branch manager to monitor negotiator progress (and discourage over-registration, if necessary) and informed other negotiators of development activities in various sectors of the city. "There is no fear of being scooped," as one negotiator put it. In contrast, negotiators with most Canadian brokerage houses tended to be secretive with details of their potential deals.

There were no sales territories, but most deals were transacted within the negotiator's city base. Management encouraged negotiators to focus their activities, to limit their client list, and to concentrate on big deals. Continental, in Nelson's words, was "not after all the business available, but all the big business." Deals completed by a negotiator outside of this branch were credited to the negotiator as usual, but for credit to the branch territory in which the deal occurred.

Continental procedures required all offices to hold sales meetings commencing no later than 8 A.M. on Monday, Wednesday and Friday of each week. These meetings were the primary forum for announcements of new development activities, for the collection of information on prospective buyers or sellers, and for discussion of proposed or current projects' sale or lease potential. The first item on the agenda of a Calgary meeting attended by the case-writer, for example, was a presentation by branch manager Steve Jannock. It began with a discussion of the marketing feasibility of a new condominium office building and whether or not the concept would sell in south-west Calgary. One negotiator noted that a rival developer was planning a similar project at the opposite end of the block. The discussion then moved to potential customers and a price estimate for such a project. Jannock pointed out that the proposal was complicated by the developer's desire for a short-term investor before proceeding. An architect's layout was then examined and suggestions were offered regarding the amount of glass space, the number and speed of elevators, and other improvements to increase the project's salability. Finally, the total credibility of the project was examined; two points of concern were that it was the developer's first effort in the condominium market, and that the architect was from out of town.

An important part of Continental's application of the agency concept was a strict investment policy. All Continental personnel were forbidden to purchase speculative real estate in Canada or any state in the U.S. in which the company maintained an active office. Infringement of the rule was grounds for immediate dismissal. McLaren explained that the logic of the policy was easy to understand: the time spent investing and developing one's own real estate holdings should be spent representing one's clients. Moreover, sophisticated clients came to respect their negotiator's advice because the latter was not plucking out the good properties for himself. Continental was one of very few real estate agencies in Canada operating with such a policy.

Continental maintained a high level of internal competition. Each negotiator's performance was charted on a graph, which was reviewed monthly before a panel of his or her peers. At the annual meeting of all Continental personnel, each negotiator's graphs were projected on a screen, and his or her performance was reviewed. Another meeting, held in the late summer or early fall, is further illustration of Continental's approach: with the chairman, president, general manager, and all branch managers present, negotiators who had not yet reached $50 000 in annual production had to account for their performance, and were offered advice for improvement by this executive team. A past Xerox salesperson who had risen quickly within Continental saw these practices as straightforward and reasonable: "One has to play on these guys' egos. It's the only way to motivate such achievement-oriented people."

Working trips were another ingredient in the Continental recipe for success. These trips were described in the company procedure manual as an incentive program to encourage negotiators to broaden their concept of commercial real estate. The manual noted that a good negotiator was expected to make many trips on his or her own, but the company would help to defray the cost of specific trips. During a negotiator's first year, western negotiators were to fly to eastern Canada and the U.S., while eastern negotiators were to fly west. In the third year, the destination was Europe; in the fourth, it was southeast Asia; and in the fifth year, the negotiator was to visit the Caribbean or Hawaii. In the course of these trips, while the negotiators were acquainting themselves with the dynamics of a new market, they were also required to update and expand the company's Buyer's Book. This book was a listing of international investors who had expressed interest in North American real estate. It included details on the clients' buying behaviour, investment criteria and history.

CORPORATE AND BRANCH MANAGEMENT

Continental operated with a lean management structure (Exhibit 1). Senior managers, including the president, general manager and branch managers, all acted as negotiators as well as administrators, and had their production charted. It was argued that few services were necessary for the effective operation of the company. The primary organizational function was the supply to negotiators of current information—applicant listings, sales data, office-space surveys, Buyer's Book—and each branch was responsible for its own surveys and record updating.

In recent years, Gordon Nelson had removed himself from management of Continental's day-to-day activities in order to spend more time as a property developer. As chairman, he remained involved in policy matters and in quite close touch with the business, informally and through quarterly board meetings.

Nelson's first replacement as president was Larry Newman, at the time branch manager in Calgary. Newman remained in Calgary after taking on his new responsibilities. He grew restless in his dual role, however, and left Continental after two years to start his own agency firm. Nelson filled the gap for a time, and then asked John Morrison to join the firm as president.

John Morrison was senior vice-president of a large insurance company at the time. He had received his B.A. from the University of Western Ontario, M.B.A. from Harvard Business School, and was a Chartered Life Underwriter. He had known Nelson for some time because of his insurance company's participation in several financing deals. Morrison was attracted by Continental's prospects, and moved to Vancouver to become president.

A few months after John Morrison's appointment, Stan Jameson, the general manager, left Continental. Jameson had been an exception in the Continental ranks. His background was as a developer rather than an agent, and he did not himself get involved in transactions. Rather, most of his time was spent travelling from branch to branch reviewing progress with individual negotiators and offering counsel and advice. He was, several negotiators mentioned, very respected in this role, and his branch visits were welcomed.

Bob McLaren, Jameson's successor, was cut from different cloth, not unlike that of his mentor, Gordon Nelson. McLaren had joined Continental after completing his M.B.A. at the University of Western Ontario. He had recently been promoted from Vancouver branch manager to executive vice-president.

McLaren was an aggressive and knowledgeable negotiator whose advice was highly valued by fellow negotiators. He continued his selling activities and was a consistently high producer, travelling about 160 000 km a year and working 70–75 hours a week. Administratively, McLaren saw his prime function as that of recruiting and training branch managers, although he could not avoid involvement in many spot problems, ranging from difficulties with deals to personnel issues. McLaren turned the monthly performance-review task over to the branch managers. On the demands of his job, McLaren commented:

> You don't enjoy success without paying the price. And you don't do it unless you want do. You have to enjoy it. You can't dedicate such physical and mental energy and sacrifice unless you get a lot of enjoyment out of what you are doing. A person who says he doesn't is a person who's not going to be successful at it.

Morrison and McLaren both felt that sales involvement and a proven sales record were important for a leadership position in Continental. The rationale was basically that of credibility, plus a latent feeling that perhaps the worst thing that could happen to Continental would be the building of "non-productive" overheads and becoming "over-administered." In this context, Morrison and McLaren had assumed a largely implicit division of management tasks. Morrison dealt with the general tasks of corporate administration and representation, McLaren with the more immediate problems of branch supervision and production.

Planning and budgeting in Continental were relatively simple procedures. Revenue by branch was estimated annually on the basis of branch input and forecasts of market activity. By far the largest cost item was negotiator commission expense and it was directly variable with revenue. Branch-office and head-office expense budgets were also prepared, and these tended to reflect a no-frills approach to operations. Only a limited amount of savings could be squeezed out of the administrative process, however, since the costs were already pared to the bone.

THE BIG BRANCHES

Vancouver

Continental's lead market, Vancouver, was beginning to emerge from a slump in office development. With 25 million square feet of existing space, compared to Calgary's 14 million square feet, Vancouver was often viewed by developers as more stable than the overheated Calgary market. Continental's Vancouver branch had maintained a relatively stable production level with a fluctuating rate of sales to leasing. The branch employed ten negotiators whose average age was 37 years.

The Vancouver branch manager, Per Ek, had less than two years with Continental when he succeeded McLaren as branch manager. Born in Sweden, Ek was raised in Switzerland and had obtained a Ph.D. in Economics from the University of Geneva. After work with a major Swiss bank, Ek moved to Montreal where he assembled properties for a consortium of European banks. Ek was brought into Continental as a European representative to supplement Gordon Nelson, who had reduced his global travelling. Ek did not see himself as a high-powered salesperson, but as a professional who specialized in large sales projects. His production graph, which bounded upward in large steps, attested to his ability. Ek believed that it was important to lead by example and, though he had hired an administrator to handle office affairs, he still found only Sunday afternoons free. With his three hats—branch manager, agent and international representative—Ek was unable to devote much time to work with individual agents.

Edmonton

The Edmonton branch consisted of eight agents, and represented an increasing proportion of Continental's total production. A year before, a group of four senior agents had left the branch, led by the previous manager, John Thompson. Those left were young (average age 32), and were managed by Cliff Baetz, who maintained a relatively relaxed atmosphere. In spite of the defections, production was only 10% below the levels of the year before, an accomplishment that was cause for a great deal of pride among the Edmonton negotiators.

At 36, Cliff Baetz was the old man of the Edmonton office. C.B., as his fellow negotiators called him, held a B. Comm. from the University of Alberta and had joined Continental in Edmonton as an assistant to the branch manager. Baetz's responsibilities included making the branch productive and setting the office's pace, but he maintained a casual, sociable atmosphere. As a point of comparison, negotiators in Edmonton sometimes wandered into the 8:00 A.M. sales meeting ten minutes late; in Vancouver, the door was locked at 8:00 A.M. Baetz noted that Edmonton's productivity per negotiator was higher than that of any other Continental office.

The Edmonton manager's laid-back nature was deceptive. His typical day began at 7:00 A.M. and stretched to 6:30 P.M.; on the two days that the casewriter was present, his lunch was two hot dogs swallowed while dialing the phone. Baetz was currently Continental's top producer. He described his job as "a pressure cooker," but he enjoyed the autonomy of his work. He liked to give his negotiators similar freedom. While Baetz admitted that he had little motivation to train his employees, he believed that few negotiators required or would tolerate direct supervision.

Calgary

The Calgary commercial-development business was in the midst of unprecedented growth and Continental had just enjoyed a superb year. Production was substantially improved over the relatively poor record of two years earlier when several key personnel had left the Calgary office, some to expand the company into Houston, others to strike out on their own. Production had dropped by over 50%. The branch had rebuilt, however, from nine negotiators to 17, with an average age of 38.

The Calgary branch manager, Steve Jannock, had ten years of experience with Continental. A former Xerox salesman, Jannock, 44, believed that more effort had to be put into retaining Continental's leading producers. "Calgary was seriously injured by Newman's departure, and Edmonton may still feel the effects of Thompson's exit," he cautioned. Talking with the commitment of a man who understood the high producers' predicament, Jannock explained, "When the investment policy removes a successful negotiator's most obvious tax shelter and participation is not offered, at some point it is no longer economical for an individual to remain in the company." The investment policy was too important a selling tool to sacrifice, according to Jannock, but something had to be done to retain Continental's "shooters." Another veteran negotiator quipped, "Gordon Nelson created a monster; he produces wealthy prima donnas that the tax system forces out of the company!"

Negotiator Management

Recruiting, training and retaining negotiators were the acknowledged keys to Continental's future growth.

Recruiting

Continental recruited from the universities and from the ranks of experienced salespeople. In recent years, university recruiting had been confined to the Universities of British Columbia, Reading (near London, England) and Western Ontario. British Columbia and Reading had courses specifically related to the real estate field, and Reading offered a Master's degree in urban land appraisal.

Recently, Xerox and IBM sales managers had been recruited into the company as junior negotiators. As well-trained, professional salespeople, these recruits brought a new style to the negotiation task. Their concentration on selling technique, combined with Continental's traditional stress on product knowledge, had produced some very satisfactory results. Negotiators with a Xerox background thought that individual negotiator productivity could be substantially improved at Continental. They identified in particular a need for instruction in more effective selling methods. As one successful, ex-Xerox negotiator put it, "Everybody here works hard, but only a handful work smart."

There was no shortage of potential recruits to Continental. As Steve Jannock noted, "I have more people phoning me for jobs than I know what to do with." The question was one of quality, of being able to succeed in the Continental milieu.

Training

An assistantship program was Continental's primary training vehicle. With the permission of the company, a negotiator could hire an assistant if he had achieved $100 000 production for two consecutive years. A second assistant could be hired if the negotiator had achieved $200 000 production over the past two years, or if he had obtained a new major office or industrial listing (over 150 000 square feet). A new assistant was paid $700 per month for the first six months, $750 per month after six months, and could be eligible for a salary of $800 per month if he or she had experience. No production bonus was allowed during the assistant's first year. One recent Western M.B.A. recruit described his initial reluctance to join Continental at $700 per month: "Hell, that was less than I was making during my summers at school!"

An assistant was hired by a single negotiator who became responsible for the assistant's training. The quality of training provided by the negotiator varied, and this factor contributed, at times, to assistant turnover. In the Calgary branch, for example, approximately five assistants had moved in and out of the office in the past two years.

For most trainees, the apprenticeship period lasted 12 months. At the end of that time, the negotiator in charge and the assistant determined a future course. On occasion, the assistants would stay on in a trainee capacity, with increased responsibilities and a cut into the bonus system. Otherwise they became full negotiators subject to the performance requirements.

Some prospective recruits were unwilling or financially unable to accept the reduction in earnings involved in an assistant position. In particular cases, if past sales experience justified it, certain recruits were permitted to enter the negotiation field directly. Their training period was typically three months, after which they became regular negotiators with $15 000 salary and a more lucrative commission rate. The junior negotiators were usually "blinkered"—assigned to a specific project or area to improve their understanding of a particular aspect of real estate development.

Apart from the assistantship program, Continental had no formal training procedures or materials. However, one senior negotiator, Brad Connelly, was assembling an extensive and detailed manual of procedures and techniques. Connelly planned to enter the consulting field eventually, providing advice on realty matters to major developers, and the manual tied in with these plans. Negotiators and branch managers alike felt that Connelly's efforts would substantially fill the present training gap in the company. One branch manager, who felt that training was critical to the company's continued success, praised Connelly's activities; he was relieved to have the responsibility off his desk.

Retraining

High turnover was characteristic of Continental's operation. Two-thirds of Continental's present negotiator group had been with the company in that capacity for less than two years. Over past years, there was an 84% probability that a negotiator would leave before his or her fifth year with the company. Part of the turnover, of course, was due to recruits who found they did not fit, or who could not produce the required $90 000 in annual commissions. Another part of the turnover, more consequential for the firm, was made up of successful negotiators who, for reasons varying from economics to personal autonomy, chose to leave.

Whether it was possible or desirable to lengthen the stay of negotiators was somewhat of a moot point at Continental. The company had implemented incentive programs aimed at stimulating continuity (Exhibit 2) and had developed a pension plan that would allow a negotiator to collect $60 000 per year on retirement and vested in ten years. These did not, however, seem to have had a major tangible impact. McLaren took a pretty hard-nosed view of the situation: "After a person has made $200 000 to $300 000 for three or four years, you can't expect him to stay." Shortly after having said this, McLaren met the casewriter at another Continental office; he had just received a message that the Toronto branch manager had resigned.

FUTURE GROWTH

There were, in the view of senior Continental personnel, two broad avenues of future growth. The first was through opening additional branches, and the second through expansion of branch volume by entry into new product areas.

Branching

New branches were generally seen as the prime growth vehicle, although it was by no means clear, on the record, that the Continental approach could be easily transferred out of the Vancouver-Calgary-Edmonton triangle. The performance of the Toronto branch had been erratic, and was attributed variously to market conditions, well-established competition, and poor management and recruiting. In spite of the difficulties, there was a general opinion in the west that an effective and energetic manager could put the operation on its feet. In the U.S., the two branches in Houston and Phoenix had been open for only a short time. Houston was, nevertheless, regarded as somewhat of a disappointment, due perhaps to the timing (relatively late in Houston's development boom) and narrow initial contact base (Continental had entered the market to work with one Canadian developer who was also entering the market). There was greater enthusiasm for the Phoenix office, which had just been opened by an aggressive negotiator. The Phoenix market was growing rapidly and had become an attractive expansion point for Canadian developers moving south.

In Bob McLaren's view, Continental should have offices established in 15 key cities within seven to ten years. The major constraints, he explained, were the availability of suitable people and his own time.

> It will take from four to seven years to build a base in a new city. By the time the lead producer peaks out in a new area, the base for effective dealing has been established. My job is to identify when a young negotiator has ripened sufficiently, place him in the new market, and help him get going. We must do this with our own people. Bringing in negotiators from outside the firm or acquiring an existing firm would bring us the worst of both worlds.

On this program, branch growth was limited by McLaren's capacity to train and supervise new managers, which amounted, in his view, to having no more than two junior branches at any one time.

New Products

An area of immediate growth potential lay in the further expansion of Continental's activities in the industrial and property-management markets.

In both Calgary and Edmonton, industrial opportunities were being pursued, but no particular priority had been given to them. Development and decision-making in the industrial market were different, Continental personnel pointed out, involving different customers and different criteria. "They are an earthy lot," one negotiator explained, "but I get along better with the tire-kickers than the oil executives." Most of the negotiators concentrating on the Calgary industrial market had not selected their placements; they had been assigned to the market. Another industrial negotiator explained, "The deals are small, you work twice as hard and make half as much." Edmonton had always had its finger in the industrial area, but, historically, only one negotiator in that office specialized in such deals.

Continental's property-management operations were headquartered in Vancouver under Ted Foster, a public accountant who had joined the company in its early years. The essential function provided was coverage of the ongoing tasks of operating an office; property-tenant relations, physical maintenance, insurance, security, etc. The major competitor was the owner himself, who was always tempted to perform the management function. Management contracts were sought by negotiators and turned over to Foster when a deal was made. In the coming year the property-management operation was expected to gross about $1 million, with Vancouver contributing about 50%, Calgary 25% and the balance from Edmonton and Toronto. The business was profitable and was growing at about 15% per year.

Another, quite different, view of growth objectives and methods was presented by a veteran representative, Dick Thorson, reflecting in some degree the thoughts of some other senior agents. His concern was that dynamic growth might cause the company to trade off quality for quantity and slip toward becoming a "brokerage" house. Using Calgary as an example, Thorson suggested that there should be only five to seven negotiators, rather than the current 17. Only these negotiators would attend the morning meetings, ensuring a free flow of information and counsel.

Each negotiator, however, would have two executive assistants and would be held accountable for the production and profit of his three-person group. To retain the senior negotiators, Thorson proposed a change in the investment policy: negotiators would still be prohibited from dealing in city-core or raw land, but a sector of land would be opened for investment. All Continental clients would be informed of the nature and extent of the investment area. Finally, Thorson would limit branch expansion to the high-growth markets in western Canada and to a few dynamic American cities.

Thorson's proposal thus preserved the firm's strategy, but recommended a fundamental change in operating method. Few negotiators were so presumptuous. Most felt that Gordon Nelson had developed a wondrous formula for success which should not be tampered with. Asked why others had not been able to duplicate Continental's methods, one negotiator replied, "Nobody else has copied the formula because nobody else has the spunk."

EXHIBIT 1   Continental's Organization Chart

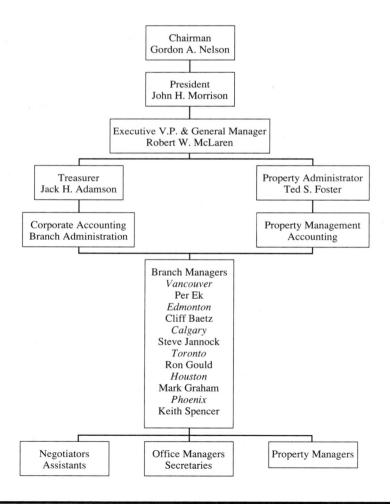

EXHIBIT 2   **Continental's Incentive Program**

Old System	Present Schedule	Prize
$ 100 000	2.5 × minimum production	Gold watch
$ 300 000	5 × minimum production	Colour television
$ 750 000	10 × minimum production	Lincoln Continental automobile
$ 1 000 000	20 × minimum production	University education for salesperson's children

Proposed 30 × minimum production

Proposed 40 × minimum production

Option to purchase 5% interest in
$5 million property
Entitled to exercise option

ATLANTIC PAPER COMPANY

J. Peter Killing

CASE 12

I n January 1991, Jack Vickers was appointed President of the Atlantic Paper Company, Australia's largest producer of linerboard and brown paper. Atlantic was a wholly-owned subsidiary of Cumberland Industries, and provided almost 50% of Cumberland's total sales volume, but its recent financial performance had not been encouraging. In spite of its historically dominant position in its businesses, the company had been losing market share to two smaller competitors since the early 1980s, and had also seen its markets shrink through the introduction of plastic products such as shrinkwrap and plastic checkout bags used in supermarkets. Vicker's predecessor Marcel Ruban had taken early retirement at age 55, having spent his last years in office struggling with unions and local governments in a successful but exhausting battle to close the company's smaller and less efficient paper mills.

Jack Vickers, age 40, had become a part of the Cumberland organization in 1988 when Cumberland acquired the Australian transport company of which he was majority owner and president. Vickers had founded the company in 1979, after completing his MBA in the United States. A series of well-executed acquisitions in the early 1980s not only tripled the size of the trucking company, but earned Vickers the reputation of being a very shrewd financial operator whose eye was firmly fixed on the bottom line.

After the 1988 takeover, Vickers continued to manage what was now the transport division of Cumberland Industries, and joined the company's board of directors. The board included, among others, Cumberland's president and chief financial officer, and the presidents of its Atlantic Paper and Diamond Cement subsidiaries. Vickers was widely seen as an "up and comer" in the organization, but as time passed, it became clear that if he were to have a chance of becoming president of Cumberland, he would first have to successfully manage one or the other of Cumberland's two major subsidiaries. In late 1990, when Marcel Ruban's retirement was announced, Vickers was taken aside by the president of Cumberland and asked if he would take over Atlantic and "get the company back on track."

THE COMPANY

In 1988, Atlantic's head office staff moved out of Cumberland's downtown office tower to much more modest offices in Acton, a suburb 20 kilometres away. The instigators of the move were Jim Smythe and John Collins, two of Atlantic's vice-presidents. Jim Smythe explained:

> The distance between Cumberland's head office and ours is not far, but psychologically it's an important gap. Their head office is full of mahogany and plush carpets. Our relatively austere offices in Acton are much more appropriate for a company that has been closing mills and laying people off for the past three years.
>
> Another advantage of the move is that we have gained a little independence from Cumberland's president and financial people, most of whom used to work for Atlantic. They still like to tell us how to run the company. Also, we took the opportunity presented by the move to eliminate about 30 technical staff, who were necessary in our expansion stage, but aren't now.

As shown in Exhibit 1, Atlantic was a functionally organized company, with five vice-presidents reporting to the president. There were currently approximately 65 employees in the Acton head office, 60 in regional sales offices, and 2 500 spread across the company's four remaining mill sites. Within the past 18 months, employment had been reduced by approximately 800 people through mill and machine closings and head office cutbacks. Two hundred of these cuts had come in the last six months.

Each of the company's mill sites is described below.

The Northern Mill

The Northern Mill was Atlantic's largest. Built on a rural site in a timber growing area approximately 200 kilometres from Acton, the Northern Mill housed three pulp mills and three paper machines. Two of the pulp mills were relatively old and small, but the third was new and very large, and due to come on stream in late 1991. With the new mill in place the company's pulp capacity would more than triple. The new pulp mill was being financed "off balance sheet," which meant that Atlantic would make lease payments of approximately $15 million per year to the (related) company that would own the pulp mill. These fixed annual payments, beginning in 1991–92, would not vary with the mill's output.

Atlantic's paper machines were highly specialized, efficient at producing only a specific type of product. Two of the paper machines on the Northern site, N1 and N2, used virgin pulp and recycled wasted paper to produce brown paper, which was sold to paper bag makers. The third machine, N3, was the largest and most efficient machine the company owned. It was used to make linerboard, which was sold to manufacturers of corrugated boxes. The efficient operation of N3 was of such importance to the company that Chris Reid, the senior vice-president to whom the mills reported, was aware of its production on a daily basis, and even Marcel Ruban usually knew if there were any problems on N3.

Because of the complex interrelationships between the pulp mills and the paper machines, and the fact that these pulp mills supplied all of Atlantic's other mill sites, the Northern site was very difficult to run well. There would be, in fact, few sites as complex in the world, once the new pulp mill was operational.

Jim Smythe, who had successfully managed the Northern Mill in the 1980s when N3 was installed, was concerned that with the addition of the new pulp mill the job of managing the Northern Mill would be beyond the capabilities of any of Atlantic's managers. The successful operation of the new pulp mill was a high priority both because of its economic importance, and the fact that the decision to build it had been made by Hector Day, currently the president of Cumberland Industries. Smythe commented, "It was difficult enough managing that site in my day, now I wonder if we have anyone who can do it." Smythe himself was reported to have been one of the two most effective Northern Mill managers in Atlantic's history.

The Senator Mill

The Senator Mill was located about 20 kilometres from Acton on the edge of the city. It was a very old mill with two active paper machines, one of which produced linerboard, and the other brown paper. The Senator Mill was plagued by hostile labour relations, and had been the site of many industrial disputes. The mill seemed to be caught in a vicious circle: its poor industrial relations record had led to even more aggressive union behaviour. Few aspiring managers in Atlantic were eager to run the Senator Mill, and it was widely believed that the current manager had now proved beyond doubt that he could not handle the unions and would soon have to be replaced. Whether a new mill manager would prove any more successful was an open question.

The Lautrec Mill

The Lautrec Mill was furthest from Atlantic's head office, about 800 kilometres, and to some within the company that was sufficient explanation of why it was so well managed. The Lautrec Mill contained one paper machine, Atlantic's only machine that could produce white papers. However, the machine was very old, and was being run constantly at speeds well above its designed capacity levels. As a result, quality was suffering in a market in which quality was becoming ever more important. Ken Mauger, the mill manager, claimed that he was "hanging on by the skin of his teeth." He explained:

> White papers is one of Atlantic's few markets that shows any growth at all. But the growth is in higher quality paper than we can make. Even for the low quality end of the market our product is marginal. We are very vulnerable. We clearly need a new paper machine. The cost will be high (about $80 million) but this company has to build a future for itself.

The Johansson Mill

In 1991 the Johansson Mill was also a single machine mill, although as recently as 1989 it had housed three machines. Located in a major urban centre, the mill specialized in the conversion of recycled waste paper (plus a little pulp) into low-grade linerboards. Formerly the site of many industrial relations problems, the mill now appeared to be stable and running without major problems.

VICKERS' FIRST WEEKS

Jack Vickers' first two weeks at Acton were devoted to meeting his senior management team, and reviewing the company's past and projected financial performance. One of the first documents he read was the company's five-year plan, dated October 1990, excerpts of which follow. He was not surprised to learn that Atlantic had met Cumberland's target of a 17.5% return on funds employed only once in the past five years, or that the most recent financial year, ended June 30, 1990, had come in at 6.7% (Exhibit 2). He was, however, startled to discover that Atlantic's plan showed that the 17.5% target would not be met in the foreseeable future.

Vickers discovered that the prime author of the five-year plan was Jim Smythe, and that much of its content was the result of a three-man task force which Smythe had headed up over a recent six-month period. Alarmed at the company's apparently bleak future, Smythe had formed the group on his own initiative, involving the market services manager and a senior accountant. The three-man group met widely with customers, suppliers, personnel in Atlantic's mills, and gathered what data they could about the competition. Jim Smythe described the results to Jack Vickers as follows:

> Our conclusion was that there was no reason to be optimistic about the future of this company. Our five-year plan may not look too good to you Jack, as an outsider, but believe me if we sit here and do nothing our future is going to be lot worse than this. Even meeting these projections is going to be a big job.
>
> Let me give you one example of the kinds of problems we face. Fibrebox Ltd. is our largest single customer. It's a well run, aggressive, growing company. They have just bought a new paper machine which will allow them to recycle their own waste. They don't need pulp to make low quality linerboard, and their box plants are now big enough that their own waste, combined with some purchased scrap paper are sufficient to supply a 40 000 ton per year machine. One of the things our task force did was to calculate Fibrebox's return on investment on that new machine. It's about 45%! There is nothing we can do in terms of pricing or anything else to make that into a bad investment for them. So we're going to lose 35 000–40 000 tons next year.
>
> We have two other big linerboard customers. Are they going to just sit and watch? So far they have done nothing, but how soon will they act?

Excerpts from Atlantic's Five-Year Plan

We have set ourselves a profitability objective of 17.5% earnings before interest and tax on total assets.

This is high compared to earlier achievements. Over the past 11 years our return before interest and taxes on total assets has ranged from 4.4% in 1982 to 18.5% in 1987. Achievement of our aim is made more difficult because of our recent $67 million investment in forest lands that currently does not yield any significant return. Our total forest assets comprise $156 million of the total funds employed in 1990/91 of $541 million, rising to $178 million out of a total of $550 million in 1995.

A 17.5% return is higher than the average return achieved by each of the various industry sectors in this country and would put us in the top 75 performers of all listed companies. This may be ambitious but we consider it an appropriate aim which will highlight the question of idle assets.

The financial projections in the five-year plan (summarized) were as follows:

Earnings Forecast, Years Ending June 30 *(millions of dollars)*

	1991	1992	1993	1994	1995
Sales	420	425	470	514	585
Profits before interest and tax	55	48[1]	70	73	89
Net profit [2]	38	27	37	40	48
Total assets	539	541	546	545	550
PBIT as a percentage of funds employed	10.2%	8.7	12.8	13.4	16.2
Deliveries forecast (thousands of tons)					
Base forecast	587	576	577	572	578
Backward integration of Fibrebox Ltd.	—	(39)	(50)	(50)	(50)
"Super Pulp" project	—	(38)	(38)	(38)	(38)
New white paper products	—	—	9	22	41
Exports	45	50	50	50	50
Total	632	549	548	556	581

[1] Profit decline due to start up of a new pulp mill.
[2] Major asset changes were the projected white paper investment and a mill closure due to the super pulp project.

This conversation triggered a series of meetings to discuss the five-year plan which lasted most of Vickers third week in the company. These meetings included Bill Leroy, Vice-President of Finance, and John Collins, Vice-President of Marketing, in addition to Vickers and Smythe. Although invited to the meetings, Chris Reid put in only a minimal appearance, explaining that he had urgent issues that had to be dealt with at the Northern Mill. The meetings touched on a wide variety of topics, and it was clear to Vickers by the end of the week that three major initiatives were being proposed to him, none of which had yet been presented to Cumberland management. These were the white papers project, the super pulp project, and the reorganization of the company. All appeared to have had their origins in Jim Smythe's task force.

THE WHITE PAPERS PROJECT

Jim Smythe explained the origin and rationale of the white papers project:

> Ken Mauger, the manager of the Lautrec Mill, had been telling us for a couple of years that we're missing out on a growth market in copier and computer paper because we can't produce the right qualities of white paper. We haven't paid too much attention because the capital required to produce the necessary quality seemed to be prohibitive.
>
> Several things have prompted us to reconsider. One is that this company can no longer afford to overlook any growing markets in related business. Another is that it looks like we're going to have to reinvest $20 million or so to upgrade Ken's existing machine, just to let him hang on to the market he's got. Maybe we should spend an extra $60 million to increase his capacity and let him produce these other grades.
>
> The task force commissioned a market research study on the white papers market which concluded that there is a market worth going after, and we think we can get 90 000 tons of new business in this area within four or five years of arriving on the market, if we get serious about it. In our geographic area Benson Industries is the only major company in the business, and its customers tell us that they would welcome a second reputable supplier.

Vickers learned that the white papers project had not yet reached the official proposal stage. No one, for instance, had contacted equipment suppliers to get exact prices, developed an in-depth marketing plan or worked out the financial implications of the proposal in other than a fairly rough fashion. Some back of the envelope calculations suggested that the financial return on the project might be in the range of 25–30% before tax. Smythe indicated that he was reluctant to talk to equipment suppliers until Cumberland's board indicated that it was willing to change its long standing policy of not competing directly with Benson Industries. Benson and Atlantic were approximately of equal size. Benson was dominant in white paper markets, and Atlantic in linerboard and brown paper.

THE "SUPER PULP" PROJECT

The super pulp idea was created about eight months before Vicker's arrival by the members of Smythe's task force. The idea, which was to use much more pulp and much less recycled waste paper in the company's linerboards, had been debated by the senior management group ever since. Technical trials carried out in the interim indicated that making super pulp linerboard would not be a problem. The company could do it. The question was whether or not it should.

The attraction of the super pulp project was that it might solve three problems at once.

Firstly, by increasing the company's need for pulp, the project would mean that Atlantic's new pulp mill would be run at capacity. Without the project it would run at 75% of capacity, primarily because the demand projections put together when the mill was planned had been too optimistic. Selling excess pulp to other companies was not a viable option as the market was poor and Atlantic's pulp was wet, which meant it was expensive to transport. Running the pulp mill below capacity would reduce its efficiency, and would mean that the large lease payment might not be offset by increased earnings.

Secondly, if the firm were to switch to super pulp linerboards, it would produce fewer tons of linerboard per year even while producing the same area. This was because the new linerboards would be thinner and lighter than existing ones of the same strength. Thus even though a square metre of linerboard would cost more to produce (as the variable cost of pulp was about 20% higher than that of recycled paper), total costs could be reduced because less machine time would be required to produce the linerboard. In practice this meant that if Atlantic switched to super pulp linerboards the Senator Mill could be closed. The net saving would be approximately $6 million per year, and the continual headaches associated with the mill would be ended.

Finally, the introduction of the super pulp linerboard might slow down the inroads which Atlantic's two smaller competitors had been making into the linerboard market. (Atlantic's market share had fallen from approximately 70% to 50% over the past seven or eight years.) Neither of these companies had access to pulp, and there was no way that either of them could produce a super pulp linerboard in the foreseeable future. If super pulp linerboard became the norm for all but the lowest grades of linerboard, these two firms would be restricted to the bottom end of the market, which was where plastic products such as shrinkwrap were making inroads and margins were the lowest.

John Collins told Vickers that he was not particularly impressed by these arguments. He commented:

> This is a production and finance driven initiative. Our customers, the boxmakers, aren't asking for it. Neither are their customers, the end users. Not much of the market really cares about box performance in a major way. Most of the time it's just a question of price. We're talking now about introducing super pulp liners at a 3% cheaper price per square metre than normal linerboard. That's a joke, because as soon as we do our competitors will put their prices 3% below ours, just as they always have.
>
> What this product could do is create a lot of confusion in the market, and we could be the big losers. We're better off to stay away from it.

Bill Leroy countered Collins' final argument by stating that the paper machines of both of Atlantic's linerboard competitors were currently at capacity, and that it would be impossible for them to take advantage of any confusion in the market. He also liked the fact that no capital investment would be required. Leroy supported the initiative, and thought its timing was ideal.

Another argument that Vickers heard concerning the super pulp project was that, by withdrawing from the wastepaper market, Atlantic would lower prices of industrial waste paper and thus help out their competitors, who placed heavy reliance on such waste. On the domestic waste collection side, some managers argued that the large wastepaper collection trucks with "Atlantic" written on the side were a significant source of goodwill for the company, necessary to offset their image in environmental circles as a company primarily interested in cutting down trees, raping the forests, and so on.

REORGANIZATION

Jim Smythe had sent an eight-page handwritten memo to Marcel Ruban shortly before he retired, suggesting that Atlantic be reorganized into four product divisions. Because of Ruban's impending retirement, of which Smythe was unaware, no action had been taken. Smythe explained the proposal to John Vickers.

> One of the conclusions that I came to as a result of our task force investigation was that Atlantic would perform much better if separate groups of people focused on each of our three product areas, and a fourth group concentrated on making pulp. Right now we all spend a lot of

time worrying about linerboard because it has the largest sales volume, but a lot of important issues in the other businesses slip by unnoticed.

The marketing group, for instance, spends all its time thinking about Fibrebox and our other two big linerboard customers, but we know very little, as the market research study revealed, about white papers. I am certain that this is also true of brown papers. Also, we have always used the same salesforce to sell all three product lines, but we could do much better with one for each product.

The biggest improvement, I have no doubt, would come from having a general manager looking after each business. Maybe we could eventually pay bonuses based on product group performance. Right now everyone here is on straight salary.

Smythe's memo contained the proposed organization charts which are shown in Exhibits 3 and 4. It also listed some further advantages and some disadvantages of his proposed reorganization.

Other Advantages

- Each product group would get more individual attention, which in turn should give faster reactions, better digestion of market intelligence, more thought to product performance and profitability, and less complex product development.

- Bringing marketing and manufacturing closer together may reduce some of the present counter productive activity.

- Promising staff members can be more readily exposed to broader business concerns, and be offered general management experience earlier in their careers.

- Reorganization may change the market's view of Atlantic as a slow moving monolith.

- Current head office staff (engineering, technical, industrial relations) can be moved to the Northern Mill where their involvement in mill operations will be useful. Other mills needing technical assistance can seek it from Northern.

- Reorganization will reduce numbers at head office by rationalization and reduction of one level of management.

Disadvantages

- More flexible attitudes will be required at the Northern Mill, Senator Mill, regional sales offices, and head office.

- This is a radical change to the traditional marketing and operations organizations. Change will be neither easy nor pleasant.

- Mill managers at Northern and Senator Mills will become site managers, responsible for managing the site, but not the product mix or output.

- The four groups are not of even size.

- Some additional marketing/sales staff may be required.

After reading Smythe's memo, Vickers asked him to elaborate on the probable reaction of Atlantic's senior employees to such an organizational change. Smythe replied:

Neither the senior marketing nor the senior operations people will support this move because it means breaking up their big functional groups. The mill managers, for instance, have long been the 'kings' in this organization. With this plan, machine managers would report directly to their own product group. On multi-machine sites like Northern and Senator the machine managers would also have a dotted line relationship to the site manager, who would be responsible for insuring that the site was properly run.

Managers without an organizational axe to grind, like Bill Leroy, believe that this is an excellent idea. (Vickers later confirmed that this was indeed the case.)

THE FOURTH WEEK

On the Monday of his fourth week in Acton, Vickers received the financial report for the six months ending December 31, 1990 (Exhibit 5). It did not make good reading. In spite of the fact that sales were as budgeted (which meant that the company had made an 8% price increase stick, its first in several years), profit before tax was only 68% of budget. Even with what looked like some creative tax accounting, earnings after tax would show less than a 10% return on shareholders equity.

In discussing this report with Chris Reid, Vickers learned that the fundamental problem was that N3, the big linerboard machine, had not been operating efficiently. Reid had made some personnel changes, but to no avail. He now wanted to bring in a very experienced "hands-on" American papermaker for two years to get the machine operating well and to raise the skill level of the machine crews. He had found such a man—but he was asking more in salary than any of Atlantic's vice-presidents were earning. This was a result of the fact, Vickers discovered, that when the man's current employer learned he was talking to Atlantic, they gave him an immediate 30% raise. Vickers told Chris Reid he would "think it over and get back to him."

Reid's request, on which he wanted to quick answer, pushed Vickers to the conclusion that it was time to decide what changes he wanted to make at Atlantic, and how he should go about them. He did not want to start making ad hoc decisions on single issues which, when added together, would make little sense.

The problem was where to start and how fast to move. In considering Jim Smythe's reorganization plan, for example, Vickers could not see how he could find four general managers in an organization that had no one with general management experience it. After living with Atlantic's senior managers for a month, he felt he could bet on Jim Smythe and Bill Leroy as good potential general managers, but as for the rest, he wasn't sure.

EXHIBIT 1   **Atlantic Paper Company Organization Chart**

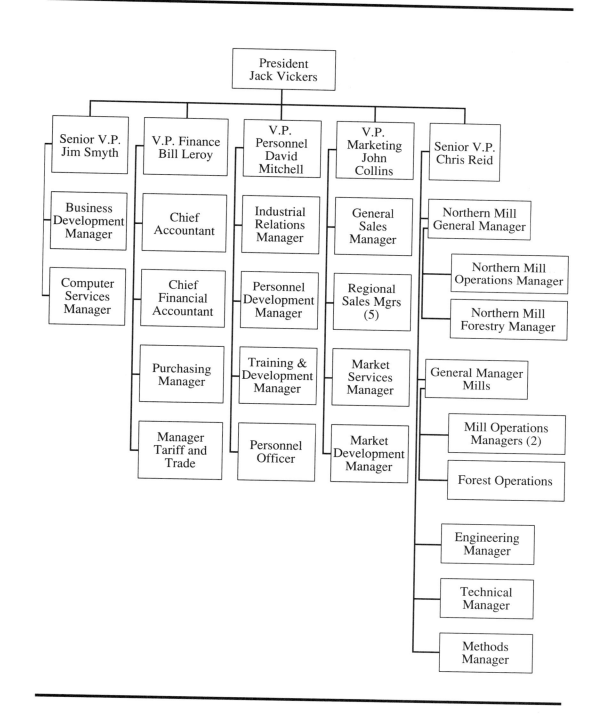

EXHIBIT 2 Atlantic Paper Company Summary Statements

12 months ending June 30	*1990*		*1989*
Earnings ($000)	**Budget**	**Actual**	**Actual**
Net sales	$ 445 420	$ 397 630	$ 420 058
Gross earnings before depreciation	94 470	68 840	92 391
Less: Depreciation	22 000	21 550	20 789
Overheads	11 670	10 960	10 514
Earnings before interest and tax	60 800	36 330	61 088
Less: Interest	11 600	7 790	10 304
Earnings before tax	49 200	28 540	50 784
Less: Income tax charge	13 400	7 030	20 759
Net earnings after tax	$ 35 800	$ 21 510	$ 30 025

Other Information

Earnings before interest and tax as a percentage of funds employed	11.2%	6.7%	12.9%
Gross margins (based on earnings before depreciation and overheads)	21.2%	17.3%	22.0%
Deliveries (tons)	685 000	640 296	715 476
Average selling price ($ per ton)	650.2	621.0	587.1
Average cost ($ per ton)	560.9	564.2	501.7

EXHIBIT 3   **Atlantic Paper Company**
Jim Smythe's Proposed Organization Chart

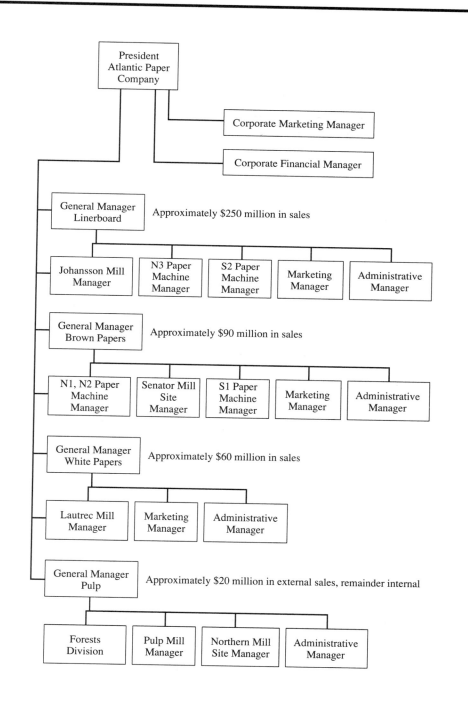

EXHIBIT 4 **Atlantic Paper Company**
Jim Smythe's Proposed Corporate Marketing Organization

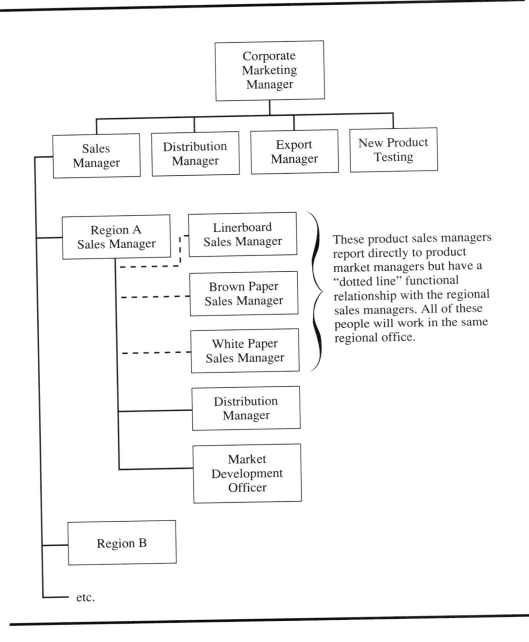

These product sales managers report directly to product market managers but have a "dotted line" functional relationship with the regional sales managers. All of these people will work in the same regional office.

EXHIBIT 5   Atlantic Paper Company Six-Month Financial Results

| *6 months ending December 31* | 1990 | | 1989 |
Earnings ($000)	**Budget**	**Actual**	**Actual**
Net sales	$ 211 550	$ 217 600	$ 214 210
Gross earnings before depreciation	51 120	40 860	39 380
Less: Depreciation	12 950	11 830	11 660
Overheads	5 950	6 190	6 130
Earnings before interest and tax	32 220	22 840	21 590
Less: Interest	4 690	4 090	3 780
Earnings before tax	27 530	18 750	17 810
Less: Income tax charge	4 920	10	3 690
Net earnings after tax	$ 22 610	$ 18 740	$ 14 120

Other Information

Annualized earnings before interest and tax as a percentage of funds employed	11.9%	8.4%	7.9%
Gross margins (based on earnings before depreciation and overheads)	24.2%	18.8%	18.4%
Deliveries (tons)	323 000	326 240	346 680
Average selling price ($ per ton)	654.9	666.9	617.8
Average cost ($ per ton)	555.2	596.9	555.6

VICTORIA HEAVY EQUIPMENT LIMITED (REVISED)

Paul W. Beamish and Thomas A. Poynter

CASE 13

Brian Walters sat back in the seat of his Lear jet as it broke through the clouds en route from Squamish, a small town near Vancouver, British Columbia, to Sacramento, California. As chairman of the board, majority shareholder, and chief executive officer, the 51-year-old Walters had run Victoria Heavy Equipment Limited as a closely held company for years. During this time Victoria had become the second-largest producer of mobile cranes in the world, with 1985 sales of $100 million and exports to more than 70 countries. But in early 1986 the problem of succession was in his thoughts. His son and daughter were not yet ready to run the organization, and he personally wanted to devote more time to other interests. He wondered about the kind of person he should hire to become president. There was also a nagging thought that there might be other problems with Victoria that would have to be worked out before he eased out of his present role.

COMPANY HISTORY

Victoria Heavy Equipment was established in 1902 in Victoria, British Columbia, to produce horse-drawn log skidders for the forest industry. The young firm showed a flair for product innovation, pioneering the development of motorized skidders and later, after diversifying into the crane business, producing the country's first commercially successful hydraulic crane controls. In spite of these innovations, the company was experiencing severe financial difficulties in 1948 when it was purchased by Brian Walters Sr., the father of the current chairman. By installing tight financial controls and paying close attention to productivity, Walters was able to turn the company around, and in the mid-1950s he decided that Victoria would focus its attention exclusively on cranes, and go after the international market.

By the time of Brian Walters Sr.'s retirement in 1968, it was clear that the decision to concentrate on the crane business had been a good one. The company's sales and profits were growing, and Victoria cranes were beginning to do well in export markets. Walters Sr. was succeeded as president by his brother, James, who began to exercise very close personal control over the company's operations. However, as Victoria continued to grow in size and complexity, the load on James became so great that his health began to fail. The solution was to appoint an assistant general manager, John Rivers, through whom tight supervision could be maintained while James Walters' workload was eased. This move was to no avail, however. James Walters suffered a heart attack in 1970, and Rivers became general manager. At the same time, the young Brian Walters, the current chairman and chief executive officer, became head of the U.S. operation.

When Brian Walters took responsibility for Victoria's U.S. business, the firm's American distributor was selling 30–40 cranes per year. Walters thought the company should be selling at least 150. Even worse, the orders that the American firm did get tended to come in large quantities—as many as 50 cranes in a single order—which played havoc with Victoria's production scheduling. Walters commented "We would rather have ten orders of ten cranes each than a single order for 100." In 1975, when the U.S. distributor's agreement expired, Walters offered the company a five-year renewal if it would guarantee sales of 150 units per year. When the firm refused, Walters bought it, and in the first month fired 13 of the 15 employees and cancelled most existing dealerships. He then set to work to rebuild—only accepting orders for 10 cranes or less. His hope was to gain a foothold and a solid reputation in the U.S. market before the big U.S. firms even noticed him.

This strategy quickly showed results, and in 1976 Walters came back to Canada. As Rivers was still general manager, there was not enough to occupy him fully, and he began travelling three or four months a year. While he was still very much a part of the company, it was not a full-time involvement.

VICTORIA IN THE 1980s

Victoria entered the 1980s with sales of approximately $50 million and by 1985, partly as a result of opening the new plant in California, had succeeded in doubling this figure. Profits reached their highest level ever in 1983, but declined somewhat over the next two years as costs rose and the rate of sales growth slowed. Financial statements are presented in Exhibits 1 and 2. The following sections describe the company and its environment in the 1980s.

Product Line

The bulk of Victoria's crane sales in the 1980s came from a single product line, the LTM 1000, which was produced both in the company's Squamish facility (the firm had moved from Victoria to Squamish in the early 1900s) and its smaller plant in California, built in 1979. The LTM 1000 line consisted of mobile cranes of five basic sizes, averaging approximately $500 000 in price. Numerous options were available for these cranes, which could provide uncompromised on-site performance, precision lifting capabilities, fast highway travel, and effortless city driving. Because of the numerous choices available, Victoria preferred not to build them to stock. The company guaranteed 60-day delivery and "tailor-made" cranes to customer specifications. This required a large inventory of both parts and raw material.

The most recent addition to the LTM 1000 line was developed in 1982, when Walters learned that a company trying to move unusually long and heavy logs from a new tract of red-wood trees in British Columbia was having serious problems with its existing cranes. A crane with a larger than average height and lifting capacity was required. Up to this point, for technical reasons, it had not been possible to produce a crane with the required specifications. However, Walters vowed that Victoria would develop such a crane, and six months later it had succeeded.

Although the LTM 1000 series provided almost all of Victoria's crane sales, a new crane had been introduced in 1984 after considerable expenditure on design, development and manufacture. The $650 000 A-100 had a 70-tonne capacity and could lift loads to heights of 61 metres, a combination previously unheard of in the industry. Through the use of smooth hydraulics even the heaviest loads could be picked up without jolts. In spite of these features, and an optional ram-operated tilt-back cab designed to alleviate the stiff necks which operators commonly developed from watching high loads, sales of the A-100 were disappointing. As a result, several of the six machines built were leased to customers at unattractive rates. The A-100 had, however, proven to be a very effective crowd attraction device at equipment shows.

Markets

There were two important segments in the crane market—custom-built cranes and standard cranes—and although the world mobile crane market was judged to be $630 million in 1985, no estimates were available as to the size of each segment. Victoria competed primarily in the custom segment, in the medium- and heavy-capacity end of the market. In the medium-capacity custom crane class, Victoria's prices were approximately 75% of those of its two main competitors. The gap closed as the cranes became heavier, with Victoria holding a 15% advantage over Washington Cranes in the heavy custom crane business. In heavy standard cranes Victoria did not have a price advantage.

Victoria's two most important markets were Canada and the United States. The U.S. market was approximately $240 million in 1985, and Victoria's share was about 15%. Victoria's Sacramento plant, serving both the U.S. market and export sales involving U.S. aid and financing, produced 60 to 70 cranes per year. The Canadian market was much smaller, about $44 million in 1985, but Victoria was the dominant firm in the country, with a 60% share. The Squamish plant, producing 130 to 150 cranes per year, supplied both the Canadian market and all export sales not covered by the U.S. plant. There had been very little real growth in the world market since 1980.

The primary consumers in the mobile crane industry were contractors. Because the amount of equipment downtime could make the difference between showing a profit or loss on a contract, contractors were very sensitive to machine dependability as well as parts and service availability. Price was important, but it was not everything. Independent surveys suggested that Washington Crane, Victoria's most significant competitor, offered somewhat superior service and reliability, and if Victoria attempted to sell similar equipment at prices comparable to Washington's, it would fail. As a result, Victoria tried to reduce its costs through extensive backward integration, manufacturing 85% of its crane components in-house, the highest percentage in the industry. This drive to reduce costs was somewhat offset, however, by the fact that much of the equipment in the Squamish plant was very old. In recent years, some of the slower and less versatile machinery had been replaced, but by 1985 only 15% of the machinery in the plant was new, efficient, numerically controlled equipment.

Victoria divided the world into eight marketing regions. The firm carried out little conventional advertising, but did participate frequently at equipment trade shows. One of the company's most effective selling tools was its ability to fly in prospective customers from all over the world in Walters' executive jet. Victoria believed that the combination of its integrated plant, worker loyalty, and the single-product concentration evident in their Canadian plant produced a convinced customer. There were over 14 such visits to the British Columbia plant in 1985, including delegations from The People's Republic of China, Korea, France and Turkey.

Competition

Victoria, as the world's second largest producer of cranes, faced competition from five major firms, all of whom were much larger and more diversified. The industry leader was the Washington Crane Company with 1985 sales of $400 million and a world market share of 50%. Washington had become a name synonymous around the world with heavy-duty equipment and had been able to maintain a sales growth-rate of over 15% per annum for the past five years. It manufactured in the U.S., Mexico and Australia. Key to its operations were 100 strong dealers worldwide with over 200 outlets. Washington had almost 30% of Canada's crane market.

Next in size after Victoria was Texas Star, another large manufacturer whose cranes were generally smaller than Victoria's and sold through the company's extensive worldwide equipment dealerships. The next two largest competitors were both very large U.S. multinational producers whose crane lines formed a small part of their overall business. With the exception of Washington, industry observers suggested that crane sales for these latter firms had been stable (at best) for quite some time. The exception was the Japanese crane producer Toshio which had been aggressively pursuing sales worldwide and had entered the North American market recently. Sato, another Japanese firm, had started in the North American market as well. Walters commented:

> My father laid the groundwork for the success that this company has enjoyed, but it is clear that we now have some major challenges ahead of us. Washington Cranes is four times our size and I know that we are at the top of their hit list. Our Japanese competitors, Toshio and Sato,

are also going to be tough. The key to our success is to remain flexible—we must not develop the same kind of organization as the big U.S. firms.

Organization

In 1979, a number of accumulating problems had ended Brian Walters' semi-retirement and brought him back into the firm full time. Although sales were growing, Walters saw that work was piling up and things were not getting done. He believed that new cranes needed to be developed, and he wanted a profit-sharing plan put in place. One of his most serious concerns was the development of middle managers. Walters commented, "we had to develop middle-level line managers—we had no depth." The root cause of these problems, Walters believed, was that the firm was overly centralized. Most of the functional managers reported to Rivers, and Rivers made most of the decisions. Walters concluded that action was necessary—"We have to change," he said. "If we want to grow further we have to do things."

Between 1979 and 1982 Walters reorganized the firm by setting up separate operating companies and a corporate staff group. In several cases, senior operating executives were placed in staff/advisory positions, while in others, executives held positions in both operating and staff groups. Exhibit 3 illustrates Victoria's organizational chart as of 1983.

By early 1984 Walters was beginning to wonder "if I had made a very bad decision." The staff groups weren't working. Rivers had been unable to accept the redistribution of power and had resigned. There was "civil war in the company." Politics and factional disputes were the rule rather than the exception. Line managers were upset by the intervention of the staff V.P.s of employee relations, manufacturing, and marketing. Staff personnel, on the other hand, were upset by "poor" line decisions.

As a result, the marketing and manufacturing staff functions were eradicated with the late-1985 organizational restructuring illustrated in Exhibit 4. The services previously supplied by the staff groups were duplicated to varying extents inside each division.

In place of most of the staff groups, an executive committee was established in 1984. Membership in this group included the president and head of all staff groups and presidents (general managers) of the four divisions. Meeting monthly, the executive committee was intended to evaluate the performance of the firm's profit and cost problems, handle mutual problems such as transfer prices, and allocate capital expenditures among the four operating divisions. Subcommittees handled subjects such as R&D and new products.

The new organization contained seven major centres for performance measurement purposes. The cost centres were:

1. Engineering; R&D (reporting to Victco Ltd.).
2. International Marketing (Victoria Marketing Ltd.).
3. Corporate staff.

The major profit centres were:

4. CraneCorp. Inc. (U.S. production and sales).
5. Victco Ltd. (supplying Victoria with components).
6. Craneco (Canadian production and marketing).
7. Victoria-owned Canadian sales outlets (reporting to Victoria Marketing Ltd.).

The major profit centres had considerable autonomy in their day-to-day operations and were motivated to behave as if their division was a separate, independent firm.

By mid-1985, Brian Walters had moved out of his position as president, and Michael Carter—a long-time employee close to retirement—was asked to take the position of president until a new one could be found.

Walters saw his role changing. "If I was anything, I was a bit of an entrepreneur. My job was to supply that thrust but to let people develop on their own accord. I was not concerned about things not working, but I was concerned when nothing was being done about it."

In the new organization Walters did not sit on the executive committee. However, as chairman of the board and chief executive officer, the committee's recommendations came to him and ". . . they tried me on six ways from Sunday." His intention was to monitor the firm's major activities rather than to set them. He did have to sit on the product development subcommittee, however, when ". . . things were not working . . . there was conflict . . . the engineering group (engineering, R&D) had designed a whole new crane and nobody including me knew about it." Mr. McCarthy, the vice-president of engineering and R&D, called only five to six committee meetings. The crane his group developed was not to Walters' liking. (There had been a high turnover rate in this group, with four V.P.s since 1983.) Recognizing these problems, Walters brought in consultants to tackle the problems of the management information system and the definition of staff/line responsibilities.

In spite of these moves, dissatisfaction still existed within the company in 1986. The new organization had resulted in considerable dissension. Some conflict centred around the establishment of appropriately challenging budgets for each operating firm and even more conflict had erupted over transfer pricing and allocation of capital budgets. In 1985–86, even though requested budgets were cut equally, lack of central control over spending resulted in overexpenditures by several of the profit and cost centres.

The views of staff and the operating companies' presidents varied considerably when they discussed Victoria's organizational evolution and the operation of the present structure.

Diane Walters, the president of Victoria International Marketing, liked the autonomous system because it helped to identify the true performance of sections of the company. "We had separate little buckets and could easily identify results." Furthermore, she felt that there was no loss of efficiency (due to the duplication of certain staff functions within the divisions) since there was little duplication of systems between groups, and each group acted as a check and balance on the other groups so that "manufacturing won't make what marketing won't sell." Comments from other executives were as follows:

> The divisionalized system allowed me to get closer to my staff because we were a separate group.
>
> We ended up with sales and marketing expertise that was much better than if we had stayed under manufacturing.
>
> If you [run the firm] with a manufacturing-oriented organization, you could forget what people want.
>
> In a divisionalized system there was bound to be conflict between divisions, but that was not necessarily unhealthy.

Some executives saw the decentralized, semi-autonomous operating company structure as a means of giving each person the opportunity to grow and develop without the hindrance of other functional executives. Most, if not all, of the operating company presidents and staff

V.P.s were aware that decentralization brought benefits, especially in terms of the autonomy it gave them to modify existing practices. One senior executive even saw the present structure as an indicator of their basic competitive stance: "Either we centralize the structure and retract, or we stay as we are and fight with the big guys." With minimal direction supplied from Brian Walters, presidents were able to build up their staff, establish priorities and programs, and, essentially, were only held responsible for the bottom line.

Other executives believed that Victoria's structure was inappropriate. As one executive put it, "The semi-independence of the operating companies and the lack of a real leader for the firm has resulted in poor co-ordination of problem solving and difficulty in allocating responsibility." As an example, he noted how engineering's response to manufacturing was often slow and poorly communicated. Even worse, the executive noted, was how the priorities of different units were not synchronized. "When you manufacture just one product line all your activities are interrelated. So when one group puts new products first on a priority list while another is still working out bugs in the existing product, conflict and inefficiencies have to develop."

The opposing group argued that the present organization was more appropriate to a larger, faster growing and more complex company. As one senior executive put it, "We're too small to be as decentralized as we are now. All of this was done to accommodate the 'Walters kids' anyway, and it's now going to detract from profitability and growth." Another of these executives stated that rather than being a president of an operating company he would prefer to be a general manager at the head of a functional group, reporting to a group head. "If we had the right Victoria Heavy Equipment president," he said, "we wouldn't need all these divisional presidents." Another continued,

> Right now the players (divisional presidents and staff V.P.s) run the company. Brian Walters gives us a shot of adrenaline four or six times a year but doesn't provide any active leadership. When Brian leaves, things stop. Instead, Brian now wants to monitor the game plan rather than set it up for others to run. As we still only have an interim president (Carter), it is the marketplace that leads us, not any strategic plan or goal.

THE NEW PRESIDENT

Individual views about the appropriate characteristics of a new president were determined by what each executive thought was wrong with Victoria. Everyone realized that the new president would have to accommodate Brian Walters' presence and role in the firm and the existence of his two children in the organization. They all generally saw Brian as wanting to supply ideas and major strategies but little else.

All but one of Victoria's executives agreed that the new president should *not* get involved in day-to-day activities or in major decision making. Instead, he should "arbitrate" among the line general managers (subsidiary presidents) and staff V.P.s as more of a "bureaucrat-cum-diplomat" than an aggressive leader. As another put it, "The company will drive itself; only once in a while he'll steer a little."

THE 1986 SITUATION

Industry analysts predicted a decline of 10% in world crane sales—which totalled 1 200 units in 1985—and as much as a 30% decrease in the North American market in 1986. Victoria's sales and production levels were down. Seventy-five shop floor employees had been laid off at Squamish, bringing total employment there to 850, and similar cuts were expected in Sacramento. Worker morale was suffering as a result, and the profit sharing plan, which had been introduced in early 1985 at Walters' initiative, was not helping matters. In spite of the optimism conveyed to workers when the plan was initiated, management had announced in October that no bonus would be paid for the year. Aggravating the problem was the workforce's observation that while certain groups met their budget, others did not, and hence all were penalized. This problem arose because each bonus was based on overall as well as divisional profits.

Many of the shop-floor workers and the supervisory staff were also disgruntled with the additions to the central and divisional staff groups, which had continued even while the workforce was being reduced. They felt that the paperwork these staff functions created was time-consuming and of little benefit. They noted, for example, that there were four or five times as many people in production control in 1986 as there were in 1980 for the same volume of production. In addition, they pointed out that despite all sorts of efforts on the part of a computer-assisted production control group, inventory levels were still too high.

Brian Walters commented on the 1986 situation and his view of the company's future:

> What we are seeing in 1986 is a temporary decline in the market. This does not pose a serious problem for us, and certainly does not impact on my longer term goals for this company, which are to achieve a 25% share of the world market by 1990, and reach sales of $250 million by 1999. We can reach these goals as long as we don't turn into one of these bureaucratic, grey-suited companies that are so common in North America. There are three keys for success in this business—a quality product, professional people and the motivation for Victoria to be the standard of excellence in our business. This means that almost everything depends on the competence and motivation of our people. We will grow by being more entrepreneurial, more dedicated, and more flexible than our competitors. With our single product line we are also more focussed than our competitors. They manage only by the numbers—there is no room in those companies for an emotional plea, they won't look at sustaining losses to get into a new area, they'll turn the key on a loser . . . we look at the longer term picture.

"The hazard for Victoria," Walters said as he looked out of his window toward the Sacramento airstrip, "is that we could develop the same kind of bureaucratic, quantitatively oriented, grey-suited managers that slow down the large U.S. competitors. But that," he said, turning to his audience, "is something I'm going to watch like a hawk. We need the right people."

EXHIBIT 1 Victoria Balance Sheet for the Years 1981–85 ($000s)

	1981	1982	1983	1984	1985
ASSETS					
Current Assets					
Accounts receivable	8 328	7 960	9 776	10 512	10 951
Allowance for doubtful accounts	(293)	(310)	(287)	(297)	(316)
Inventories	21 153	24 425	24 698	25 626	27 045
Prepaid expenses	119	104	156	106	129
Total current assets	29 307	32 179	34 343	35 947	37 809
Advances to shareholders	1 300	1 300	1 300	1 300	1 300
Fixed assets: property plant and equipment	6 840	6 980	6 875	7 353	7 389
Total assets	37 447	40 459	42 518	44 600	46 598
LIABILITIES AND SHAREHOLDERS' EQUITY					
Current Liabilities					
Notes payable to bank	7 733	8 219	9 258	10 161	11 332
Accounts payable	9 712	11 353	10 543	10 465	10 986
Accrued expenses	1 074	1 119	1 742	1 501	1 155
Deferred income tax	419	400	396	408	345
Income tax payable	545	692	612	520	516
Current portion of long-term debt	912	891	867	888	903
Total current liabilities	20 395	22 674	23 418	23 943	25 237
Long-term debt	6 284	6 110	6 020	6 005	6 114
Total liabilities	26 679	28 784	29 438	29 948	31 351
Shareholders' Equity					
Common shares	200	290	295	390	435
Retained earnings	10 568	11 385	12 790	14 262	14 812
Total shareholders' equity	10 768	11 675	13 080	14 652	15 247
Total liabilities and shareholders' equity	37 447	40 459	42 518	44 600	46 598

EXHIBIT 2   **Victoria Income Statement for the Years 1981–85** ($000s)

	1981	1982	1983	1984	1985
Revenue					
Net sales	$63 386	$77 711	$86 346	$94 886	$100 943
Costs and Expenses					
Cost of sales	49 238	59 837	63 996	71 818	75 808
Selling expense	7 470	9 234	10 935	11 437	13 104
Administrative expense	2 684	3 867	5 490	5 795	7 038
Engineering expense	1 342	1 689	1 832	1 949	2 109
Gross income	2 652	3 084	4 093	3 887	2 884
Income taxes	1 081	1 281	1 630	1 505	1 254
Net income	$ 1 571	$ 1 803	$ 2 463	$ 2 382	$ 1 630

EXHIBIT 3   **Victoria Organizational Structure, 1979–83**

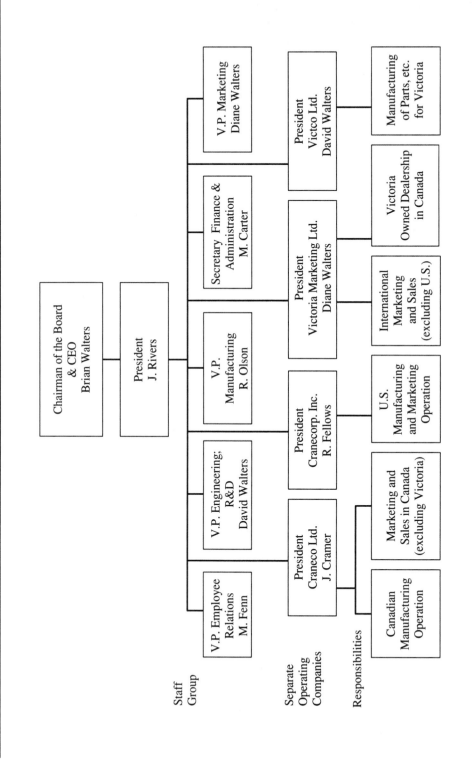

EXHIBIT 4 Victoria Organizational Structure, Late 1985

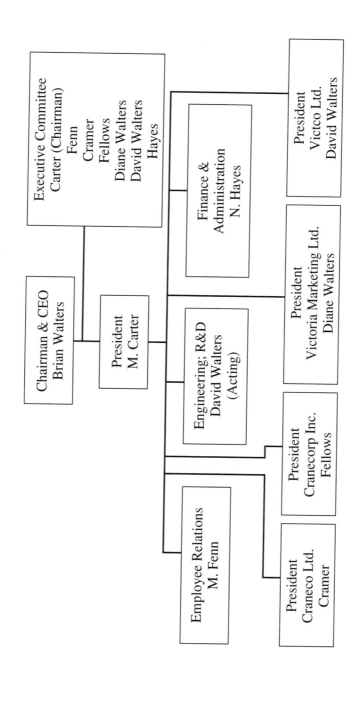

UNIVERSITY HOSPITAL—"FINDING A BETTER WAY." [1]

Roderick E. White and Mary M. Crossan

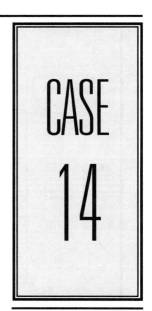

CASE

14

In the fall of 1987, University Hospital (UH) had just completed, with the assistance of outside consultants, an extensive strategy review culminating in a formal strategic plan. The original stimulus for the plan had been to better understand the growth patterns and potential of the hospital's services in order to forecast the need for and justify a significant expansion of the hospital's facilities. However, the final document had gone beyond this original intention, raising questions about the hospital's "service portfolio" and its future potential.

The strategic plan had seven key recommendations (Exhibit 1), several of which represented significant departures from past practice. As part of the planning process, the hospital's services had been put into different categories, a portfolio approach, with apparent implications for future emphasis and resource allocation. As one UH vice-president commented:

> The plan has forced us to establish some priorities for our different services. Not everything we do is, or will be, world-class, and the plan will help us allocate our increasingly scarce resources, capital and operating funds, towards our premier services.

---

[1] UH's motto; attributed to Thomas Edison.

Further, the plan recommended organizing business units around these "service clusters" (or product lines), and continuing the planning process as an ongoing, in-house activity.

As Pat Blewett, President and CEO of UH, reviewed the report and its recommendations, he was satisfied with both the process and the results. Blewett was widely recognized as a highly positive, entrepreneurial type of administrator willing to try new ideas and promote innovative services. Results had been impressive. New services had contributed substantially to UH's growth and cash flow. However, the facility was straining within its existing physical space. In addition, UH, like other hospitals in the province of Ontario, had to cope with increasing budgetary pressures from the Ministry of Health, while demand for all services continued to grow. Blewett hoped the recommendations from the strategic plan would allow the hospital to deal with these issues while maintaining the institution's innovative and entrepreneurial spirit.

BACKGROUND

While a separate institution, UH was part of a larger health sciences complex of the University of Western Ontario. UH had been an educational and research, as well as a health care delivery facility since opening in 1972. The newest of the three major acute care hospitals in London, Ontario, a community of about 300 000 in southwestern Ontario, UH was established, owned and operated by the London Health Association (LHA).

Founded in 1909, the LHA's activities had changed dramatically over the years. Originally, it had operated a tuberculosis sanatorium on the outskirts of the city. As the number of tuberculosis patients declined, the LHA made plans to diversify into chest diseases and purchased property adjacent to the University for a new hospital. However, in the decade of the 1960s, the University was growing rapidly, especially in the health sciences, and wanted a full-fledged teaching/research hospital attached to the University. The LHA was persuaded to undertake this more ambitious task, but stipulated that their institution would remain administratively separate from the University.

Planning for the new facility began in 1966. An innovative spirit was evident from the outset. Hospitals tend to be very traditional institutions, but the planning group, in its efforts to create an outstanding medical facility, were willing to deviate from conventional practices. The UH motto, "Finding a better way," was applied to facilities design, organizational practice, as well as patient care and research activities. Using a philosophy of form follows function, the hospital layout was guided by an analysis of function. The result was revolutionary with physicians' offices, research areas, inpatient and outpatient departments, and teaching space all on the same floor. Essentially each of the floors operated as a specialized mini-hospital sharing support services within a larger hospital setting. UH's deviation from accepted hospital practices were wide ranging from the use of noise-deadening carpeted floors, a hospital blasphemy at the time, to the decentralized organizational structure with an unconventional division of tasks.

The Health Care Environment

Canada's health care system was one of the most comprehensive in the world, providing equal access to all Canadians. The publicly funded system was the responsibility of the provincial governments, although a substantial portion of the funding came from the federal level by way of transfer payments. In Ontario, the Ministry of Health (MOH) was the department concerned with hospitals. Health care costs accounted for 32% of the province's $32 billion budget, the single largest category of expenditure with the most rapid growth. As a result, the province was becoming increasingly active in its efforts to contain these costs. Examples included the banning of extra billing by doctors, cuts in the number of medical residency positions and provision for the MOH to take over any hospital in a deficit position.

Health care funding had evolved in a piecemeal fashion into an extremely complex and often ambiguous system. Basically, the MOH contracted with the hospitals to provide services, in an approved plant, at an approved ("global") budget. Further, the Ministry expected each hospital to show an excess of revenue over expenses sufficient to provide for a reasonable accumulation of funds for future capital requirements. Program, service reductions, or bed closures which related directly to patient care required the agreement of the Ministry. However, under pressure to balance budgets, some hospitals were reducing services without the formal agreement of the Ministry. Using a universal formula based largely on history, the Ministry arrived at a hospital's global operating budget. Most MOH revenues were *not* directly tied to actual expenditures or the provision of services. New programs could be initiated by the hospital, but incremental capital and/or operating costs were incorporated into the existing global funding base. Additional funds were forthcoming only if approved by the Ministry.

In the approval of new programs, District Health Councils had a prominent voice. They provided the forum for ensuring that changes met the health care needs of the *local* community. The Thames Valley District Health Council (TVDHC) was responsible for the 18 hospitals in the London area. New program proposals submitted to TVDHC were very diverse, ranging from a $400 000 request from UH for a four-bed epilepsy unit, to Victoria Hospital's $94 million expansion request. Evaluating programs on a regional basis, based on local community need, did not allow much consideration of the type of care provided or the referral base they served. UH frequently went outside this process, appealing directly to the Ministry, or failing that, by funding projects from their own accumulated surplus.

The government's influence upon hospitals extended well beyond the control of global operating budgets and new programs. It also affected the supply of nurses, residents, and physicians by controlling the number of available positions in nursing and medical schools, by influencing the certification of immigrants, and by limiting the number of hospital residency positions funded. The MOH had recently reduced, province-wide, the number of medical residency positions for physicians doing post-graduate specialty training. Essentially, medical residents learned a specialty while providing patient care in a hospital, freeing physicians to do teaching, research and other activities. Reduction in residency positions created a gap in the provision of service in larger, teaching hospitals, and would ultimately lead to a decline in the number of indigenously trained medical specialists and researchers.

Pressures on the health care system were increasing partly because of an aging population. Demand for basic services was expected to increase into the 21st century. Further, increasingly sophisticated and expensive new medical technologies not only improved existing services, but also developed new treatments for previously untreatable illnesses, all at a cost, however. While gross measures of productivity, like patient days in hospital per procedure, had been improving, the increasing sophistication of treatments appeared to be increasing costs at a faster rate than offsetting gains in productivity. Further, most gains in productivity came about by requiring fewer personnel to do the same tasks, rather than reducing the number of tasks. The increasing stresses and turnover that naturally resulted were present in all hospital health care professionals, but especially evident in the exodus from the nursing profession. Although not as severe in the London area, it was estimated 600–800 beds in Toronto hospitals were closed because of lack of nursing staff. Shortages of staff existed in other areas; like occupational and physical therapists, radiologists, and pharmacists.

The province's basic approach to managing demand (and costs) appeared to be by limiting supply. As a result, waiting lists were growing, especially for elective procedures. Certain serious, but not immediately life threatening conditions, had waiting lists for treatment of six months to a year, and were getting longer.

Social and political expectations also put pressures on the system. Universal, free access to a health care system offering equal, high-quality care to all had become a societal expectation and a political sacred cow. Politically acceptable ideas for fundamentally restructuring the industry were not obvious. There was no apparent way to reconcile increasing demand and costs with the governmental funding likely to be available. As a result, many observers felt that the health care system was out of control. And the Ministry was under tremendous pressure to control costs and account for its expenditures, while at the same time providing more, new and enhanced services. Without an overall approach to the health care situation, it was not clear how the Ministry would allocate funds in the future. Choices between high technology, expensive procedures, like heart transplantation and intensive care for premature infants, and basic care for the aged were difficult to make and politically sensitive.

UNIVERSITY HOSPITAL

UH was a well-designed and maintained facility. It was located in north London, Ontario. Rising from a three-floor service podium, each of its seven tower floors was divided into two basic components—one an inpatient area, and the other an outpatient, office, research and teaching area. Each inpatient area, except paediatrics, had a corresponding outpatient department for initial assessment follow-up, and the performance of minor procedures. UH had 463 inpatient beds with an average occupancy rate of over 90%, which effectively meant 100% utilization. The occupancy rate and number of beds had been fairly constant over the past few years. Although space was severely constrained within the hospital, there was a land bank available for future expansion.

In the past, UH had employed some creative solutions to its problem of space constraints. Services had been reviewed to determine whether they could be more effectively provided in one of the other London hospitals, or, as in the case of the Occupational Health Centre, whether they could be better served in an off-site location. Some specialization had already occurred within the city. For example, since another major acute-care hospital specialized in maternity, UH did not duplicate this service. However, UH did have an in-vitro fertilization program (popularly known as test-tube babies).

In a major move during 1986, the Robarts Research Institute (RRI) was opened adjacent to UH. A separate but affiliated institution with its own board, the RRI specialized in heart and stroke research. Moving researchers from UH to this new facility helped to alleviate, at least temporarily, some of the hospital's space pressures. The five-floor, 69 000-square-foot institute housed 35 laboratories. By the end of 1987, it was expected 80 RRI researchers would be active in conducting basic research into stroke and aging, heart and circulation, and immunological disorders relating to transplantations.

UH housed some of the latest medical technology. For example, a magnetic resonance imaging (MRI) machine costing $3 million was added in 1986. One of the most powerful machines in Canada, the MRI provided unparalleled images of all body organs. Interestingly, neither funding for the total capital cost nor the majority of the ongoing operating costs for this advanced technology instrument was assumed by the Ministry. However, this had not deterred Blewett, and UH was considering other high technology equipment like a $3 million gamma knife which would enable neurosurgeons to operate without having to cut the skin surface.

Mission and Strategy

UH's mission involved three core activities: research, teaching and patient care. And in this way it did not differ from other university affiliated teaching hospitals. What made it more unique was the emphasis on innovative, leading edge research. Clinical and teaching activities were expected to reflect and reinforce this focus. This strategy had implications for UH's product/market scope and its service portfolio.

Product/Market Scope

UH attempted to serve the needs of three related, but different markets: teaching, research and the health care needs of the community. Local community and basic teaching needs generally required a broad base of standard services. On the other hand, research needs argued for focus and specialization of products offered with a physician's clinical activities related to their research and necessarily drawing from a large patient referral base.

With three different markets service focus was not easy to achieve. The initial design of UH had included only a small emergency service because another hospital in the city specialized in trauma. However, in response to local community pressure, a larger emergency department was incorporated. Balancing the product/service portfolio under increasing space constraints, funding pressure and demand for basic health care services was becoming ever more challenging.

Overall UH's mix of cases had a high proportion of acute cases—very ill patients requiring high levels of care. UH had approximately 1% of the approved hospital beds in Ontario, as well as 1% of discharges and patient days in acute care public hospitals. However, when broken down by the acuity/difficulty of the procedure, UH's tertiary focus was clear (Table 1).

Geographically, 81% of UH's admitted patients came from the primary service area of Southwestern Ontario, with one-third of all patients originating from the hospital's primary service area of Middlesex County. Fifteen percent of all patients came from the secondary service area, which consisted of all parts of Ontario outside the primary region. The remaining 4% of patients came from outside the province of Ontario. However, because these cases tended to be more acute than the norm they accounted for a disproportionate share of patient days, approximately 6% and an even larger proportion of revenues. Exhibit 2 provides a breakdown of current patient origin by service. For the future the strategic plan had identified services with high, out-of-province potential:

TABLE 1   UH Market Share of Ontario Patients by Acuity*

	UH Share	Number of Cases
Level I: Primary	0.7%	8 092
Level II: Secondary	1.4	2 616
Level III: Tertiary	4.2	2 783
Examples:		
heart transplant	66.0	31
liver transplant	30.8	175
kidney transplant	27.0	71
craniotomy (age > 18 yrs)	15.7	388

* As classified by a scheme developed in the U.S. designed to reflect intensity of nursing care required. Higher level indicates more acute.

- transplantation
- neurosciences
- cardiology/cardiovascular surgery
- orthopaedics/sport injury
- in vitro fertilization
- diabetes
- epilepsy
- occupational health care

To help manage the service/product portfolio, the strategic plan called for the following designation of products: *Premier Product Lines* were designated on the basis of the world-class, cutting-edge nature of the service; *Intermediate Product Lines* represented those services that were approaching premier status or that stood alone as a service entity; *Service Support Clusters* were services that supported the intermediate and premier product lines; *Ambulatory/Emergency Services* included outpatient clinics, emergency services and regional joint venture arrangements; and *Diversification/Collaboration Ventures* were stand alone services that generated revenue for UH. The services for premier and intermediate categories are listed in Exhibit 3. A more detailed profile of the premier product lines is provided in Appendix A.

Product Innovation

Developing new and improved leading edge treatments for health problems was a key element of UH's mission relating to research and teaching. And while the institution, over its relatively brief history, had participated in a number of medical innovations this success did not appear attributable to formal planning. Rather new programs and services developed at UH in a seemingly ad hoc fashion. As Ken Stuart, Vice-President Medical, observed, "New services happen because of individuals—they just grow. There is some targeted research, but it is not the route of most (activities) because it would stifle people's ideas. They need to fiddle with things and be able to fail." The development of the Epilepsy Unit, outlined in Appendix B, describes an example of this process.

Blewett commented on the development of new programs at UH:

> The fact that the hospital is so small—everyone knows everyone—I can get around. Everyone knows what's going on in the hospital. ... People just drop in to see me. Someone will come down and tell me that they've found a real winner and they just have to have him/her, and so we go out and get them. There's always room for one more; we find a way to say yes.
>
> When it impacts other resources, Diane (Stewart, Executive Vice-President) becomes involved. She says it's easy for me to agree, but her people have to pick up the pieces. In order to better identify the requirements for new physicians and new programs Diane came up with the idea of the Impact Analysis (a study of how new or expanded programs affected hospital staffing, supplies and facilities). But even when the study is done we don't use it as a reason to say no; we use it to find out what we have to do to make it happen.

Diane Stewart, the Executive Vice-President, was sensitive to the need for continued innovation. She had stated, "We like to leave the door open to try new things. We go by the philosophy that to try and fail is at least to learn." A UH vice-president commented:

> People here are well read. When ideas break, anywhere in the world, they want them. There is a lot of compromising. But things get resolved. It just takes some time. We haven't learned the meaning of the word "no." But we're at a juncture where we may have to start saying no. We're just beginning to be [in the tight financial position], where many other hospitals have been for several years.

Revenues and Costs

UH's revenues and costs could not be neatly assigned to its major areas of activity. As shown in Exhibit 4a, in 1983 73% of UH's sources of funds were a "global allocation" from the MOH, and by 1987 this amount had been reduced to 70%. For the most part these funds were not attached to specific activities, acuity of patients or outcomes. Over the past few years, UH, like all other hospitals, had simply been getting an annual increase in its global allocation to off-set inflation. The stipulation attached to MOH funds was that there could be no deficit.

Some small part of MOH funding was tied to activity levels. Increases in outpatient activity did, through a complex formula, eventually result in increased funding to the hospital. Further, the Ministry had established a special "life support fund" to fund volume increases for specified procedures. However, this fund was capped and the number of claims by all hospitals already exceeded funds available, so only partial funding was received. The MOH also funded the clinical education of medical students and interns. This accounted for most of the $5.8 million in revenue from MOH programs (Exhibit 4a).

Approximately 30% of UH's revenues did not come directly from the Ministry of Health through its global funding allocation. A large percentage of these self-generated revenues originated from servicing out-of-province patients. For patients from other provinces the MOH negotiated with the paying provinces, a per diem charge for services provided. Even so, as out-of-province patients generated incremental revenues above and beyond the global allocation, they were a very attractive market. For out-of-country patients, UH could set their own price for services provided, thereby ensuring that the full cost of providing health care was recovered. But, as shown in Table 2, the out-of-province and out-of-country revenue appeared to have reached a plateau at around 14% of total revenue. There was also a sense the mix of this component was shifting away from out-of-country patients towards out-of-province.

TABLE 2   UH Revenue Breakdown

Fiscal Year	MOH Global Base	Other Revenue	Out-of-Province & Out-of-Country
1983	74.6%	25.4%	7.4%
1984	73.7	26.3	8.7
1985	72.1	27.9	11.3
1986	69.3	30.7	13.8
1987	70.5	29.5	13.9

Additional funds also came from the University Hospital Foundation of London and other entrepreneurial activities. The numerous fund-raising appeals by the Foundation included sales of operating room greens in sizes ranging from doll-size through to a small child, and a specially produced record and music video. The Foundation was a separate financial entity and funds flowing to UH appeared as an addition to UH equity (and cash) with no effect on revenues.

Salaries, wages and benefits made up the single largest cost category. (The base salary of medical staff, who were employees of the University, were not directly included in this number.) As a proportion of total revenues these costs had declined marginally over the last five years. Other costs had, however, increased, in particular medical supplies and drugs. Much of this increase was due to the MOH's unwillingness to pay for certain drug therapies. For example, drugs used to prevent rejection of transplanted organs were not paid for by the MOH because the drugs were considered experimental, and therefore the cost of these drugs had to be covered under the hospital's global budget. Similar funding limitations had evolved with other drugs and medical apparatus, e.g., implantable defibrillators. The boundary between clinical research and clinical practice was often difficult to draw. Research funding bodies, like the Medical Research Council, would not pay for medical procedures beyond the purely experimental stage. And often the MOH would not immediately step in, and fund procedures after research grants expired.

On balance UH had never recorded a deficit year. However, its operating surplus had been decreasing (Exhibit 4a). Blewett felt the key to UH's future financial success was reduced reliance on Ministry funding. (UH's reliance on Ministry funding was already less than most hospitals.) UH was actively pursuing opportunities with the potential to generate funds. One recent development was the Occupational Health Centre (OHC), which opened in 1986 as a separate private, for-profit organization to provide occupational health care services to the business community. By the end of 1987, it had 30 companies with 11 000 employees as clients. However, like most startups, the OHC had required an initial infusion of cash, and was not expected to generate net positive cash flow for several years.

Not all of the activity undertaken at UH was reflected in its financial statements and operating statistics. Research grants and many of their associated costs were not included in the hospital's statements, even though they were administered by the University, and much of the activity was conducted at UH. During 1986–87, UH physicians and researchers were involved in over 200 projects with annual funding of $9.5 million. Table 3 lists the services most involved in research. In an effort to capitalize on the revenue potential of the innovations developed at UH, an innovations inventory was being compiled and the potential for licensing explored. It was expected this activity, if it demonstrated potential, would be spun out into a private, for profit corporation.

TABLE 3 UH Clinical Services with Largest Research Budgets

Service	Amount ($000)
Transplantation & Nephrology	$1 979
Gynaecology	1 454
Neurology	1 105
Endocrinology	923
Cardiology	678

SOURCE: *Research Annual Compendium*, not including the Robarts Research Institute.

Staffing and Organization

UH was a large and diverse organization employing 2 600 personnel. There were 128 medical clinicians and researchers, 70 residents, 44 interns and research fellows, 875 nursing staff, 140 paramedical, 312 technical, 214 supervisory and specialist, 444 clerical and 379 service staff.

The relationship with UH's medical staff was especially unique. *All* UH physicians held joint appointments with UH and the University, and were technically University employees. As well, they did not have a private practice outside of University Hospital. As a consequence, all patients (except those admitted through the emergency department) were referred to UH by outside physicians. At most other hospitals, physicians were not salaried employees. They had hospital privileges, and spent part of their time at the hospital and the rest at their own clinics/offices, usually separate from the hospital. These physicians billed OHIP directly for all patient care delivered. At UH, the "GFT"[2] relationship with physicians was very different. They were paid a base salary by the University. Physicians negotiated with the Dean of Medicine and Department Chairperson for salaries in excess of this base. This negotiated portion was called the "if earned" portion. UH physicians were expected to make OHIP billings from clinical work inside the hospital at least up to the level of their "if earned" portion. Any additional billings were "donated" to the University, and were placed into a research fund. Although arrangements varied, the physicians who contributed their billings usually had some say in the allocation of these research funds.

Because of this GFT relationship, the medical staff at UH generally developed a stronger identification and affiliation with the institution. Even so, retaining medical staff was not easy. Most could make significantly higher incomes if they gave up their teaching and research activities, and devoted all their efforts to private practice. While the salary of UH physicians was

---

[2] Geographic Full-Time.

competitive with similar institutions in Canada, many research hospitals in the U.S. were perceived to offer higher compensation and often better support for research. To further complicate matters, the available number of University positions in the medical faculty and the dollar amount of the salary had been frozen for several years. As a result, the base salary for any net new positions or salary increases were funded entirely by UH.

Structure

The physicians were by nature highly autonomous and independent. Nominally at least medical staff were responsible through their clinical service head (e.g., Neurology) or a department head (e.g., Neurosciences) to Ken Stuart, Vice-President Medical. The role of service and department head was a part-time responsibility rotated amongst senior clinicians in the particular specialty. The heads of services and departments in the hospital often, but not always, held parallel appointments in the Faculty of Medicine at the University.

The division of services and departments was in most instances determined by traditional professional practice. However, "product offerings" which crossed traditional departmental boundaries were common. At UH, the only one with formal organizational recognition was the multi-organ transplant service (MOTS). It had its own medical head, manager and budget. Other multi-disciplinary units, like the Epilepsy Unit, did not have formal organizational status, even though the strategic plan recommended organizing around product lines (or business units).

In general, the hierarchy could best be described as loose and collegial. Although it varied from individual to individual, most physicians, while they might consult with their service and department heads when confronted with a problem or pursuing an opportunity, felt no requirement to do so. Typically they dealt directly with the persons concerned. Most chiefs of services supported this *laissez-faire* approach, since they wanted to encourage initiative and did not wish to become overly involved in administration, coordination and control.

At an operational level, the primary organizational difference between UH and traditional hospitals was its decentralized approach. Each floor acted as a mini-hospital. A triumvirate of medical, nursing and administrative staff were responsible for the operation of their unit. In many hospitals, nurses spent much of their time doing non-nursing tasks including administrative duties like budget preparation, coordinating maintenance and repairs, etc. At UH, a service coordinator located on each floor handled non-nursing responsibilities for each unit and interfaced with centralized services like purchasing, housekeeping, and engineering. Whenever possible, the allied health professionals, such as psychologists, occupational therapists and physiotherapists, were also located on the floors. In traditional hospitals, hiring, staff development, quality assurance and staff assignment of nurses were done on a centralized basis. At UH, a nursing manager, located in each service, handled the nursing supervision responsibilities. A nursing co-ordinator handled the clinical guidance and supervision of the nurses.

Organizationally service coordinators and allied health professionals reported through their respective managers to the newly created, and as yet unfilled, position of Vice-President Patient Services. Nurses reported through nursing managers to the Vice-President Nursing. In practice, the physicians, nurses and service coordinators on each floor formed a team which managed their floor. Ideally, integration occurred, and operational issues were addressed at the floor level, only rarely referred up for resolution.

Non-medical personnel working in centralized laboratories and services, but not directly involved in patient care reported to the Vice-President Administration. Activities dealing with financial, accounting and information were the responsibility of the Vice-President Finance. While final hiring decisions for non-physician positions were decentralized to the units concerned, job description, posting and initial screening was done in the human resources department. In addition, some employee education and health services were handled through this department. The hiring of physicians, even though technically University employees, was usually initiated within UH. Typically, service or department heads would identify desirable candidates. If the person was being hired for a new position (as opposed to a replacement), then after discussion of the physician's plans, an impact analysis would be prepared identifying the resources required. Generally, Pat Blewett was very involved in the recruitment of physicians.

UH was considered progressive in its staffing and organization, having recorded many firsts among Canadian hospitals. Over the years, they had been one of the first to introduce service coordinators, paid maternity leave, dental benefits, 12-hour shifts, job-sharing, workload measurement and productivity monitoring. The concern for employees was reflected in UH's relatively low turnover, in the 9% range. Exit interviews indicated very few people went to another health care job because they were dissatisfied with UH. Aside from normal attrition, the biggest reason for leaving was lack of upward job mobility, a situation caused by UH's flat structure and low turnover.

Committees at all levels and often crossing departments were a fact of life at UH, and reflected the organization's decentralized and participative approach to decision-making. Diane Stewart, for example, was a member of 48 different hospital and board committees. Medical staff were also expected to be involved, as Ken Stuart explained:

> Committee work is not a physician's favourite activity. But it's important they be involved in the management of the hospital. I balance committee assignments amongst the medical staff and no one can continually refuse to do their part. This is a demand UH makes of its GFT physicians that other hospitals do not.

UH's management group had recently undergone a reorganization, reducing the number of direct reports to Pat Blewett from five to three. Now the Vice-President Human Resources and the Vice-President Administration, along with the Vice-Presidents of Patient Services and Nursing, reported to the Executive Vice-President, Diane Stewart (Exhibit 5). The reorganization centered control of operations around Stewart, allowing Blewett to concentrate on physicians, external relationships and the future direction of UH.

Budgets

There were five groups that submitted budgets to administration: support services, nursing, allied health, diagnostic services, and administrative services. The annual capital and operating budgetary processes involved a lot of meetings, and give-and-take. As one manager described:

> ... The budget of each department is circulated to the other departments within our service. We have a meeting with ... V.P. Administration and ... V.P. Finance and all the department heads. Although the department heads are physicians, often the department managers will either accompany or represent the department head. In that meeting we review each department's budget, questioning any items which seem out of place. The department will either remain firm on its budget, back down, or decide to postpone the expenditure to the following year. People do back down. If we can't get our collective budgets within the budget for our service, the vice-presidents will either make trade-offs with the other service categories, or speak with the de-

partment heads privately to try and obtain further cuts. The majority of cuts are made in the meeting. ... It works because the department heads are fiscally responsible, and there is a lot of trust between the departments and between the departments and administration.

Operating budgets were coordinated by the service coordinator on each floor, but really driven by the plans of the medical staff. Each year physicians were asked about their activity levels for the upcoming year; these were translated into staffing and supplies requirements, in terms of number of hours worked and the physical volume of supplies consumed. Costs were attached and the overall expense budget tabulated later by the finance department. In the last fiscal year, when the overall budget was tabulated, it exceeded the estimated revenues of the hospital by over $10 million, roughly 10%. Ross Chapin, Vice-President Finance, explained what happened:

> We went back to each of the clinical services and looked at their proposed level of activity. The hospital had already been operating at 100 plus percent of its physical capacity. Most of the services had not taken this into account in preparing their plans. They had assumed more space and more patient beds would be available. Since this just wasn't going to happen, at least in the short term, we asked them to redo their budgets with more realistic space assumptions. As a result our revenue and expense budgets came more into line.

While the activity of the medical staff drove the operating expenditures of the hospital, physicians were not in the ongoing budgetary loop. If expenditures were exceeding budget, physicians might not even be aware, and if aware, had no incentive to cut expenses and reduce activity levels in order to meet budget. Aside from the number of physicians and the limits of their own time, the major constraint on expenditures was space and the availability of support services. A patient could not be admitted unless a bed was available; an outpatient procedure could not be conducted unless a consultation room was free and the needed support services, e.g., radiology, physical therapy, etc., could be scheduled.

Because of MOH funding and space constraints, the hospital had a set number of inpatient beds. The allocation of beds amongst services was determined by a committee made up of the manager of admitting, several of physicians and chaired by the Vice-President Medical. Since bed availability affected the activity level of the services and their physicians, this allocation was a sensitive area. Services would often lend an unused bed to another, usually adjacent, service. However, the formal reallocation of beds was done infrequently. And when done, was based on waiting lists (by service) and bed utilization rates.

New Programs

While capital and operating budgets for ongoing activities originated with the managers on the floors, the medical staff usually initiated requests for new programs and equipment. Money to fund large outlays associated with new or expanded programs would be requested from the MOH, or might be part of a special fund raising campaign. Private charitable foundations had made significant contributions to the Epilepsy Unit, the MOTU and the MRI facility. When proposals for a new program or the addition of a new physician were made, an impact analysis was undertaken. These studies detailed the resource requirement: space, support staff, supplies, etc. of the initiative, and summarized the overall financial impact. The analysis did not, however, identify the availability or source of the required resources should the initiative be pursued. As one vice-president explained:

The impact analysis might show that if we bring on a new orthopaedic surgeon, we'll need two more physical therapists (PTs). But there is no space (and probably no money) for the PTs. Quite often the physician is hired anyway, and the PTs currently on staff have to try and manage the additional work load. We *know* what a new physician will need beforehand, but we don't always ensure it's there before they come on board.

Recently a new physician had arrived after being hired, and office space was not available.

Basis for Success

UH attributed its success to several factors. A primary factor was the GFT status of the medical staff, which cultivated a high degree of loyalty and commitment to the hospital, and supported the integration of excellence in teaching, research and practice. The ability of the medical staff to attract out-of-province patients contributed to the hospital's revenues. The strong entrepreneurial orientation of management, its ability to identify and create additional sources of revenue, and a widely shared understanding of the mission of UH helped to foster commitment to the organization's goals.

Early in its development, UH had attracted physicians/researchers capable of developing major internationally recognized research and clinical programs, like Doctors Drake and Barnett in neurosciences and Dr. Stiller in transplantation. These physicians and their programs had developed international recognition, and generated patient referrals from all over the country and around the world.

UH's product portfolio required a delicate balance. It was natural for products to evolve and mature. As innovative procedures became more commonplace, they tended to diffuse to other hospitals. Indeed, UH contributed to this process by training physicians in these procedures as part of their teaching mission. As a consequence, UH's patient referral base would shrink, and so too would out-of-country, out-of-province revenues from maturing service. UH required a constant inflow of innovative, internationally recognized clinical procedures in order to sustain its out-of-province referral base.

THE STRATEGIC PLAN

UH did not have an internal ongoing strategic planning process. In 1985, a change occurred. UH signed an affiliation agreement with the Hospital Corporation of Canada (HCC), an affiliate of the Hospital Corporation of America (HCA), and a large, publicly owned international health care company, which gave UH access to HCA strategic planning expertise. For UH's existing service portfolio, the consultants assessed underlying demand, UH's share of market, its capability base and abilities relative to other research and teaching hospitals. They did not specifically consider MOH funding policy.

Senior management wanted a process that would enable people to buy into the emerging plan, so they conducted a series of planning sessions. The first information session was conducted in the fall of 1986, when general information about the health care environment was presented to the chiefs of services and administration. In December, a day-long retreat was held to disseminate information, and to provide some education on key strategic concepts such as market share and product life cycle. In January 1987, a second retreat was held. The Chiefs of Services were asked to come prepared to make a presentation on the direction of their department, resource requirements and priorities. Blewett commented on the meeting:

> The chiefs did an outstanding job. They really got into it, using business ideas to look at their services and where they are going. They were talking about market share and product life cycles. I believe it gave them a new way to think about things. Really, the chiefs were presenting to each other and they wanted to do a good job and make their best case. A lot of information sharing occurred.

In late February, the consultants' initial recommendations were presented to administration. One of the recommendations was to adopt a portfolio approach to planning. A preliminary designation of products into portfolios of premier, intermediate and service support clusters was provided. The initial criteria used to determine premier status were:

- geographic "draw"
- consensus as a priority
- "leading edge" service
- future orientation of its people

Subsequent meetings with the medical staff led to some modifications of these designations. Blewett reflected on the process of identifying the product/service portfolio.

> I never thought we would do it. But when it came down to making the hard decisions, it didn't take that long. I give a lot of credit to the planners and to our administrative person, who kept in close contact with everyone, and made sure that concerns were taken care of. ... The GFTs are committed to this institution, therefore it's easier to mobilize these people. ... We also made it clear that services could move between categories, which provides some incentive.

Indeed, Sport Medicine had not initially been categorized as a premier service, but in the final version of the plan was placed in this category.

The final strategic plan, a 150-page document, was approved by both the Medical Advisory Committee of the hospital and by its Board of Directors. As Blewett reflected on the process, he was pleased with the results of the effort which had taken over a year to complete. Blewett knew many of his senior managers had applauded the direction the report had taken in providing a more solid foundation on which to make difficult resource allocation decisions. However, he was concerned the plan not be used as a reason to say "no," to stifle initiative and the emergence of new areas of excellence. He wondered how an ongoing planning process would have affected the evolution of the epilepsy unit described in Appendix B. With this in mind, he was wondering where to go from here: How could the plan, its recommendations and following activities be used to help guide the hospital?

EXHIBIT 1   UH Key Recommendations from the Strategic Plan

1. Pursue a Service Cluster/Product Line Development Approach

Product line management is a system that organizes management accountability and operations around discrete service or product lines. Service clusters are those groups of services that are provided to distinct market segments.

By shifting management focus to product line development, hospitals can increase their market share by improving the efficiency of their services and by tailoring services to specific market needs.

2. Adopt an Appropriate Bed Complement for UH in the 1990s

To facilitate the implementation of a service cluster or product line concept for University Hospital, it will be essential to adopt an appropriate bed complement (for each service).

3. Address Facility Considerations through a Medical Mall Implementation Strategy

The purpose of the medical mall is multifold:

- It compartmentalizes functions and services to allow an optimum level of capital expense by type of service.
- It targets and controls traffic by patient type while ensuring convenience and accessibility.
- It provides a "one-stop" location for multiple levels of inpatient and outpatient support services.

4. Pursue a Networking Strategy as Part of the Role of Tertiary Care

Pursuit of a networking strategy asserts that the role of University Hospital in tertiary care should represent a "hub" within the Canadian and international health care system.

As such, options have been developed to ensure University Hospital is able to accept patients who need to be "stepped-up" from community hospitals and outpatient settings, and also to "step down" patients who no longer require UH's intensity of services.

EXHIBIT 1   (continued)

5. Adopt a Diversification Strategy

To encourage management to investigate which type of integration makes most sense for UH, given its tertiary nature and commitment to research and education. Diversification efforts can be adopted by an institution in basically three ways. Through vertical integration, horizontal integration or geographic dispersion.

6. Implement an Organizational Enhancement Strategy

Due to the complexity and dynamic nature of University Hospital, ongoing strategic planning and administrative support and leadership will be essential. The recommended organizational enhancement strategy has, as its focus, to

- Pursue process planning and implementation by adopting an ongoing annual planning cycle.
- Assign responsibility/authority for successful ongoing strategic planning.
- Address management/medical staff succession.
- Exploit the benefits of University Hospital's relationship with HCA.

At the heart of this strategy is the need to formalize and integrate current planning mechanisms into an ongoing process.

7. Continue an Aggressive Financial Strategy: Preserve/Enhance Financial Resources

The objectives of this recommendation are twofold:
- To enhance financial resources.
- To preserve financial resources.

EXHIBIT 2 UH Patient Origin by Service—1986 (percent)

	Origin			
	Primary	*Secondary*	*Tertiary*	
Service	*(S-W Ont.)*	*(Remainder of Ont.)*	*Canada (except Ont.)*	*International*
Cardiology	71.9	22.3	3.9	1.9
Cardiovascular and Thoracic Surgery	61.4	28.8	7.8	2.1
Chest Diseases	88.1	10.8	0.6	0.5
Dentistry	89.1	10.8	0.0	0.1
Endocrinology	83.2	15.4	0.0	1.5
Gastroenterology	80.1	15.7	2.5	1.0
General Surgery	87.5	11.1	0.6	0.8
Gynaecology	70.9	24.4	3.8	1.0
Haematology	92.2	6.8	0.0	1.0
Immunology	90.0	10.0	0.0	0.0
Internal Medicine, Infectious Diseases	85.6	10.1	0.2	2.0
Nephrology	76.8	20.4	0.2	2.5
Neurology	70.0	26.2	2.4	1.4
Neurosurgery	42.6	36.3	2.4	18.6
Ophthalmology	75.9	23.7	0.0	0.4
Orthopaedic Surgery	85.6	13.4	0.3	0.7
Otolaryngology	92.2	7.0	0.4	0.0
Paediatrics	42.6	45.0	0.0	12.4
Plastic Surgery	86.8	12.4	0.2	0.6
Psychiatry	91.0	6.7	0.3	2.0
Rheumatology	91.9	7.7	0.0	0.4
Urology	92.9	7.1	0.0	0.0

SOURCE: UH Strategic Plan.

EXHIBIT 3   UH Services by Strategic Category

Premier Product Lines

Cardiology/Cardiovascular Surgery
    Arrythmia Investigation and Surgery
    V.A.D.

Clinical Neurological Sciences (Neurology/Neurosurgery)
    Epilepsy Unit
    Stroke Investigation
    Multiple Sclerosis
    Aneurysm Surgery

Multiple Organ Transplant Centre (Adult and Paediatric)
    Kidney   Pancreas
    Liver   Small Bowel
    Heart   Bone Marrow
    Heart/Lung   Whole Joint and Bone
    Other

Reproductive Biology
    I.V.F. Clinic

Intermediate Product Lines

Chest Diseases	Dentistry
Endocrinology/Metabolism	Gastroenterology
General Internal Medicine	General Surgery
Haematology	Immunology
Nephrology	Ophthalmology
— Dialysis Unit	Otolaryngology
Orthopaedic Surgery	Plastic/Reconstructive Surgery
Paediatrics	Psychiatry
Physical Medicine and Rehabilitation	Urology
Rheumatology	

EXHIBIT 4A UH Statement of Revenues and Expenses for the Year Ended March 31 ($000s)

	1983	1984	1985	1986	1987
Revenue					
MOH allocation	$47 067	$51 527	$56 329	$61 103	$ 69 502
Inpatient services	5 355	7 482	9 986	13 945	14 771
Accommodation differential	1 548	1 624	1 746	2 277	2 537
Outpatient services	1 692	2 069	2 033	2 428	3 135
MOH programs	4 908	5 083	5 405	5 503	5 811
Other revenue	3 626	3 471	4 079	4 510	4 836
	64 196	71 256	79 578	89 766	100 592
Expenses					
Salaries and wages	35 779	39 480	43 505	47 450	53 581
Employee benefits	3 869	4 441	4711	4 866	5 628
Supplies and other services	10 312	11 751	13 640	15 289	18 960
Ministry of Health programs	4 978	5 376	5 701	5 976	6 099
Medical supplies	3 679	3 915	4 842	5 506	6 547
Drugs	2 226	2 079	2 871	3 846	5 220
Depreciation	2 444	2 818	3 121	3 398	3 843
Bad debts	192	205	165	197	141
Interest	75	137	144	122	420
	63 554	70 202	78 700	86 650	100 439
Excess of revenue over expenses from operations	642	1 054	878	3 116	153
Add (deduct) unusual items:					
debenture issue cost					(154)
gain on asset sale					466
Excess of revenue over exp.	642	1 054	878	3 116	465

Operating Statistics

	1983	1984	1985	1986	1987
Inpatient days (000s)	137.5	138.5	139.7	140.4	142.0
Inpatient admissions (000s)	11.8	11.9	12.5	12.9	13.1
Average inpatient stay (days)	11.7	11.6	11.2	10.9	10.8
Occupancy (per cent)	89.5%	89.9%	90.3%	91.0%	90.9%
Outpatient visits (000s)	96.5	101.9	108.4	113.1	122.4
Total patients seen	n/a	n/a	221 090	233 688	254 001
Equivalent patient days	n/a	n/a	208 932	214 980	222 137
Bookings ahead:					
urgent				294	584
elective				650	724
UH employees:					
Number of beds:					
approved	421	424	424	428	436
rated	451	451	451	463	463

EXHIBIT 4B   UH Balance Sheet as of March 31 ($000s)

Assets	1983	1984	1985	1986	1987
Integrated Funds[1]					
Current:					
Cash and securities	$ 2 795	$ 1 580	$ 1 562	$ 1 799	$ 1 541
Accounts receivable:					
province	3 095	3 341	4 324	6 068	7 508
other	2 299	3 119	3 742	6 394	7 006
Inventories	1 005	1 147	1 130	1 127	1 064
Prepaid expenses	101	109	99	78	100
Total current assets	9 231	9 296	10 857	15 466	17 219
Funds available to purchase plant property and equipment	2 099	3 701	3 086	2 764	6 800
Fixed assets:					
Property plant & equip.	36 884	37 873	38 511	40 325	48 223
Capital leases	173	144	141	40 249	48 114
	37 057	38 017	38 652	40 325	48 223
	48 387	51 014	52 596	58 555	72 242
Special Funds[1]					
Cash and deposits	19	21	35	40	90
Marketable securities (cost)	4 256	5 042	5 948	7 105	7 817
Accrued interest	57	103	108	123	141
Mortgage receivable	59	56	53	49	46
Advance to integrated fund	1 264	1 004	744	734	1 775
	5 655	6 227	6 888	8 051	9 869
	54 042	57 241	59 485	66 606	82 112

[1] Revenue and expenses relating to the day-to-day activities of the Hospital are recorded in the statement of revenue and expenses and the integrated fund statement of assets. Activities relating to funds made available to the LHA under conditions specified by the donor are recorded in the special funds statement. Most of these monies were donated to the LHA prior to the establishment of the Foundation.

EXHIBIT 4B (continued)

Liabilities and Equity	1983	1984	1985	1986	1987
Integrated Funds					
Current:					
Accounts payable	$ 2 941	$ 4 490	$ 4 153	$ 5 618	$ 6 987
Accrued charges	2 401	2 074	2 580	2 988	3 668
Current portion of leases and loans	417	401	400	260	307
Total current liabilities	5 759	6 965	7 133	8 866	10 962
Long-term:					
Debentures[2]					5 629
Advances from special funds	1 265	1 004	744	734	1 775
Capital lease	175	141	95	18	12
	1 440	1 145	839	752	7 417
Less principal due	417	401	400	260	307
	1 023	744	439	492	7 109
Integrated equity	41 605	43 305	45 025	49 196	54 170
	48 387	51 014	52 597	58 554	72 241
Special Fund[3]					
Equity	5 656	6 227	6 888	8 052	9 870
Total equity and liabilities	54 042	57 241	59 485	66 606	82 111

[2] In February 1987 the Hospital issued debentures to finance the new parking garage and attached office facility.

[3] The hospital has received the following advances from the Special Fund, repayable with interest:

Year	Amount	Purpose
1983	$1 264 000	New telephone system
1986	$ 250 000	Establishment of Occupational Health Centre
1987	$1 400 000	Finance MRI building.

EXHIBIT 4C **UH Statement of Changes in Equity for the Year Ended March 31**

Statement of Equity	*1983*	*1984*	*1985*	*1986*	*1987*
Integrated Funds					
Balance beginning of year	$40 386	$41 605	$43 305	$45 025	$49 196
Add (deduct) MOH settlements	(1 114)				
	39 272	41 605	43 305	45 025	49 196
Donations & grants	1 692	646	842	1 054	4 509
Excess of revenue over expenses	641	1 054	878	3 117	465
	2 333	1 700	1 720	4 171	4 974
Balance end of year	$41 605	$43 305	$45 025	$49 196	$54 170
Special Funds					
Balance beginning of year	$ 5 044	$ 5 651	$ 6 227	$ 6 888	$ 8 052
Add:					
Donations and bequests	1	1	11	409	835
Net investment income	606	575	650	755	983
Balance end of year	$ 5 651	$ 6 227	$ 6 888	$ 8 052	$ 9 870
Represented by:					
Non-expendable funds	$ 492	$ 492	$ 492	$ 492	$ 492
Expendable funds	5 139	5 734	6 396	7 560	9 378
	$ 5 651	$ 6 227	$ 6 888	$ 8 052	$ 9 870

EXHIBIT 5 UH Organization Chart

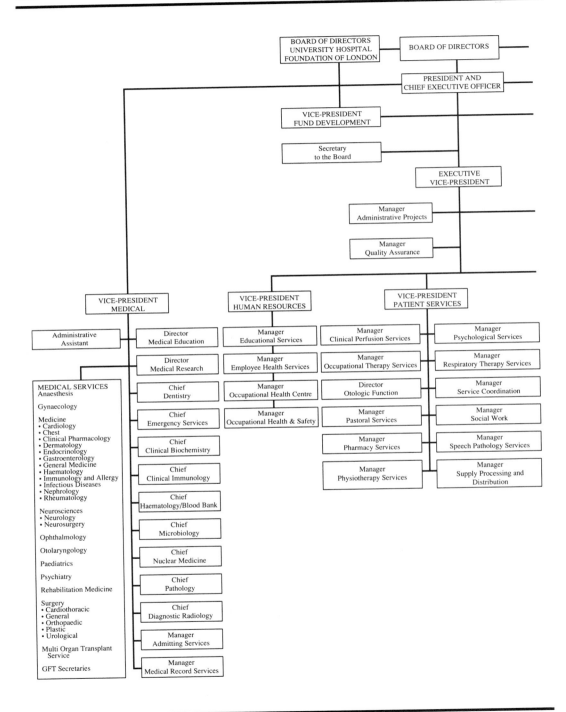

EXHIBIT 5   UH Organization Chart (continued)

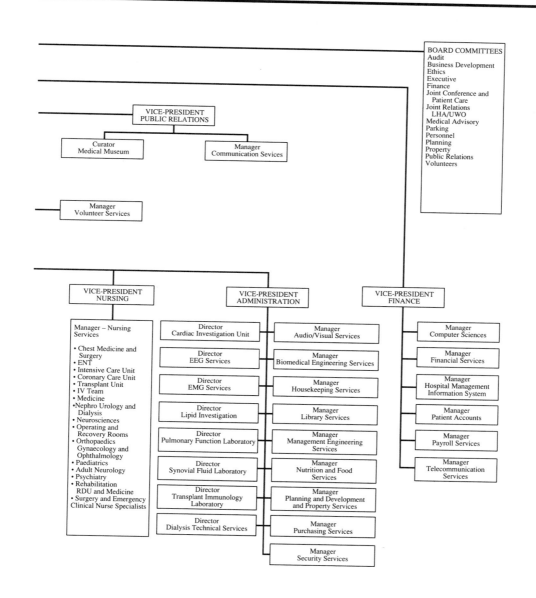

APPENDIX A   UH Profile of Premier Service Categories

The premier product lines fell under four categories: cardiology/cardiovascular surgery, clinical neurological sciences, multiple organ transplant, and reproductive biology. More detailed descriptions follow.

CARDIOLOGY/CARDIOVASCULAR SURGERY

The two major programs in cardiology/cardiovascular surgery were Arrythmia Investigation and Surgery, and the Ventricular Assist Device (VAD). Arrythmia investigation received a major breakthrough when in 1981, the world's first heart operation was performed to correct life-threatening right ventricular dysplasia. In 1984, UH entered into a collaborative relationship with Biomedical Instrumentation Inc., a Canadian research and development firm based near Toronto, to produce a sophisticated heart mapping device, which greatly advanced the surgical treatment of patients suffering from life-threatening heart rhythm disorders. The computer-assisted mapping system, which fit over the heart like a sock, enabled doctors to almost instantaneously locate the "electric short circuit" in the hearts of patients afflicted with cardiac arrhythmias. Physicians were then able to more easily locate and destroy the tissue which caused the patient's heart to beat abnormally.

The ventricular assist device (VAD), which UH began using in 1987, was functionally no different from some life support machines, such as the heart-lung machine already in use. In assisting the heart to pump blood, the VAD was used for patients waiting for transplants, those needing help after open heart surgery, and hearts weakened after a severe heart attack. The VAD worked outside the patient's body, carrying out approximately 50% of the heart's work. When the patient's heart recovered sufficiently or when a donor organ became available for those who required a transplant, the pump could be disconnected without difficulty. Other than UH, there was only one other hospital in Canada using the VAD.

CLINICAL NEUROLOGICAL SCIENCES (CNS)

There were four major programs in CNS: The Epilepsy Unit; Stroke Investigation; Multiple Sclerosis; and Aneurysm Surgery.

The Epilepsy Unit, discussed at length in Appendix B, was one of only a few of its kind in North America. The demand for its services had extended the waiting time for a bed to over a year.

A four-bed Investigative Stroke Unit was established at UH in 1983 to improve the diagnosis and treatment of stroke. In 1986, UH and the University of Western Ontario collaborated in the development of the Robarts Research Institute, which focused its efforts on stroke research.

The Multiple Sclerosis (MS) clinic at UH conducted exploratory research to study the causes and incidence of MS, a chronic degenerative disease of the central nervous system. One study involved 200 MS patients in 10 centres, coordinated by UH, to determine whether cyclosporin[1] and prednisone, either alone or in combination with repeated plasma exchange treatments could prevent further deterioration in MS patients.

Aneurysm Surgery became a centre for excellence and internationally renowned early on, when in 1972, Dr. Charles Drake pioneered a technique for surgically treating a cerebral aneurysm. In October of

---

[1] Cyclosporin was the drug originally used to minimize the bodies' rejection of transplanted organs. Because of its transplantation experience, UH had considerable expertise with this drug and immunology in general.

1979, vocalist Della Reese underwent neurosurgery at UH. She returned to London the following year to give a benefit concert to raise funds for UH.

MULTIPLE ORGAN TRANSPLANT CENTRE

The first kidney transplant at UH was performed in 1973, followed by its first liver transplant in 1977. In 1979, UH was chosen as the first centre in North America to test the anti-rejection drug Cyclosporin A. In 1981, the first heart transplant at UH was performed. In that same year, UH became the site of the Canadian Centre for Transplant Studies. In 1984, Canada's first heart-lung transplant was performed at UH.

In 1984, the provincial government announced that they would partially fund a multi-organ transplant unit (MOTU) at UH. The 12-bed MOTU, which opened in 1987, was one of the first units of its kind in the world. With the help of leading-edge computer technology, transplant patients were closely monitored for the first signs of organ rejection. A highly specialized team of transplant experts including surgeons, physicians, nurses, technologists and physiotherapists joined together in the MOTU to care for transplant patients.

REPRODUCTIVE BIOLOGY

The primary work in Reproductive Biology was the In-Vitro Fertilization (IVF) program. The program was launched in 1982, with the first birth occurring in 1985. By 1987, the 100th child was born to parents who previously had been incapable of conceiving a child. The pregnancy rate was 27% using this method, with a birth rate of 22%. These results were comparable to those of well-established clinics world-wide. It was anticipated that with the combination of continually increasing experience together with basic science and clinical research interests in IVF, the success rate in the program would continue to increase. There was a two-year waiting period to participate in the program.

APPENDIX B   The Process of Innovation at UH

THE EPILEPSY UNIT

Research and service innovations had been important to UH. This appendix described how one of these came about.

The epilepsy unit probably had its genesis when Dr. Warren Blume, a neurologist, joined Dr. John Girvin, a neurosurgeon at UH in 1972. Girvin had trained under a founding father in epilepsy treatment at the Montreal Neurological Institute (MNI). Blume had done postgraduate work in epilepsy and electroencephalography (EEG)[2] at the Mayo clinic. Girvin was unique among neurosurgeons in that he had also gone on to obtain a Ph.D. in neurophysiology.

In 1972, the primary treatment for epilepsy was through drug therapy. However, there were many patients whose epilepsy could not be effectively treated this way. For those patients, the only hope was a surgical procedure to remove that part of their brain which caused the epileptic seizure. This required an

---

[2] The mapping of electrical activity in the brain.

EEG recording of a patient's seizure to identify the focus of the problem. There were few individuals trained in the use of EEG to study epilepsy. However, Blume had this expertise. Furthermore, Girvin had the training in neurosurgery to carry out the surgical procedure. Neither physician, however, was recruited specifically to do work in epilepsy. It was an interest they both shared and developed over time.

There were a number of factors that united Blume and Girvin, providing the impetus for the dedicated Epilepsy Unit that was eventually opened in May of 1986. One factor was the integration within UH of neurosurgery and neurology under the umbrella of neurosciences. In most hospitals the two departments were separate, neurosurgery being part of surgery and neurology being its own service. At UH, they were integrated organizationally and located on the same floor. Many attribute this unique relationship to the leadership and friendship of Doctors Barnett and Drake, the original Chiefs of neurology and neurosurgery.

In 1974, a young Italian boy and his father arrived on the doorstep of UH seeking help to control the boy's epilepsy; the precipitating factor that brought Blume and Girvin together to work on their first case experience. It was a complex case, requiring the expertise of both Blume and Girvin. The surgery was successful, and Blume and Girvin realized that by pooling their expertise, they could make a significant contribution to the field. Prior to that time, Blume's efforts had been focused on providing EEG readings for epileptic patients that would either be treated with medication or referred to the MNI for possible surgical treatment. Girvin's efforts had been directed at neurosurgery in general, having no special contact with epileptic patients.

Blume and Girvin began to draw together a team. The technique of removing part of the brain for the treatment of epilepsy was based on the fact that most human functions were duplicated in both temporal lobes of the brain. In the early days of surgical treatment of epilepsy at the MNI, there was no method of ensuring that both temporal lobes were functioning normally. As a result in some cases where a malfunctioning temporal lobe could not duplicate the function of the part of the brain that had been removed, patients were left with serious brain dysfunction like loss of memory capacity. Later, a procedure was developed, whereby neuropsychologists were able to assess the level of function of one temporal lobe, while the other temporal lobe was anaesthetized. It so happened that a neuropsychologist with this expertise was working at U.W.O.'s psychology department. She was asked to join the team. For Blume and Girvin, adding a neuropsychologist was essential to their ability to deal with more complex cases. The addition of full-time researchers also served to enhance the team's capability.

Capability was further enhanced, when in 1977, Blume and Girvin were successful in obtaining funding to purchase a computer that would facilitate the recording and reading of the EEG. This was a significant step, since to obtain funding, they positioned themselves as a Regional Epilepsy Unit. This was the first formal recognition of their efforts as an organized endeavour. The computerized monitoring could benefit from a dedicated unit; at the time, beds and staff were still borrowed from other departments as needed. Epileptic patients were scattered around the neurosciences floor.

As the volume of patients increased, it became increasingly apparent that a unit was needed. In order to identify the focus of the brain that triggered the epileptic seizure, it was necessary to record a seizure. As a result, EEG recording rooms were tied up for several hours in the hope that a patient would have a seizure. There were a number of problems with this approach. The patient had to have a seizure while in a recording room, and the patient or technologist had to activate the recorder. It was estimated that over 50% of seizures were missed using this method. Furthermore, leaving the patient unattended without the benefit of medication to control their seizures was dangerous. A unit that would provide full-time monitoring in order to get the vital EEG recordings, and ensure patient safety was needed.

Blume, Girvin and the manager of EEG developed a proposal for a four bed epilepsy unit. The beds that they had been using on an ad hoc basis were the neurosciences overflow beds which "belonged" to Paediatrics. Paediatrics was located on the same floor as EEG, so when Blume, who was also a member of the department of paediatrics, heard that Paediatrics was downsizing, he had approached the chief of Paediatrics to negotiate for four beds. As well, the Paediatric nurses, who had been responsible for the overflow beds, had become comfortable with providing care for epileptic patients, and it was agreed that they would provide continued support for the unit. Blume and Girvin approached Blewett with a plan requiring funding of $400 000 for equipment and renovations. There was no provision for an annual budget, since Paediatrics was prepared to cover the nursing salaries and supplies.

Blewett and his senior management group supported the plan, and it was submitted as a new program to the TVDHC for funding in February 1984. The proposal was ranked tenth, which meant it was not one of the top few submitted to the Ministry for consideration. A revised proposal was resubmitted the following February. In the meantime, Blewett, Girvin and Blume met with the Assistant Deputy Minister of Health to make a plea for funding; to no avail. They subsequently received news that the TVDHC had given the proposal a ranking of sixth. Blume and Girvin did not lose hope, and were persistent in their efforts to obtain funding. After exhausting all alternatives, Blewett decided to fund it out of the hospital's operating surplus. However, compromises were made in the plans by cutting the budget back as far as possible. The Board approved the allocation, and shortly thereafter, the unit was opened.

STRATEGY— MANAGEMENT PREFERENCES

TWILL ENTERPRISES LIMITED

Joseph N. Fry with William R. Killeen

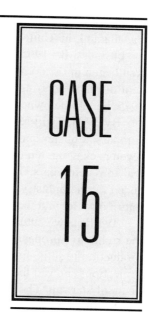

CASE

15

Ken Shelstad leaned forward in his chair, flashed a great smile and said, "Look, I love what I'm doing! I'm at it 70 hours a week—but that's the limit, after that I feel fuzzy and I can't concentrate. I enjoy every minute! Hell, I own half this company and we're making money. Lots of it! Profits, I love 'em!"

Shelstad, 51, was President of Twill Enterprises Limited, a growing and prosperous company in the printing and packaging industry. He was clearly in his element, but he expressed some misgivings about the future as he pushed the company into one of its most aggressive expansion projects. The issues, he thought, were not so much in the market opportunity as in his and his peoples' ability to handle the anticipated growth. "What concerns me," he said, "is that the company may be outgrowing me. I used to know exactly what was going on in every department. Lately, I feel like I've lost some of that control. The consultants have been telling me for years that I should change the way I run things. Maybe they are finally right."

COMPANY BACKGROUND

In 1945, Barry Shelstad, Ken's father, purchased a small Toronto-based producer of business forms and labels, and started Twill Enterprises. Over the next 20 years, Barry Shelstad built the business by internal growth, and by the careful acquisition of similar small companies in Canada and the United States. With time Barry Shelstad brought his sons John and Ken into the business. By 1965 John, the eldest, was the president, and in 1974 he became chairman. Ken began in the company as a salesman, moved up through the ranks to become vice-president of manufacturing, and in 1974 became president. When Barry Shelstad passed away in 1975, he left the ownership of the company in equal shares to the two brothers.

By 1988, Twill revenues were over $150 million, and the company's product range encompassed blister and flexible packaging, labels and business forms. The company operated seven packaging, ten business form and seven label plants at various locations in North America. In recent years, Twill's growth had been somewhat higher than the 5–7% rates experienced by the industry, and profitability had been consistently higher than the 2–3% after tax return on sales and the 4–7% return on average assets of comparable firms.

Twill's new venture was in the rigid plastic container business. Ken Shelstad had acquired the rights to European technology, which promised greater design flexibility and lower cost production in some lines of jars and bottles than was currently in place in North America. His projections showed the new lines would add over $40 million to Twill's revenues within three years of start-up. The capital investment implications of the venture were sizeable, however, and for the first time ever Shelstad had run into difficulty working out financial arrangements with Twill's long-time bank. "They wanted to know who the project manager was going to be," said Shelstad, "and when I told them, first, that it was none of their business, and, second, that it was going to be me, they wanted to have a consultant hired to monitor the operation. Well, there was no way I was going to operate with some jerk looking over my shoulder, so we got financing elsewhere." At the time of this case, Twill had made commitment for land in Toronto, and for the purchase of the major items of equipment.

INDUSTRY CHARACTERISTICS

The markets in which Twill operated were fiercely competitive. Typically, a few large competitors would account for about 70% of the sales in a region, and the balance would be filled by literally hundreds of small companies. Most products were made to customer specifications so operations took on job shop characteristics. Profitability was a reflection of efficient manufacturing operations and local pricing, customer and product mix decisions. Raw materials usually represented over 60% of direct product costs.

Price, delivery, quality and service tended to become equated among local producers. Often a competitive edge was decided by the reputation of the producer for especially good service, and the personal relations between the supplier firm personnel and their customers. The larger suppliers had somewhat more of an advantage with larger accounts because the scope of their operations allowed them to meet the national requirements of their customers.

Twill was fortunate to have focused its operations in Toronto, one of the two largest centres for printing concentration in North America (Chicago being the other). On the downside, this created a fiercely competitive environment, in which suppliers had to offer a high degree of sophistication, technical capability and a range of production options. The challenge was to make more complicated products with faster response times and lower costs.

The outlook for industry demand in Twill's market areas was generally positive. Demand tended to follow the fortunes of the economy as a whole, and in recent years had been outpacing this indicator. Existing competitors had reacted by expanding their capacity, and new entrants had been attracted to the industry. Competition would continue to be intense and there was some concern that an economic downturn would leave suppliers in a state of serious overcapacity.

TWILL'S STRATEGY

Goals

The Shelstad's goals for Twill were for it to continue to operate as a large, successful, growing, family firm. Twill had been owned and run by the Shelstad family for nearly 45 years. Ken had three sons working for the firm, and while they were still in their early 20s, he hoped they would provide for family succession.

The Shelstads were known as prudent, successful businessmen. They had built Twill with a conservative growth strategy. Typically, whether acquisition or internal expansion was involved, Twill started new projects and followed them to completion before progressing to a new venture. Twill's recent plastic container expansion represented a more aggressive step than had been typical for the company.

Product Market Strategy

Twill had always chosen to expand into markets in which it could be profitable by exploiting its competitive strengths—in particular, high-service levels, low-cost production, and in-house capabilities. When a market opportunity was uncovered (usually in the form of a neglected niche with high prices and low customer satisfaction), Twill was quick to respond. Table 1 provides a general review of Twill's market position.

TABLE 1   **Twill Market Position**

	Blister and Flexible Packaging	Labels	Business Forms
Expect overall market growth[1]	4–6%	1–3%	3–4%
Industry key Success factors	Product development Range of technical capabilities Quality and service Cost control	Personal relationships Service reputation Cost control	
Twill share of served market[2]	12%	19%	10%
% Twill revenues	Over 50%	About 15%	About 35%
Plants[3]	7	7	10

[1] Management estimate.

[2] Twill did not compete in all product formats or geographic regions in North America. The market share estimates are based on Twill's sales in its served markets.

[3] Some of Twill's plants occupied the same site and even the same building. They had distinct plant managers, however.

In recent years, Twill had experimented with a variety of plastic container products. Their strategy had been to "test the waters" with product entries based on sub-contracted production. Over time, the company had developed its understanding of the market. In 1989, Twill planned to start up its own production facilities in Toronto. The new facility represented a major step by Twill into a highly competitive market. The Shelstads were confident, however, that their current competitive advantages would transfer readily into the new market.

Competitive Strategy

Twill aimed to be competitive in price and distinctive in service. The company had always endeavoured to ensure that customers got the product they wanted, when they wanted it. To this end, Twill offered their own in-house design and typesetting service, and employed a large direct sales organization and delivery fleet.

The Shelstads ran a no-nonsense, low-cost operation. Money was spent where it was necessary—on equipment modernization and maintenance. Otherwise, there were few frills at a Twill plant. Parking lots were not paved, and offices were not carpeted. The salesforce shared spartan office space, which kept costs to a minimum and "forced" them to stay on the road. Expediting and cost control were inbred habits throughout the organization.

Recently Twill had been attempting to supplement its low-cost emphasis with a greater concern for quality. The aim was to eliminate situations in which substandard but usable products would be sent to customers. Under the current program, such a client could be informed of quality problems, given a sample, and asked for their approval prior to shipment.

TWILL'S ORGANIZATION

The practice of management at Twill had remained relatively unchanged for 20 years. Growth had added to the complexity of the business, but to this point had not forced any significant change in basic management structures or systems and style. There were, however, continuing questions about how best to handle the inherently and increasingly complicated operations of the company, as will be illustrated in the following description of the way in which the organization worked.

Management Structure

Twill was managed through a functional structure as outlined in the partial organization chart in Exhibit 1. The senior managers in the structure—John and Ken Shelstad, Larry Dixon, Vice-President of Sales and Marketing, and Doug Burgess, Vice-President of Production—had been in their positions since 1974. Each senior manager, based on long experience, would step outside of their strict functional responsibilities to handle specific projects, and often, day-to-day activities. Together they nurtured an intense, "hands-on" style of management.

Top-level coordination was handled through a management committee. The committee consisted of six members—the Shelstads, Doug Burgess, Larry Dixon, Tim O'Dowda, and Jeff Bak. The group attempted to meet weekly (schedules limited this number to about 30 meetings annually) for two to four hours. John Shelstad set an agenda but new topics could be informally introduced. No minutes were taken. The group's role was to develop strategy; day-to-day operations were not discussed. Final decisions rested with the Shelstads, but no decisions were made without the assistance and input of the committee.

John and Ken Shelstad's roles in the management structure were vastly different. The older brother, John, had a number of outside interests and limited his involvement to strategic issues. Ken, on the other hand, was highly involved in all of the company's activities—from the management committee to daily decision making. As one manager observed: "Twill gets its pulse from Ken. He commands respect and he gets it. He's very dynamic. He drives this company. But there is a problem—I think people are losing contact with him."

Another added an ominous note: "Ken is going to kill himself. He pushes himself too hard. He recently delegated the monthly cheque signing. Umpteen hundred a month and he used to sign—and check—every one. That's 15 hours minimum right there."

From time to time, Twill had attempted to modify its structure and decentralize its operations through the use of general management positions. These attempts had been unsuccessful, however, for a variety of reasons that ranged from incapable personnel to corporate culture to head office interference. Twill's experience with its Denver plant was a prime example.

Twill had purchased a profitable business in Denver, and had put a "general manager" in charge. Within one year, however, the revenues and profits of the Denver operation had declined to the point where consideration was being given to shutting it down. The cause of the problem was not clear. The manager may not have been competent, head office might have stifled him—or whatever; head office did take over, the manager was fired, and another notch was marked against a general manager concept.

Management Systems

Twill's job shop operations were inherently complex, and worked under the pressure of tight delivery schedules and cost containment. The following description of order processing gives some idea of the manner in which the operating problems were handled by the company.

ORDER PROCESSING In 1971 Twill had implemented an on-line electronic data interchange (EDI) system. Orders were either brought, phoned, or mailed in, and then keyed into a terminal at the order department. By 1987, three separate systems were in use, reflecting the differing information needs of the major product lines—packaging, labels and business forms.

An EDI file was created for each client. After entering an order, a delivery slip was created and sent to shipping. Stock items were shipped immediately. Made-to-order product delivery dates were confirmed by the order department representative, who acted as an interface between manufacturing and the salesman or client.

Each salesperson at Twill (over 100 in all) had a corresponding representative in the order department. The order department people served as the vital link between sales and production, and helped to maintain the excellent relations between these two departments. This was a significant accomplishment since the processing of a job was very complex.

When a new product order was received, it passed through some or all of the order, graphics, art, typesetting, scheduling, plant and shipping departments. There was no set pattern within these departments because of the iterative steps required to process each order. The graphics people, for example, could theoretically handle one order dozens of times.

Each department at this level of the organization had its own hierarchy. The order and art departments reported to the sales vice-president, while graphics, typesetting, and scheduling reported to the production vice-president. Budget authority did not necessarily follow these lines: the graphics budget, for example, was set by sales, yet that manager reported to production personnel.

The complex nature of Twill's structure was also apparent in the sales organization. It was separated as two distinct entities, but in fact operated as a single salesforce. The salesforce for the packaging division was arranged geographically, while the labels and forms salesforce was arranged along product lines. In both cases, large single accounts were handled by a few national salespeople. In spite of these formal differences, each salesperson tended to be a generalist, selling all products to their individual customers.

CONTROL Budgets and standards were the way of life at Twill. In production, for example, standard objectives included waste, productivity, safety and cost. These standards were set by discussion with everyone right down to the machine operators who were paid piecework rates related to the standards. Meeting standards was both a corporate goal and an individual goal at Twill. The value system created by the Shelstads dictated that meeting standards would result in a reward and security.

In larger scope, Twill's planning and accounting system was based on 18 separate profit centres, representing individual products, product ranges, or plant/product combinations. Monthly reports were prepared which identified the contribution of each product at each profit centre. Ken Shelstad and Doug Burgess followed these monthly reports very carefully, and were quick to pick up on any problems that they observed.

But the pursuit of control at Twill went much deeper than this. Both Ken and Doug personally reviewed the monthly general ledger, in which every transaction of the company was entered and allocated to the profit centres. By combining this with the ledger overview, they could examine activities down to the level, for example, of specific orders, customers or purchases. It was a common occurrence for either Ken or Doug to question a plant manager, for example, about costs that were only slightly off standard or about a specific purchase transaction.

Ken explained the ledger reviews as a type of policing: "You can cross-check the allocations and make sure costs are being charged against the right profit centre and you can identify potential problems right at the start. Just the other day I picked off a cheque for $300 that had been issued to one of our competitors—I had to go down and ask why the hell we were doing business with them." Doug Burgess was proud of the fact that, as he put it: "We ask more questions and discover more horror stories than any other company. That is what has led to our success." Despite his claims, Burgess, at the time of the interview, had been unable to review his ledger, which was literally hundreds of pages deep, for two months. Time was a problem.

Staffing

Twill had always strived to take care of its employees through internal promotion, job security and profit sharing. Twill encouraged employees to move up through the ranks. In addition, as Doug Burgess explained: "No one has ever been laid off. Jobs have been eliminated but we've always been able to shift people around." Pay was above industry averages, and a pension plan was currently under consideration. Every six months, all staff above, including the supervisory level, received a bonus based on company profits. This system was highly reliant on the Shel-stads' credibility since actual profit figures were not revealed.

In 1986, Twill had initiated a Management Assistant Program. "We've got to increase our management team," said Larry Dixon, "our recent management assistant hirees are a step in this direction." In 1987, two young men were hired to assume various roles in the organization, with the goal of assuming management (and ultimately, executive) positions within a few years. Slow development from within was essential. Twill's culture dictated that managers ask questions, be nitpickers, work long hours, and get involved in everything. Only by having moved up through the ranks could one develop the essential experience and attitudes. Initiative was the trait most often looked for in personnel, and the trait which most often led to promotions.

KEY MANAGER VIEWS

The casewriter interviewed ten key Twill employees to secure their views about the issues facing Twill. These managers were cooperative and candid in their remarks.

It is worth noting that these interviews were frequently interrupted. The diversity of roles and the informal nature of management meant that senior people were inextricably involved in the problems of the day. For example, during an interview with Larry Dixon, Ken Shelstad and Jeff Bak dropped into the office, unannounced, seeking pricing information for Denver. Three hours later, Ken interrupted a meeting with Doug Burgess, this time to discuss a firewall at one of the new plants under construction. Within 30 minutes, Ken was back for an answer to a shipping problem—no space was available for a loaded truck in the yard.

Doug Burgess

Doug Burgess had been vice-president of production since 1969. He was an extremely hard worker, a detail-man, and a man with a lot of authority.

> I'm very cognizant of my authority, and sure, I like power. I really enjoy it when Ken is away. Don't misunderstand me, because I respect Ken a lot. I think he is Twill's biggest asset. He's also our biggest drawback.
>
> I don't like detail! It's the culture of the company though. Things have to get done and I'm the one who does it. What I like is solving problems and developing people.
>
> I usually work 8 to 8, with a little weekend work. It ends up being a 70-hour week and it's been steady like this for the last ten years. I'm definitely at my limit and I've been actively trying to cut back by delegating a fair bit. I'm tied to my desk too much right now. I get bored with the paperwork.
>
> I see a couple of things occurring within ten years. Personally, I believe that I'll be managing more generalities, rather than specifics. We must manage towards growth. This may require us to also move towards general managers, with much more sales involvement. I realize that our strength has been in production but there has been a shift in recent years towards sales.
>
> Twill has had difficulties with general managers. A real general manager wants autonomy and we haven't provided it. At Excelon, our Canadian poster plant, we tried a general manager and he delegated too much. He basically abdicated his office. I fired him. The new guy starts next week—with much less authority. In our plastic container start-ups, one guy was given a general manager title but he never grabbed all the reins. He still has the title but he certainly doesn't run the area.

It's been difficult to change things because the people have been here for too long. We were here when you could check on everything. Now we can't. Another justification for our structure is our results. Both our space utilization and inventory turnover are excellent. We're making money in areas other companies are not.

I acknowledge that we've done little to develop managers here but we're now at a junction in our history where something has to be done. I believe we'll have to develop from within. Jeff Bak is an exception because he's such a nitpicker that he fit right into the Twill culture.

Larry Dixon

Larry Dixon was vice-president of sales and marketing, and nominally had profit and loss responsibilities for 17 (of 18) profit centres. He worked 60-hour weeks, with the majority of his time spent in meetings. When he started at Twill in 1959, he worked 80- to 90-hour weeks.

I enjoy what I'm doing so I don't mind the long hours. I get my kicks from the diversity—of the job and the organization. The success of the company has also been an incentive. Many people work hard and don't get the rewards. To use a cliché, at Twill we've seen our hard work bear fruit.

In the early sixties I was general manager of business forms but over the years I've grown from a generalist to a specialist. We all have. Twenty years ago the four of us did everything. We can't anymore. The day-to-day work is diminishing because it has to diminish. Likewise, we've got to increase our management team. The recent management assistant hirees are an admission of this.

Managing is getting things done through people. We're getting more people to get more done. Perhaps general managers will be that way in the future, but we have not been successful with this concept. The main reason is that we're all "hands-on" managers and we can't let go. After thirty years of experience, I've seen situations that allow me to understand things better than others. So I get involved to make things happen right.

We've also discussed creating the positions of senior V.P.'s for sales and production and bringing in more V.P.'s (or some other title). I don't know what will happen. We do recognize that we must pass on authority and give people responsibilities for areas.

Each year the six of us (on the Committee) go down to a management retreat in Florida for four days in September. This year we are each assuming another's role and providing recommendations to achieve given goals. I want to do a bang-up job on my production role, so I'm putting in 40 hours on the task. I'm sure the others will do the same. Sure it's a challenge but it's supposed to give each of us a better base of knowledge at Twill.

Jeff Bak

Jeff Bak, the vice-president of finance, was responsible for all accounting functions including payables, cost accounting, payroll, and credit.

I've only been here for four and a half years. I guess that makes me the new kid on the block. I've had to adjust somewhat to fit in with these guys but it hasn't been difficult.

My role here is mainly administrative. The finance title is really a misnomer. When I arrived here the payables were screwed up so I spent half my time fixing them. Last year, half my time was spent in Denver. I still spend one day a week there. Ken thought this was too much time away but it had to be done. We had purchased this plant and the operations were not in good shape. Doug Burgess was already on another plant project so I was given this one.

I like getting responsibilities for these projects. I get a kick out of finding something that's not right, making it right, and then backing off. Denver is a prime example. It's at a point now where production is all set—all we need are sales. I'm a hired hand here. They gave me Denver, so I turned it around.

Another role of mine at Twill is to sit on the management committee. Ken and John are very good at getting the opinions of other people, so that is the ultimate purpose of the meetings. They end up deciding things, because we can't have decision by committee. After all, it is their company!

John and Ken have proven they are knowledgeable businessmen. Twill has been successful and I don't foresee any problems with the new plastic container expansion. This is what keeps things exciting around here—growth. I don't want to get bored and as long as we keep growing I won't get bored.

As for general managers, well, it seems that all of our attempts with them have been mistakes. I don't foresee a change in our organizational structure for just that reason. I also believe that a reorganization is generally done to wake people up. We don't need to be woken up at Twill.

Tim O'Dowda

Tim O'Dowda, the packaging sales manager, has been with Twill for 16 years. He oversees the sales of packaging products, one of Twill's core product lines, representing one-half of the company's annual sales. Eighty percent of his time is spent in his office, and seven sales managers report directly to him.

Twill has always been a strong manufacturing company. It's been dominated by four individuals for 20 years—John and Ken Shelstad, Larry Dixon and Doug Burgess. I think the major strength of this company is the dominance of these four individuals. I also think it's our major weakness.

Inside the management committee, Ken and Doug are the two major players and they haven't got a sales bone in their bodies! Ken is the autocratic king at Twill in my opinion, but he's on overload now. He's the best internal auditor I've ever seen. He's always reading. It's amazing, I thought he was at his limit ten years ago but he keeps on going. He really isn't a good delegator, either of tasks or authority. If someone makes a decision he'll end up questioning it.

Doug Burgess. I've never met anyone who works harder than Doug. His detail is incredible. He's on overload too. He's got no social life. He's also a real taskmaster—I sure wouldn't want to work for him. This has led to quite a turnover in production. In sales, I've lost one person in ten years, so I know that they don't have the depth of quality that we have.

Twill is unique because of the domination of these two men. They're always involved in new plants and construction. Ken really gets his jollies there. They get involved in all the materials purchasing—and I mean *all*. They are tough buyers. I couldn't sell to them.

We've had growing pains. An example right now is a salary problem we're having with our salesforce. Hay Associates have been in here to try and fix things up. Some of the salespeople are pulling in a lot more than their managers. One 24-year-old made $48 000 last year. That's obscene and he knows it. This is one control system that I've got to get a hold on.

One thing we've done in the last year is install Crosby's QYS culture at Twill. The management committee took Crosby's three-day course in Florida. Doug Burgess actually took it first and got hooked. If someone else had brought it back, say, Larry, I'm sure it wouldn't have caught on. Anyways, it's certainly helped. Errors in the sales department alone have been reduced 75%. We're at the "confrontation stage" as Crosby describes it. We're policing everybody and some people don't like it. This will only last another three months though.

Twill has to expand. There are too many opportunities out there. I want to double my sales force. I also believe that we'll have to go divisional and "general-managerized" within ten years. But we're too people-poor now. There's also a low level of trust. General managers have only stepped on the toes of the vice-presidents, especially Doug's and Larry's, so it's been difficult to change the organizational chart. I started in production and I would love the opportunity to be general manager of packaging and oversee everything in that area. We'll see. I think that Ken's kids are going to end up running the company eventually so they'll probably be the ones forced to change the structure around here.

Bruce Roberts

In 1987, Twill began a new hiring program to enhance their managerial staff. The new so-called management assistants were to complete a rotation with each member of the management committee during their first two years with Twill. Bruce Roberts, 27, was the first of two assistants hired.

> I remember going through the interview process last year. There I was, sitting in this boardroom with eight guys that run Twill. That's the way things work around here. Everyone seems to get involved in everything. "Hands-on" is a very appropriate term here, especially when applied to Ken and Doug.
>
> We were hired with the impression that John and Ken Shelstad were looking for people to step into the upper management at Twill within ten years. They're not going to last forever and they're trying to develop people that can assume their roles. Seeing firsthand how hard these guys work makes me question whether that's where I want to end up.
>
> It has been quite a learning experience thus far. At times it gets frustrating though. I'm currently trying to solve a problem we have with our branch dealers. Twill bought them years ago and they represent about $20 million in annual sales. But they are losing money, very little, mind you, but at Twill any loss is a shock. I've been on this now for six months but my project boss, Tim O'Dowda, had been on it for two years. I can't find a solution. It's really a no-win proposition. I've suggested two alternatives, sell or franchise, and boy, was I shot down by Ken! "No way," he said, "find an answer that I want to hear." Ever since he's been checking on me weekly. He's interested but he's really provided no help.

CROSSROADS

Ken Shelstad was quite aware of the pressures and cross-currents in Twill. In fact, some flipcharts in his office summarized his position. One sheet identified the "Corporate Success Factors" as: (1) low-cost production; (2) maintaining account relationships; and (3) broad service. However, in small print at the bottom of the sheet, the following words jumped out: "Get competent people at all levels."

A second sheet, entitled "Power Thinking," provided a laundry list of the major personal concerns facing Ken Shelstad. These included questions about himself, his brother, his family, and the business. These sheets had been on Shelstad's wall for over a year, and he acknowledged their importance. He, and the others, had to give considerable thought to all of these issues. Management could tire, and they would find themselves short of suitable replacements. People could limit the growth. And an economic downturn could severely impact the performance of both the new and existing products. Ken Shelstad and Twill faced an interesting future.

"I know what you are thinking," said Shelstad, smiling again, "I've had smart guys tell me to change our management structure before. And in general I agree—we must free up our time. Why, general managers would allow this simply by taking the phone calls we currently get! But it's not that simple. Our plant and distribution setup makes the general management concept difficult. We have a tough time finding good people—the general management pool is small, and most of the prospects don't even know how to spell profit. And we are smarter than they will ever be. I do have an answer though, when people get pushy. I say, 'Look, let's compare tax returns.'"

EXHIBIT 1   Twill's Simplified Organization Chart

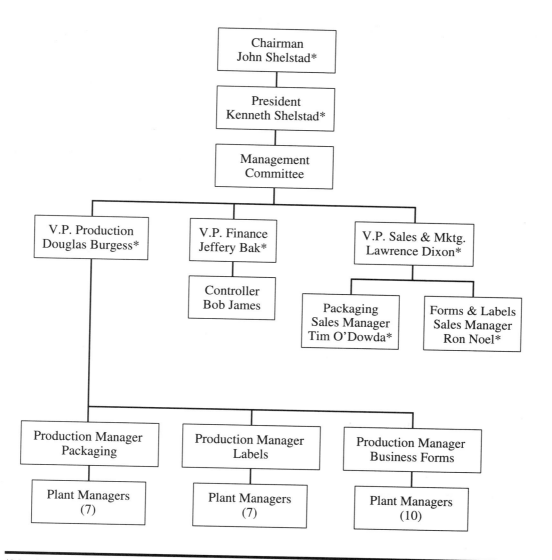

AER LINGUS – ATS (A)

J. Peter Killing

On July 15, 1985, Denis Hanrahan was flying from Dublin to Toronto, as he had many times over the past 11 months, to meet with Klaus Woerner, the owner and president of Automation Tooling Systems (ATS), a robotics firm based in Kitchener, Ontario. Mr. Hanrahan's job was to expand the "non-airline" activities of Aer Lingus, and ATS was a company in which he wanted to acquire an equity position.

The negotiations between Denis and Klaus had been friendly but protracted, and it appeared that they were finally nearing an end. The deal, which both sides had agreed to verbally, was that Aer Lingus would purchase 75% of the shares of ATS, and that Klaus would stay on and manage the company. The price that he would receive for his shares would depend on the earnings of ATS in the years ending September 30, 1985, and 1986. If ATS met the profit forecast that Klaus had prepared for it, he would receive a total of $4.6 million in cash, and retain a 25% interest in the company.

AER LINGUS

Aer Lingus was the Irish international airline, wholly owned by the Irish government. Like many airlines, Aer Lingus had difficulty producing a consistent high level of earnings (Table 1). The early 1980s in particular were not good years for the airline (nor for any other), and only the consistent profitability of the group's hotels, airline related businesses (maintenance and overhaul of the other firm's aircraft, training of flight crews and so on), and financial and commercial businesses kept the company's overall losses in check.

TABLE 1 Aer Lingus Financial Results[1] Years Ending March 31
(millions of Irish pounds)[2]

	1985		1984		1983		1982		1981	
	Revenue	Profit	Revenue	Profit	Revenue	Profit	Revenue	Profit	Revenue	Profit
Air Transport Ancillary Operations	281	.5	270	1.4	244	(2.7)	218	(11.2)	164	(15.9)
Airline Related	110	12.7	82	11.1	66	9.0	62	8.6	47	7.5
Hotel & Leisure	79	11.7	82	7.7	82	6.0	71	7.8	54	7.7
Financial & Commerical	33	5.4	24	4.5	11	3.6	8	2.0	6	1.3
Net Profit After Head Office Expenses, Interest, Tax[3]	11.6		4.9		(2.5)		(9.2)		(13.6)	

[1] In 1985 the group total assets stood at £285 million. A breakdown of assets employed in each business area was not publicly reported.
[2] Canadian dollars per Irish pound: 1981—1.90; 1982—1.75; 1983—1.54; 1984—1.41; 1985—1.44
[3] The company earned a positive net profit in each of the four years preceding 1981.

A small group of managers under the leadership of Gerry Dempsey were responsible for managing and expanding Aer Lingus's non-airline activities. Denis Hanrahan, second in command, commented:

> We all recognize that the airline business is a cyclical one, and our goal is to create a stable base of earnings which will see the airline safely through the bottom of the cycles. We have been successful so far so we don't know if the government would bail us out if we did make continued heavy losses, and we don't want to have to find out! The mission of our "ancillary activities" is to increase the Group's reported earnings and to strengthen its balance sheet.

The "financial and commercial" results in Table 1 include a data processing firm, an insurance company, a helicopter company, a hospital management firm, a land development company, and a 25% interest in GPA, formerly Guiness Peat Aviation. Many of these firms, with the exception of the hotels, were founded by former Aer Lingus employees. Although most of the companies were performing well, the undoubted star was GPA. A manager explained:

> In 1975 or so, Tony Ryan, our New York station manager, was transferred back to Ireland and asked to lease out a 747 which we did not need for the winter. In looking at the leasing market, he thought he saw a very good business opportunity, and he convinced us and a related British company to each put up 45% of the capital required to start an aircraft leasing company. He kept the remaining 10%. As things have developed, he was certainly right about the opportunity. In the ten intervening years, we have received almost 20 million Irish pounds from that business, and our initial investment was only 2.2 million! We still own 25% of the company, and now have firms like Air Canada and the General Electric Credit Corporation as partners. GPA is one of the Irish success stories of the past decade.

THE MOVE INTO ROBOTICS

In 1983, Denis Hanrahan began an informal search for a new area of investment which could provide healthy financial returns to Aer Lingus for at least the next decade. By January 1984, he had concluded that robotics was an extremely interesting field. Robots had been used in Japan since the 1960s but were not adopted in Europe and the U.S. until the late 1970s. Many analysts expected a robotics boom, with growth rates as high as 30% per annum, as Western firms strove to catch up.

Although robot manufacturing appeared to Denis to be an overcrowded field, he was excited about the possibility of becoming a developer of the ancillary technology and components that were required by firms wanting to install robot-based flexible manufacturing assembly lines. His figures suggested that the market value of ancillary systems was at least equal to the value of the robots themselves. Although the volume of business being done in this new area was impossible to quantify with any degree of precision, it appeared to be growing quickly and offer high margins. There were as yet no major companies in the business. Denis described Aer Lingus's initial entry into the field:

> The first company we looked at was in the UK. We quickly decided that it was too big, too sexy, and considering its size, depended too heavily on a single supplier of robots. One thing you have to watch out for in this business is guys in very classy suits who know more about doing deals and driving for the initial public offering which is going to make them rich than they do about robotics. It turned out that we were right about that company, as it went bankrupt afterwards.
>
> The company we did buy was Airstead Industrial Systems of the UK. This is a very small company, much smaller that ATS, but it has the rights to distribute Seiko robots in England. Seiko, in addition to producing products such as watches and Epson computer printers, is a prominent robot manufacturer and doing very well in some fast growing niches.

After the acquisition of Airstead, Aer Lingus dispatched an analyst to North America to examine six companies that Seiko had identified as the most promising North American robotics systems firms. On August 15, Denis received a telex containing a thumbnail sketch of ATS, indicating that it was the best of the three firms the analyst had seen to date, and was worth a closer look. On August 28, Denis was in Kitchener for his first meeting with Klaus Woerner.

KLAUS WOERNER AND ATS

Born in Germany in 1940, Klaus Woerner emigrated to Canada at age 20 after serving an apprenticeship in the tool and die business. He subsequently worked for a variety of manufacturing firms in Canada but, tired of the "hierarchies and rigidities of large corporations," founded ATS in 1978. The new company was not successful, however, until Klaus turned it away from manufacturing and into systems work. The move into robotics was made in late 1981.

By the summer of 1984 ATS had grown to employ 44 people, including 26 tool makers, 15 hardware and software designers, and three in sales and administration. Denis was encouraged to see that Klaus was a technically oriented hands-on manager whose elegant and creative solutions to systems problems played a major role in the company's success. Klaus, Denis observed, was more at home on the shop floor than talking to accountants, bankers or lawyers. In his summary of their first meeting, Denis made the following points:

1. Woerner was an easy individual to get along with, though I would anticipate that he is used to getting his own way. He is the key decision-maker in the company, although he does solicit the opinions of his senior colleagues.

2. The company currently turns over approximately $3.5 million per year, and expects to double its sales this year on last year, after a number of years of relatively slow growth. Woerner reports a current backlog of $3 million.

3. The major financial problem with the business is that there is a significant working capital requirement. I have heard a rule of thumb that suggests 40% of turnover is required in this business, but Klaus thought that was far too high. The practical problem is that the final payment of 30% of systems costs tends to be delayed for several months after completion of the work while fine tuning is being performed.

4. Woerner recently came very close to selling ATS to Berton Industries,[1] a major Canadian corporation in the automotive components business. One hundred percent of ATS was to be acquired and, depending on results, it would have been valued at $3–4 million. Woerner got very concerned, however, at what he perceived to be the inordinate length of time being taken in detailed negotiations, and at the aggressive attitude of the other party's attorneys. In addition, Berton would not give him any assurances about future investment in ATS, and apparently Woerner learned that plans had been made to move ATS to another location without any consultation with him. When the president of Berton then ignored Woerner's request that a number of written commitments be made within one week, the deal was off.

5. Woerner's proposal was that Aer Lingus would take 50% of the company for an undetermined amount, 50% of which would be left in the company, and that he would take 50% out. I indicated to him that 50% would probably be the minimum share that we would require, and it could be that we would want considerably more. However, any deal that we would do would be structured in such a way that he and his key people would be committed to staying with the company. He had no difficulty with this point, and conceded that he was not wedded to the 50-50 formula, which was clearly an ideal going-in position from his point of view.

6. On balance, I found ATS to be very impressive. Though operating in cramped facilities, it does appear to have a real technical depth, and undoubtedly has an established customer base. The company appears to be an appropriate size to take over since it is neither so small as to be extraordinarily risky nor so big as to be extraordinarily expensive.

The meeting ended with the two men agreeing to continue discussions, and to try to reach a gentlemen's agreement reasonably quickly rather than getting bogged down in protracted technical or legal discussions. Woerner promised to send some financial information as soon as he could get it together, although he warned that his business plan should not be taken too literally as "these things are more exercises than necessarily forecasts of reality."

SUBSEQUENT MEETINGS

Over the next six months, Denis Hanrahan held a number of meetings with Klaus Woerner, bringing with him on occasion Gerry Dempsey and Larry Stanley, two of Aer Lingus's ancillary business managers. Both men subsequently supported Denis's view that ATS would be a good acquisition. This positive feedback was also strengthened by comments from Seiko's

---

[1] Disguised name.

North American sales manager, who stated that in ten years ATS would be "one of the top three robot systems integrator firms in North America" if it grew to its potential. The meetings with Klaus also yielded more information about his expectations and the operations of ATS. The following excerpts are taken from Denis Hanrahan's notes and comments on various meetings, all of which were held in either Kitchener or Toronto.

Meeting of November 6

Present: G.P. Dempsey, Denis Hanrahan, Klaus Woerner, and Peter Jones,[2] who was Klaus Woerner's personal financial advisor and company accountant.

1. Woerner outlined his expectations for growth of the automation and robotics industry and for ATS. It seems clear that they have not done very much forward planning. Woerner quoted Laura Conigliaro of Prudential-Bache as suggesting growth from $250 million in 1984 to $1 billion by 1987, but these figures were not very convincing since they related to the total industry rather than to the sub-segment in which ATS is involved.

2. Woerner stated that he expected ATS revenues to total $4 million for the year ending September 1984, $6 million for 1985 (rather than the $5 million he had earlier been projecting), and to reach $10 million in three years' time. He believed that growth to $10 million could be financed through a combination of retained earnings and bank debt.

3. Northern Telecom, a major Canadian multinational firm, apparently accounts for approximately 40% of ATS revenues. Woerner indicated that this proportion would fall to one-third in 1985 due to the growth of ATS. He stated strongly that in spite of the company's high dependence on Northern Telecom he could, if necessary, survive a total loss of Northern's business by falling back on traditional non flexible production line work ("hard" automation). However, he expressed the view that Northern Telecom could not break the relationship with him since they were dependent on ATS for maintenance and software updates.

4. There was an extensive discussion on the subject of control. Woerner's recent negotiations with Berton have left him very uneasy about the behaviour of large corporations, and he again expressed his strong preference for a 50-50 partnership. Dempsey responded that our whole approach to subsidiares was to work in partnership with the management of them, and that this approach was not altered whether the shareholding was 2%, 50%, or 99%. Woerner appeared to implicitly accept that we might go to 75% or higher of the equity as long as we were concerned only with issues such as overall earnings and growth rather than the detailed operating practices involved. Dempsey suggested that Woerner should write to us in simple nonlegal terms outlining those issues upon which he believed he would require assurance from us. Woerner accepted this suggestion.

5. Woerner also expressed concern that his was a small company in danger of being "trampled on" by Aer Lingus. While he was happy enough with the people he currently knew in Aer Lingus, he felt that these individuals could change and he could thus find himself exposed to changes of policy or personality. Dempsey responded that we could not fully reassure him on this issue. We now had a wide range of relationships with subsidiaries over a long period of time; this had not occurred historically, and he saw no reason why it should happen in the future.

---

[2] Disguised name.

6. There were no specific discussions on the matter of price. Dempsey stated on a number of occasions that it was purposeless to discuss price until the financials were available and had been reviewed. Woerner concurred.

7. The meeting ended on a positive and progressive note. It was agreed that we would appoint Peat Marwick to review the affairs of ATS, and they would contact Jones as necessary. Also Jones would shortly produce a three-year forecast for ATS.

Meeting of January 10

The next meeting between Klaus and Denis included Bill Harcourt[3] of Peat Marwick Mitchell. During this meeting the ATS financial statements and projections (Exhibits 1 and 2) were given to Denis. These were to have been sent to Ireland several weeks earlier.

Denis learned during this meeting that Klaus had not written the promised letter concerning his specific issues of concern because he preferred to discuss them face to face. Further discussion ensued during which Klaus reiterated his general unease at the prospect of being controlled, and repeated his desire for a 50-50 deal. While still not raising any specific concerns, Klaus repeatedly referred to the Berton deal and how lucky he was to have avoided it. Denis commented after the meeting:

> All of this was territory that we had covered several times previously with him, and we essentially just covered it again. It was clear that, as the discussion progressed, Klaus began to get more comfortable, and his fears began to recede. I have no doubt that after I depart from Canada he begins to get uneasy again at the unknown. He reiterated that he was quite comfortable working with Mr. Dempsey or myself, but that the could naturally have no assurance that we would be around forever.
>
> In the earlier part of the meeting when Klaus was appearing very reluctant, Bill Harcourt asked him directly if he, in fact, wanted to sell ATS. Klaus replied that he didn't really want to—he had devoted all of his time in the last few years in building up the company, and wished to continue to do so in the future—but because ATS would not be producing large amounts of cash in the short term he had no choice. He believes that ATS can and must grow very rapidly to forestall the competition—the opportunities are there, and if ATS does not take advantage of them, someone else will. In this vein he mentioned that he had just revised his estimate of the current year's sales from $6 million to $9 million.
>
> The other reason that Klaus feels that he has to sell ATS is that important customers like Northern Telecom are nervous of becoming too dependent on him, as long as he does not have a major corporate backer. Klaus told us in the meeting that Northern had in fact deliberately cut back their orders to him for this reason, and we independently checked that this was indeed the case.

The meeting ended on a very friendly note with Denis again encouraging Klaus to make up a list of his specific concerns so that they could be addressed, and Klaus inviting Bill Harcourt to visit the ATS plant before the next meeting so that he could develop a better understanding of what they were doing.

Meetings of January 24 and February 20

The meetings of January 24 and February 20 were devoted to discussions of a deal whereby Aer Lingus would acquire 75% of ATS' stock, with Klaus Woerner holding the remaining

---

[3] Disguised name.

25%. At the January 24 meeting, Klaus appeared to accept the idea that he would sell the 75% of the company, but apparently as a result of his earlier negotiations with Berton, was adamant that ATS was worth at least $6 million. In the February 20th meeting, Denis finally agreed that ATS could be worth $6 million if the company met Klaus's new projections for it, but at that moment it was not. As a consequence, Denis proposed that the amount paid to Klaus should depend on the company's performance in 1985 and 1986. The details, spelled out in a letter from Denis to Klaus following the February meeting, were as follows:

1. We propose that a valuation be established for ATS as of September 30, 1986. This valuation will be calculated by taking 3.5 times the pretax income for the fiscal year ended September 30, 1985, and adding to it 3.5 times the incremental pretax income earned in the fiscal year ending September, 1986. By incremental income here, I mean the excess of pretax income in fiscal 1986 over that earned in fiscal 1985.

2. In determining pretax income, research and development costs shall be charged at the rate contained in your financial projections or at a higher rate if so incurred. Profit sharing to employees shall be charged at 10% of pretax income before profit sharing or such higher rate as may be incurred. In addition, we would require the company to maintain a key-man insurance policy on yourself in the amount of $5 000 000, and the cost of such coverage would be borne as a charge before striking pretax income.

3. On the basis of the pretax income figures outlined above, the company would have a total value of $6 835 000 as of September 30, 1986.

4. Under the above formula, the maximum value that we would be prepared to put on ATS would be $7 000 000, even if the results are better than projected.

5. It is our view that the company is in need of significant additional funds to allow it to develop to the sales and income levels in your projections. Accordingly, we are willing to inject $2 000 000 into ATS for agreed working capital and investment use in the form of a secured debt with a 10% interest rate. It would be our intention to make available $750 000 at time of closing, $750 000 at time of completion of the 1985 audit, and the remaining $500 000 as needed by the company on an agreed basis during 1986.

6. It would be our intention that this loan would be used to purchase treasury stock from ATS at the end of 1986, using the valuation for the company as established by the formula outlined above. In other words, if the company was valued at $6 835 000, the $2 000 000 loan would convert to give us 22.6% of the enlarged equity in the company. The attraction of this arrangement from your point of view is that it provides you with the money now to grow, but that the shares are ultimately purchased in ATS at the valuation achieved in 1986 rather than at a current valuation. Depending upon the ultimate valuation of the company, the percentage of its enlarged equity that would be bought by the $2 000 000 referred to above would vary. It would then be our intention to purchase directly from you existing shares held by you in ATS such as would give us 75% of the then enlarged equity of the company. In the example quoted above, we would need to purchase 67% of your shareholding to give us a total of 75% of the enlarged equity. Using the value above, this would cost $4 600 000. In other words, what you would receive would be $4 600 000 in cash plus 25% interest in the $2 000 000 injected by us: for a total of $5 100 000, which is 75% of $6 835 000.

7. We propose that you would be paid for these shares as follows: on closing, $500 000; in March 1986 and March 1987, further payments of $500 000; in March 1988 and March 1989, further payments of $1 000 000 each; the balance, payable on March 1990. To the degree that the final value of the company is larger or smaller than the $6 835 000 figure, the above payments would be prorated.

MOVING FORWARD

On March 16, Bill Harcourt phoned Denis to report that the had met with Klaus, subsequent to the February 22 meeting. Denis recalled the discussion:

> Apparently Klaus was initially very unhappy with the limit of $7 million that we put on the company, although he is now willing to live with it, and in fact has become very positive about doing a deal with Aer Lingus. He appears to have overcome his hesitance and concern at another party becoming the majority shareholder of ATS. This may be due to the fact that he has taken advice from a friend name Bob Tivey, who is retired president of Monarch Canada.[4] Some minor improvements are required, however.
>
> One of these is that Klaus wants us to increase the $500 000 coming to him on closing so that he can pay employee bonuses—these will come out of his own pocket—and have more for himself. He also wants us to pay interest on the portion of the purchase price which remains unpaid until the earn-out is completed. Finally, he would like a personal contract which will last five years, and include a good salary, plus a bonus that is 2% of pretax earnings, and a car.
>
> Other news included the fact that Klaus is in the process of hiring a financial person, and is considering a second-year registered industrial accountancy student. Bill suggested that he discuss this matter in some detail with us, as it might be advisable to opt for a more high-powered person. Bill also told me that Klaus was facing an immediate decision with respect to new premises for ATS—the major question being whether the company should rent or buy. Purchase cost will be close to $1 million.

Shortly after his phone call, Denis received a letter from Klaus, which began, "I wish to advise you that as I am prepared to accept the proposal as outlined ... subject to the following changes." As expected, the most important of the requested changes were an increased initial payment, the payment of interest on the unpaid portion of the purchase price, and a five-year employment contract.

After some negotiation, Aer Lingus agreed to increase its initial payment to allow Klaus to pay employee bonuses, and to increase the initial funds going to his own pocket by approximately 50%, which was less than he had requested, but was deemed satisfactory.

In early April, Klaus travelled to Ireland for a meeting with the Chief Executive of Aer Lingus, and later that month the Aer Lingus board approved the purchase of a 75% shareholding of ATS on the terms which had been agreed with Klaus.

At the end of April, Denis was once again in Kitchener, where he and Klaus held a most amicable meeting. Denis learned that Klaus and Bob Tivey had prepared a new business plan which they had used to obtain an increase in the ATS credit line. Also, Klaus had decided to proceed with the acquisition, his only objection being that eight board meetings a year was too many. Denis concluded his notes on the meeting with the following:

> We discussed at length the need for ATS management to develop credibility with me, and for me to develop credibility on ATS subjects in Dublin, which he seemed to accept. All in all, the discussions were satisfactory and straightforward, and have put to rest a significant number of my fears concerning Mr. Woerner's independence and his unwillingness to accommodate the requirements of a major corporate shareholder. In my view, he will accept direction, provided that the direction is fast-paced and is seen by him as being responsive to ATS's needs.

---

[4] Disguised name.

Due to some apparent foot-dragging on the part of Klaus's lawyers and intervening vacations, it was July before Denis arrived in Kitchener to review the drafts of the sale contracts, and bring the deal to a conclusion.

THE MEETING OF JULY 16

Klaus attended this meeting with Ron Jutras, his new financial controller, who had been hired without consultation with Aer Lingus, and Bob Tivey, who was acting as a consultant to Klaus. Denis recalled the meeting as follows:

They opened the meeting by tabling a number of requirements which they said were critical to the deal going ahead. These were:

1. A reluctance to hand over control to us before the valuation date of September 1986.
2. A five-year guaranteed contract for Klaus, with a ten-year period before we can force him out of share ownership.
3. A degree of protection against the possibility that one off costs may depress 1986 earnings—specifically a *minimum* buyout price of $6 million!

I was very distressed to find such a total about-face on something that we had agreed three months earlier, and when faced with this, Klaus acknowledged that he was changing his mind, but said that he could not afford the possibility of one bad year depressing his buyout price. As for the contract length, Klaus was very emotional when the possibility of anything shorter than a five-year contract was raised.

The question facing me as I sat in that meeting was how to react. Was it time to give up on this long and apparently fruitless process, or should I continue—and if so, how?

EXHIBIT 1   ATS Financial Statements (C$000)

	1980	1981	1982	1983	1984
Sales	332	765	1 210	1 753	4 168
Cost of Sales	187	491	902	1 450	3 197
Gross Margin	145	274	308	303	971
Overheads	58	127	188	243	451
Operating Profit	87	147	120	60	520
Interest	2	10	20	26	71
Tax	11	22	4	0	18
Net Profit	74	115	96	34	431

Balance Sheets

	1980	1981	1982	1983	1984
Fixed Assets	106	211	308	390	517
Current Assets	113	282	384	457	1 300
Current Liabilities	(35)	(129)	(209)	(252)	(390)
Working Capital	78	153	175	205	910
	184	364	483	595	1 427

Funded by:

	1980	1981	1982	1983	1984
Share Capital	1	6	5	3	3
Revenue Reserves	79	114	177	(160)	164
Shareholder's Funds	80	120	182	(157)	167
Loan Capital	104	244	301	752	1 260
	184	364	483	595	1 427

EXHIBIT 2 Projected ATS Financial Statements* (C$000)

		1985	1986	1987	1988
Sales		8 000	11 000	14 000	17 000
Cost of Sales		5 920	8 360	10 920	13 260
Gross Margin		2 080	2 640	3 080	3 740
Overheads		1 040	1 430	1 750	2 210
Operating Profit		1 040	1 210	1 330	1 530
Interest		70	120	200	300
Tax		427	480	497	541
Net Profit		543	610	633	689
Dividends (Projected)		0	0	250	300

Projected Balance Sheets	1984	1985	1986	1987	1988
Fixed Assets	517	680	1 030	1 310	1 860
Development				1 000	1 000
Current Assets	1 300	2 417	4 904	5 740	6 580
Current Liabilities	(390)	(760)	(1 720)	(1 886)	(2 260)
Working Capital	910	1 657	3 184	3 854	4 320
	1 427	2 337	4 214	6 164	7 180

Funded by:					
Share Capital	3	750	2 000	2 300	2 700
Revenue Reserves	164	707	1 317	1 701	2 090
Shareholder's Funds	167	1 457	3 317	4 001	3 790
Loan Capital	1 260	880	897	2 163	3 390
	1 427	2 337	4 214	6 164	7 180

* These projections were prepared by Klaus Woerner and Peter Jones.

EXHIBIT 3   Revised ATS Income Projections* (C$000)

	1985	1986	1987	1988
Sales	8 000	14 000	20 000	30 000
Gross Margin	2 080	3 360	4 400	6 000
	(26%)	(24%)	(22%)	(20%)
General & Admin.	862	1 190	1 578	2 159
Income	1 218	2 170	2 822	3 841
Profit Sharing	120	217	282	384
Pretax Income	1 098	1 953	2 540	3 457
Tax at 45%	494	879	1 143	1 556
After Tax Income	604	1 074	1 397	1 901

* These revisions were dated February 20, 1985. They were prepared by Klaus Woerner, working with Bill Harcourt.

VISIONING AT XEROX CANADA

Mary M. Crossan and Nick Bontis

CASE

17

On June 15, 1994, Diane McGarry, Chairman, CEO and President of Xerox Canada, asked Bryan Smith, a consultant working for the company, if he would join her outside the conference room for a brief tête-à-tête. They had been meeting with her leadership team[1] since 8:00 A.M. to craft the organization's new vision statement.

It was now past 11:30 A.M. and the "visioning" session was scheduled to end at noon. During the previous three and a half hours, some progress had been made, but Smith felt that more time would be needed to give the decision its due process. Smith suggested that they extend the allotted time into the afternoon or postpone the session. However, McGarry was hesitant to delay the final selection of the vision statement because it was very important to her. As they both returned to the conference room, McGarry contemplated her next move.

XEROX CORP.

Xerox Corp. was a global player in the document processing market. Its activities encompassed the designing, manufacturing and servicing of a complete range of document process-

---

[1] Consisting of 23 senior managers (many of which were McGarry's direct reports).

Mary M. Crossan and Nick Bontis of the Western Business School prepared this case. Copyright © 1995, The University of Western Ontario. This material is not covered under authorization from CanCopy or any reproduction rights organization. Any form of reproduction, storage or transmittal of this material is prohibited without written permission from Western Business School, The University of Western Ontario, London, Canada N6A 3K7

ing products. Xerox copiers, duplicators, electronic printers, optical scanners, facsimile machines, networks, multifunction publishing machines and related software and supplies were marketed in more than 130 countries.

Xerox Corp. had won many accolades in the United States, Australia, Belgium, Brazil, Canada, Colombia, France, Hong Kong, India, Ireland, Japan, Mexico, the Netherlands and the United Kingdom, reflecting its prestigious standing in the business world. In 1980, Fuji Xerox won the Deming Prize, Japan's highest quality award. The major U.S. award was the Malcolm Baldrige National Quality Award, which Xerox Business Products and Systems won in 1989. Then in 1992, Rank Xerox won the first European Quality Award. The pursuit of these awards often incited organizations to participate in the visioning process. Vision statements were a critical element in the evaluation process.

XEROX CANADA

Although Xerox Corp. controlled its Canadian subsidiary from a regulatory perspective, it often allowed the smaller organization enough latitude to pursue its own initiatives (this included developing its own vision statement). The parent considered its Canadian subsidiary as a laboratory for strategic experiments. With this unofficial mandate, the Canadian operation had developed a solid reputation for the implementation of various employee-inspired programs. Xerox Canada was also known for its publicly displayed corporate ideals. A senior manager described the company's situation this way:

> Our company is very well known and respected in the business community for integrating its various "corporate concepts."[2] In fact, CEOs of other large multinational enterprises often marvel at the way we are able to harmonize our numerous strategic initiatives into a coordinated effort. They often sit in our boardroom and just admire the programs we proudly display on our walls. Many of these strategic initiatives are sponsored by our parent company in Stamford, Connecticut, while others are independently developed by our own employees here in Canada.

One of the main themes in Xerox Canada's philosophy deals with "satisfied customers." To further improve service to its customers, Xerox Canada announced an organizational restructuring that would create special customer business units in order to maintain closer ties with the marketplace. This restructuring was McGarry's responsibility.

McGarry's Arrival in Canada

McGarry was promoted to the top position in Canada in October 1993 because she was recognized as a team player who prided herself on open communication. Her leadership skills and risk-taking attitude were exactly what Xerox Canada needed during this restructuring period. In the first 60 days in her new position, she visited 14 cities across Canada and talked to thousands of employees, customers, and suppliers in order to "get to know Canada." She came back from this trip with a better understanding of the company, the domestic market, Canada's economy and its government. McGarry's most important mandate since her arrival in late 1993 was to bring this restructured design to life and make it work in Canada.

---

[2] Including Xerox's signature, philosophy, priorities, cultural dimensions (see Exhibit 1).

While the restructuring took place, Xerox Canada employees continued to develop and support innovative strategic initiatives. Many of these programs, including the new employee evaluation system, went on to become worldwide initiatives that eventually helped shape the culture and the values of the whole organization.

Employee-Inspired Initiatives

A commitment to community involvement was basic to the company's business philosophy. Xerox Canada contributed $1.3 million in 1994 to charities and nonprofit organizations across Canada. About 65% of the contributions were focused on projects which support Information Technology Literacy which includes the Xerox Aboriginal Scholarships program for aboriginal students studying programs which could lead to a career in information technology. The remaining funds were focused on community programs such as the United Way, matching employee gifts to post-secondary institutions, and the Xerox Community Involvement Program (XCIP). The XCIP offered financial support to community organizations in which employees volunteer on a regular basis.

In addition to its sense of community involvement, Xerox Canada shared the public's concern about the environment and integrated that concern into its business activities. The company was dedicated to protecting the environment as a responsible corporate citizen. In its marketing materials, Xerox described itself as setting standards for its products that went beyond many government requirements for health, safety and environmental protection in the countries in which it operated. The company was proud to communicate its commitment to the philosophy of sustainable development, which meant meeting the needs of the present without compromising the needs of future generations.

Another very successful program that symbolized the progressive culture of the organization was a new collaborative, performance-feedback process: COMIT (Communication of Objectives and Measurements and ensuring our success through Inspection and Teamwork). COMIT's objective was to extend beyond Xerox Canada's standard business results by incorporating its five key priorities with eight new cultural dimensions (see Exhibit 1 for details). Senior management hoped the union of these 13 elements would allow the COMIT process to affect the behaviours of the employees and to create a more empowered and dynamic organizational culture. Although Xerox Canada could be criticized for its overzealous pursuit of these and other programs, which went above and beyond its operational duties, the company never ignored its pledge of boundless service to its customers. In the 1994 Annual Report, Diane McGarry stated:

> We focus on what will make a difference for our customers—anticipating their needs, satisfying and exceeding all their expectations, and creating relationships that will serve them into the next century.

During the restructuring period, McGarry also familiarized herself with the most recently developed employee-inspired initiatives to get a better sense of what important issues interested the employees of Xerox Canada. The following describes three more employee-inspired programs developed at Xerox Canada:

> *Xerox chez moi*—in this work-from-home or work-from-anywhere program, nearly 750 staff "telecommuted" as part of a work-at-home experiment that began company-wide in March

1994. Reaction so far was favourable. Employees claimed that they got double and triple the work done without normal office interruptions.

Keeping customers forever—the objective of this program was to get customers and keep them forever. The advent of CBUs provided for a system that allowed service employees to build loyal and long-term relationships in which customers felt satisfied.

Xerox flexplace—ninety percent of surveyed employees said that being able to balance the needs of both family life and the needs of the business was a key factor in the satisfaction of an employee. This program offered a wide range of flexible work arrangements, including the opportunity for men to nurture new babies while on a parental leave.

As the restructuring continued and new initiatives were launched, the parent company watched over McGarry closely. This prompted her to re-examine not only her contribution to the organization, but the contribution of every other employee as well. The genesis of the visioning process had emerged. Senior management felt that a new vision statement would convey the ideals of the corporation, encompass present attitudes, and continue to align employees in their operational activities and in their innovative efforts.

THE VISIONING PROCESS

By mid-1994, Diane McGarry's leadership transition into Xerox Canada was running smoothly. Business performance was favourable (see Exhibit 2) and customers and employees alike were supporting new developments in the organization. Furthermore, corporate insiders predicted that Xerox Canada was slowly becoming the jewel of the Xerox Corp. empire worldwide.

As Xerox Canada moved comfortably into the latter half of the 1990s, McGarry believed that a vision statement for the company should be developed to help integrate all of the company's diverse activities. Previous vision statements for Xerox Canada were not widely known throughout the organization and had been practically forgotten by most employees since McGarry's arrival in Canada. Although McGarry recognized that Xerox Canada already had several important "corporate concepts" such as the signature (THE DOCUMENT COMPANY), the philosophy, five priorities and eight cultural dimensions (see Exhibit 1), she believed that it was imperative to synthesize a vision statement for the company that would coordinate all of the concepts, initiatives and activities of the organization. This was considered a critical exercise early in her tenure and one she felt would prove to be highly insightful.

McGarry invited her leadership team to Niagara-on-the-Lake for a two-day corporate retreat. The first scheduled item on the program was a four-hour session to create the new vision statement. McGarry also brought in a management consultant, Bryan Smith, who had prior experience with visioning with several other large corporate clients.[3] Smith had also done some prior consulting with Xerox Canada and was, therefore, somewhat familiar with the company's history.

Several weeks prior to the meeting, McGarry asked each team member to review the company's earlier vision statements. Approximately 90% of the team members had been through a

---

[3] In fact, he had published an article on the topic: Bryan Smith, "Vision: A Time to Take Stock," *Business Quarterly* (Autumn 1989), pp. 80–84.

visioning process at least once in their careers. The last time any of the participants had been through this process was during David McCamus' tenure in the early 1990s. Bryan Smith also played a significant role during McCamus' tenure and had earned a solid reputation for himself amongst the senior managers by running several successful workshops and joint projects. Current members of Xerox Canada's leadership team were already familiar with Smith's work and respected his contributions. McCamus' team had developed the following vision statement during the early 1990s:

> Our raison d'être is to create a dynamic growth oriented business by providing superior customer satisfaction through quality products and innovative services supported by an inspired team of skilled individuals.

When Richard Barton took over the leadership position from McCamus in 1991, he personally developed a vision statement which was subsequently confirmed by his management team at a meeting in August 1991. This statement was printed on the 1992 COMIT documents for all employees:

> We will know we have reached the desired state of Xerox when The Document Company is the leader in providing Document services that enhance business productivity.

Now that McGarry was in charge, she felt that it was necessary not only to create a new vision statement, but to seek input from her direct reports and their subordinates. She wanted this to be a team effort. The first task she had her team accomplish was to seek feedback from Xerox Canada's largest customers on what their needs were. The following describes some of the comments received from customers:

- we want someone with skill, expertise, resources and the creativity that is needed to take cost out of operations, and add speed and quality;
- we want someone to identify what our needs are, recommend solutions, and work every step of the way to ensure success;
- we need software that will allow us to access information and respond far more quickly than we could in a paper-based environment.

As the visioning session approached, McGarry's team reflected on the organization's recent accomplishments and carefully considered the values that motivated the employees to work each and every day. At the start of the visioning session, the team members collectively selected the criteria that they would use to help guide the process. The three chosen criteria ensured that the statement would be: (1) clear; (2) motivating; and (3) inspiring. The brainstorming session commenced once the criteria were set. Each participant was asked to write down three words on a flip chart to help spark the brainstorming process. At this point, the tone of the session was very positive and there was a tremendous amount of energy and excitement in the conference room. Soon after, the participants were asked to create and write down one vision statement that included their three key words.

Eventually, twenty-four individual statements (one from each member of the leadership team plus McGarry) were posted around the room on flip charts. Participants were asked to read out their own statements twice while emphasizing the key words. The whole group cheered after each participant was finished. Smith then facilitated the session by grouping the statements together and removing duplication.

JUNE 15, 1994, 11:32 A.M.

McGarry had allotted four hours for the whole visioning process. Each of the participants had brainstormed ideas all morning and it was becoming increasingly difficult to select the "one statement." After three and a half hours, they had only narrowed it down to about half a dozen possibilities (see Exhibit 3 for the final statements). Many participants became discouraged as time elapsed and the tone of the session turned 180 degrees as their energy drained away. Although the morning had started off with a bang, now there were concerns that the rest of the two-day retreat would be consumed by this visioning process. Other planned activities risked being cancelled.

By 11:32 A.M., McGarry was becoming concerned with the team's progress. She asked Smith to join her outside the conference room for a brief private meeting. She told Smith that she was hesitant to extend the session past noon because she realized that continued discussion of the vision statement would preclude work on other scheduled initiatives. However, she recognized that the visioning process deserved a dedicated commitment by the whole group and a concerted amount of time and effort. Furthermore, Smith suggested that it was going to be very difficult to assimilate all the agreed-upon suggestions thus far into one coherent statement within the next half hour. On the other hand, Smith also knew that time pressure could facilitate the creative process. McGarry returned to the conference room with Smith and spoke to her team.

EXHIBIT 1   Xerox Canada's Priorities, Philosophy and Cultural Dimensions

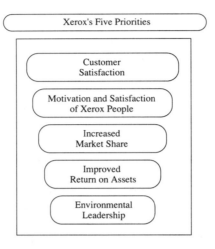

Xerox's Five Priorities

Customer Satisfaction

Motivation and Satisfaction of Xerox People

Increased Market Share

Improved Return on Assets

Environmental Leadership

XEROX'S PHILOSOPHY IS STATED AS: "We succeed through satisfied customers. We aspire to deliver quality and excellence in all we do. We require premium return on assets. We use technology to develop product leadership. We value our employees. We behave responsibly as a corporate citizen."

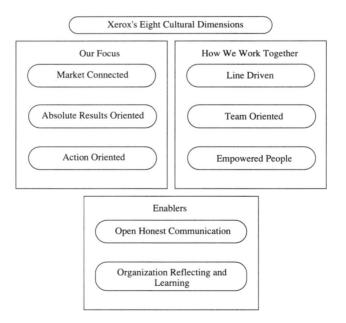

Xerox's Eight Cultural Dimensions

Our Focus

Market Connected

Absolute Results Oriented

Action Oriented

How We Work Together

Line Driven

Team Oriented

Empowered People

Enablers

Open Honest Communication

Organization Reflecting and Learning

EXHIBIT 2   **Historical Business Performance** ($ millions)

Operational Highlights	1994	1993	1992	1991	1990
Revenues: Sales	767.1	722.3	656.7	651.1	641.9
Revenues: Service and Rental	302.9	310.3	307.1	281.2	274.3
Revenues: Finance	101.7	112.1	115.5	119.0	122.8
Total Revenues	1 171.7	1 144.7	1 079.3	1 051.3	1 039.0
Net Earnings	88.8	25.8	61.1	39.5	35.7
Total Assets	1 601.3	1 706.8	1 717.5	1 686.9	1 904.8
Shareholder's Equity	670.7	676.3	610.9	578.0	569.3
Cash Flow from Operations	182.3	95.1	35.4	317.4	139.1
Number of Employees	4 315	4 775	4 802	5 017	5 059
Return on Equity	13.4%	3.9%	10.4%	6.8%	6.4%

SOURCE: Company reports.

Xerox Canada Monthly Stock Close

Note: Monthly close stock prices of XXC.B on the TSE.
SOURCE: Casewriter's illustration (data taken from Bloomberg).

EXHIBIT 3 Final Remaining Vision Statements

Fast, focused and fun.

Providing personal and professional
development while exceeding
our customers' expectations.

To provide our customers with
innovative products and services
that fully satisfy their needs.

To boldly go where no
company has gone before.

To maintain 15% growth
and 20% return on equity.

Employee energy and quality work
keeps customers for life.

Xerox, a market-driven,
customer-focused company.

FIFTH COLUMN (A)

Christopher K. Bart and Kate Button

CASE 18

The plane touched down at Bombay airport precisely on time. Olivia Jones made her way through the usual immigration bureaucracy with little irritation and was finally ushered into a waiting limousine, complete with uniformed chauffeur. Her excitement at being in India for the first time was insurmountable. As she cruised the dark city streets she asked her chauffeur why so few cars had their headlights on at night-time. She was told this was because most drivers believe that headlights use too much petrol! Finally, she arrived at her hotel, a black marble monolith, grandiose and decadent in its splendor, towering above the bay.

The goal of her four-day trip was to sample and select swatches of woven cotton from the mills in and around Bombay to be used in the following season's youthwear collection of shirts, trousers and underwear. She was thus treated with the utmost reverence. Her hosts were invariably Indian factory owners, or British agents for Indian mills. For three days she was ferried from one air-conditioned office to another, sipping iced tea or chilled lemonade, poring over leather bound swatch catalogues which featured every type of stripe and design possible. On the fourth day, Jones made a request which she knew would cause some anxiety in the camp. "I want to see a factory," she declared.

After great consultation and several attempts at dissuasion, she was once again ushered in a limousine and driven through a part of the city she had not previously seen. Gradually, the hotel and the western shops dissolved into the background and Jones entered downtown Bombay. All around was a sprawling shantytown, constructed from sheets of corrugated iron and panels of cardboard boxes. Dust flew in spirals everywhere among the dirt roads and open drains. The car crawled along the unsealed roads behind carts hauled by man and beast alike, laden to overflowing with straw or city refuse—the treasure of the ghetto. Several times she was forced to halt and wait while a lumbering white bull passed across the road before her.

Finally, in the very heart of the ghetto, the car came to a stop. "Are you sure you want to do this?" asked her host. Determined not to be faint hearted, Jones got out of the car.

An unlikely sight indeed! White skinned, blue eyed and blonde, complete with a city suit, stilettoes and a briefcase. It was hardly surprising that the inhabitants of the area found her an interesting and amusing subject, as she picked her way along the dusty street and stepped gingerly over the open sewers.

Her host led her down an alley, between the shacks and open doors and inky black interiors. Some shelters, Jones was told, were restaurants, where at lunch time the townspeople would gather on the rush mat floors and eat rice together. In the doorway of one shack there was a table which served as a counter, laden with ancient cans of baked beans, sardines and rusted tins of fluorescent green mushy peas. The eyes of the young man behind the counter were smiling and proud as he beckoned her forward to view his wares.

Jones turned another corner to find an old man, clad in a waist cloth, sitting in a large tin bucket in the middle of the street. He had an empty tin can in his hand with which he poured water from the bucket over his head and shoulders. Beside him two little girls played in brilliant white nylon dresses, strewn with ribbons and lace. They posed for her with smiling faces, delighted at having their photograph taken in their best frocks. The men and women moved around her with great dignity and grace.

Finally her host led her up a precarious wooden ladder to a floor above the street. At the top Jones was warned not to stand straight as the ceiling was just five feet high. There, in a room not 20 feet by 40 feet, 20 men were sitting at treadle sewing machines, bent over yards of white cloth. Between them on the floor were rush mats, some occupied by sleeping workers awaiting their next shift. Jones learned that these men ran a 24-hour rotation—12 hours on and 12 hours off every day for six months of the year. For the remaining six months they would return to their families in the countryside and work the land, planting and building with the money they had earned in the city. The shirts they were working on were for an order she had placed four weeks earlier in London, an order of which she had been particularly proud for the price she had succeeded in negotiating. Jones reflected that this sight was the most humbling experience of her life.

Eventually she left the heat, dust and din of the little shirt factory and returned to her cosseted world in the air-conditioned limousine with seats of black leather.

"What I've experienced today and the role I've played in creating that living hell will stay with me forever," she thought. Later in the day, she asked herself whether the rape of a nation and its people was a necessary sacrifice to enable the British customer to purchase shirts at £12.99 instead of £13.99, and for the company still to make its *mandatory* 56% margin? Was this the result of many years of training as a strong negotiator?

Once Jones returned to the UK she considered her position and the options open to her as a buyer for a large retail chain. Her dilemma was twofold: could ambitious employees afford to exercise a social conscience in their careers; and could career-minded individuals truly make a difference without jeopardizing their own futures?

BUSINESS SCOPE AND COMPETITIVE ADVANTAGE

PART

6

COOPER CANADA LIMITED

Donald H. Thain

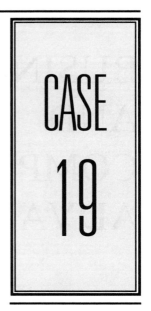

CASE 19

In late 1982 CCM Canada, a manufacturer of bicycles, skates and hockey equipment, was put into receivership and the business put up for sale. While CCM's competitors had noted the company's accumulating problems with some satisfaction and relief, they were now faced with new questions: Who would acquire the assets of CCM? What would be the impact on the competitive structure of the industry?

In the meantime, the CCM receiver was pressing for action. John Cooper, vice chairman of Cooper Canada Ltd., one of the interested competitors, described the situation:

> Our people visited the CCM plant and offices last week and they had no sooner returned than the receiver called wanting to know how soon we could make a bid. He said that speed is critical because he expects other bids at any moment and that the creditors want action since CCM's situation worsens every day. We will have to act fast . . . we have a meeting set for next Monday to make an offer if we want to. It is too bad we are under such time pressure but that's the way this deal is.

Cooper was interested only in the skate and hockey equipment part of the CCM business. Here, some elements of the fit between Cooper and CCM's winter goods business were obvious. Cooper could completely outfit a hockey player except for sweaters and skates. CCM's skate line was still one of the most respected in the business. The value of CCM's competing

Donald H. Thain of the Western Business School prepared this case. Copyright © 1992, The University of Western Ontario. This material is not covered under authorization from CanCopy or any reproduction rights organization. Any form of reproduction, storage or transmittal of this material is prohibited without written permission from Western Business School, The University of Western Ontario, London, Canada N6A 3K7

lines of hockey sticks and protective equipment, however, was less clear. The bicycle line was of no interest but Cooper had made arrangements with another prospective buyer to pick up this part of the CCM operation in a joint bid. The question facing Cooper management, under time pressure, was whether they wished to proceed with their side of a bid and, if so, with what price and conditions?

THE SKATE AND HOCKEY EQUIPMENT INDUSTRY

There were four basic product lines in the industry: skates, protective equipment (e.g., helmets, gloves, pads) sticks and apparel. Cooper management estimated the industry's 1981 value of shipments for these lines were as follows:

	($000)	%
Ice skates	78 000	47
Hockey equipment	31 500	19
Hockey sticks	29 000	18
Apparel	27 000	16

The overall demand for hockey related products had grown slowly in the 1970s and little or no growth was expected in the 1980s. Population trends in the prime hockey-playing age groups were not favourable and participation rates were under pressure. A major problem with participation was the increasing cost of equipping a player: from $100 to $200 for beginners including used equipment and up to $1500 for a professional.

The rapidly changing technology of hockey equipment was one reason for the high cost of equipment. Product innovation was driving toward lighter, safer and more comfortable gear. As a 1982 article in the Maple Leaf Gardens program described it:

> Space-age hockey equipment is speeding up the game and cutting down on injuries. Technological breakthroughs are sending the NHL where it has never gone before—to lighter, cooler, stronger, tighter-fitting one-piece body protection; aluminum or fibreglass and plastic laminated sticks; and zircon-guarded, carbon-bladed skates encased in ballistic and nylon-wrapped boots.
>
> Leaf trainer Danny Lemelin thinks skates have 'changed most dramatically' in the past few years. He points out that most are four ounces lighter because of the plastic blade holder and nylon boot. This space-age equipment has speeded up the game and cut down on injuries. And, it's made the felt and fibre shin, shoulder, elbow and pant pads, one-piece ash sticks and leather tube skates, so popular only a decade ago, obsolete...
>
> The evolution turned revolution in NHL gear is the by-product of by-products. New foams, plastics, nylon and fibreglass, (many invented in Korea during the fifties to keep fighting forces warm and protected) have made things 'lighter and stronger,' says one long time equipment manufacturer. All these new inventions have been developed to conform to the game of hockey...

Canadian brands had established an international reputation for product excellence, and exports of hockey equipment had increased from $20 million in 1971 to $41.5 million in 1980. Skates represented the largest export product. The United States was the largest market, but Scandinavia and western Europe were also strong. Japan and Australia were newly developing markets.

The market shares of the major competitors in the industry by-product line are given in Exhibit 1. The skate business was dominated by three firms, Warrington Industries Ltd. (with three brands—Bauer, Lange and Micron), CCM and Daoust. Cooper was the primary company in hockey equipment. The stick business was shared by half a dozen significant competitors, of which the largest was Sherwood-Drolet. Cooper and Sport Maska were the two most significant competitors in apparel. A brief description of the companies that Cooper considered interested and capable of bidding for CCM is given in Appendix A.

Skates

The demand for skates in Canada had for several years fluctuated between 1 and 1.3 million pairs. There were two basic types of skate boots, sewn and molded. Leather had been the first boot material and was still used in most high quality, high-priced skates. Over 90% of NHL players wore leather skates.

However, in the 1970s molded boots had entered the market and in the low priced market particularly had become competitive with leather booted skates.

Information on the total Canadian hockey-skate market and the shares of major competitors segmented by sewn and molded boots is presented in Exhibit 2. Hockey skates could also be segmented by price point as follows:

Range	Retail Price	1982 Estimated Share (units)
High	More than $200	15%
Medium	$120–$180	20%
Low	Less than $90	65%

Industry observers noted that the high- and low-end market shares were increasing and the medium range decreasing. The breakdown of CCM's total unit skate sales in the high, medium and low price ranges was approximately 60%, 25% and 15% respectively and that of Bauer, the largest brand, was thought to be 20%, 30% and 50% respectively.

Skate blades were another factor in the market. They were available from three sources in Canada. The largest manufacturer, the St. Lawrence company of Montreal, sold mainly to CCM and Daoust. Canpro Ltd., owned by Warrington, sold mainly to Bauer, Micron and Lange. CCM manufactured their own Tuuk blades and sold some to other skate makers. While blade technology had changed significantly in the late 1970s with the introduction of plastic mounts to replace tubes, the major current change was the trend back to carbon steel from the newer stainless steel.

Hockey Equipment

Hockey equipment included all items on the list shown in Table 1, which also shows the range of typical retail prices. Continuous research and development was necessary to ensure that these items provided maximum protection and comfort. Cooper dominated the market with a 69% share.

TABLE 1   Price Ranges for Hockey Equipment

	Typical Retail Price Range	
Item	*Men's*	*Boys'*
Pants	$40–130	$30–60
Gloves	50–140	25–70
Helmet	27–45	27–45
Cooperall	115–125	98
Shin pads	20–75	20–75
Elbow pads	19–50	7–25
Shoulder pads	25–70	14–40

Sticks

The composition of sticks was continually changing. What had started out as a one-piece blade and handle developed into a two-piece solid-wood handle and blade, and later a laminated handle and curved blade with fibreglass reinforcement. The most recent development was an aluminum handle with a replaceable wooden blade. Changes were intended to improve strength and passing and shooting accuracy. Sherwood-Drolet led in this market with a 25% share.

Apparel

Differences in prices of sweaters and socks were due basically to the material used in the product. The most popular sweater materials were polyester and cotton knits because of their strength and lightness. Designs of sweaters were fairly standard, with lettering and cresting done separately. Socks were a standard product with little differentiation. Sport Maska controlled 42% of this market because of its quality product, excellent distribution, and good rapport with dealers.

Distribution

Skates and hockey equipment were sold in a wide range of retail outlets including specialty, independent, department, discount, chain and catalogue stores. Although specific numbers were not available, the split of business between these outlets followed a common retail pattern. The specialty independents and chains dominated in the higher priced items where product knowledge and service were essential. The mass merchandisers were dominant in the lower priced product areas.

In Canada the most common route from manufacturer to retailer was through distributors who used sales agents. Manufacturers wanted agents who would represent their product aggressively, seek out new orders and provide them with market feedback. Usually these agents either were, or had been, actively involved in sports. However, since the agents sold multiple lines, it was difficult to control their activities and level and mix of sales. Most companies used a sales force of 10 to 12 reps to cover most of Canada. A few small companies utilized wholesalers to supplement their sales force.

Retail outlets had experienced little real growth in sales and were finding themselves with increasing inventories. Therefore, retailers started carrying shallower stocks, ordering more frequently and relying on manufacturers or distributors to provide back-up inventories. This trend meant that bargaining power had shifted from the manufacturers to the retailers, who were trying to gain volume discounts and delivery advantages by reducing the number of suppliers.

Promotion

Three types of promotion were used: company and product promotion, media advertising, and trade show participation. Product and image promotion seemed to be the most effective avenue for stimulating sales. Because professional players set industry trends it was important to get popular players to use and endorse products. To recruit these players, professional "detail men" from sports equipment manufacturers were assigned to players to make sure their equipment fit perfectly and that the player was loyal to the brand. It was also important to get as many players as possible wearing the products so that the brand name would enjoy good exposure during televised games. Therefore, the detail men also tried to work through team trainers to supply most of the team with the brand. While some competitors used financial incentives to push a product, Cooper relied on high quality, fast service in fitting and repairs and intensive sales efforts, and was not involved with special deals or endorsement contracts.

Media advertising was primarily confined to the larger firms. Print advertising in the concentrated population areas was the most common approach.

Trade shows significantly influenced retail buyers. Many sales took place at the shows, bookings were made for orders and sales were made on follow-up calls by sales reps. The Canadian Sporting Goods Association organized two shows annually.

COOPER CANADA

In 1946, Jack Cooper left Eaton's to join General Leather Goods Ltd., as its first and, until 1951, only salesperson. Subsequently, Cooper and Cecil Weeks bought out the company's original owner and changed the name to Cooper-Weeks. In 1954, Cooper acquired Cecil Weeks' interest and the company became the exclusive Canadian manufacturer of Buxton Leather goods. In the following years the company grew through internal development and acquisitions to encompass a wide range of leather and sporting good products. In 1970, the company changed its name to Cooper Canada Ltd. and went public. By 1981, revenues were almost $63 million, but Cooper experienced its first loss in years. Cooper management expected a return to profitability in 1982 in spite of a recession and high interest rates. Financial statements for Cooper Canada from 1977 through 1981 are presented in Exhibits 3 and 4.

In 1982 Cooper was engaged in two major lines of business; sporting goods (hockey equipment, apparel, golf bags, baseball gloves, inflated goods, etc.) and leather goods and finishing (wallets, carrying bags, etc.). The relative scale and performance of these businesses is illustrated in Table 2. Cooper also had a significant sales and distribution operation in the United States as indicated by the geographic segmentation of the business in Table 2.

TABLE 2 Cooper Canada Revenues and Profits by Business Segment, 1981 ($000s)

	Industry Segments		
	Sporting Goods	*Leather Goods & Finishing*	*Consolidated*
Revenue	$46 913	$16 076	$62 827
Operating profit	7 434	1 678	8 939
Identifiable assets	28 703	8 001	40 870*

	Geographic Segments		
	Canada	*United States*	*Consolidated*
Revenue	$57 122	$11 321	$62 827
Operating profit	7 823	1 289	8 939
Identifiable assets	30 403	6 301	40 870*

* Includes corporate assets of $4 549.

Management Goals

Jack Cooper, "the chief," and his two sons, John and Don,[1] owned 82% of the company's outstanding common stock. Jack Cooper, who retained voting control, was chairman and chief executive officer and Henry Nolting was president and chief operating officer. John Cooper was vice chairman and deputy chief executive officer. They worked closely together, meeting for frequent discussions daily. The company's organization is shown in Exhibit 5.

Management's immediate concerns were to increase sales and margins; to implement a badly-needed information system; to strengthen control activities in marketing, production, and finance; to reduce short-term bank debt and high-interest expenses; to bring the leather goods division from a loss to a profit; and to iron out troublesome technical and production problems in J.B. Foam, a manufacturer of plastic foam pads and products that had recently been purchased and moved to Cooper's Toronto plant.

Long-term goals called for further development of sporting goods to increase growth and utilize the great strengths of the Cooper name. Additions to the product line were sought

---

[1] Don, who had managed the leather goods division for several years, left the company in 1980 and started a women's sportswear retailing company. He remained a director.

through new product development and/or acquisition. Cooper was also developing more export markets for its sporting goods products.

Performance

Growth had always been foremost among Jack Cooper's goals. Sales had increased continuously since 1969, except in 1975. However, earnings had fluctuated widely over the same period. Earnings dropped in 1979 because of problems in absorbing the purchase of Winnwell Sports. And in 1981, high interest rates, the recession and the disposal of Cooper's unsuccessful production operations in Barbados all hurt the bottom line. However, interim 1982 figures indicated much stronger performance. Although there was little growth in sales, tight inventory and cost controls implemented by Henry Nolting had helped to increase earnings.

Marketing

Cooper products covered a wide range of quality and price points. In hockey equipment, for example, the Cooper line ranged from high end items, used by top professional teams around the world, to medium-low for the beginning player. In baseball equipment and supplies, the quality and price covered a medium-high to low range, appealing to younger and more experienced players, but not professionals.

Hockey equipment was the company's major line and future growth area. To keep its competitive edge, Cooper employed eight people to work full time on product development, with a priority on hockey products. The aim was product leadership, giving athletes the best possible effectiveness and protection. An example of the product development work was Cooper's latest product, the Cooperall, an elasticized body garment which held all the protective pads in place. Cooperalls represented a major innovation and had given Cooper a clear lead on competitors who were currently trying to copy the product.

Distribution of Cooper goods was through its 25-person sales force, which provided the most extensive national coverage of any company in the industry. Sales reps were organized on a geographic basis and were paid on a salary-plus-bonus-minus-expenses system, with no upper limit on bonuses. The total customer base was around 1 600. Because Cooper and CCM had been competitive across a wide product line and Cooper accounts usually sold Bauer skates, significant overlap of Cooper and CCM accounts was not extensive. Sales were distributed equally throughout the East, Ontario, and the West. National coverage by its own sales force gave Cooper an advantage over its competitors, few of whom had such coverage. However, a concern was that 90% of sales were made to 20% of accounts and almost 40% of sales were made to only 20 major customers.

Cliff Gabel, executive vice-president, sporting goods, reported that the sales force was enthusiastic about adding skates to their line. While no one in the Cooper organization had any in-depth experience in the skate business, Mr. Gabel, who was widely known and highly respected in the industry, had maintained a good relationship with several key marketing managers at CCM, some of whom were now retired. He believed that one man in particular, who had an outstanding reputation as perhaps the "best skate man around," would welcome the opportunity to help Cooper take over and manage CCM should the opportunity arise. A respected and now retired manager from the Bauer Company who was a good friend of John Cooper was also thought to be available.

Cooper was the largest national advertiser in the sporting goods industry and had won awards for the quality of its television and print ads. The latest campaign had featured the Cooperall and was aired during the 1982 Stanley Cup telecasts.

Manufacturing and Distribution

Cooper had two manufacturing facilities. A plant in west Toronto did the bulk of the work but an older woodworking plant in Cambridge produced hockey sticks, baseball bats, and canoe paddles. Each facility manufactured hundreds of separate products that involved thousands of parts, requiring control procedures that were complex and numerous.

There was an excess of relatively expensive manufacturing space in the Toronto plant because it was built larger than necessary in 1976. In addition, several products, previously produced in Canada, had since been contracted to offshore manufacturers at lower costs. These manufacturers were primarily in the Orient and did contract work for most of Cooper's competitors. As a result, Cooper's designs were widely and easily copied by the other companies.

In distribution, Cooper chose to act as a "stockhouse," filling as many customer orders as possible on request. Speedy response was a major factor in maintaining customer loyalty. Cooper had a policy of providing a fill rate of 90% in non-peak seasons and 80% in peak seasons. This required substantial working capital, as Cooper's line encompassed over 12 000 stock-keeping units (SKU's). The sporting goods division carried 65% to 80% of the total company inventory. Sporting goods' finished goods inventory reached as high as $18 million each April for deliveries of fall lines. A company objective was to reduce year-end inventories from $23.7 million in 1981 to a more manageable $18 million by the end of 1982. One manager indicated that a recent reduction in the past company policy of producing 120% of forecast sales to a level of 100% of forecast sales would be a major factor in reducing inventory.

Information Systems

A monthly report of sales and gross profit for each SKU and product line was available to each product manager. Quarterly reports provided by cost accounting attempted to determine actual margins realized by each division on each product line. Product managers were also provided with a report on the inventory of each SKU. Product managers were expected to make decisions on pricing and provide input on production levels based on the information provided by these reports.

Product managers were evaluated on the basis of sales, market share, and product margins. The market share was expected to be maintained or increased to achieve sales growth. Product line margins were compared to the company average. However, a major argument of the department and product managers, particularly for leather goods, was that allocated overheads were not fair or accurate. The cost accounting department had struggled with this problem for years.

Financing

A bank operating loan and other term loans were the company's major sources of financing. Banking services for Canada were provided by the Canadian Imperial Bank of Commerce (CIBC) and for Cooper International by Marine Midland Bank of Buffalo, New York. The CIBC provided an operating loan to a maximum line of $16 million at 0.25% above prime and a term loan at 0.75% above prime to be paid in $1 million per year installments in the first five years and $2 million per year thereafter. The bank prime rate was currently 12% but had been as high as 20% in mid-1982.

A combination of high working capital requirements and high interest rates in the early 1980s had prompted Cooper to seek to minimize capital expenditures without adversely affecting manufacturing or productivity. The payback requirement approval of capital expenditures was 2.5 years or better. Typical annual capital expenditures were additions of new dyes and molds and the purchase of manufacturing equipment.

CCM

Incorporated in 1899 as the Canadian Cycle and Motor Company, CCM was Canada's oldest sporting goods manufacturer. Over its history, CCM had been engaged in three separate businesses; bicycles; automobiles; and skates, hockey sticks and equipment.

The skate business was entered in 1905 to even out the seasonal sales and production of bicycles. Originally CCM manufactured high quality blades and riveted them to the best available boots purchased from George Tackaberry of Brandon, Manitoba, to make the skates used by virtually all professional and high-level amateur hockey players. Later, to fill out the line, it purchased lower quality boots from two small shoe companies in Quebec and its hockey equipment from other manufacturers. By 1967, all winter goods were manufactured by the company in what was then a large, modern, efficient plant, in St. Jean, Quebec.

Through industry-leading product innovation, CCM became the world's premier hockey skate manufacturer. For years, customers in Europe equated Canada with hockey and hockey with CCM.

Performance

Starting in 1961 CCM went through an unfortunate series of ownership and management changes. This resulted at various times in serious labour problems, in inadequate attention to marketing and distribution, and in general to a deterioration of the company's reputation for quality and service. Despite sales growth in recent years, profitability had been erratic and in 1982 devastatingly poor, since an operating loss of $4.3 million was expected.

The company's financial position, as at September 30, 1982, was summarized by the interim receiver as follows:

> CCM owes two secured creditors $33 million—the Royal Bank $28 million and the Enterprise Development Board $5 million—while the liquidation value of the company is $11.6 million less than its total debts of $41 million.

Preferred creditors are owed $1.2 million and product liability claims amount to almost $13 million–$12 million of which rests on the resolution of a New York civil suit lodged by a hockey player who suffered an injury while wearing a CCM helmet.

The financial information available to Cooper on CCM's winter goods operation is presented in Exhibits 6 and 7.

Marketing

CCM's world-class strength was in leather skates. Like other leading skate manufacturers, CCM concentrated heavily on supplying skates to professional players because they were the trend setters. Three special pro detail men were employed to sell and service these players, who were often given custom-fitted skates free of charge.

Up to the mid-seventies, when it began to slide, CCM's share of the Canadian and world-wide hockey skate markets had been approximately 60%, 30% and 20% of the high, medium and low priced markets respectively. Because of its domination of the top end of the market, "Supertack," its long-established premium brand name was better known around the world than CCM. Although skate sales were the largest contributor to fixed costs, they declined from 68% of winter goods sales in 1980 to 58% in 1982. At the same time, protective equipment sales roughly doubled from 14% to 26%, with gross margins of 24%. Total gross margin as a percent of sales decreased from 27.8% in 1980 to 26.6% in 1982.

Distribution

From 1945 to 1982 CCM's dealer network had shrunk from 2 500 to 1 500 and its sales force from 21 to 12. All dealers sold the total CCM line but spent most of their time on winter goods. Up to 1970 the sales reps had been paid salary plus car and expenses and had been encouraged to service dealers and customers. However, industry sources reported that by 1982, the sales reps were strictly on a commission basis and, pressured to get orders through as many dealers as possible, spent little time on service.

Although CCM's reputation for service was suffering, its reputation for quality had been maintained fairly well. A quick survey of a few present or past CCM dealers in November 1982 indicated that approximately one third said they would never carry CCM again; one third would consider carrying CCM again if they could be assured of delivery and service; and one third would stick with CCM through thick and thin because they were enthusiastic about the product and the name.

Manufacturing

Early in November Henry Nolting, president, and Jerry Harder, vice-president of manufacturing of Cooper Canada Ltd, visited CCM's winter goods plant in St. Jean. Following are excerpts from their reports on the visit:

The woodworking facility is not modern, looks somewhat like ours as far as equipment and machinery are concerned, and it is not surprising that they do not turn a profit in that part of

their operation. The roof in the stick-making facility is leaking and that part of their plant is badly maintained.

The protective equipment manufacturing had nothing in it which we do not know, there is nothing innovative being done and, as far as I am concerned, it is worth very little.

The skate manufacturing operation seems reasonable despite the fact that there are no great innovations. The boot-making part is something which is easily transferable to our location, Jerry feels he would like to have it and can run it. The whole layout seems relatively simple but modern enough and efficient. The equipment is not new but in good repair.

The existing machine shop is old and dirty and there is nothing in it which I would like to buy. They have, at present, approximately 100 people working, but cleaning up work in process. The people are very slow, they seem to be puzzled, unenthusiastic and listless.

There seems to be a lot of old stock in the finished goods warehouse.

The major lasting machines are leased from United Shoe Machinery which is normal in this trade. They say they have 3 000 plus pairs of lasts (many are specials for individual players) at about $25 per pair. The lasts I saw were in very good repair.

The R&D department has two employees. They have had tremendous problems with their Propacs (copies of Cooperall) and are constantly trying to improve the product. They are working very closely with the Quebec Nordiques in perfecting this product. They have never done any helmet-related work at that facility.

We think their sporting goods division lost approximately half a million dollars each year, in '80 and '81, sharing equally in the total company loss of $4.3 million at end of September '82.

The offices are in terrible condition. They are old and in an unbelievable mess.

The president's assessment of the situation is that somebody will buy the assets and he feels that they might go for book value. His opinion is that nobody could pick it up for less.

Not counting raw material storage we would need at least 25 000 sq. ft., which excludes cutting, to accommodate the skate-making operation. This is equal to 42 of our present 600 sq. ft. bays. To give you another perspective, this area would be slightly larger than the whole area now devoted to apparel. Because of the size, we would have to do major relocations of our existing floors (in Toronto plant). Also, we must be careful of the existing electrical supplies—I would make a cautious estimate of a $25 000 rewiring charge.

Organization

As a result of natural attrition and dim prospects, the CCM organization had shrunk to skeleton status. While it was reportedly limping along, many of the best and most experienced managers had either retired or moved on to better opportunities.

DECIDING TO BID

In reviewing a list of possible bidders for CCM (Appendix A), John Cooper felt that the strongest competitive threats would be Warrington and Sport Maska. Both companies had strong management teams, well-established distribution systems and adequate financial strength. In addition, both companies were Canadian-owned and would not face possible delay and veto of their offer by the Foreign Investment Review Agency. Of further concern was the realization that the St. Jean plant represented up to 200 politically sensitive jobs and that the Quebec government might become involved directly or indirectly in the proceedings. Immediate decisions and actions were essential, however, if Cooper wanted to acquire CCM. Two questions puzzled John Cooper: "If we don't buy CCM, who will? And how will it affect our business?"

EXHIBIT 1   **Products and Estimated Market Shares of Major Competitors in the Canadian Hockey Equipment Market, 1981**

Company	Skates	Hockey Equipment	Sticks	Apparel
Cooper		69	7	31
Canadien		7	12	
CCM	25	7	6	
D & R		7		
Jofa		3		
Koho		2.5	10.5	
Sherwood			25	
Victoriaville			11	
Louisville			6.5	
Titan			11	
Maska				42
Bernard				11
Sandow				10
Bauer*	33			
Lange*	5			
Micron*	13			
Daoust	17			
Orbit	5			
Roos	1			
Ridell	1			
Others		4.5	11	6
	100%	100%	100%	100%
($ 000 000s)	$78	$31.5	$29	$27

* Brands of Warrington Industries Ltd.
SOURCE: Rough estimates by Cooper product managers.

EXHIBIT 2   **Canadian Hockey Skate Production** (000s of pairs)

Year	Sewn	Molded	Total
1977	1 050	50	1 100
1978	775	150	925
1979	1 050	250	1 300
1980	850	300	1 150
1981	970	400	1 370
1982 (forecast)	750	300	1 050
1983 (forecast)	900	350	1 250

EXHIBIT 2 (continued)
1982 Factory Sales and Market Shares of Leading Competitors
(000s of pairs)

	Sewn	%	Molded	%	Total	%	($000)	%	$ Average of Total
Bauer	305	42.9	50	13.7	355	32.9	$20 265	35.4	$57.08
Micron	—	—	185	50.5	185	17.2	8 690	15.2	46.97
Lange	—	—	100	27.3	100	9.3	3 280	5.8	32.80
Daoust	205	28.7	—	—	205	19.0	9 780	17.0	47.70
CCM	147	20.6	6	1.6	153	14.2	12 050	21.0	78.76
Orbit	55	7.8	25	6.8	80	7.4	3 205	5.6	40.06
Totals	712	100	366	100	1 078	100	$52 270	100	$53.13

EXHIBIT 2   1982 Hockey Skate Sales by Geographic Market (000s of pairs)

Manufacturer	Canada	U.S.	Europe	Far East	Total
Canadian	785	238	67	15	1 105
Non-Canadian	—	312	233	25	570
Totals	785	550	300	40	1 675

SOURCE: Estimates based on industry information and casewriter's estimates.

EXHIBIT 3   Cooper Consolidated Statement of Income and Retained Earnings
Years Ended December 31 ($000s)

	1981	1980	1979	1978	1977
Net Sales	62 827	62 183	55 810	49 429	42 803
Less: Operating costs	57 049	55 901	51 844	44 364	38 538
Net Before Depreciation, etc.	5 778	6 282	3 966	5 064	4 265
Less: Deprec. & amortization	724	746	748	626	609
Long-term debt interest	1 905	934	1 022	929	778
Other interest	2 933	2 866	2 068	1 138	941
Add: Foreign exchange gain	105	369	107	216	173
Earnings, discontinued operation	929	—	—	—	—
Less: Income taxes					
Current	14	176	20	525	518
Deferred	208	48	454	21	58
Net Income, Operations	818	1 977	455	2 039	1 650
Add: Extraordinary item	(1 543)	76	—	—	—
Net Income	(725)	2 053	455	2 039	1 650
Shares Outstanding					
Common ($000s)	1 486	1 483	1 483	1 404	1 388
Net income per share	(0.49)	1.38	0.31	1.45	1.18

EXHIBIT 4   Cooper Consolidated Balance Sheet as at December 31 ($000s)

	1981	1980	1979	1978	1977
ASSETS					
Current					
Short-term bank deposit	—	1 790	—	22	95
Accounts receivable	9 726	10 625	10 315	9 185	8 340
Inventories:					
Raw materials	6 177	8 792	13 064	5 675	5 535
Work in progress	1 593	1 758	1 817	1 006	1 379
Finished goods	15 954	11 669	10 530	10 937	10 839
Prepaid expenses, etc.	580	691	545	886	630
	34 030	35 325	39 271	27 714	26 897
Fixed Assets at Cost					
Buildings	6 179	6 145	6 145	6 117	6 078
Machines, equipment, etc.	4 191	4 521	4 171	3 354	3 174
Dies, moulds, etc.	235	567	619	435	284
Land	91	91	91	90	90
Less: Accumulated depreciation	5 351	5 104	4 518	4 000	3 712
	5 345	6 220	6 508	5 998	5 914
Investment in non-consolidated subsidiaries	1 122	—	—	—	—
Deferred income taxes	373	581	533	—	—
	40 870	42 126	46 312	33 713	32 889
LIABILITIES					
Current					
Bank indebtedness	10 373	15 853	17 423	8 283	6 955
Accts. payable	3 463	3 380	6 380	3 153	3 576
Income & other taxes payable	1 002	695	641	352	314
Long-term debt due	16	233	603	1 134	1 059
	14 854	20 161	25 057	12 924	11 905
Long-Term Debt					
Bank loans	9 000	4 000	5 375	5 875	6 900
10% s.f. debs. due 1990	1582	1 892	1 920	2 053	2 148
6.5% mortgage, due 1992	248	265	273	291	280
Notes payable to shareholders	—	125	437	504	—
Less: Amount due 1 yr.	16	233	603	1 134	1 059
Deferred Taxes	—	—	—	418	397
SHAREHOLDERS' EQUITY					
Capital Stock					
Common	3 403	3 392	3 392	2 764	2 716
Retained Earnings	11 799	12 524	10 471	10 016	9 600
	40 870	42 126	46 312	33 713	32 889

EXHIBIT 5   **Cooper Organization Chart**

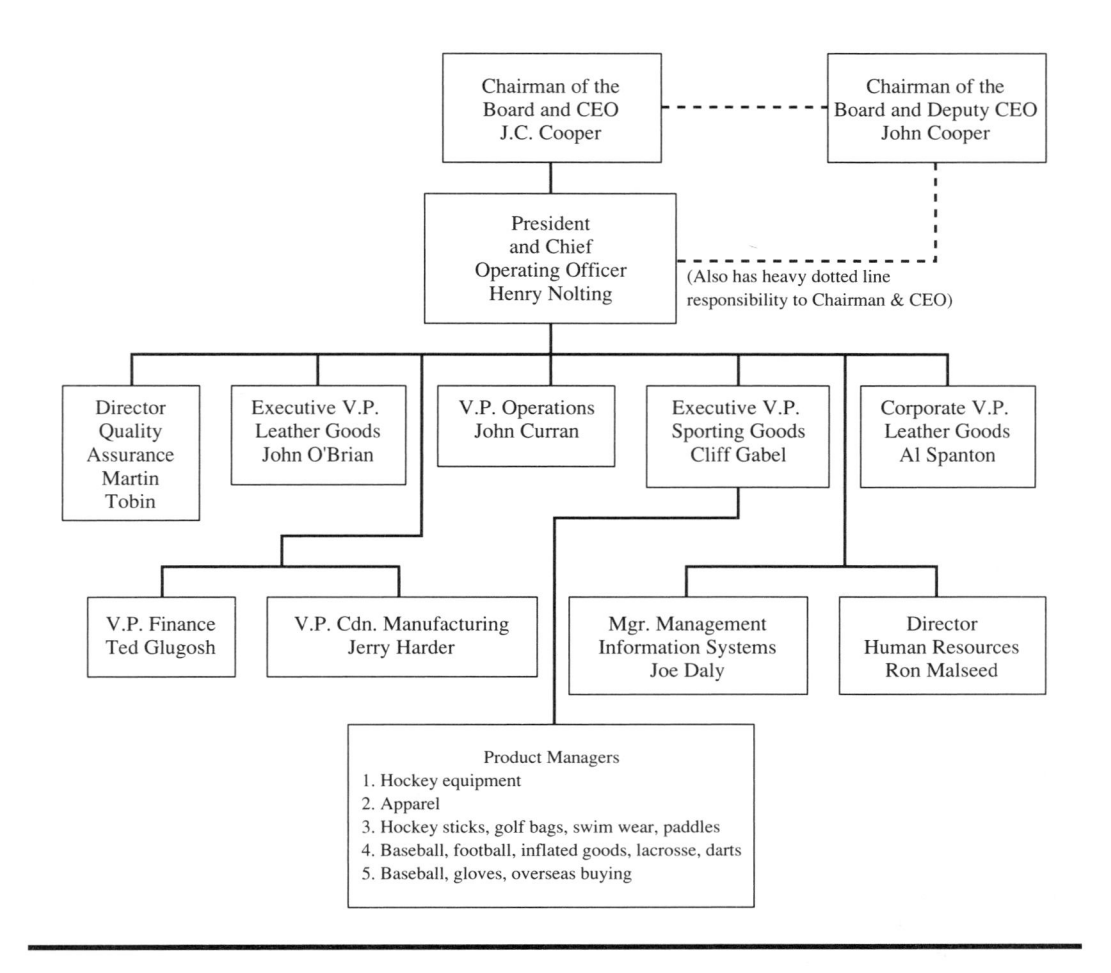

EXHIBIT 6   CCM Inc. Winter Goods Operations ($000s)

	Actual Year Ended		Projected Year Ending	
	Sept. 30/80	*Sept. 30/81*	*Sept. 30/82*	*Dec. 31/83*
Sales				
Skates	17 148	16 530	14 304	16 500
Sticks	1 413	2 307	1 445	2 000
Helmets	1 774	1 814	1 714	2 000
Protective	3 681	5 047	6 455	6 000
Sundries	1 250	838	787	1 000
	25 266	26 536	24 705	27 500

Gross Margins		%		%		%		%
Skates	5 985	35.0	5 604	34.0	4 577	32.0	5 940	36.0
Sticks	(230)	(16.3)	(30)	(1.3)	(267)	(18.5)	—	—
Helmets	415	23.4	424	23.4	492	28.7	600	30.0
Protective	482	13.1	934	18.5	1 556	24.1	1 350	22.5
Sundries	381	30.5	262	31.3	215	27.3	300	30.0
	7 033	27.8	7 194	27.1	6 573	26.6	8 190	29.8

Expenses

Selling	1 291
Administration	661
Warehouse and distribution (Not Available)	1 086
Financial	618
	3 656
Net before income taxes	4 534

SOURCES: 1980–82 from audited financial statements.

1983 projections estimated by CCM management.

EXHIBIT 7   Summary of CCM Winter Goods Assets (at Cost) October 29, 1982 ($000s)

Inventories		
Finished goods		
Skates	1 861	
Sticks	407	
Helmets	264	
Protective	1 476	
Sundries	349	
		4 357
Raw Material		
Skates	1 264	
Protective	798	
Blades	1 604	
		3 666
Work in Process		
Skates	216	
Sticks	250	
Protective	234	
Blades	25	
	725	
		8 748
Fixed Assets		
St. Jean	1 200	
Hudson	70	
Nylite	867	
		2 137
Total		10 885

SOURCE: CCM management estimates.

APPENDIX A
Competitors in the Skate and Hockey Equipment Industry

There were many manufacturers of hockey equipment, helmets, skates and sticks in Canada. There were seven businesses that Cooper management considered capable and perhaps interested in the CCM winter goods assets.

1. *Canadian Hockey Industries.* CHI was a small company that made high quality hockey sticks. Its use of fibreglass technology and other materials such as graphite, plastics, laminates and aluminum had resulted in the most unique stick line in the market. It also marketed a full line of hockey equipment, including a helmet, but no skates or apparel.

    Located in Drummondville, Quebec, it had sales of $10 million in 1981, which had been growing rapidly for the past five years. In the factory it employed approximately 120 workers. It was owned by Amer industries, a Finnish company which also owned Koho.

2. *Koho.* Koho was owned by Amer industries Finland, and shared marketing, distribution and some hockey stick manufacturing with Canadian hockey Industries. It was thought to be the largest hockey stick manufacturer in the world. It also manufactured and marketed hockey equipment and helmets, but no skates or apparel.

    Koho had sales of approximately $14 million from about 800 or 900 dealers, serviced by six or seven commission agents who primarily sold Koho and Canadian. Major accounts included large department stores, e.g., Eatons, Simpsons, and Sears, sporting goods chains, e.g., Collegiate Sports, and other stores such as Canadian Tire.

    Sticks were manufactured in the Canadian plant in Quebec; sticks and some hockey equipment were manufactured in Finland and some hockey equipment was purchased in the Orient.

    Koho's organization in Canada was headed by a sales manager who reported to a president for North America. The United States also had a sales manager who reported to the North American president. This president reported to the head office of Amer, a very large and profitable Finnish corporation that was involved with ship building, steel, food and tobacco.

3. *Jofa.* A Volvo-owned company, Jofa manufactured and marketed hockey equipment, hockey sticks and skates, but not apparel. It had one factory in Sherbrooke, Quebec, and others in Sweden. The rest of its products were purchased in the Orient.

    Sales of $10 million were achieved through 700 and 800 dealers and approximately seven commissioned sales agents. Major accounts included large department stores and sporting goods stores and Canadian Tire.

    The organization of the company was thin, with one director of marketing responsible for all of North America. Supporting him was a sales manager and a small number of commissioned sales agents.

4. *Sherwood-Drolet.* Sherwood-Drolet was a Quebec company, 80% owned by an American firm, ATO Inc. ATO was the world's largest integrated producer of fire protection equipment and also owned Rawlings and Adirondack sporting goods in the United States.

    Sherwood, a producer of high quality hockey sticks, had been an industry leader in sales and in the introduction of new materials and production processes. It had one of the most automated plants in the industry, enabling it to produce large volumes of sticks of consistent quality. In 1981 its share of the Canadian market was 25%.

Sales of approximately $15 million came from approximately 600 dealers. The company's direct sales were aided by 10 sales agents who sold to 300 dealers.

5. *Hillerich and Bradsby*. Hillerich and Bradsby's head office and manufacturing facility were located in Wallaceburg, Ontario. The company was a wholly owned subsidiary of H & B, Louisville, Kentucky, the world's top baseball bat manufacturers. Besides producing the Louisville hockey stick and being a market leader in brightly coloured goalie sticks, it was making aggressive inroads into the baseball glove and accessory markets. It had also earned a good name for itself in manufacturing golf clubs that were sold primarily through club professionals. The plant employed 62 people.

Sales in 1981 were about $6 million. H & B distribution system included warehouses in Richmond, B.C., Dorval, Quebec, Winnipeg, Manitoba, and Concord, Ontario. The sales were achieved primarily by commission sales agents through approximately 400 dealers. Management was reportedly very strong.

6. *Warrington Industries*. Warrington produced Bauer, Micron, and Lange skates. Bauer had been in the skate business for many years, and was CCM's major competitor. This Canadian owned company was located in Kitchener, Ontario, and produced only skates and shoes. It employed 400 in the skate business and 150 in the shoe business.

Sales of approximately $30 million were generated by 12 to 15 agents through a dealership of 1200 stores. Warrington was in turn owned by Cemp Investments, a firm representing the interests of the Bronfman family.

7. *Sport Maska*. Maska was a high quality hockey-jersey manufacturer. Good distribution resulted in Maska being exclusive suppliers to the NHL. Besides hockey jerseys and apparel, its business consisted of spring and summer ball uniforms and apparel, soccer jerseys and leisure wear. The plant in St. Hyacinthe, Quebec, employed approximately 175 people.

Sales in Canada were achieved by approximately nine commissioned agents through 120 to 1500 dealers across Canada. The agents did not carry Maska exclusively. It was distributed coast to coast across the United States through the use of commission agents. Recently, Maska had purchased Sandow, another Canadian athletic apparel company, and had consolidated the manufacturing into its own plant.

Sport Maska was a private company that appeared to be profitable and to have a strong equity base. Industry sources felt that the management team, directed by president Denny Coter, was strong and had good depth.

IMASCO LIMITED: THE ROY ROGERS ACQUISITION

Joseph N. Fry and Kent E. Neupert

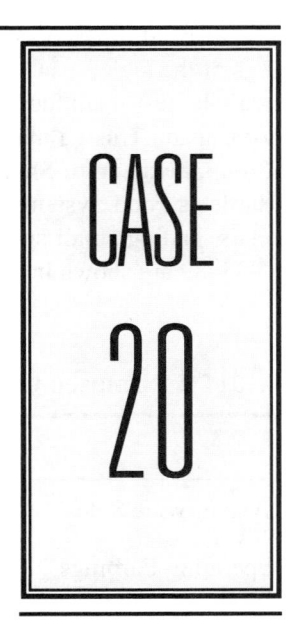

CASE 20

In January 1990, Purdy Crawford, the chairman, president and CEO of Imasco Limited, was reviewing an acquisition proposal from one of Imasco's operating companies, Hardee's Food Systems, Inc. (Hardee's) to purchase the Roy Rogers restaurant chain. Bill Prather, Hardee's CEO, was coming to Montreal the following day to present the proposal to the Imasco board. Prather thought the acquisition would permit Hardee's to expand rapidly into markets where they had very little presence. While Crawford was inclined to support Prather's proposal, he wanted to carefully weigh its broader impact for Imasco as a whole. The probable price of more than $390 million represented a substantial commitment of funds, at a time when growth in the U.S. fast food business was slowing.

IMASCO BACKGROUND

Imasco was a diversified Canadian public corporation with consolidated revenues of $5.7 billion in 1989 and net profits of $366 million. Imasco's founding and largest shareholder was B.A.T Industries (B.A.T), which had maintained a relatively constant 40% equity ownership over the years. B.A.T was a very large diversified British company with roots, like Imasco, in the tobacco business. The balance of Imasco shares were widely held.

In 1990, Imasco's operations were focused on four major operating companies, "the four legs of the table," as Crawford referred to them. The companies were: Imperial Tobacco, Canada's largest manufacturer and distributor of cigarettes; CT Financial, the holding company for Canada Trust, a major Canadian retail financial services business; Imasco Drug Retailing Group, made up of Shoppers Drug Mart in Canada and Peoples Drug Stores in the U.S.; and Hardee's Food Systems, Inc. in the U.S. A fifth, smaller company was The UCS Group, Canada's leading small space specialty retailer. Highlights of Imasco's operations for the years 1985–89 are shown in Table 1.

TABLE 1 Imasco Operating Highlights ($ million unless otherwise noted)

	1989	*1988*	*1987*	*1986*	*1985*
System-wide Sales	14 715.6	13 836.5	12 951.5	11 132.2	8 371.8
Revenues	5 724.7	6 000.6	5 924.4	5 596.6	5 110.2
Operating Earnings	692.0	636.7	578.4	455.6	464.1
Total Assets	5 378.0	5 310.2	5 656.6	5 505.5	2 905.7
Earnings before Extraordinary Items	366.1	314.3	282.7	226.4	261.6
EPS before Extraordinary Items	2.87	2.51	2.24	1.92	2.40
DVDS/Share	1.12	1.04	0.96	0.84	0.72

IMASCO DIVERSIFICATION ACTIVITIES

Imasco Limited was created in 1969 as a corporate entity to encompass and oversee the tobacco, food and distribution businesses of Imperial Tobacco Limited, and to manage a program of further diversification. The aim was to build a broadly based corporation that would rely less on the tobacco business and be better received in the stock market.

Paul Paré was the first president, chairman and CEO of Imasco, and the person with prime responsibility for its diversification program up to his retirement from the chairmanship in 1987. Paré's 38-year career began in the legal department of Imperial Tobacco and led to senior positions in the marketing areas. He became President and CEO in 1969 and Chairman in 1979. Except for a two-year stint with the Department of National Defence, his career was always in the tobacco industry. Paré's approach to diversification in the early years had been a conservative one. He preferred to make a number of relatively small investments, and build or divest the positions as experience dictated.

Crawford, Paré's successor, pictured the first ten years of diversification as a process of experimentation and learning. He described the evolution of thought and action: "Imperial's first attempt at diversification had been through vertical integration." Crawford explained: "Although it appeared logical that if Imperial bought a tinfoil company and made foil wrap themselves there were economies to be realized, we quickly learned that making cigarettes and making tinfoil are two different things." Imperial knew little about the highly specialized tinfoil business, and also discovered that "the competition didn't like the idea of buying tinfoil from us."

Upon reflection, management determined that they were "in the business of converting and marketing agricultural products." Crawford recounted: "It made sense then that the next acquisition was a winery. Unfortunately, we failed to take into consideration provincial liquor regulations which made it impossible to operate at a sufficient scale to be profitable."

Management then broadened its perspective and decided that they were best at marketing. This led to acquisitions that "embodied exciting new marketing concepts," such as two sporting goods companies, Collegiate and Arlington, and a discount bottler and retailer of soft drinks called PoP Shoppes. These investments were held for several years, but they failed to live up to their promise and were subsequently sold off. Other acquisitions, in food processing and distribution, for example, were quite successful, but not on a scale of importance to Imasco. These were later divested when Imasco refocused its efforts.

For the most part, these early diversification moves involved the acquisition of several small companies, and subsequent restructuring of them into a larger enterprise. Most of these acquisitions were then later divested. For example, Imasco's three food companies, which were sold in the late 1970s and early 1980s, were originally ten different companies. Amco Vending, sold in 1977, was built up from eight separate vending companies across Canada. Other businesses which were grown and later sold included wines, drycleaning, and video tape services.

With time, Paré's team built an understanding of its capabilities, sharpened its sense of mission, and focused its acquisition criteria. The mission was to "create shareholder value as a leading North American consumer products and services company." Based on their learning, the criteria for acquisitions were formalized. Imasco would acquire companies that (1) were well positioned in the consumer goods and services sector of the economy; (2) had a capable management team in place, or were able to be smoothly integrated into an existing operating division; (3) had above average growth potential, and were capable of making a meaningful and immediate contribution to profits; and (4) were North American based, preferably in Canada. Crawford noted that "perhaps the most important end result of approximately ten years of experimentation was that we developed a clear vision of what the company was and was not."

As Imasco became more focused and confident of its skills, the acquisitions became less frequent and larger in size, and the diversification from tobacco more significant. Imasco's acquisitions and net investments are given in Exhibit 1. The most significant events of the 1980s are described below in the review of the present-day Imasco operating companies. The net result of 20 years of diversification was that Imasco increased its revenues tenfold and its earnings twentyfold. Moreover, its reliance on tobacco for corporate earnings went from 100% in 1970 to 48% in 1989. A twenty year review of Imasco performance is given in Exhibit 2.

Corporate Management

While Imasco's diversification policy was directed from the central office, its operations were not centralized. The corporate management structure was decentralized and rather flat. Only 50 people staffed the head office in Montreal. The various companies, with operations across Canada and most of the U.S., were encouraged to aggressively pursue the development of their businesses and related trademarks. Management believed that "combining the experience and expertise that flow from the individual operating companies creates a unique opportunity to add value to all of its (Imasco's) operations and assets." Accordingly, Imasco saw its greatest strengths as the high degree of autonomy, and clear lines of authority and responsibility, which existed between Imasco's head office (the Imasco Centre) and the operating companies. While each company's CEO operated with the widest possible autonomy, they also contributed to the development of the annual and five-year plans, and "to furthering Imasco's overall growth objectives." The role of the Imasco Centre was to guide Imasco's overall growth without interfering with the operating companies. The 1988 business plan stipulated that "the role of the Imasco Centre is to be a source of excellence in management dedicated to achieving overall corporate objectives, and supporting Imasco's operating companies in the fulfilment of their respective missions and objectives."

It was very important to Imasco that any acquisition be friendly. While it was not formally stipulated in the acquisition criteria, it was evident in Imasco's actions, such as the aborted acquisition of Canadian Tire in 1983.

In June of that year, Imasco initiated an acquisition attempt of Canadian Tire, but later withdrew the offer. Imasco had outlined a proposal to the members of the Billes family, majority shareholders in Canadian Tire, and the management of Canadian Tire in which Imasco would purchase as many of Canadian Tire's outstanding common and Class "A" shares as would be tendered. Imasco stipulated the offer was conditional on family and management support. Imasco expected the cost of the acquisition to be about $1.13 billion.

Several days later, Paré issued a press release in which he stated:

> We at Imasco are obviously disappointed with the reaction of the senior management group at Canadian Tire to purchase all of the outstanding shares of the company. We stated at the outset that we were seeking both the support of the major voting shareholders and the endorsement of management. It now appears that such support and endorsement are not forthcoming. In light of this and in view of the announcement made ... by the trustees of the John W. Billes estate, we have concluded that one or more of the conditions to our offer will not be satisfied. Therefore, we do not propose to proceed with our previously announced offer.

In explaining Imasco's rationale for withdrawing the offer, Paré continued:

> Throughout the negotiations, we have been keenly aware of the essential ingredients that have made Canadian Tire one of the retail success stories in Canada. These ingredients include the able leadership of the management group, the unique relationship between management and the associate-dealers, and the employee profit-sharing and share-ownership plans. As we have mentioned on several occasions, it was our intention to preserve these relationships and the formulas that have so obviously contributed to the success of the Canadian Tire organization.

OPERATING COMPANIES

Imperial Tobacco

Imperial Tobacco was the largest tobacco enterprise in Canada, with operations ranging from leaf tobacco buying and processing, to the manufacture and distribution of a broad range of tobacco products. The manufacture and sale of cigarettes constituted the largest segment of its business, representing 89.4% of Imperial Tobacco's revenues in 1989. Highlights of Imperial Tobacco's operations for the years 1985–89 are shown in Table 2.

TABLE 2   Imperial Tobacco Operating Summary
($ million unless otherwise noted)

	1989	1988	1987	1986	1985
Revenues	2 385.6	2 018.1	1 926.0	1 754.6	1 701.8
Revenues, Net of Sales and Excise Taxes	896.2	862.0	816.2	712.0	757.5
Operating Earnings	334.0	308.0	279.1	208.1	243.7
Operating Margins (%)	37.3	35.7	34.2	29.2	32.2
Market Share–Domestic	57.9	56.2	54.4	51.5	52.6
Capital Employed*	558.1	496.4	513.9	594.6†	587.0†

* Capital employed of each consolidated segment consists of directly identifiable assets at net book value, less current liabilities, excluding income taxes payable and bank and other debt. Corporate assets and corporate current liabilities are also excluded.

† Reflects fiscal year ending March 31.

Over the years, Imperial had concentrated on building its market share in Canada from a low of 36% in 1970 to 57.9% in 1989. Revenues in 1989 reached an all time high of almost $2.4 billion, in spite of a 4% decline in unit sales to 27.5 billion cigarettes. The market share gains had been achieved by focusing on the strength of Imperial Tobacco's trademarks, particularly the continued growth of its two leading Canadian brands, Player's and du Maurier. Together these two brands held 47.4% of the market in 1989.

Imperial Tobacco had production and packaging facilities in Montreal and Joliette, Quebec, and Guelph, Ontario, and leaf processing facilities in Joliette and LaSalle, Quebec, and Aylmer, Ontario. Imperial continually modernized its production facilities to the point that management claimed them to be "the most technologically advanced in the tobacco industry in Canada." The distribution and promotion of Imperial Tobacco's products to wholesalers and retailers was carried out through a nationwide sales staff operating out of the sales offices and distribution centres in St. Johns, Moncton, Montreal, Toronto, Winnipeg, Calgary and Vancouver.

Imasco Enterprises (Including Canada Trust)

Imasco Enterprises Inc. (IEI) was wholly-owned through Imasco Limited and three of its other companies, making it an indirect wholly-owned subsidiary. In 1986, Imasco announced its intention to acquire all of the outstanding common shares of Genstar Corporation (Genstar) through IEI. At the time, Imasco's primary objective was to gain entry into the financial services sector by assuming Genstar's 98% ownership position in Canada Trust. Genstar had purchased Canada Trust in 1985 for $1.2 billion dollars and merged it with Canada Permanent

Mortgage Corporation, which Genstar had purchased in 1981. This merger created Canada's seventh largest financial institution with $50 billion in assets under administration.

Once acquired, Imasco intended to sell off all of Genstar's nonfinancial assets. Within the year, all of the shares were acquired at a cost of approximately $2.6 billion. This was the first acquisition orchestrated by Crawford.

In addition to Canada Trust, Genstar had holdings in an assortment of other businesses. Most of these, such as the cement and related operations, Genstar Container Corporation, and Seaspan International, were sold off. The cost of those assets retained, including Canada Trust, was about $2.4 billion, of which all but $150 million was attributed to the Canada Trust holding. The balance of the amount was accounted for by a variety of assets which included Genstar Development Company, Genstar Mortgage Corporation, a one-third limited partnership in Sutter Hill Ventures, a portfolio of other venture capital investments, and certain other assets and liabilities. Genstar Development Company was involved in land development in primary Canadian metropolitan areas, such as Vancouver, Calgary, Edmonton, Winnipeg, Toronto and Ottawa. U.S.-based Sutter Hill Ventures had capital investments in over 43 different companies. Most of these investments were in the areas of medical research, biotechnology, communications and computer hardware and software. Highlights of investments in IEI are shown in Table 3.

TABLE 3 Investments in Imasco Enterprises, Inc. ($ million)

	1989	1988	1987*
Equity in Net Earnings of Imasco Enterprises	152.5	142.1	126.5
Investment in Imasco Enterprises	2 700.2	2 655.4	2 613.5

* Financial information is shown beginning with 1987 to reflect the acquisition of Canada Trust in 1986.

CT Financial was the holding company for the Canada Trust group of companies. In 1989, Canada Trust was Canada's second largest trust and loan company, and a major residential real estate broker. The principal businesses of Canada Trust were financial intermediary services, such as deposit services, credit card services, mortgage lending, consumer lending, corporate and commercial lending, and investments. It also offered trust services, real estate services and real estate development. Canada Trust operated 331 financial services branches, 22 personal and pension trust services offices, and 275 company operated and franchised real estate offices. Total assets under the administration of Canada Trust at the end of 1989 were $74.1 billion, comprising $32.7 billion in corporate assets, and $41.4 billion in assets administered for estate, trust and agency accounts. Total personal deposits were estimated to be the fourth largest among Canadian financial institutions. The return of common shareholders' average equity was 17.3% compared with an average of 7.7% for Canada's six largest banks. Highlights of CT Financial operations are shown in Table 4.

Imasco Drug Retailing

SHOPPERS DRUG MART
Shoppers Drug Mart provided a wide range of marketing and management services to a group of 633 associated retail drug stores located throughout Canada, operating under the trademarks Shoppers Drug Mart (585 stores), and Pharmaprix in Quebec (48 stores). The Shoppers Drug Mart stores also included the extended concepts of Shoppers Drug Mart Food Baskets and Shoppers Drug Mart Home Health Care Centres.

TABLE 4   Operating Performance Data for CT Financial
($ million unless otherwise noted)

	1989	*1988*	*1987**
Assets under Administration	74 096.0	67 401.0	60 626.0
Corporate Assets	32 666.0	29 219.2	25 514.8
Deposits	30 403.0	27 319.5	23 859.0
Loans	24 201.1	22 661.7	19 679.3
Net Earnings Attributed to Common Shares	240.2	232.0	201.0
Return on Common Shareholders Average Equity (%)	17.3	19.0	19.4

* Financial information is shown beginning with 1987 to reflect the acquisition of Canada Trust in 1986.

In 1989, Shoppers Drug Mart was the largest drug store group in Canada with about 33% of the retail drug store market. In system wide sales, it ranked first and fifth among all drug store groups in Canada and North America, respectively. In the past, competition had come primarily from regional chains and independent drug stores, but food stores with drug departments represented a growing challenge. During 1989, management had emphasized strengthening the productivity and profitability of existing stores, particularly the former Super X Drugs and Howie's stores, recently converted to Shoppers Drug Mart stores.

The Shoppers Drug Mart operating division utilized licensing and franchise agreements. Under the licensing arrangement, each Shoppers Drug Mart was owned and operated by a licensed pharmacist, called an Associate. In Quebec, Pharmaprix stores used a franchise system. In return for an annual fee, each Associate of a Shoppers Drug Mart store and Franchisee of a Pharmaprix store had access to a variety of services, such as store design, merchandising techniques, financial analysis, training, advertising and marketing. Highlights of Shoppers Drug Mart operations are shown in Table 5.

TABLE 5 Shoppers Drug Mart Operating Summary
($ million unless otherwise noted)

	1989	*1988*	*1987*	*1986*	*1985*
System-wide Sales	2 597.7	2 355.6	2 073.4	1 775.0	1 522.3
Revenues	136.2	114.9	95.7	86.6	73.4
Operating Earnings	70.6	57.1	51.3	48.9	42.5
Operating Margins (%)	51.8	49.7	53.6	56.5	57.9
Average Sales per Store	4.1	4.2	4.1	3.9	3.6
Number of Stores	633	613	586	543	431
Capital Expenditures	24.0	28.0	27.6	23.3	16.4
Capital Employed*	204.1	209.8	194.2	117.9†	106.8†
Depreciation	26.6	20.6	17.9	13.0	11.8

* Capital employed of each consolidated segment consists of directly identifiable assets at net book value, less current liabilities, excluding income taxes payable and bank and other debt. Corporate assets and corporate current liabilities are also excluded.

† Reflects fiscal year ending March 31.

PEOPLES DRUG STORES Peoples Drug Stores, Incorporated (Peoples) operated 490 company owned drug stores in the U.S. during 1989. The stores were primarily operated from leased premises under the trade names Peoples Drug Stores, Health Mart, and Rea and Derick. Imasco had built the Peoples operating division from several acquired drug store chains in six eastern U.S. states and the District of Columbia.

After a disappointing performance in 1986, Peoples began a comprehensive plan to revitalise the chain and focus on areas of market strength. Earnings steadily improved, with operating earnings of $8.0 million in 1989, compared with operating losses of $8.3 million in 1988 and $22.5 million in 1987. The turnaround involved restructuring, including the divestment of Peoples' Reed, Lane, Midwest, Bud's Deep Discount, and other smaller divisions. During 1989, a total of 326 drug stores were sold, 21 were closed, and 13 opened for a net decrease of 334 stores. At the beginning of 1990, only five Bud's stores remained to be sold. The result was a concentration on People's strongest markets, primarily, the District of Columbia, Maryland, Virginia, West Virginia and Pennsylvania. The highlights of Peoples operations are shown in Table 6.

TABLE 6   Peoples Drug Stores Operating Summary
($ million unless otherwise noted)

	1989	1988	1987	1986	1985
Revenues	1 207.2	1 841.6	1 850.2	1 922.5	1 737.3
Operating Earnings	8.0	(8.3)	(22.5)	0.1	52.5
Operating Margins (%)	0.7	(0.5)	(1.2)	—	3.0
Average Sales per Store (US $)	2.1	1.8	1.7	1.7	1.5
Number of Stores	490	829	819	830	824
Capital Expenditures	12.4	41.9	29.1	32.7	58.5
Capital Employed*	369.4	523.5	703.6	819.5†	653.5†

* Capital employed of each consolidated segment consists of directly identifiable assets at net book value, less current liabilities, excluding income taxes payable and bank and other debt. Corporate assets and corporate current liabilities are also excluded.

† Reflects fiscal year ending March 31.

The UCS Group

In 1989, The UCS Group operated 531 stores in Canada from leased premises. The stores carried a wide variety of everyday convenience items, including newspapers and magazines, cigarettes and smokers' accessories, confectionary, snack foods, gifts and souvenir selections. The retail outlets were all company-operated, and included UCS newsstands in shopping centres, commercial office towers, airports, hotels, and other high consumer traffic locations. The UCS group operated 531 stores in five divisions: Woolco/Woolworth, Specialty Stores, Hotel/Airport, Den for Men/AuMasculin, and Tax and Duty Free. Highlights of The UCS Group operations are shown in Table 7.

TABLE 7   The UCS Group Operating Summary ($ million unless otherwise noted)

	1989	1988	1987	1986	1985
Revenues	286.1	256.6	235.3	206.0	187.8
Operating Earnings	8.3	7.5	6.7	6.6	5.5
Operating Margins (%)	2.9	2.9	2.9	3.2	2.9
Average Sales per Stores ($000)	543	489	461	432	410
Average Sales per Sq.Ft. ($)	790	718	675	651	629
Number of Stores	531	525	524	494	460
Capital Employed (Est.)*	41.4	45.6	40.7	37.6†	57.2†

* Capital employed of each consolidated segment consists of directly identifiable assets at net book value, less current liabilities, excluding income taxes payable and bank and other debt. Corporate assets and corporate current liabilities are also excluded.

† Reflects fiscal year ending March 31.

Hardee's Food Systems

Imasco's move to make a major investment in a U.S.-based company arose in part from the greater opportunity offered by the U.S. economy for potential acquisitions of an interesting nature and scale, and in part from the constraints on Canadian acquisitions posed by the Foreign Investment Review Act (FIRA). The purpose of FIRA was to review certain forms of foreign investment in Canada, particularly controlling acquisitions of Canadian business enterprises, and diversifications of existing foreign controlled firms into unrelated businesses. For several years, Imasco came under the control of FIRA due to B.A.T's 40% ownership of Imasco. In later years, however, Imasco was reclassified as a Canadian owned enterprise.

Imasco's involvement with Hardee's and the U.S. restaurant business developed slowly. Imasco first became acquainted with Hardee's in 1969 when its pension fund manager was on holiday in South Carolina. The manager and his family were so fond of the Hardee's hamburgers that upon returning to Montreal, he investigated Hardee's as a possible pension fund investment. The following year, Imasco made a relatively small investment in Hardee's.

Later, when Hardee's was looking for expansion capital, it approached Imasco. In March 1977, Imasco invested $18.2 million in convertible preferred shares which, if converted, would give Imasco a 25% position in Hardee's. Between March 1980 and January 1981, Imasco converted their preferred shares and purchased the outstanding common shares at a cost of $114.1 million. At this time, Hardee's was the seventh largest hamburger restaurant chain in the U.S. Later, Imasco made additional investments in Hardee's to facilitate growth and acquisition.

By 1989, Hardee's Food Systems, Inc. (Hardee's) was the third largest hamburger restaurant chain in the U.S., as measured by system-wide sales and average unit sales volume. In number of outlets, it ranked fourth. With its head office in Rocky Mount, North Carolina, Hardee's restaurant operations consisted of 3 298 restaurants, of which 1 086 were company-operated and 2 212 were licensed. Of these restaurants, 3 257 were located in 39 states and the District of Columbia in the U.S., and 41 were located in nine other countries in the Middle East, Central America, and Southeast Asia. Average annual unit sales for 1989 were $1 060 300, compared with $1 058 000 in 1988. Highlights of Hardee's operations are shown in Table 8.

TABLE 8   Hardee's Operating Summary ($ million unless otherwise noted)

	1989	1988	1987	1986	1985
System-wide Sales	4 146.7	4 058.9*	4 059.1	3 721.6	3 248.4
Revenues	1 786.5	1 756.9	1 801.7	1 642.0	1 457.0
Operating Earnings	118.6	130.3	137.3	129.0	117.1
Operating Margins (%)	6.6	7.4	7.6	7.9	8.0
Average Sales per Restaurant (US $)	922	920	877	837	801
Capital Expenditures	155.3	209.9	217.0	135.6	99.9
Depreciation	78.9	78.0	75.5	63.0	53.4
Restaurants Company Owned	1 086	1 070	995	893	876
Restaurants Franchised	2 212	2 081	1 962	1 818	1 662
Total Restaurants	3 298	3 151	2 957	2 711	2 538
Capital Employed**	618.3	587.7*	777.5	668.1†	555.4†

* Includes sale and leaseback of properties.

** Capital employed of each consolidated segment consists of directly identifiable assets at net book value, less current liabilities, excluding income taxes payable and bank and other debt. Corporate assets and corporate current liabilities are also excluded.

† Reflects fiscal year ending March 31.

Hardee's had encouraged multi-unit development by licensees. In some cases, Hardee's granted exclusive territorial development rights to licensees on the condition that minimum numbers of new licensed restaurants in the area be opened within specific periods of time. As of December 31, 1989, Hardee's had license agreements with 234 licensee groups operating 2 205 restaurants. The ten largest of these licensees operated 1 213 restaurants, representing 55% of the licensed restaurants in the chain, and the two largest operated 738 licensed restaurants, or approximately 33% of the licensed restaurants.

Hardee's restaurants were limited-menu, quick-service family restaurants, and featured moderately priced items for all meals. These products were principally hamburgers, roast beef, chicken, turkey club, ham and cheese and fish sandwiches, breakfast biscuits, frankfurters, french fries, salads, turnovers, cookies, ice cream, and assorted beverages for both take-out and on-premise consumption. Recent additions to the Hardee's menu included a grilled chicken sandwich, Crispy Curl fries, and pancakes. These new products followed a series of initiatives taken in 1988, which included being the first hamburger chain to switch to all vegetable cooking oil in order to lower fat and cholesterol levels in fried products. Hardee's also introduced more salads and more desserts to the menu.

Fast Food Merchandisers, Inc. (FFM) was an operating division of Hardee's that furnished restaurants with food and paper products through its food processing and distribution operations. All company-operated Hardee's restaurants purchased their food and paper products from FFM. Although licensees were not obligated to purchase from FFM, approximately

75% of Hardee's licensees purchased some or all of their requirements from FFM. FFM operated three food processing plants and eleven distribution centres. FFM also sold products to other food service and supermarket accounts.

THE PROPOSED ROY ROGERS ACQUISITION

The U.S. Food Service Industry[1]

Over the past twenty years, Americans spent a rising portion of their food dollars at restaurants. More two-income families, fewer women as full-time homemakers and a decline in the number of children to feed made dining out increasingly popular. In 1989, U.S. consumers spent $167 billion at 400 000 restaurants. This excluded an estimated $61 billion spent at other food and beverage outlets, such as employee cafeterias, hospitals, ice-cream stands and taverns. Although sales growth for the restaurant industry outpaced the economy in recent years, industry analysts noted indications of outlet saturation. In 1989, franchise restaurant chains expected to have U.S. sales of $70.4 billion, up 7.4% from the year before. However, on a per unit basis, 1989 sales for franchise chain units averaged $737 000, up only 4.3% from the previous year. Analysts pointed out that this rise corresponded to increases in menu prices.

Quick service or "fast food" restaurants had led industry growth for several decades, and were expected to do so over the near term. However, industry analysts cautioned that, as the average age of the American consumers increased, a shift away from fast food restaurants toward mid-scale restaurants might occur. Increased emphasis on take-out service and home delivery would help to maintain momentum, but analysts expected that fast food sales and new unit growth would not be up to the 6.6% compound annual rate from 1985 to 1989. McDonald's 8 000 U.S. outlets had sales of $12 billion, or about 7% of total U.S. restaurant spending. Chains that emphasized hamburgers, hot dogs, or roast beef were the largest part of the U.S. franchise restaurant industry, with 1989 sales of $33.8 billion from 36 206 outlets. McDonald's U.S. market share in the segment was about 36.1%, followed by Burger King (19.2%), Hardee's (9.9%), and Wendy's (8.5%).

Nature of Operations

The large hamburger chains generated revenues from three sources: (1) the operation of company owned restaurants; (2) franchising, which encompassed royalties and initial fees from licensees operating under the trade name; and (3) commissary, consisting of food processing and the distribution of food, restaurant supplies and equipment essential to the operation of the company and franchised outlets. Profitable operation of company-owned restaurant operations called for high unit sales volume and tight control of operating margins.

Franchising had been the major chains' initial growth strategy. This enabled them to increase revenues, establish a competitive position, and achieve the scale necessary for efficient

---

[1] Industry figures in U.S. dollars.

commissary and marketing operations. In 1989, there were 90 000 franchise operations accounting for 40% of U.S.restaurant operations. In 1989, McDonald's operating profit from franchising ($1.2 billion) substantially exceeded its profit from company operated restaurants ($822 million).

It was often the case that in a franchising relationship, the cost of the land, building and equipment were the responsibility of the franchisee. The franchisee also paid a royalty, typically 3–6% of sales, and were charged 1–5% of sales for common advertising expenses. In return, the franchisee got brand name recognition, training and marketing support. However, some of the larger chains had taken an alternate approach by owning the land and the building. Not only did such an approach provide lease revenue but it also allowed the company to maintain some control over the franchisee's facilities.

Competition

Fast food restaurants competed with at-home eating, other restaurant types, and each other. To build and maintain unit volumes, top chains developed strategies to differentiate themselves by target market, style of operation, menu and promotional approach, among other methods.

MCDONALD'S McDonald's was the leader of the fast food restaurant business. The chain began in the early 1950s in California. The McDonald brothers discovered that a combination of assembly line procedures, product standardization and high volume made it possible to offer exceptional value, providing consistent quality food at a reasonable price. The potential of their concept was recognized by Ray Kroc, a paper cup and milkshake mixer salesman. He acquired the operations, and provided the leadership for the formation and subsequent growth of the McDonald's corporation.

McDonald's had traditionally targeted children, teens and young families, and focused its menu of products around hamburgers and french fries. Scale, experience and simplified operating procedures permitted McDonald's to operate at significantly lower costs than its competitors. In the late 1970s, the company broadened its target market to follow demographic shifts and increase unit volumes. The menu was expanded to include breakfast line and chicken items, and the hours of operation were increased. The emphasis on simplicity and efficiency was maintained, and the company continued its rigorous dedication to quality, service and cleanliness. This strategy was supported by the largest promotional budget in the industry. McDonald's typical arrangement with franchisees was that it owned the property, which the franchisee then leased. Highlights of McDonald's operations are shown in Table 9.

BURGER KING Burger King had been a subsidiary of Pillsbury until December 1988, when Grand Metropolitan PLC acquired Pillsbury and its holdings, which included Burger King. Burger King's traditional market target market had been the 25–39 age group, but it was trying to improve its appeal to the family trade. The key element of Burger King's competitive strategy had been to offer more product choice than McDonald's. Burger King's food preparation system was centred around a hamburger that could be dressed to customer specifications, with onions, lettuce, tomato, etc. Burger King had been the first hamburger chain to diversify significantly into additional hot sandwich items, but this had resulted in somewhat longer service times and higher food preparation costs.

In 1989, Burger King's profits were $48.2 million, down 49% from the previous two years. Its market share was 19.2%, down from 19.9% in 1987. Average unit sales in 1989 were $1.05 million. Burger King had four different CEOs during the past ten years, and was having problems with its marketing program, changing advertising campaigns five times in two years. Additionally, Burger King had experienced problems with their franchisees prior to the acquisition by Grand Metropolitan, but these were beginning to subside with the ownership change.

TABLE 9   McDonald's Operating Summary (US$ million unless otherwise noted)

	1989	1988	1987
Revenues	6 142.0	5 566.3	4 893.5
Depreciation	364.0	324.0	278.9
Operating Income	1 459.0	1 283.7	1 161.9
Operating Profit Margin (%)	23.7	23.1	23.7
Interest Expense	332.0	266.8	224.8
Pretax Income	1 157.0	1 046.5	958.8
Net Income	727.0	645.9	596.5
Net Income Margin (%)	11.8	11.6	12.2
Earnings Per Share	1.95	1.72	1.45
Dividend Per Share	.30	.27	.24
Market Price Year End	34.50	24.06	22.00
Price/Earnings Ratio	17.7	14.0	15.2
Shareholders Equity	3 549.0	3 412.8	2 916.7
Total Common Shares Outstanding (million)	362	375	378

SOURCE: *Worldscope 1990.*

WENDY'S Wendy's also targeted the young adult market. Like Burger King, it provided food prepared to specification, and had broadened its initial emphasis on hamburgers to cover a variety of items, including chili and a self-service buffet and salad bar. In 1989, Wendy's 3 490 restaurants' had average unit sales of $.79 million. This was an increase from $.76 million and $.74 million in 1988 and 1987, respectively. Highlights of Wendy's operations are shown in Table 10.

TABLE 10 Wendy's Operating Summary (US$ million unless otherwise noted)

	1989	1988	1987
Revenues	1 069.7	1 045.9	1 051.1
Depreciation	56.4	57.3	55.4
Operating Income	51.3	44.0	0.1
Operating Profit Margin (%)	4.8	4.2	NIL
Interest Expense	22.3	16.9	24.2
Pretax Income	36.9	43.8	(12.8)
Net Income	30.4	28.5	4.5
Net Income Margin %	2.8	2.7	0.4
Earnings Per Share ($)	.25	.30	.04
Dividend Per Share ($)	.24	.24	.24
Market Price Year End ($)	4.63	5.75	5.63
Price/Earnings Ratio	18.5	19.2	140.6
Shareholder Equity	428.9	419.6	412.2
Total Common Shares Outstanding (million)	96	96	96

SOURCE: *Worldscope 1990.*

HARDEE'S Hardee's was the third largest hamburger-based fast food chain in the U.S., in terms of total sales and unit sales volume; and fourth in outlets. Approximately 30% of Hardee's sales were at breakfast, and it was a leader in the breakfast trade. The other major sales category was hamburgers, with 34% of sales.

The demographic profile of Hardee's customers was skewed slightly to males. Children and 25- to 34-year-olds were two groups that had been targeted for higher penetration. The introduction of ice cream in 1987 had spurred a 98% increase in visits by children under 13. Packaged salads and the broadening of menu selections were expected to help attract 25- to 34-year-olds.

Hardee's management was highly regarded in the food service industry for taking a very shaky firm in 1972–73 and turning it into a good performer. In 1979, Hardee's was cited by *Restaurant Business* magazine as a prime example of a corporate turnaround. In 1981, Jack Laughery, Hardee's CEO through the turnaround period, was awarded the Food Manufacturer's Association gold plate award for exemplary involvement in the food service industry. In 1990, Laughery was Hardee's Chairman, and Bill Prather was the President and CEO.

Hardee's Acquisition of Burger Chef

In 1981, Hardee's was relatively small in the industry, and decided it had to expand quickly just to keep pace with its larger competitors. Competition had intensified, and the ability to support heavy fixed promotional costs became increasingly critical. Hardee's viewed an acquisition as a way to build a stronger market share base to support an increased television campaign.

Burger Chef, acquired by General Foods in 1968, had 1981 sales of $391 million. General Foods had nurtured it into a profitable regional chain. However, due to management changes at General Foods and the acquisition of the Oscar Meyer company, Burger Chef was no longer important to General Food future plans.

Imasco and Hardee's saw this as an opportunity. The Burger Chef chain was made up of about 250 company units and 450 franchised units, located primarily in the states of Michigan, Ohio, Indiana, Iowa and Kentucky. Most of the locations complemented Hardee's markets. Imasco purchased Burger Chef in 1981 for $51.8 million. During the next three years, they converted the sites to Hardee's at a cost of about $80 000 per unit. The acquisition of Burger Chef created two more market areas for Hardee's overnight. By 1986, the stores in these areas were, and still are, the most profitable in the entire Hardee's system. Similarly, in 1972, Hardee's had expanded their market base by acquiring Sandy's Systems, a fast food chain of about 200 restaurants for $5.7 million.

The Roy Rogers Opportunity

The Roy Rogers restaurant chain was owned by the Marriott Corporation (Marriott), and was located in the northeastern U.S. In Baltimore, Washington, D.C., Philadelphia and New York, it was second only to McDonald's in number of locations. Roy Rogers restaurants were well known for fresh fried chicken and roast beef sandwiches. In 1989, Roy Rogers system-wide sales[2] were $713 million, up from the previous year's $661 million. In 1988, revenues were $431 million, up from $399 million in 1987. Operating earnings in 1988 were $43.7 million, up from $38 million the year before. The chain had 660 units, up from 610 the previous year, with average annual unit sales of $1 081 000.

Marriott was a leader in the hotel lodging industry and had extensive restaurant holdings. In 1988, Marriott began to refocus on lodging. As a result, it had reevaluated its other holdings, among these the Roy Rogers chain. In 1988, Marriott had talked to Hardee's about the possible sale of Roy Rogers. However, Marriott was not yet committed to selling the chain and the two companies were unable to agree on a sale price. In late 1989, Marriott announced it was again interested in selling Roy Rogers.

Prather contacted Marriott about the details. Marriott was offering to sell 648 of its Roy Rogers units, of which 363 were company owned and 285 were franchised. These units were in attractive market locations that would not otherwise be available. However, Marriott wanted to retain several sites located on various turnpikes and interstate highways. Additionally, Marriott had a 14-point contract to which any purchaser had to agree. The contract addressed such things as Marriott's concern for Roy Rogers franchisees and indemnification against future litigation.

Prather saw this as the opportunity he had been waiting for and began putting together an acquisition proposal. Before he could make a serious offer to Marriott, he had to first get the approval of Crawford and the Imasco board. While preparing the proposal, Prather had reflected on what it was like to work in the Imasco organization. He had built his career in the food service industry, coming up through the ranks, starting as an assistant store manager. Until 1986, he had been the Number Three man at Burger King, Vice President in charge of World Operations. Prather had spent 14 years with the company, when it was owned by Pillsbury. Pillsbury, a highly centralized company, had required that any expenditures over $1 million had to be authorized by the head office. He thought how much this contrasted with Imasco. For him, Imasco

---

[2] System-wide sales reflect retail sales figures of both company-owned and franchisee stores. Revenues reflect retail sales of only company-owned stores, in addition to royalties received from franchisees.

was "like a breath of fresh air," a decentralized organization in the best sense. He had a great working relationship with Crawford and the others at the Centre, in contact by phone every couple weeks or as required. There was easy and open access with no surprises.

Prather had received preliminary approval from Crawford to proceed with the negotiations. Marriott had structured the Roy Rogers sale in two rounds. In the first round, all those parties who were interested in the chain were interviewed, "much like a job interview," Prather recalled. It was during this first round that Marriott expressed their concerns for their franchisees, and assessed the capabilities and sincerity of those interested in buying the chain. To Prather, "the first round was a screening process just to get into the game."

Prather made it through the first round, but there were three or four other interested groups still in the running. During the next round, the terms of the sale would be negotiated. Although the rumoured price had initially been $390 million, Prather thought that it might be more. Prather felt he could convince Marriott that Hardee's offered the best means of exit, given Marriott's concern for the franchisees, and that a solid offer of $420 million would convince them to sell Roy Rogers to Hardee's.

Prather figured conversion to Hardee's outlets would cost $80 000 to $115 000 per unit, depending on local conditions. He weighed this against the average "from scratch" start-up cost of $1.2 million per site. Additionally, Roy Rogers' menu, which included their popular fresh fried chicken, would complement Hardee's current menu. However, he was not sure it would be an "easy sell" in Montreal. Imasco's 40%-shareholder, B.A.T, was in the midst of fighting off a takeover bid from Sir James Goldsmith (see Appendix). Prather knew that Crawford and the board would be concerned about Goldsmith's run at B.A.T, but the Roy Rogers deal was just what he needed to solidify Hardee's number three industry position.

EXHIBIT 1   Imasco Acquisitions: Distinguishable Eras in Acquisition Size

1963–77

Canada Foils
Growers Wine
Simtel and Editel
S&W Foods: C$18.4 million
Uddo & Taormina (Progresso): C$32.5 million
Pasquale Brothers (Unico): C$4 million
Grissol: C$12.2 million
Collegiate: C$1.4 million
Arlington Sports
Top Drug Mart and Top Value Discount
Tinderbox: US$1.4 million
PoP Shoppes investment: C$10.5 million
Canada Northwest Land Ltd. investment
Hardee's Food Systems investment: US$15 million
— Includes Imperial Tobacco Limited acquisitions

EXHIBIT 1 (continued)

1978–86

Shoppers Drug Mart (Koffler's): C$66.6 million
Further Hardee's investment: C$15 million
Hardee's totally acquired: US$76 million
Burger Chef: US$44 million
Peoples Drug Stores: C$398 million
Rea & Derick Drug Stores: C$114 million
Genstar: C$2.4 billion

EXHIBIT 2   20-Year Financials: Imasco Ltd. and Tobacco Business
($ millions unless noted)

	Imasco Ltd.				Tobacco Business			Imasco Ltd.		
Year	Total Revenues	Operating Earnings	Net Earnings Before Extra-ordinary Items	Earnings Per Common Share[4,5]	Tobacco Operating Earnings/ Total Operating Earnings (%)	Tobacco Revenue	Tobacco Operating Earnings	Stock Price High[6]	Stock Price Low[6]	Annual Dividend[5] Per Common Share
1970[1]	582.2	37.3	15.7	.20	.88	435.2	32.7	16.13	12.00	0.10
1971[1]	569.6	40.6	17.7	.22	.88	418.0	35.9	20.50	15.25	0.125
1972[1]	625.6	48.1	22.2	.28	.84	430.4	40.4	28.38	19.00	0.137 5
1973[1]	717.1	56.0	28.0	.36	.81	446.9	45.4	34.75	25.75	0.15
1975[3]	1 030.3	78.5	36.8	.47	.79	610.5	62.0	33.25	18.75	0.193 75
1976[2]	941.2	74.9	36.5	.47	.81	560.1	60.7	32.00	26.00	0.162 5
1977[2]	1 031.6	74.7	34.9	.45	.81	605.4	60.9	27.25	20.63	0.169
1978[2]	1 049.4	84.2	43.1	.55	.81	655.0	68.3	31.63	24.00	0.18
1979[2]	1 161.5	114.8	56.4	.70	.69	741.4	78.8	40.75	29.75	0.205
1980[2]	1 150.5	132.1	68.2	.83	.75	826.7	99.1	47.25	38.25	0.25
1981[2]	1 423.7	168.8	89.6	1.07	.73	952.9	123.2	38.25	21.25	0.30
1982[2]	2 190.7	247.0	124.2	1.39	.63	1 120.2	156.0	44.50	29.50	0.35
1983[2]	2 713.9	300.3	156.8	1.73	.61	1 242.9	182.3	37.50	18.00	0.40
1984[2]	2 873.2	339.6	194.2	2.03	.60	1 358.9	205.2	36.25	29.88	0.50
1985[2]	4 353.2	432.0	234.1	2.25	.52	1 451.1	224.0	28.25	17.38	0.645
1986[2]	5 325.1	465.9	261.7	2.40	.53	1 769.8	246.0	35.00	22.63	0.75
1987[1]	5 924.4	578.4	282.7	2.24	.48	1 926.0	279.1	46.00	24.25	0.96
1988[1]	6 000.6	636.7	314.3	2.51	.48	2 018.1	308.0	29.50	23.75	1.04
1989[1]	5 724.7	692.0	366.1	2.87	.48	2 385.6	334.0	40.50	27.63	1.12

[1] January – December Fiscal Year.
[2] April – March Fiscal Year.
[3] Reflects 15-month period from January 1974 to March 1975.
[4] Before extraordinary items.
[5] Prior to 1980, adjusted to reflect three stock splits; after 1980, 2 for 1 stock splits July 1980, November 1982, and March 1985.
[6] Not adjusted for stock splits.
SOURCE: Imasco Limited.

APPENDIX   IMASCO Limited, 1990

In the summer of 1989, Sir James Goldsmith formed a syndicate of investors under the name of Hoylake Investments Limited to mount a takeover attempt on B.A.T, Imasco's largest shareholder. Goldsmith's argument was that B.A.T was being valued by the market at less than the sum of its parts, and that the true value would only be realized by the "unbundling" of B.A.T. The stakes in the bid were enormous—it was estimated that Hoylake and its partners would have to put up over $25 billion to carry through on the transaction. Hoylake's intentions with respect to the block of Imasco's shares that B.A.T owned were unknown. Imasco's position was that, while it was an "interested observer," it was not directly involved in the proceedings and would only monitor developments related to the offer. While the specifics of Goldsmith's case are not pertinent here, the general arguments are. These are given below as excerpts from Goldsmith's letter to B.A.T shareholders dated August 8, 1989.

THE KEY QUESTIONS

The case for this bid must rest on the answer to simple questions. Has the existing management placed B.A.T in a position to compete successfully? Are the subsidiaries growing healthily, or are they failing relative to their competitors? Have shareholders' funds been invested in a wise and progressive way which adds value to the shares of the company? Is the conglomerate structure able to provide strength and innovation over the longer term to its diversified subsidiaries? In short, is B.A.T in a state to compete in the modern world and to face the future with confidence? Or has it been managed in a way which could lead to progressive senescence and decay? That is the crux of the argument.

CONGLOMERATION — B.A.T'S FAILURE

It is our case that B.A.T's management has sought size rather than quality or value; it has used shareholders' funds to acquire totally unconnected businesses, about which it knew little, and which are being damaged by having been brought under the control of B.A.T's bureaucratic yoke.

THE CAUSE OF FAILURE

Before presenting the case in factual detail, I would like to explain why such a state of affairs can occur. It is not that the men in charge are malevolent. Not at all. No doubt they are serious administrators. The problem originates from their belief that tobacco was a declining business, and that the company should diversify into other industries. This logic sounded compelling. The flaw was that B.A.T's management knew something about tobacco, but little about the businesses of the companies that it was acquiring. Also there exists a very natural conflict of interest between management and shareholders. Management wishes its company to be big. The bigger it is, the greater the respect, power and honours that flow to management. Shareholders, on the other hand, want value. They do not seek size for the sake of size. They want growth to be the result of excellence, and thereby to improve the short- and long-term value of their investment. Some conglomerates have performed well under the leadership of their founders. But that ceases when the flame of the founder is replaced by the dead hand of the corporate bureaucrat. That is why great conglomerates often have been well advised to de-conglomerate before they retire.

PURPOSE OF THE OFFER

1. We intend to reverse B.A.T's strategy. Instead of accumulating miscellaneous companies within B.A.T, we intend to release them and, as described below, return the proceeds to you.

2. We would concentrate B.A.T's attention on running its core business, tobacco. That is the process which we have described as "unbundling."

CONSEQUENCES

Of course, you will be concerned to know the consequences for the companies being released, and for those who work within them. Will those companies suffer? Will jobs be sacrificed? Would their future be jeopardized, for example, by a reduction in the level of investment in research, development and capital equipment? That is what you may have been led to believe. The reality is the opposite. Instead of vegetating within B.A.T, those companies would either return to independence, or they would join more homogeneous companies. Such companies have the skills which would contribute to future development, and a true mutuality of interest would result. This would lead to increased opportunity for employees, greater long-term investment, productivity and growth. The real danger to employees is that they should remain trapped within B.A.T, and condemned to slow but progressive relative decline. Ultimately that would lead to employee hardship, despite the benevolent intentions of existing management.

CONCLUSION

To summarize, the flawed architecture of the tobacco-based conglomerates was exposed, first with the acquisition of Imperial Group by Hanson in 1986, and late last year when the management and directors of RJR/Nabisco recognized that shareholder values could only be properly realized by a sale of the company.

Size is often a protection against change, but these same basic structural defects have now been revealed, and the logic of unbundling B.A.T has become inescapable.

BRITISH AIRWAYS PLC.

Joseph N. Fry, Roderick E. White and
Bruce Lanning

CASE
21

In the summer of 1994, executives at British Airways (BA) were reviewing their investment in faltering USAir and its implications for BA's global leadership strategy. Following many setbacks, BA had purchased 25% of USAir's equity for US$400 million in early 1993 to secure a marketing partner and access to a route structure in the United States. Now, 16 months later with USAir still not profitable, BA's options varied from severing the marketing relationship and writing-off the investment to injecting further cash.

In prospect, BA's investment in USAir and an accompanying code sharing authority were viewed as a tremendous coup—so much so that the combination prompted accusations of unfair competition by several major U.S. carriers.[1] Code sharing with USAir allowed BA to expand its presence in the U.S. market from 17 airports to 59 by May 1994. In addition, 23 more USAir markets were scheduled to begin code sharing with BA later in 1994.

It had taken BA almost two years to acquire its partial share in USAir. The U.S. Departments of Transport (DOT) and Justice (DOJ) had scrutinized the proposed equity alliance/

---

[1] A code sharing authority allowed two carriers to "link" their connecting flights using the same flight number, thus giving the impression of a through flight. Consequently, code share flights were listed earlier on travel agents' computer reservation systems (CRSs), received more exposure, and had greater probability of being booked. In reality, passengers transferred airline and aircraft where the two airlines' flights connected.

code share pact, causing delays and imposing conditions. DOT/DOJ were concerned by the possibility of BA exercising tacit control over USAir following completion of the equity alliance/code share pact. Explicitly, DOT/DOJ were concerned by the potential for price fixing. Frustrated by the delays, BA had terminated negotiations, only to re-open them six months later with a revised offer. This second offer was amended over a five-month period before it was finally acceptable to the U.S. DOT and DOJ.

In hindsight, the competitive damage feared by the U.S. majors had not materialized. The passenger traffic on BA's North Atlantic route exceeded 4 million one-way trips before code sharing. After one year of phasing in code sharing on the North Atlantic route, BA's cumulative incremental traffic totalled 6700 passengers.[2] Alternately, daily incremental traffic arising from code sharing had only reached 60 passengers in each direction by May 1994. Current annualized incremental revenue equalled approximately US$2 million, less than three-one hundredths of a percent of BA's 1994 revenue. Finally, BA's decision to invest in USAir was clouded by the continuing poor performance of USAir: loss of US$1 229 million in 1992 was followed by loss of US$393 million in 1993 and US$197 million in the first quarter of 1994.

BA was among a number of participants in the airline industry that believed the industry was tending toward a few globe-spanning confederations or partnerships which would dominate international air travel. Under this scenario, those airlines that failed to make the leap to a global carrier were expected to serve as regional carriers and suffer lower profitability.

Accordingly, BA had invested US$1.5 billion in the period 1992–93 to acquire partial ownership of strategically located airlines world-wide. A global network was created using equity alliances—25% of Qantas covering the Asia-Pacific region, 49% of Deutsche BA in Germany, 49.9% of TAT in France, and 25% of USAir—to feed traffic from strategic markets to BA's inter-continental routes. Because the U.S. market represented 29% of global passenger traffic and the North Atlantic routes 28% of international passenger traffic, an alliance with a U.S. airline was critical to BA's strategy. The alliance with USAir completed a major portion of BA's global network, and would supposedly capture additional U.S. passenger "feed" between the U.S.A and Europe.

TRENDS IN GLOBAL DEMAND

The globe could be segmented into six key air travel markets: three intra-regional markets (North America, Europe and the Asia-Pacific region) and three inter-regional markets (the North Atlantic, trans-Pacific and Asia-Europe). North America was the largest of these markets in terms of revenue passenger-kilometres (the number of passengers multiplied by the distance flown—RPK).

High GDP growth in the Asia-Pacific countries was spurring high air travel growth in the Asia-Pacific, trans-Pacific and Asia-Europe markets. As a result, over the next 20 years the North America-Europe-Japan proportion of total global demand would decrease while the Asia-Pacific region proportion increased. Air traffic within and to/from the Asia-Pacific region was expected to experience 41% of world-wide RPK growth and increase from 25% to 31% of world-wide demand by 2013. International carriers were scrambling to position themselves

---

[2] *Air Transport World*, June, 1994, p. 174.

in these fast growing markets. North America was expected to maintain high proportions of world-wide RPK growth (20%) despite lower annual growth rates due to its large base of RPK traffic. Table 1 details predicted changes in travel consumption.[3]

TABLE 1   1993 Regional Traffic Data and 20-Year Regional Forecast: 1994–2013

Geographic Region	1993 Passenger Traffic (1)	1993 Revenue Passenger-Km (RPK) Traffic (1)	Forecast Average Annual Incremental RPK Traffic (2)	Forecast Average Annual % Change 1994–2013 (2)
Intra Asia-Pacific	130 338	173 028	37 800	6.8
North America	390 259	546 027	36 500	4.0
Trans-Pacific	24 066	165 153	21 400	6.8
Intra Europe	158 754	121 425	18 000	4.4
North Atlantic	33 846	217 665	15 800	4.4
Asia-Europe	16 292	130 337	14 200	7.2
Between The Americas	20 737	48 604	6 100	5.5
Europe-Latin America	5 038	32 433	4 000	4.8
Intra Latin America	28 426	20 324	3 000	5.6
Europe-Africa	10 289	41 690	3 100	4.3
TOTAL	818 045 *thousands*	1 496 686 *millions*	160 300 *millions*	5.2 *percent*

SOURCES: (1) IATA, *World Air Transport Statistics, 1994*; (2) Boeing, *1994 World Market Outlook.*

Other trends of particular note concerned customer mix and expectations. By 1994, business travellers were voluntarily moving (or being pushed by their company controller) to economy-class fares. Compounding this trend were proportionately fewer business travellers in the airlines' customer profile—55% of all travel was business-related in 1984; 52% in 1991; but only 37% in 1994. Facsimile machines, tele- and video-conferencing, return to one-person sales presentations in place of team presentations, and flatter organizational structures were changing business-related demand.

The shift in customer profile toward the leisure traveller created significant revenue yield and cost management implications for airlines. Business travellers had traditionally returned a higher yield to the airlines per passenger because of premiums paid for upper-class seats, short-notice bookings and flights during the premium mid-week period. Increasing proportions of leisure travellers meant all fares should rise to correct reduced yields—but leisure travel was sensitive to pricing. If fares rose, load factors would plummet and excess capacity rise.

---

[3] Columns one and two include passenger and RPK data for 147 carriers, excluding Aeroflot, as compiled by the International Air Travel Association (IATA), the airline industry trade association. The RPK data from IATA accounts for 83% of 1993 world-wide traffic. The third and fourth columns of Table 1 relate to average annual change in RPK traffic and average annual percent change in RPK traffic, as predicted by Boeing Commercial Airplane Group. Differences in reporting methods make data in columns one and two not directly comparable with columns three and four.

Furthermore, balancing operations was made more complicated by the nature of leisure travellers. They were cyclical, following the health of the economy and generating seasonal peaks (50–70% extra travellers) in November and August.

Finally, as business and leisure travel became increasingly international, airlines were forced to respond to customers changing expectations. The physical reality of "hopping" from one continent to another was incredibly tiring. Low fares were important but so were convenient connections, elapsed travel time, in-bond transit of people and baggage through international hubs, and prompt delivery to the final destination. Combinations of real and perceived customer expectations regarding "seamless air travel" created a need for global networks of airlines.

ECONOMICS OF THE AIRLINE INDUSTRY

Airline industry profitability was very volatile. The six-year period 1984–89 witnessed record industry operating profits of US$39 billion; 1989 posted an industry net profit of US$3.5 billion. In stark contrast, the industry reported cumulative net losses of US$20 billion for the period 1990–93. The Gulf War and the 1990–91 recession had stalled traffic growth and resulted in airlines discounting fares to stimulate demand. Meanwhile, fuel prices spiked upward. The airlines cost structure prevented them from shedding costs as quickly as yields fell.

BA was consistently profitable during this four year drought, an exception among major carriers. Superior performance was attributed to BA's route structure centred on the Heathrow hub giving it a strong market position, and 1988 Thatcherite privatization which had forced BA to rationalize operations in the late-1980s.

Table 2 compares key inter-regional data reflecting yield and cost differences. The Pacific Rim carriers had the lowest labour costs in the industry. Singapore Airlines had a very different revenue tonne-kilometre composition from the others which, with its lower labour costs, gave it radically lower revenue/RTK and cost/ATK.[4] U.S. carriers experienced relatively high labour as a percentage of their operating costs, but rationalized higher costs over much larger system networks. The result was that even the highest cost U.S. carriers were cost competitive internationally.

The conditions necessary to improve an airline's profitability can be presented very simply. It was necessary to achieve either (1) a greater load factor for a constant revenue yield, (2) higher fares and hence greater revenue yield for a constant load factor, (3) lower operating costs or preferably (4) higher load factor and revenue yield combined with lower operating costs. (See Glossary at end for definitions.)

---

[4] Note introduction of Revenue Tonne-Kilometres (RTK) and Available Tonne-Kilometres (ATK) reflect combined passenger and cargo tonnage multiplied by the distance flown. These measures are used similarly to RPK and ASK introduced earlier.

TABLE 2   Comparison of 1993 Revenue and Cost Data for Selected Major Carriers

Measure	Canadian Industry	U.S. Industry	British Airways	USAir	Japan Airlines	Singapore Airlines
Passenger revenue yield/ RPK	8.0¢	8.1¢	9.4¢	10.7¢	11.5¢	10.1¢
Passenger load factor	67.0%	67.7%	70.0%	59.2%	65.2%	71.4%
Salaries & benefits/operating cost	29.8%	34.9%	27.9%	39.7%	—	21.7%
Revenue yield/RTK	79.1¢	82.7¢	75.5¢	est. 105¢	107.0¢	48.4¢
Operating expense/ATK	45.0¢	44.7¢	46.3¢	est. 66¢	71.9¢	31.7¢
Achieved weight load factor	55.8%	54.5%	66.5%	59.2%	64.1%	69.5%
Break-even weight load factor	56.8%	54.1%	61.3%	61.7%	67.2%	65.5%
Operating margin (%)	–1.0%	1.7%	7.9%	–1.1%	–2.7%	9.6%
Net profit margin (%)	–9.4%	–2.6%	4.5%	–5.6%	–2.6%	13.0%

Note: Currency values in U.S. Funds, 1.324 C$ = 1US$; 1£ = 1.48US$; 1.57SI$ = 1US.
SOURCE: Carriers' 1993 Annual Reports & IATA *World Air Transport Statistics, 1994.*

Actually achieving profitability was much more complicated. Load factors could be stimulated in the short term by effective promotion and pricing but cutting fares eroded revenue yield. Skillful balancing of the trade-off between load factors and yield was vital to airline competitive advantage and profitability. On the other hand, cost reductions were dependent upon increasing productivity of labour and equipment without diminishing passenger service and safety. Underlying the factors above was a second level driving cost and yield management performance. These were: (1) a non-variable cost structure, (2) cost management hobbled by dependence on several key inputs, (3) incremental advantages between airlines on their yield management and (4) limited route structure economies available to reduce unit costs.

BA must understand these underlying issues if it were to make an accurate analysis of the U.S. airline industry and USAir's future prospects. There were a limited number of avenues available to reverse USAir's plight. BA's understanding of U.S. industry cost structure and yield management opportunities would determine how it decided its future involvement with USAir.

Cost Structure

A large proportion, 82%, of airline operating costs were fixed or semi-variable; only 18% of operating costs were truly variable—travel agency commissions, ticketing fees and meals. Semi-variable costs could be varied only by large and expensive "steps" over the medium- and long-term. The implications were that once an airline determined its route structure—the combination of destinations, frequencies and aircraft—fuel, crew and ground staff costs were fixed. Almost the same amount of fuel was used whether a plane flew empty or full; crew and ground staff size were determined by the type of aircraft, not the passenger load. Of the 82% fixed and semi-variable operating costs, approximately 38 points related to provision of airborne transportation; the balance, 44 points, related to ground service—maintenance, provision of hubs and administration.

Yield Management

The industry's cost structure pressured carriers to sell more seats on each flight at higher yields—contribution to profit was increased by improving load factors and/or revenue yield per RPK. By 1993, the airline industry was increasing load factors and total revenue with millions of new passengers annually, most of whom were vacationers. The industry set a new record in 1993 with 2 000 billion RPKs travelled. Increased volumes of travellers reduced aircraft over-capacity and increased load factors, however, leisure travellers paid lower fares through advance bookings and group rates which reduced yields per RPK and in turn required further increases to load factors.

"Yield management," optimally balancing load factor and yield to maximize operating profit, was entrusted to sophisticated computer software embedded in the computer reservation system (CRS) operated by each major airline. Yield management software constantly reviewed bookings data for each flight to forecast demand and attempt to optimize final load factor and yield. Sophisticated algorithms calculated the opportunity on individual flights to charge selectively discounted fares within a class of service, to offer different classes of service (e.g., first, business, economy, excursion), and to vary fares with advance purchase conditions and with restrictions such as limited return or exchange privileges. By varying fares and classes of service, yield management attempted to optimize load factor and yield combinations on every flight, and in turn, maximize system-wide net revenue.

Industry conditions had resulted in steady declines in revenue yield per RPK of approximately 2% per year. This trend was expected to continue downwards unabated. Recent attempts by American Airlines (AA) to increase yields with simplified fares had been fruitless— the industry lacked pricing discipline; it would not limit the availability of discounted fares; individual airlines simply scrambled for market share.

Cost Management

Given the downward pressure on fares and intense competition for patronage, airline management placed priority on reducing operating costs. Unfortunately, two principal operating costs, fuel and labour (13% and 39% of costs respectively for U.S. carriers) offered limited opportunity for reduction. Both were non-variable costs dictated by route structure and fleet configuration. Fuel efficiency was closely monitored and modifications such as "hush-kitting" to improve efficiency were introduced, but oil price spikes could not be fully hedged. Accordingly, fuel costs occasionally increased to a much greater degree than fares could be supplemented with fuel surcharges.

Furthermore, as a service industry and because of the critical nature of flying safety, labour was a large part of costs and good labour relations were vital. High frequencies of employee/customer interaction and error-free mechanical records required highly trained staff to preserve customer patronage and confidence. Moreover, the older, larger carriers could not easily introduce more flexible and efficient work rules due to restrictive collective agreements. These carriers consequently struggled to compete with the younger airlines' higher labour productivity and efficiency ratios, and subsequently lower unit costs.

The age of active fleets of aircraft was closely watched. Newer aircraft offered significant efficiency and productivity savings due to reduced fuel and flight crew costs. So, not only did an airline have to match the capability of its fleet to its route structure to be efficient, it had to replace aircraft to take advantage of efficiency improvements offered by newer aircraft. However, delivery queues, previous lease commitments and limited cash flow made wholesale fleet changes impossible. A Boeing 747-400 cost US$150 million. Revamping fleets could be accomplished only as cash flow allowed.

Looking forward, significant reductions in labour costs would remain elusive: favourable fuel prices, not increased labour productivity, accounted for reduced 1993 operating costs. Furthermore, employee stock ownership initiatives with associated wage and benefit concessions at UAL, TWA, and Northwest were not expected to add lasting value to operations. Finally, increasing interest rates and fuel prices and the increasing need to replace aging aircraft foretold of greater airline indebtedness. Only those airlines able to increase productivity quickly—more quickly than nose-diving fares—could look forward to profitable operations.

Route Structure Economies

North American airlines generally had structured their operations around so-called "hub and spoke" networks since the hub structure was introduced by AA in 1982. Spokes fed passengers from outlying points into a central airport (hub) where passengers connected with other flights to other hubs, often travelling another spoke to their final destination. For passengers, hubs created the inconvenience of a transfer but offset the inconvenience with greater frequency of flights and lower fares.

Hubs were the most cost efficient method of distributing services over a large network—20% less costly system-wide than point-to-point service—and dramatically reduced the number of flights and aircraft necessary to serve the U.S. market versus a continent-wide system offering point-to-point service with equivalent frequency.

Airlines had been able to generate extra cost efficiencies in the mid-1980s by expanding their operations. By increasing the number of flights offered within a fixed route structure or alternately, by expanding the route structure with new destinations, airlines had stimulated passenger traffic faster than they increased costs. Additional flights from existing hubs were inexpensive to add because 55–70% of usual costs did not apply—the costs were already "sunk" into a previously established hub and trained ground crew. The allure of low break-even load factors and additional passenger "feed" was a powerful incentive to expand operations.

However, by the early-1990s, route structure economies were no longer valid options to "grow out of" the industry recession. Instead, the airlines were left to stimulate traffic on specific routes through marketing promotions—an expensive proposition. Stimulation amounted to discounting fares, offering frequent flyer plans and increasing service.

AERO-POLITICAL CONSIDERATIONS AND MARKET INTERFERENCE

Every nation has a history of using its airline(s) to achieve social and technological objectives, and undeniably, the motives influencing government engagement in an airline overlap into an expression of national pride. This mix of purpose and emotion required delicate negotiation between the airlines and their respective governments, and then between governments. The major influences—government subsidization, the social needs of developing nations, restrictive bilateral agreements, congestion, and government policy—are outlined below.

Government Subsidization

Subsidization of state-owned *flag carriers* was a major component of the continuing international over-capacity problem. The prestige associated with a flag carrier prevented serious debate regarding termination of unprofitable national airlines in many countries. As an example of government subsidization and market interference, Air France received US$3.7 billion in 1994 from the French and European Community governments for capital refinancing after 1993 losses of US$1.9 billion on revenues of US$12.9 billion.

Developing Nations with Social Needs

In developing countries, governments weighed the social role of aviation against the interests of private capital. Pressing internal development requirements would not be met by external, private airlines; governments were forced to operate and subsidize airlines. Naturally, these airlines attempted to expand internationally to equalize balance of payments and underwrite internal operations, adding to global over-capacity.

Bilateral Agreements, Cabotage and Fifth Freedom Rights

Bilateral negotiations between two countries determined what airline rights would be traded to balance economic and material benefits. Negotiations centred upon *cabotage* and six negotiable rights, the so-called *six freedoms of the air*. Negotiations received great emphasis because export of air service to foreign passengers typically repatriated 60–70% of fares, subsequently improving a country's balance of payments, GDP and overall transportation system. As a result, governments jealously protected airline(s) during negotiation of reciprocal agreements.

Cabotage was the right of an airline to carry "local traffic in a foreign market." As a general rule, cabotage was strictly prohibited. For example, Lufthansa was unable to board passengers originating in Atlanta for Dallas on its Frankfurt-Atlanta-Dallas service. Similarly, UAL could not board and deliver traffic between Munich and Frankfurt.

The *fifth freedom of the air* allowed carriers the privilege of boarding passengers in one foreign country for transport to another foreign country. Fifth freedom privileges acquired by the U.S. government following World War II were extremely important to U.S. carriers in Europe. Compact European geography allowed those with fifth freedoms to serve several major European cities on a single flight, for example New York-London-Frankfurt. Conversely, European carriers making a trip of similar distance and configuration, say Frankfurt-Atlanta-Dallas, were unable to board passengers on the Atlanta-Dallas leg. European carriers required, but could not obtain, cabotage privileges to carry "local traffic within a foreign (U.S.) market." This aberration in commercial access between carriers of different nations was created using the prevailing fifth freedom and cabotage privileges contained in the bilateral agreements. As an aside, there was a consensus that the U.S. government's position on multilateral agreements and *open skies* (relaxation of the *six freedoms*) would eventually force free trade on air service.

A related issue was limits to foreign ownership of airlines. With foreign ownership of airlines currently capped in many countries at 25% of voting stock and 50% of total equity, national legislatures were being pressured by airlines to relax restrictions and allow ingress of foreign equity. Existing equity restrictions would eventually be relaxed and foreign direct investment would be possible.

Congestion

Airport facility capacity constraints and landing rights became a contentious issue in the 1990s. It was practically impossible to gain access to major airports. New competitors were often denied access to important airports and routes while the incumbents further monopolized those airports. London-Heathrow, New York-JFK, Tokyo-Narita, Chicago-O'Hare, Paris-Orly, Hong Kong, Singapore: all were operating beyond design capacity and would grow more congested in the foreseeable future. Furthermore, access to airport gates as they became available was controlled either by local governments and airport authorities (in the U.S.) or by the airport's incumbent airlines.

The Walking Wounded

United States bankruptcy law allows insolvent firms to shelter themselves from creditors under a section titled Chapter 11. This provides the firm's management a moratorium period under the supervision of the bankruptcy court while financial reorganization is attempted. Theoretically, Chapter 11 preserves creditors' wealth more effectively by allowing restructuring rather than simply "shutting the doors."

Use of Chapter 11 provisions had become an exit strategy in the U.S. airline industry. Exit was very difficult as excess aircraft suitable for most routes were readily available—on-going airlines could demand unreasonably low prices for used aircraft. Also, routes were overcrowded and therefore less valuable than several years earlier. Facing a hostile environment, several airlines had slipped into Chapter 11, and by using the moratorium on their outstanding liabilities, had conducted a managed withdrawal over several years. The largest U.S. carriers claimed that Chapter 11, by delaying final bankruptcy decisions, promoted persistence of endemic over-capacity.

Furthermore, by freezing creditors' claims, Chapter 11 could drastically lower a firm's breakeven point. As a result, those airlines sheltering in Chapter 11 could survive on "artificially" low fares while they attempted to boost their load factors to self-sufficient levels. Other airlines were forced to match fares, disrupting industry pricing and further weakening those not yet in bankruptcy. Continental, TWA, Eastern and Pan Am operated domestic and international routes under bankruptcy court protection in the 1989–92 period. Only Continental and

TWA reorganized successfully, but all four had aggressively discounted their fares while under Court protection.

COMPETITIVE DEVELOPMENTS

In light of eroding yields, constant effort was made to increase load factors through better service—more attentive personnel, greater frequency of flights, more convenient connections and larger networks. This became an increasingly costly endeavour as service improvements had limited sustainable advantage. Airlines routinely matched each other's offerings on fares, frequent flyer plans, and service enhancements with the result that aircraft seats were reduced to a commodity. Industry competition in the 1990s centred on:

- a variety of alliances forming expansive global networks,
- the relative capabilities of computer reservation systems, and
- the relative attractiveness of frequent flyer plans.

Marketing and Equity Alliances and Code Sharing

By 1994, international route expansion was being accomplished by marketing alliances and code sharing, outright purchase of routes having become relatively expensive or not possible. Alliances were less capital intensive and quicker to assemble, and therefore, more effective avenues to international route expansion. For instance, marketing alliances allowed both UAL and Delta to complete worldwide route structures connecting all key markets during 1992. This would have been a drawn-out process if route acquisition alone had been pursued.

Alliance arrangements ranged from arm's length marketing partnerships to minority equity purchases and swaps, resulting in varying degrees of mutual commitment, complexity, stability and reversibility. The most common alliance (with the least mutual commitment) was a marketing agreement between carriers involving preferential exchange of traffic. For example, Canadian Airlines International (CAI) had a marketing agreement with Lufthansa under which CAI traffic to a variety of European destinations was booked onward from Frankfurt on Lufthansa. In return, Lufthansa traffic to Canada was booked to its final destination on CAI. Marketing alliances were volatile with partners and terms changing often. At one time, Air Canada had marketing alliances with Qantas, Air New Zealand and Lufthansa; these airlines were now allied with CAI.

Intermediate levels of commitment involved code sharing while the greatest mutual commitment with significant penalties for withdrawal was an equity alliance. Lufthansa and UAL had extensive code share arrangements without equity encumbrances while BA used equity alliances to secure "permanent" code share partnerships. Delta, Swissair and Singapore Airlines had one of the most complex equity alliances, requiring mutual exchange of 5% of each airline's equity and coordinated purchase of common aircraft and specialized maintenance. Their ultimate aim was creation of an integrated global operation. Table 3 illustrates typical carrier alliance networks.

TABLE 3   Alliances of Selected Carriers

	AA	*UAL*	*Delta*	*NWA*	*CO*	*BA*	*USAir*
Equity	Canadian	—	Singapore Airlines	KLM	Air Canada	Deutsche BA	British Airways
			Comair			GB Airways	
			Skywest			Qantas	
			Swissair			TAT	
						USAir	
Marketing only	British Midland	ALM Antillean	Aero-mexico	Alaska Airlines	Air France	Aero-mexico	All Nippon Airways
	Gulf Air	Air Canada	Aeroflot		Alitalia	Aer Lingus	Alitalia
	LOT Polish	Aloha	Austrian	USAir	SAS	Korean Air	Northwest
	Qantas	Ansett	Korean Air		Maersk Air	Qantas	
	South African	British Midland	Air New Zealand	America West	America West	Cathay Pacific	
		China Southern	Malev		Malaysia Airlines	Malaysia Airlines	
		Emirates	Sabena				
		Iberia	Varig				
		Cyprus Airways	Vietnam Airlines				
		Thai Inter-national	Virgin Atlantic				
		Lufthansa					

SOURCE: *Air Transport World.*

BA/USAir Code Sharing Arrangements

Code sharing by European carriers with U.S. carriers circumvented U.S. cabotage barriers by linking two carriers' intra-regional flights using one of the carrier's international flights. Code sharing did not require an equity partnership but BA deliberately withheld code sharing from USAir until the equity purchase was completed. Code sharing between USAir and BA in conjunction with an equity position was intended to create a stable platform for BA to build passenger traffic to and from the U.S. market to points around the world. BA clearly preferred more permanent marketing partners as it established a global network. USAir's flights would integrate into BA's route structure, and conversely, BA's flights into USAir's route structure.

For fiscal 1995, BA was estimating US$105 million incremental revenue from its global marketing/equity alliances detailed as follows: US$30–35 million was attributed to incremental code sharing traffic; another US$30–35 million to cross-linked FFPs attracting incremental traffic; and US$40 million to cost reductions through shared marketing and purchasing. A large proportion of these savings were anticipated originating in the USAir alliance, a dubious prospect given the results of the first 12 months of code sharing.

Moreover, dependence upon code sharing to build and channel passenger volume was risky as code sharing authorities were temporary. The U.S. Department of Transport (DOT) issued or renewed orders authorizing code sharing for one-year periods. The existing BA-USAir authorities on 65 airports expired 17 March 1995. In addition, approval of outstanding BA-USAir applications for code sharing authorities in another 65 U.S. and seven foreign destinations was being delayed by U.S. DOT.

Computer Reservation Systems

American Airlines' Sabre division originated computer reservation systems (CRSs) as an intentional competitive hurdle. Over time, all of the largest airlines developed proprietary CRSs to administer coordination of booking and ticket distribution activity, yield and cost management, and internal operations such as accounting. Smaller airlines cooperated in joint systems, or licensed another airline's CRS.

By 1994, CRSs were no longer effective in differentiating performance and distribution activities. Systems differences were insignificant when compared to disruptions caused by market rivalry and airlines operating under Chapter 11 protection.

Frequent Flyer Programs

Frequent flyer programs (FFPs) rewarded passengers with free trips and other benefits based on kilometres flown. First introduced by American Airlines, this marketing innovation favoured large carriers with extensive route systems on which customers could more readily accumulate mileage and select desirable reward destinations. As the power of FFPs became apparent, all major North American airlines quickly followed AA's lead. By 1994, most large European and Asian carriers had initiated their own FFPs or allied with North American carriers' FFPs. Like CRSs, FFPs were a mature innovation offering little or no advantage.

THE U.S. MARKET SITUATION—POINT-TO-POINT CARRIERS ATTACK

AA, Delta and UAL—the "Big Three"—competed with increasing difficulty in the U.S. due to their unadaptable cost structures, full-service philosophy and hub orientation. Attacks by lower cost, higher productivity point-to-point carriers, particularly Southwest Airlines of Dallas, created intense competition in the short-haul market.

Over time, each of the Big Three had focused its operations on a unique hub and spoke network resulting in limited competition at many airports. For example, at Dallas/Fort Worth International Airport, AA had a market share of over 60% and Delta accounted for a large part of the remainder; at Chicago-O'Hare, UAL and AA dominated. The result of unique networks and hub dominance was restriction of competition which enabled the airlines to charge fares as much as 20% higher than fares in openly contested markets.

The "Southwest Effect"

The only continuously profitable major North American airline, Southwest Airlines, avoided operating an expensive hub and spoke system. Instead, Southwest offered high frequency "no frills" point-to-point service in high volume, short-haul corridors, not unlike a bus route. It was the antithesis of the Big Three.

Southwest fundamentally changed the U.S. short-haul air travel industry with regard to its demand characteristics, cost structure and industry barriers. By not offering expensive service options like food and CRS listings and by reducing payment of expensive travel agency commissions with toll-free in-house reservation desks, Southwest kept costs low. Meanwhile, it boosted load factors by attracting customers from other forms of transportation—bus, auto, train—with fares 50–70% below full-service competitors. The diseconomies of point-to-point flying were overcome by focusing on high volume corridors and maintaining the lowest costs of the U.S. major airlines.

By 1993, the Southwest and its imitators had stolen a significant share of the U.S. domestic market from the Big Three. Full-service hub-oriented carriers like AA, Delta, and UAL could not compete profitably at the prevailing short-haul fares. As a result, they reduced flights and gates serving short-haul markets and re-emphasized long-haul and international routes. Market share of the Big Three slipped to 57% in 1993, down from 70% three years earlier.

The major airlines' hub and spoke operations could not compete effectively on short haul-high volume routes with high frequency, no frills point-to-point service. The majors' route and cost structures were poorly suited to frequent, short flights with many take-off and landing cycles. Hubs were interdependent and had to mesh connecting flights flawlessly. A congestion delay at one airport could inconvenience passengers and disrupt airlines/hubs for the balance of the day. Time delays had to be built into hub schedules, reducing productivity of personnel and equipment. Increasing productivity on short-haul flights required greater utilization of aircraft and crew which required de-linking flights from hubs and interdependent schedules and flying point-to-point instead.

This presented the full service airlines with a dilemma: their extensive networks required hub systems to achieve economies—corrupting the hub system with hybrid point-to-point and hub route structures could dangerously increase costs, diminish service frequency, disrupt on-time connections and de-stabilize connector systems feeding into long-haul and overseas routes.

The Big Three had yet to respond to attacks on the short-haul market. Instead, they dealt with their non-competitive unit costs on short-haul operations with layoffs, wage rollbacks and concessions, allying with regional carriers, and retreating to long-haul and international routes—a route structure better suited to full-service, high cost operations. By mid-1994, Continental and USAir had responded directly to the Southwest challenge with fundamental route structure changes. In addition, UAL had announced introduction of *Shuttle by UAL* with point-to-point service beginning in the Fall of 1994. It was yet to be determined if hub-oriented airlines could change to point-to-point service and achieve Southwest's industry-low cost structure. To date, airlines had found imitating Southwest's point-to-point route structure very expensive.

USAIR: PERFORMANCE AND PROSPECTS

USAir was the weakest of the eight major U.S. airlines: its cost structure was non-competitive with low cost and financially restructured airlines; its equity was severely depleted from losses estimated to reach US$2.4 billion by the end of the three years 1991–93; its operations focused on business travel in the short-haul Eastern U.S. market; its fleet was older than most; and its labour unions were not yet convinced of a pressing need to give concessions to improve productivity.

USAir was also different than its U.S. competitors from an operations perspective. Its history as a conglomeration of smaller commuter airlines—Allegheny, Piedmont, PSA, Suburban and Pennsylvania—made it unique and gave it a different competitive focus. USAir operations were isolated in the Eastern U.S. commuter market, allowing it to offset higher operating costs associated with flying short-haul routes through congested airports with higher traffic volumes and the ability to extract premium net yields per RPK.

Following 1991, USAir lost control of its unit costs in comparison to other major U.S. carriers. Costs per ASK had risen more than 9% in the past two years while its competitors had held or reduced their costs. Furthermore, USAir's fares were subjected to constant promotions, eroding their once industry-high net yields.

Until 1993, the other U.S. airlines had been content to focus in other markets, not challenging USAir on the Eastern U.S. short-haul routes. However, in Fall 1993, Southwest Airlines (LUV) inaugurated high frequency service to Chicago and Cleveland from Baltimore/Washington International Airport with fares 75–80% below those offered by USAir. USAir responded by matching most fares and increasing the frequency of its service.

Then, in October 1993, Continental Airlines (CAL) announced route changes centred on the high volume Eastern U.S. corridors, primarily adopting the low-cost, no-frills point-to-point system. By early-1994, Continental Lite (CALite) accounted for 15% of CAL's domestic route structure with its "Peanuts Fares." CAL planned to convert 50% of its domestic route to point-to-point service by mid-1994.

USAir responded by introducing "Project High Ground" and "Quick Turns" in the first quarter of 1994 to introduce point-to-point service and enhance productivity. It immediately started conversion of 25% of its daily flights to point-to-point service. By late-April, USAir reported 20% more ASKs flown without adding assets due to point-to-point conversions, and that it was on target for a breakeven operating profit in the second quarter.

With competition escalating in its traditional market, it was probable that USAir would continue to suffer losses. Whereas LUV and CAL had low cost structures and could subsidize low and below-cost fares from operations elsewhere, USAir's high cost structure, limited cash reserves, and base in the Eastern U.S. business travel market left it vulnerable. USAir was forecasting pretax losses of US$350 million for 1994.

Exhibit 1 contains comparative performance data on the U.S. majors and BA. BA ranked first in international RPK and passenger counts, whereas USAir ranked 50th with minimal international traffic or route structure, principally Frankfurt, Paris and Mexico City. The Foreign Revenue section presents 1993 regional revenues where available, or otherwise notes regions in which the airlines have active international operations. Foreign Revenue Growth indicates year-over-year international revenue by company, where available.

Following release of USAir's 1993 losses in March, BA announced it would not invest further in USAir until the outcome of USAir's efforts to reduce operating costs was known. However, with US$400 million already invested in USAir, and US$1.5 billion invested in equity alliances globally, could BA afford to ignore the situation?

GLOSSARY OF COMMON MEASUREMENTS OF PERFORMANCE AND ACTIVITY

1   *Revenue Passenger Kilometres (RPK)* The number of revenue passengers carried multiplied by the distance flown.

2   *Available Seat Kilometres (ASK)* The number of seats available for sale multiplied by the distance flown.

3   *Passenger Load Factor* RPK expressed as a percentage of ASK

4   *Revenue Yield* Passenger revenue from scheduled operations divided by scheduled RPKs.

5   *Unit Costs* Operating costs from scheduled operations divided by scheduled ASKs.

6   *Available Tonne-Kilometres (ATK)* The number of tonnes (2 204 lb.) of capacity available for carriage of revenue load (passenger and cargo) multiplied by the distance flown.

7   *Revenue Tonne-Kilometres (RTK)* The revenue load in tonnes multiplied by the distance flown.

8   *Breakeven Weight Load Factor* The load factor required to equate total traffic revenue with operating costs.

EXHIBIT 1   1993 Performance Data: U.S. Carriers and British Airways

	AA	UAL	Delta	NWA	CAL	BA	USAir	South-west
RPK Traffic *(millions)*								
International	46 419	62 647	36 532	40 977	17 465	75 044	3 960	—
Rank	4	2	9	7	16	1	50	—
Domestic	109 883	99 879	96 813	52 572	50 649	5 042	52 720	30 481
Total	156 302	162 526	133 345	93 549	68 113	80 086	56 681	30 481
Rank	1	2	3	4	6	5	7	(16)
Passenger Traffic *(thousands)*								
International	14 305	10 942	8 202	7 481	5 076	22 367	—	—
Rank	3	5	10	13	20	1	—	—
Domestic	68 240	58 730	76 829	36 640	33 551	5 766	52 774	36 955
Total	82 545	69 672	85 032	44 121	38 627	30 595	53 678	36 955
Rank	2	3	1	5	6	9	4	(7)
Passenger Load Factor %								
International	63.3	70.7	64.5	71.1	67.4	70.0	69.1	—
Domestic	59.2	65.1	61.6	63.6	61.8	68.9	58.6	68.4
Total load factor %	60.4	67.1	62.3	66.7	63.2	69.9	59.2	68.4
Breakeven load factor	~ 58.	65.6	65.5		65.2	61.3	61.7	

EXHIBIT 1 (continued)

	AA	UAL	Delta	NWA	CAL	BA	USAir	South-west
Cost Structure (US¢)								
Revenue Yield/RPK	8.3	7.8	8.4		7.1	9.4	10.7	7.3
Unit Cost/ASK	5.1	5.8	5.9	5.2	4.9	7.3	6.9	5.2
Foreign Revenue (US$ millions)								
Asia-Pacific	362	✔	✔	✔	✔			
Europe	1 659	✔	✔	✔	✔	3 603		
Latin America	1 888	✔	✔		✔			
Middle-East			✔					
Africa						1 332		
The Americas						3 003		
Mid-East, India, Asia-Pacific						1 390		
Foreign Revenue Growth (US$ billions)								
1991	2.67	3.87	1.18		1.1	5.50	n/a	n/a
1992	3.68	4.86	1.95		1.2	5.03	n/a	n/a
1993	3.91	5.56	2.58		1.1	5.74	n/a	n/a
Financial Data (US$ millions)								
Operating revenue	14 737	14 511	11 997	8 650	3 284	9 328	7 083	2 296
Operating profit (loss)	374	263	(575)	272	112	734	(75)	291
Operating profit margin	2.5%	1.8%			3.4%	7.8%		12.7%
Net expense and interest	(688)	(310)	(76)		(122)	(289)	(274)	32
Income before taxes and accounting changes	(314)	(47)	(651)		(11)	445	(350)	259
Net income	*(110)	(50)	(1 002)	(115)	(39)	423	(393)	169
Less preferred dividend	*60	33	110		—	157	74	5
Net income to stockholders	*(170)	(83)	(1 112)		(39)	266	(467)	164
Total assets less current liabilities	13 509	7 944	8 898		2 797	8 365	4 641	2 097
Long-term debt; redeemable preferred stock	(7 290)	(3 529)	(3 799)		(1 579)	(5 563)	(3 203)	(639)
Deferred credits & other liabilities	(3 051)	(3 212)	(3 186)		(497)	(98)	(1 651)	(404)
Total stockholders equity	3 168	1 203	1 913		721	2 350	(213)	1 054

Note: Reported in U.S. funds.

* Net income, dividend and net income apply to AMR Corp. 1993 Consolidated Statement, AA's parent.

** CAL emerged from Chapter 11, April 28, 1994.

SOURCE: Airline Annual Reports.

COMPETING IN THE NORTH AMERICAN MARKET

PART

7

DAMARK PACKAGING INC.: WRAPPING UP MEXICO

Mary M. Crossan, David Ager and
Luvy Gonzalez de Wilson

CASE

22

In early June, 1994, William (Bill) Steel, vice-president of Damark Packaging Inc. (Damark) of Markham, Canada, reflected on the implications of accepting the order he had just received from Dr. Roberto Silva Nieto, whose company, SINIE, held the exclusive Mexico distribution rights for Damark's products. Dr. Silva reported that he had received an urgent request from a client for US$1 million in shrink wrap packaging equipment. He was calling Bill to offer Damark the order, but said he would need a quick reply because he would have to get back to his client within the week, and that he would need time to pursue other suppliers if Damark was not prepared to handle the order. For Damark, the order would represent a fundamental shift in the primary source of the company's sales, such that over 50% of total corporate revenues would originate from Mexico. Although the order satisfied Damark management's objective to expand through foreign markets, Bill was uncertain about the future viability of the Mexican market and he was worried that Damark was foregoing opportunities that were sustainable in the long run. Specifically, Bill wondered whether Damark's long-term survival would be better ensured by focusing on more stable markets such as those in Europe or by increasing the company's efforts in the United States.

Although almost 25% of Damark's sales currently originated in Mexico, Bill had always looked upon Mexico as an experiment. Clearly, he could no longer do so, and he would need to decide if and how Mexico fit into the company's long-term plans.

Mary M. Crossan, David Ager of the Western Business School and Luvy Gonzalez de Wilson of the Instituto Tecnológico des Estudios Superiores de Monterrey prepared this case. Copyright © 1995, The University of Western Ontario. This material is not covered under authorization from CanCopy or any reproduction rights organization. Any form of reproduction, storage or transmittal of this material is prohibited without written permission from Western Business School, The University of Western Ontario, London, Canada N6A 3K7

THE SHRINK WRAP PACKAGING INDUSTRY

Shrink wrapping is a packaging process whereby a product or a bundle of products is surrounded by a loose-fitting sheet of plastic film[1] and fed along a conveyor belt through a heated chamber where the plastic film, activated by the heat, shrinks so that it forms a tight skin around the product or bundle. It was discovered that shrink film offered several advantages: it provided good protection from water, dust and bugs; it allowed the merchandise to be clearly displayed; and it offered, depending on the quality of plastic film that was used, rigidity so that the group of products could be held together for easier transportation.

Shrink wrapping also provided a versatile form of packaging. It was used for food products such as frozen and canned goods, printed materials, toys and games, and industrial products such as oil filters and jugs of windshield wiper fluid. Exhibit 1 presents a number of products that have been packaged using the shrink wrapping process.

Packaging: Industry Overview

Packaging was a multi-billion-dollar industry in North America. Sales trends for the industry reflected trends in the unit sales of goods, particularly foods, beverages and personal products, although pharmaceuticals and industrial products were also important. The most recent development was a move away from expensive, elaborate, fancy packaging toward lower cost packaging which used less material. End customers in the industry insisted on innovation in packaging design, help with planning their filling and packaging production lines, and prompt service. Competition in the industry was described as fierce, with several different packaging materials vying for a position in the market.

Shrink Wrap Packaging: Industry Overview

As a sub-sector of the packaging industry, shrink wrapping competed against alternative packaging such as glass, metal, paperboard, Styrofoam and other formats of plastic packaging.

Shrink wrap packaging had been introduced in the late 1960s, although almost a decade had passed before it became popular as a viable alternative to traditional packaging formats. Three phenomena have been credited with increasing the awareness and popularity of shrink wrap packaging.

The first phenomenon was the Tylenol scare that had erupted in 1978 when Johnson & Johnson found that someone had laced a shipment of Tylenol tablets with cyanide. Pharmaceutical companies responded to the crisis by quickly developing a tamper-evident package. Shrink wrapping provided an easy, cost effective solution to their problem. Bill described the situation in the industry in 1978:

> Pharmaceutical companies went crazy for six months after the incident buying shrink wrap packaging equipment. If someone had wanted to give the shrink wrap packaging industry a kick in the rear end to get it started, he couldn't have come up with a better plan.

---

[1] Plastic film used in shrink wrapping was a thin sheet of plastic that resembled cellophane wrap, but possessed unique, physical properties.

The second phenomenon occurred in the mid- to late-1980s. Traditionally, plastics had been considered the "bad boys" in the packaging industry. However, by the late 1980s plastic had become a more desirable substance in terms of disposal than cardboard. First of all, because of its compressibility, it consumed much less space. In addition, it burned fairly easily. And finally, it was a stable substance which, when buried, did not fall apart like paper or cardboard and leech many unpleasant chemicals into the water table. These findings had led consumers to put pressure on retailers to replace corrugated cardboard with an alternative packaging medium.

The third phenomenon was the emergence of warehouse clubs such as Price Club and COSTCO. Almost 90% of all the merchandise sold in these stores was shrink wrapped. The strategy behind these organizations was to sell bundles of products, rather than one product, and therefore offer the consumer better prices. Shrink wrapping allowed these stores to bundle several products (e.g., 12 cans of peas) together securely and at the same time clearly display the product to the consumer. Because most companies spent large amounts of money on labels, it was important that they not be hidden inside boxes where they would have little opportunity to influence the customer's buying decision. The warehouse clubs spawned an entirely new industry that specialized in supplying custom packaged merchandise. Most often, these new companies used shrink wrapping equipment to bundle products together.

Shrink Wrap Packaging: Industry Structure

The industry consisted of shrink wrap film manufacturers, shrink wrap equipment manufacturers, distributors and end-users (consumer goods manufacturers, custom packaging companies and retail operations).

The industry mechanism was simple. Independent[2] distributors purchased plastic film and shrink wrap packaging equipment from manufacturers and sold it to end customers. Distributors preferred to carry films manufactured by DuPont and WR Grace (operated under the name Cryovac in Canada) because end customers, who had come to associate films manufactured by these two companies with quality and reliability, were prepared to pay a premium for them. In addition, both companies were very active in research and development and were responsible for most of the innovations in the industry both in terms of applications and films. Other plastic film manufacturers, which didn't enjoy the same position as DuPont and WR Grace, were forced to compete on the basis of price in order to convince distributors to carry their products. These second-tier film manufacturers were known to sell their films at prices 20 to 45% less than those charged for DuPont and WR Grace films.

Shrink wrap packaging equipment manufacturers competed on the basis of price. The two largest manufacturers were Shanklin and Weldotron, each of which enjoyed annual sales in excess of US$20 million. These two companies were the exception. Most equipment manufacturers had sales of less than US$2 million.

The manufacturers were divided into two groups: those which manufactured machines capable of process speeds of 60 products per minute or greater, and those whose machines oper-

---

[2] While some film and equipment manufacturers maintained their own sales forces, most sold their product through distributors.

ated at speeds of less than 60 products per minute. Very few manufacturers did both. Damark manufactured machines that fell in the latter category. As a result Bill did not consider Shanklin and Weldotron to be competitors. He explained:

> We tend not to think of them (Shanklin and Weldotron) as competitors because in excess of 95% of their market are machines that we don't make. They might do the same thing—they might make a form-fill-seal machine—but it operates at a much higher level. It's one that will do 150 packages a minute.
>
> Shanklin and Weldotron could probably serve the '60 products per minute or less' segment of the market but it would require a complete re-organization of their manufacturing operation to focus on slower, non-custom machines. The profits are so lucrative in the upper segment of the market that I don't believe they have much interest in the lower segment.

In 1994, annual sales in North America of shrink wrap packaging equipment were estimated to be the following:

Country	Number of Manufacturers	Sales of Machines that Operate at Speeds of Less Than 60 Products per Minute (C$)	Sales of Machines that Operate at Speeds of Greater Than 60 Products per Minute (C$)	Total Industry Sales (C$)
Canada	43	$2 000 000	$1 000 000	$3 000 000
United States	172	$16 500 000	$45 500 000	$62 000 000
Mexico	?	?	?	?

Distributors

Distributors sold both plastic film and shrink wrap packaging equipment, although they earned their primary income through the sale of plastic film. As one distributor explained:

> I can almost afford to give the machines away as long as the customer buys the film.

Distributors played a critical role in the industry. Many sold the equipment of several different manufacturers and the end customer often left the decision of what equipment best suited their needs to the distributor. Many manufacturers agreed that given the choice between the best machine in the market or the best distributor in the market, without a doubt, the best distributor was the obvious choice because as the leader in the industry, end customers gravitated to this person regardless of the equipment he or she sold. As well, the leaders almost always sold the leading films in the industry and as such were closely involved in new film and new applications research. Information on future trends in the industry were extremely important to manufacturers for both new product development and market forecasting.

Distributors expected manufacturers to promote the equipment in trade magazines and to attend trade shows. They also expected manufacturers to provide a high level of sales support before, during and after a sale was made. The sales support requirement was particularly important in the case of larger, more expensive machines which often required a significant amount of custom design work.

THE MEXICAN SHRINK WRAPPING EQUIPMENT MARKET

Dr. Silva described the Mexican shrink wrapping equipment market:

> In the eighties, the market for shrink wrapping equipment in Mexico was characterized by slow, steady annual growth of about 5%. Industries such as the egg industry were end-users, but there was no real force pushing growth as corrugated paper dominated the packaging industry and the companies that did use plastic, such as Cerveceria Cuauhtemoc-Moctezuma (brewery), required machines that handled 75 to 120 packages per minute.
>
> By mid-1991, there were rumours that U.S. discount retailers were planning to enter the Mexican market. In June, 1991, Comercial Mexicana, a large Mexican retailer, formed a strategic alliance with Price Club. Two weeks later, CIFRA, the largest Mexican retail conglomerate, announced a joint-venture with U.S. retail giant Wal-Mart to open a version of Sam's Club stores called Club Aurrera in Mexico. One year later, the first Club Aurrera opened in Mexico City and became the second largest store, in terms of sales, in the Wal-Mart empire. These retailing successes led CIFRA and Wal-Mart to expand rapidly, with several new store openings planned in the coming years. These new U.S. retailers offered Mexican consumers, many of whom had previously travelled to the U.S. to purchase foreign manufactured products, the opportunity of acquiring this merchandise without the expense of a trip. The potential for growth of discount retailers in Mexico was expected to drive the demand for shrink packaging equipment in Mexico. By 1992, the annual growth in the shrink packaging industry was projected at 20%.

According to Dr. Silva, the packaging industry in Mexico relied on trade shows as its primary means of promotion, followed by trade magazines and direct selling. Promotion, although necessary in Mexico, was not as critical because the market was far from being saturated.

A practice that frustrated Dr. Silva was that of Mexican equipment manufacturers who would by-pass their distributors and sell direct to the client, a client that very often had been obtained through the distributor. This occurred because most people who bought shrink wrapping equipment were looking for only one thing, the lowest price. Although the contractionary monetary policies of the government that had fuelled this attitude were expected to continue, Dr. Silva believed that in the future, companies would pay more for packaging equipment in response to the North American Free Trade Agreement (NAFTA) that had forced Mexican companies to manufacture globally competitive products. Dr. Silva believed that the only way Mexican manufactured goods could meet international standards was through the adoption of world class technology and machinery.

DAMARK PACKAGING

Damark Packaging Inc. was founded in 1980 in Toronto, Canada, by William Steel and Derek Camden. The company was established to design and manufacture automated sleeve wrap packaging equipment, which was suitable for packaging a broad range of items including: industrial, consumer and pharmaceutical products. Prior to founding Damark, both men had worked for a Canadian company that was one of only three in the world which designed and manufactured automated shrink wrap packaging machines.

By 1983, sales of the shrink wrap packaging equipment had led the company to grow to five employees and had resulted in annual revenues of approximately C$600 000–C$700 000.

It was at this time that Allied Automation of Dallas, Texas, made a bid to purchase Damark from Bill and Derek. Shortly thereafter, Damark became the research and development department for Allied Automation. Bill and Derek were retained by Allied to continue to manage the Canadian subsidiary.

By 1990, Allied Automation had undergone several changes that led Bill and Derek to make a bid to repurchase Damark from its U.S. parent. As William Steel described the situation:

> The recession hit them and they (Allied) went into a tail spin. The last thing they needed was a foreign based subsidiary.

In the sales agreement, Allied agreed to turn all Canadian assets[3] over to Bill and Derek. Allied also agreed to continue to act as a distributor for Damark's product in the U.S. When Damark was repurchased in June 1991, annual sales were approximately C$1.8 million and the company had grown to 20 employees.

Upon repurchasing the company Bill and Derek, motivated by a strategy to increase the size of the company in terms of sales and profits, relocated Damark from Toronto to Markham, and redesigned the Damark product line. Most U.S. manufacturers were trying to build the sleeve wrap packaging equipment more cheaply, often by removing features from the machines or by replacing better quality components with cheaper components of poorer quality; however, Damark management chose to use the best quality materials and components in their machines and to incorporate more features into each. They reasoned that because of the forthcoming North American Free Trade Agreement (NAFTA) between Canada, the U.S. and Mexico, and the 15% difference in production costs between Canadian shrink wrap packaging manufacturers and their U.S. counterparts, there was no way that Damark would be able to compete on the basis of price. Instead, the company would compete on the basis of quality equipment. Bill and Derek decided that any promotional material would emphasize the fact the Damark's equipment was made of superior components and offered many more features than the machines of most of its competitors. To reinforce the quality concept, Damark offered 10-year warranties on most of its equipment.

Bill and Derek had also realized that, if Damark expected to experience sales growth and increased profitability, the company could not depend on the stable Canadian market. Instead Damark would need to expand into foreign markets. By 1994 Damark had focused its efforts on selling equipment in the United States and Mexico. While Damark had also sold equipment in Greece, Saudi Arabia, Nicaragua and Panama, these sales were unsolicited, and had come as a result of an advertisement in a trade magazine or someone having seen Damark's booth at a trade show. Both Bill and Derek considered such sales to be bonuses.

Initially, the company's expansion strategy appeared to be effective and by November 1994, Bill estimated that sales for fiscal year 1995 would reach C$2.6 million. Damark's Income Statement and Balance Sheet for 1992, 1993 and 1994, and year-to-date figures for fiscal 1995 appear in Exhibit 2.

---

[3] The Canadian assets consisted primarily of manufacturing equipment, raw materials, work-in-process, and finished goods inventory.

Internal Organization and Operations

Damark was run by William Steel and Derek Camden and their spouses. Phyllis Steel, who worked as a Chartered Accountant at a firm in Toronto, served as the company's accountant, and Lorraine Camden managed the company's human resource function. Exhibit 3 presents the company's organization chart. While Derek was designated as the company's president, Bill explained that this was purely for psychological reasons:

> If you are in sales and marketing and your card says President, you have no excuse for hesitating on a deal. If on the other hand your card says Vice President you always have the option of telling the client that you must check with the President first.

Managing the company required an enormous amount of time, and left both Bill and Derek with little time to think about strategic issues or the development of formal management systems. When they had sold Damark to Allied Automation in the early 1980s, part of what had motivated them to sell the company had been their belief that they would acquire management systems. Much to their disappointment this had not occurred. As Bill described it:

> Apart from our accounting system, most information travels through the company informally by word of mouth. As a result, it is very difficult to develop an idea about costs or the actual time it takes to put an order through the plant.

In early 1994, in response to the company's increased activity, Bill hired a person to be responsible for shipping and receiving and the collection of accounts receivable.

Manufacture of Packaging Machines

Damark's manufacturing process was not complex. Raw steel was fabricated in-house according to order specifications, or in some cases the stamped pieces were received from a local company. These pieces were then painted and were shipped to one of three assembly areas where the equipment was built.

Bill organized the company's products, as detailed in Exhibit 4, into three broad categories:

- Smaller semi-automatic systems
- Larger semi-automatic systems
- Automatic systems

The smaller semi-automatic systems required little or no custom work and were manufactured at the rate of 28 to 33 per month. Because these machines sold so quickly and with such consistency, they were manufactured without prior orders. On the other hand, the larger semi-automatic systems and the automatic systems often required a significant amount of custom work and their manufacture was begun once an order had been received. However, production of the latter two categories was usually backlogged because of the more complicated engineering required for their construction, and because of the unpredictability of orders. Unfortunately, hiring more plant workers would not alleviate this problem, as it originated in the design rather than the manufacturing department. Damark had once tried to find a solution by hiring a recent engineering graduate to design two in-feed mechanisms; however, when the product he developed had been impossible to manufacture, management had been forced to terminate his contract. Damark had also considered hiring an experienced design engineer at

C$80 000 a year, a price that Bill believed Damark could not afford. Another option had been to hire experienced design engineers on a contractual basis. Although this would be less expensive, it would require time on the part of Derek and Peter Ellis (Mechanical Design Manager), spent training this person to ensure that they understood how the equipment worked and appreciated the company's manufacturing capabilities, in order to avoid an experience similar to that which had occurred with the recently graduated design engineer.

Sales and Promotion

Damark sold its equipment almost exclusively through distributors because the volume of equipment the company sold was insufficient to sustain a sales force. This practice was typical of the industry. As Bill explained:

> The salespeople would starve to death if they relied exclusively on selling our equipment to make a living.

The company provided support to its distributors by advertising in trade magazines, participating in trade shows, working closely with customers on custom orders, and responding quickly to customer requests for assistance.

Damark management had found that it could service its clients quite well from its head office in Markham. Often a client required the greatest level of support when the system was being designed and installed. After the machine was operational, most repairs and routine maintenance could be performed by an in-house technician. Specialized repair technicians were not necessary because of the simplicity of the design.

The equipment was very well known and was highly regarded in the "less than 60 units per minute" segment of the Canadian shrink wrap packaging equipment market. Bill believed that Damark controlled in excess of 60% of this segment of the market. As a result, Damark had little trouble finding Canadian distributors to carry its product, and it was able to work closely with the larger plastic film manufacturers in Canada to develop new applications for shrink wrap packaging films and machines. Unfortunately, the company had not experienced the same reception in the United States.

DAMARK IN THE UNITED STATES

In 1991, shortly after their repurchase of the company, Damark's management team realized that any future growth would have to come from the U.S. Anxious to proceed, Bill and Derek located four film and equipment distributors spread throughout the U.S. and arranged for these companies to sell Damark products to U.S. clients. Bill described the results of this strategy as marginal and explained the company's performance:

> We met with limited success (few repeat customers) and we were very disappointed, especially when it was clear that, despite the fact that the benefits of our products far exceeded those of our U.S. competitors, their products continued to be selected over ours. Between Derek and me, we were spending about 10% of our time concentrating on the U.S. market. This was clearly insufficient. Further exacerbating the situation was our lack of a physical presence in the U.S. that resulted in our being perceived as foreign.

The shrink wrapping equipment business in the U.S., especially at the low end, required that you constantly be at the door step of the customer. It didn't matter how good your prices and products were, if you weren't there you were forgotten and if you weren't American, you were immediately at a disadvantage.

We concluded that in order to expand we needed to spend more time there, as having a physical presence in the U.S. was essential.

In late 1992, Bill and Derek decided that Damark would establish a presence by founding a new company called Damark U.S. They would hire a manager for this project who would work with U.S. distributors to convince them to sell Damark's machines.

In June 1993, Damark U.S. opened its doors. Bill and Derek had hired John Salamone, a colleague of theirs from Allied Automation who had recently left that company. By November 1994, the new company was supplying machines to over 16 U.S. distributors. Bill, who estimated that 20% of Damark's sales and 10% of Damark's profits came from the U.S. operation, explained, "Damark U.S. was profitable, and it seemed to have turned the corner."

DAMARK IN MEXICO[4]

The Monterrey Trade Show

In early 1992, Damark was invited by Industry Canada to participate in the Canadian Government Trade Show at Cintermex in Monterrey, Nuevo León, Mexico. Bill described his initial reaction:

Prior to receiving the invitation to participate in the trade show, Mexico wasn't even on the list of countries that Damark was considering in its expansion plans. My and my partner's perception of Mexico was of a country where labour rates were low, people didn't speak English and manufacturing equipment and systems were antiquated. I knew that shrink wrap packaging equipment was being manufactured in Mexico and that this equipment was much less expensive than our own. Apart from the above, neither I nor my partner knew much about Mexico.

Despite their lack of knowledge about the Mexican market, Bill and Derek decided to participate in the trade show. Bill explained their decision:

We had committed ourselves to growing the company through expansion into foreign markets. The Mexico trade show represented an opportunity to see what was in Mexico with a minimum drain on corporate resources.

In February 1992, Bill arrived at the Monterrey trade show armed with a small shrink wrap packaging machine and some brochures that described Damark and its products. Bill described what ensued:

The first day at the trade show exceeded my wildest expectations. All my brochures were gone, I had received offers from four companies to distribute Damark products in Mexico and I had sold the shrink wrap packaging machine and had been paid in U.S. dollars.

---

[4] Exhibit 5 presents some leading economic indicators for Mexico, and Exhibit 6 presents a discussion of the history of the country's economy.

It had become obvious to me that there was a lot more potential in Mexico than I had originally imagined. In addition, the people I had talked to were telling me that despite the fact that
Damark machines were more expensive, the reasons for the higher price were obvious and they
were prepared to pay more for a better quality product.

While in Monterrey Bill was invited to visit a number of manufacturing operations in
which he had observed the following:

These people were using equipment that looked as if it had been made out of Meccano. It was
no wonder that they were anxious to put our equipment in their plant.

The people Bill met with all conveyed the same message:

If we are going to be a part of NAFTA, like we believe that we are, we are going to have to
start producing products of a higher quality than we are producing right now. It's pretty hard to
ship consumer products in Mexico. As barriers drop and we are required to compete against
foreign imports and as we try to expand by moving outward, we are going to have to go for
higher quality product ourselves. One of the ways we are going to do that is in improving the
packaging. In order to improve our packaging we are going to need something (equipment) of
a high quality to move us to that level.

Although there was some less expensive U.S. shrink wrapping equipment of similar quality in Mexico, Bill thought that his Canadian company would have an advantage in future
sales. He sensed that Mexicans, in general, preferred to do business with Canadians over
Americans because Canadians shared their dislike of high pressure U.S. sales tactics. Bill concluded that:

Canada is in the same boat as Mexico vis-à-vis the United States and I believe that Mexicans
find comfort in that.

After the trade show, Bill appointed two of the four Mexican distributors that had approached him at the trade show to represent Damark products in Mexico.

In May 1992, Bill attended a second Mexican trade show, this time in Mexico City. Although he had been optimistic about prospects in Mexico after the Monterrey trade show,
three months had passed and Bill had not yet received an order. During the Mexico City trade
show, Dr. Roberto Silva Nieto, president and owner of SINIE a packaging machinery and
plastic film company, approached Bill regarding the distribution of Damark products in Mexico. Dr. Silva had approached Bill at the Monterrey show, but Bill had decided against appointing SINIE to represent Damark in Mexico because SINIE represented Allied Automation
(Damark's former parent) in Mexico. Despite his previous reluctance to do so, and in response
to the dismal performance of the first two Mexican distributors, Bill appointed SINIE Damark's exclusive distributor in Mexico.

Up to 1988, SINIE had exclusively handled national brands of equipment and material. As
the Mexican economy had opened and doing business with foreigners had become easier, Dr.
Silva decided to start importing machinery in a move that proved to be an excellent growth
strategy for the company because foreign partners tended to honour their distribution contracts, a practice which was less common in Mexico.[5] By 1992, SINIE was handling several

---

[5] In order to guarantee a sale, some Mexican equipment manufacturers and film manufacturers would by-pass their
distributor and sell direct to the end user in order to be able to offer the end user a more competitive price on the
product. In most cases the end user was a client that the distributor located and with whom the distributor had established a relationship.

U.S. brand name products including Afisamatic, Allied Automation, APV Rockford, Clamco, and Shanklin and had offices in the three largest industrial centres in Mexico: Monterrey, Mexico City and Guadalajara. Combined these three centres accounted for over 80% of all the industrial activity in the country.

Appointing SINIE appeared to be the break that Damark needed. After only six months in Mexico Damark had sold over C$250 000 worth of shrink wrap packaging equipment. By June 1994, Bill estimated that over 25% of Damark's sales originated in Mexico, and this most recent request from Dr. Silva could push that figure to well over 50%. Specifically, the most recent order was broken down as follows:

- Category 1 Packaging Machines — 20 units
- Category 2 Packaging Machines — 10 units
- Category 3 Packaging Machines — 45 units
- Category 4 Packaging Machines — 17 units

Through his association with SINIE and the various sales of shrink wrap packaging equipment that had been made to Mexico, Bill had learned a great deal about doing business in the Mexico, but most importantly he had come to understand how Mexicans used the word mañana. Literally translated mañana meant tomorrow. Very often, when used in a business context by Mexicans, the word meant "sometime in the future." Often Bill had received telephone calls from Dr. Silva who was calling to say that "mañana" he would receive an order for equipment. In the majority of cases it wasn't until three weeks later that the client actually placed the order.

FUTURE GROWTH

Bill commented that both he and his partner were particularly interested in seeing Damark's future growth coming in part from Europe, in particular the United Kingdom. As former Britons, both men knew the culture and the market, and because of the heavy concentration of people in areas they were confident that Damark's prospects looked favourable. As well, such an operation would give them an excuse to travel to Europe at least once or twice a year.

The two partners were also excited about what was happening in Europe in the shrink wrapping industry. As Bill explained:

> Europe tends to be a couple of years ahead, not in technology but in the application of technology. This could definitely help us in our North American operation. As well, it's almost as if people over in Europe get together and fix the price and then go away and build the machines, because prices appear to be incredibly high.

On several occasions, Damark had made attempts to penetrate the European market; yet, despite the favourable aspects, the company had not succeeded. The phenomenon seemed very strange, because both men were perceived as British, although clearly some factor was working against them. Bill commented:

> All we knew was that we if we were to seriously pursue the European market, we would have to devote a considerable amount of time and energy to understanding 'how' the market over there worked. Time right now is non-existent.

Most of the time the partners felt stretched and wondered whether they might not be better off by selling the company. They had talked about the flexibility and freedom they would have "to do other things" if they were to sell the company. And yet, they had put so much energy and time into building Damark that they desired passing it along to their children. In fact, both men's daughters, aged 14 and 15, had indicated an interest to take over the business in the future.

In spite of their desire for growth, whether it be Canada, the United States, Mexico or Europe, Bill and Derek considered other options:

> Damark almost needs to take six months where we don't manufacture anything and instead, think about where the company is headed in the future.
>
> Perhaps we should bring someone in from outside to help us to put better systems in place. Maybe then we could better understand our costs and keep better control of our inventory.

THE DECISION

In order to deal with the situation temporarily, Bill had considered accepting part of the Mexican order, but was informed by Dr. Silva that the end client insisted on dealing with only one supplier. Bill was certain that Dr. Silva would find a U.S. company which was prepared to fill the entire order, if Damark refused it, and in the process Damark would lose its status as a preferred supplier. Bill had long known that the distributor was the key to succeeding in any market, and SINIE had proven to be an exceptional distributor. He did not know how he could continue in Mexico without SINIE.

As Bill reflected on Dr. Silva's request and on the opportunity this presented for Damark, two employees from the plant came to the door with a "problem" that needed to be resolved immediately. As he left his office, he wondered whether Mexico was the right place for Damark. Perhaps the company would be better off focusing on the U.S. Then again, Mexico had provided much greater returns for the effort than had the U.S. Why would Damark abandon such a lucrative market? Then there was always Europe, and after all, because he and his partner had always sought some sort of venture in the UK, perhaps by abandoning Mexico, they could realize their dream. More confused than ever, Bill left his office for the plant.

EXHIBIT 1 **Products Packaged Using Shrink Wrap**

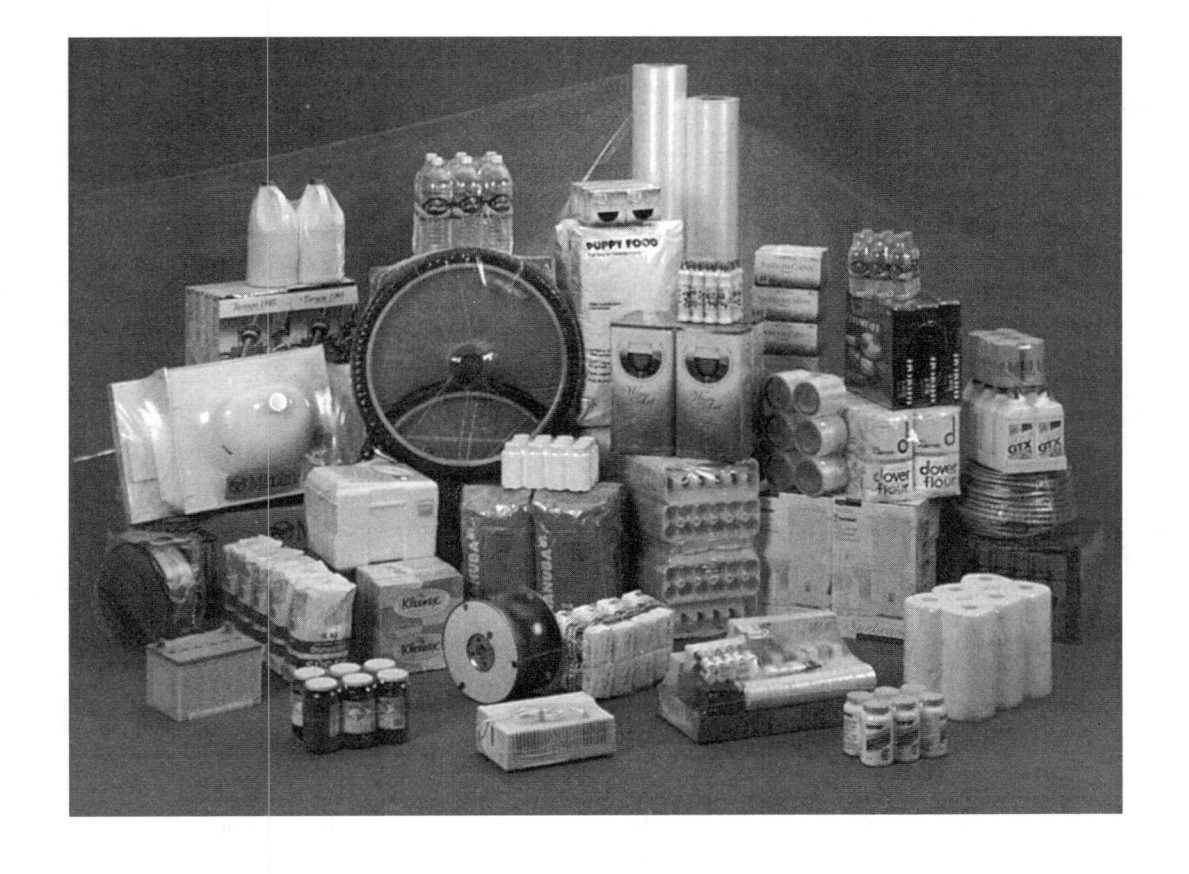

EXHIBIT 2   Year End Balance Sheet 1992 –95

	1992[6] (9 mths)	1993	1994	1995[7] (3 mths)
CURRENT ASSETS				
Cash	(77 972.70)	(11 719.27)	36 684.76	(9 775.98)
Accounts receivable	323 424.02	276 374.87	301 720.82	417 563.76
Allowance for doubtful accounts	(10 000.00)	(10 000.00)	(10 000.00)	(10 000.00)
Inventory	207 663.47	113 712.87	104 271.83	120 890.84
Prepaid expenses	13 377.93	9 789.82	18 216.32	23 097.70
Total current assets	456 492.72	378 158.29	450 893.73	541 776.32
Fixed assets net	32 607.53	24 064.63	19 989.51	28 185.06
Other assets	(7 523.14)	(7 523.14)	(7 523.14)	(7 523.14)
Total assets	481 577.11	394 699.78	463 360.10	562 438.24
CURRENT LIABILITIES				
Bank loan	91 000.00	110 000.05	140 000.07	110 000.07
Accounts payable	126 151.87	155 793.94	123 572.56	157 666.83
Deposits on hand[8]	17 335.00	27 519.57	54 829.55	95 829.55
Accrued liabilities	4 799.15	1 327.36	13 689.65	19 568.51
Taxes payable	0.00	0.00	0.00	(1 448.00)
Total current liabilities	239 286.02	294 640.92	332 091.83	381 616.96
LONG-TERM LIABILITIES				
O.D.C.[9] Grant	47 138.98	40 320.57	34 487.62	31 961.35
Note payable Allied	40 033.54	0.00	0.00	0.00
Due shareholders	8 572.79	19 972.79	0.00	0.00
Total long-term liabilities	95 745.31	60 293.36	34 487.62	31 961.35
SHAREHOLDERS' EQUITY				
Equity	49 254.41	49 254.41	29 254.41	49 254.41
Retained earnings	97 291.37	(9 488.91)	67 526.24	99 605.52
Total liabilities and Shareholders' Equity	481 577.11	394 699.78	463 360.10	562 438.24

[6] 1992 figures are for the period June 1991 (when the company was repatriated) to February 1992 (the company's year end).

[7] 1995 figures are estimates of year to date figures taken at May 31, 1994.

[8] Customers will advance Damark a certain percentage of the contract price on custom orders.

[9] O.D.C.–Ontario Development Corporation.

EXHIBIT 2 (continued)
Income Statement Year End 1992–95

	1992[10] (9 mths)	1993	1994	1995[11] (3 mths)
Sales:				
Manufactured products	1 743 547.60	1 601 970.84	1 901 816.94	597 956.23
Imported prod. U.S.	17 827.50	10 567.50	622.50	0.00
Imported prod. other	0.00	0.00	0.00	0.00
Parts & service	137 318.44	123 921.14	159 188.62	53 190.73
Less discounts taken	(3 909.88)	(4 262.32)	(6 669.87)	(2 170.93)
Total revenue	1 894 783.66	1 732 197.16	2 054 958.19	648 976.03
Cost of Goods Sold[12]	766 822.98	756 414.87	839 562.84	268 227.17
Gross profit	1 127 960.68	975 782.29	1 215 395.35	380 748.86
Operating expenses				
Manufacturing	585 773.16	544 882.16	697 190.38	207 970.25
Engineering	139 748.62	122 641.94	133 365.24	40 801.18
Sales	90 539.45	110 661.70	107 981.92	21 788.97
Administration	205 162.74	208 406.71	218 741.49	61 318.66
Total expenses	1 021 223.97	986 592.51	1 157 279.03	331 879.06
Earnings (loss) from operations	106 736.71	(10 810.22)	58 116.32	48 869.80
Net Interest	(13 354.63)	(15 573.09)	(13 084.93)	(3 071.05)
U.S. exchange gain (loss)	433.41	1 617.45	11 875.00	(1 884.67)
Net earnings (loss)	93 815.49	(24 765.86)	56 906.39	43 914.08

[10] 1992 figures are for the period June 1991 (when the company was repatriated) to February 1992 (the company's year end).

[11] 1995 figures are estimates of year to date figures as May 31, 1994.

[12] Includes materials costs only. Assembly and fabrication wages are included in the Manufacccturing line item under OPERATING EXPENSES.

EXHIBIT 3 **Company Organization**

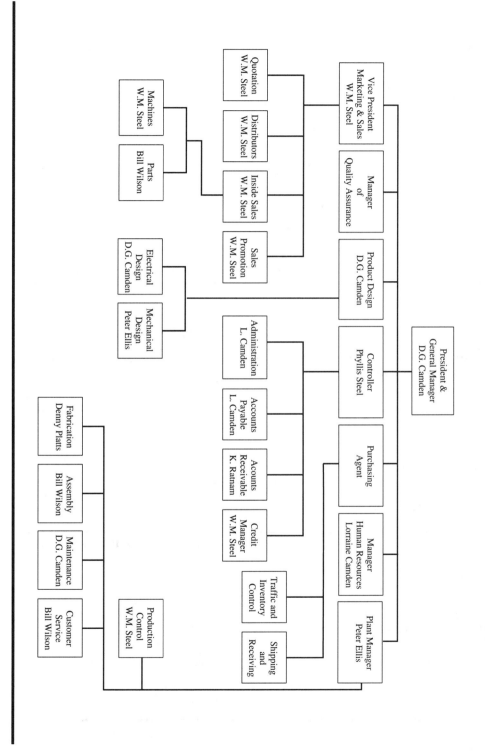

EXHIBIT 4 **Product Information**

Categories of Packaging Machines

Smaller semi-automatic systems

Category	Net Distributor Price (C$)	Margin (%)	Quantity Manufactured (per month)	Manufacturing Time Required
1	3 500	10 – 15	16 – 18	26 hours
2	7 500	15 – 20	12 – 15	40–50 hours

Larger semi-automatic systems

Category	Net Distributor Price (C$)	Margin (%)	Quantity Manufactured (per month)	Manufacturing Time Required
3	12 000 – 15 000	20	3 – 4	Depends on level of customization

Automatic systems

Category	Net Distributor Price (C$)	Margin (%)	Quantity Manufactured (per month)	Manufacturing Time Required
4	35 000 – 40 000	25	2	Depends on level of customization

Note: Margins were estimated by Bill Steel after consideration of materials and manufacturing costs.

EXHIBIT 4 (continued) Product Information

Sales and profit breakdown by country

	Canada	United States	Mexico	Other[13]
Sales (%)	45	20	25	10
Profit (%)	40	10	30	20

Product mix by country (in percent)

Category	Canada	United States	Mexico
1	26.8	25.1	7.3
2	23.3	21.9	
3	27.4	24.7	92.7
4	22.5	28.3	

Order turn around times — November 1994

Category	Turn Around Times Considered to be Acceptable	Damark Turn Around Times
1	2 – 3 weeks	4 weeks
2	2 – 4 weeks	5 – 6 weeks
3	4 – 6 weeks	8 – 10 weeks
4	12 weeks	16 + weeks

[13] There is no distributor involvement in "other" sales.

EXHIBIT 5 Economic Structure—Mexico

Economic Indicators	1980	1981	1982	1983	1984	1985	1986	1987	1988	1989	1990	1991	1992	1993
GDP Billions of New Pesos	4.5	6.1	9.8	17.9	29.5	47.4	79.2	193.3	390.5	507.6	686.4	865.1	1 019.2	1025.3
Real GDP growth %	8.3	7.9	–0.6	–4.2	3.6	2.6	–3.8	19.	1.2	3.3	4.5	3.6	2.6	0.6
Consumer price inflation %	26.4	27.9	58.9	101.8	65.5	57.7	86.2	131.8	114.2	20.0	26.7	22.7	15.5	9.7
Population millions	69.66	71.35	73.02	74.67	76.31	77.94	79.57	81.20	82.84	84.49	86.15	87.84	89.54	91.21
Exports U.S.$ billions	15.570	19.646	21.214	21.819	24.407	22.112	16.347	20.887	20.765	23.048	27.131	27.318	27.618	30.190
Imports U.S.$ billions	19.460	24.068	15.128	8.023	11.788	13.993	11.997	12.731	19.591	24.438	29.969	38.124	48.160	49.627
Current account U.S.$ billions	–10.750	–16.061	–6.307	5.403	4.194	1.130	–1.673	3.968	–2.443	–3.958	–7.117	–14.896	–24.806	–23.393
Trade balance U.S.$ billions	–3.385	–3.846	6.795	13.762	12.941	8.451	4.599	8.433	1.668	–0.645	–4.433	–11.329	–20.667	–18.891
Treasury Bill Rates %[a]	22.46	30.77	45.75	59.07	49.32	63.20	88.01	103.07	69.15	44.99	34.76	19.28	15.62	14.9
Exchange rate New Pesos: U.S.$[b]	n/a	n/a	n/a	0.1503	0.1852	0.3102	0.6374	1.3782	2.2731	2.4615	2.8126	3.0184	3.0949	3.1156

[a] Period averages in percent per annum.
[b] Average for the year.

SOURCE: International Financial Statistics, International Monetary Fund.

EXHIBIT 6   Mexico's Economy—Historical Perspective

Before it joined the General Agreement on Tariffs and Trade (GATT) in 1986, Mexico was a closed-economy. The protection of domestic industry was the main principle underlying all government economic policy. If a product could be manufactured in Mexico, it was, even if it was more expensive and of lower quality than similar products available internationally. The Mexican government implemented several economic policy tools to ensure the achievement of this goal. High tariffs (often over 100%), restrictions on foreign ownership and investment, import permits, and export requirements succeeded in dampening foreign interest in Mexico.

From 1958 to 1970, Mexico thrived. The country's gross domestic product (GDP) grew at an average annual rate of approximately 6.8%, with GDP per capita growth of 3.2% annually. Consumer price inflation over the same period averaged only 2.9% per year. The ratios of public-sector deficits and public external debt to GDP were low and stable, and real interest rates were positive. During this period neither the current-account deficit nor the balance of payments exceeded 3% of GDP.

According to the statistics, all should have been well in Mexico. Unfortunately, this was not the case. Wealth in the country was very unevenly distributed with 30% of the population controlling over 65% of the country's annual income. To correct this inequity and to reduce the widespread poverty in Mexico, President Echeverría (1970–76) and his successor President López Portillo (1976–82) attempted to increase the country's economic growth by pursuing a policy of higher government expenditure. In theory, such a policy would

> permit a more plentiful 'trickle down' to those on the lowest incomes; higher public expenditure, and, in particular, higher welfare spending and transfer payments, would soften the rigours of an inegalitarian system.[14]

Increased government spending throughout the 1970s and early 1980s was financed through foreign borrowing. The discovery of the large Capecha oil fields in the State of Chiapas in the late 1970s allowed the government to intensify its expenditures by borrowing more furiously from foreign banks that were ready and anxious to lend money to Mexico because they anticipated rising oil revenues for the country.

When oil prices began to fall in the early 1980s, the Mexican economy was destabilized with large increases in inflation and the current account deficit. Under pressure from the international financial community, the Mexican government responded with severe import restrictions and high domestic interest rates.

In 1982, investors, anticipating a devaluation of the currency, moved out of pesos into more stable currencies. This put strains on the government as it used foreign currency reserves to maintain the country's fixed exchange rates. Oil prices softened further, the global recession peaked, interest rates increased, and private capital in international markets disappeared. On August 15, 1982, the Mexican government announced that it was no longer able to meet its interest obligations on its US$88 billion foreign debt. The government signed an agreement with the International Monetary Fund (IMF) that rescued the country, but forced it to introduce a program of economic reforms. Public expenditures were reduced, taxes were increased and

---

[14] The Economist Intelligence Unit, *Mexico: Country Profile* (New York: Business International Limited, 1992), p. 10.

some small public service enterprises were closed. Exchange controls were abolished, and the currency was devalued by over 100%. Prices for public services and administered prices (for foodstuffs) were brought into line with production costs or international prices. The group who suffered most was Mexico's middle class. Real wages fell and savings were all but wiped out. Unlike Mexico's elite class, this group did not have the luxury of investing abroad in order to insulate their savings from currency devaluations.

The debt crisis of 1982 forced Mexico to abandon its inward-looking policies of protection and state regulation in favour of new policies that stressed a more outward-focused development strategy that would be led by the private sector.

The results from 1983–85 showed a resumption in real growth and a decrease in inflation from over 90% in 1982–83 to approximately 60% in the following two years. The public sector deficit as a share of GDP was halved. The fall in the real exchange rate stimulated export growth and reduced the level of imports from US$25 billion in 1981 to US$9 billion 1983. From 1985–87 real GDP fell to 3% and inflation accelerated to over 130%. Oil prices softened and Mexico neared crisis once again. A new debt repayment plan was introduced by the IMF that tied Mexico's debt repayment schedule to the health of the country's economy.

Upon assuming office December 1, 1988, President Carlos Salinas de Gortari introduced the first of what was to become a series of pacts among government, labour and employers' organizations. The intention of these pacts was to reduce inflation without causing a recession. These pacts used publicly-controlled prices, minimum wages and the nominal exchange rate as the tools to eliminate the economic distortions that had led to inflation in the past. Fiscal and credit policies were tightened and a more equitable tax system was introduced. Tariffs were reduced, as was the number of products subject to import licenses. Another significant element of the government's strategy to curb inflation was a reduction in the money supply growth rate. In 1982, when foreign capital disappeared, the Mexican government borrowed from domestic banks. After 1988, government borrowing was done predominantly through bonds.

In 1989, the Salinas government introduced its National Development Plan (1989–94), which committed the government to the liberalization of foreign trade and investment policies. These changes were intended to force Mexican enterprises to introduce stricter efficiency standards and new technologies in an effort to render Mexican products more competitive on domestic and world markets. The government sought foreign investment as a means of complementing domestic capital in this plant modernization process. It introduced a new tax policy that protected the lowest income groups without adversely affecting public finances. Finally, it introduced subsidy policies that were intended to increase the purchasing power of the needy.

The Salinas government appeared to have ushered in a new era of improved performance of the Mexican economy. Inflation fell from 52% in 1988 to approximately 7% in the first seven months of 1994. Most of the fall was attributed to the government's wage and price restraints and its trade liberalization policies that had culminated in the North American Free Trade Agreement (NAFTA), effective January 1, 1994. The public sector deficit was reduced from 12.5% of GDP in 1988 to a surplus of 0.1% of GDP in 1993. A reduction in interest rates through the liberalization of markets and lifting of interest controls and cash reserves had also had a positive influence on the economy.

The country's 1993 current account deficit, fueled by growth in imports, led to a merchandise trade deficit (1993 US$13 billion, 1994 estimated at US$18 billion) that was expected to be US$27.8 billion or 8% of GDP in 1994. While foreign capital inflows had acted to cover the shortfall, the bulk of these inward flows had been in the form of portfolio investment, money going to both the stock market and to government securities such as Treasury Certificates (CETES), both of which were intrinsically volatile and were required to offer high rates of return in order to continue to attract capital inflows and avoid capital outflows.

Finally, in August of 1994, the country elected Ernesto Zedillo of the PRI party to replace outgoing President Carlos Salinas. President-elect Zedillo had committed to political reform and to continuing the economic programs that had been begun by his predecessor, although he planned to place more emphasis on job creation and addressing the problem of poverty. The new president would also need to resolve the conflict that had erupted in the southern Mexican state of Chiapas where rebel leaders had attracted world attention through their demands for democratic reforms within the state.

UNA CERVECERIA POR FAVOR: LABATT BUYS INTO MEXICO

Joseph N. Fry and David Ager

CASE

23

O$_{n}$ Wednesday, July 6, 1994, John Labatt Limited of Toronto, Canada, and Fomento Económico Mexicano S.A. (FEMSA) of Monterrey, Mexico, announced an agreement whereby Labatt would acquire 22% of the beer division of FEMSA for US$510 million. In a news release issued to the media and investment analysts, Labatt indicated that the partnership with FEMSA allowed Labatt "to use financial capacity and know how to meet the company's growth and strategic objectives."[1] George Taylor, Labatt's president, further explained the decision:

> It is, we believe, an unparallelled investment opportunity ... growth in today's global beer market requires the right partnership, and with this alliance we have clearly positioned ourselves for growth.[2]

Analyst reaction to Labatt's acquisition was positive, and although some questioned whether Labatt had paid too much for the 22% stake in FEMSA, most agreed that shareholders would be pleased in five or six years when the company began to reap the benefits from the enormous upside potential of the Mexican beer market that, according to Labatt president George Taylor, was expected to grow 5–7% per year. Others were comfortable with the obser-

---

[1] John Labatt Limited, "A Winning North American Brewing Partnership," July 1994, p. 11.

[2] Marina Strauss, Labatt Puts Down Roots in Mexico, *The Globe and Mail*, July 7, 1994, p. B1.

vation that Labatt was returning to its brewing roots after several years of having diversified into and divested out of other sectors. On the Toronto Stock Exchange, Labatt stock gained 37 cents to close at $20.62 after the deal was announced.

Some controversy over the decision persisted, however, and in the fall of 1994 many investors were reviewing the deal and attempting to decide whether the Mexican brewery acquisition represented a good strategic move for Labatt.

JOHN LABATT LIMITED

Founded in 1847, in London, Ontario, by John Kinder Labatt, Labatt was one of Canada's oldest companies and had been established to produce, distribute and sell beer in Canada. In the late 1950s, Labatt expanded into the U.S. through a partnership with the General Brewing Corp. of California. In 1964–65, the company underwent a re-organization whereby Labatt became a holding company for four main subsidiaries: Labatt Breweries of Canada Limited; General Brewing Corporation (U.S. brewing operations); Labatt International Limited (international and property operations); and Labatt Industries Limited (directed biotechnical interests). This was the first of several corporate re-organizations that the company would undergo over the next 25 years as it pursued an aggressive acquisition and development strategy in Canada and the U.S. In addition to beer assets, Labatt acquired subsidiaries involved in the processed foods, dairy and packaging industries as well as the Toronto Blue Jays baseball club, the Toronto Argonauts football club, a stake in the Skydome stadium, sports networks, and a company that specialized in rock concert promotion. By 1989, Labatt had become a conglomerate and described itself as a broadly based North American food and beverage company.

In 1990, Labatt adopted a new strategy which was outlined in its report to shareholders:

> With the increasing globalization of its core business, John Labatt's long-term objective is to concentrate on fewer, larger businesses and to grow internationally.

Specifically, the company planned to build on its strengths in brewing and expand its broadcast and entertainment business.

By 1992, Labatt had disposed of its food related businesses. In 1993 it distributed ownership of its Canadian dairy operations commonly referred to as Ault Foods Limited to its shareholders, and sold its U.S. dairy holdings.

By 1994, Labatt was organized into two segments: brewing and broadcast, sports and entertainment. The brewing segment comprised several divisions: Labatt Breweries of Canada; Labatt's USA; and Labatt Breweries of Europe. The company also pursued selected international activities through Labatt Breweries International. Exhibit 1 presents segmented financial results for Labatt for the most recent 10 years.

In 1994, in addition to acquiring a stake in FEMSA Cerveza, Labatt announced its intention to acquire a stake in Madison Square Garden which included an arena, the New York Rangers hockey team, the New York Knicks basketball team and a regional sports cable-television network, a deal expected to fetch in excess of US$1 billion. Labatt also announced its intention to sell its majority interest in BCL Group, which promoted concerts, a move which confused analysts because, in 1993, Labatt had increased its interest in BCL to 75% from 45%. The sale of

BCL Group was expected to generate revenues of approximately C$50 million. Many analysts questioned this decision because of the quick turnabout. Lorne Stephenson, a spokesman for Labatt, said that "the decision to raise the stake in BCL and then try to reduce it was the result of 'strategic rethinking.'"[3]

Labatt's had also recently announced its intention to spin off some of its sports and entertainment holdings worth approximately C$1 billion. According to analysts, this most recent announcement was yet another signal that Labatt's strategy was focusing ever more on its profitable beer roots.

LABATT'S BREWING BUSINESS

Labatt's brewing division had become a national player throughout the 1960s by acquiring production facilities across Canada. In 1987, the division had acquired the Latrobe Brewing Company of Latrobe, Pennsylvania, and in addition, had added a new operating unit, Labatt Breweries of Europe, which was established to direct expansion into the UK and Continental Europe.

Throughout the corporation's expansion, the brewing division had continued to deliver consistent profits. Since 1989 earnings from John Labatt's brewing segment had grown from C$144 million to C$260 million. Table 1 presents segmented financial data from the company's brewing division.

TABLE 1 Segmented Financial Data From Labatt's Brewing Division (C$ millions)

	Net Sales		EBIT		Net Assets Employed	
	1994	*1993*	*1994*	*1993*	*1994*	*1993*
Labatt Canada	$1 245	$1 241	$ 283	$ 239	$ 495	$ 534
Labatt's USA	$ 228	$ 180	$ 4	$ 5	$ 74	$ 67
Tariff	—	—	$–4	$–8	—	—
Birra Moretti	$ 134	$ 130	$–1	$–3	$ 203	$ 180
Labatt UK	$ 74	$ 42	$–2	$–8	$ 110	$ 75

SOURCE: John Labatt Limited 1994 Annual Report.

Labatt Breweries of Canada

BEER DEMAND IN CANADA High provincial and federal taxes on beer, declining per capita consumption in recent years, demographic changes and a general shift in public taste away from alcoholic beverages had resulted in flat growth in the Canadian brewing industry. In addition,

---

[3] Marina Strauss, "Labatt Making Investors Nervous," *The Globe and Mail*, August 13, 1994, p. B3.

the distribution and sale of alcoholic beverages in Canada were regulated and for the most part conducted by the provincial governments, thereby reducing the number of points of sale and limiting potential market penetration. By 1994, the size of the Canadian beer market was estimated to be 21 million hectolitres (hLs).

COMPETITION Through a series of mergers and acquisitions the Canadian brewing industry had become rationalized and, in 1994, was dominated by two players: Labatt (44.2%) and Molson Breweries (48.9%). Since 1990, consumers had begun looking for different and distinctive-tasting beers, a trend which had spawned the growth of regional brewers and microbrewers, although combined, these smaller players controlled less than 5% of the Canadian market.

Competition in the Canadian brewing industry took the form of advertising and marketing, with the two major Canadian brewers spending millions of dollars annually to retain and capture market share. New product introductions such as "ice beer" and "dry beer" were common in Canada, although they were quickly copied and had, therefore, not resulted in a significant change in a brewer's overall market share. Price competition was limited in Canada because of constraints imposed on pricing through government regulation and because of federal and provincial alcohol taxes.

Molson Breweries of Canada (Molson), the country's largest brewer, was controlled by three groups: the Molson Group of Companies (40%), Elders IXL Ltd. of Australia (40%) and Miller Brewing Company of the U.S. (20%). Miller had only recently acquired its stake in Molson Breweries of Canada, when, in March 1993, it had paid C$360 million or 7.7 times earnings before interest and taxes (EBIT) for its stake in the Canadian brewer. Molson Companies Limited explained that the ownership structure was intended to assist Molson to adapt to the changing global marketplace and would enable the company to access the enormous U.S. market, something that was impossible without a powerful U.S. partner. The Molson Group of Companies had pursued a diversification strategy parallel to archrival Labatt. In 1994, the company brewed ale and beer, sold retail merchandise, and made cleaning products. Coincidentally, the company had recently announced its intention to narrow its focus to two core businesses: brewing and chemical specialties.

Canadian brewers operated at a disadvantage on several dimensions in comparison to their U.S. counterparts. In response to geographic and demographic forces in conjunction with government regulation and intervention, the Canadian brewing industry consisted of a series of small and medium-sized production plants across the country. The average brewery size in Canada was estimated at 1.24 million hL, much smaller than the average size of a U.S. brewer that was estimated at 3.0 million hL. Supplies such as malting barley were purchased in the U.S. on the open market, whereas Canadian brewers had to purchase at a (premium) price set by the Canadian Wheat Board. As a result, most Canadian beer imported in the U.S. competed in the premium segment of the market because the cost disadvantage made it difficult for Canadian brewers to compete in the price sensitive segment of the U.S. market.

GOVERNMENT Government involvement in the Canadian brewing industry had always been significant. Until recently, brewers had been required to brew beer within a province in order to list it for sale there. This requirement was eliminated as a result of several complaints launched by U.S. brewers and adjudications by the General Agreement on Trade and Tariffs (GATT) panel that ruled that inter-provincial trading policies in Canada were inconsistent with international trading policies. As a result of this change, Labatt breweries closed three of its 12 breweries between 1992 and 1994, although it maintained its domestic sales volume at approximately 8.3 million hL.

In all Canadian provinces, beer was distributed through both government owned stores (e.g., LCBO Stores in Ontario) or regulated retail outlets (e.g., The Beer Stores in Ontario, which were owned by Labatt, Molson, and Northern Breweries). The exceptions were in Quebec, where grocery stores were allowed to sell beer, and Newfoundland, which allowed beer to be sold in corner stores and also allowed the establishment of privately owned liquor stores. Alberta was in the process of planning the privatization of its liquor retailing system.

Government regulations often imposed other constraints on pricing. Many provinces had minimum price mark-ups, set minimum allowable prices, and required uniform pricing throughout the province. Canadian beer consumers paid among the highest taxes in the world for their beer, with an average "tax bite" of 53% of the retail price of a bottle of beer.

Finally, under the Canada–U.S. Free Trade Agreement that had taken effect in 1988, tariffs on brewing products shipped between the two countries were to be reduced to 0% over 10 years. This agreement had been reached despite repeated protests on the part of the industry and a one-day strike by brewery workers who were convinced that without pre-1988 tariff protection the Canadian industry would cease to exist.

Italy

Labatt International, a division of Labatt Breweries, began operating in Italy in 1989 when it acquired a 77.5% interest in a joint venture with Birra Moretti S.p.A. of Italy. Birra Moretti, in turn, acquired Prinz Brau S.p.A., another Italian brewery, which was integrated to form the fourth largest brewing group in Italy. In 1992, Labatt acquired the 22.5% minority interest in Birra Moretti to achieve full ownership.

Despite poor industry growth, nationwide discounting by competitors, deepening recession, and successive upsets in Italy's political, economic and industrial environments, Labatt had continued to make sales volume gains in Italy, although earnings had been negative in 1994 and 1993. Its main strategy was to establish a premium position for its brands rather than competing on price simply to gain volume. The company believed that this strategy, which was driven by creative advertising and promotional programs, was proving to be successful and expected its first operating profit from its activities in Italy in the coming year.

The United Kingdom

The six largest brewers in the United Kingdom (UK) controlled over 75% of the domestic market. The UK brewing industry was referred to as a complex monopoly. Brewers had vertically integrated to include not only beer production but also wholesale and retail outlets for beer distribution. This allowed brewers to control the products that were for sale and their prices. The result was that independent suppliers faced difficulties in distributing and selling their products.

Labatt first entered the UK in 1988 when it began marketing its Canadian draught products through Greenall Whitley pubs. By 1993, Labatt UK held interests in partnerships and joint ventures owning approximately 300 pubs. In all, Labatt brands were marketed through approximately 12 000 pubs, in addition to sales through outlets for off-premise consumption. However the trading environment in the UK was difficult and was expected to remain so; total industry volume in the UK, for example, had declined 1% in 1993. Labatt's strategy was to continue to focus its activities on augmenting its strong brand franchises and building a solid pub estate. Labatt had yet to earn an operating profit from its UK activities, recording losses of C$2 million and C$8 million in 1994 and 1993 respectively, although the company was confident that the coming year would be different.

Labatt USA

While Labatt had actively exported its portfolio of brands to the U.S. since the early 1960s, it wasn't until 1989 with the acquisition of the Latrobe Company that it established a brewing presence in the U.S. Since then it had exploited a niche position with the Rolling Rock brand primarily in the northeastern U.S. where it maintained a strong competitive presence.

BEER DEMAND IN THE U.S. Overall, U.S. beer shipments declined for a third year in a row in 1993, and there was little hope for growth in the future. Despite this fact, the U.S. brewing market, estimated to be 237 million hL in size in 1994, still represented the largest single beer market in the world. Product segmentation was increasing and new products like "Ice Beer" were being launched at an ever-increasing rate. In spite of slowing overall demand, the industry remained profitable with the acceptance of new premium products as consumers began to trade up to premium beers that offered something different, something that was not mass-produced and was more full-bodied in taste. Much of this demand was being met by a plethora of specialty beers and imports.

COMPETITION Stagnant growth and poor prospects for the future had turned the mass market segments of the U.S. brewing industry into a gruelling battleground for market share. Three brewers accounted for nearly 80% of the market: Anheuser-Busch (46%), Miller Brewing (23%), and Coors Brewing (11%). While there were several smaller brewers operating throughout the U.S., they operated on a regional basis because they lacked both the production capacity (minimum 26 million hL) and the financial resources (Anheuser-Busch spent in excess of US$300 million in advertising in 1993) to support a national brand.

Two strategies had been adopted for increasing market share: launching new, niche- targeted products and price competition.

Imports accounted for 4.4% of all beer sales, with Heineken of the Netherlands representing the top position, accounting for 29.4% of all beer imports in the U.S. Canada was second at 25.8%, followed by Mexico at 18.4%. The top three imported brands in the U.S. were Heineken (2.7 million hL), Corona Extra (1.2 million hL), and Molson Golden (0.62 million hL). The import segment was expected to experience volume growth of 5.5% in 1994.

The microbrew segment of the U.S. brewing industry that had at one time been considered insignificant, was expected to experience a 50% growth in volume in 1994. Although it accounted for less than 2% of the entire U.S. industry, with overall beer sales showing little growth, the four largest U.S. brewers had begun to aggressively enter the micro segment through the purchase of significant stakes in microbrewers and through the development of "micro-style" brands.

One industry analyst explained the growth in both the import and microbrew segments of the U.S. brewing industry:

> There is a synergy between the imports and the microbrews. They are driven by the same sort of consumer motivation—the taste for something different, something that is not mass-produced and more full-bodied in taste.

Labatt and FEMSA Cerveza's combined sales volumes in the U.S. for all of their brands represented approximately 2.7 million hL[4] in 1994.

SUPPLY AND DISTRIBUTION

In the U.S., the brewing infrastructure of plant locations and distribution systems was a function of market size, geography and transportation costs, not state legislation. Breweries could ship product across state lines. As a result, breweries were located in 26 of the 49 mainland states. The average new brewery built in the United States was in the 8–10 million hL size.

GOVERNMENT

Unlike Canada, in the U.S. the government only influenced prices to the extent that excise and sales taxes were levied on beer. Wholesale and retail prices were set by the members of the distribution and retail network in response to market conditions and supply. While beer could be shipped across state lines, 27 states had packaging and labelling requirements that favoured U.S. producers and discriminated against imported products.

FOMENTO ECONOMICO MEXICANO, S.A. de C.V. (FEMSA)[5]

FEMSA was a sub-entity of Valores Industriales, S.A., more commonly known as VISA. VISA, Mexico's fifth-largest publicly traded company, was founded in 1890 as Cerveceria Cuauhtemoc. Through the years the brewery expanded into other industries, and in 1936, VISA was created as a holding company to manage the portfolio of enterprises. FEMSA was the result of a consolidation of VISA's food related activities and was engaged in the production and distribution of beer and soft drinks, as well as the production of packaging materials used mainly in the bottled beverage industry. FEMSA was organized into four divisions: Beer, Retail, Coca-Cola FEMSA and Packaging.

The Retail division was responsible for the management of the over 700 OXXO convenience stores located throughout Mexico. Coca-Cola FEMSA was the largest Coca-Cola franchise in the world, and was responsible for the production and distribution of Coca-Cola, Sprite and Fanta Orange throughout Mexico. The packaging division's major products were beverage cans, crown bottle caps, glass bottles, labels, and cardboard boxes and its mission was to produce these at prices that were cost competitive at international levels. The beer divi-

---

[4] *A Winning North American Brewing Partnership*, John Labatt Limited, July 1994.

[5] Information for this section is taken from: *Annual Report 1993*, Fomento Económico Mexicano, S.A. de C.V.; *A Winning North American Brewing Partnership*, John Labatt Limited, July 1994 (this public document was provided to all Labatt's shareholders and was reported widely in Canada's press); Carlos Laboy, *Special Report: The Mexican Beer Industry*, Bear Stearns & Co Inc, New York: February 16, 1994; and *Siempre Los Mejores, Edición Especial, Diciembre* 1993.

sion, FEMSA Cerveza, was responsible for the production and distribution of beer throughout Mexico and the rest of the world.

Management

The brewing division was a consolidation of two Mexican brewers: Cerveceria Cuauhtemoc and Cerveceria Moctezuma. FEMSA management had proved itself in the mid-1980s when, in an aggressive move, it acquired Cerveceria Moctezuma, a Mexican brewer that had experienced significant financial and operational difficulties between 1980 and 1985 and whose debt of US$338.4 million represented 481.3% of total capitalization.[6] The mid-1980s was a time of economic collapse in Mexico, and while most companies were busy defending their own financial and operational health, Cuauhtemoc was aggressively expanding by acquiring Moctezuma. At the same time, however, Modelo, its prime competitor, began to compete aggressively on the basis of price. Although FEMSA lost market share to Modelo, by the end of the 1980s both Modelo and FEMSA emerged as the key competitors in the Mexican beer market. FEMSA's accomplishment, and its ability to absorb Moctezuma, led some analysts to suggest that FEMSA's management's experience might be a hidden corporate asset.

Recent Developments

Between 1988 and 1993, FEMSA had invested US$950 million as part of a capital expenditure program designed to modernize its manufacturing and distribution facilities.[7] At the end of fiscal 1993 the company's long-term debt totaled N$2 345 million or US$752.7 million. Of this amount N$1 844 million or 78.6% was denominated in U.S. dollars and German Marks.[8]

FEMSA had also acquired Bancomer, one of Mexico's largest financial services companies. Proceeds from the sale of 49% of Coca-Cola FEMSA, S.A. de C.V. had been used to purchase Bancomer. Exhibit 2 presents financial data for FEMSA for fiscal 1992 and 1993 and segmented financial information for the period 1991 to 1993. Financial statements in Mexico were restated in terms of the purchasing power of the Mexican peso as of the most recent year-end as required by the *Instituto Mexicano de Contadores Publicos*. High inflation and significant changes in prices had been common in Mexico for several years. By restating financial statements, it became possible to compare financial statements between fiscal periods and between companies. Because of the process involved in restating financial statements most Mexican companies only did so for the current and the past year's statements.

The Chairman of the Board of FEMSA stated in the 1993 annual report that the company would:

> continue to pursue our objective of identifying and carrying out strategic joint ventures that will improve our position in the industries and markets where we operated and will open new opportunities for growth.

---

[6] Carlos Laboy, *Special Report: The Mexican Beer Industry,* Bear, Stearns & Co. Inc, New York: February 16, 1994, p. 5.

[7] *Annual Report 1993, Fomento Económico Mexicano, S.A. de C.V.,* p. 6.

[8] *Annual Report 1993, Fomento Económico Mexicano, S.A. de C.V.,* p. 65.

Philip Morris, corporate parent of Miller Brewing, had acquired a 7.93% stake in FEMSA in 1992, and prior to Labatt's acquisition of a position in FEMSA Cerveza in July 1994, it was believed that FEMSA was continuing discussions for the possible sale of a strategic stake in FEMSA Cerveza with Philip Morris, Coors and other international brewers.

FEMSA Cerveza's Export Division

FEMSA Cerveza operated an export division that distributed the company's products in over 55 countries around the world. The principal objectives of the export division were to generate volume for the company and to provide a source of foreign currency. The latter was important because some of the company's inputs needed to be acquired from outside the country. This, combined with the instability of the Mexican peso, created a need for FEMSA to develop a stable source of foreign currency.

Over 95% of FEMSA's exports, primarily under the Tecate and Dos Equis brand names, were destined for the U.S. Wisdom Import Sales Co. was acquired by FEMSA in 1986 and was the company's exclusive importer in the U.S. Wisdom distributed FEMSA products throughout the country although its strength lay in the U.S. south and southwest. FEMSA Cerveza's sales from exports totalled US$56.8 million in 1993, up 6% from 1992.

THE MEXICAN BREWING INDUSTRY

Demand

The Mexican beer market, which was estimated to be 41 million hL in size in 1994, was almost twice as large as Canada's. Unlike the Canadian and U.S. brewing industries that had experienced flat growth for several years and were expected to continue to stagnate in the future, Mexican beer output had grown at compound annual growth rates in excess of 6% throughout the 1980s and into the early 1990s and was expected to continue to grow at the same rate in the foreseeable future. Improving economic conditions coupled with the fact that over 45% of the population was under the age of 18 (the legal drinking age) led analysts to conclude that the demand side of the beer equation would be positively influenced in the future. In addition, per capita consumption rates in Mexico (44.2 litres per person) were half those in Canada (78.3 litres per person) and the U.S. (87.4 litres per person).

Competition

The Mexican beer market was essentially a duopoly shared almost equally between FEMSA Cerveza (49%) and Grupo Modelo, S.A. de C.V. (Modelo) (51%),[9] known internationally for the Corona brand. FEMSA had enjoyed a dominant position in the northern and southern regions of the market, while Modelo had led in the central and Metropolitan Mexico City markets. Table 2 presents each company's relative regional market share.

---

[9] Carlos Laboy, *Special Report: The Mexican Beer Industry*, Bear, Stearns & Co. Inc., New York: February 16, 1994, p. 1.

TABLE 2 Regional Market Share

	North	Central	Metropolitan Mexico City	South
Mexico City				
FEMSA	63.4%	30.7%	27.2%	54.8%
Modelo	36.6%	69.3%	72.8%	45.2%

SOURCE: FEMSA

FEMSA was considered to be more aggressive than Modelo as reflected in FEMSA's broader (and expanding) brand portfolio, the company's emphasis on the growing nonreturnable segment of the market and management's high degree of financial sophistication. As explained below, the distribution characteristics of the market made it unlikely that domestic or foreign competitors would be able to independently penetrate the market in a meaningful way in the near future and explained the relatively low (less than 1%) presence of imports in the market. It also explained Anheuser-Busch's March 1993 investment of over US$477 million to acquire 17.77% of Modelo. Table 3 presents Mexican domestic beer shipments and Mexican beer exports by company.

TABLE 3 Mexican Domestic Beer Shipments (millions of hL)

	1993	1992	1991	1990	1989	1988
FEMSA	19.1	19.1	18.9	18.7	18.3	15.9
Modelo	20.7	20.0	20.0	18.4	18.1	15.1
TOTAL	39.8	39.1	38.9	37.1	36.4	31.0

SOURCE: ANAFACER

Mexican Beer Export (millions of hL)

	1993	1992	1991	1990	1989	1988
FEMSA	0.65	0.60	0.68	0.69	0.61	0.70
Modelo	1.85	1.75	1.37	1.41	1.46	1.90
TOTAL	2.50	2.35	2.05	2.1	2.07	2.6

SOURCE: ANAFACER

Production and Distribution[10]

FEMSA and Modelo operated production facilities spread throughout the country. FEMSA's production facilities ranged in size from 0.36 million hL to 6.0 million hL, whereas Modelo's ranged in size from 0.5 million hL to its plant in Mexico City that had a production capacity of 11.1 million hL.

The most significant barrier to entry in the Mexican beer market was its distribution system. The nature of the retail system and the prevalence of returnable presentations required far-reaching distribution capabilities. FEMSA's distribution network consisted of 274 wholly-owned distribution centres which operated a fleet of 3 100 trucks and moved 73% of the brewery's volume. In addition, the company's product was also delivered to retailers through 122 franchised third-party distribution outlets which operated 1 500 trucks. Modelo operated in much the same way as FEMSA with 88% of its product being distributed through 82 majority-owned distributors and the remainder through third-party distributors. In total, Modelo claimed to operate a fleet of 6 379 trucks and service vehicles.

FEMSA and Modelo distributed their product to over 348 000 retailers in Mexico, many of whom (in excess of 80%) had exclusive arrangements with one producer or the other. Each company also operated its own chain of retail outlets (FEMSA's operated under the name of OXXO).

Supermarkets accounted for less than 5% of total industry sales. This was not surprising for two reasons. First, supermarkets were frequented by upper-middle class and upper class Mexicans who accounted for approximately 18% of the population and second, Mexican culture and tradition had accustomed most people to do their shopping in neighbourhood *tiendas* which were "Mom and Pop" types of operations.

Government Involvement in the Industry

The primary influence of the Mexican government on the brewing industry was in the form of pricing controls. The government, in an attempt to bring down inflation, had instituted PACTO that was an agreement between business, labour and government aimed at controlling wage and price increases.

Price wars between the two brewers throughout the 1980s and then the inclusion of beer as food in the *Pacto de Solidaridad Económica (Pacto)*[11] introduced in December 1987, had resulted in real producer beer prices being fixed at levels about 35% below pre price war levels. Most recently there had been a modest improvement in the real producer price of beer.

The number of retail outlets authorized to sell beer was regulated by the Mexican government through licences which were granted to beer producers who, in turn, authorized specific dealers to carry their products under their permits. This practice further reinforced the closed nature of the Mexican distribution system for beer.

---

[10] This section is taken from: Carlos Laboy, *Special Report: The Mexican Beer Industry*, Bear, Stearns & Co. Inc, New York: February 16, 1994, p. 22–24.

[11] The *pacto* was an agreement among government, industry and labour which froze wages, prices and the exchange rate. It was designed to fight against inflation.

TERMS OF THE LABATT-FEMSA PARTNERSHIP[12]

Financial

Under the terms of the partnership negotiated between Labatt and FEMSA, Labatt would acquire 22% of FEMSA Cerveza for US$510 million, and would receive the right to acquire an additional 8% within three years. The price of the remaining stake, worth US$185 million at the July 6, 1994, valuation, would be determined by a formula based on the July 6, 1994, purchase price and future market prices of the stock.

The acquisition was financed by cash on hand of C$300 million, drawdown of a bank loan facility by C$300 million, and issuance of commercial paper of C$100 million. The bank loan facility was new and involved a revolving extendable facility at floating rates with a minimum term of three years, and could be drawn in U.S. or Canadian dollars.

FEMSA would continue to hold 51% of FEMSA Cerveza and intended that 19% of the equity of its brewing division be placed in the Mexican and International markets in a registered public offering.

In addition, the companies would merge their U.S. operations to form a U.S. specialty beer company. Under the negotiated arrangement, Labatt would receive 51% control of the new entity, while FEMSA would receive 30%. The remaining 19% would go to "additional partners," when they could be found. Exhibit 3 presents the Labatt/FEMSA partnership.

Markets and Brands

In Mexico, both partners would jointly select the best portfolio of U.S. and imported brands for Mexico. All of Labatt's Canadian, U.S. and European brands and brewing technology would be made available to FEMSA Cerveza. Labatt would also bring its brand management skills to Mexico, where Labatt executives believed the company's experience in "pull" marketing in diverse cultural markets would produce significant results.

Labatt and FEMSA would form a U.S. Specialty Beer Company that was expected to become the largest of its kind in the U.S., focusing on the fast growing and profitable specialty beer segment. Both partners would work together to seek and develop additional quality, specialty brands that would complement their own brands in order to achieve faster growth in the U.S. Under the partnership agreement, Labatt USA (Labatt's U.S. division) and Wisdom (FEMSA's U.S. import company) were merged into a U.S. specialty company to service the high-end U.S. specialty market. The merged entity would be managed jointly by both companies and would give each company access to the other's wholesaler and distribution networks (Labatt had traditionally been strong in the U.S. northeast, and FEMSA in the U.S. south and southwest).

In Canada, Labatt would position a portfolio of FEMSA Cerveza's brands throughout the country, aiming to become the leading Canadian importer of Mexican beer.

---

[12] This section is taken from: *A Winning North American Brewing Partnership*, John Labatt Limited, July 1994.

FEMSA Cerveza Management Structure[13]

Under the partnership agreement, FEMSA would appoint the chairman and Labatt the vice chairman for FEMSA Cerveza; 11 of the directors would be appointed by FEMSA, five of the directors by Labatt and two directors would be publicly appointed. The current FEMSA Cerveza CEO, would retain his position, although he would now be advised by a six-member management committee, three members to be appointed by FEMSA and three members by Labatt. Finally, a management interchange program between the two companies would be initiated.

REACTION TO THE PARTNERSHIP

On August 24, 1994, Dominion Bond Rating Service (DBRS) downgraded the debt securities of Labatt. DBRS cited several reasons for the downgrade including relatively flat growth in the Canadian beer market and low returns to invested capital in other Labatt divisions such as sports and entertainment. While DBRS felt that the brewing alliance with FEMSA Cerveza would have many positive implications for Labatt, DBRS was concerned that the additional debt the company had assumed to finance the acquisition would result in a weakening of Labatt's balance sheet and coverage ratios. The consolidated statement of earnings and consolidated balance sheet appear in Exhibit 4.

DBRS managing director, Doug Sawchuk, explained:

> It's still a reasonable rating ... they (Labatt) went from an above-average rating to an average rating ... It's just the fact that they had an above-average balance sheet before and they're using some of that strength, which has been given away to do this acquisition.[14]

THE POISON PILL

On July 20, 1994, Labatt's board of directors proposed a "poison pill" takeover defence. According to Labatt, the poison pill had been designed to encourage the fair treatment of all shareholders in connection with any takeover attempt. Under the takeover defence, shareholders would receive rights to purchase Labatt stock for 50% of the prevailing market price. Since Brascan Limited of Toronto, Canada, sold its 37% stake in Labatt in late 1993, Labatt shares had been widely held. Analysts did not feel that the poison pill was unusual.

> It (the poison pill) is not a big issue one way or the other ... Every other consumer stock without a controlling shareholder has a poison pill, even Molson (Canada's largest brewer) has a poison pill.[15]

However, a number of institutional investors disagreed with the proposal. Some were philosophically opposed to poison pills, while others were expressing displeasure with management's recent decisions to spin off the $1 billion entertainment holdings; purchase a 22%

---

[13] This section is taken from: *A Winning North American Brewing Partnership,* John Labatt Limited, July 1994.

[14] Marina Strauss, "DBRS Downgrades Labatt Debt: Mexican Expansion Plans, Flat Beer Sales Growth Cited," *The Globe and Mail,* August 25, 1994, p. B4.

[15] Paul Brent, "Labatt Brews Up Poison Pill Plan," *The Financial Post,* Thursday, July 21, 1994, p. 3.

stake in Mexican brewer FEMSA Cerveza; and managements' interest in acquiring New York's Madison Square Gardens and Toronto's Maple Leaf Gardens.

On September 13, 1994, shareholders rejected Labatt's poison-pill plan 52% to 48%. This event represented the first time in Canadian history that investors had rejected such a plan. In response, George Taylor, Labatt's president commented:

> We hear that our strategy is faulty, perhaps misguided, and too bold ... Perhaps this is the Canadian way—in the United States, in Europe and in Mexico, our success received applause not only from the financial communities but from every other major world brewer.[16]

DEVELOPMENTS IN MEXICO

On August 21, 1994, Mexicans elected PRI candidate, Ernesto Zedillo to become the country's next President. His election had come after several of the most turbulent months that the country had experienced since the revolution that had culminated in the PRI first assuming power in the 1920s, a position it had held ever since.

On January 1, 1994, the day that the North American Free Trade Agreement (NAFTA) took effect, Indian peasants in the southern state of Chiapas had risen in armed rebellion. Led by the Zapatista National Liberation Army (EZLN), the Indians claimed that they had been cheated of their land, denied basic services and had had their culture eroded. Many people claimed that the roots of the rebellion lay in poverty, racial discrimination and the failure of regional and social policy. Others claimed that Guatamalan guerillas were behind the situation and were using it to destabilize Mexico.

On March 23, shortly after the uprising in the state of Chiapas appeared to have been brought under control, Luis Donaldo Colosio, the presidential candidate for the PRI party, was shot at a rally in Tijuana. In the days that followed, many stories emerged in the press suggesting that the assassination might have been conceived by ultra-conservatives within the PRI party who were allegedly opposed to the economic and political reforms that Colosio was promising to continue if he were elected.[17]

On March 28, Ernesto Zedillo, Mexico's former education Minister, accepted the presidential candidacy for the PRI. Many people in the country questioned the political skills and abilities of Zedillo because of the previous bureaucratic positions he had held and the limited time available for him to prepare for the position of President. This gave rise to speculation that one of Mexico's two other national political parties might be elected to power, although neither had any experience in running the country.

Many investors were concerned with events in Mexico: Chiapas, bombings in Mexico City, kidnappings, and the assassination of the presidential candidate. By April 1994, the peso had been devalued to 8% below its January level and interest rates had been raised to 18%, double the figure of two months before.

Appendix A contains economic data on Mexico and a brief discussion of the country's political and economic history.

---

[16] Marina Strauss, "Labatt Shareholders Reject Poison Pill," *The Globe and Mail*, September 14, 1994, p. B5.
[17] "Mexico's Whodunnit," *The Economist*, New York: October 15, 1994, p. 53.

CONCLUSION

In the aftermath of the poison-pill debate, the FEMSA deal remained in the spotlight. Was it or was it not a sound move in furthering Labatt's future as a global brewer?

EXHIBIT 1 Segmented Financial Results
John Labatt Limited

Net Sales (millions of C$)

	1994	1993	1992	1991	1990	1989	1988	1987	1986	1985
Brewing	1 769	1 672	1 564	2 043	1 920	1 818	1 633	1 424	1 274	1 149
BS&E[18]	630	—	—	—	—	—	—	—	—	—
Entertainment	—	546	374	—	—	—	—	—	—	—
Dairy	—	—	2 110	—	—	—	—	—	—	—
Food	—	—	—	3 327	3 354	3 606	—	—	—	—
Agri products	—	—	—	—	—	—	2 450	2 018	1 605	1 075
Packaged food	—	—	—	—	—	—	1 024	811	702	579

Earnings Before Interest Restructuring Charges and Income Taxes (millions of C$)

	1994	1993	1992	1991	1990	1989	1988	1987	1986	1985
Brewing	260	218	181	109	174	157	140	118	93	78
BS&E	32	—	—	—	—	—	—	—	—	—
Entertainment	—	56	58	—	—	—	—	—	—	—
Dairy	—	—	62	—	—	—	—	—	—	—
Food	—	—	—	90	90	106	—	—	—	—
Agri products	—	—	—	—	—	—	91	93	92	72
Packaged food	—	—	—	—	—	—	64	61	51	31

Capital Expenditures (millions of C$)

	1994	1993	1992	1991	1990	1989	1988	1987	1986	1985
Brewing	103	191	122	104	98	78	77	54	55	61
BS&E	20	—	—	—	—	—	—	—	—	—
Entertainment	—	12	5	—	—	—	—	—	—	—
Dairy	—	—	45	—	—	—	—	—	—	—
Food	—	—	—	87	108	160	—	—	—	—
Agri products	—	—	—	—	—	—	71	57	35	16
Packaged food	—	—	—	—	—	—	61	47	26	34

---

[18] BS&E is an acronym for the Broadcast, Sport and Enyertainment division.

EXHIBIT 1   (continued)

Net Assets Employed (millions of C$)

Brewing	960	1 146	799	727	717	516	527	386	343	317
BS&E	308	—	—	—	—	—	—	—	—	—
Entertainment	—	283	140	—	—	—	—	—	—	—
Dairy	—	—	629	—	—	—	—	—	—	—
Food	—	—	—	1 319	1 233	1 110	—	—	—	—
Agri products	—	—	—	—	—	—	657	664	404	278
Packaged food	—	—	—	—	—	—	651	623	372	343

Stock Price (1985–94)

	1994	*1993*	*1992*	*1991*	*1990*	*1989*	*1988*	*1987*	*1986* [19]	*1985*
High	26.25	30.38	27.88	26.00	27.50	24.38	29.75	25.00	16.06	12.63
Low	20.50	24.25	22.25	18.38	20.50	20.63	20.13	14.25	10.88	8.75
Dividend Record (C$ per share)	0.82	3.82	0.795	0.77	0.73	0.685	0.62	0.547	0.502	0.472
Dividend Record (millions of C$)	88	344 [20]	83	84	73	50.6	45.5	39.64	32.31	28.18
Dividend as % of Net Profits	56.8	NA	82.2	77.1	43.2	37.5	32.4	31.6	31.8	34.5

SOURCE: John Labatt Limited, Annual Reports 1984–93.

---

[19] Stock prices prior to 1986 have been adjusted to refiect the 1986 2 for 1 stock split.

[20] Large dividend payout to shareholders as a result of the sale of Labatt's food-related assets.

EXHIBIT 2 Financial Statements
Fomento Económico Mexicano, S.A. de C.V. and Subsidiaries
(amounts in millions of New Pesos (N$) and millions of US dollars)

CONSOLIDATED INCOME STATEMENT
For the years ended December 31

	1993		1992	
	N$	US$	N$	US$
Sales	7 571	2 430	7 090	2 275
Gross profit	3 515	1 128	3 122	1 002
Operating expenses	2 718	872	2 382	764
Income from operations	777	249	710	227
Income tax, tax on assets and employee profit sharing	348	111	359	115
Income before extraordinary items	243	78	289	93
Net income for the year	684[21]	219	552	177

CONSOLIDATED STATEMENT OF FINANCIAL POSITION
For the years ended December 31

	1993		1992	
Assets	N$	US$	N$	US$
Current assets	1 895	608	1 832	588
Investments and other assets	21	6	42	13
Property plant and equipment	7 981	2 561	7 711	2 474
Other	226	72	139	44
Total assets	10 123	3 249	9 724	3 121

CONSOLIDATED STATEMENT OF FINANCIAL POSITION
For the years ended December 31

	1993		1992	
Liabilities and stockholders' equity	N$	US$	N$	US$
Current liabilities	1 226	394	1 718	551
Long-term liabilities	2 345	753	2 679	860
Stockholders' equity	6 115	1 963	4 874	1 564
Total liabilities and stockholders equity	10 123	3 249	9 724	3 121

Note: Mexican peso figures for 1992 and 1993 have been restated in U.S. dollars using 1993 average annual exchange rate, because 1992 figures were restated in terms of the purchasing power of the Mexican peso as of 1993 year-end. This practice was commonly referred to as "Accounting for Changing Price Levels."
SOURCE: *Annual Report 1993, Fomento Económico Mexicano, S.A. de C.V.*

---

[21] In 1993 the sale of Coca-Cola FEMSA shares resulted in N$353 million gain that was recorded as an extraordinary item.

EXHIBIT 2   (continued)
Segmented Financial Information—Fomento Económico Mexicano, S.A. de C.V.
(millions of Average New Pesos and millions of US$)

Sales	1993		1992		1991	
	N$	*US$*	*N$*	*US$*	*N$*	*US$*
Brewing	4 089	1 312	4 072	1 306	4 077	1 308
Retail	1 061	340	872	279	737	236
Coca-cola FEMSA	1 838	589	1 601	513	1 468	471
Packaging	1 214	389	1 104	354	1 056	339

Operating Profit	1993		1992		1991	
	N$	*US$*	*N$*	*US$*	*N$*	*US$*
Brewing	449	144	443	142	438	140
Retail	20	6	31	10	25	8
Coca-cola FEMSA	277	88	247	79	230	73
Packaging	187	60	156	50	142	45

Cash Flow From Operations	1993		1992		1991	
	N$	*US$*	*N$*	*US$*	*N$*	*US$*
Brewing	379	121	504	161	459	147
Retail	14	4	30	9	25	8
Coca-cola FEMSA	245	78	181	58	199	63
Packaging	194	62	175	56	171	54

Total Assets	1993		1992		1991	
	N$	*US$*	*N$*	*US$*	*N$*	*US$*
Brewing	6 542	2 099	6 196	1 988	5 950	1 909
Retail	396	127	366	177	230	73
Coca-cola FEMSA	1 384	444	1 172	376	1 024	328
Packaging	1 440	462	1 327	425	1 268	407

Note: Mexican peso figures for 1991, 1992 and 1993 have been restated in U.S. dollars using 1993 average annual exchange rate, because 1991 and 1992 figures were restated in terms of the purchasing power of the Mexican peso as of 1993 year-end. This practice was commonly known as "Accounting for Changing Price Levels."

SOURCE: *Annual Report 1993, Fomento Económico Mexicano, S.A. de C.V.*

EXHIBIT 3 Labatt/FEMSA Partnership Structure

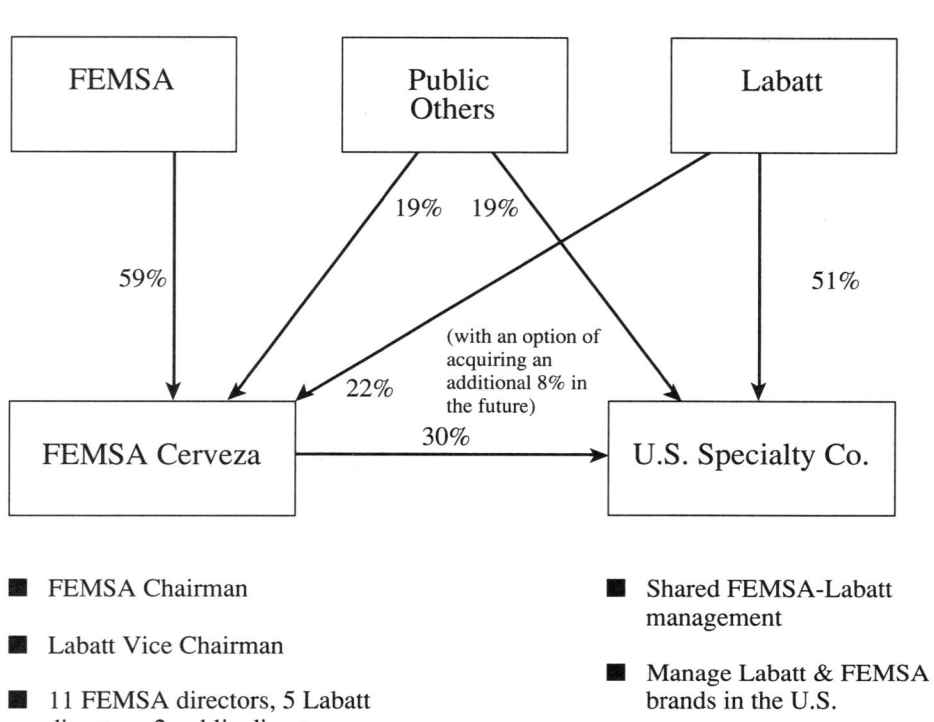

- FEMSA Chairman

- Labatt Vice Chairman

- 11 FEMSA directors, 5 Labatt directors, 2 public directors

- Current FEMSA Cerveza CEO, retains leadership role

- CEO advised by 6 member management committee (3 FEMSA, 3 Labatt)

- Labatt-FEMSA management interchange program

- Shared FEMSA-Labatt management

- Manage Labatt & FEMSA brands in the U.S.

- Utilize Labatt USA and Wisdom existing management & distribution network

- Utilize Labatt USA's and Wisdom's national wholesaler and distribution presence

- Jointly seek other brands for portfolio

SOURCE: A Winning North Americam Brewing Partnership, John Labatt Limited, July 1994.

EXHIBIT 4   John Labatt Limited
Consolidated Statement of Earnings[22] (millions of C$)

	1994	1993	1992	1991	1990	1989	1988
Net sales	2 321	2 135	3 837	4 760	4 681	4 857	4 611
Operating costs	2 085	1 896	3 562	4 602	4 450	4 661	4 390
Earnings before interest, income taxes and restructuring charges	292	274	301	199	264	263	295
Income taxes	85	64	37	50	72	57	85
Earnings before share in partly owned business	151	130	93	108	159	129	142
Net earnings	155	(70)[23]	101	109	169	135	141

John Labatt Limited
Consolidated Balance Sheet[24] (millions of C$)

Assets	1994	1993	1992	1991	1990	1989	1988
Current assets	1 102	1 187	1 634	1 234	1 184	1 227	964
Fixed assets less depreciation	813	784	1 027	1 257	1 181	1 002	992
Other assets	621	597	520	647	581	528	582
Total assets	2 536	3 020	3 320	3 138	2 946	2 757	2 538

Liabilities	1994	1993	1992	1991	1990	1989	1988
Current liabilities	721	932	836	913	628	683	736
Non-convertible long-term debt	610	630	646	416	544	533	482
Deferred income taxes	86	141	90	133	130	143	162
Convertible debentures and shareholders' equity	1 119	1 317	1 748	1 676	1 644	1 398	1 158
Total liabilities	2 536	3 020	3 320	3 138	2 946	2 757	2 538

---

[22] Over the period 1988 to 1993, John Labatt divested itself of several of its business. This explains the significant drop in net sales over the period.

[23] In 1993, John Labatt incurred a loss from discontinued operations of C$203 million as a result of provisions for estimated future liabilities from businesses sold in prior years, and a provision to write down the assets of its U.S. dairy business.

[24] Over the period 1988 to 1993, John Labatt divested itself of several of its businesses. This explains the significant drop in net sales over the period.

APPENDIX A   Economic Indicators—Mexico

Economic Indicators	1980	1981	1982	1983	1984	1985	1986	1987	1988	1989	1990	1991	1992	1993
Trade balance US$ billions	−3.385	−3.846	6.795	13.762	12.941	8.451	4.599	8.433	1.668	−0.645	−4.433	−11.329	−20.677	−18.891
Current account US$ billions	−10.750	−16.061	−6.307	5.403	4.194	1.130	−1.673	4.247	−2.374	−5.825	7.451	−14.888	−24.806	−23.391
Foreign reserves (less gold) US$ billions	2.960	4.074	0.834	3.913	7.272	4.906	5.670	12.464	5.279	6.329	9.863	17.726	18.942	25.110
Consumer price inflation %	26.4	27.9	58.9	101.8	65.5	57.7	86.2	131.8	114.2	20.0	26.7	22.7	15.5	9.8
Treasury Bill rate %[a]	22.46	30.77	45.75	59.07	49.32	63.20	88.01	103.07	69.15	44.99	34.76	19.28	15.62	14.93
Total external debt US$ billions	N/A	75.25	87.61	93.78	95.87	96.9	101.0	109.4	100.8	95.5	97.4	101.7	113.4	124.0
Exchange rate New Pesos: US$[b]	0.0230	0.0245	0.0564	0.1201	0.1678	0.2569	0.6118	1.3782	2.2731	2.4615	2.8126	3.0184	3.0949	3.1156

[a] Period averages in percent per annum.
[b] Average per year.

SOURCE: *International Financial Statistics Year Book 1994*, International Monetary Fund.

Mexico Economy—Historical Perspective

Before it joined the General Agreement on Tariffs and Trade (GATT) in 1986, Mexico was an inward-looking country. The protection of domestic industry was the main principle underlying all government economic policy. If a product could be manufactured in Mexico, it was, even if it was more expensive and of lower quality than similar products available internationally. The Mexican government implemented several economic policy tools to ensure the achievement of this goal. High tariffs (often over 100%), restrictions on foreign ownership and investment, import permits, and export requirements, succeeded in dampening foreign interest in Mexico.

From 1958 to 1970, Mexico thrived. The country's gross domestic product (GDP) grew at an average annual rate of approximately 6.8%, with GDP per capita growth of 3.2% annually. Consumer price inflation over the same period averaged only 2.9% per year. The ratios of public-sector deficits and public external debt to GDP were low and stable, and real interest rates were positive. During this period neither the current-account deficit nor the balance of payments exceeded 3% of GDP.

According to the statistics, all should have been well in Mexico. Unfortunately, this was not the case. Wealth in the country was very unevenly distributed. To correct this inequity and to reduce the widespread poverty in Mexico, President Echeverría (1970–76) and his successor, President López Portillo (1976–82) attempted to increase the country's economic growth by pursuing a policy of higher government expenditure. In theory, such a policy would

> permit a more plentiful "trickle down" to those on the lowest incomes; higher public expenditure, and, in particular, higher welfare spending and transfer payments, would soften the rigours of an inegalitarian system.[25]

Increased government spending throughout the 1970s and early 1980s was financed through foreign borrowing. The discovery of the large Capecha oil fields in the State of Chiapas in the late 1970s allowed the government to intensify its expenditures by borrowing more furiously from foreign banks that were ready and anxious to lend money to Mexico because they anticipated rising oil revenues for the country.

When oil prices began to fall in the early 1980s, the Mexican economy was destabilized with large increases in inflation and the current account deficit. Under pressure from the international financial community, the Mexican government responded with severe import restrictions and high domestic interest rates.

In 1982, investors, anticipating a devaluation of the currency, moved out of pesos into more stable currencies. This put strains on the government as it used foreign currency reserves to maintain the country's fixed exchange rates. Oil prices softened further, the global recession peaked, interest rates increased, and private capital in international markets disappeared. On August 15, 1982, the Mexican government announced that it was no longer able to meet its interest obligations on its US$88 billion foreign debt. The government signed an agreement with the International Monetary Fund (IMF) that rescued the country, but forced it to introduce a program of economic reforms. Public expenditures were reduced, taxes were increased and some small public service enterprises were closed. Exchange controls were abolished, and the currency was devalued by over 100%. Prices for public services and administered prices (for foodstuffs) were brought into line with production costs or international prices. The group that suffered most was Mexico's middle class. Real wages fell and savings were all but wiped out. Unlike Mexico's elite class, this group did not have the luxury of investing abroad in order to insulate their savings from currency devaluations.

The debt crisis of 1982 forced Mexico to abandon its inward-looking policies of protection and state regulation in favour of new policies that stressed a more outward-focused development strategy that would be led by the private sector.

The results from 1983–85 showed a resumption in real growth and a decrease in inflation from over 90% in 1982–83 to approximately 60% in the following two years. The public sector deficit as a share of GDP was halved. The fall in the real exchange rate stimulated export growth and reduced the level of imports from US$25 billion in 1981 to US$9 billion 1983. From 1985–87, real GDP fell to 3% and inflation accelerated to over 130%. Oil prices soft-

---

[25] The Economist Intelligence Unit, Mexico: Country Profile, (New York: Business International Limited, 1992), p. 10.

ened and Mexico neared crisis once again. A new debt repayment plan was introduced by the IMF that tied Mexico's debt repayment schedule to the health of the country's economy.

Upon assuming office on December 1, 1988, President Carlos Salinas de Gortari introduced the first of what was to become a series of pacts among government, labour and employers' organizations. The intention of these pacts was to reduce inflation without causing a recession. These pacts used publicly controlled prices, minimum wages and the nominal exchange rate as the tools to eliminate the economic distortions that had led to inflation in the past. Fiscal and credit policies were tightened and a more equitable tax system was introduced. Tariffs were reduced, as was the number of products subject to import licences. Another significant element of the government's strategy to curb inflation was a reduction in the money supply growth rate. In 1982, when foreign capital disappeared, the Mexican government borrowed from domestic banks. After 1988, government borrowing was done predominantly through bonds.

In 1989, the Salinas government introduced its National Development Plan (1989–94), which committed the government to the liberalization of foreign trade and investment policies. These changes were intended to force Mexican enterprises to introduce stricter efficiency standards and new technologies in an effort to render Mexican products more competitive on domestic and world markets. The government sought foreign investment as a means of complementing domestic capital in this plant modernization process. It introduced a new tax policy that protected the lowest income groups without adversely affecting public finances. Finally, it introduced subsidy policies that were intended to increase the purchasing power of the needy.

The Salinas government appeared to have ushered in a new era of improved performance of the Mexican economy. Inflation fell from 52% in 1988 to approximately 7% in the first seven months of 1994. Most of the fall was attributed to the government's wage and price restraints and its trade liberalization policies that culminated in the North American Free Trade Agreement (NAFTA) that came into effect on January 1, 1994. The public sector deficit was reduced from 12.5% of GDP in 1988 to a surplus of 0.1% of GDP in 1993. A reduction in interest rates through the liberalization of markets and lifting of interest controls and cash reserves had also had a positive influence on the economy.

The country's current account deficit, fuelled by growth in imports which led to a merchandise trade deficit (1993 US$13 billion, 1994 estimated at US$18 billion) was expected to be US$27.8 billion or 8% of GDP in 1994. While foreign capital inflows had acted to cover the shortfall, the bulk of these inward flows had been in the form of portfolio investment, money going to both the stock market and to government securities such as Treasury Certificates (CETES), both of which were intrinsically volatile and were required to offer high rates of return in order to continue to attract capital inflows and avoid capital outflows.

Finally, in August 1994, the country had elected Ernesto Zedillo of the PRI party to replace outgoing President Carlos Salinas. President-elect Zedillo had committed to political reform and to continuing the economic programs that had been begun by his predecessor, although he planned to place more emphasis on job creation and addressing the problem of poverty. The new president would also need to resolve the conflict that had erupted in the southern Mexican state of Chiapas where rebel leaders had attracted world attention through their demands for democratic reforms within the state.

Purchasing Power Parity Estimates of GNP

Country	PPP estimates of GNP per capita United States = 100		Current International dollars[26]
	1987	*1992*	*1992*
Mexico	31.6	32.4	7 490
Canada	91.0	85.3	19 720
United States	100	100	23 120

SOURCE: World Development Report 1994: Infrastructure for Development, The World Bank.

---

[26] The "international dollar" has the same purchasing power over total GNP as the US dollar in a give year..

MR. JAX FASHION INC.

J. Michael Geringer and
Patrick C. Woodcock

CASE

24

It was 6:30 A.M., Monday, January 16, 1989. Dawn had not yet broken on the Vancouver skyline, and Louis Eisman, President of Mr. Jax Fashion Inc., was sitting at his desk pondering opportunities for future growth. Growth had been an important objective for Eisman and the other principle shareholder, Joseph Segal. Initially the company had focused on the professional/career women's dresses, suits and coordinates market, but by 1986 it had virtually saturated its ability to grow within this market segment in Canada. Growth was then sought through the acquisition of four companies: a woolen textile mill and three apparel manufacturing companies. The result of this decade-long expansion was a company that had become the sixth largest apparel manufacturer in Canada.

In the future, Eisman felt continued growth would require a different approach. A good option appeared to be expansion into the U.S. market. Strong growth was forecast in the women's professional/career market, Mr. Jax's principal market segment, and the recently ratified Free Trade Agreement (FTA) provided an excellent low tariff environment for expansion into the U.S. Yet, Eisman wanted to ensure the appropriate growth strategy was selected. He was confident that, if the right approach was taken, Mr. Jax could become a major international apparel company by the end of the next decade.

THE INDUSTRY

The apparel industry was divided into a variety of market segments based upon gender, type of garment and price points. Based on price points, the women's segments ranged from low-priced unexceptional to runway fashion segments. Low-priced segments competed on a low-cost manufacturing capability, while the higher quality segments tended to compete on design and marketing capabilities. Companies in the higher priced segments often subcontracted out manufacturing.

The professional/career women's segment ranged from the medium to medium-high price points. During the late 1970s and early 1980s, this segment had experienced strong growth due to the demographic growth in career-oriented, professional women. In the U.S., it had grown by 50% annually during the first half of the 1980s, but had slowed to about 20% in 1988. Experts predicted that by the mid-1990s, growth would drop to the rate of GNP growth. The U.S. professional/career women's segment was estimated to be $2 billion in 1988. The Canadian market was estimated to be one-tenth this size and growth was expected to emulate the U.S. market. Yet, the exact timing of the slowing of growth was difficult to predict because of extreme cyclicality in the fashion industry. During difficult economic times, women tended to delay purchases, particularly in the mid-priced, fashionable market sectors. Then during times of economic prosperity, women who would not otherwise be able to afford fashionable items tended to have more resources to devote to these items.

Competition

Some of the more prominent Canada-based companies competing in the professional/career women's segment included the following.

JONES NEW YORK OF CANADA Jones New York of Canada, a marketing subsidiary of a U.S.-based fashion company, was thought to share the leadership position with Mr. Jax in the Canadian professional/career women's market. The company focused exclusively on marketing clothes to this market segment. Manufacturing was contracted out to Asian companies.

THE MONACO GROUP The Monaco Group had become a major Canadian designer and retailer of men's and women's fashions during the 1980s. By 1988, the company had sales of $21 million and a rate of return on capital of over 20%. The company designed their own fashion lines, which were merchandised through their own retail outlets as well as major department stores. Manufacturing was contracted out to Asian companies. Recently, the company had been purchased by Dylex Inc., a large Canada-based retail conglomerate with 2 000 retail apparel stores located in both Canada and the U.S.

NYGARD INTERNATIONAL LTD. Nygard International Ltd., with revenues of over $200 million, was Canada's largest apparel manufacturer. Approximately one-third of their sales and production were located in the U.S. This company had historically focused on lower priced clothing, but they had hired away Mr. Jax's former designer to create the Peter Nygard Signature Collection, a fashion line aimed at the professional/career women's market. This new line had been out for only six months, and sales were rumored to be moderate.

Additional competition in this Canadian segment included a wide variety of U.S. and European imports. These companies generally manufactured garments in Asia and marketed them in Canada through independent Canadian sales agents. Historically, most had concentrated their marketing resources on the rapidly growing U.S. market, yet many had captured a significant share of the Canadian market based upon strong international brand recognition. Prominent U.S.-based competition included the following companies.

LIZ CLAIBORNE Liz Claiborne, as the originator of the professional/career women's fashion look, had utilized their first-mover advantage to build a dominant position in this segment. This company, started in 1976, grew tremendously during the late 1970s and early 1980s, and by 1988 they had sales in excess of US$1.2 billion, or nearly two-thirds of the market. Claiborne generally competed on price and brand recognition, a strategy copied by many of the larger companies which had begun to compete in this segment. To keep prices low, Claiborne contracted out manufacturing to low-cost manufacturers, 85% of which were Asian. The company's large size allowed them to wield considerable influence over these manufacturing relationships. Recently, the company had diversified into retailing.

J.H. COLLECTIBLES J.H. Collectibles, a Milwaukee-based company with sales of US$200 million, had one of the more unique strategies in this segment. They produced slightly upscale products which emphasized an English country-sporting look. Using facilities in Wisconsin and Missouri, they were the only company to both manufacture all of their products in-house and to produce all of them in the U.S. In addition to providing stronger quality control, this strategy enabled J.H. Collectibles to provide very fast delivery service in the U.S. Limiting distribution of their product to strong market regions and retailers also enabled them to maintain production at levels estimated to be at or near their plants' capacities.

JONES OF NEW YORK Jones of New York, the parent company of Jones New York of Canada, was a major competitor in the U.S. market. In fact, the majority of their US$200 million in sales was derived from this market.

EVAN-PICONE Evan-Picone was a U.S.-based apparel designer and marketer which had become very successful in the slightly older professional/career women's market. This company also contracted out their manufacturing function, and had annual sales in excess of US$200 million.

In addition, there were a myriad of other apparel designers, marketers and manufacturers competing in this segment. They included such companies as Christian Dior, Kasper, Pendleton, Carole Little, Susan Bristol, J.G. Hooke, Ellen Tracy, Anne Klein II, Perry Ellis, Adrienne Vittadini, Tahari, Harve Bernard, Norma Kamali, Philippe Adec, Gianni Sport, Regina Porter, and Herman Geist.

Profitability in this segment had been excellent. According to data from annual reports and financial analyst reports, Liz Claiborne led profitability in the apparel industry with a five-year average return on equity of 56% and a 12-month return of 45%, and J.H. Collectibles had averaged over 40% return on equity during the last five years. This compared to an average return on equity in the overall apparel industry of 12.5% in the U.S., and 16% in Canada during the past five years.

Distribution

The selection and maintenance of retail distribution channels had become a very important consideration for apparel manufacturers in the 1980s. The retail industry had gone through a particularly bad year in 1988, although the professional/career women's segment had been relatively profitable. Overall demand had declined, and retail analysts were predicting revenue increases of only 1–2% in 1989, which paled beside the 6–7% growth experienced in the mid-1980s. The consensus was that high interest rates and inflation, as well as somewhat stagnant demand levels, were suppressing overall profitability.

Although initially considered a mild downturn, recent market indicators suggested that this downward trend was relatively stable and long lasting. Industry analysts had begun to suspect that permanent market changes might be occurring. With baby boomers reaching their childbearing years, further constraints on disposable income might result as this group's consumption patterns reflected increasing emphasis on purchases of homes, or the decision by many women to permanently or temporarily leave the workforce to raise their children. In addition, the effects of rampant growth in the number of retail outlets during the 1980s were beginning to take their toll. Vicious competition had been eroding margins at the retailer level, and the industry appeared to be moving into a period of consolidation. As a result of these developments, a shift in power from the designers to the retailers appeared to be underway.

To counter the retailers' increasing power, some apparel designers had been vertically integrating into retailing. The attractiveness of this option was based on controlling the downstream distribution channel activities, and thus enabling an apparel company to aggressively pursue increased market share. The principal components for success in the retail apparel industry were location, brand awareness and superior purchasing skills. The apparel companies which had integrated successfully into retailing were the more market-oriented firms such as Benetton and Esprit.

The Free Trade Agreement

Historically, developed nations had protected their textile and clothing industries through the imposition of relatively high tariffs and import quotas. Tariffs for apparel imported into Canada averaged 24.5%, and 22.5% into the U.S. Tariffs for worsted woolen fabrics, one of the principal ingredients for Mr. Jax's products, were 40% into Canada, and 22.5% into the U.S. Import quotas were used to further limit the ability of developing country manufacturers to import into either country. Despite these obstacles, Canadian apparel imports had grown from 20% to 30% of total shipments during the 1980s; most of which came from developing countries. Shipments into Canada from the U.S. represented an estimated $200 million in 1988, while Canadian manufacturers exported approximately $70 million to the U.S.

The FTA would alter trade restrictions in North America considerably. Over the next ten years, all clothing and textile tariffs between the two countries would be eliminated, but stringent "rules of origin" would apply. To qualify, goods not only had to be manufactured in North America, but they also had to utilize raw materials (i.e., yarn, in the case of textiles, and fabric, in the case of apparel) manufactured in North America. Unfortunately, these "rules of origin" favoured U.S. apparel manufacturers as 85% of the textiles they used were sourced in the U.S., while Canadian manufacturers utilized mostly imported textiles. To ameliorate this disadvantage, a clause was appended to the agreement which allowed Canadians to export $500 million worth of apparel annually into the U.S. that was exempt from the "rules of origin" but would have a 50% Canadian value-added content. There was much speculation as to how this exemption would be allocated when, in approximately five years, exports were projected to exceed the exemption limit. Experts expected the companies successfully demonstrating their ability to export into the U.S. would have first rights to these exceptions.

Many industry experts had contemplated the consequences of the FTA. There was some agreement that in the short-term, the FTA would most severely impact the lower priced apparel segments in Canada because of the economies of scale which existed in the U.S. market (i.e., the average U.S. apparel manufacturer was ten times larger than its Canadian counterpart). Yet, long-term prospects for all segments were restrained because the industry was slowly being pressured by the Canadian government to become internationally competitive. The question was when international negotiations would eliminate more of the protection afforded to the industry. It was with this concern in mind that Eisman had been continuously pushing the company to become a major international fashion designer and manufacturer.

Overall, Eisman considered the FTA a mixed blessing. Competition in Canada would increase moderately over time, but he felt that the lower tariff rates and the company's high-quality, in-house woolen mill presented a wonderful opportunity for potential expansion into the U.S. market.

MR. JAX FASHIONS

In 1979, a venture capital company owned by Joseph Segal acquired a sleepy Vancouver-based apparel manufacturer having $3 million in sales, 70% of which was in men's wear. Segal immediately recruited Louis Eisman, a well-known women's fashion executive, who proceeded to drop the men's clothing line, and aggressively refocus the company on the career/professional women's market segment.

Eisman appreciated the importance of fashion, and for the first three years he designed all of the new lines. In 1982, he recruited an up-and-coming young Canadian fashion designer, yet he continued to influence the direction of designs considerably. He travelled to Europe for approximately two months annually to review European trends and procure quality fabrics appropriate for the upcoming season. He personally reviewed all designs. The combined women's fashion knowledge and designing abilities provided Mr. Jax with a high-quality, classically designed product which differentiated it from most other Canadian competition. In 1989, the designer resigned, and Eisman recruited a New York-based fashion designer, Ron Leal. Leal had excellent experience in several large U.S. design houses and, unlike the previous designer, he brought considerable U.S. market experience and presence.

Eisman's energy and drive were also critical in establishing the merchandising and distribution network. He personally developed relationships with many of the major retailers. He hired and developed sales agents, in-house sales staff, and in 1983, recruited Jackie Clabon who subsequently became Vice-President of Marketing and Sales. The sales staff were considered to be some of the best in the industry. Clabon's extensive Canadian sales and merchandising experience, combined with Eisman's design and marketing strength, provided Mr. Jax with considerable ability in these critical activities.

Initially, acceptance by Eastern fashion buyers was cool. The fashion "establishment" was highly skeptical of this new Vancouver-based apparel designer and manufacturer. Thus, Eisman focused on smaller independent retail stores, which were more easily swayed in their purchasing decisions. As Mr. Jax gained a reputation for high quality, classical design and excellent service, larger retail chains started to place orders. By 1988, Mr. Jax's products were sold in over 400 department and specialty stores across Canada. Major customers included The Bay, Eaton's, Holt Renfrew and Simpson's, and, although initial marketing efforts had been aimed at the smaller retailer, the majority of Mr. Jax's sales were now to the larger retail chains. The apparel lines were sold through a combination of sales agents and in-house salespersons. Ontario and Quebec accounted for 72% of sales. In addition, two retail stores had recently been established in Vancouver and Seattle; the Vancouver store was very profitable, but the Seattle store was very unprofitable. Industry observers had suggested a number of factors to explain the two stores' performance differences. These factors included increased competition in U.S. metropolitan areas due to increased market density, lower levels of regulation and other entry barriers, greater product selection, and more timely fashion trend shifts compared to the Canadian market, which often exhibited lags in fashion developments of six months or more. Mr. Jax also had a local presence in Vancouver, which was believed to have helped their store by way of reputation, ancillary promotions, and easier access to skilled resources.

Many industry experts felt that Mr. Jax's product line success could be attributed directly to Eisman. He was known for his energy and brashness, as well as his creativity and knowledge of the women's fashion market. In his prior merchandising and marketing experience, he had developed an intuitive skill for the capricious women's apparel market. This industry was often considered to be one of instinct rather than rationality. Eisman was particularly good at design, merchandising and marketing (Exhibit 1). He worked very closely with these departments, often getting involved in the smallest details. As Eisman said, "It is the details that make the difference in our business." Although Eisman concentrated a great deal of his effort and time on these functions, he also attempted to provide guidance to production. The production function had been important in providing the service advantage, particularly in terms of delivery time, which Mr. Jax held over imports. By 1988, Mr. Jax's professional/career women's fashion lines accounted for $25 million in revenues and $3 million in net income (Exhibit 2).

Diversification through Acquisitions

In 1986, Segal and Eisman took Mr. Jax public, raising in excess of $17 million although they both retained one-third of equity ownership. The newly raised capital was used to diversify growth through the acquisition of four semi-related companies.

SURREY CLASSICS MANUFACTURING LTD. Surrey Classics Manufacturing Ltd., a family-owned, Vancouver-based firm, was purchased for $2 million in 1986. This company was principally a manufacturer of lower priced women's apparel and coats. The acquisition was initially made with the objective of keeping the company an autonomous unit. However, the previous owner and his management team adapted poorly to their position within the Mr. Jax organization, and, upon expiration of their noncompetition clauses, they resigned and started a competing company. Unfortunately, sales began to decline rapidly because of this new competition and the absence of managerial talent. To stem the losses, a variety of designers were hired under contract. However, Surrey's poor cash flow could not support the required promotional campaigns and the new fashion lines faired poorly, resulting in mounting operating losses.

In late 1988, Eisman reassigned Mr. Jax's Vice-President of Finance as interim manager of Surrey Classics. As Eisman stated, "The company needed a manager who knew the financial priorities in the industry and could maximize the effectiveness of the company's productive capacity." Several administrative functions were transferred to Mr. Jax, including design, pattern making, sizing and scaling operations. Marketing and production continued to be independent operations housed in a leased facility just outside of Vancouver. Surrey Classics now produced a diversified product line which included Highland Queen, a licensed older women's line of woolen apparel, and Jaki Petite, a Mr. Jax fashion line patterned for smaller women. During this turnaround, Eisman himself provided the required industry specific management skills, which demanded a considerable amount of his time and attention. Eisman kept in daily contact and was involved in most major decisions. During this time Surrey's revenues had declined from $12 million in 1986 to $10.8 million in 1988, and net income had dropped from $100 000 in 1986 to a loss of approximately $2 million in 1988. Eisman felt that in the next two years Surrey's operations would have to be further rationalized into Mr. Jax's to save on overhead costs.

WEST COAST WOOLEN MILLS LTD.

West Coast Woolen Mills Ltd. was a 40-year-old family-owned, Vancouver-based worsted woolen mill. Mr. Jax acquired the company for $2.2 million in 1987. Eisman was able to retain most of the previous management, all of whom had skills quite unique to the industry. West Coast marketed fabric to customers across Canada. In 1986, its sales were $5 million, profits were nil, and its estimated capacity was $10 million annually. The company was the smallest of three worsted woolen mills in Canada, and in the U.S. there were about 18 worsted woolen manufacturers, several being divisions of the world's largest textile manufacturing companies.

Both Mr. Jax and West Coast had mutually benefited from this acquisition. The affiliation allowed Mr. Jax to obtain control of fabric production scheduling, design and quality. In particular, Mr. Jax had been able to significantly reduce order lead times for fabric produced at this subsidiary, although the effects of this on West Coast had not been studied. West Coast benefitted from increased capital funding which allowed it to invest in new equipment and technology, both important attributes in such a capital intensive industry. These investments supported the company's long-term strategic objective of becoming the highest quality, most design-conscious worsted woolen mill in North America. This objective had already been reached in Canada.

Mr. Jax was presently fulfilling 30% to 40% of its textile demands through West Coast. The remainder was being sourced in Europe. By 1988, West Coast's revenues were $6.5 million and profitability was at the break-even point.

OLYMPIC PANT AND SPORTSWEAR CO. LTD.

and Canadian Sportswear Co. Ltd. Mr. Jax acquired Olympic Pant and Sportswear Co. Ltd. and Canadian Sportswear Co. Ltd., both privately owned companies, in 1987 for $18.3 million. The former management, excluding owners, was retained in both of these Winnipeg-based companies.

Olympic manufactured lower priced men's and boys' pants and outerwear as well as some women's sportswear. Canadian Sportswear manufactured low-priced women's and girls' outerwear and coats. Canadian Sportswear was also a certified apparel supplier to the Canadian Armed Forces, and, although these types of sales made up a minority of their revenue base, such a certification provided the company with a small but protected market niche. The disparity in target markets and locations between these companies, and Mr. Jax dictated that they operate largely independently. The expected synergies were limited to a few corporate administrative functions such as finance and systems management.

Combined revenues for these companies had declined from $35 million in 1986 to $30 million in 1988. Both of these companies had remained profitable during this period, although profits had declined. In 1988, combined net income was $1.2 million. Management blamed declining revenues on increased competition and a shortage of management because of the previous owners' retirement.

The Corporation's Present Situation

Diversification had provided the company with excellent growth, but it had also created problems. The most serious was the lack of management control over the now diversified structure (Exhibit 3). By 1988, it had become quite clear that without the entrepreneurial control and drive of the previous owners, the companies were not as successful as they had been prior to their acquisition. Therefore in late 1988, Eisman recruited a new CFO, Judith Madill, to coordinate a corporate control consolidation program. Madill had extensive accounting and corporate reorganization experience, but had limited operating experience in an entrepreneurial environment such as the fashion industry. Madill suggested that corporate personnel, financial, and systems management departments be established to integrate and aid in the management of the subsidiaries. Eisman was not completely convinced this was the right approach. He had always maintained that one of Mr. Jax's competitive strengths was its flexibility and rapid response time. He thought increased administrative overhead would restrict this entrepreneurial ability, and that extra costs would severely restrict future expansion opportunities. Thus, he had limited the administrative expansion to two industrial accountants for the next year.

Consolidation was also occurring in the existing organization. Eisman was trying to recruit a vice-president of production. Mr. Jax had never officially had such a position, and, unfortunately, recruiting a suitable candidate was proving to be difficult. There were relatively few experienced apparel manufacturing executives in North America. Furthermore, Vancouver was not an attractive place for fashion executives because it, not being a fashion centre, would isolate him or her from future employment opportunities. Higher salaries as well as lower taxes tended to keep qualified individuals in the U.S. Yet, a manager of production was badly needed to coordinate the internal production consolidation program.

Originally, production had been located in an old 22 000-square foot facility. By 1986, it had grown to 48 000 square feet located in four buildings throughout Vancouver. Production flow encompassed the typical apparel industry operational tasks (Exhibit 4). However, the division of tasks between buildings made production planning and scheduling very difficult. Production problems slowly accumulated between 1986 and 1988. The problems not only restricted capacity, but also caused customer service to deteriorate from an excellent shipment rate of approximately 95% of orders to recently being sometimes below the industry average of 75%. Mr. Jax's ability to ship had been a key to their growth strategy in Canada. Normally, apparel manufacturers met between 70% and 80% of their orders, but Mr. Jax had built a reputation for shipping more than 90% of orders.

Consolidation had begun in the latter part of 1987. An old building in downtown Vancouver was acquired and renovated. The facility incorporated some of the most modern production equipment available. In total, the company had spent approximately $3.5 million on upgrading production technology. Equipment in the new facility included a $220 000 Gerber automatic cloth cutting machine to improve efficiency and reduce waste; $300 000 of modern sewing equipment to improve productivity and production capacity; a $200 000 Gerber production moving system to automatically move work to appropriate work stations as required; and a computerized design assistance system to integrate the above equipment (i.e., tracking in-process inventory, scheduling, planning and arranging and sizing cloth patterns for cutting). The objectives of these investments were to lower labour content, improve production capacity, and reduce the time required to produce a garment.

In the last quarter of 1988, Mr. Jax had moved into this new head office facility. The building, which was renovated by one of Italy's leading architects, represented a design marvel with its skylights and soaring atriums. The production department had just recently settled into its expansive space. However, the move had not gone without incident. The equipment operators had difficulties adapting to the new machines. Most of the workers had become accustomed to the repetitive tasks required of the old technology. The new equipment was forcing them to retrain themselves and required additional effort; something that was not appreciated by many of the workers. In addition, the largely Asian work force had difficulty understanding retraining instructions because English was their second language.

To further facilitate the implementation of the consolidation program, an apparel production consultant had been hired. The consultant was using time-motion studies to reorganize and improve task efficiency and effectiveness. An example of a problem which had resulted from the move was the need for integration between overall production planning, task assignment, worker remuneration, and the new Gerber production moving system. If these elements were not integrated, the new system would in fact slow production. Unfortunately, this integration had not been considered until after the move, and the machine subsequently had to be removed until adjustments were made. The adjustments required converting workers from a salary base to a piece rate pay scale. The consultants were training all the workers to convert to piece rate work, and to operate the necessary equipment in the most efficient manner. Three workers were being trained per week. The conversion was expected to take two years.

Despite these ongoing problems, production appeared to be improving, and operational activities were now organized and coordinated with some degree of efficiency. Eisman was hopeful that production would gain the upper hand in the fight to remedy scheduling problems within the next six months.

Opportunities for Future Growth

Despite problems such as those detailed above, Mr. Jax's revenues and profits had grown by 1 500% and 500% respectively over the past eight years. Furthermore, Eisman was extremely positive about further growth opportunities in the U.S. market. During the past two years, Eisman had tested the Dallas and New York markets. Local sales agents had carried the Mr. Jax fashion line, and 1988 revenues had grown to US$1 million, the majority of which had come from Dallas. Follow-up research revealed that retail purchasers liked the "classical European styling combined with the North American flair."

This initial success had been inspiring, but it had also exposed Eisman to the difficulties of entering the highly competitive U.S. market. In particular, attaining good sales representation and excellent service, both of which were demanded by U.S. retailers, would be difficult. Securing first-class sales representation required having either a strong market presence or a promising promotional program. In addition, Mr. Jax had found U.S. retailers to be extremely onerous in their service demands. These demands were generally a result of the more competitive retail environment. Demands were particularly stringent for smaller apparel suppliers because of their nominal selling power. These demands ranged from very low wholesale prices to extremely fast order-filling and restocking requirements. Eisman recognized that Mr. Jax would have to establish a focused, coordinated and aggressive marketing campaign to achieve its desired objectives in this market.

Eisman had studied two alternate approaches to entering the U.S. market. One approach involved establishing a retailing chain, while the other involved starting a U.S.-based wholesale distribution subsidiary responsible for managing the aggressive promotional and sales campaign required.

Establishing a retail chain would require both new capital and skills. Capital costs, including leasehold improvements and inventory, would be initially very high, and an administrative infrastructure as well as a distribution and product inventorying system would have to be developed. Yet, starting a retail chain did have benefits. The retail approach would provide controllability, visibility and rapid market penetration. It was the approach taken by many of the aggressive apparel companies in the women's professional/career market segment, such as Liz Claiborne, Benetton, and Esprit. Furthermore, Mr. Jax's marketing strength fit well with this approach. It was estimated that the initial capital required would be about $10 million to open the first 30 stores, and then cost $300 000 per outlet thereafter. Sales revenues would grow to between $300 000 and $750 000 per outlet, depending upon the location, after two to five years. Operating margins on apparel stores averaged slightly less than 10%. Experts felt that within five years the company could possibly open 45 outlets; five the first year, and ten each year thereafter. In summary, this option would entail the greatest financial risk, but it would also have the greatest potential return.

The alternative approach was to establish a U.S. distribution subsidiary. This alternative would require capital and more of the same skills the company had developed in Canada. In general, the company would have to set up one or more showrooms throughout the U.S. The location of the showrooms would be critical to the approach eventually implemented. Exhibit 5 illustrates regional apparel buying patterns in North America.

A wholesale distribution approach could be carried out in one of two ways: either on a regional or national basis. A regional approach would involve focusing on the smaller regional retail stores. These stores tended to attract less competitive attention because of the higher sales expense-to-revenue ratio inherent in servicing these accounts. The approach required the new distributor to provide good-quality fashion lines, and service the accounts in a better manner than established suppliers. An advantage to this approach was that regional retailers demanded fewer and smaller price concessions compared to the larger national chains. The obstacles to this approach included the large sales force required and the superior service capability. Even though Mr. Jax had utilized this strategy successfully in Canada, success was not assured in the U.S. because of the very competitive environment. These factors made this approach both difficult to implement and slow relative to other approaches. Experts estimated fixed costs to average $1 million annually per region, of which 75% would be advertising and 25% other promotional costs. Additional operating costs would consist of sales commissions (7% of sales) and administrative overhead costs (see below). Revenues would be dependent upon many factors, but an initial annual growth rate of $1 million annually within each region was considered attainable over the next five years. In summary, this approach would minimize Mr. Jax's risk exposure, but it would also minimize the short term opportunities.

The national approach was also a viable option. The greatest challenge in a national strategy would be the difficulty in penetrating well established buyer/seller relationships. Floor space was expensive, and national chains and department stores tended to buy conservatively, sticking with the more reputable suppliers who they knew could produce a saleable product and service large orders. They also tended to demand low prices and rapid reorder terms. In summary, the national approach provided significant entry barriers, but it also provided the greatest potential for market share growth. Clearly, if economies of scale and competitive advantage in the larger North American context was the desired goal, this had to be the eventual strategy.

The principal costs of this approach would be the advertising and promotional expenses. National apparel companies had advertising expenditures of many millions of dollars. In discussions with Eisman, industry advertising executives had recommended an advertising expenditure of between $3 and $5 million annually in the first three years and then, if successful, increasing it by $1 million annually in the next two successive years. Additional operating costs would be required for sales commissions (7% of sales) and administrative overhead. The results of this approach were very uncertain and two outcomes were possible. If the approach was successful, Eisman expected that one or two accounts grossing $1 to $2 million annually could be captured in the first two years. Eisman then felt the sales would expand to about $5 million in the third year, and increase by $5 million annually for the next two successive years. However, if the expected quality, design or service requirements were not sustained, sales would probably decline in the third year to that of the first year and then virtually disappear thereafter.

Both the national and regional approaches would require an infrastructure. Depending upon the approach taken, the head office could be located in a number of places. If a national approach was taken, Mr. Jax would have to locate in one of the major U.S. apparel centres (e.g., New York or California). Eisman estimated that the national approach would require a full-time Director of U.S. Operations immediately, while the regional approach could delay this hiring until required. Such a managing director would require extensive previous experience in the industry, and be both capable and compatible with Mr. Jax's marketing, operating and strategic approach. To ensure top-quality candidates, Eisman felt that a signing bonus of at least $100 000 would have to be offered. The remuneration would be tied to sales growth and volume, but a continued minimum salary guarantee might be necessary until the sales reached some minimum volume. In addition, a full-time sales manager would be required. Eisman estimated that the subsidiary's administrative overhead expense would be $500 000 if a regional approach was taken, versus $1 million for a national approach in both cases. These overhead costs would then escalate by approximately $0.5 million annually for the first five years.

Eisman had now studied the U.S. growth options for over six months. He felt a decision had to be made very soon, otherwise the company would forgo the window of opportunity which existed. The new FTA environment and the growth in the professional/career women's market segment were strong incentives, and delaying a decision would only increase the costs as well as the possibility of failure. Eisman realized the decision was critical to the company's evolution toward its ultimate goal of becoming a major international fashion company. The challenge was deciding which approach to take, as well as the sequencing and timing of the subsequent actions.

EXHIBIT 1   Mr. Jax Fashion's President Helping in a Promotional Photo Session

EXHIBIT 2 Mr. Jax Fashion Inc. Financial Statements

Income Statement (000s)

	1981	1982	1983	1984	1985	1986	1987 9 months	1988
Sales	4 592	4 315	5 472	7 666	13 018	24 705	53 391	72 027
Cost of sales	2 875	2 803	3 404	4 797	7 885	14 667	38 165	49 558
Gross profit	1 717	1 512	2 068	2 869	5 133	10 038	15 226	22 469
Selling & gen. admin.	1 172	1 117	1 458	1 898	2 434	4 530	9 071	18 175
Income from operations	545	395	610	971	2 699	5 508	6 155	4 294
Other income	22	25	25	10	16	564	418	117
Loss from discontinued operation								(554)
Income before taxes	567	420	635	981	2 715	6 072	6 573	3 857
Income taxes–								
Current	150	194	285	432	1 251	2 874	2 746	1 825
Deferred	47	2	(5)	28	24	57	245	(195)
Net income	370	224	355	521	1 440	3 141	3 582	2 227
Share price						$7.5–	$8–	$7.5–
						$11	$18	$14

Note: In 1987, the accounting year end was changed from February 1988 to November 1987. This made the 1987 accounting year nine months in duration.

Balance Sheet (000s)

	1981	1982	1983	1984	1985	1986	1987	1988
Assets								
Current Assets								
Short-term investments	—	—	—	—	—	5 027	1 794	495
Accounts receivable	709	874	961	1 697	2 974	6 430	16 133	14 923
Inventories	464	474	684	736	1 431	3 026	15 431	16 914
Prepaid expenses	11	15	20	22	201	398	404	293
Income taxes recoverable	—	—	—	—	—	—	—	1 074
Prop., Plant & Equip.	318	349	424	572	795	4 042	7 789	13 645
Other Assets						273	526	513
Total Assets	1 502	1 712	2 089	3 027	5 401	22 196	42 077	47 857
Liabilities								
Current Liabilities								
Bank indebtedness	129	356	114	351	579	575	1 788	4 729
Accounts payable	490	435	678	963	1 494	3 100	4 893	6 934
Income taxes payable	126	58	86	153	809	1 047	546	
Deferred Taxes	84	86	81	109	133	217	462	267
Shareholder Equity								
Share equity	127	7	13	5	4	12 252	26 577	26 577
Retained earnings	546	770	1 125	1 446	2 347	5 005	7 811	9 350
Total Liabilities	1 502	1 712	2 097	3 027	5 401	22 196	42 077	47 857

Note: Years 1981–84 were estimated from change in financial position statements.

EXHIBIT 3 Mr. Jax Fashion's Organization Chart

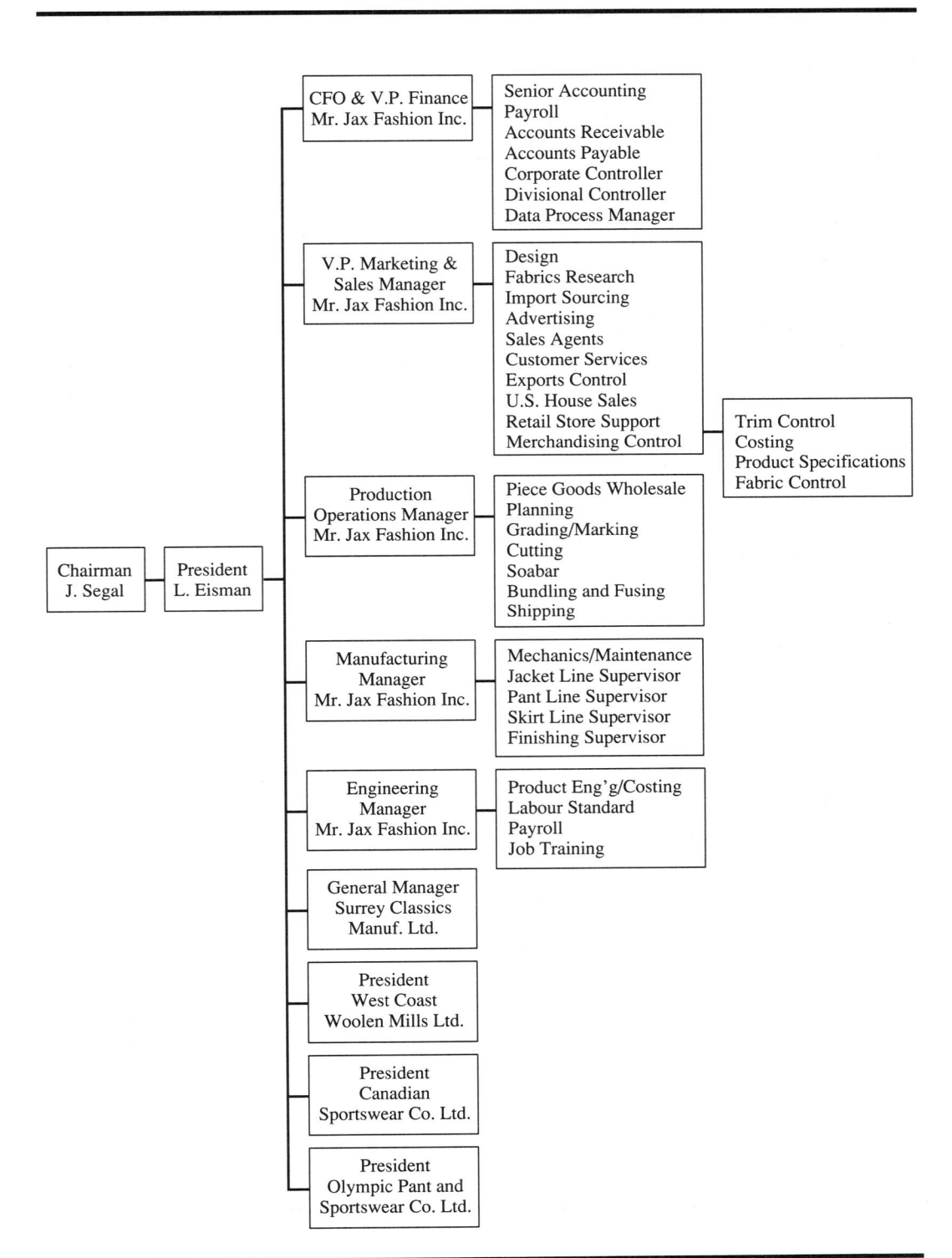

EXHIBIT 4   Mr. Jax Fashion's Production Flow Chart

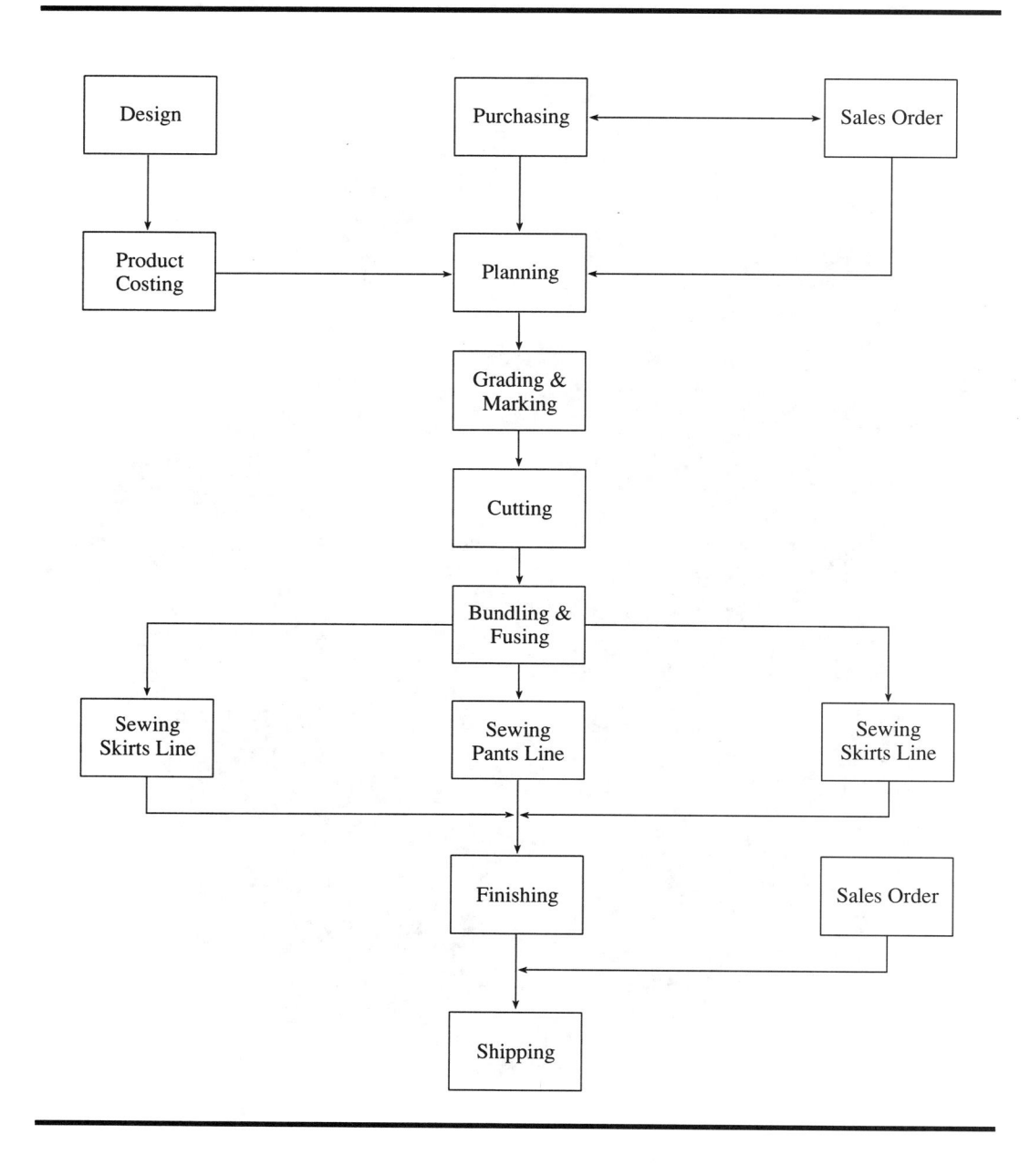

EXHIBIT 5 North American Apparel Consumption by Region

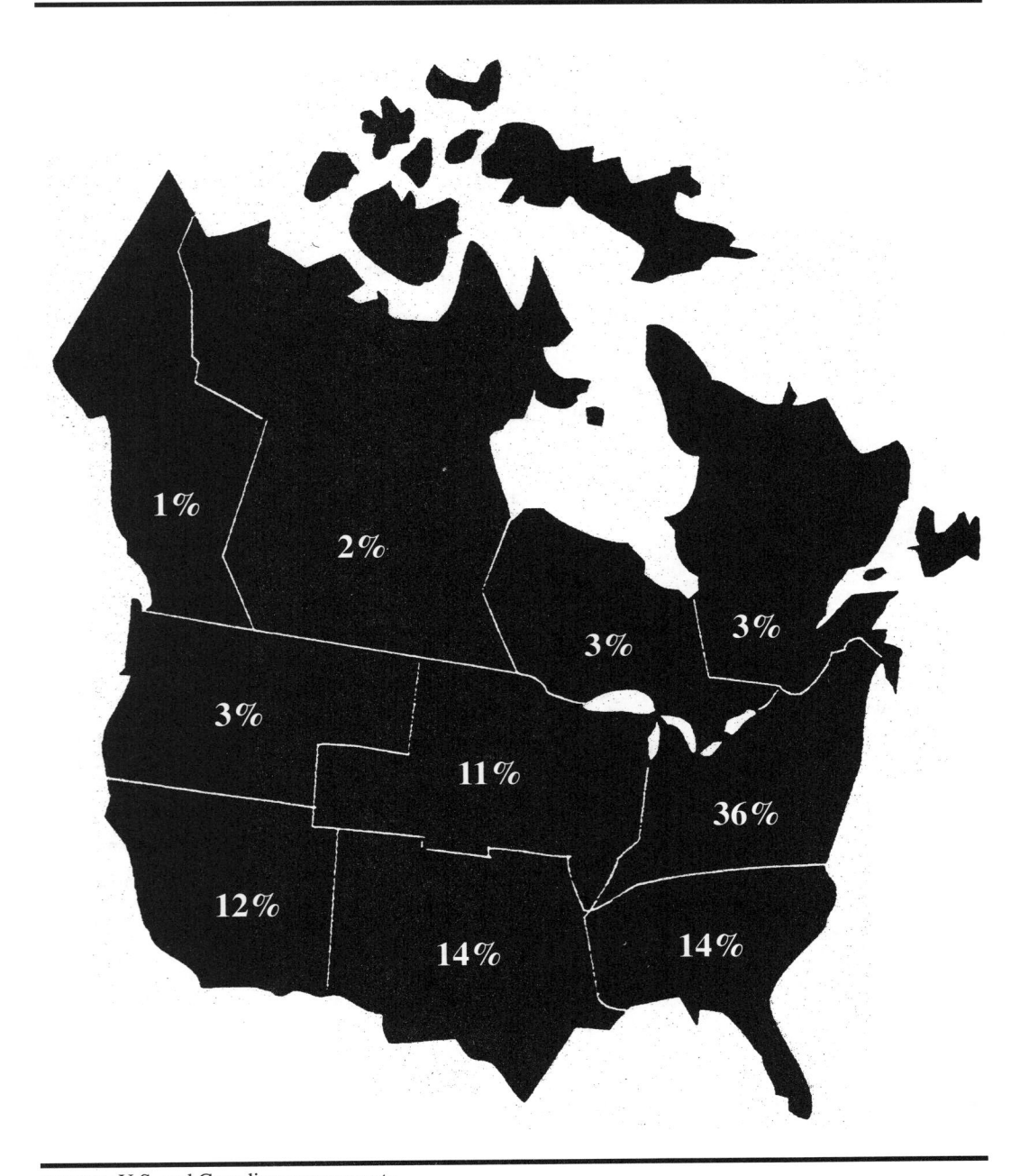

SOURCE: U.S. and Canadian governments.

BANK OF MONTREAL (A): A VISION FOR THE FUTURE

Roderick E. White and
Catherine Paul-Chowdhury

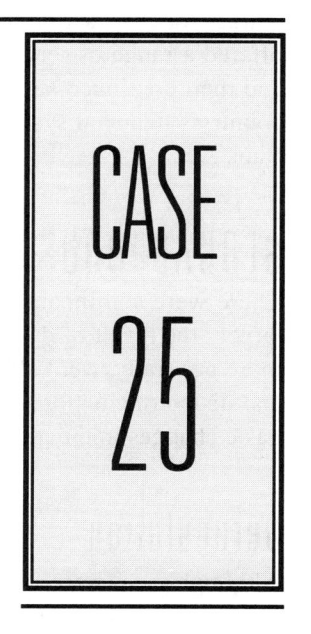

Reflecting on the business he had inherited in 1989, over two years earlier, Bank of Montreal Chairman and CEO Matthew Barrett was pleased with the progress so far. Problem areas were being addressed and the Bank was improving its position and performance in the Canadian market. However, many opportunities, particularly in the U.S. had still to be realized. Mr. Barrett felt that, given the fundamental changes occurring in the financial services industry, incremental improvements in the existing business were necessary but would not suffice. He wanted to present the employees of the Bank with a challenge—a vision of the future they could create.

CANADA'S BANKS

Canadian banking was a mature, relatively stable industry dominated by six large chartered banks: the Royal Bank (RBC), Canadian Imperial Bank of Commerce (CIBC), Bank of Montreal (BMO), Bank of Nova Scotia (BNS), Toronto Dominion Bank (TD) and the National Bank. (See Exhibit 1 for a summary of the major Canadian banks.) All but the National Bank ranked among the 65 largest banks in the world and among the 12 largest in North America in terms of shareholders' equity. These six Schedule I banks held about 90% of the Canadian market for bank services. While the depth of coverage varied, each was national in scope and offered a range of services. The Bank of Canada used these banks to enact monetary policy, and their continued strength was viewed as a critical factor in maintaining the stability of the country's financial system. For this reason, their activities were federally regulated under The Bank Act.

GLOBAL INDUSTRY TRENDS

There were significant differences among the banking sectors in major industrial countries, largely the result of different regulatory regimes. But banks worldwide, and financial services more generally, were affected by several interrelated major trends: deregulation, globalization and disintermediation. These trends were the result of dramatic improvements in technology, basic changes in the global economy, more demanding customers and regulatory changes.

Deregulation

Although there were differences among countries, regulation had traditionally limited foreign control and cross-ownership of the "four pillars" of the financial services industry: banking, investment banking, trust and insurance. In major industrialized countries, regulations were most restrictive in the U.S. and Japan, followed by Canada and the UK. Banks in Germany and France were comparatively unconstrained by separate pillar regulation.

Increased competition from foreign financial institutions, many of which were not subject to the same regulatory constraints in their home countries, and from domestic non-bank providers of financial services had supplied the impetus for deregulation of the banking industries in many countries, including the UK, Canada and, to a lesser extent the U.S. Beginning in the early 1980s, deregulation typically broadened the powers of banks, allowing them to enter into other financial services businesses.

In Canada, banks were federally regulated. Investment dealers were provincially regulated and trust and insurance companies fell under both federal and provincial jurisdiction. Harmonizing these different regulatory regimes was a challenge. The small number of major Canadian banks allowed substantial cooperation between banks and regulators. Certain policies were adopted without regulation, and deregulation had been orderly and relatively quick. In 1987, banks were allowed to acquire or form securities dealers. By 1991, banks and federally incorporated trust and insurance companies, with certain restrictions and subject to regulatory approval, could offer a similar range of services as well as competitive products and cross ownership was permitted. The remaining regulatory separation of banking from insurance and trust was expected to erode gradually. These regulatory changes presented the banks with opportunities to expand their range of services, to become universal banks, provided that they had the resources to invest either in de novo development or in acquisition.

In the U.S., state regulation of chartered banks and the existence of over 11 000 banks gave rise to a more rule-based environment, and a slow pace for deregulation. In Western Europe, banks were looking forward to expanded geographic powers with the scheduled economic union in 1992, when banking would become an open industry across most European countries. In leading European countries such as Germany, banks were already able to offer a wide range of products and services in their home markets. This freedom had resulted in the development of large financial services conglomerates, or "universal banks."

Globalization

Banks were an important part of a country's economic infrastructure. Accordingly, restrictions on foreign ownership had been commonplace. Retail activities including deposit-taking, and consumer and small business lending were intrinsically local. Historically, these factors had combined to make retail banking a national, or even community-based business.

Corporate and institutional banking, however, had been and was increasingly international. Early in Canada's history, domestic banks provided a conduit for the foreign investment which financed major infrastructure projects (e.g., CP Railway).[1] As the economy developed, lending to foreign governments, foreign financial institutions and corporations doing business internationally took banks beyond their own borders. As international trade and investment became increasingly important, banks followed their customers into foreign markets. Often restricted from deposit-taking, and lacking the distribution networks and local knowledge to be effective in retail and small to mid-sized commercial segments, these "suitcase" banks had tended to focus on large corporate and institutional clients outside of their domestic markets. Many foreign banks, along with investment banks, also competed for government business. The result was a proliferation of competitors and increased competition in the large corporate, institutional and government market segments.

Prior to the 1980 revision to Canada's Bank Act, foreign banks operated in Canada exclusively on a suitcase basis. The revisions allowed the chartering of foreign-owned, "Schedule II" banks. By 1992, approximately 55 Schedule II banks had been incorporated. None had established a significant presence in the retail banking business. They focused mainly on corporate, institutional and government customers. Furthermore, these foreign-owned subsidiaries were initially limited to no more than 16% of the domestic assets of the entire Canadian banking system, and required permission of the Minister of Finance to open additional branches. The implementation of the Canada–U.S. Free Trade Agreement (FTA) in 1989 removed U.S.-controlled Schedule II banks from these restrictions.[2] The ceiling on other foreign-owned banks was lowered to 12% of domestic banking assets. Schedule I banks had to be widely held, with no investor group owning more than 10%, and foreign ownership limited to 25%. (The FTA removed U.S. investors from this 25% limit.)

While businesses and their banks were strengthening their presence internationally, technological and product innovations were linking money centres around the world, resulting in the globalization of financial markets. Record inflation and interest rates during the late 1970s and early 1980s had forced money managers and securities issuers to become increasingly sophisticated and agile, shopping worldwide for the best rates. Advances in electronic communi-

---

[1] The Bank of Montreal, Canada's first bank (chartered in 1817) was very active in arranging international financing for railways. (See: Darroch, J.L., *Canadian Banks and Global Competitiveness*. Kingston: McGill-Queens University Press, 1994.)

[2] The FTA provided for national treatment of banks from the partner country. It did not harmonize the regulatory regimes. Thus Canadian owned banks were subject to U.S. regulations in that country and vice versa.

cations allowed investors and traders to scan markets worldwide in seconds for information and the best prices. Complex products known as derivatives allowed institutions to hedge their international positions to manage their risk exposures and those of their clients. Globalization of the financial markets significantly increased the level of sophistication of the banks' corporate clients, and necessitated the development of new skills and complex information systems within the banks.

Another factor reinforcing the globalization of the banking industry was the development of common international standards for capital adequacy. In 1988, the Bank for International Settlements (BIS) member countries agreed to require a minimum risk-weighted capital-asset ratio of 8% on their banks by 1992. This was in response to the concern that the failure of an undercapitalized bank in one country could cascade through the network of international relationships and threaten the global financial system. More sophisticated and pervasive international standards were expected.

Disintermediation

The major function of banks had been to serve as an intermediary between suppliers of funds (depositors) and users of funds (borrowers). In this capacity, the banks absorbed the risk of default by the borrower and earned a "spread," the difference between the cost of funds and interest earned. Now, instead of depending on bank loans for financing, major corporations were turning directly to the capital markets and large suppliers of capital to meet their needs. With the emergence of large pools of capital in the pension fund and mutual fund industries, large users of capital were able to bypass bank intermediaries and directly access the suppliers of capital. This resulted in declining demand for the traditional bank lending services in the already competitive large corporate market segment. (See Exhibit 2 for information on all commercial debt.)

Increasingly, individuals invested their savings in non-deposit products[3] often outside the banking system. Money market and other mutual funds, many offered by non-bank institutions, were very popular. Private pension plans, another form of non-bank savings, were now commonplace. U.S. banks had, until the early 1970s, been limited to paying 4% on savings accounts. Money market funds offering twice that return had attracted a large share of consumer savings. Even though U.S. banks now offered competitive products and rates, they had never fully recovered their position. The banks' declining share of consumer savings is shown in Exhibit 2. Consumers were directing large portions of their savings to non-bank funds, which large corporate and institutional customers were accessing directly.

Related to disintermediation was the recent trend toward the securitization of assets. Securitization involved packaging large pools of assets with similar properties (e.g., risk, income streams) and selling the package in the form of a debenture-like security. Increasingly, banks were securitizing their mortgage and credit card portfolios. Typically, they were sold to pension funds, insurance companies, or any institution with large amounts of capital to invest. Banks were also considering selling or securitizing parts of their loan portfolios. Banks were,

---

[3] Deposit products were distinguished by being guaranteed by a government agency—for example the Federal Deposit Insurance Corporation (FDIC) in the U.S.

in effect, disintermediating themselves. However, this practice allowed banks more flexibility in managing their loan portfolios. It removed the loans from the banks' books and improved their capital ratios,[4] or made capital available for other purposes. However, since the assets most appropriate for securitization were the high quality ones, a bank pursuing indiscriminate securitization risked being left with a high risk, low quality portfolio of loans.

BANKING BUSINESSES

Historically, commercial banks had been distinguished from other financial institutions by their ability to accept deposits and use those funds to make commercial (as well as personal) loans. Over time, a variety of other lending products and for-fee services had been added. Banks addressed three broad market segments: retail, commercial, and corporate and institutional.

Retail and Commercial

Retail banking was a distribution-based business. It involved offering deposit products and cheque-processing services, as well as providing loans and residential mortgages for individuals, and commercial loans and current accounts for medium to small sized businesses. Through the same network of branches, banks also offered other financial services such as credit cards and mutual funds. Personal deposits provided much of the funding for the banking industry, and when gathered through an efficient distribution network, were lower cost than funds available in the wholesale market. Canada's major banks managed retail branch networks of national scope. Even so, many aspects of retail banking were local activities. A branch's performance was closely tied to the economic performance of its community and the region.

Canada was home to 7400 bank branches that, in urban areas, served approximately 2500 people per branch. When credit unions, trust companies and *caisses populaires* were included in the calculation, Canada had more financial institution retail branches per capita than any other country in the world, leading to observations that it was "over-branched."

Retail banking was becoming increasingly complex, as rapidly evolving technology opened up a wide array of non-branch distribution alternatives. Traditional bricks-and-mortar branch networks had been the cornerstone of banks' distribution strategies. But the importance of these branches had been eroded in recent years by the widespread use of automated banking machines (ABMs), and the emergence of telephone banking and point-of-sale terminals. In some instances, technology was advancing faster than consumer acceptance of it; for example, in the area of home banking. The banks had to manage their investment in electronic distribution in such a way as to be neither behind nor too far ahead of their clients' expectations.

To further complicate the issue, different groups of retail clients exhibited different preferences for branches and alternative delivery channels. Considerable market research had been done on usage patterns, revealing two extreme types of retail customer: branch-dependent and

---

[4] The risk assumed by banks, measured by capital ratios, was of concern to regulators. Securitization was an easy way to improve capital ratios, although doing so did not necessarily positively affect the risk profile of the bank.

self-service oriented. These groups corresponded roughly to the client's age, with people under the age of 35 preferring not to frequent branches, and pre-baby boomers valuing highly the personal service and social interaction associated with branch banking. Dramatic as the changing technology and its associated opportunities appeared to be for banks, the balance between bricks and mortar and electronic banking still seemed to be tipped in favour of traditional branch banking. No "branchless" retail banks yet existed.[5] Consumers still appeared to want a branch presence, even though they might not frequent it. Electronic distribution was a complement, not yet a substitute, for bricks and mortar in the delivery of conventional retail banking services.

The commercial banking business targeted companies that could be serviced through the branch network, typically small to mid-sized firms, loosely defined as having revenues of less than $500 million.[6] In larger centres, certain branches specialized in this segment. The main product offerings to this segment included lines of credit and operating services. Firms of this size did not have ready access to the capital markets and relied heavily on the credit provided by their banks. They valued the strength and stability of the banking relationship, and were prepared to pay for this support. For this reason, margins in the commercial business were relatively high in comparison to the larger corporate market. Heavy competition in Canada, however, had driven the margin on these loans to approximately 300 basis points compared with 400 basis points in the U.S. and 500 basis points in the UK. The thin margins in Canada made it virtually impossible to lend money profitably without a low-cost retail deposit base and an established branch system to service commercial customers.

Retail banking was transaction-intensive. It required processing a huge number of mostly small dollar transactions. To compete effectively in this business required a time-sensitive, efficient back-office operation. The major Canadian banks had moved most of their back-office transaction processing out of the branches and consolidated this activity in a few regional centres. A rough measure of overall operational efficiency is provided in Exhibit 3.

All the banks had made enormous strides in reducing their processing costs. During the 1970s, much of the improvement was driven by simple automation or computerization of manual functions. With these opportunities already exploited, further improvements required re-engineering and restructuring the underlying work flows and utilizing technology as appropriate.

Processing for some of the corporate and institutional lines of business was similarly transaction-intensive (e.g., payroll services, trade finance services). However, corporate lending involved fewer and larger transactions than retail banking, making it less affected by processing-related economies.

Corporate and Institutional

Corporate banking involved the provision of a wide range of products and services to large corporations, as well as governments and other financial institutions. Often these clients had direct access to the capital markets, and were wooed by banks worldwide. The range of their alternatives and the size of their transactions made these clients price-sensitive and sophisti-

---

[5] UK's Midland Bank had launched a branchless banking unit in 1989 called First Direct.

[6] $500 million was the upper limit used by the Bank of Montreal. Other banks used limits as low as $150 million.

cated in their requirements. The trends toward deregulation, globalization and disintermedia-tion had left margins on corporate lending thin, and often it was only the provision of other services which made relationships with these clients even marginally profitable. In any coun-try, corporate banking was typically conducted from a few large money-centre locations.

It was difficult to assess the relative profitability of the Canadian banks' retail and corpo-rate businesses. The banks did not break out their revenues or profitability along these lines for public reporting purposes. Internally, each had its own criteria for differentiating between small and large business customers. The banks also faced revenue and cost allocation issues. While corporate lending typically took place in central banking offices, a corporate client's nightly deposits of cash, for example, were made at the local branch level. The banks' infor-mation systems were unable to track the corporate transactions at the branch level and allocate costs and revenues accordingly. However, the loan losses associated with large corporate lend-ing could be identified, and in Canada they had been considerable.

Historically, the large corporate business segment in Canada had not been a financially re-warding area. The Canadian banking industry appeared to over-commit to specific sectors: oil and gas in the early 1980s; commercial real estate in the late 1980s. When these sectors expe-rienced difficulties, the banks were left with large problem loans. Given the relatively small size of the Canadian economy and their own large size, it was difficult for the major banks to avoid lending to specific sectors. Another contributing factor was the industry's pricing prob-lems. Loans were not priced to reflect their inherent risks, and the thin margins were not enough to cover unexpectedly high levels of nonperforming loans. As a result, over the full economic cycle, most Canadian banks realized inadequate returns on their Canadian large cor-porate lending businesses.

The corporate segments in Canada and the U.S. had some significant differences. These differences were largely due to the much greater size and depth of the U.S. market. In Canada, the primary source of competition for the limited number of large corporate clients was the other Schedule I banks. In the U.S., customers and competitors were far more numerous and more specialized, making the industry less well-defined. This diversity allowed well-managed banks to find profitable niches.

In the U.S., the corporate and institutional markets were served by a few purely corporate banks like J.P. Morgan, and a much larger number of banks offering some mixture of corpo-rate and institutional banking services as well as retail banking.[7] The U.S. represented a more attractive market than Canada for corporate banking because of the greater availability of good lending opportunities combined with better risk assessment and greater pricing disci-pline. Because the U.S. had an active secondary market for loans, rates were set by the market, and were appropriate to the risk of the underlying asset.

Traditional financing in the form of different types of loans generated spread income for the banks. Interest rate volatility and competition had, however, significantly narrowed banks' spreads over the past decade. Increasingly, banks on both sides of the border were actively at-tempting to shift their revenues from spread to fee income. Banks offered a range of fee-based treasury, operating and, in some cases, trust services to their large corporate clients. Treasury

---

[7] There were also banks, like Banc One that specialized in personal and commercial branch banking and chose to do no large corporate or institutional business.

services included foreign exchange, money market and risk management. Operating services included cash management, payments, securities services and trade finance. A bank's institutional clients including Schedule II banks, insurance companies, pension funds and mutual funds were particularly heavy users of operating services. Because operating and treasury services were typically processing-intensive or required significant capital investment in information systems and facilities, banks with larger transaction volumes had a potential cost advantage. Banks also charged fees for corporate advisory work related to their business services. Because they tended to be highly specialized, advisory services were not subject to any particular size-related advantages.

INVESTMENT BANKING

Historically, legislation in Canada and the U.S. had separated the businesses of banking and investment banking. In 1987, however, Canadian regulators responded to changes in the global competitive environment, and allowed Canadian banks to engage in investment banking activities and to own investment banks. Investment banking was attractive to the banks for two reasons. First, it allowed banks to recapture some of the corporate and retail clients that they were losing through disintermediation. Secondly, in a good year, investment banking provided returns well in excess of the 15% ROE commonly sought by the banks. Five of Canada's six largest banks purchased investment dealers, while the sixth, the TD, chose to develop these capabilities in-house. Made in 1987 through 1988, these acquisitions were generally priced at more than two times book value, in what was widely considered to be a sellers' market.

The Canadian markets were dominated by several large investment dealers, summarized in Exhibit 4, of which all but one offered a full range of institutional and retail services. These firms were capitalized in the $100 to $300 million range, and each considered itself a top-tier supplier in the Canadian market. Despite their different strengths and areas of dominance, the firms were perceived outside of Canada as being relatively undifferentiated. In addition to the major full-service investment dealers, Canada was home to a handful of small boutiques specializing in areas including M&A, research and small-capitalization companies.

After the first wave of acquisitions following deregulation, the 1989–91 period saw considerable consolidation in the Canadian securities industry. Pemberton Securities, one of the last full-service regional brokers, was bought by Dominion Securities in 1989. Midland Capital found itself too small to compete, and merged with Walwyn Stodgell. Several U.S.-owned securities dealers exited the industry. Pru-Bache Canada sold its retail operation to Burns Fry. Merrill Lynch Canada sold its retail businesses to Wood Gundy, and both U.S. dealers withdrew from Canada. Dean Witter sold its Canadian operations to Midland Walwyn.

Despite the closure of their Canadian retail and trading operations, a number of the major Wall Street firms had begun competing for Canadian corporate finance/M&A business on a suitcase basis, sometimes in partnership with Canadian investment dealers. They offered prospective clients great depth of experience in specialized product segments and extensive international distribution networks, as well as the underwriting capacity associated with capitalizations many times greater than those of their Canadian rivals.

Table 1 ranks the major underwriters of Canadian corporate debt and equity issues, and illustrates the recent emergence of strong U.S. competitors in the Canadian market.

TABLE 1   Underwriters of Canadian Corporate Securities Issues* ($ millions)

Rank 1991	Rank 1990	Underwriter	Total – 1991	Debt	Equity
1	1	RBC Dominion Securities	3 559	1 995	1 564
2	4	Burns Fry	2 730	1 483	1 247
3	3	Wood Gundy	2 563	1 449	1 114
4	11	Goldman Sachs (U.S.)	2 246	1 590	659
5	2	Scotia McLeod	2 185	1 146	1 039
6	5	Nesbitt Thomson	1 633	681	952
7	14	Merrill Lynch (U.S.)	1 510	1 415	95
8	6	Gordon Capital	1 415	555	860
9	—	Morgan Stanley (U.S.)	1 181	1 110	71
10	7	TD Securities	993	568	425

* All Canadian corporate issues including domestic and international, public and private.

SOURCE: *Financial Post*, June 29, 1992.

A fully integrated investment dealer had both retail and institutional businesses. The institutional side consisted of equity and fixed income sales and trading, research and investment banking. Investment banking included corporate and government finance and M&A advisory work. Securities originated through corporate and government finance transactions were then distributed by the institutional and retail sales forces as public offerings or private placements. Investment banking and large corporate banking clients were the same large organizations. Activities such as the private placement of debt were common to both commercial and investment banking, and illustrated the blurring of boundaries between them.

Both banking and investment banking earned revenues through some combination of spread and fee businesses. In banking, spread referred to the difference in interest rates paid on deposits and received from loans. In an investment bank's fixed income and equity trading businesses, the spread was the difference in the price at which a security was purchased and sold. Investment banks were required by law to maintain capital reserves in proportion to the size and riskiness of the businesses. Investment bankers had their firms' capital at stake for much shorter periods of time than did banks. The transactions they managed were less frequent than those conducted by banks and they yielded higher margins. However, the risks associated with underwriting had increased during the 1980s and early 1990s with the emergence of bought deals[8] and the diminishing use of "market out"[9] clauses. The potential risk in many deals often exceeded the equity base of the investment bank. Having the backing of a large chartered bank was viewed as an advantage.

---

[8] In a bought deal, investment dealers purchased the entire issue, legally assuming all of the risks associated with pricing and distribution. These deals could be brought to market much more quickly than "best effort" underwritten deals. The timing did not however, allow investment dealers their usual "pre-marketing" period to informally determine where and for what price securities could be placed.

[9] Market out clauses released investment dealers from the legal obligation to underwrite an equity issue if the market conditions were to change in such a way that they could not profitably underwrite and distribute the securities.

Investment banks also earned commission income on the sale of securities to retail and institutional investors. Commissions, particularly on institutional sales, had diminished over the past decade under competitive pressure. Earnings in the investment banking business were highly volatile, and tended to be counter-cyclical. Investment dealers made significant trading profits on interest-rate fluctuations. They also commanded considerable corporate finance fees when a firm needed to look for external financing.

The size of an investment dealer was important for long-term success in three ways. First, a large retail network represented superior distribution capabilities to reach the small investor. This was often a consideration in awarding underwriting business. Second, a firm with a strong capital base was able to assume larger trading and underwriting positions, allowing it to deliver superior or unique service to its clients. Third, since some investment dealer costs were fixed (e.g., research) a larger firm was able to spread these costs over a bigger base of business. During peak periods in the industry, investment dealers earned after-tax returns of over 20% on their regulatory equity bases. Nevertheless, analysts believed that few, if any, of the Canadian banks had achieved double-digit ROEs on their costs of acquisition.

Integration was widely considered to be key in making the investment by banks in securities dealers profitable. Integration on at least two fronts was possible. The banks could use their considerable retail presence, their branch networks, to direct business to their investment bank. (Chartered banks were prohibited from directly giving investment advice to their customers.) They could, in theory, even share retail facilities. The other potential area of integration was between large corporate and institutional banking and investment banking. These businesses shared the same customer base and even overlapped in some of their service offering. CIBC was moving most aggressively in this respect, having announced its intention to combine the two divisions into one Corporate and Investment Bank. The other banks had maintained separate entities, but continued to search for points of integration. Profound differences in culture and compensation practices, however, made the marriage of corporate and investment banking difficult.

Investment Banking—U.S.

In the U.S., banks' entry into investment banking had proceeded more slowly. The participation by U.S. commercial banks in securities activities had been restricted since 1933 by the Glass Steagall Act. Permissible activities were generally limited to underwriting and dealing in government securities and in certain money market instruments. Some commercial banks also offered M&A advice, privately placed many types of securities, and engaged in investment banking activities outside the U.S. By the late 1980s, legal interpretation of the laws had been relaxed, allowing underwriting and dealing activities for bank holding companies to include a wider array of securities: commercial paper, municipal revenue bonds, mortgage-backed securities and consumer receivable-related securities. By the early 1990s, certain well-capitalized U.S. and foreign banks (including four major Canadian banks) had obtained rulings which had further extended their activities to include underwriting and dealing in corporate debt and equity securities. These activities were still considered to be "bank ineligible" and had to be carried out separately through what was known as a "Section 20 subsidiary." Underwriting could not exceed 10% of the subsidiary's gross revenues.

As is clear from Table 2, the U.S. capital markets were much larger than their Canadian counterparts. The U.S. market was dominated by the large, Wall Street based "bulge bracket" firms: Merrill Lynch, Goldman Sachs, First Boston, Lehman Brothers, Morgan Stanley and Salomon Brothers. These firms also dominated international equity issues and were a major presence in the international and Eurobond market. In the past decade, the only bank to have emerged as a significant competitor to these firms was JP Morgan.

TABLE 2   Comparison of U.S. and Canadian Securities Markets (US$ billions—1992)

Activity	U.S.	Canada
Public Debt Underwriting	314	4
Corporate Debt Trading	5 384	300
Equity Underwriting	81	9
Equity Trading	2 100	102
M&A Activity	124	6

SOURCE: Booz Allen.

Only the few well-capitalized, large firms offered a full range of services in terms of products, clients and geographic location. Notable in this group were Merrill Lynch with capital of $12 billion, and Smith Barney Shearson. Others were more specialized. Large investment banks including Goldman Sachs, Morgan Stanley and Salomon Brothers with capital bases in the $4–$5 billion range, focused on global corporate finance and institutional distribution. Smaller regional firms capitalized in the $100–$200 million range including Alex Brown and Piper Jaffray, focused on equity origination and distribution through retail and institutional channels, and municipal finance. Other firms specialized in functions including M&A, institutional equity distribution, research and proprietary trading.

THE U.S. BANKING MARKET

With mature markets in their businesses at home and a history of international presence, Canada's Big Six Banks were looking with renewed interest at foreign markets. The U.S. was particularly attractive. It represented a market of over 250 million people with a GDP of $5.7 trillion compared to Canada's population of 27 million and US$593 billion GDP. It was the headquarters to 383 of the world's largest 1 000 corporations. Despite well-publicized difficulties, the U.S. economy was sound and dynamic, and was expected to remain so during the coming decade.

Canada and the U.S. already enjoyed a significant degree of economic integration. Their two-way trade flow was valued at approximately US$200 billion, an estimated 60% of which was intra-company. The U.S. accounted for 80% of Canadian exports. The Canada–U.S. Free Trade Agreement (FTA) was expected to further strengthen economic ties, and increase demands for seamless financial services on both sides of the border. The possible extension of the FTA to Mexico (NAFTA) promised an even larger market and corresponding opportunities.

Because of their different regulatory histories, the U.S. banking industry differed from its Canadian counterpart in certain key respects. It was much less concentrated. As shown in Exhibit 5, the six largest U.S. banks accounted for about 22% of banking assets. They were also more heterogeneous. J.P. Morgan was exclusively a corporate bank; Citicorp, Chemical Bank and Chase were predominately corporate banks; Nationsbank was largely a retail bank. On the corporate side, banks had been restricted from participating in underwriting activities, although there had been some easing of this restriction. Since U.S. banks were already active in trust businesses, deregulation focused primarily on allowing banks to enter a wider range of investment banking activities and to broaden geographic distribution in the retail business, within and across state lines.

On the retail side, the U.S. banking system had evolved under state regulations which had tightly restricted branching and interstate expansion, resulting in a highly fragmented industry and no competitors with national scope in the retail market. Regulation was largely a state prerogative. In some so-called unit banking states (e.g., Illinois, Texas), branching activities within the state had been severely limited. Over the past decade, however, these regulations had been relaxed to allow bank holding companies the ownership of multiple banks within and outside their home states. Deregulation had proceeded at different rates in different states and regions, but was followed quickly by waves of consolidation and the emergence of regional and super-regional banks. There were an estimated 11 806 insured commercial banks in the U.S. in 1991, compared to 14 478 in 1980. Almost 2 000 banks had been acquired between 1983 and 1991. A separate bank charter was still required in each state but Congress was considering abolishing this requirement to allow for true nationwide branch networks. During 1991–92, mega-mergers created three bank entities with asset bases greater than that of the Bank of Montreal: Bank of America/Security Pacific, NCNB/C&S/Sovran (now Nationsbank), and Chemical/Manufacturers Hanover.

Over the last decade, the U.S. financial system had experienced significant difficulties. Reasons varied, but many institutions in the search for higher returns had taken on high yield investments without being aware of or able to manage the accompanying risks. Since 1985, 1 200 banks had failed. In 1991, there were 1 000 problem banks, representing 16% of the country's banking assets. Largely as a consequence of "disorderly" deregulation in the early 1980s and management ineptitude, the entire savings and loan industry was threatened with extinction. It was expected that by the turn of the century the number of banks would decline a further 25%, and the number of Savings and Loans would decline by two-thirds. With this high level of uncertainty, banks with strong capital positions and overall financial stability had a competitive advantage in mergers and acquisitions, and in attracting customers.

As the U.S. began to look more like Canada from a regulatory perspective, it presented a number of potentially attractive opportunities for Canadian banks: to leverage branching expertise in a large, highly fragmented market; to capitalize on their financial strength and stability in the turbulent U.S. financial system; to take advantage of transborder business opportunities associated with the Free Trade Agreement; and to further integrate banking and investment banking. As Table 3 suggests all the major Canadian Banks had a long and continuing involvement in the U.S. corporate market.

TABLE 3 **Earning Assets of Canadian Banks at Risk in the U.S.** (C$ billions)

Institution	1988	1989	1990	1991	% of 1991 Total Assets
Bank of Montreal	20.3	22.6	23.6	25.1	25.6%
Bank of Nova Scotia	13.4	14.5	16.8	17.4	19.6%
Toronto Dominion	n.a.	7.3	8.1	8.5	14.7%
CIBC	11.4	10.3	11.0	13.2	10.7%
Royal Bank	6.7	7.2	8.1	8.7	7.3%

SOURCE: Bank Annual Reports.

In the U.S. retail banking market, however, the success of Canadian banks had been limited. The TD had entered the California market in 1971 but exited in 1985. CIBC established the California Canadian Bank in 1982 but sold this business, including 11 retail branches in 1985. In 1991, Canada Trust acquired for $217 million a savings and loan association with 67 retail branches and 16 mortgage lending offices located primarily in New York state and Massachusetts. Of the banks, only the Bank of Montreal with its 1984 purchase of Chicago's Harris Bank had a retail presence in the U.S. Even so, Harris Bank was primarily a corporate bank.

THE BANK OF MONTREAL

With an average asset base of $94 billion in 1991, the Bank of Montreal was the third largest bank in Canada in terms of assets, and the 11th largest in North America on the basis of shareholders' equity. The Bank benchmarked its performance primarily against the other five big Canadian banks through profitability, productivity and prudential measures. The management team had set minimum performance standards for each of these measures as the average of the "big six," and its goal was to rank first or second in each of the measures. Management had also recently begun tracking the Bank's performance with respect to a broader group of North American banks. Table 4 and Exhibit 6 show the Bank's performance compared to its Canadian competitors.

Total revenues were just below $4 billion in 1991. Net interest income, the difference between the amount charged on loans and the interest cost of funds (including provision for loan losses), made up the largest part of the Bank's revenue. But as shown in Table 5, other operating revenues had grown to over 31% of total revenues. Operating revenues were made up of operating services (28%), credit card (15%), securities (15%), foreign exchange (11%), loan fees (8%) and trust income (12%). Non-interest expenses were 65.2% of revenues. The largest non-interest expense was for salary and benefits (55% of total expenses) followed by computer and communications costs (11%), with premises costs third at 6%.

TABLE 4 Bank of Montreal Performance (October 31, 1991)

Measure		BMO	Big Six Average	BMO Rank
Profitability	ROI[+]	47.4%	51.8%	3
	ROE	15.0%	14.0%	3
	Earnings Growth	13.9%	3.8%	2
Productivity	Expenses/Revenues	65.2%	60.7%	6
	Capital Adequacy[*]	8.82	8.92	4
	Asset Quality—1[**]	0.53	0.65	1
Prudential	Asset Quality—2[*+]	49.05	45.27	4
	Senior Debt Rating[##]	AA-	AA	3
	Liquidity[++]	31.9	19.9	1

[+] to a shareholder, includes: capital gain + dividend + dividend reinvestment
[*] Capital/Risk Adjusted Assets (regulatory requirement of 8%)
[**] Provisions for Credit Losses/Net Loans + Acceptances
[*+] Gross NPL/Equity + Allowance for Credit Losses
[##] Composite of S&P and Moody's Ratings
[++] Cash + Securities/Assets
SOURCE: BMO documents.

TABLE 5 Bank of Montreal Revenues and Expenses ($ millions)

	1988	1989	1990	1991
Net Interest Income (TEB)	2 612	2 600	2 606	2 776
Other Operating Income	1 095	1 076	1 158	1 249
Adjustments	(53)	(90)	(111)	(30)
Total Revenues	3 654	3 586	3 653	3 995
Non-Interest Expense	2 297	2 330	2 453	2 605
Provision for Credit Losses	390	1 181	169	337
Provision for Income Taxes (TEB)	461	109	506	452
Net Income (after minority interests)	500	(39)	522	595

SOURCE: BMO Annual Report.

The Bank of Montreal was organized around four major lines of business, or pillars.[10] They were Personal and Commercial Financial Services (PCFS), Corporate and Institutional Financial Services (CIFS), Nesbitt Thomson (NT) in investment banking and Harris Bankcorp, its U.S. subsidiary based in Chicago. The domestic PCFS business was by far the largest pillar, accounting for over half of total revenues, CIFS and Harris each contributed just over 20% of revenues and NT roughly 6%.

---

[10] In addition to these pillars the Bank of Montreal owned Banco de Montreal S.A., a commercial and investment bank subsidiary in Brazil. It had a small impact on overall revenues and income but because of the volatility of earnings and the increasingly restrictive Brazilian regulatory environment, BMO was looking for ways to reduce its position with this subsidiary.

PCFS

Canadian retail and commercial businesses within the Bank comprised Personal and Commercial Financial Services, or PCFS. In Canada, these clients were served through a network of approximately 17 000 employees based in 1 274 branches and 1 221 automated banking machines. The Bank offered a full range of deposit and loan products, mortgages, credit cards and operating services to these segments. One of every two Canadian households had some type of business with the Bank of Montreal. Yet its market share in several key product lines fell short of its "natural" market share of approximately 15%, based on the Bank's share of branches or industry expenses. The Bank's market share in key retail business segments is summarized in Table 6.

TABLE 6   BMO PCFS 1991 Market Share in Key Business Segments

Product/Service	Bank Market (%)	Overall Market* (%)
Personal Loans	14.3	10.4
Residential Mortgages	14.0	7.2
Credit Cards	19.2	16.5
Personal Deposits	16.2	8.7
Retail Operating Deposits	17.6	11.9
Personal Term Deposits	14.6	6.4
Mutual Funds	21.1	3.8
Commercial Lending	10.8	n.a.

* Includes banks, trust companies, credit unions and mutual funds.
SOURCE: BMO internal documents.

Since the late 1980s, BMO had distinguished itself from its Canadian competitors by segmenting its retail network into 250 communities. These communities consisted of groups of branches within limited geographic areas. Decision making was decentralized, where possible, to the community level. PCFS had achieved consistent, high levels of profitability. Because of the large branch network, non-interest expense as a proportion of total revenues was higher than the bank average. Even so, this pillar accounted for a disproportionate share of the Bank's net income and had a ROE higher than the Bank's average.

CIFS

The Bank's corporate businesses were grouped under Corporate and Institutional Financial Services, or CIFS. The Bank served its corporate clients through 19 offices located in Canada, the U.S., Mexico, UK, China, Hong Kong, Taiwan, Korea, Singapore and Japan. It offered a range of lending products, operating services including payments, securities services and trade finance, and treasury services including the management of cash, foreign exchange and risk.

BMO had a significant corporate presence in the U.S. Of the approximately 1 100 CIFS employees, 250 were based in the U.S. While the majority were located in Chicago and New

York, 24 were based in Houston and 17 in Los Angeles. Over 90% of these individuals were professionals and senior management. The Bank served over 250 U.S. companies, with committed credit facilities in excess of $16 billion.

This business had a comparatively small number of large transactions. As a consequence, non-interest expenses as a proportion of revenues were well below the bank average. However, as with most other banks, large provisions for loan losses (mostly for problem LDC loans and, more recently, Canadian originated commercial real estate loans) had substantially affected the profitability of the CIFS business. Returns from the U.S. business were better, but overall returns were, except for the best years, still below the Bank's overall target of 15% ROE. During years when large loans losses were booked negative, profitability resulted. Table 7 provides the recent history on loan losses.

TABLE 7   Provision for Loan Losses ($ millions)

	1988	1989	1990	1991
Business and other*	53	32	52	216
LDC	238	1 000	–21	–60
Other	4	43	23	–4
Harris**	60	70	70	90
Individuals	35	36	45	95
Total	390	1 181	169	337

* Includes both commercial and corporate business.
** All of Harris, including individuals.
SOURCE: BMO Annual Report, 1991.

In an effort to enhance profitability, the CIFS group was developing more sophisticated approaches to risk management and the pricing of large corporate loans. However, as one executive stated, "The industry has hooked corporate Canada on poorly priced credit." It was difficult to raise prices if competitors did not do likewise.

Investment Banking

BMO participated in the Canadian investment banking business primarily through its partially owned subsidiary Nesbitt Thompson. The Bank had purchased 75% of Nesbitt Thomson, a full-service securities dealer, in 1987 for $292 million, or approximately 2.5 times book value. In the early 1970s, Nesbitt was a small Montreal-based dealer on the brink of financial collapse. The firm had been bought out by a small group of employees. By 1987, this group had built the firm into Canada's fifth largest securities dealer in terms of equity capital. In 1985, Nesbitt had purchased an ailing U.S. regional brokerage firm and began to rebuild it. This firm, however, was sold when BMO purchased Nesbitt to comply with U.S. banking regulation. Consequently, Nesbitt did little business outside of Canada.

The cornerstone of Nesbitt's strategy was its commitment to research. Its research department was consistently ranked among the top two in Canada. Its strong corporate culture emphasized long-term employee commitment, individual entrepreneurship, integrity and professionalism in client service, and tireless competition. However, Nesbitt remained small compared to other bank-affiliated securities dealers, particularly Dominion Securities and Wood Gundy. Like most investment banks, Nesbitt's profits were highly cyclical. The period following the October 1987 stock market crash was not a good time for this industry. Recent Nesbitt results are summarized in Table 8. Even with the profit improvement in 1991, ROE was still below the bank's 15% target.

TABLE 8   Nesbitt Thomson Results 1988–91 ($ millions)

	1988	1989	1990	1991
Net Interest Income	26	33	30	58
Non-Interest Revenues	137	128	126	154
Total Revenues (NII + NIR)	163	161	156	212
Non-Interest Expense	146	141	149	174
Income Tax	5	7	2	16
Net Income	12	13	5	22
Average Assets ($ billions)	1.4	1.6	1.8	2.6

SOURCE: BMO annual reports.

Harris Bankcorp

The Bank of Montreal was unique among Canadian banks in its ownership of a significant U.S. bank. Harris Bankcorp was a Chicago-based bank with assets of US$13 billion. It was purchased in 1984 for US$546 million in cash, about 1.4 times book value.[11] The Chicago area market, or Chicagoland as it was called, was the hub of the Midwest region, the country's industrial heartland. The region had a population twice the size of Canada's and a gross state product almost twice Canada's GDP. The Midwest had been decimated by recession and changing patterns of investment in the early 1980s. However, by the early 1990s, the region's economy was growing significantly faster than the national average.

Illinois remained one of the most restricted banking markets in the country. The state had a history of unit banking. Until recently each bank location had to be separately chartered and all banking activity had to take place in a single office. Regulations had been relaxed over the past decade to permit growth through multibank holding companies, the purchase of banks in other Midwest states and, most recently, expanded branch networks within the state. Despite a wave of consolidation, the Illinois market remained highly fragmented. Some 290 commercial

---

[11]Harris had a 1991 book value of approximately $820 million, and recent acquisitions had been priced in the 2 to 2 1/2 times book range.

banks and thrifts were located in the Chicago area alone. A summary of Harris' major Chicagoland competitors is shown in Exhibit 7.

From its inception in 1882 until a 1960 merger with Chicago National Bank introduced it to the retail business, Harris had been exclusively a corporate and institutional bank. It had a nationwide scope, with offices in San Francisco, St. Louis and New York and "suitcase bankers" serving corporate clients across the country. Its long history of corporate banking meant that Harris' market share in such businesses as foreign exchange and cash management was much greater than would be expected for a Chicago bank of its size.

Harris supplied a broad range of products and services to retail, commercial and corporate clients. Indeed, few banks of Harris' size competed in as many businesses. This degree of diversification had been a strength until structural changes in the industry began to reward specialization. The bank held a respectable national position in its corporate agency, foreign exchange, portfolio management, cash management and custom clients businesses. In Chicagoland, it held a top-tier position in private/personal banking, the commercial mid-market, employee trust, indenture trust, personal trust and banking relationships with large firms in selected industries, like futures, agri-business and mid-west financial institutions.

Since the Bank of Montreal had purchased Harris, the relationship had been at arm's length. Revenue growth had been steady during the intervening time, but profitability had been variable with ROE ranging from 6.08% in 1987 to 12.70% in 1991. Nonetheless, Harris had avoided the dramatic fluctuations experienced by many of its competitors. Table 9 summarizes Harris' recent performance, and Exhibit 8 compares Harris' performance to its major competitors.

TABLE 9   Harris Bankcorp Results (C$ millions)

	1988	1989	1990	1991
Net Interest Income	477	478	480	526
Non-Interest Revenues	291	284	306	335
Total Revenues (NII + NIR)	768	762	786	861
Provision for Loss on Loans	60	71	70	90
Non-Interest Expense	509	529	546	582
Income Tax	80	66	74	72
Net Income	120	96	96	117
Average Assets ($ billions)	14.0	13.5	14.0	14.7
ROE (Harris Annual Report)	12.6%	7.3%	10.6%	12.7%

SOURCE: BMO Annual Reports.

Harris divided its business lines into its Corporate Bank, Investment Bank, Personal Bank and Community Banks. The corporate banking business included lending and advisory services, cash management, as well as corporate and institutional trust (40% of the corporate bank's business). The so-called investment bank was composed of treasury services for corporations. Corporate business including treasury services accounted for over 60% of revenues and an even larger share of income. The personal (or private) bank served high income individuals and also included the credit card business. The community banks were separately chartered retail banks in the Chicago suburbs.

Consolidation in the U.S. banking industry threatened Harris's competitive position. Harris' overall position in terms of asset size had eroded from the 39th largest bank holding company in the U.S. in 1984 to the 42nd by 1991. The bank was becoming disadvantaged with respect to its larger and increasingly specialized competitors, especially in markets where size was important, including electronic banking and many corporate and institutional trust services. Harris was also active in personal trust. During the 1986–88 period, these services along with personal banking and financial advisory services were brought together as a package of private banking services targeted at high income individuals. By 1991, this area was formally recognized as an area of strength and steps were being taken to expand this business.

Following state banking regulatory changes in 1982, Harris purchased a number of suburban community banks. Harris pursued a strategy of buying strong, well-run, community-oriented banks. These banks retained their local decision-making authority and operated independently from Harris and each other. During the late 1980s, as prices escalated, Harris' acquisitions of community banks slowed. However, this strategy came to a sudden, unexpected halt in 1991 when Harris was notified that it was in violation of the Community Reinvestment Act.[12] Harris would be unable to make further acquisitions until it conformed with CRA requirements.

The setback in Harris' community banking business and the challenges in the trust businesses coupled with the major changes taking place within the U.S. banking industry raised questions about the future of Harris within the BMO. In the current market, Harris was a very saleable commodity and at current premiums the Bank would realize a considerable gain on any sale.

CONCLUSION

The Bank of Montreal had an improving profit picture but faced mature, competitive markets in two of its major Canadian businesses—PCFS, and CIFS/Investment Banking. Sustaining high levels of performance in these businesses would not be a simple proposition. Technology was driving profound changes in PCFS distribution systems. But investment in technology was costly, and the risks were substantial. The Bank spent approximately $250 million annually, an amount equal to its available cash flow, to develop and maintain its information systems. The key to profitability in the CIFS business appeared to be a deepening of client relationships to include a wide range of services including investment banking. But Nesbitt Thomson was an entirely separate organization from BMO CIFS, and was itself quite a small competitor in a consolidating industry.

Harris Bankcorp, an asset which differentiated BMO from its Canadian competitors, was in a strategically vulnerable position in a dynamic, competitive market. But Harris and the attractive U.S. midwest market offered many opportunities.

---

[12]The CRA was a federal fair lending Act. It required a retail bank to reinvest in certain ways back into the "community" in which it operated.

Mr. Barrett faced a broad range of possibilities across the Bank's major businesses. He knew that if major investments or additional acquisitions were to be made, the Bank could access capital through the debt and equity markets, with the following caveats. He could not risk a level of earnings dilution which would be unacceptable to shareholders, and he could not risk damaging the Bank's credit rating. The market usually accepted a 5% dilution of earnings with only minor effect on a firm's share price. Beyond that, management needed to convincingly demonstrate the financial wisdom of any initiatives. Any action that materially increased risk levels, or damaged capital or profitability ratios, could jeopardize a bank's credit rating.

With so many demands upon the Bank's resources, Matthew Barrett felt a need to provide some sort of vision that would help people in the Bank define strategic priorities. He believed that if the Bank was to remain a strong competitor into the next century, it was important to align the energies of its people and capital with a coherent, compelling vision for the future.

EXHIBIT 1   Major Canadian Banks by Size Measures (1991)

Bank	Assets ($ billions)	Number of Employees	Number of Branches*	Number of ABMs	Net Interest & Other Income (TEB) ($ millions)	Net Income (available to common s/h) ($ millions)
Royal	130	50 547	1 747	3 981	5 168	983.5
CIBC	119	34 593	1 529	2 754	4 469	710.0
BMO	94	32 130	1 274	1 221	3 658	543.7
BNS	89	29 616	1 329	1 280	3 066	554.6
TD	69	24 003	908	1 858	2 591	376.0
National	37	13 937	662	496	1 213	152.7

* Including international operations and securities subsidiaries.

Note: Combined assets of the six largest banks represented 84.5% of assets in the Canadian banking system.

SOURCES: Annual Reports, Nesbitt Thomson, "The Bank Analyzer," DBRS, Bank of Canada Review.

EXHIBIT 2   Banks' Share of Canadian Commercial Debt

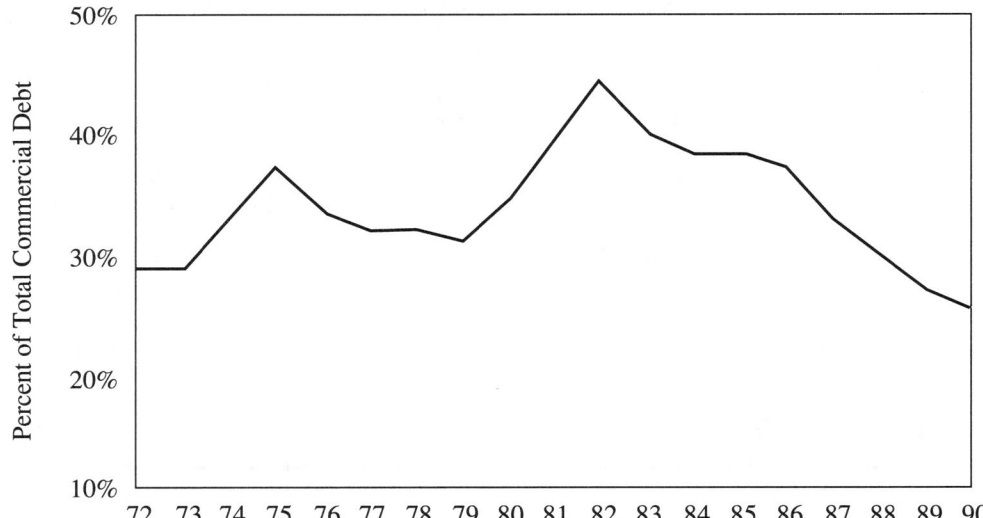

EXHIBIT 3   Operational Efficiency of Major Canadian Banks

Bank	Productivity Ratio Non-Interest Expenses/Revenue (%)			
	1985	*1987*	*1989*	*1991*
Royal Bank	56.7	55.9	55.9	62.3
Canadian Imperial Bank of Commerce	55.8	56.6	58.2	60.5
Bank of Montreal	63.4	65.0	65.0	64.2
Bank of Nova Scotia	55.6	53.0	55.9	58.0
Toronto Dominion Bank	46.6	45.7	51.0	55.0

SOURCE: Nesbitt Thomson, "The Bank Analyzer."

EXHIBIT 4 **Major Canadian Investment Banks (1991)**

Size

Institution	Assets ($ millions)	Employees	Retail Outlets	Ownership
RBC—Dominion Securities	9 400	n.a.	70+	majority by RBC
Wood Gundy	n.a.	1 860	36	majority by CIBC
Scotia McLeod	n.a.	1 790	59	wholly by BNS
Nesbitt Thomson	2 767	1 500	36	majority by BMO
Burns Fry	3 000	1 550	28	majority by employees
Gordon Capital	1 300	n.a.	0	50% Gordon Investment Co.; 50% employees
Richardson Greenshields	2 333	1 670	55	majority by James Richardson & Sons
Midland Walwyn	668	1 700	73	publicly held

SOURCES: Annual Reports

EXHIBIT 5 **Major U.S. Banks Ranked by Assets (1991)**

Rank (1990)	Bank	Assets (US$ billions)	Number of Employees	Number of Branches	ROA(%) 5 yr average	ROA(%) 1991	ROE(%) 1991
1 (1)	Citicorp	216.1	86 000	425	0.1	0	8.8
2 (6)	Chemical Bank	138.9	43 169	653	0	0.1	0.4
3 (2)	Bankamerica	115.5	54 369	1 347	0.6	1.0	15.8
4 (7)	Nationsbank	110.3	57 177	1 864	0.6	0.2	2.7
5 (4)	J.P. Morgan	103.5	13 323	6	0.4	1.1	20.2
6 (3)	Chase Manhattan	98.2	36 210	365	–0.1	0.5	9.8

Note: Combined assets of the six largest banks represented 21.8 % of assets in the U.S. banking system.

SOURCES: "Hundred Largest Commercial Banking Companies," *Fortune,* June 1, 1992, American Banker.

EXHIBIT 6   **Performance of Major Canadian Banks**

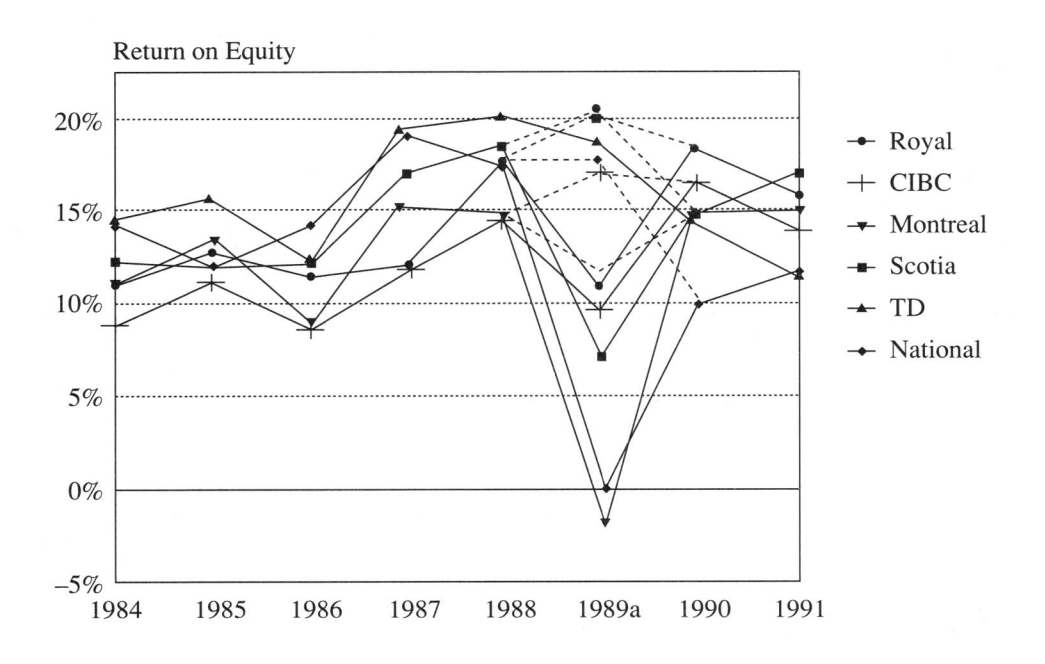

Return on Equity

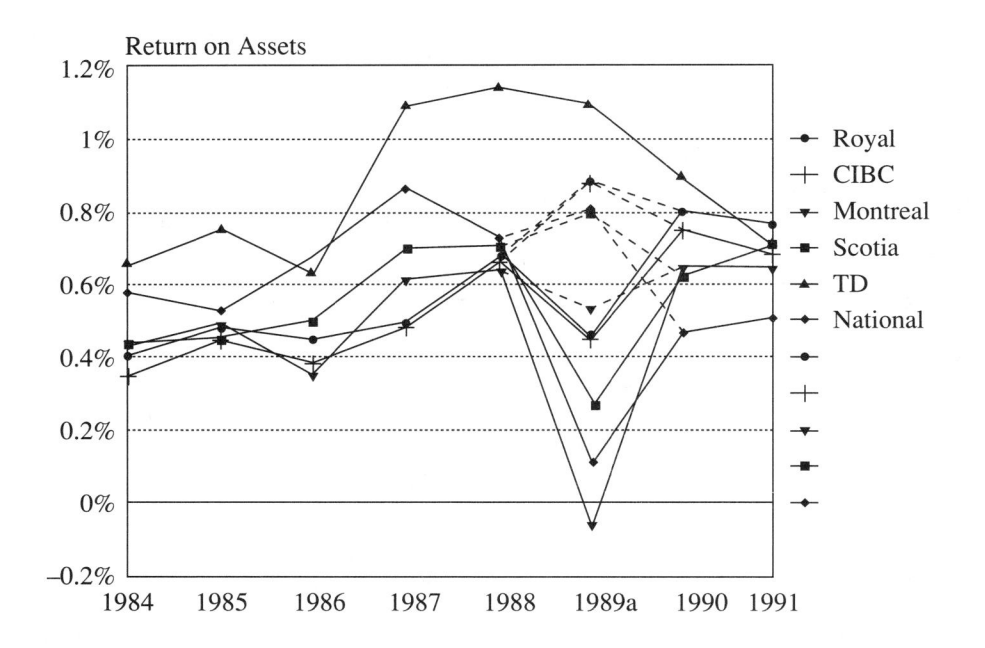

Return on Assets

ᵃ 1989 reported with and without special provisions for LDC loan losses.

SOURCE: Nesbitt Thomson, The Bank Analyzer

EXHIBIT 7 **Major Retail and Mid-Market Banks in Chicago Area (1991)**

Bank	Assets (US$ billions)	Branch of Retail Outlets	ROA 5 yr Average	ROA (%) 1991	ROE (%) 1991	Market Share (%) Mid-Consumer	Commercial
Citicorp	216.9	425*	0.1	0.2	8.8	13	—
First Chicago	49.0	67	0.3	0.2	3.3	20	14
NBD	29.5	417*	0.6	1.0	14.0	2	7
Continental	24	0	–0.1	–0.3	10.0	—	10
Harris	14.5	40	0.6	0.7	12.1	5	15
Northern Trust	13.2	26	0.7	1.0	17.3	2	10

* System-wide total branches, most are outside the Chicago/Illinois area.

SOURCES: "Hundred Largest Commercial Banking Companies," *Fortune,* June 1, 1992, "Bank Management," *American Banker,* October 1992.

EXHIBIT 8 **Performance of Chicagoland Banks**

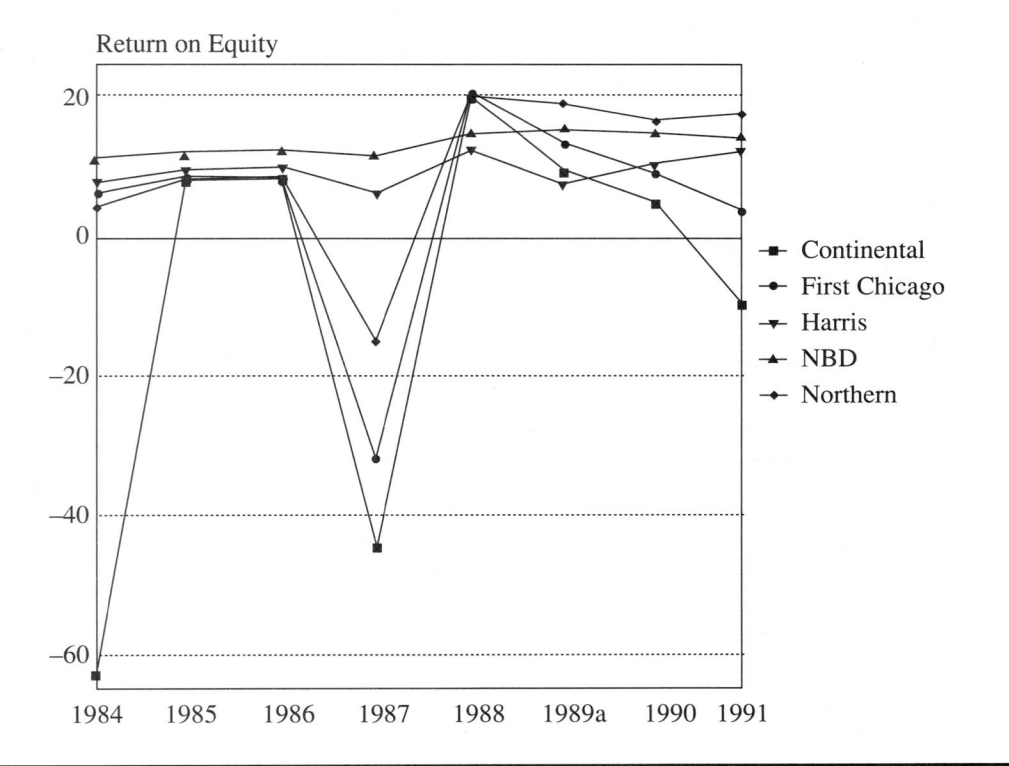

EXHIBIT 8   (continued)

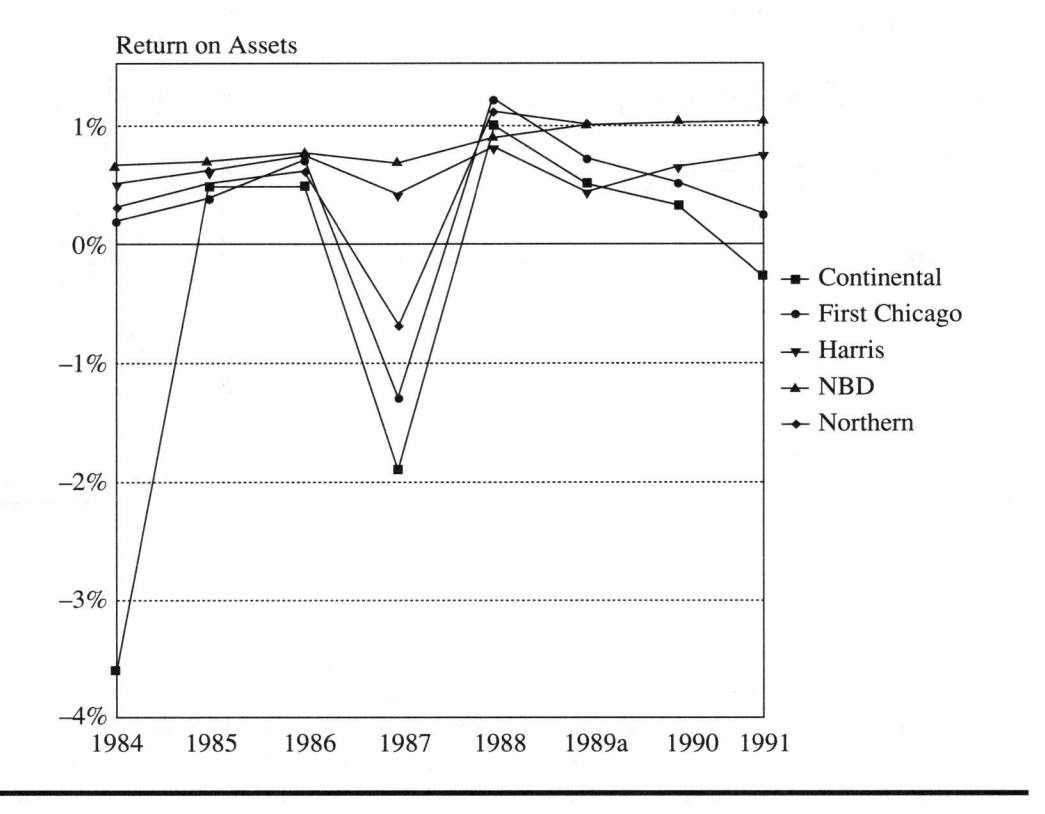

Return on Assets

Continental
First Chicago
Harris
NBD
Northern

THE GE ENERGY MANAGEMENT INITIATIVE (A)

Joseph N. Fry and Julian Birkinshaw

CASE

26

In August 1992, Raj Bhatt, Business Development Manager for GE Canada, met with executives from GE Supply, a U.S.-based distribution arm of GE. The purpose of the meeting was to discuss new business opportunities in Energy Efficiency, an industry that focused on the reduction of energy usage through the installation of energy-efficient technologies. Bhatt had recently gained prequalification for GE Canada to bid in a $1 billion program to install energy-efficient technologies in all federal government buildings. He was confident that GE's expertise in lighting, motors, appliances and financing was sufficient to win at least some of the contracts. Furthermore, he saw the program as a stepping stone to building a new GE business to service the Energy Efficiency needs of a range of clients.

The GE Supply executives informed Bhatt that they had already established a position in the U.S. Energy Efficiency industry, through a joint venture with a new Energy Service Company (ESCo), and had retained the services of a full-time consultant to develop *the* business. They were interested in the Federal Buildings Program that Bhatt had been working on, but felt that it would be more efficiently run through a division of GE Supply, rather than as a locally managed Canadian venture. The meeting posed a dilemma for Bhatt. He was encouraged by the level of interest that already existed for Energy Efficiency within GE, but at the same time held certain misgivings about folding the Federal Buildings Program into GE Supply's

Joseph N. Fry and Julian Birkinshaw of the Western Business School prepared this case. Copyright © 1994, The University of Western Ontario. This material is not covered under authorization from CanCopy or any reproduction rights organization. Any form of reproduction, storage or transmittal of this material is prohibited without written permission from Western Business School, The University of Western Ontario, London, Canada N6A 3K7

nascent business. Specifically, he was concerned that a lot of interesting Energy Efficiency opportunities existed in Canada which a U.S.-focused business would not be in a position to exploit. Bhatt left the meeting uncertain how to proceed.

GENERAL ELECTRIC (GE)

GE, with $60 billion in revenues in 1991, was among the top ten industrial corporations in the world. From the early days of Thomas Edison, it had grown to be a diversified 54-business corporation by the early eighties. With 400 000 employees and a very strong corporate planning division, it exemplified the traditional strategic planning oriented corporation of the 1970s.

In 1980, Jack Welch, the incoming CEO, made a series of sweeping changes. The corporate planning department was eliminated, layers of management were eliminated and the concepts of empowerment and customer focus became the new drivers behind GE's activities. Of the 54 businesses that Welch inherited, some were sold and others were amalgamated, leaving just 13. Welch's stated position was that the major criterion for holding on to a business was that it was number one or number two worldwide in its chosen industry.

The corporate structure under Welch was simplified and decentralized. Each division was autonomous, and was further subdivided into a number of operating companies. The head office for each division was in the U.S., but on average, 25% of GE's revenues came from its non-U.S. operations. International operations, including Canada, were structured under the Vice Chairman of International Operations, but operating authority was held by the relevant division of GE. Thus, the lighting plant in Oakville, Ontario, reported to GE Lighting in Cleveland, Ohio, with only a secondary line of reporting through GE Canada.

Welch was committed to creating a more open and candid management style at GE. A central thrust of this commitment was the "Work-Out" program, which he described as follows:

> The ultimate objective of Work-Out is clear. We want 300 000 people with different family aspirations, different financial goals, to share directly in this company's vision the decision-making process and the rewards. We want to build a more stimulating environment, a more creative environment, a freer work atmosphere, with incentives tied directly to what people do.[1]

Through a series of workshops and facilitated sessions, Work-Out's objective was to challenge the accepted practice at every level in every business. Work-Out sessions had already realized large cost savings by identifying nonessential practices that had gone undetected for years, but equally important, they had created a new level of creativity and enthusiasm among employees.

GE Canada

GE Canada was the longest-established international subsidiary of GE, with operations in 12 of the company's 13 businesses. In the 1970s, GE Canada operated as a "miniature replica" of its parent company: all functions were represented in Canada, and typically a full line of products was made, primarily for the Canadian market but with some exporting possibilities. The

---

[1] *Harvard Business Review*, (September 1989), pp. 112–120.

Canadian CEO was fully responsible for the profits of the Canadian operating divisions, and separate financial statements were prepared (GE held a 92% stake in GE Canada).

In the eighties, Jack Welch embarked on a major structural change to GE's North American business. Consistent with the increasingly global business environment that was taking shape, Welch recognized that maintaining separate country organizations could not be justified. Instead, an integrated organizational model emerged that became known as "direct-connect."[2] Essentially, this meant creating 13 strategic business units, and organizing them according to the global demands of the business rather than national interests. Typically, the general manager's role was eliminated in Canada, so that business leaders or functional managers reported directly to their business headquarters in the U.S., rather than through the Canadian organization. For example, the marketing manager for GE Lighting's Canadian operations reported directly to the GE Lighting marketing manager in Cleveland, Ohio. Profit responsibility was held by the global business unit. This arrangement ensured that business activities were effectively coordinated on a global basis. It also furthered Welch's objective of removing layers of management and empowering employees.

Matthew Meyer, CEO of GE Canada, had a vastly different role from his predecessors. With all operations reporting straight to their U.S. divisional bosses, Meyer was directly responsible only for the activities of a very small number of employees. He had vice-presidents in finance, environmental affairs, legal, human resources and government affairs. These managers were responsible for all the uniquely Canadian issues that cropped up, such as new legislation, tax accounting, government grants and so on. In addition, there was a small business development group, consisting of three managers. Traditionally, this group had been involved in feasibility studies and new market development for the business units in Canada. Following the shift to a "direct-connect" structure, the role had become primarily one of looking for opportunities to leverage the strengths of Canadian activities on a global basis. They were also concerned with identifying new business opportunities in Canada. Bhatt, one of the business development managers, explained:

> Canada is a relatively small marketplace. Consequently, most U.S.-based business leaders have a limited awareness of the opportunities here because they have either a U.S. or a global focus. The role of business development is to attempt to identify investment or market opportunities here that they might find valuable.

There was some discussion among business development managers over the extent to which they should actively "sell" business opportunities to the GE businesses. Some felt that a proactive strategy of promoting Canadian opportunities was appropriate; others preferred to investigate only those cases where business development's involvement had been solicited. The recent decision to promote the Vice-President of Business Development, but not replace him, added further to the uncertainty over the group's role.

---

[2] The integration process was smoothed by the buy out of minority shareholders in GE Canada in 1989. The 1989 Free Trade Agreement further streamlined the change.

Raj Bhatt

Bhatt was only 29. He had worked at GE for just one year, following a successful period at Northern Telecom and an MBA at the University of Western Ontario.

> Business development is quite a challenging experience. There are lots of good opportunities in Canada, but it is sometimes difficult to achieve the level of interest and buy-in necessary to attract the appropriate attention. The Oakville lighting plant, a global manufacturing mandate, is a planned $144 million investment and is certainly our biggest success so far, but there have been a lot of ideas that failed to materialize.

The business development manager typically held that post for only two years, after which he or she was expected to take a line position in one of the businesses. Bhatt had been given a number of attractive options, but had turned them down because he was afraid that his involvement was critical to a number of projects. Specifically, he was concerned that the Energy Efficiency business opportunity he had championed up to now would die because no one else had the knowledge of, or the enthusiasm for, that particular opportunity.

ENERGY EFFICIENCY

Energy Efficiency covered the multitude of ways that energy usage could be optimized, including conservation, use of efficient appliances and off peak usage. Energy Efficiency was originally conceived in the early 1970s as a response to rising oil prices. It recently saw a resurgence due to the environmental movement and the increasing need for cost competitiveness in the late eighties. Although strongly motivated by public opinion and government pressure, Energy Efficiency initiatives were usually sponsored by the energy supply utilities. They recognized that they could more effectively keep their investment down by reducing demand than by building expensive new power stations. There were also obvious benefits to consumers (in reduced costs) and to the environment.

The growth in utility-sponsored programs for Energy Efficiency was responsible for the formation of many Energy Service Companies (ESCos). These companies aimed to meet the demands and needs of their customers by utilizing these programs. Under the most common arrangement (called a performance contract), the ESCo would install energy efficient technologies at no upfront cost to the client. The costs would be recouped from the savings realized. Such an arrangement could be very lucrative, but the ESCo bore all the risk in the event that the promised savings never materialized.

Th ESCo Industry in Canada

The Canadian ESCo industry was among the most advanced in the world. Both federal and provincial governments had active energy-management programs to promote "green" issues, and had targeted Energy Efficiency as a critical industry. Ontario Hydro and Quebec Hydro had budgets for Energy Efficiency of $800 million and $300 million respectively, in comparison to the C$1.5 billion budget for all U.S. utilities combined.

As a result of the utilities' involvement, the Canadian ESCo industry was growing very rapidly; 1989 revenues of $20 million had grown to $100 million by 1992, and one estimate put the total market potential in the billions of dollars. Three major segments could be identified, each accounting for approximately one third of the total volume. They were *commercial,* which consisted primarily of office buildings, hospitals and other public buildings; *industrial,* which consisted of factories and production plants; and *residential,* which consisted of single-family dwellings. So far the commercial sector had been the most rewarding to ESCos, largely due to the similarities between (for example) one hospital and another. Industrial also had potential, but required knowledge of the specific process technology used in each case.

Over the past decade, the ESCo industry in Canada had experienced mixed fortunes, as companies struggled to understand the dynamics of the market. Lack of technical and risk management experience, flawed contracts, lack of financial strength and energy price collapses had all led to very low levels of profitability among major players. The recent upsurge of interest in Energy Efficiency, however, had pushed the industry onto a more steady footing. Furthermore, a shake-out had occurred, leaving between five and ten serious competitors in Canada.

ESCo Strategies

ESCos saw themselves as undertaking three useful functions with commercial and industrial customers. First, they could undertake energy audits of client sites and advise what forms of energy management were most appropriate. Second, they could engineer and provide access to a wide range of energy-efficient technologies that would normally be hard to get hold of. Third, they could install new energy-efficient equipment, under a performance contract or similar. In the Canadian industry, there were several hundred consulting engineers that participated in energy audits, but only seven "full-service" ESCos that undertook all three functions.

Of the three functions, programs such as performance contracting offered the greatest potential return to ESCos, but also the highest degree of risk. Following an installation, it took between five and ten years before the financial benefits were realized. ESCos were paid at the time of installation by their financing partners, who recovered their costs over the lifetime of the project, but in the event that the project was badly estimated, the shortfall in revenue would have to be made up by the ESCo. Access to capital at a reasonable cost was thus critical. Some ESCos had parent companies with deep pockets. The audit and supply functions, while less lucrative, were important elements of the ESCo's business because they established legitimacy in the eyes of the customer. Many commercial clients were extremely sceptical of the estimated energy savings provided by ESCos, but if they agreed to an energy audit, there was a greater likelihood they could be sold on the merits of an installation. The credibility of the guarantee provided by the ESCo was thus of great importance.

THE GE ENERGY MANAGEMENT INITIATIVE

The Initial Opportunity

As GE Business Development Manager, Raj Bhatt received a communication from the federal government inviting ESCos to seek to be prequalified for the implementation of performance contracts in 50 000 federal buildings in Canada. The program had a potential total value of $1 billion, which was to be split into a number of smaller contracts. Bhatt was struck by the potential fit between GE's areas of expertise and the requirements of the program. ESCos had to be able to provide energy-efficient lighting, motors and controls and provide financing for the project; GE was a leading supplier of many of the required products and had a large financing division. Unlike rival firms that would have to form consortia between electrical and financing companies, GE could do many things in-house.

Bhatt submitted a proposal for the Federal Buildings Program and, along with a number of other consortia, achieved "prequalification," meaning the right to bid on subsequent contracts that fell under the Federal Buildings umbrella. This success underlines the magnitude of the opportunity that GE was facing in the ESCo industry. Rather than limiting GE's involvement to the one-off Federal Buildings Program, Bhatt thought there was potential for an ongoing GE business to meet the expected surge in demand for energy management services. He began to think through the best way of proceeding.

The GE Canada Executive Meeting

Bhatt's first move was to meet with the GE Canada executive group and get their reaction to his idea for an Energy Management Business. Attending were Matthew Meyer, Chairman & CEO, Mike Kozinsky, Vice-President of Finance, and Scott Larwood, Vice-President of Government Relations. Larwood had already been heavily involved in the Federal Buildings Program and was in favour of Bhatt's proposal.

BHATT:	GE Canada is very well-positioned to start an Energy Management business. We have a broader range of relevant products and services than any other ESCo, and the Ontario and Quebec Hydro programs are among the most advanced in the world.
KOZINSKY: (FINANCE)	But this is a systems business. We have never been very good at systems implementation.
BHATT:	I realize that we may have to find partners. We are working with a small ESCo on the Federal Buildings project which will do all *the* installation work. We can identify suitable future partners as things progress.
KOZINSKY:	But what is our experience in being a prime contractor? This seems to be very different from any business we have been involved with before.
LARWOOD : (GOVERNMENT RELATIONS)	That's not quite true. The Apparatus Technical Service (ATS) business in Power Systems manages service contracts, and there is a lot of project experience in the States.
MEYER (CEO):	But there seems to be a considerable risk here. What happens if we pull down a load of asbestos when we're changing a lighting system? GE is an obvious target for legal action.
KOZINSKY:	And you stated earlier that there is some downside financial risk if the performance contract does not yield the expected savings.

BHATT:	True, but the estimates are conservative. The overall financial projections are very promising, and involve very little up-front cost. Apart from the salaries of three or four employees, most costs are on a contract-by-contract basis.
MEYER:	Have you given any thought as to how this business would fit into the GE structure?
BHATT:	One of the strengths of GE Canada is that it already taps into all the different businesses. I would like to see the Energy Management business based in Canada, and drawing from the other GE businesses as required.

Bhatt received a lot of questioning and cautioning on various aspects of the proposal, but there was consensus at the end that the project was worth pursuing. Meyer recommended that Bhatt investigate the level of interest in the U.S. businesses and at the corporate level before any formal proposal was put together.

The GE Supply Opportunity

In discussion with U.S. colleagues, Bhatt discovered that three U.S. divisions were attempting to establish their own ESCo-like initiatives. Two of them were at about the same stage of development as Bhatt. The third, GE Supply, which was a division of GE Industrial and Power Systems, was more advanced. They had been working with an ESCo for a number of months, and had retained a well-connected consultant to advise them. Up to now, the ESCo had assumed all the risk, with GE providing their name, their products and some servicing expertise, but the division was planning to create a joint venture with the ESCo in the near future.

On hearing about the GE Supply initiative, Bhatt went to Connecticut to visit the GE Supply executives to discuss their respective plans. Present at the meeting were Bhatt, Doug Taylor, CEO of GE Supply, and Fred Allen, manager of the Energy Management business.

TAYLOR (CEO):	Last week we signed a formal alliance agreement with Wetherwell Inc. to run for 18 months. We are now actively looking for contracts.
ALLEN : (ENERGY MANAGEMENT)	But the U.S. market requires some education. How is the market in Canada?
BHATT:	There is a very promising opportunity that we are working on right now. Basically, the federal government is looking for bidders on a $1 billion program, and we have already gained prequalification.
ALLEN :	That beats anything we've got down here. I think there could be some real opportunities for us to work together. We have gained quite a lot of experience over the past 12 months, and combined with your market, we could have a winning combination.
BHATT:	I am certainly interested in exploring opportunities. How do you see a Canadian Energy Management business fitting with your business?
TAYLOR:	We could manage the Canadian business out of our office here.

BHATT: That causes me some concern. The business relies on close coordination with utilities and government bodies, and a strong local presence would definitely be necessary. I must admit, we considered that management of at least part of the business should be in Canada. The opportunities in Canada are unmatched.

TAYLOR: Well, there is some strength to your argument, but I don't see why this business should not fit the normal model.

Bhatt had some misgivings when the meeting came to a close. The business depended on close ties with government bodies, provincial utilities and local contractors to be really successful, and he felt that these would be lost if there was not a strong Canadian presence. Under the "direct-connect" system, he felt that would be more difficult to achieve.

EXHIBIT 1   GE Structure (North America)

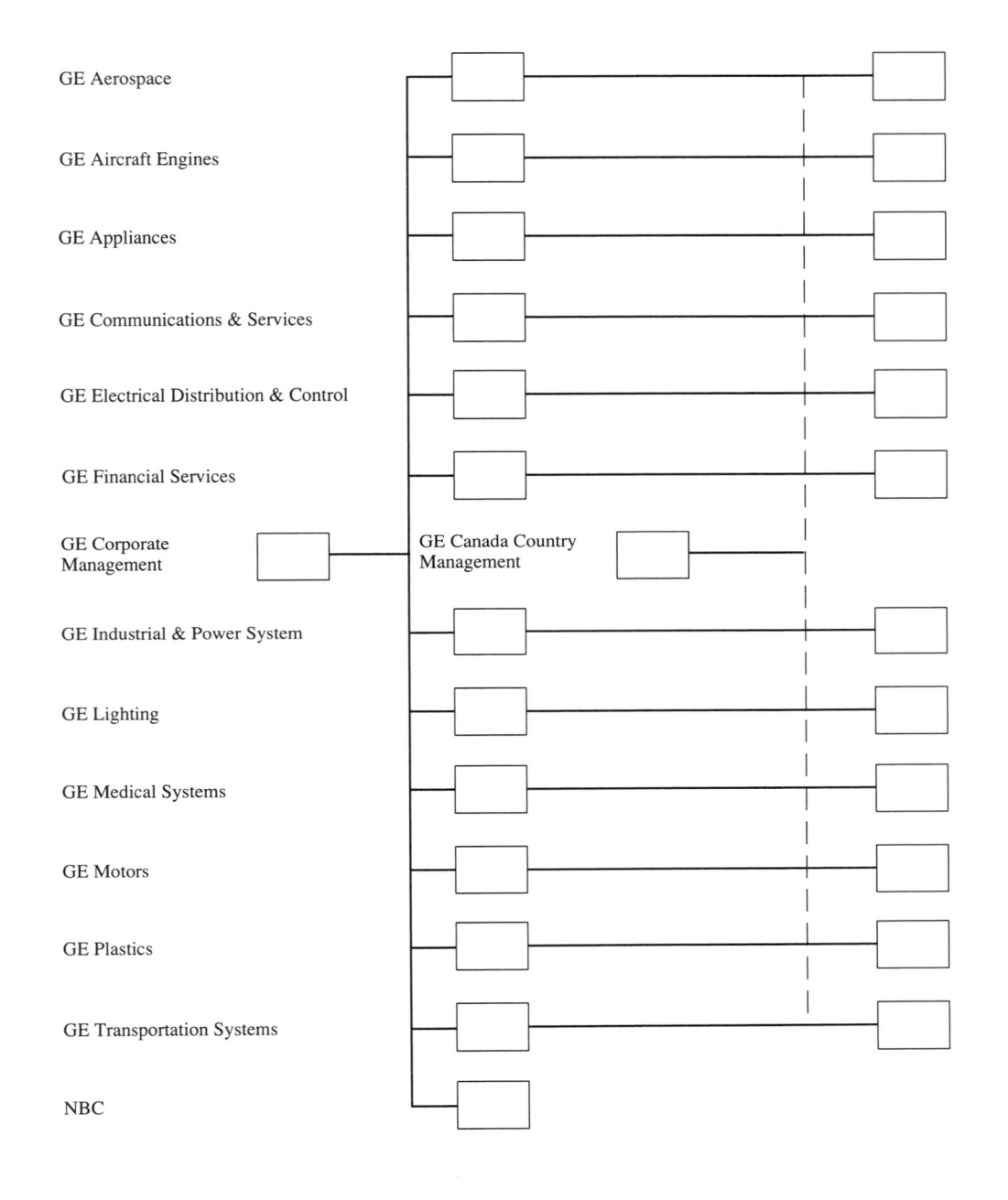

GE Aerospace

GE Aircraft Engines

GE Appliances

GE Communications & Services

GE Electrical Distribution & Control

GE Financial Services

GE Corporate Management

GE Canada Country Management

GE Industrial & Power System

GE Lighting

GE Medical Systems

GE Motors

GE Plastics

GE Transportation Systems

NBC

COMPETING IN FOREIGN MARKETS

DIALOGUE: A RUSSIAN JOINT VENTURE

Peter J. Killing and Carl Fey

CASE

27

In November 1987, Joe Ritchie was in Russia meeting with Pyotr and Tanya Zrelov to discuss the creation of a joint venture to produce and distribute computer equipment and computer software in Russia and abroad. Ritchie, an American, had no previous business experience in the computer industry or the Soviet Union, but was keen to create a venture with the Zrelovs, whom Ritchie judged to be extremely bright, hardworking and trustworthy. The Zrelovs' plan called for Ritchie to contribute up to US$5 million for a minority (perhaps 25%) share in the joint venture.

THE SITUATION IN THE USSR IN 1987

Mikhail Gorbachev became General Secretary of the Communist Party in 1985 and was handed a country rapidly approaching an economic crisis. The USSR's Net Material Product[1] had decreased from 4.3% in 1976–80 to 1.6% in 1987. External debt had increased in the

---

[1] Net material product is a measure commonly used in Eastern Block countries to measure output from the "productive sphere." The measure is based on the Marxian distinction between productive and unproductive work. All manufacturing and a few services (e.g., tourism) are considered part of the "productive sphere."

USSR from US$28.9 billion dollars in 1985 to US$39.2 billion dollars in 1987. To try to prevent the USSR from entering into an economic crisis, Gorbachev started a program of wide-sweeping economic reforms called *Perestroika*. This was accompanied by *Glasnost*, a program of increased political freedom for the Russian people. As part of *Perestroika*, in 1987 the Soviet Union passed a new law on foreign investment that allowed Western firms to form joint ventures in all of its republics. The law provided joint ventures with several advantages over other types of business, the most important of which was a two-year tax holiday which began the first year the joint venture made a profit. Russia, which had a population of over 140 million, was the largest of the Soviet republics and was judged by most people to be the most attractive to foreign investment. The largest cities in Russia were Moscow and St. Petersburg, with over 8.5 and 4.5 million people respectively. Russia had a Gross National Product (GNP) of US$1 268 billion in 1987. GNP per capita was US$8 556. Inflation was 5.6% and unemployment was 0%. Russia covered 6.6 million square miles of land which is almost twice the size of the United States. However, investing in the Soviet Union was clearly risky and presented many problems because the Soviet Union did not possess a market economy.

JOE RITCHIE

A philosophy major in college, Joe Ritchie's first jobs after graduation were as a bus driver and a policeman. Then in 1977, at the age of 30, Ritchie and three friends decided to start a small commodities-trading firm named Chicago Research and Trading (CRT). He had so little money when he started the company that he had to wear a borrowed suit to business meetings. Ten years later, CRT had become the world's largest options-trading company and the envy of the rest of the industry due to its fast growth and consistent excellent performance. There were two apparent keys to CRT's success. First, the company's trading was based on mathematical models which had been developed by Ritchie, who was described as a "natural math genius" despite never having taken an advanced math course. Second, Ritchie created a unique atmosphere at CRT which made people feel relaxed, empowered and part of a team. By 1987, Ritchie had accumulated substantial personal wealth.[2]

In the mid 1980s, Ritchie was taken with the idea of starting a joint venture in a country emerging from communism. In 1985, he made three trips to China, but in spite of many meetings with potential partners, he did not find anyone whom he thought appropriate. In July 1987, Ritchie took a trip to Russia, primarily as a vacation, but also out of interest to see how Russia was changing. In the back of his mind he was still searching for an appropriate partner for a joint venture. Ritchie recalled:

> I wanted to start a joint venture with Russia, not solely to make money, but because I was intrigued by the chance to show that business can work well without people pursuing their own unbridled self interest. I wanted to demonstrate another way of organizing people, which I have found works very well in the U.S., but which is quite different from the way most U.S. companies work. I wanted to show that you can follow the golden rule, treat people well, and think about what is good for society; and still do well in business.

---

[2] Much of the information for this paragraph was obtained from "Money Machine," *Wall Street Journal*, February 8, 1988.

Ritchie did not actively pursue finding a joint venture partner, and he did not meet anyone by chance who would make a good partner. He did, however, find Russia interesting and decided to return in September 1987. This time John Nikolopolus, a friend of Ritchie's who was an American journalist currently living in Russia, told Ritchie that he thought he knew a couple who would be ideal for Ritchie to start a joint venture with. On September 10, Nikolopolus arranged for Ritchie and Tanya and Pyotr Zrelov to meet. From the very beginning Joe Ritchie and the Zrelovs got along well, and Ritchie thought he might have found the partner he was looking for. The Zrelovs intrigued Ritchie because they looked like young lovers, despite being in their early 40s. Ritchie was impressed by the way this couple worked side by side very peacefully with each other. They appeared to be excited about discovering their new world, and they seemed to be the type of people who would rather lose money than let down a friend or participate in an unethical act. These were exactly the type of people Ritchie had been seeking.

Ritchie, believing that people are what make a business work, considered that finding the correct people to run the joint venture was his most important task and that deciding what the joint venture would do was secondary. As a result, Ritchie was willing to start a joint venture in whatever field these "ideal people" thought made sense, as long as it seemed to have some promise for the future. Ritchie explained his focus on trust as follows:

> If you are going to start a joint venture with someone in a country that is as physically and culturally distanced from the U.S. as Russia is and you think that you are going to successfully exercise much control over the business, you are dreaming. That is why I knew that if I were going to make a venture with Russia work, I had to find a partner that I implicitly trusted, so that trust became a non-issue. This was the case for the Zrelovs.

Thus, once Ritchie had found the correct people to work with he gave them trust and autonomy. Ritchie believed that if employees want to cheat you, they will find a way, and therefore there is no point in trying to make many complicated agreements and exert tight control over employees. Such tactics, according to Ritchie, made people less productive. Further, he believed that empowering employees could often act as a stronger control mechanism than exerting tight control over them, because they would feel that they did not want to let down the owner who he had placed so much trust in them.

PYOTR AND TANYA ZRELOV

Because the Zrelovs were well connected and Nikolopolus was confident that they would be able to find good organizations to serve as the Russian partners for the joint venture. Pyotr Zrelov was the designer and director of information systems at Kamaz, Russia's largest truck manufacturer. Tanya Zrelova was a computer scientist at the Russian Academy of Sciences. They both had Ph.Ds in computer science and were in their mid 40s. Pyotr and Tanya Zrelov, both friendly and outgoing, were hard workers who were willing to take risks. They also appeared to be natural leaders.

DEVELOPING THE RELATIONSHIP

Nikolopolus had arranged for Ritchie and the Zrelovs to meet at a telecommunications company where Pyotr Zrelov had some negotiations dealing with the purchase of new telecommunications systems for Kamaz. They did not know that this meeting was set up or that Ritchie was interested in their running his joint venture. To the Zrelovs, it simply appeared as if Ritchie and his colleagues were waiting in the telecommunications firm for a later appointment. After Ritchie had observed the Zrelovs in negotiation, he decided he liked what he saw. When the Zrelovs were finished, Ritchie introduced himself, explained that he was interested in starting a joint venture, and stated that he would like to get to know the Zrelovs better, as he thought they might be good people to run this joint venture.

The Zrelovs and Ritchie talked for two hours at the telecommunications company. From the very first meeting, the Zrelovs and Ritchie got along very well. They discovered that they all not only wanted to be in business, but that they wanted to help make the world a better place to live as well. At the end of their discussion, they agreed to meet for dinner two days later. At Ritchie's request, John Nikolopolus accompanied him to this meeting and many of Ritchie's future meetings in Russia. Nikolopolus served not only as a language translator, but more importantly, as a cultural translator, explaining to Ritchie what different Russian actions really meant. At dinner the Zrelovs persuaded Ritchie to extend his trip to Russia and come to visit the Kamaz factory, 1000 km from Moscow. Ritchie accepted this offer. At the time, Ritchie thought that the Zrelovs would propose a joint venture for manufacturing trucks. Certainly, this was not an area that Ritchie knew anything about and it was not the first field in which he would have chosen to start a joint venture. However, Ritchie was primarily concerned about finding the correct partners for his joint venture, and not about what the joint venture would do.

Pyotr Zrelov had recently been assigned the large task of implementing from the start an information system at Kamaz. He thought it would make sense to develop this project on a larger scale by participating in a joint venture, which could bring in additional expertise to assist with this project and also provide a similar service for other companies.

When Ritchie arrived at Kamaz, he was pleasantly surprised that the Zrelovs wanted to start a joint venture that would produce computer equipment and computer software rather than trucks. Fortunately, Ritchie knew much more about computers than trucks. In addition to starting the joint venture to serve the needs of Kamaz, the Zrelovs argued that there were other good reasons to start a joint venture to produce and distribute computer software and computer equipment. Russia had many highly skilled computer programmers who would be willing to work for very low salaries by Western standards. Further, the Zrelovs argued that these computer programmers currently did not have access to adequate computing equipment or an environment with enough freedom to reach their creative potential. The Zrelovs also recognized the vast need for personal computer equipment in Russia. They expected that the market for personal computer equipment in Russia to expand rapidly in the next few years. Ritchie thought that the Zrelovs' ideas and logic sounded good.

After spending three days at Kamaz, Ritchie had to return to the U.S., but he told the Zrelovs to develop further their ideas about the joint venture, and promised to return to Russia within two months.

The November Visit

On November 5, 1987, Ritchie returned to Russia, and the Zrelovs further explained their ideas for the joint venture including who the Russian partners would be. The Zrelovs proposed that the Russian partners would be Kamaz, Vneshtechnika, Moscow State University, Central Institute for the Study of the Economy and Mathematics, General Demonstration Computer Center of the Central Exhibition Center of the USSR, and the Space Research Institute. Ritchie was impressed that the Zrelovs had found such well-known and influential partners for the joint venture; but as far as he was concerned, his real partners were the Zrelovs, and it would be up to them to manage the others. Ritchie commented:

> If we go ahead with this, our joint venture will be one of the first, in fact maybe *the* first, U.S./Soviet joint venture in existence. Time is of the essence. There are *four* personal computers in Moscow State University right now. Four! If Pyotr walks in there in three months with 100 personal computers that we have shipped in from the U.S., he can completely captivate the best computer people in the place, and have them all working for him.

At the end of the visit, the Zrelovs asked Ritchie if he would sign the statement of intent shown in Exhibit 1.

EXHIBIT 1 Protocol of Intentions between Kamaz (USSR) and CRT (USA) on the Subject of Forming the Joint Stock Company Dialogue

Moscow, 27 October 1987

Taking into consideration the importance of forming a joint venture on the territory of the USSR and trying to promote further cooperation and mutual understanding between the U.S. and the USSR, Kamaz and CRT are establishing the following intentions:

1. Object

The main item of cooperation is to form on the territory of the USSR the joint venture company and for it to produce personal computers and different software and to sell these products in the USSR, the U.S. and in markets in third world countries.

2. The Main Product

The main products of the joint stock company are personal computers and different software for them (made to order or worked out by Soviet participants for their own aims).

3. Organization of the Joint Venture

The starting capital is needed for us to form a joint venture. The amount of starting capital would be discussed on the next negotiations taking into consideration the necessity of providing the main activities of the joint venture.

EXHIBIT 1 (continued)

The stock of the partners should be not less than 51% and the stock of the firm should be not more than 49% of the starting capital. (*Joe Ritchie interpreted this to mean that firm employees could never own more than 49% of the firm.*)

3.1 From the side of USSR the following organizations are shareholders of the joint venture: Kamaz, Moscow State University, Space Research Institute, Central Institute for the Study of the Economy and Mathematics, All Union Foreign Trade Organization "Vneshtechnika," and the General Demonstration and Testing Computer Center of the Exhibition of Economic Achievements of the USSR. The participation of these organizations is determined by the charter of the joint stock company. The number of these organizations is determined in the charter of the joint venture. The number of shareholders could be increased.

3.2 The Soviet side would offer the following as stock:

- People for producing software
- Capacity for producing personal computers
- Office for the representatives of CRT during the time of their stay in Moscow

3.3 CRT would offer the following as stock:

- Starting capital
- The delivery of the first lot of personal computers (300)
- Organization of the trade
- Teaching and consulting in the field of trade
- Equipping the office in Moscow

4. The Planning of the Amount of Production

Year	Personal Computers	Software (in Mil. Rubles)	Others
1988	3000	.5	1.4
1989	5000	1.0	3.0
1990	5000	3.0	5.7
1991	10000	10.0	10.0

5. Organization of the Main Activities of the Joint Venture

The following items would be used during the preparation of the charter of the joint venture:

- The property of the joint venture will be estimated in rubles at agreed upon prices taking into consideration the prices of the world market.
- The joint venture will be planning its activities proceeding from the demand on the trading markets and currency resources of the partners.

- Foreign trade operations will be done by the joint venture itself or with the help of the Soviet foreign-trade organizations. The realization of the products to the Soviet consumers will be done with the help of the Soviet trade organizations and will be estimated in rubles in agreed upon prices taking into consideration the prices on the world market.
- In general the personnel of the joint venture will be formed from the Soviet citizens. Management of the joint venture will be done by the administration board and the board of directors.
- The setting of the personnel will be done by mutual consent of the both sides.
- The administration board is the leading authority of the joint venture. The economic operation of the joint venture will be controlled by the board of directors. Only citizens of the USSR could be either head of the administration board or board of directors.
- Conditions of paying salary, work and rest are regulated according to Soviet laws.
- The application of the same laws is extended to the foreign citizens except in the question of paying the salary. This item would be specially discussed.
- While signing the contract the list of positions and quantity of the foreign specialists to be involved in the work of the joint venture will be also specially discussed.
- The responsibility of the joint venture is limited with all of its property. The work of the joint venture will be organized according to the laws of the USSR, according to the charter of the contract about forming the joint venture.

KENTUCKY FRIED CHICKEN IN CHINA

Allen J. Morrison and Paul W. Beamish

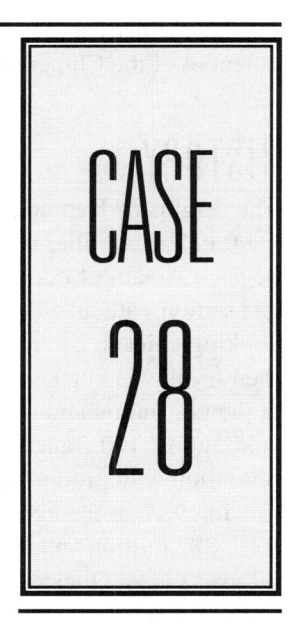

CASE

28

In late September 1986, Tony Wang leaned back in his leather chair in his Singapore office and thought of the long road that lay ahead if Kentucky Fried Chicken (KFC) were ever to establish the first completely Western-style fast food joint venture in the People's Republic of China. Wang, an experienced entrepreneur and seven-year veteran of KFC had only two months previously accepted the position of company vice-president for Southeast Asia with an option of bringing the world's largest chicken restaurant company into the world's most populous country. Yet, as he began exploring the opportunities facing KFC in Southeast Asia, Wang was beginning to wonder whether the company should attempt to enter the Chinese market at this time.

Without any industry track record, Wang wondered how to evaluate the attractiveness of the Chinese market within the context of KFC's Southeast Asia region. Compounding the challenge was the realization that although China was a huge, high profile market, it would demand precious managerial resources and could offer no real term prospects for significant hard currency profit repatriation—even in the medium term. Wang also realized that a decision to go into China necessitated selecting a particular investment location in the face of great uncertainty. It was equally clear that while opportunities and risks varied widely from city to city, the criteria for evaluating suitable locations remained unspecified. With limited information to go on, Wang realized that a positive decision on China would be inherently risky—both for the company and for his own reputation. And while Wang was intrigued by the enormous potential of the Chinese market, he also knew that many others had failed in similar ventures.

HISTORY

The origins of Kentucky Fried Chicken can be traced to Harland Sanders, who was born in 1890 in Henreyville, Indiana. When Sanders was a boy, he dropped out of the sixth grade and began a stream of odd jobs, concentrating eventually on cooking. In time he opened his own gas station with an adjoining restaurant. In the 1930s, Sanders developed a "secret" recipe for cooking chicken by first applying a coating containing a mixture of 11 herbs and spices and then frying the chicken under pressure. This "southern fried chicken" eventually became a hit at the gas station and in 1956 Sanders decided to franchise his novel concept. By 1964, he had sold almost 700 franchises. Much of Sanders' success in this pioneer industry lay in his near obsession with product quality and a commitment to maintaining a focused line of products.

In 1964, at the age of 74, Harland Sanders finally agreed to sell the business in exchange for US$2 million and a promise of a lifetime salary. The sale of the business to John Brown, a 29-year old Kentucky lawyer, and his financial backer, Jack Massey, 60, was accompanied by the assurance that Sanders would maintain an active role in both product promotion and quality control of the new venture.

With new, aggressive managers and a rapidly evolving American fast food industry, KFC's growth soared. Over the next five years, sales grew by an average of 96% per year, topping US$200 million by 1970. This same year almost 1000 new stores were built, the vast majority by franchisees.

A key element in this rapid growth was Brown's ability to select a group of hard-working entrepreneurial managers. Brown's philosophy was that every manager had the right to expect to become wealthy in the rapidly growing company. By relying heavily on franchising, the company was able to avoid the high capital costs associated with rapid expansion while maximizing returns to shareholders. Rapid sales growth provided promotion and opportunities to purchase stock for company managers as well as the opportunity for franchisees to improve margins by spreading administrative costs over a broader base of operations. This was critically important given the high fixed costs associated with each store. Volume, both at the individual store level and within a franchisee's territory, was thus essential in determining profitability. Profitability, in turn, assured the attractiveness of KFC to potential future franchisees.

In 1971, Brown and Massey sold KFC to Heublein Inc. for US$275 million. Heublein, based in Farmington, Connecticut, was a packaged goods company which marketed such products as Smirnoff Vodka, Black Velvet Canadian Whisky, Grey Poupon Mustard, and A1 Steak Sauce.

Challenges at Home and Abroad

The establishment of KFC's international operations began just prior to the company's acquisition by Heublein. KFC opened its first store in the Far East in Osaka, Japan, in 1970 as part of Expo-70. By 1973, KFC had established 64 stores in Japan, mostly in the Tokyo area. KFC also moved quickly into Hong Kong, establishing 15 stores there by 1973. Other areas of expansion included Australia, the UK and South Africa.

Shortly after the acquisition, KFC's small international staff was merged with Heublein's much larger international group in Connecticut. In spite of Heublein's efforts to impose rigid operational controls, KFC country managers were frustrated by the imposition of U.S. store designs, menus, and marketing methods on culturally divergent host countries. Resistance to corporate control grew and led many stores to develop their own menus: fried fish and smoked chicken in Japan, hamburgers in South Africa and roast chicken in Australia. In some cases, local managers seemed to know what they were doing; in other cases, they clearly did not. After heavy losses, KFC pulled out of Hong Kong entirely in 1975. In Japan, operations also began on shaky grounds with losses experienced throughout much of the 1970s.

In addition to poor relations between country managers and corporate staff, the 1970s presented a much more challenging environment for KFC in the United States. The fast food industry was becoming much more competitive with the national emergence of the Church's Fried Chicken franchise and the onset of several strong regional competitors. Important market share gains were also being made by McDonald's hamburgers.

With the Heublein acquisition, many top managers who had been hired by Brown and Massey were either fired or quit, resulting in much turmoil among the franchisees. By 1976, sales were off 8% and profits were decreasing by 26% per year. To make matters worse, rapid expansion had led to inconsistent quality, poor cleanliness and a burgeoning group of disenchanted franchisees who represented over 80% of total KFC sales. At one point, even white-haired Harland Sanders was publicly quoted admitting that many stores lacked adequate cleanliness while providing shoddy customer service and poor product quality.

Turning Operations Around

In the fall of 1975, with rapidly deteriorating operations both at home and abroad, Heublein tapped Michael Miles to salvage the chain. Miles was initially brought in to head up Heublein's international group, which by this point was dominated by KFC. Miles had come to Heublein after managing KFC's advertising account for ten years with the Leo Burnett agency. At Heublein, he had risen to vice-president in charge of the Grocery Products Division. While he had little international experience, he had developed a strong reputation for strategic planning. His challenge in late 1975 was to install consistency in international operations by increasing both corporate support and control. One of his first decisions was to move KFC-International back to Louisville where it could begin to develop a degree of autonomy within the corporation. Within 18 months, Miles was asked to manage KFC's entire worldwide turnaround, including operations in the U.S.

The basic thrust of Miles' strategy was a return to back-to-basics in terms of menu selection and commitment to quality, service and cleanliness (QSC). The back-to-basics strategy was supported by a new series of staff training programs, random inspections of company-owned and franchise stores and a new "we do chicken right" advertising program. The goal was to focus consumer awareness on a sleeker, more customer-oriented KFC which would make one product—chicken—better than any of its competitors.

The results of the turnaround strategy were dramatic. By 1982, KFC had become Heublein's fastest growing division, with real growth of 2.3%. From 1978 to 1982, sales at company-owned stores jumped an average 73%, while franchise unit sales rose by almost 45%. Much of this growth came from KFC's international operations where company units outnumbered even McDonald's outside the U.S. While chicken is eaten almost everywhere in the world, the same is not true of beef which has been poorly received in many countries. This provided KFC with a considerable advantage in penetrating foreign markets. Nowhere was this more true than in the Pacific Rim, where by 1982, KFC had nearly 400 stores in Japan. In Singapore alone, KFC had 23 franchised stores.

Acquisition by R.J. Reynolds

Although KFC had made dramatic progress, growth was limited by restricted expansion capital at Heublein. Most of the profits generated by KFC were being used to revive Heublein's spirits operations which were themselves facing flat sales and increased competition. By 1982, KFC was receiving only US$50 million per year in expansion funds compared with the US$400 million being spent by hamburger giant McDonald's. KFC also had one of the lowest ratios of company-owned to franchise stores in the industry. Many franchise stores were slow to upgrade facilities and it was understood that major investments would be required to assure the integrity of the overall KFC network.

In the late summer of 1982, R.J. Reynolds of Winston-Salem, N.C., acquired Heublein for US$1.4. billion. The acquisition was supported by Heublein directors fearful that the company might be taken over and sold in pieces. Reynolds had been seeking expansion possibilities in the consumer products industry where its marketing skills and huge cash flow could best be put to work. Although hugely profitable, Reynolds' tobacco operations were being attacked by soaring taxes and consumers' declining interest in smoking. The acquisition of Heublein was only part of a group of companies Reynolds acquired during the late 1970s and early 1980s, including Del-Monte Corp. in 1979, Canada Dry and Sunkist Soft Drinks in 1984, and Nabisco Brands in 1985.

Soon after the acquisition, Mike Miles left the company to become president of Dart and Kraft. He was succeeded as CEO of KFC by Richard Mayer who had worked with Miles on the turnaround. Mayer had put in a 10-year stint at General Foods where he rose to become head of the Jell-O product group. Mayer characterized the acquisition as "marvellous."

International Expansion

The heavy financial backing of Reynolds resulted in further growth for KFC. Betting that health-consciousness consumers would increasingly shift consumption to chicken, Reynolds designed an ambitious worldwide expansion plan that promised US$1 billion in funds over five years. Much of this expansion would come outside the U.S. where markets remained largely untapped.

As was the case with domestic operations, franchising played a major role in KFC's international growth. Franchising became the mode of choice in many markets where political risk and cultural unfamiliarity encouraged the use of locals. Another advantage with franchising was that KFC could be assured a flow of revenues with little investment, thus leveraging existing equity. This was a particularly attractive option internationally where potential deviations of franchisees from KFC operating procedures could be more easily isolated.

The downside of a reliance on franchisees was that it permitted an erosion of system integrity. Local franchisees typically controlled a portfolio of companies, with KFC sales representing only a portion of revenues. Local franchisees, driven by a desire to maximize profits, often cut corners or "milked" operations. While this type of strategy would generally not compromise short-term profitability, it often led to the deterioration of operations over the longer term. This problem was only exacerbated internationally where control was more difficult to maintain.

Southeast Asia Operations

By 1983, KFC had established 85 franchise stores in southeast Asia, including 20 stores in Indonesia, 27 stores in Malaysia and 23 stores in Singapore. This area was recognized as the Southeast Asia Region, one of five separate geographic regions within the corporation. Harry Schwab headed the Area office, where he served as a company vice-president. Schwab had been successful in managing KFC's South African operations where he eventually built a chain of 48 company-owned stores and 95 franchise stores. After returning to Louisville to assume the position of KFC vice-president for international franchising, he was given the added responsibility of supervising the company's Southeast Asia area. Exhibit 1 presents a partial map of Asian Pacific nations.

THE CHINESE MARKET

After a 10-year absence, KFC moved back into Hong Kong in 1985. During KFC's long absence from Hong Kong, McDonald's, Burger King, Wendy's and Pizza Hut had entered the market, providing the local population with a taste for Western fast food. After preparing a new Cantonese version of the "we do chicken right" advertising campaign, KFC opened the first of its 20 planned stores. During its first week of operation, the store sold more than 41 000 pieces of chicken, the most that any startup ever sold during its first week of operation. With renewed confidence that management had finally learned how to balance the need for corporate control with the demands for local responsiveness, the company began contemplating a much more ambitious move into the Chinese mainland.

The initial discussions over the feasibility of entering the huge Chinese market were held in early January 1985 between Richard Mayer and Ta-Tung (Tony) Wang, a former executive of KFC. Tony Wang was born in Sichuan province in the People's Republic of China in 1944. When Tony was five years old, the family made its way to Taiwan where in 1968 he graduated from Chong-Yuan University with a degree in engineering. He later moved to the United States, and in 1973, completed a masters degree in management science from Stevens Institute of Technology in New Jersey. Wang then attended New York University where in 1975 he earned a post-master's certificate in international business management.

Upon completion of his studies in 1975, Wang accepted a position in Louisville with KFC. A series of promotions culminated with his assuming the position of Director of Business Development for the company. In this position, Wang reported directly to Mayer where the two developed a close personal relationship. Yet by 1982, Wang was feeling increasingly uneasy at KFC. Although KFC had completed a dramatic turnaround, Wang felt strongly that the company had been too conservative in penetrating international markets. Wang's conviction was that the company was afraid to take real investment risks, particularly in the Far East where American managers were culturally out of touch. In his capacity as director of business development, Wang also saw some of the enormous profits that many of his projects were generating for franchisees. In Wang's view he was merely a bureaucrat, "enriching a conservative, ethnocentric corporation." He plotted his departure. This eventually led to the establishment of QSR Management Company where Wang served as president. QSR was principally engaged in franchisee operations of Wendy's restaurants in Northern California. The company also provided management consulting to other franchisees of major fast food companies.

The Tianjin Experience

In spite of QSR's highly profitable operations in California, Wang remained convinced of the enormous potential for American-style fast food in the Far East. In the summer of 1984, the mayor of Tianjin (the third largest city in China with a population of 7 million) visited San Francisco and spoke to a small group of Chinese-Americans about investment opportunities in his city. Wang attended the meeting and was later invited by the mayor to serve as an advisor on improving the food service industry in Tianjin. Wang's counter-proposal was to serve not only as an advisor but as an investor in a joint Chinese-American-style fast food restaurant. The mayor welcomed the idea. Primary backing for the project came from a group of Chinese-American investors in the San Francisco bay area; additional backing was provided by Don Stephens, the chairman of the Bank of San Francisco. With this support, Wang reached a 50-50 joint venture agreement with a local Tianjin partner to establish "Orchid Food," the first ever Chinese/U.S. joint venture in the restaurant industry in China. The combination take-out/80-seat restaurant was hugely successful from its first day of operation with revenues averaging 100% above break even.

Buoyed by this success, Wang began reflecting on the tremendous potential that KFC had in China. Wang's interests were in bringing KFC into China through personally winning the franchise rights for key regions of the country. Barring this, he would try to convince his friend, Richard Mayer, to become a partner in a three-way deal involving Wang, KFC, and a local and as yet undetermined partner. In a letter to Mayer in mid-January 1985, Wang argued that the time was right for KFC to move "aggressively" into China:

> I am totally convinced that KFC has a definite competitive edge over any other major fast food chains in the U.S. in developing the China market at the present time. In spite of the fact that McDonald's is trying to establish a relationship there, it will be a long while before beef could become feasibly available. On the other hand, the poultry industry is one of the top priority categories in China's agriculture modernization and it is highly encouraged by the government. It is my opinion that KFC can open the door in China and build an undisputable lead by first establishing a firm poultry-supply foundation.

Movement into China was also being encouraged by KFC's parent, R.J. Reynolds, itself interested in penetrating the vast Chinese market for cigarettes. Executives at RJR had long realized that, unlike North American demand, the demand for cigarettes was soaring in Third World and communist countries. American cigarettes, in particular, faced almost unlimited demand. China seemed like the perfect market for the company.

Mayer approached Wang's offer to bring KFC into China with great interest. On the one hand, Wang had a long and productive history with KFC; Mayer could trust him. He was aggressive and had a proven track record of successfully negotiating with the Chinese. He was also Chinese—he spoke perfect Mandarin and felt at ease in either Beijing or Louisville. If anyone could get KFC into China, it seemed that Tony Wang was the person. On the other hand, Mayer had considerable concerns about turning over such a strategically important market to a franchisee. Experiences in other international markets had shown the perils of relying on franchisees. The granting of franchise rights could also jeopardize KFC's ability to expand later in other regions of the country. According to Mayer, China was "too important to not be developed as a company operation."

Tony Wang himself was beginning to have serious doubts about his ability to move KFC into China by relying on his own resources. His experience in Tianjin had only reemphasized his conviction that major changes in the attitudes of Chinese employees would almost certainly be required for operation under the KFC banner. These changes could only be achieved through time consuming training programs, suggesting heavy pre-start-up costs which Wang could not adequately support. Wang was also concerned about the up-front money needed to find and negotiate a partnership, to sign a lease and to gain operating permits. By late fall of 1985, it was becoming increasingly clear to Wang that China was "too big a market for individuals."

Changes in Management

It was in April 1986 that Mayer decided to make his move. He telephoned Tony Wang with several announcements: Steve Fellingham was being promoted to head up all of KFC's international operations. Fellingham had over 10 years' experience in KFC-International and was widely respected as someone who would move much more aggressively internationally by relying less on franchisees and more on joint ventures with local partners. This observation was confirmed by Mayer. Mayer also announced that KFC was buying up its Singapore franchisee which now operated 29 KFC stores. This would result in considerably more administrative responsibilities for KFC's Southeast Asia regional office. Finally, Mayer was moving Harry Schwab out of Singapore, and restructuring the Southeast Asia region. The job of running the region was Tony's, if he wanted it. Mayer also expressed his encouragement that Wang pursue the China option according to his best judgement and efforts.

After some soul-searching, Wang accepted the position and, in the summer of 1986, officially became vice-president of KFC Southeast Asia with headquarters in Singapore. According to Wang, he accepted the job because of the "personal challenge to develop KFC in China." Wang viewed this opportunity of establishing the first Western-style fast food operation in China as an historic opportunity—both personally and for the company as a whole. He also realized that with this very visible challenge came high personal risks should the venture fail.

With the assumption of responsibility for all KFC operations in Southeast Asia, Wang began to see the decision to invest in China in a different light. The singular objective of getting into China would now have to be balanced with other investment opportunities in the region. KFC had enormous growth potential throughout Southeast Asia. The national markets of the region, while together smaller than the entire Chinese market, had already been exposed to Western-style fast food; patterns of demand for KFC's products were well understood. Compared to China, targeting these markets for growth had certain appeal. Control over partners and employees would be rather simple to maintain, leading to rapid growth and higher returns. Hard currency was also readily available. China, in contrast, would demand a huge amount of scarce managerial resources. The primary constraint was the limited number of Chinese-speaking KFC managers—many of whom were already being pushed to the limits in Hong Kong and Singapore. As a consequence, by the late summer of 1986, Wang was beginning to wonder whether committing these resources to China would be in the best interests of the region for which he was now responsible. Exhibit 2 presents selected national economic and population statistics for the Southeast Asia region as well as KFC location and sales figures.

The China Option: Investigating Alternatives

Wang's reaction to the ambiguity surrounding the China option was to investigate the Chinese market more thoroughly. Here, the principal question facing Wang was the intended geographic location of the first Chinese store. The location decision would potentially have a dramatic effect on profitability, future expansion elsewhere in China and managerial resource commitments—all vital considerations in a go/no-go decision.

In considering where to establish the first store, Wang initially thought of Tianjin. Through his earlier experiences, he had developed excellent contacts within the municipal government of Tianjin and he appreciated that Tianjin was one of three municipal governments in China that were administered directly by the Central Government in Beijing. (The other two were Shanghai and Beijing.) Yet, he also recognized that the city had several shortcomings. First, Tianjin lacked a convenient supply of grain-fed chickens. Experience in Hong Kong—where in 1973 KFC had entered the market using fish meal-fed chickens—suggested that Chinese consumers placed a high value on freshness and taste. This would be particularly important with a product prepared in a way which was unfamiliar to the Chinese. Another problem with Tianjin was that the city was not generally frequented by Western tourists. While Wang anticipated that most sales would be from soft currency renminbi (RMB), some hard foreign currency sales would be essential for profit repatriation and/or the purchase of critical supplies such as chicken coating, packaging, promotion materials, and so on.[1] Finally, and perhaps most importantly, Tianjin would be unable to provide KFC with the profile necessary to facilitate eventual national market penetration. In fact, Tianjin was generally regarded in China as a gateway to its larger sister, Beijing, only 85 miles to the west.

Other cities presenting viable alternative locations for KFC's entry into China included Shanghai, Guangzhou and Beijing. The location of each is noted in Exhibit 1.

SHANGHAI As China's largest city, Shanghai is home to some 11 million people, almost 9 000 factories and the country's busiest harbour. Metropolitan Shanghai is widely regarded as China's most prosperous business centre. The city alone accounts for approximately 11% of

---

[1] Like virtually all communist economies, the Chinese economy operates through two separate currencies: renminbi, or the "People's Currency," which is used by local Chinese for the purchase of goods and services; and FEC (Foreign Exchange Certificate) which is used by foreigners to represent the value of hard currency while in China. FEC is required at all hotels, taxis, restaurants and shops which cater to foreigners. A black market for FEC existed in most large Chinese cities.

China's total industrial output and almost 17% of the country's exports. It is also one of three self-administered municipalities.

Shanghai has a long history of involvement with Westerners. The Treaty of Nanking, thrust upon the Chinese by the British during the middle of the nineteenth century, set Shanghai aside as one of five Chinese port cities open to foreign trade. Western commerce and cultural influence flourished. Foreign gunboats continued to patrol the river until well into the 20th century. Complete expulsion of foreigners came in 1949 with the communist victory over the Nationalist Chinese army. However, since then the city has maintained an interest in international business and trade. Today, the city is the home of a large variety of Western hotels, business facilities and tourists.

Shanghai also had the benefit of providing easy access to a seemingly ample supply of quality chickens. In fact, through joint ventures a Thailand-based company—the Chia Tai Group—had established ten feed mills and poultry operations in the region and was the largest poultry supplier in Shanghai. KFC's Southeast Asia office had good relations with Chia Tai and was currently negotiating with one of the company's divisions as a potential franchisee in Bangkok.

While Shanghai remains a major centre for business, its noise and pollution have discouraged tourists. For KFC, the sheer population of a host city is important, although less so than the mix of potential customers. While Shanghai could provide KFC with eagerly sought-after media exposure, the operation would also need to promise an adequate return in FEC before an investment could be justified. Here, the concern was whether or not Western business people would be attracted to KFC or would prefer to frequent more fashionable restaurants. Clearly, no one knew.

GUANGZHOU Another alternative was the city of Guangzhou, located in southeast China only a short distance from Hong Kong. Guangzhou, historically know as Canton, is one of 14 special coastal cities set apart in 1984 as preferential treatment centres for foreign investment. As such, Guangzhou was given greater autonomy in approving foreign investment projects, reducing tax rates and encouraging technological development. By the end of 1986, about 80% of the almost US$6 billion foreign investment in China had been located in these open coastal cities. In addition, Guangzhou is the capital of Guangdong Province, which contains three of the country's four "Special Economic Zones" (SEZs), designed specifically to attract foreign investment. The SEZs were initially set up as part of the broad economic reforms that were launched in China in the late 1970s.

Guangzhou was frequented by Western business people as well as by tourists who visited the city on one-day excursions from Hong Kong. Due to its proximity to Hong Kong—less than 75 miles away and easily accessible by road or train—an operation in Guangzhou could easily be serviced out of the company's Hong Kong office. The Chinese in this region were also more familiar with Western management practices and culture. In fact, the people in Guangzhou speak Cantonese—the same language spoken in Hong Kong. Cantonese Chinese is quite different from the Mandarin Chinese spoken elsewhere in China. Preliminary investigations also indicated that little difficulty would be anticipated in locating an adequate supplier of chickens.

BEIJING Another location that warranted closer inspection was Beijing, China's second most populous city (after Shanghai) with nine million citizens. Since its establishment as the Chinese capital by the Mongols in the thirteenth century, Beijing has remained the political and cultural centre of China. For example, although China spans a breath of 3 000 miles, the entire nation runs according to Beijing time—an indication of the power of the central government. As the nation's capital, Beijing also sports a subway and freeway system and an international airport complete with airconditioning and moving sidewalks.

Chinese citizens from all over the country pour into Beijing eager to attend meetings or to represent their factories or districts before the authorities of the central government. The city is also the educational capital in the country with university campuses ringing the city. These factors all contribute to the relatively high levels of affluence and the intellectual enlightenment of the population—critically important in generating RMB sales. Beijing is also a tourist centre for Western visitors anxious to see the Forbidden City, Summer Palace, and nearby Ming Tombs and Great Wall. This would mean a ready supply of FEC currency. Finally, without doubt a start-up in Beijing would grab the people's attention and would communicate the tacit approval of the central authorities, thus facilitating future expansion outside the city.

Beijing could provide considerable advantages to a company eager to expand throughout China. A preliminary investigation indicated that several poultry producers were operating just outside the city. Yet, politically and operationally, Beijing would be more of a gamble than alternative locations. High profile operations heightened the possibility of government interference for political purposes.

Weighing the Decision

In his heart, Tony Wang knew he was a man who liked taking risks, and clearly, China qualified as the risk of a lifetime. However, it was also clear that the location of the first store could mitigate much of the obvious risk of moving into China. Left undetermined was whether the low risk alternatives were worth pursuing. What was needed was to weigh the possibility of reducing the risks against the potential benefits that could be achieved through the investment.

Clearly, Wang had staked out a position as the person who could bring KFC into China. However, he now had different responsibilities which also demanded his attention and for which he would surely be evaluated. He was certain that there would be little second guessing by Richard Mayer if he recommended that after careful consideration, KFC should hold off for the present from China. He also realized that, because there were no competitors as yet in China, the present time could be the most opportune time for making the move. Indeed, even if a Chinese location were selected, it would likely take years of negotiations before operations could start. To delay any further risked ceding the market to others. The challenge to Wang would be in balancing these possible risks with the possible returns.

EXHIBIT 1   **Partial Map of Pacific Asian Countries**

EXHIBIT 2 Selected Country Statistics Southeast Asia and China (1986)

	Population (millions)	Life Expectancy	GNP per Capita (US$)	Annual Real GNP Growth Rate	# of KFC units	KFC Sales (US$000 000)
Thailand	52.6	64	790	5.3 %	4	1.5
Singapore	2.6	73	7 450	7.3 %	26	15.0
Malaysia	16.1	68	1 830	1.8 %	53	27.0
Indonesia	166.6	55	500	1.2 %	25	6.8
Hong Kong	5.4	76	7 030	12.1 %	4	2.7
PRC	1 054.0	69	300	7.9 %	—	—

CAE ELECTRONICS

Mary M. Crossan and Barbara Pierce

CASE

29

In August 1993, after having spent one year and $500 000 on a bid for three power plant simulators for the Korean Electric Power Corporation (KEPCO), valued at over $50 million, Allan Abramovitch, Manager for Power Plant Simulators at Canadian Aviation Electronics (CAE Electronics), was reconsidering how aggressively his firm should continue to pursue the contract. Allan's recommendation would be considered by CAE management, who would ultimately make the final decision. CAE's initial approach had been to go after KEPCO's business aggressively. Each new request for information, however, provided an opportunity to re-evaluate the bidding strategy, and there had been many. As well, it was evident that KEPCO might start the bidding all over, as it appeared that none of the proposals would meet their new budget. This was an opportune time to revisit the bidding strategy. Abramovitch was growing increasingly uncomfortable with the nature of this project and was beginning to worry about the potential implications, even if CAE did win the contract.

CANADIAN AVIATION ELECTRONICS

Since its founding in 1947, Canadian Aviation Electronics (CAE Inc.) had become a diversified high-tech company with sales in excess of $1 billion (Exhibit 1). Its portfolio of international

Mary M. Crossan and Barbara Pierce of the Western Business School prepared this case. Copyright © 1994, The University of Western Ontario. This material is not covered under authorization from CanCopy or any reproduction rights organization. Any form of reproduction, storage or transmittal of this material is prohibited without written permission from Western Business School, The University of Western Ontario, London, Canada N6A 3K7

companies, eight in all, was divided into two product groups: Aerospace and Electronics, and Industrial Products. CAE Electronics, based in Montreal, came under the Aerospace and Electronics group. Although it designed and manufactured shipboard machinery control systems, supervisory control and data acquisition systems (primarily for utility companies), and airborne magnetic anomaly detection systems for anti-submarine warfare forces, these products represented less than 10% of CAE Inc.'s total sales. The major products designed and manufactured by CAE Electronics were training simulators (65% civil aviation simulators, 13% military aviation simulators and 13% power plant simulators). Simulators were an important training tool in settings where mistakes made by inexperienced trainees could have dangerous or costly consequences. Simulation provided a safe, cost-efficient and effective supplement to live training for pilots, cabin crews, air traffic controllers or power plant operators. Examples of CAE Electronics' products are provided in Exhibits 2 and 3.

By 1993, CAE Electronics was the world leader in flight simulators with 65% of the total market share. It was known as the innovator in the industry, reinvesting 20% of its sales on research and development activities each year. It had ISO 9001 QA Certification for Avionics, Naval, Nuclear and Space. Over half of its 3400 employees were scientific and technical personnel. Of the remainder, 1125 worked in manufacturing and 450 in management and administration. CAE's customers included international and regional airlines, defense forces, power utilities, government agencies, research establishments and space agencies. In total, there was a 70/30 split between sales for commercial and military applications. Eighty-five percent (85%) of its products were exported to 43 countries: 49% sold in the Americas, 30% in Europe and 21% in Africa, Asia and the Pacific.

Nuclear Power Plant Simulators

CAE had carved out a niche in the design and construction of simulators for the CANDU nuclear power plant. Simulators for nuclear power plants were constructed using the control panels and equipment of the actual power plant. Manipulating the controls, however, activated sophisticated computer programs rather than a nuclear reactor. These programs could be adjusted to mimic actual operations and appeared to the operators exactly the same as real installations.

In 1970, CAE developed its first power plant simulator for the Pickering Ontario nuclear plant using CANDU technology. Supplying training simulators to Ontario Hydro for subsequent plants became an attractive, although relatively small, component of its business. In 1983, CAE entered the U.S. market. Although the first few programs were difficult, requiring some upfront entry investment on the part of CAE, the company subsequently developed strong management and technological capability in the area of power plant simulators.

As indicated in Exhibit 4, from a peak of $38.8 million in 1987, CAE had experienced a slump in new orders for power plant simulators. This decline was primarily due to a decline in the number of nuclear plants being constructed. CAE had considered getting out of the business, but was persuaded that changes in the regulatory environment would generate substantial demand for power plant simulators. Furthermore, since changes in the airline industry were having an adverse effect on the demand for CAE's other product lines, CAE felt it was important to keep a diversified portfolio of products.

INDUSTRY TRENDS

While CAE Electronics had experienced steady sales and profit growth in flight simulators, there were two disturbing trends which it felt might influence future sales growth. First, there was the major world-wide slump in the airline industry resulting in a major decline in the sale of flight simulators. In an attempt to attract passengers to fill empty seats, airlines had been slashing fares. As a result, profits in the industry had quickly eroded. Those companies that had managed to survive were slashing costs and deferring major capital expenditures, hoping to ride out the downturn and wait until better times returned. In spite of the lack of profitability in the industry, the future did not look entirely bleak. Passenger volume was expected to grow 5% a year throughout the 1990s. As well, it was expected that 4 000 new long-range wide-bodied aircraft would be required by the year 2010 to meet the increasing demand for business travel in world markets.

Second, military spending was being cut, particularly in the U.S. With cold war tensions removed and major national economies in recession, governments saw military budgets as a potential source of spending restraint. It was difficult to determine if this trend would result in permanent reductions to military spending, but, in the near term, it was definitely a factor to consider. On the other hand, the U.S. Department of Defense had identified simulation as one of its seven major technological thrusts in order to reduce its expenditures; simulator training costs averaged US$600 per hour, while training on a military aircraft could cost US$10 000 per hour. The U.S. National Training and Simulation Association had forecast a doubling of the U.S. Army's simulation budget by 1994.

Although CAE Electronics was still in the process of filling orders made in previous years, the order book for the next five years was beginning to show the effects of these trends. CAE's perspective on this industry upheaval was captured in its annual report:

> (In)... the commercial airline industry, there will be no quick fixes to the problems of overcapacity and tight financing. The industry's turnaround will take at least another two years. But air travel itself will continue to grow. And once the airline industry undergoes its unprecedented change, it will be a stronger, healthier, and more profitable industry.
>
> And as for the defense forces, potential conflict between two rival superpowers no longer threatens. Unfortunately, however, the promise of peace has also dimmed. Rising nationalism is fostering greater regional hostilities. New nations are stillborn amid bloody ethnic conflicts. Greater instability endangers the Middle East, Africa, regions of Asia, Eastern Europe, and former republics of the Soviet Union. The new world has precious little order. In fact, the challenge for defense forces throughout the world has grown in complexity, rather than diminished.

CAE was advised that new regulations being planned in the U.S. would require simulators for every nuclear plant, potentially creating a large number of new orders. In addition, CAE felt there would be continuing demand for fossil fuel power plant simulators and existing installations would always require updating and modification. Exhibit 5 provides Ontario Hydro's estimates for nuclear and fossil training simulator demand for the 1990s. Other market studies indicated that there were 30 active nuclear power plants in the U.S. that would be required to have operator training simulators in the near future.

REPUBLIC OF KOREA (ROK)

The Republic of Korea (ROK) or South Korea was located on the southern portion of the Korean peninsula, adjacent to the Democratic People's Republic of Korea (North Korea). Despite continued tensions and mutual suspicion resulting from years of disputes and confrontations between the two countries, there were hopes of renewed political harmony, if not eventual reunification. However, having seen the price West Germany had paid in its reunification with East Germany, the South Koreans had become more cautious and concerned about reunification with the Northern communist population of 21 million, with an expected price tag of hundreds of billions of dollars.

One of the most densely populated countries in the world, South Korea's population of over 43 million covered a geographic area equal in size to Portugal, the state of Indiana, or twice the size of the province of Nova Scotia. Over one quarter of the population lived in the capital city of Seoul located near the North/South border.

At the end of the Korean war in 1953, South Korea (hereafter Korea) was one of the poorest countries in the world with GNP per capita of less than US$100. With its capital city, Seoul, levelled, Korea literally began rebuilding from the ground up. In what has been termed an "economic miracle," Korea transformed itself from an agrarian to an industrially based economy with economic growth averaging 10% through 1990. Korea achieved NIC (Newly Industrialized Country) status by 1970, and was expected to achieve advanced country status by the late 1990s.

Technology Transfer

One key to Korea's phenomenal growth was its aggressive accumulation of technology from higher income countries. When Korea entered the race to industrialize, like other developing countries, it suffered from a significant deficit in industrial technology. Korea could never have hoped to become competitive through its own R&D or basic research activities alone. It had neither the time nor the capability. It was forced instead to borrow, license and imitate technology to compensate for its initial position.

At first, borrowing, licensing and imitation were sufficient. Low wage levels and government subsidization allowed Korean products to compete on a global basis. Koreans became extremely proficient in acquiring technology from other countries and using it to manufacture products for export. These products were often priced lower than the same product manufactured in the country where the technology originated.

Eventually, as productivity and economic benefits increased, so did worker demands for a greater share of the gains. Mounting wage pressure began to erode the competitive position of labour-intensive Korean products prompting Korean companies to explore product and process innovation for increases in productivity and competitiveness. This emphasis on product and process innovation signalled a significant change in industrialization policy. Not only did technology need to be transferred, but after transfer, it needed to be improved upon to enhance productivity. While it was not uncommon for the first plant in an industry to be built on a turnkey basis with little Korean involvement, the development of subsequent plants relied heavily on the involvement of local engineers and technicians who assumed an expanding role. This growing capability eventually reduced reliance on the initial foreign investor. The "apprentices" graduated to assume full journeyman status. Koreans had added the ability to develop and enhance technology to their existing ability to acquire it.

As Korea became more successful, its wage advantage deteriorated further and, by the late 1980s, it began to emphasize the development of technology-intensive industries. Koreans expected significant changes in the near future given the new emphasis in economic development, and the change in political leadership. In particular, the development of technology was high on the agenda of the Korean government. A recent survey by the Korea Industrial Technology Association (KITA) showed that in spite of Korea's impressive improvements in technology over the previous two decades, it still lagged far behind the United States and Japan. As a result, foreign companies were required to have a high level of "localization" in manufactured products, i.e., finished products could not be imported to Korea but instead a significant proportion of the product had to be manufactured and preferably sourced in Korea. As well, foreign companies wishing to do business in Korea were required to submit a detailed plan to the government on how they planned to transfer technology to Korean companies. The government hoped that the transfer of technological knowledge to Korea would fuel economic growth through productivity increases and new product introduction. This technology-based strategy was considered critical to Korea's long-term economic success since it increasingly felt the effects of being sandwiched between the lower labour cost economies of China and Taiwan, and the high value added economies of Japan and the United States. Korea's aspirations were to match the technological development of the G7 group.

Government's Role in the Economy

Korea's economic success had been attributed to a number of factors: "strong leadership, creative policies tailored to concrete situations, a deep understanding of international opportunities, sound utilization of domestic resources and, most important, sacrifice and hard work on the part of the Korean People."[1] The government exercised significant controls on business activities to achieve planned economic results. In 1962, Korea began a series of five-year economic plans which initially focused the country's efforts on the development of heavy industry and labour-intensive manufacturing with a strong export orientation. The "export first" principle was strongly enforced by the government. For example, sales of domestic colour television sets were prohibited until 1980, forcing manufacturers to focus on overseas markets. The strong export orientation was coupled with a high level of restrictions on imports. For example, there was a ban on 258 Japanese import products ranging from cars to appliances. In recent years, the government had been willing to ease import restrictions somewhat but only permitted imports and foreign investments which it felt would contribute to Korean economic development, improve its balance-of-payments position or bring in advanced technology.

Most companies in Korea were small and closely held by family groups. However, during the early stages of economic reform, certain economic sectors, such as the auto industry, received preferential treatment from the government in terms of better access to capital, lower interest rates, R&D support and tax incentives. Given the limited capital available, these in-

---

[1] Richard Ibghy, Taieb Hafsi, *South Korea's National Strategies 1962 to 1988*; Monographs on International Business and Economics; National Library of Canada.

dustries developed into highly leveraged, very large diversified multinational conglomerates known as *chaebols* (pronounced chi-bols) (Exhibit 6, Exhibit 7). Most notable among the *chaebols* were Hyundai, Daewoo, Lucky-Goldstar and Samsung. These octopus-like conglomerates, which were predominantly family-owned, were an indispensable part of the Korean economy which they clearly dominated. For example, Samsung's revenues of US$17 billion in 1986 ranked it 35th in the world and represented 14% of Korea's GNP. The taxes paid by Samsung represented 5% of the government's total tax revenue.

The Korean government invested heavily in the development of human resources. At over 10% of GNP, Korea's investment in education was second only to the United States. Children in the United States attended school for a net 158 days per year while Korean students attended for 250 days. Much of this investment was directed at acquiring scientific and technical knowledge. Between 1960 and 1980, employment of general managers only doubled while the employment of engineers increased tenfold.

The new President, Kim Young-Sam was expected to have a significant impact on the country. President Roh Tae-Woo, a former general, had stepped down after completing his maximum five-year term in office. Although the Roh administration had already made inroads into political reform, it was felt that there was a long way to go. It was only in 1980 that 200 students were killed and 1 000 injured in the Kwangju uprising. It was a wave of similar demonstrations in 1987 that brought down Roh's predecessor, Chun Doo-Hwan. Roh himself had faced three weeks of demonstrations throughout the nation in response to the fatal beating of a university student by riot policemen.

The recent election was the first since the Second World War, in which none of the Presidential candidates had a military background. President Kim Young-Sam promised sweeping changes to clean up the corruption that was considered rampant in the country. The situation had been ripe for perks and kick-backs given the heavy involvement by the government in developing the economy, coupled with weak measures on the financial side to track investments. The head of one of Korea's major companies stated that "we pay as much in extortion—legal, semi-legal and illegal extortion—as we do in legitimate taxes."[2]

Korea was Canada's fifth largest trading partner with trade between the two countries projected to reach $12 billion by the end of the decade. By 1991, two-way trade had reached $4 billion and Canada was third on the list of foreign investors in Korea. Many countries viewed Korea as a gateway to other Asian countries, particularly China. Although history had shown that both Japan and China had been Korea's aggressors, there were much closer geographic, ethnic and linguistic ties between Korea and China. While there still remained a great deal of animosity between Korea and Japan, China viewed Korea much like a "little brother," a role that Korea was anxious to grow out of. Korea's fear of dependence on Japan was evidenced by the ban on Japanese cars that persisted three years after the ban on other foreign cars had been lifted.

CAE'S KOREAN OPERATIONS

CAE had been very successful in penetrating the Korean market for flight simulators. Korean Air Lines (KAL), part of the Hanjin chaebol, had been very pleased with CAE's products and

---

[2] "Corruption: The Cost of Politics," *Far Eastern Economic Review,* March 30, 1991.

service. CAE representatives had developed long-term relationships with KAL personnel in what one CAE employee referred to as the need to build "off-shore friendships." Despite the 12-hour time difference, the team of CAE employees in Canada who supported the KAL simulators, made themselves available 24 hours a day to discuss any concerns. CAE also placed a Korean-speaking employee on the team to facilitate communication between the two companies. Although the CAE team observed that the Koreans were very conscious of hierarchy and titles, they often spoke directly to the Korean-speaking CAE employee in spite of his lower status in the company.

CAE's experience in Korea with power plant simulators was more limited. It had acted as a contractor through Atomic Energy of Canada Limited (AECL) to supply a CANDU digital control system to KEPCO when it had purchased a CANDU power plant a few years previously. This was very much an arms length transaction, in which CAE had little contact with its Korean counterparts, although the equipment had worked well and KEPCO was pleased with the installation.

KEPCO POWER PLANT SIMULATOR BID

In early 1991, KEPCO initiated a bid process for three power plant simulators. The process began with a high degree of information exchange between the parties involved. An informal request for information was issued asking potential bidders for generic technical specifications and an approximate price. Based on its submission, CAE was asked to make a presentation to KEPCO in Korea. The CAE contingent arrived jetlagged to what appeared to be an "executive triathalon." On the Friday they arrived, they were handed plant drawings, and asked to develop a fully functional set of plant-specific models on the workstation they had brought with them. They were then asked to demonstrate their customized model on Saturday. In one day, they did the best they could on a task which would normally take two months, and came up with the demo as requested.

Based on the information received during the presentation round, KEPCO sent out an unofficial request for proposals (RFP). This RFP was developed by combining the best technical specifications from each of the original informal submissions. The CAE bid team found this approach interesting, since in many cases it appeared as if KEPCO had not fully understood the nature of the components they were requiring; when in doubt, they had indicated a company's proprietary name for a particular component. As the informal process moved toward a more formal request, the stakes were getting higher; technical requirements were escalating, the acceptable price was dropping and there seemed to be no limit to the amount of technology transfer demanded.

When the formal request for quotation (RFQ) came, it allowed for only one week to respond, as KEPCO needed to meet some internal deadlines. The procedure was that proposals would first be screened on the basis of their technical strength, and those meeting the first test would then be evaluated on price.

KEPCO required foreign companies to partner with a Korean "prime" contractor. Most of CAE's competitors had chosen to partner with one of the chaebols; Hyundai was partnering with ABB-CE (U.S.), Lucky-Goldstar with Westinghouse (U.S.), Samsung with S3 Technologies (U.S.), Daeyong with General Physics International (GPI) (U.S.) and Daewoo with Thomson CSF (France). As was the custom, CAE had engaged a consultant in Korea. The consultant used his knowledge of the market and competition plus his influence through a network of contacts to bridge geographic and cultural differences. The consultant had recommended that CAE partner with Iljin Electronics, which was a much smaller company than the Korean conglomerates, yet was comparable in size to the divisions of the other companies Iljin would be competing against. As well, given that Iljin was much smaller than CAE, CAE would not be overshadowed by its Korean counterpart. The consultant also assured CAE that Iljin had solid contacts within KEPCO.

The playing field had shifted throughout the bidding process. All potential partnering relationships had to be approved by the Korean government to ensure that the government's policies for localization and technology transfer were being met. The Daewoo-Thomson partnership did not receive approval, because Thomson, one of CAE's biggest competitors in flight simulators, was unwilling to meet the requirements for technology transfer. As well, since GPI could not come to an agreement with Daeyong, it decided to partner with Hyundai. Hyundai was released from its initial agreement with ABB-CE (U.S.) when ABB-CE decided not to participate in this competitive procurement.

Iljin Electronics

Iljin Electronics was a division of Iljin Electrics and Machinery, which was founded in 1967 as a non-ferrous metal manufacturer. Iljin had grown into a diversified company with sales of over $250 million. While still maintaining a strong position in non-ferrous metals, it was also involved in manufacturing industrial machinery and electrical equipment, construction, and electronics and communications. Iljin Electronics was established in 1983 to focus on electronics and communications, including computer networking, factory automation, computers and facsimile. With sales of $35.7 million and assets of $21.7 million, it employed 170 people.

From a somewhat difficult beginning, CAE's relationship with Iljin had developed over time. The partnership experienced some turbulence early on when Iljin "strongly recommended" that CAE bid on a smaller deal with Korean Gas. Iljin advised CAE that it was not likely to win the bid, but that CAE needed to bid to establish credibility in the Korean market. However, CAE won the bid, then ended up losing money on the project. What started out as a ten-month project ran six months over schedule, creating a great deal of frustration between the project managers at Iljin and CAE.

With respect to the KEPCO proposal, it was apparent to CAE that all of the Korean prime contractors, not just Iljin, were moving into a new area of expertise. Therefore, while Iljin was very responsive to CAE's input, there were some questions about how the project would be implemented should CAE and Iljin win the bid.

Localization

The project was divided almost equally between hardware and software. CAE was bidding solely on the software which represented approximately $25 million of the $50 million project. For the software portion, KEPCO required localization of 50% on each of the first two simulators and 80% on the third. The percentages pertained to cash flow but inferred technical performance. Each new power plant required a software package to replicate the plant. As a result, each power plant required the development of new software. However, CAE was continually developing tools and modelling techniques to support the software development process. The localization requirement referred to software development. It was not apparent at this point how CAE would fulfil not only its obligations for quality, cost and delivery, but also meet the localization requirement.

Technology Transfer

The requirements for technology transfer had escalated with each iteration of the process. Originally, the transfer of technology was such that it would enable KEPCO to do its own maintenance on the simulator which quickly evolved into maintenance of simulators for all similar power plant simulators. The requirements seemed to escalate incrementally, with the most recent request being a complete transfer of technology including the basic software source code for the tools and modelling techniques which KEPCO could then use to develop software for any simulator.

Opinion at CAE was mixed concerning the potential threat from the transfer of technology. Views ranged from truly significant to nonexistent or manageable. Those who felt the threat was significant pointed to how quickly the Koreans had been able to pick things up during the process of putting the request for information and request for proposal together. They suggested that others were underestimating the Koreans in the same way that many North Americans had underestimated the Japanese in their early years of technological development. With respect to power plant technology, the example was given of the Romanians who bought their first and second plants, and produced the last three themselves.

Others felt that the risk was negligible, suggesting that the Korean partner was really not capable of assimilating the technology. One person stated that "intellectual transfer of technology would be extremely difficult. It took 15 years to develop at CAE; they can't possibly learn it in two to three years, especially not in English." Another person suggested that "even after the extensive in-house training that CAE was required to offer, if an engineer could get a working knowledge of the technology, he was likely to get promoted into a position that did not utilize the knowledge." Finally, several people suggested there was little threat given CAE's rate of innovation; "if CAE could stay one step ahead of its direct competitors, surely it could stay ahead of a new entry into the field."

In general, risk to intellectual property in Korea was considered to be high. The laws regulating monopolies and enforcing fair trade had only been enacted in 1980. However, it was widely recognized that legislation guarding against inappropriate transfer of technology was not enforced. The Canadian Embassy, who had often interceded on behalf of a Canadian company registering a violation, indicated it had not won any of the cases that had been put forth. Infractions were most notable in consumer products where watches, audio and video cassettes, garments and electronics products were often copies of more expensive branded products.

CAE had previous experience in the Korean market with its KAL flight simulators and their contribution to the CANDU reactor project with AECL. In these deals, however, there had been no requirement for offset or any local work requirements. CAE had worked closely with its Korean customers in the past but partnering with a Korean company and engaging in this level of technology transfer presented new territory for CAE.

Although S3 Technologies was a strong competitor in the area of power plant simulators, CAE was confident it was well positioned to be competitive on the bid with respect to both technology and pricing given that it had won the last two contracts awarded worldwide. In addition to its success in recent contracts, CAE's experience in Korea with the sale of flight simulators had been quite positive. Finally, it had a great deal of confidence in its consultant who was well connected with KEPCO.

CAE was concerned about the potential competitive repercussions of losing the bid, since the nuclear simulator would provide one of its competitors with a potential advantage in bidding for a follow-on contract with KEPCO to supply a simulator for its CANDU nuclear plant. Since CAE had built all the simulators for the CANDU plant project, it was confident of winning the Korean Wolsong II CANDU simulator.

The project had been costed out, and it was clear that margins were shrinking with each round in the bidding process. At this stage, it was evident that from a financial standpoint, the returns would be low. Abramovitch had to weigh the project's risks associated against the financial and non-financial returns to assess how aggressively CAE should continue pursuing the project.

To complicate matters, KEPCO had received budget approval of only US$13.7 million. CAE, Iljin and the Korean consultant believed that KEPCO would either have to lower its technical specifications, reduce the number of plants, or seek a higher budget. At this stage, all that was clear was that the process would be delayed.

EXHIBIT 1   CAE Revenues and Earnings

Consolidated

	1992	*1991*	*1990*
Total Revenue	1 045 812	1 097 728	1 119 546
Operating Earnings	73 287	69 754	61 370

Aerospace and Electronics

	1992	*1991*	*1990*
Total Revenue	966 293	1 021 296	1 028 554
Operating Earnings	63 092	62 410	48 460

Industrial Products

	1992	*1991*	*1990*
Total Revenue	79 519	76 432	90 992
Operating Earnings	10 195	7 344	12 910

EXHIBIT 2   CAE'S Simulator Products

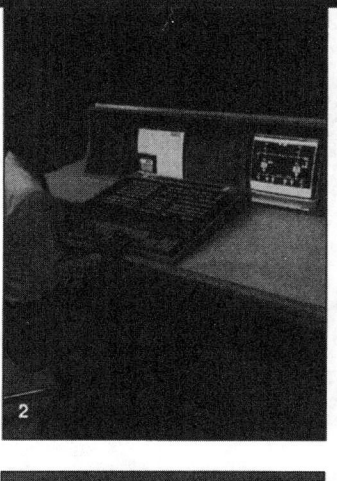

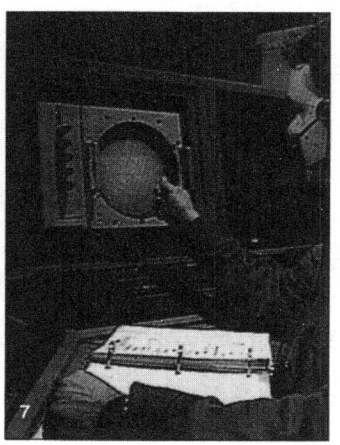

CAE Electronics
C.P. 1800 Saint-Laurent,
Québec, Canada H4L 4X4
Tel (514) 341-6780
Tlx 05 824856
Fax (514) 341-7699

Where new frontiers become reality

1. Helicopter Simulators
2. Energy Management and Control Systems
3. Magnetic Anomaly Submarine Detection Systems
4. Helicopter Research & Development Facilities
5. Civil Flight Simulators
6. Tactical Aircraft Systems Support
7. Air Defense Anti-Tank System Trainers

8. Power Plant Control Systems and Simulators
9. Telerobotics
10. Flight Training Devices
11. C-5B Galaxy Weapon System Trainers
12. Naval Integrated Platform Management Systems
13. Air Traffic Control Systems

EXHIBIT 3 CAE'S Power Plant Simulator Products

GOAL: Maximum Power Availability with Maximum Efficiency

SOLUTION: A CAE Power Plant Training Simulator

Essential Benefits for Utilities

Faster start-ups, reduced downtime, high plant efficiency and reduced training costs are just a few of the benefits which result from a CAE Power Plant Simulator. And the mark of the utility moving to this type of training is a complete dedication to provide optimum service and safe operation at the most economical rate.

CAE Offers More Than the Competition

CAE Electronics provides innovative and flexible solutions using custom designed systems to meet each utility's specific needs. We've been involved with simulation systems for more than thirty years, and real-time computer-based control systems for over twenty-five. You can count on us to find the solutions which exactly meet your nuclear or fossil-fueled power plant requirements.

CAE's Experience is Unique

Among all major manufacturers, CAE is the only one to have supplied simulators for BWR, PWR and CANDU reactor types. Current orders bring the number of nuclear simulators supplied by CAE to major utilities in the U.S. and Canada to 12.

Whether your requirements are for nuclear or fossil-fueled power plant training simulators, CAE will provide you with a customized training environment designed for your specific needs.

CAE ELECTRONICS LTD.

A subsidiary of CAE Industries Ltd.

C.P. 1800 Saint-Laurent, Québec, Canada H4L 4X4 Tel. (514) 341-6780 TLX 05 824856 TWX 610-422-3063 FAX (514) 341-7699

EXHIBIT 4   CAE Electronics Orders Received

	Nuclear Simulator Order ($ millions)	Total CAE Orders ($ millions)	Percentage
1984	22.6	131	17%
1985	35.4	206	17%
1986	10.0	196	5%
1987	38.8	297	13%
1988	0	315	0%
1989	11.4	367	3%
1990	3.7	363	1%
1991	7.8	335	2%
Overall	129.7	2 210	5.9%

EXHIBIT 5   Potential Training Simulator Market

	Canada	U.S.	Other
Nuclear Training Simulator	2	0	25
Nuclear Simulator Updates	7	75	?
Fossil Training Simulator	8	12	50

EXHIBIT 6 Korean *Chaebols*—The Top 15

Group	Core Firms	Family Ownership	Debt Ratio
Samsung	Samsung Shipbuilding[*]	98.3	544.2
	Samsung Electronics	30.7	398.1
	Samsung Petrochemical[*]	83.0	474.3
Hanjin	KAL	28.4	644.3
	Hanjin Shipping	91.2	C.I.
	Hanil Development	24.1	354.1
Daewoo	Daewoo Corp.	14.9	290.8
	Daewoo Electronics	7.1	251.5
	Daewoo Shipyard[*]	83.9	296.3
Hyundai	Hyundai Motors	29.9	453.0
	Hyundai Electronics[*]	100.0	568.9
	Hyundai Petrochemical[*]	100.0	171.8
Lucky	Lucky Ltd.	10.8	176.2
	Goldstar	15.3	344.6
	Goldstar Electron[*]	100.0	991.9
Ssangyong	Ssangyong Cement	20.7	170.8
	Ssangyong Oil Refinery	44.7	186.4
	Ssangyong Motor	17.3	282.2
Sunkyong	Yukong Ltd.	26.3	398.0
	SKI	30.4	412.6
	SKC[*]	84.1	881.3
Hanil	Hanil Synthetic Fiber	47.7	235.7
	Kyungnam Woolen Textile	40.8	207.3
	Kukje Corp.	43.2	C.I.
Kia	Asia Motors	36.8	303.5
	Kla Machine Tool	89.6	889.1
	Kla Steel	66.7	456.1
Daelim	Daelim Motor[*]	100.0	C.I.
	Daelim Ceramic[*]	100.0	154.8
	Daelim Concrete[*]	66.3	171.6
Kumho	Kumho	19.8	309.6
	Kumho Petrochemical	23.4	78.5
	Asiana[*]	57.5	C.I.
Hyosung	Hyosung Corp.	17.2	374.3
	Hyosung Heavy Ind[*]	62.5	624.7
	Tongyang Nylon	26.8	262.1
Doosan	Oriental Brewery	36.3	470.8
	Doosan Machinery	58.8	262.4
	Doosan Glass	38.2	354.0
Exposives	Korea Explosives	31.5	178.3
	Hanyang Chemical	29.3	187.1
	Kyongin Energy	44.3	442.6
Dongkuk Steel	Dongkuk Steel	42.2	95.4
	Korea Iron & Steel	63.7	120.5
	Dongkuk Ind.[*]	83.6	546.4

[*] C.I. means Capital Impairment.
[*] Those in asterisks are unlisted affiliates (OBSE).
[*] The figures are based on the end of 1990.
[*] Family ownership encompasses family members, and affiliates, excluding shares held by executives of those groups.

SOURCE: Office of Bank Supervision and Examination, *Far Eastern Economic Review*, May 30, 1991, p. 52.

EXHIBIT 7   **Korean *Chaebols* Major Statistics of the Samsung Group** (billion won)

	1976	1980	1986
Employment (000s)	25.8	75.0	147.2
Sales	455.3	2 385.5	14 615.8
Domestic sales	237.6	1 136.8	7 241.1
Exports	217.7	1 248.7	7 374.7
Capital	50.9	392.3	1 101.9
Fixed assets	110.3	697.1	2 948.4
Long-term liabilities	72.8	782.0	5 168.4
Net profit after tax	10 370	10 850	161 150
Tax	68.1	254.5	717.1
R&D Expenditure	1.9	9.8	163.1
Training expenses			10.9
Exchange rate (WON/US$)	484	659.9	861.4

SOURCE: The Office of the Secretary to the Chairman, Samsung Conglomerate, *Samsung Osipynyonsa* (A 50-Year History of Samsung), Seoul, Samsung Group, 1988.

ESCORTS LIMITED—1993

Jay Anand and Andrew Delios

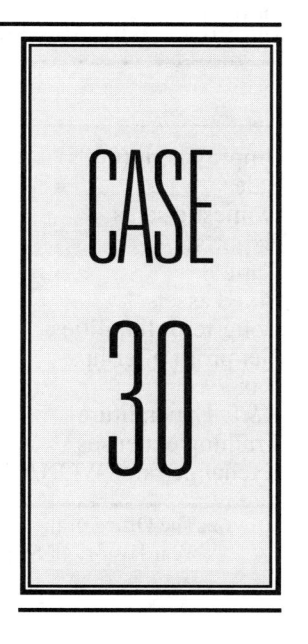

CASE

30

In mid 1993, Mr. Rajan Nanda, the Chairman and Managing Director of Escorts Ltd. (Escorts) in Faridabad, India, was reviewing the performance of the company. In the first two years following the introduction of India's economic liberalization program, Escorts' profits had declined while revenues were stagnant (see Exhibit 1). The Chairman, concerned about Escorts' performance, had charged the newly created Corporate Strategic Planning Department with formulating a plan of response and charting a new strategic direction for the company.

Escorts, the 18th largest company in India (see Exhibit 2), was founded by H.P. Nanda on October 17, 1944. During its first five decades the company grew steadily and was either the market leader or the second largest producer in each of its markets. Escorts was primarily a manufacturing company producing farm and construction equipment, motorcycles and auto-parts, though it had recently entered the financial and telecommunication sectors. In 1993, The Escorts group of companies had revenues of Rs. 16.5 billion (US$513 million); Escorts Ltd.'s revenues were Rs. 9.82 billion.

COMPANY HISTORY

On October 17, 1944, Escorts Agents Ltd., founded by two brothers, Yudi and Hari Nanda, began operations as a private bus service in Lahore, India. In 1947, during the partition of

India in which Lahore became a part of Pakistan, all the assets of the company were lost. The Nandas were forced to start from scratch and they reestablished Escorts in Delhi as an agency house serving foreign manufacturers in India. Yudi and Hari Nanda were, respectively, the Managing Director and Chairman of Escorts Agents, as the company was then known. In 1948, Yudi Nanda founded Escorts (Agriculture and Machines) Ltd., a separate entity from Escorts Agents Ltd. After Yudi Nanda's death in 1952, the two companies were merged in 1953.

In Escorts' first international alliance, the company served as Westinghouse's franchisee for domestic appliances in India. With the recognition of the opportunities in the Indian rural economy, the company quickly forged a number of additional marketing alliances with German corporations like MAN, AEG, Haniel & Leung and Knorr Bremse for sophisticated electrical and mechanical engineering equipment. Another series of alliances with American corporations like Minneapolis Moline, Wisconsin and Massey-Ferguson facilitated entry into agricultural tractors, implements and engines. Escorts provided the marketing and service activities in these alliances, beginning the development of a strong dealer network across all of India.

In 1954, Escorts participated in its first industrial venture, manufacturing piston rings and liners in partnership with Goetze Werke of Germany. Subsequent collaborations with Mahle of Germany in 1960, for the production of pistons, and with Ursus of Poland, for the assembly of tractors, solidified Escorts' backward integration from the distribution to the manufacture of industrial products. In January 1960, Escorts Agents Pvt. Ltd. was incorporated as a public company under the name of Escorts Ltd.

Throughout Escorts' early years, focus was on the company's strength as a broadly based marketing and service network which had extensive access to India's large and widely dispersed population. The tractor business exemplified Escorts' customer focus. In the 1950s, Escorts instituted a policy of on-site service. Escorts offered to repair and service tractors at the customer's farm. To provide this service, dealers were located in small towns near the villages in which the tractors were used.

Escorts stimulated the development of the tractor market through its customer focus. In the 1950s and 1960s, Indian farmers, unaware of the benefits of mechanization, were reluctant to adopt tractors. Escorts sought to change this aversion to mechanization. A private Institute of Farm Mechanization was established at Azadpur, Delhi. Customers, many of them newcomers to the use of automated farm machinery, were trained, free of cost, by Escorts when they purchased a tractor.

Escorts combined this service and market orientation with extensive manufacturing capabilities. In 1993, Escorts had 20 manufacturing plants located throughout India. Though the technology employed in these plants was competitive within India, the technology was attained through a series of international alliances (see Appendix A for a description of an alliance with Yamaha). Company growth during the 1960s and 1970s occurred through product diversification, and the company moved into a number of new industries.

Diversification

In the 1960s and 1970s, Escorts grew in a controlled market: manufacturers were only able to produce products for which they held a license. A number of acts and policies institutionalized the government's efforts to control production. The Monopoly and Restrictive Trade Practices

(MRTP) Act prevented large companies from obtaining exclusive control of any one market. Sales of any one firm in a particular market were limited; thus individual company growth was shunted away from concentration in any one product area. The Foreign Exchange Regulation Act (FERA) controlled the amount of foreign trade, limiting international competition in India's domestic markets.

Finally, a licensing authority controlled growth across sectors in the economy. The licensing authority determined which areas in the economy were to be prioritized, and, by the issuance of licenses, who was able to produce in the different markets. Market mechanisms were distorted, and industry became widely known as a system of "know-who, not know-how." To grow and to receive licenses for production, companies had to curry favour with government officials. Companies which possessed the majority of licensed capacity for a product could control prices by restriction of output. Competitors were not free to enter this monopolized market and, perversely, a system which had overt mechanisms for preventing the formation of monopolies, implicitly supported the formation of monopolies through its licensing system.

Escorts' growth during this period was primarily achieved by product line diversification. After growth in the 1970s and 1980s, Escorts' licensed capacity was far greater than its productive capacity, and the number of foreign partners was large (see Exhibit 3).

A Moment of Crisis

Through the 1970s and 1980s, Escorts' revenues, profits and share price increased steadily. However, in 1983, the price of Escorts' shares began to climb perceptibly faster on stock exchanges across India. From a January price of Rs. 40, shares doubled to Rs. 80 in May 1983. Hostile takeovers were unheard of at this time in India, and Escorts' managers suspected that they were being green-mailed at this time, though, in fact, a takeover of Escorts was being attempted by Swraj Paul, a London-based nonresident Indian (NRI).

Escorts was susceptible to a stock market raid partly because of the country's expropriatory tax laws. High marginal tax rates, which frequently exceeded 60%, left little in retained earnings for the internal financing of growth, and at times, even forced companies to sell shares to meet their tax liabilities. Thus, frequent share issues had diluted the stock holdings of the founding Nanda family. In the 1980s, the Nanda family held just 15% of the total equity capital of the company.

Two government-controlled Indian financial institutions, Unit Trust of India (UTI) and Life Insurance Corporation (LIC), jointly controlled over 50% of Escorts' equity. The dominant presence of these financial institutions in Escorts was not unusual among Indian companies. Other large and prominent companies, such as DCM (a conglomerate), TELCO, and Tata Steel (see Exhibit 2), had substantial chunks of equity (40% or more) owned by financial institutions.

Investment in Indian companies by financial institutions was strictly for the purpose of financing growth. Generally, these institutions followed a non-interventionist policy, supporting management but not seeking control over management. However, the weak ownership position of the founding families of many of India's larger companies made them vulnerable to hostile takeovers.

NRIs, like Swarj Paul, were in a favourable position to invest in Indian businesses because of the foreign exchange problems faced by the Indian economy. NRIs were encouraged by the Indian government to invest foreign funds in India to help improve the country's balance of payments position. However, this investment was to be portfolio investment, rather than investment for management control. Thus, individual NRIs were restricted to a 1% ownership position in any one Indian company, though this restriction was easy to circumvent. NRIs could purchase shares through a series of different companies and thereby, in a circuitous manner, attain a controlling interest.

Escorts, led by the efforts of H. P. Nanda, resisted Swarj Paul's takeover attempt. Appeals to the government and to other industry leaders to deal with the threat of NRI control of Indian companies did not bring immediate results. Finally, Escorts found an ally in Rajiv Gandhi, the Prime Minister's son and, at that time, the General Secretary of the Congress Party. Rajiv Gandhi's efforts and influence eventually resulted in total NRI holdings in any Indian company being restricted to 5% of the company's outstanding shares. This ruling helped prevent the takeover of Escorts, though a long three-year battle between the Nandas, Swraj Paul, the Reserve Bank of India, and the government of India remained before the situation was finally resolved in Escorts' favour. The Nanda family purchased back Swarj Paul's shares at a premium.

These events left an indelible mark on Escorts. Management at Escorts remained sensitive to their susceptibility to a takeover, and later strategies reflected the desire not to increase their exposure to this threat. By 1993, equity held by financial institutions remained high, but had dropped to 48%, while the Nandas' holdings had increased to 20%.

ESCORTS: PRE-LIBERALIZATION

Organizational Structure

Prior to 1991, the Escorts group of companies comprised a number of subsidiary and associate companies, technical collaborations, and joint ventures. Twenty separate business entities existed in the Escorts group. These entities were organized under a broad directive which divided marketing and manufacturing functions. Each entity had a separate mandate that may or may have not been related to the mandate of another entity. Thus, considerable overlap existed between these business entities. A typical example was tractors.

Historically, Escorts had been India's largest producer of tractors in the 25 to 50 hp range. Prior to 1993, tractors were produced by two separate divisions: one was a farm equipment manufacturing division, and the other was a manufacturing joint venture first with Ford, and then with Ford New Holland which was taken over by Fiat-Agri. The first division operated two manufacturing plants, the second, one plant. Both the divisions had complete autonomy in sourcing, manpower and other administrative decisions, and acted as profit centres. Both division heads reported directly to H. P. Nanda, then the Managing Director and Chairman of Escorts. The divisions produced tractors under the Escorts and Ford names, and these brands were sold through a third division, the Farm Equipment division, responsible only for the distribution and sale of tractors.

Like the two manufacturing divisions, the farm equipment division acted independently and reported on its own profitability. A fourth division in the broader area of farm equipment, Escorts Claas Limited, a wholly owned subsidiary, was involved in the manufacture of harvester combines. Output from this independent venture was also marketed through the Farm Equipment division.

This system, which separated manufacturing and sales, was utilized in a similar manner across each major product area. Twenty separate entities existed, each with its own division head who reported to the Chairman. Under this system, despite the separation and independence of operations, it became difficult to apportion responsibility between divisions for the failure to meet goals and targets.

Collaborations

Escorts had routinely partnered with foreign companies in technical collaborations and equity joint ventures. Foreign participation benefited Escorts in a number of ways. Escorts swiftly acquired manufacturing capability; often it used an internationally recognized brand name like Yamaha or Ford; and Escorts received technology and product feature upgrades as long as the venture was in existence. Escorts' most successful ventures were the 1990 joint venture with Yamaha, Japan for the manufacture of motorcycles; J.C. Bamford, UK, for the manufacture of earthmoving equipment (1979); Ford, U.S., for the manufacture of low power (less than 50 hp) tractors (1969); Mahle of Germany for the production of piston rings (1959); and Goetze of Germany for the production of pistons (1954).

By the 1980s, through these and other alliances with companies based in England, Germany, Japan, Poland and the U.S., the Escorts group of companies was large. The individual businesses produced or distributed tractors, industrial equipment, two-wheelers, and construction equipment (see Exhibit 3). While each of these products was manufactured for the transport industry, the trends within each product line and the competitive environment faced by each of these businesses were different.

BUSINESSES

Tractors and Farm Equipment

During its three decades of serving the Indian tractor market, Escorts had sold over 500 000 tractors to the farmers of India. Tractors produced under the Ford name had sold 300 000 units and Escorts brand tractors, 200 000 units. Ford tractors were larger and operated at the 50 hp level. Tractors sold under the Escorts name ranged between 25 and 47 hp. Tractors in India tended to be smaller and less expensive than those sold in North America, Europe and Australia, making the Indian market quite unique. The usage patterns of tractors in India differed as well. Tractors purchased in Western markets were usually used exclusively on the farm, and often in conjunction with a variety of application specific implements. In India, a tractor had to be as versatile as a pickup truck. Less than 50% of the time, a tractor was used directly for farming purposes; the majority of the time, the tractor acted as a mode of transportation, moving people and goods from one place to another along the nation's rural roads and highways.

The majority of tractors produced by Escorts and other manufacturers in India like Eicher were sold in the north of India. Escorts' tractor sales were concentrated in three northern states: 28.5% of tractor sales were in Uttar Pradesh, 16.8% in Punjab and 12.5% in Haryana. These states were engaged more in wheat than rice production and Escorts' tractors were designed for use in the relatively drier fields used in wheat production. For example, the tractors' brake systems and horsepower levels made them unsuitable for use in wet paddy fields. However, as agricultural patterns changed in India, Escorts expected tractor requirements to change. Agriculture was becoming more sophisticated, and more market niches were being created, leading to larger markets for more specialized equipment. For example, the wheel base of an Escorts' tractor would have to be widened and clearances increased for it to be suitable for cotton farming. Other agricultural innovations would require further modifications. Uniformity in tractors was expected to decrease in the move toward application-driven designs.

A joint venture, Escorts Claas Ltd., produced harvester combines for domestic and international markets. Domestic sales accounted for half of the revenues of this subsidiary and were to South Indian markets. South-East Asian markets were the primary destination for export sales. ECL planned to continue concentrating on these regions with volumes increasing to five times present levels in the coming years. A redesigned model of the current combine was to be introduced to northern Indian markets in 1995–96.

The farm equipment/tractor industry had a number of strong competitors. In the 1990s, Mahindra had displaced Escorts and assumed the market leader position. Mahindra had displaced Escorts through technical innovations, such as a better designed engine which had greater fuel and power efficiency, and through a marketing innovation, a 3-cylinder 30 hp engine which had a more powerful and attractive image than the standard 2-cylinder 30 hp engine. Mahindra, which had a technology relationship with International Harvester, held a 24.9% share in the tractor market and produced other transportation-related equipment like jeeps and engines. The company had a turnover almost double that of Escorts at Rs. 21 billion.

Escorts, currently the number two producer, held a 21.1% share, which was split between Escort branded and Ford branded tractors: 9.2% of the market was held by the Ford 50 hp model; 11.9% of the market was held by the Escorts brand, with 35 hp models accounting for 60% of sales within the group, 25 hp models 25%, and 45 hp models 15%.

The number three producer was Tractors and Farm Equipment (TAFE), which produced tractors more applicable to paddy farming, and received technology support from Massey-Ferguson. TAFE's share was 17.2%. Punjab Tractors, the fourth largest competitor, received some support from the Punjab government and had several external collaborators. In the past few years, the share of Punjab Tractors had increased from 10.9% to 14.1%. Eicher competed in the 18–25 hp range with technology acquired from Germany a number of years ago. Eicher had an 11.1% market share. Hindustan Machines Tools (HMT) with a 10.2% share was the last major producer in this market. HMT had a collaborative agreement with Zetor of the Czech Republic. Several smaller manufacturers competed for the remainder of this market.

Bi-Wheelers

The bi-wheeler market was composed of three segments: motorcycles, scooters and mopeds. In 1993, Escorts participated solely in the motorcycle segment which it had entered in the early 1960s, though the moped segment would be entered in 1994. In the early 1970s, the Escorts (Rajdoot) motorcycle, Escorts GTS, became widely known after being depicted in the 1972 blockbuster movie, *Bobby*. The GTS, ridden by the hero of the film and known as the Bobby, was a generational icon widely desired by school boys and university students growing up in 1970s India. The Rajdoot 175cc, the traditional Escorts motorcycle, was, as measured by unit sales, the most successful motorcycle line in India. It was the only motorcycle brand in India to have sold more than a million units.

In 1985, Escorts introduced a new 100cc motorcycle. This motorcycle, the Yamaha RX 100, was developed in a collaborative venture with Yamaha of Japan. Yamaha provided the technology for production of the Yamaha RX 100, and Escorts provided the land, factory and distribution system. In 1990, Yamaha became an active partner in this venture. The partnership, initiated by Escorts in 1981, was one of many collaborations between Indian and Japanese companies for the manufacture of motorcycles. Also in the mid 1980s, the three other major Japanese motorcycle manufacturers—Suzuki, Kawasaki and Honda—became active in the Indian market. By the time Escorts' application to produce 100cc motorcycles was sanctioned, several other joint ventures such as Hero Honda, TVS Suzuki and Bajaj Kawasaki were operating and selling motorcycles.

In 1993, Escorts' position in the motorcycle segment was strong. Production of the Yamaha RX 100 cc motorcycle had been 95% indigenized and Escorts was searching for a partner to develop a four-stroke engine, to counter similar product developments by Hero Honda and Bajaj Kawasaki. Recently, however, there had been an industry-wide downturn in sales (see Exhibit 6). Further, with liberalization, foreign investment in the automotive sector was subject to automatic approval and competition was expected to intensify. Escorts was formulating plans to move into the scooter segment in a collaboration with a foreign partner.

Other Businesses

Escorts produced a variety of component parts for automobiles, motorcycles, tractors and construction machinery in its components businesses. This portion of Escorts' business, more than any other, enjoyed substantial and growing overseas demand for its product.

A fourth business area was industrial and construction equipment in which Escorts manufactured and marketed a diverse range of construction, road building and material handling equipment.

A variety of other business areas completed the Escorts group of companies. Railway ancillaries, financial services, telecommunications (Escorts was planning to form a joint venture with First Pacific, a Hong Kong-based firm, to provide cellular services in India) and health care (included in the group of companies was the Escorts Heart Institute and Research Centre) were a few of the other industries in which Escorts competed.

LIBERALIZATION

The Indian economy had been slowly liberalizing through the 1980s, but it was not until 1991 that changes were initiated to make the market truly accessible and desirable to foreign investors. Changes in industrial policy at this time were designed to attract foreign direct investment and to encourage technology collaboration agreements between Indian and foreign firms. The changes substantially abolished industrial licensing, facilitated foreign direct investment and technology transfer, and opened up areas previously reserved for the public sector to the private sector. The areas still reserved for the public sector were those of national strategic concern such as defense, railways and atomic energy.

Liberalization in trade policy resulted in the dismantling of the system of export and import licensing, and included a scaling down of tariff barriers. Most goods could now be imported freely, with quantitative restrictions on imports of capital goods and intermediate products almost completely removed. Tariff reductions were substantial. Prior to July 1991, tariff rates were as high as 300%. By 1993, the average tariff rate was 65%. For capital goods, tariff rates were lower at 20–40% and for goods and equipment used for export-oriented projects, tariffs were nil.

The initial results of liberalization were positive. GDP growth increased from less than 1% in 1991–92, to a projected 5.3% in 1994–95. The dollar value of imports and exports grew by 25% in this same period, while foreign direct investment (FDI), led by firms based in the United States, tripled. In addition, numerous multinationals had established a presence in India in the early 1990s (see Exhibit 4). Sectorally, FDI was distributed across many industries, with primary sectors such as fuels, oil refining and power receiving the largest share of FDI (see Exhibit 5).

Shortly after liberalization, interest in the stock market surged. Investors from all walks of life emerged and the Bombay Stock Index more than doubled from its January 24, 1992, position at 2200, to its peak of 4500 in April of the same year. However, the euphoria of investors was smothered under the weight of falling stock prices in the late-April 1992 stock scandal and crash of the Bombay Index. Investors suffered substantial losses in the index's rapid 1500 point decline. The index continued to decline slowly and rested at the 2500 level in early 1993.

Many of the investors caught in the crash represented India's large and emerging middle-class. These individuals purchased the bulk of consumer products such as white goods, electronic equipment, bi-wheelers and four wheelers. However, as a result of the crash, their purchasing power was diminished and consumption of these products declined. The poor financial health of these consumers was exacerbated by the reluctance of banks to lend during 1992 when the rupee was devalued and inflation continued to be high.

Escorts' managers attributed the poor performance of Escorts to this decline in the stock market, the concomitant decline in purchasing power of middle-class consumers, and a sector specific decline in the automotive industry. Supporting this explanation was the sluggish motorcycle market in 1991 and 1992 (see Exhibit 6), although by 1993 this market had rebounded. Overall, the economic picture was positive and strong growth was expected through the mid-1990s.

ESCORTS: POST-LIBERALIZATION

Liberalization in India had stimulated growth across most sectors; however, Escorts suffered through two years of stagnant growth and declining profits immediately following liberalization (see Exhibit 1). Also, Escorts had recently lost its market leader position in the tractor market to Mahindra, a company which had performed well following liberalization (see Exhibit 2). In 1993, the Corporate Strategic Planning Department (CSPD) was created. The department was charged with the task of navigating Escorts through its period of adjustment, and with charting Escorts' future course through the uncertain waters of the Indian economy.

Growth Opportunities

The CSPD recognized that liberalization had created several new opportunities, along with new threats, in the various markets in which Escorts participated. For example, the domestic tractor market was opened to foreign competitors. However, despite the size and growth potential of the agricultural sector in India, Escorts did not expect a large number of new entrants to this industry. New competitors required a distribution system which reached into India's numerous villages and agricultural communities, and they required a product suitable for the small scale of Indian agriculture (see the Appendix B for a description of Escorts' unique distribution system). The 25–50 hp tractor models which were sold in India were difficult for foreign competitors from Western markets, who produced 100–125 hp tractors, to emulate. Tractor manufacturers based in countries like Japan and Taiwan produced tractors suitable for rice cultivation on very small, terraced paddy fields. Also, new entrants to the tractor industry had to contend with the considerable goodwill Escorts had created during its years of serving rural agricultural markets.

The bi-wheeler segment, already a global industry, was expected to become much more competitive in future years. Escorts had to become more competitive in this sector by better utilizing its distribution system, and by developing motorcycles which were technologically competitive with those of similar size sold in world markets. Escorts sold 16 000 to 18 000 motorcycles in international markets, accounting for about 20% of this division's sales. However, exports of these motorcycles were restricted by Yamaha, its joint venture partner.

Automotive components was Escorts' most globally competitive business. Growth in this area was expected to come from both domestic and international markets. Telecommunications was also seen as a key growth area by Escorts, though it was a new business area for Escorts. Further, Escorts believed that as it moved through the 1990s, leadership in markets would be related to technical strengths. Accordingly, a Research Centre employing 220 engineers and technicians (total employment at Escorts was approximately 25 000 people) had been recently established with the mandate to upgrade existing products and develop new products in anticipation of consumer needs.

A PLAN OF RESPONSE

Management at Escorts' CSPD had evaluated these changes in the Indian economy against Escorts' current position and strategy. Clearly, conditions in India had changed; new opportunities had opened up, and a general sense of optimism pervaded the business community. However, Escorts' recent performance had been poor, and the industries in which it competed were becoming more dynamic while evolving in different directions.

Escorts had to respond to these diverse changes, and several options existed. The company could choose to consolidate its assorted businesses; it could grow aggressively in new product areas like telecommunications; or it could expand the scope of its current businesses. While the managers in the CSPD had to select one of these three options, or develop another, they also had to decide on the focus of the company. Whichever of these options was chosen, it would set the company's strategic direction for the years to come.

EXHIBIT 1 **Summary of Escorts Ltd.'s Operations (1984–93)** Rs. Crores

	1984	*1985*	*1986*	*1987*	*1988–89*	*1989–90*	*1990–91*	*1991–92*	*1992–93*
Total Income	328	378	385	482	783	770	976	1 093	982
Cost of Sales	307	350	361	450	736	711	891	1 038	930
Interest	8	11	16	20	26	24	25	34	43
Profit Before Tax	13	18	9	13	21	35	53	21	9
Tax	5	1	1	0	3	12	20	8	0
Profit After Tax	9	17	8	7	18	23	33	13	9
Dividend	3	3	3	5	9	10	12	10	7
Retained Profits	6	14	5	2	10	12	22	3	2

Notes: 1. 1 Crore equals Rs. 10 000 000. Exchange rates varied considerably during this nine-year period. At the end of 1993, US$1 equaled Rs. 30.77.

2. Escorts Ltd. is the largest company in the Escorts group. In the Escorts group of companies, agribusiness accounted for 46% of revenues, bi-wheelers for 20%, automotive components for 22%, construction equipment for 8%. The remaining 4% came from a variety of activities.

SOURCE: Company records.

EXHIBIT 2 **India's Top 25 Companies by Sales (1993)**

Rank	*Company*	*Industry*	*Sales*	*1993 % Rise (fall)*	*Pretax Profit*	*1993 % Rise (fall)*
1	ITC	Conglomerate	37 408	26.0	4 219	31.1
2	Tata Steel	Steel	33 521	20.3	5 450	(6.8)
3	Reliance Industries	Conglomerate	31 086	35.1	8 809	53.3
4	Tata Engineering (TELCO)	Vehicles	28 758	(4.9)	3 276	(21.2)
5	Hindustan Lever	Consumer Products	20 868	17.5	2 177	22.7
6	Larsen & Toubro	Engineering	18 875	34.8	3 058	1.5
7	Grasim Industries	Textiles	17 480	18.8	2 800	5.4
8	Associated Cement	Cement	15 202	7.3	1 807	(39.2)
9	Mahindra & Mahindra	Vehicles	14 252	23.7	1 204	(4.7)
10	Bajaj Auto	Vehicles	12 430	2.4	2 109	2.7
11	Century Textiles	Textiles	11 969	9.0	2 422	(15.3)
12	Southern Petro	Fertilizers	11 676	14.6	1 447	32.1
13	Gujarat State Fertilizer	Fertilizers	10 515	3.1	2 064	6.7
14	JK Synthetics	Textiles	10 142	1.7	1 134	(25.8)
15	Hindalco Industries	Aluminum	9 755	14.0	2 748	35.0
16	Ballarpur Ind.	Conglomerate	9 586	9.7	1 604	8.6
17	Ashok Leyland	Vehicles	9 544	(7.4)	1 196	3.9
18	Escorts	Conglomerate	9 385	(11.4)	697	(2.1)
19	MRF	Tires	8 469	13.9	869	8.5
20	Indian Rayon	Textiles	8 092	22.3	1 772	26.2
21	Bombay Suburban	Utility	7 976	40.3	1 236	66.4
22	Peico	Electronics	7 970	7.0	721	(23.3)
23	Crompton Greaves	Electrical Products	7 804	8.3	773	6.1
24	ICI India	Chemicals	7 792	10.1	823	(11.0)
25	Indian Aluminum	Aluminum	7 617	15.6	968	10.4

Note: All monetary values are in millions of rupees.

SOURCE: *Economic Times*, Research Bureau.

EXHIBIT 3   A Profile of Escorts' Product Lines (1990s)

Product/Business	Collaboration	Licensed Capacity	Installed Capacity	Quantity Produced (1993)
Agricultural Tractors	Fiat Geotech, Italy		28 000	
	Ursus, Poland			
	Ford, U.S.	42 500	15 500	27 876
Harvester Combines	Claas OHG, Germany		100	
Motorcycles	Yamaha, Japan			
	Cekop, Poland	500 000	210 000	114 702
Pistons	Mahle GmbH, Germany	3 750 000	4 500 000	3 839 920
Piston Rings	Goetze AG, Germany	Delicensed	34 800 000	31 931 587
Shock Absorbers	Fichtel & Sach, Germany		2 875 000	1 658 979
	Aygyst Bilmstein GmbH			
Telescopic Front Fork	Kayaba, Japan	2 781 250		counted in shocks
Struts	Kayaba, Japan			
Railway Ancillaries	Knorr Bremise, Germany	N.A.	N.A.	35 000
Carburetors (for 4 wheeled vehicles)	Mikuni, Japan	N.A.	600 000	N.A.
Clutch Assemblies	Fuji, Japan	N.A.	10 000 000	N.A.
CDI Magnetos	IIC, Japan	N.A.	100 000 sets	N.A.
Hydraulic Products, Automatic Valves	Herion-Werke, GmbH	N.A.	30 000	N.A.
Cranes	Faun, Germany	413	200	217
	R & R, Germany			
Excavator Loaders	J.C. Bamford Excavators Ltd.		900	646
Compactors	Dynapac, Sweden	875	30	16
VSAT Satellite Communication Systems	Hughes Network Systems	N.A.	N.A.	N.A.
Telecommunications	JS Telecom Bosch, France	62 500 lines	62 500 lines	10 750 lines

SOURCE: Company records.

EXHIBIT 4   **Examples of Multinationals in India**

Market		Multinational	Brand
Consumer Durables	Passenger Cars	Suzuki General Motors Daimler Benz Peugeot	Maruti - Suzuki Opel - Astra Mercedes - Benz Peugeot 309
	Motorcycles	Suzuki Kawasaki Honda Yamaha	Suzuki Kawasaki Bajaj Hero Honda, Kinetic Honda (scooter) Escorts Yamaha
	White Goods/ Home Appliances	General Electric Bosch Sanyo Phillips	Godrej - GE IFB Bosch BPL - Sanyo Whirlpool, Electrolux, National
Consumer Non-Durables	Soaps and Detergents	Unilever Proctor & Gamble Henkel	Surf, Lux, Le Sancy, etc. Camay, Head & Shoulders, etc. Henko
	Personal Care	Colgate-Palmolive Ciba-Geigy Reckitt & Colman Gillette	Colgate Cibaca Dettol Gillette
	Food and Beverages	Unilever Nestlé Cadbury Schweppes PepsiCo Coke Kelloggs	Lipton, Brooke Bond, Wall's Nestle, Cerelac, Polo Cadbury Pepsi, Pizza Hut, Kentucky Fried Chicken Coca-Cola Kelloggs
	Apparel	Coats Viyella Benetton Lacoste	Louis Phillippe, Van Heusen Benetton Lacoste

SOURCE: Economic Coordination Unit, Government of India, *India: Business Perspectives,* 1994.

EXHIBIT 5   **Sectoral Distribution of FDI approvals (early 1990s)**

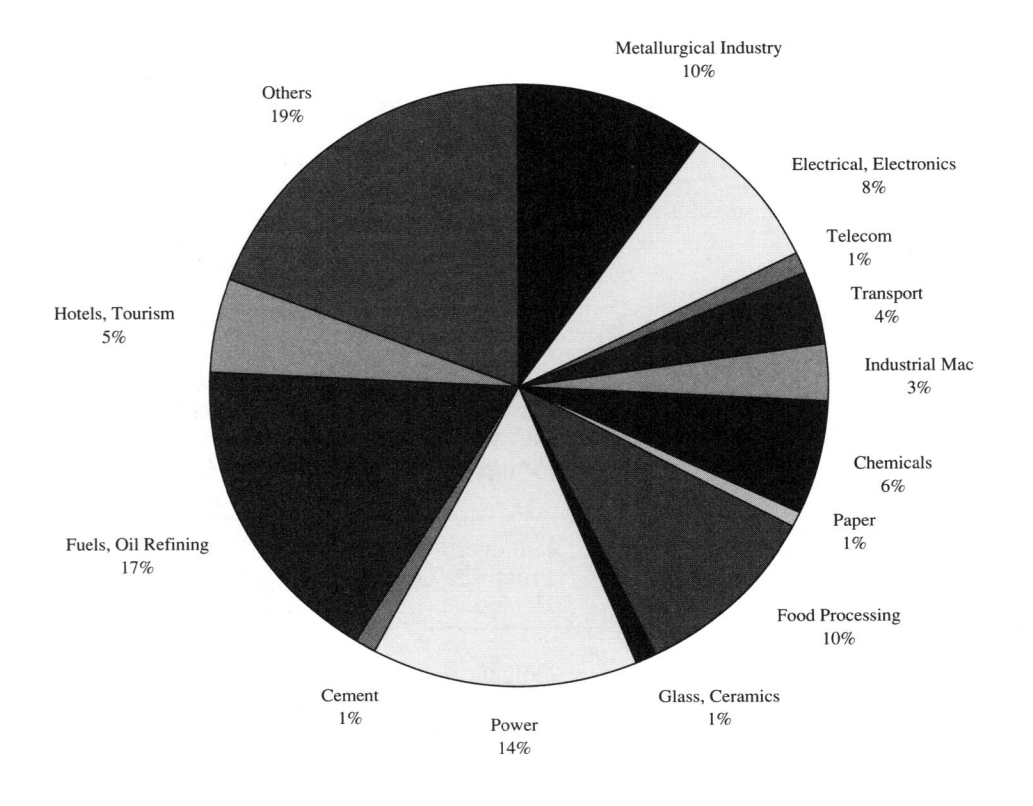

Metallurgical Industry	9.56%	Food Processing	9.77%
Electrical, Electronic	7.89%	Glass, Ceramics	1.32%
Telecom	1.33%	Power	14.03%
Transport	3.56%	Cement	1.11%
Industrial Machinery	2.51%	Fuels, Oil Refining	16.83%
Chemicals	6.49%	Hotels, Tourism	5.02%
Paper	1.15%	Others	19.58%

SOURCE: Economic Coordination Unit, Government of India, *India: Business Perspectives,* 1994.

EXHIBIT 6   Trends in the Motorcycle Market in India

	1981–85	*1986–89*	*1990*	*1991*	*1992*	*1993*
Rajdoot 350*	4 204	—	—	—	—	—
Rajdoot 175cc*	337 948	331 960	85 516	53 502	46 789	58 310
Escorts HD (GTS)*	6 320	—	—	—	—	—
Yamaha RX 100*	0	126 356	68 509	64 100	46 483	56 399
Bajaj KB100/4S	0	65 723	49 083	33 252	34 015	42 134
Ideal Jawa 250cc	150 680	5 848	0	630	2 519	5 866
Enfield/Explorer	111 818	28 185	26 967	17 130	17 677	16 360
Hero Honda	13 292	120 058	135 001	127 803	148 134	183 671
TVS Suzuki AX100	39 482	37 043	33 746	30 085	53 120	87 220
TOTAL**	762 011	1 405 522	471 429	373 417	397 019	466 936

Notes: 1. * Indicates products of Escorts group.
2. ** Total does not include other smaller manufacturers not listed in the table.
3. Total motorcycle sales were forecasted to increase by 100 000 units in 1994 and 1995. By 1996, annual sales of motorcycles in India were forecasted to be 700 000 units.
4. Demand for mopeds was similar to that for motorcycles, while demand for scooters was approximately double that of motorcycles.

SOURCE: Company records, Government of India documents.

APPENDIX A   Escorts – Yamaha Joint Venture

Escorts had two plants manufacturing motorcycles. One plant, located in Faridabad, was wholly designed and operated by Escorts. The other plant in Surajpur commenced operations in 1986. Originally, the Surajpur plant was operated by Escorts and produced Yamaha motorcycles under a licensing agreement with Yamaha. In 1990, a new plant was established in the Surajpur location.

Yamaha participated more actively in designing and operating this plant. The plant employed a new, younger workforce and new forms of work organization were introduced. Training was a common theme in this plant. Senior managers, technical personnel and supervisors underwent extensive training which included short two to six week stints in Japan. Workers received two weeks, training prior to going on to the shop floor. Thereafter, a group of new workers would undergo further training in which they were directed by a group of ten Japanese and ten Indian trainers. The cycle between shop-floor and off the shop-floor training was repeated for several months. Formal training continued throughout the employment span of the worker, with monetary rewards accompanying the acquisition of new skills.

The plant followed a typical Japanese design with work organized on a cellular basis. Work teams were responsible for each cell, and workers were trained to perform a multitude of tasks within a cell. Each machine operator was responsible for and able to work a number of machines unlike in the Faridabad plant where one worker was assigned to just one machine. Just-in-time practices were also adopted.

The results of the Surajpur plant, in comparison to the Faridabad plant, were impressive (see table). The Surajpur plant was much more efficient than the plant in Faridabad, and produced nearly the same number of motorcycles with a workforce 6.4 times smaller.

TABLE Comparison of Surajpur and Faridabad Plants, 1990

Plant	Annual Output (# of Motorcycles)	Number of Workers	Output per Worker	Change Over Time	Inventory Inputs
Surajpur	77 500	625	124	30–60 minutes	15–30 days
Faridabad	96 000	4 000	24	8 hours	3–6 months

SOURCE: Transnational Corporations and Management Division, *Transnational Corporations and the Transfer of New Management Practices to Developing Countries*. New York: United Nations.

APPENDIX B Escorts Dealers' Development Association Limited

Distribution in India was challenging. The nation's urban population was concentrated in the 21 cities which had populations greater than one million people. The rural population was less concentrated. Hundreds of millions of people lived in the 640 000 villages that dotted India's countryside. Escorts' distribution channels had to reach into both rural and urban segments as its two main product areas, farm equipment and bi-wheelers, had greater sales in rural and urban regions, respectively.

Escorts' extensive dealer network had grown incrementally during the company's 50 years of operations. More than 500 dealers serviced the farm equipment customer segment and 700 dealers retailed bi-wheelers. These dealers, dispersed across this large and populous nation, were welded together into a large, cohesive network termed the Escort Dealers' Development Association Limited (EDDAL). This network permitted Escorts to constantly upgrade the quality of tractor and motorcycle dealerships while imparting a sense of unity to the dealers.

The philosophy behind the network was one of assistance and mentorship. Larger dealers helped smaller dealers. Through EDDAL financial assistance, training programs, and managerial education programs were offered to dealers. In this sense, EDDAL was a mutual benefit association which promoted the shared business interests of all the dealers.

Of the 14 directors in this association, 11 were dealers themselves. From the 191 dealer members that comprised EDDAL when it was formed in 1977, membership had increased to 818 by 1993. Funding for EDDAL came from the dealers themselves, who contributed a set amount for each unit sold, and from Escorts, which contributed a larger set amount. EDDAL's cash reserve was greater than Rs. 1 crore. Most recently, in response to the increased acceptance of debt purchasing by Indian consumers, Escorts was encouraging EDDAL member dealers to jointly establish refinancing programs to assist with the financing of bi-wheeler purchases.

MANAGING STRATEGIC CHANGE

PART

9

WESTMILLS CARPETS LIMITED
(CONDENSED)

Joseph N. Fry

CASE

31

"**W**e are in quite a pickle with Westmills, and in dire need of a rescue program," said Derek Mather, Senior Vice-President of Canadian Enterprise Development Corporation Ltd. (CED), a venture capital company with a major equity position in the Calgary-based carpet manufacturer.

> Our losses are continuing and the prospects for early relief are poor since the market is soft and our operations disorganized. The banks are very nervous. Garry Morrison, whom we groomed for a year, has just resigned after two months as president. Harry Higson, his predecessor, is filling in on a stopgap basis, but neither Harry, the board, nor the banks want this to continue for more than a few weeks. The balance of the management team look promising but are as yet untested.
>
> As shareholders, we (CED) have to sort out our options and position on this investment, but the matter, for me, is a personal one as well. I've just been asked to step in as president, at least until we are in position to hire a new man. I'd appreciate your views on where to go from here.

THE CANADIAN CARPET INDUSTRY

The carpet industry in Canada, as it is presently known, had its beginnings in the late 1950s with the introduction of carpet tufting technology from the United States. Tufting was a low cost, flexible process for producing carpets of various qualities and styles. The new production capability coincided with expanding affluence in the Canadian marketplace and a prolonged boom in residential construction. Carpet sales grew dramatically in the 1960s and early 1970s, reaching a volume of 74 million square metres in 1975.

The growth of the Canadian market slowed in 1976 and 1977 with total sales of 76.5 million and 78.6 million square metres respectively. Nevertheless, Canadian consumption of 3.4 metres per capita was approaching that of the United States.

Between 85% and 90% of Canadian sales were domestically produced. Imports were limited to the less price-sensitive segments of the market by a tariff of 20% plus $.375 per square metre.

Carpet Manufacture

A tufted carpet was made in three principal sequential production steps: the tufting itself, dyeing and finishing. Equipment and process flexibilities were such that in each step there were a number of design options (Figure 1). By pursuing combinations of these options, carpet mills,

FIGURE 1   Main Steps in Tufted Carpet Manufacture

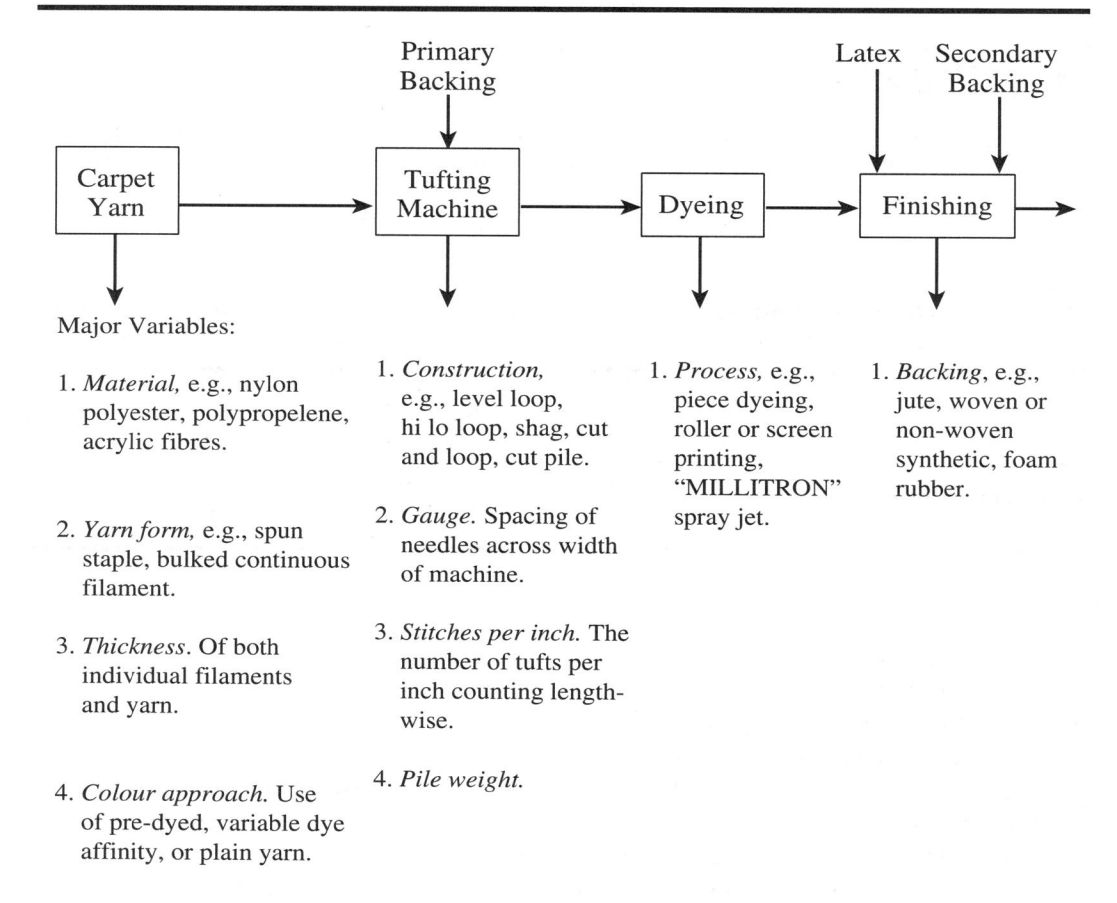

within the constraints of their particular equipment configuration, could produce a variety of carpet lines. A major mill might produce over 25 different products and each of these would be produced in 10 to 15 different colours. This capacity for diversity had the effect of complicating both manufacturing operations and the nature of competition in the industry.

As noted in Figure 1, there was a variety of construction possibilities open for the design of carpets for particular functional and/or aesthetic purposes. A level loop pile design made with relatively coarse nylon yarn might be developed for a heavy-traffic commercial application, for example, or a plush, cut pile design of fine yarn might be produced for a high fashion location. Different carpet designs implied different materials costs and processing efficiency. The actual design decision was thus a mixture of craft, science and economics, as aim was taken at a particular target product market and a balance was struck between fashion, function and production costs.

The value added in carpet manufacture was relatively low in relation to the total value of the finished product. Purchased materials typically amounted to 75% or more of total costs, plant labour 5% and general overhead 20%. Production scheduling was a critical function in carpet mills—the challenge was to maintain customer service on the one hand and avoid excessive inventories, with their built-in working-capital demands and fashion risks, on the other hand.

Carpet Marketing

The Canadian carpet market was comprised of three major segments; retail, residential contract and commercial contract. An approximate division of the market into these categories is given in Table 1.

TABLE 1   The Canadian and Western Canadian Carpet Markets by Segment, 1977 (estimated volume in million square metres)

	Retail	Residential Contract	Commercial Contract	Total
Canadian market	51.0 (65%)	14.0 (17.8%)	13.4 (17.2%)	78.5
Western Canadian	8.8 (40.2%)	7.6 (34.7%)	5.5 (25.1%)	21.9

SOURCE: Canadian Carpet Institute, casewriter's estimates.

Retail Market

The typical retail customer was a homeowner purchasing a relatively small amount of carpet for first-time or replacement installation. The rough order of importance of purchase criteria in the retail market was generally cited as colour, style (texture), price, dealer service and guarantees. There was a very low awareness of brand names in the market, with perhaps only Harding (a carpet manufacturer) and DuPont (fibre supplier) having any significant recognition. Similarly, consumers had very little knowledge of the technical characteristics of carpets and the variables that would influence wear and care.

The retail market was serviced by a wide variety of outlets, including department stores, specialty floorcovering dealers, promotional carpet warehouses, furniture stores and home decoration centres. These outlets, depending upon their volume, their proximity to the mill and the manufacturer's distribution strategy, were in turn supplied directly from the mill, by mill-owned distributors or by independent distributors. The approximate proportions of the retail market serviced by mill-direct, mill-owned distributor and independent distributor were for Canada 35%, 45% and 20% respectively, and for western Canada 25%, 40% and 35%. The trend in the previous decade had been for the mills to seek greater control of their distribution by implementing mill-direct or mill-owned distribution programs.

RESIDENTIAL CONTRACT This market consisted of home/apartment/condominium builders and mobile home manufacturers. It was serviced directly or through contract dealer/installers. Builder preferences tended toward basic carpet styles at price points below those popular in the retail and commercial markets. Order sizes were quite large and price competition was severe, with orders switching on differentials as low as 5 to 10 cents a metre. Assuming price and style competitiveness, service elements—and particularly the dependability of delivery—were important in maintaining mill/account relationships (Table 2).

TABLE 2   Ranking of Channel Service Aspects by Segment

Service Item*	Retail	Residential Contract	Commercial Contract
Speed of delivery	2	4	
Delivery when promised	1	1	1
Update of samples	4		3
Complaint handling	3	2	
Notification of price changes			4
Regular representative contact		3	2

* Original lists contained many additional items such as mill warranties, co-op advertising, salesperson personality, etc.
SOURCE: Westmills research files.

COMMERCIAL CONTRACT The commercial market consisted of new or replacement installations in offices, hotels, retail outlets, schools, etc. The majority of commercial business was controlled by specialty installation firms that purchased directly from the mills. Unlike residential contract sales, the product was usually specified for particular projects by architects and interior designers on the basis of information from many sources (building owner, project manager, architect, etc.). The most popular styles were patterned multi-colour carpets with specific wear characteristics for the intended use.

Competitive Structure

There were 28 firms engaged in the manufacture of tufted carpet in Canada in 1977. These firms could be divided into three categories on the basis of their scale, scope of activities and degree of integration in marketing and manufacturing.

GROUP 1 This group consisted of firms with sales of $20 million or more, wide product lines and, in most cases, yarn spinning and substantial captive distribution operations. Operating results for the five firms in this group are summarized in Table 3. Together these firms accounted for somewhat less than 50% of the carpet market.

TABLE 3 **Summary Performance of Major Carpet Firms ($000 000s)**

		1977	*1976*	*1975*
Harding Carpets	Sales	$73.0	$74.5	$58.7
(as of Oct. 31)	Profit before tax	(.2)	3.0	2.1
Celanese Canada	Sales	37.6	39.0	47.7
Carpet Division	Profit before tax	(5.5)	(4.1)	.9
(as of Dec. 31)				
Peerless Rug	Sales	40.0	37.8	32.4
(as of Feb. 28)	Profit before tax	.6	.9	(.7)
Peeters Carpets	Sales	22.0(est)	22.0 (est)	20.0
Westmills	Sales	21.7	23.1	21.7
(as of Aug. 31)	Profit before tax	(1.5)	(2.4)	(.7)

SOURCE: Corporate financial reports.

GROUP 2 This group consisted of approximately eight firms with sales ranging from $10 to $20 million. They were generally somewhat more specialized than the Group 1 firms in product line or geographic market coverage. Most were private firms or divisions of U.S. manufacturers, with the result that specific financial data are not available.

GROUP 3 The balance of the industry consisted of small firms specializing in particular product, channel or geographic markets. Firms with sales as low as $2 million were apparently viable operations. Such firms might use pre-dyed yarns exclusively in order to limit operations to tufting and minimal finishing.

As the total market grew in the 1960s and early 1970s, entry had been relatively easy. By 1977 there was substantially more capacity in the Canadian industry than was justified by current demand. Excess capacity, coupled with a fragmented industry structure and the dynamics of style obsolescence, had led to fierce competition, price cutting and a deterioration of industry profitability.

Style competition was a major aspect of rivalry in the industry, stemming from a heterogeneous and fashion-conscious market on the one side and flexible manufacturing on the other. The benefits of design innovations were frequently short-lived, however, as other manufacturers "knocked-off" the popular styles. The time lag before a new innovation could be imitated by competitors was as short as six to nine months. With lasting product advantages difficult to achieve, success in specific markets often turned on price and a mill's ability to deliver high quality and excellent service.

WESTMILLS' BACKGROUND

Westmills Carpets Limited was incorporated in February 1966 in Kelowna, British Columbia. The company was (and remained through 1977) the only carpet manufacturer in the west. The intention was to capitalize on the fast-growing mass housing markets in British Columbia and Alberta through the manufacture of a relatively narrow range of tufted carpet products. Westmills commenced production in September of 1966 and by 1969 had sales of $2.4 million.

Early Growth

After some start-up difficulties, Westmills capitalized on the emerging popularity of shag carpet to fully establish its operations. Growth accelerated and facilities were expanded. In 1970, a distribution centre was opened in Winnipeg. In 1971, the Kelowna distribution facility was enlarged and sales were commenced in Ontario. In 1972, the capacity of the Kelowna plant was almost doubled.

The pace of activity increased even further in 1973 as the company moved to become a national manufacturer and distributor. "We felt we were an awfully clever carpet company," Derek Mather recalled, "and that we might as well be clever on a national scale."

In January 1973, Westmills acquired Globe Mills of Meaford, Ontario, in a move to reduce its dependence on outside yarn suppliers. In February, Westmills was converted to a public company. "This provided additional equity money for the company and an opportunity for the original investors to realize a profit," Mather explained. Financial statements for Westmills from 1973 onward are given in Exhibits 1 and 2.

Later in 1973, Westmills acquired the assets of Centennial Carpets in Trenton, Ontario. Further, to expand the company's marketing base, major exclusive distributors were appointed in Quebec and Ontario. By the end of 1973, Westmills had manufacturing plants in Kelowna, Meaford and Trenton and distribution facilities in Vancouver, Calgary, Winnipeg and Trenton.

"In retrospect it was overconfidence, but we felt awfully good about ourselves at that time," said Mather. Markets remained buoyant in early 1974. In Kelowna, however, the company was becoming entangled in changing political jurisdictions with different views and rules affecting plant effluent. Since this posed uncertainties and constraints on operation and expansion, a decision was made to move all dyeing operations to Calgary. This transfer to a purchased 13 000 square foot plant was initiated during the year. Distribution in Calgary continued to be handled through a separate 8000 square foot facility. The fiscal year (to August 31, 1974) closed strong, with the company booking record sales and profits.

Decline

In the last quarter of 1974, the carpet market across Canada turned soft and Westmills' fortunes started to sag. For the first time, the company faced significant price and style competition and found itself overextended.

In 1975, the Kelowna plant was completely closed and all manufacturing equipment was moved to Calgary for installation on an ongoing basis in 1975 and early 1976. The Trenton manufacturing facility and distribution centre were also closed. Sales volumes were maintained near $22 million but gross margins slipped from 23.4% in 1974 to 16.5% in 1975 and a before-tax loss of $715 000 was incurred (Exhibit 1).

Markets remained soft in 1976 and Westmills further consolidated facilities and attempted to reduce costs. The Winnipeg distribution centre was closed; now all carpet manufacturing and distribution was handled out of Calgary. Cost reductions were hampered by the need to re-establish production with an untrained labour force earning in most cases $1.50 more per hour than workers in eastern mills; quality declined, deliveries became erratic, inventory grew and market credibility slipped. In fiscal year 1976, the company experienced a before-tax loss of $2.4 million.

Mather explained,

> Through this period we (the board) were slow to realize that there was something fundamentally wrong with the company and the way it was being run. The market problem, withdrawing from carpet manufacture in the east, and the plant relocation from Kelowna to Calgary, all confused our perception of the real situation.

Management Changes

As poor operation results continued, the Westmills board moved to strengthen management. Mather commented,

> Harry's [Harry Higson, the president] difficulty was in building a team; he couldn't develop strong men around him. As a result, he was working under tremendous pressure and his health was beginning to suffer. The scale of operation wasn't for him and he realized it. But improving management meant going outside. There was no one in a functional job that was near strong enough to step up.

Mr. Garry W. Morrison was hired as executive vice-president in late 1976. Morrison, aged 32, was an American citizen and now a Canadian landed immigrant. He held a B.Sc. in Textile Technology, an M.B.A. and had had seven years of management experience with U.S.-based Riegel Textile Corporation. At Riegel, Morrison had moved quickly through management ranks. Just prior to moving to Westmills, he had been a significant figure in the turnaround of a Canadian division of Riegel. His initial job at Westmills was to back up Harry Higson, but it was generally assumed he would become president in the not too distant future.

Morrison set out to learn the business, address some of the more pressing issues and recruit a second echelon of management.

OPERATING CHANGES From January through August 1977, steps were taken to improve Westmills' financial condition, to cut operating costs and to bolster the product line. The vacant Trenton and Kelowna plants were sold; the former for $915 000 cash and the latter for $200 000 cash plus mortgage receivable for $1 million. The cash proceeds were used to reduce Westmills' long-term indebtedness to its banks and the mortgage was assigned to the banks as additional security. Inventories were reduced by fiscal year-end to about $4.3 million in an attempt to reduce the pressure on interest costs and working-capital levels. Salaried and hourly personnel were cut and more stringent guidelines were introduced for administrative, travel and other expenses. Five new high-end commercial carpet lines and six new residential lines were designed and prepared for introduction in the fall selling season. This brought the total Westmills product range to 34 lines.

MANAGEMENT ADDITIONS In August 1977, Mr. J. William Ford joined Westmills as secretary-treasurer and chief financial officer. Ford, aged 33, was an American citizen and a Canadian landed immigrant. He was also married to a Canadian. He had known and worked with Garry Morrison at Riegel's Canadian subsidiary. Bill Ford's background included undergraduate and graduate studies in management at Virginia Polytechnic and Clemson University; service with the U.S. Army including combat experience and decoration in Vietnam; and experience in senior financial positions in two Canadian-based textile companies. Ford explained his move to Westmills: "Garry didn't pull any punches in describing the situation, but we'd been through a difficult turnaround before and I knew I could work with him. It seemed like a great challenge and opportunity."

At the time, Higson and Morrison were also engaged in negotiations with David Hirst, which would lead to Hirst joining Westmills as vice president of manufacturing in January 1978. Hirst, aged 54, was born in Yorkshire and educated in the UK at Batley Technical College (Textile Engineering) and Bradford Technical College (Cloth Manufacture). He had moved to Canada in 1957 and worked in a variety of carpet-mill plant supervisory and general management positions. Hirst was well known in technical circles in the industry and highly regarded for his capability in carpet design and particularly for designing around equipment constraints. Prior to committing to Westmills, David Hirst had visited Calgary to review the operation and recalled, "It was clear to me that there were also significant opportunities to improve productivity and quality. I welcomed the challenge."

A third senior manager was also hired by Westmills in this period to assume the top marketing position. By the time of the case, however, it was apparent that this appointment was not working out and that the marketing/sales function would have to be covered by James W. Hamilton, the current general sales manager. Hamilton, aged 36, had 18 years' experience in sales and sales management in the floorcovering business. He had started with Westmills in 1971 as a contract sales representative in Vancouver and shortly thereafter had been moved to Toronto to "open up" the east for Westmills. This he had done very successfully and after a short sales management stint with another company had been persuaded by Harry Higson to come back to Calgary and address the now apparent sales problems in the west. He had been general sales manager since mid-1976. Jim Hamilton knew the grassroots workings of the carpet business and had a reputation as a top-flight sales rep and sales manager.

For fiscal year 1977, however, there were no miracle cures. The year closed with another significant loss having to be booked—this time about $1.5 million pretax. Working capital was at a perilous level and the banks were becoming increasingly uneasy about their position. Now the financial as well as operating foundations of the business were deteriorating and the very survival of the firm was coming into question.

THE RECOVERY PLAN

Through the latter part of the 1976–77 fiscal year, Westmills had been working on a recovery plan, which took form at the beginning of the 1977–78 period. The essence of the plan was to reduce the company's product/market base somewhat, but maintain or improve volume by achieving greater penetration in the commercial and retail markets in western Canada. At the same time, steps would be taken to relieve financial pressure through the sale and lease-back of the Calgary plant. Projections for the 1978 fiscal year, which management regarded as conservative, are given in Exhibits 3 and 4. Significant parts of the new plan follow.

Marketing

In late 1977, Westmills distributed carpets through nearly 3 000 accounts across Canada, but primarily in the west. Geographic, customer type and product type segments, and Westmills share therein, are given in Table 4.

TABLE 4 Westmills' Position in the Canadian Carpet Market, 1976 (volumes in millions of square metres)

| | Western Market | | | Eastern Market | |
	Retail	Residential Contract	Commercial Contract	All Segments	Total
All Product Volume	8.8	7.6	5.5	56.6	78.5
Westmills' Volume Share (%)	.51 5.8	1.76 23.1	.25 4.6	.80 1.4	3.32 4.2
Solid Colour Volume	4.4	4.6	1.8	n/a	
Westmills' Volume Share (%)	.40 9.1	1.41 30.6	.20 11.1	n/a n/a	

SOURCE: Company and casewriter's estimates.

Under the plan for 1977–78, sales in the west were to be emphasized. Representation would be maintained in Quebec, but at a minimum level. There was some anticipation of better results in Ontario through a new sales agency arranged by Garry Morrison. This latter activity had been debated in the company as not fully consistent with the western focus, but Morrison had prevailed, arguing that the incremental volume was essential.

SEGMENT AND PRODUCT EMPHASIS Westmills' traditional market in the west had been residential contracts. The new carpet lines mentioned previously had been developed as part of a program to increase Westmills' retail and commercial market penetration. Most were multi-coloured lines developed from pre-dyed acrylic–nylon blends. The reasons for emphasis on pre-dyed yarns in the new products were market preferences and the limitations of Westmills' post-tufting colouring capabilities. It should be noted that many dealers in the west serviced more than one and perhaps all three segments, although most had a particular emphasis in their trade. It was also true that certain carpet styles could suitably be used by purchasers in one or more of the segments. The ultimate market mix of a mill could thus be only roughly estimated.

As a complement to the new product lines, Westmills was readying a foam backing application process in the Calgary plant. Foam-backed carpet accounted for about 20% of carpet sales by volume, and was particularly popular in lower-priced print and multicolour styles. Since foam-backed carpet was easier and less expensive to install than jute-backed carpet, it had a specific advantage in the "do-it-yourself" market and in certain residential contract applications. Westmills intended, at least initially, to put foam backing on selected current solid-colour lines to build volume at minimum incremental investment.

PROMOTION Westmills' sales force numbered 23 representatives, each covering a specified geographic territory or, in the major cities, a specific account list. The sales reps were paid a guaranteed minimum of $16 000, plus a commission which varied from 1% to 3% of sales, depending on the carpet line. Each sales rep had a $200 per month car allowance and a travel and entertainment budget. The average gross earnings of the sales force were about $30 000. No changes were anticipated in the size or nature of the sales organization, although certain specific personnel adjustments were foreseen.

A major promotional expense was the cost of samples, sample kits, "waterfalls," etc., for use by the sales reps, in trade showrooms and in retail stores. While as much of the sample cost as possible was recovered from the trade, the net cost of sampling a new line was in the order of $50 000. Overall, sampling expense in 1976–77 was about $420 000. Only incidental amounts were spent on media advertising.

DELIVERY AND CUSTOMER SERVICE Westmills' 8 000-square-foot Calgary distribution centre housed the majority of the finished goods inventory as well as the customer service and shipping departments. This facility had never operated to management's satisfaction and was believed to be the weak link responsible for mounting customer complaints about late or mistaken delivery. There were plans for 1977–78 to reduce the space used by half, to relocate personnel to the plant (making changes and reductions in the process) and to ship more goods directly from the plant. One objective of the move was to reduce finished goods inventory by $1 million.

Manufacturing

Westmills' manufacturing costs had recovered somewhat from the effects of relocation and the coincident plateauing of sales. Efficiency had improved through 1976–77, but costs were still about 20% higher than those incurred by similar mills in the U.S. (after adjustments for differences in input costs).

A consultant hired by Westmills noted that the high costs in the plant were due to production scheduling problems, low equipment utilization (in dyeing) and inappropriate equipment utilization (in finishing). The production process, in short, was not as yet running in a smooth and balanced fashion. Regarding quality, the consultant commented,

Off quality in manufacturing is approximately double what one would expect . . . Part of this may be due to operational reasons . . . some must be attributed to attempts to utilize substandard fibres and blends in the carpet yarns (creating problems at Globe as well as Calgary) . . . some is due to the high personnel turnover in Calgary.

While identifying these problems, Wilson noted that if Westmills could achieve the "U.S. level" costs it would be competitive with any mill in Canada and could dominate the west in the demand segments which fit its yarn and carpet production capabilities.

The 1977–78 plan anticipated the following changes.

1. Reducing plant direct labour.

2. Shifting the product line to achieve greater utilization of Globe Mills' spinning capacity, and having Globe seek external contracts.

3. Implementing more stringent quality control, with the goal of reducing "second" yardage from 7% to 4.5%.

4. Changing certain dye and chemical formulations to cheaper equivalently effective materials.

5. Eliminating a 4 000-square-foot warehouse currently housing raw materials and off-quality or slow-selling goods.

The aggregate savings were forecast to be slightly more than $1 million on a volume base equivalent to 1976–77. Morrison wrote, "We are performing major surgery on our operations to reduce their size to conform with sales volumes dictated by the marketplace." Westmills would still retain the capacity, however, to produce about 4.6 million metres of carpet, provided there were no unusual product-mix demands.

Finance

As part of the recovery plan, Westmills was pursuing financial arrangements that would "reduce long-term debt, improve working capital and generally put us in a better situation financially." The main elements of this plan were the sale and lease-back of the Calgary plant and the discounting and sale of the Kelowna mortgage.

Discussions with potential purchasers of the Calgary plant indicated that a $3 million price might be acceptable, with a lease-back based on an 8–10% capitalization rate. It was probable that one year's lease cost in advance would have to be maintained in a trust account. Negotiations were underway, with an anticipated closing in January or February 1978. Other discussions regarding the mortgage on the Kelowna property indicated that the mortgage might be sold for something in the order of $900 000 cash. It was anticipated that this, too, would close early in the new year.

THE CRUNCH

As Westmills moved through January and February of 1978, it became increasingly apparent that events were not unfolding as anticipated. Sales were substantially below forecast and losses were accumulating at a distressing rate (Exhibits 3 and 4). Garry Morrison had left the company to be replaced on an interim basis by Harry Higson. The company's plight became well known in the industry and it was losing credibility as a continuing supplier. Management was working, as Jim Hamilton put it, somewhere between desperation and chaos.

Westmills, seen from outside, was on the verge of collapse. Within the company the difficulties were recognized, but there was a resilience in management's attitude that offered at least the possibility of continuity and survival. The question they were asking was not whether, but how. An assessment by various managers of their areas of operation follows.

Marketing—Jim Hamilton

The problems Jim Hamilton was facing in the marketplace were, in simple form, credibility, product and reliability in quality and delivery. "Right now," he said, "we have a terrible image in the market."

Credibility

Hamilton commented,

> Most of our accounts have been real good and have tried to support us; but they have heard rumours of us folding and they are really very concerned about the availability of goods. Some have come to us saying they just have to protect themselves by adding other suppliers. Others just won't do business with us; they say we are too shaky. Naturally our competitors are taking as much as they can and have kept prices real keen.

PRODUCT The new product programs had not met expectations. The foam-backed solid-colour carpets had encountered market and salesperson resistance and took an inordinate time to run in the plant. The new multi-colour retail lines had been based on yarn imported from the United States; the depreciation of the dollar had sharply increased materials costs, forcing Westmills into a noncompetitive situation. No Canadian supplier had the capacity to supply on a reliable basis. Further, there was resistance at the retail level to purchasing samples and inventories, at least in part because of Westmills' uncertain position. It was too early to evaluate the contract lines, as the selling cycle in this market was considerably longer.

In spite of these difficulties, as Hamilton notes, "We have a good basic line in solid-colour goods, particularly for residential contract. We make a good solid-colour fabric. What we don't have are reasonable upgrades to cover the higher price points."

QUALITY/DELIVERY RELIABILITY Good intentions to the contrary, Westmills was not living up to its promises to customers. The "mechanics" of order processing, commitment, scheduling, production and shipping were, in Hamilton's words, the "worst ever." He commented, "We are missing delivery dates and we are having quality problems; we have had to issue a pile of credit notes for problems we have created. I have a 4000-square-foot warehouse full of seconds to dispose of. How do I do this without upsetting the market?"

As a result of the foregoing, Hamilton was having trouble with sales-force morale. "There has been a tendency in this company to treat salesmen as a necessary evil anyway," he noted, "and now we aren't giving them product and service. How am I supposed to keep good men?"

Manufacturing—David Hirst

In the plant, Hirst was confronted with problems of morale, production scheduling and control, and product quality. His first test was immediate: on the very day he arrived in Calgary for work (having moved his family across the country), Garry Morrison had announced his resignation as president, to the surprise of all.

MORALE There was a bad morale problem in the plant, David Hirst noted, stemming from inadequate direction and control of work and further instability rising from concerns that there was "every possibility ... (we) ... may not be there tomorrow."

In his first weeks at the plant, Hirst had had a chance to assess his supervisory staff and was quite pleased, with the exception of one or two areas where he anticipated making changes. But overall he felt he could build on the strengths and experience of these people and that the problems being experienced were more the result of the context they had been working in than of particular personal shortcomings. In light of this assessment, Hirst felt his first priority was to earn the respect of the plant personnel, establish that one person was in control and from this foundation isolate and address the operating problems.

PRODUCTION SCHEDULING The production scheduling of Westmills had fallen into progressive disarray as market pressures, new-product development, quality problems and financing difficulties had accumulated, driving operations into a vicious circle of deterioration. Hirst commented, "We are dealing in chaos...the tufters are being scheduled on the spot by telephone calls, slips of paper that people walk in with...there is no way we can operate efficiently like this...sales and customer service just don't see the costs...how can they make the promises they do?" Such were the difficulties of coordination between sales, customer service, manufacturing and delivery that one sales rep had recently verified that an order he had placed for 2500 square metres of carpet had, quite simply, been lost.

The key to manufacturing efficiency in a carpet plant, Hirst pointed out, was proper scheduling and integration of equipment loads through the entire production process. This was quite impossible in the current circumstances and it was essential, as he put it, "to reduce the interference factors."

QUALITY The sources of product quality problems were not all known but there principal contributing factors: the quality of the incoming yarns from Globe Mills, certain product designs, and deficiencies in training and experience in Calgary.

The limitations of Globe Mills had not been fully appreciated or considered in some product designs, with the result that it was stretching its capabilities to make certain yarns. Hirst, among others, agreed that Globe did a good job on yarns within its range and that the core problem was one of not balancing capabilities and efficiency in Globe and Calgary when designing fabrics.

Certain product designs, as well, were ill-fitted to the Calgary plant. An internal memo commented that one of the new multi-colour lines "makes our inadequacy in the multi-coloured area only too evident."

On training an experience, Hirst noted that "Calgary is not exactly a textile centre and there is little access to trained workers." Westmills was thus forced to hire in a booming, resource-based economy with the attendant high wage-rates and worker mobility. Substantial progress had been made in developing a stable work force, but it was clear from the kind of problems arising from the plant floor that a great deal of training and experience were yet necessary.

Hirst weighed the circumstances:

Sure we have problems. We have limitations in our equipment in Meaford and Calgary. But, with the exception of multi-colour, we can produce volume and quality and make carpets that sell. We can do more than has been done with what we have now. I guess, coming from York-shire, if that's all you have, use it well. The job can be done...I have no reservations.

Control and Finance—Bill Ford

In early 1978, Bill Ford was working to improve the quality and use of the company's information systems and at the same time doing battle day-to-day for cash to meet immediate obligations.

INFORMATION SYSTEMS On arriving at Westmills, Ford had reviewed the control and financial systems and found that "a lot of good things had been started, but they were still in a half-fin-ished state." The computer facility had been applied to the financial side of the business for such tasks as payroll and receivables accounting and financial reporting. These areas, he felt, were in pretty good shape.

The problems lay more in the lack of development and use of operating and cost account-ing systems. Here there were shortcomings in most areas, from order entry through manufac-turing cost control to inventory control. The general frame-work for a workable system was in place but the actual work being done was not up to a reasonable standard in either effective-ness or efficiency. The matter was further complicated by a lack of understanding and commu-nication between accounting and the line managers and supervision. "There was a problem of attitude and capabilities both inside and outside the accounting department," Ford noted, "and it has been necessary to change some personnel and segment the general and management ac-counting functions." Work was proceeding to improve the control system, but in the prevailing circumstances progress had been fairly slow.

CASH FLOW Westmills' cash position in early 1978 was so tight that Bill Ford was personally mon-itoring all receipts and approving all disbursements. The noose was drawing tighter every day.

On the receipts side, sales were down and collections were becoming more difficult. To prop up sales, credit had been granted in questionable circumstances. Difficulties with deliver-ies and quality claims had led to a flurry of credit notes being granted in the field, which meant a very complicated reconciliation of accounts. Some accounts were deferring payment until such matters were clarified; others, sensing weakness, were simply being very slow to pay. On the payables side, suppliers were getting tougher about terms and some had put Westmills in COD for orders incremental to existing balances.

Ford described the situation: "I'm in daily discussions with the banks. They are very skep-tical and very close to pulling the plug. If they did now, my guess is that they might end up 10–15% out of pocket. They have asked for a meeting within the next few days."

Derek Mather and CED

Derek Mather, aged 45, had started his business career as an investment analyst for Sun Life Assurance Co. In 1962 he had joined CED as an investment officer and was currently senior vice-president. In his time at CED, Mather had been involved in recruiting and screening of new corporate ventures and the monitoring of venture investments. He had been a member of Westmills' board of directors since 1967. These jobs, he pointed out, had not brought him into direct operating management.

> I see my own involvement as a dubious solution...a solution with many flaws. Although I've been on the board for many years, I don't know the industry from a technical standpoint, nor do I know the market particularly well. I don't have the high level of skills in the business which I think financial people, considering an investment, would demand.

The countervailing problem at the moment was the expected difficulty of finding an experienced and credible presidential candidate. Mather commented, "I don't think we've got a hope of finding a guy like that in this present environment. I think whatever solution we are able to work out at this time...and by that I mean the next few days...will be a patchwork solution...if we were to go out and try to hire a new man we'd just be wasting out time." He continued, "It may be, from a banker's point of view, that if CED is prepared to supply additional equity capital and personnel, then that degree of shareholder commitment would be impressive."

CED was currently Westmills' major shareholder, holding approximately 40% of the 1 100 984 common shares issued and $402 000 worth of the $1.144 million in unsecured convertible debentures (convertible to common shares at $2.50). Westmills common stock was currently trading on the Toronto Stock Exchange at from $.70 to $.90.

On CED's future involvement, Mather and Gerald Sutton, CED's president, were of one mind: within reason, CED must stick with the investment and do what was necessary to revive the company. Sutton explained, "We took Westmills public and in so doing reduced our holdings, recaptured our initial investment and made a profit. Under the circumstances we can't just withdraw from this situation; we have a moral responsibility to the public." Mather added, "The business community in the west knows we started this company...we can't have them say we walked away when times got tough."

EXHIBIT 1   Westmills' Consolidated Operating Results for Fiscal Years Ending August 31 ($000s)

	1977	1976	1975	1974	1973
Net sales	$21 678	$23 056	$21 725	$22 823	$14 407
Cost of sales	17 886	19 594	17 506	17 098	10 622
Depreciation	712	660	638	347	188
Total	18 598	20 254	18 144	17 445	10 810
Gross margin	3 080	2 802	3 581	5 378	3 597
%	14.2%	12.1%	16.5%	23.4%	25.0%
Marketing expenses	2 625	2 478	2 141	3 063	1 933
Administration	876	900	610	—	—
Financing:					
Long-term	756	681	597	309	133
Short-term	308	514	333	156	37
Extraordinary costs	—	635	615	—	—
Total	4 565	5 208	4 296	3 528	2 103
Net income before tax	(1 485)	(2 406)	(715)	1 849	1 494
Income tax	(305)	(361)	(309)	798	651
Net income	(1 180)	(2 045)	(405)	1 051	842
Extraordinary items	314	—	96	96	—
Net profit	(866)	(2 045)	(309)	1 147	842

SOURCE: Company documents.

EXHIBIT 2   Westmills' Consolidated Balance Sheets for Fiscal Years Ending August 31 ($000s)

	1977	1976	1975	1974	1973
Current Assets					
Cash	$	$	$	$ 77	$ 169
Accounts receivable	3 880	3 874	4 506	3 480	2 337
Inventories	4 584	6 198	5 316	6 033	3 857
Prepaid expenses	253	227	169	168	173
Income taxes recoverable	—	—	354	—	—
	8 717	10 296	10 345	9 757	6 536
Current Liabilities					
Short-term borrowings	4 497	4 230	2 576	2 463	421
Accounts payable, accrued liabilities	2 458	2 796	3 421	3 279	2 164
Income and other taxes	195	255	236	231	519
Current portion, LT debt	470	402	397	653	442
	7 620	7 683	6 630	6 626	3 546
Working capital	1 097	2 613	3 715	3 131	2 990
Net fixed assets	6 644[1]	7 811	8 075	7 841	3 887
	$ 7 741	$10 424	$11 790	$10 972	$ 6 877
Long-term debt[2]	4 989	6 500	5 461	4 459	4 873
Deferred income taxes	408	713	1 074	948	586
Shareholders' equity:					
Common stock	3 362	3 362	3 362	3 362	3 362
Retained earnings	(1 018)	(151)	1 893	2 203	1 056
	$ 7 741	$10 424	$11 790	$10 972	$ 6 877

[1] Includes mortgage receivable of $1 000 000 on sale of Kelowna plant.
[2] The structure of the long-term debt as of August 31, 1977 was as follows:

9.5% First mortgage on land and buildings; payments $9 000 per month, including interest	$1 017 950
Term bank loans at 1.5% over prime; payments $30 000 per month plus interest. Secured by assignment of mortgage receivable plus a charge on land, buildings and equipment	$1 556 000
12% Series A debentures, due 1980; payments $22 000 per month including interest. Secured by charge on land, buildings and equipment ranking with bank term loan	$1 444 775
12% Convertible, redeemable unsecured debentures. Series A and B Semi-annual interest	$1 441 000
	$5 459 725
Less current portion of long-term debt	$ 470 705
	$4 989 020

SOURCE: Company documents.

EXHIBIT 3   Westmills' Forecast Profit and Actual Experience, 1977–78 ($000s)

	Recovery Plan Pds. 1–6	Forecast FY 1978	Estimated Actual Pds. 1–6
Square metres (000s)	1 550	3 340	1 230
Net sales	$10 217	$ 22 138	$ 7 966
Cost of sales	8 712	18 611	6 888
Gross margin	1 505	3 527	1 078
Percent net sales	14.7%	15.9%	13.6%
Marketing	968	2 029	893
Administration	412	871	432
Finance-interest	415	777	461
Total	1 795	3 677	1 786
Operating income (loss)	(290)	(150)	(708)
Taxes recoverable	(96)	(201)	(106)
Income (loss before extraordinary items)	(194)	51	(602)
Extraordinary Items:			
Sale of mortgage (net)	(48)	(48)	—
Sale of plant (net)	92	892	—
Income tax recovery	356	356	—
Net profit (loss)	$ 1 006	$ 1 251	$ (602)

EXHIBIT 4 Westmills' Balance Sheet Forecasts and Actual Experience, 1977–78

($000s)

	Recovery Plan Forecast		Estimated Actual
	End Period 6	*End 1978 FY*	*End Period 6*
Current Assets			
Accounts receivable	$4 750	$4 500	$4 191
Trust account	300	300	—
Inventories:			
Raw material	1 600	1 600	1 355
Work in process	650	650	1 087
Finished goods	1 425	1 176	1 947
Total inventory	3 675	3 426	4 389
Prepaid expenses	225	316	156
Total current assets	8 950	8 632	8 736
Mortgage	—	—	1 000
Net fixed assets	3 691	3 495	5 427
Total	$12 641	$12 127	$15 163
Liabilities & Shareholders' Equity			
Bank indebtedness	5 501	4 507	5 701
Accounts payable	1 847	2 198	1 943
Taxes payable	225	214	220
Current portion:			
Long-term debt	—	—	470
Current liabilities	7 573	6 919	8 334
Long-term debt	1 441	1 441	4 785
Deferred taxes	278	173	302
Shareholders' Equity:			
Common shares	3 362	3 362	3 362
Retained earnings	(13)	232	(1 620)
Total	$12 641	$12 127	$15 163

DELTA AGROCHEMICALS, INC.

J. Peter Killing and Joyce Miller

CASE 32

Based in Denver, Colorado, Consolidated Western Holdings (CWH) was a large Fortune 500 listed industrial company. From its beginnings in the 1940s as an oil and gas venture, CWH had steadily expanded its oil operations and had diversified through acquisition to become a major participant in the chemical industry. The company also owned and managed coal mining operations around the world and had acquired a collection of small, but growing, high technology, energy-related businesses in the United States.

CWH's chemical business consisted of four divisions, each run as an autonomous profit centre. The smallest and newest of these was the Western Biotechnology ("Westec") business, managed by John Finlayson. In May 1991, however, Finlayson was considering moving to Delta Agrochemicals, Inc. ("DeltaAg"), a much larger sister division in the agricultural chemicals business. Finlayson knew the senior managers of DeltaAg well, as he been a member of the division's internal management board since the mid-1980s.

Because of his success in building Westec, Finlayson was widely viewed as a competent manager, and he was sure that if he asked for a transfer to DeltaAg, it would be approved. Although the move would not be a promotion, Finlayson thought that the change would be an interesting one as DeltaAg faced a number of major issues. He added, "I now have someone here who can run Westec with only minor consultation with me, and I am spending so much time working on DeltaAg issues that I think I might as well move over there full time." DeltaAg's head office was about two kilometres from Westec's. Both were located in St. Louis, Missouri.

THE AGROCHEMICALS BUSINESS

Agrochemical companies discovered, developed, registered and sold products for controlling pests (insecticides), plant diseases (fungicides) and weeds (herbicides). Traditionally, it had been a high growth, high margin business, and gross margins in the 60% range were not uncommon. By the 1990s, however, industry profit was eroding as costs skyrocketed and growth flattened. In many countries, the industry was not able to increase its prices sufficiently to offset cost inflation. Moreover, the food supply in the developed world was broadly in surplus, and arable land was being taken out of production. At the same time, mounting public concern about the environmental effects of agrochemicals was delaying registration of new products. Over the long term, no more than 1–2% growth per annum was expected in existing markets.

Some industry observers felt that there was strong market potential in centrally planned and developing countries, but the question was when and where such growth would occur. Hot spots like South East Asia looked very promising, but Eastern European countries were problematic. In terms of crops, it was widely believed that wheat production was likely to decline, while rice and maize, for example, would increase. Eighty percent of the world agrochemicals market was believed to be found in less than 20 countries.

Overall, the market for agrochemical products was highly fragmented, with more than 40 separate product categories each worth more than $100 million. Herbicides, for example, were sold for approximately 10 different crops, including cotton, rice, maize, soya beans, sugar cane, sugar beets and so on. Within any of these general crop areas were a variety of individual product categories. In the maize segment, for example, there were separate herbicide products available to: (1) kill grass before it emerged; (2) kill grass after it emerged; (3) kill broad-leafed weeds before they emerged; and (4) kill broad-leafed weeds after they emerged. Delta had products in most, but not all, of these product categories.

Expectations were that the fight for market share would continue to intensify. All major companies were spending heavily on research and development. The key to success was to find new "active ingredients" with novel effects for controlling pests, diseases or weeds, and then to get these to the market ahead of the competition. It was, however, a long and expensive process. Gestation periods of 7–10 years were not uncommon as companies took their new products through toxicology tests, metabolism tests, studies of crop residue, environmental impact assessments and so on. Detailed field studies had to be performed before a product could be offered for sale in an individual country and this was both time-consuming and expensive in most major markets. The registration process could cost up to $50 million per product, and of course, it cost the same whether the product turned out to be a world beater or a lacklustre "me too" offering.

A further hurdle facing agricultural chemical producers was the 1988 American legislation that required products, which had been introduced when registration standards were less stringent, to be re-registered, at great cost. The result was that poorly performing old products were taken off the market. For companies like DeltaAg, however, which had a range of successful older products, re-registration was an expensive necessity. Other countries were expected to follow the American lead.

DELTA AGROCHEMICALS, INC.

With almost $2.5 billion in sales in 1990, DeltaAg had a 14% share of the world agrochemical market. The company's product line, which consisted of more than 2 000 individual chemical formulations, was built on 35–40 active ingredients, seven or eight of which accounted for 80% of sales. The company manufactured its active ingredients in a few key plants in North America and Europe, and shipped them to more than 50 formulation plants around the world where final formulation, packaging, and labelling took place. DeltaAg's products were sold in more than 100 countries, and the company had its own selling organization in 45 countries. DeltaAg's largest markets were the United States, Canada and France.

In the mid-1960s, shortly after CWH acquired DeltaAg, the company developed a "blockbuster" weed killer, Melinor, which sold well in many markets around the world and fuelled the company's growth for the next ten years. Then in the late 1970s, DeltaAg acquired a mid-sized French company and a British firm which specialized in insecticides. These acquisitions, combined with strong market growth, brought DeltaAg's sales volume to approximately $1.4 billion by the mid-1980s. In 1988, DeltaAg purchased the agrochemical division of another major American company, which was particularly strong in corn and wheat protection. In addition to growth by acquisition, DeltaAg had been introducing new products at a record rate. George Hill, DeltaAg's research director, commented:

> We spent a decade looking for another blockbuster like Melinor, without success, and then changed our strategy to go for incremental development of existing products. This worked extremely well and by the early 1980s, we were introducing two new products per year, which is remarkable by industry standards. As late as 1979, Melinor accounted for 80% of the company's gross margin—thanks to our new products it is now down around 10–15%.
>
> We are currently spending about $300 million on research and development. The budget is split into three equal parts—one third for invention, one third for the development and registration of new products, and one third for the reformulation and re-registration of existing products.

1988—STRATEGIC AND ORGANIZATIONAL CHANGES

In 1988, DeltaAg underwent a major strategy review. Under the direction of Alan Jemison, who had been the president of DeltaAg for five years, the management team set an objective of becoming "the world's leading agricultural chemical company." Profitability targets were established: the immediate goal was a 16% operating profit to sales ratio (compared with 10% in 1987) and by 1997, the return on assets was to reach 36%, approximately double the 1987 figure. Growth would be at a rate 50% greater than the market. All of these objectives were considered ambitious but achievable—and in the words of the strategy document, they would require "increasingly selective decisions aimed at steering all activities toward the areas of highest reward."

As a first step in implementing the new strategy, countries were divided into six categories, with a different DeltaAg objective established for each. These objectives ranged from "defend dominant position" to "improve market share rapidly." At the same time, three broad product categories were created, namely: "products of key strategic importance," "high price, high margin specialties," and products with "commercial or technical limitations." Again, different objectives were set for the products in each category.

The 1988 strategy was accompanied by organizational changes. Cost saving reductions were made in the St. Louis head office, particularly in the marketing areas. About 80 of St. Louis' 600 employees were laid off. In addition, a new vice-presidential layer of management was added (see Exhibit 1) in order to free up the senior vice-presidents to concentrate on the long term future of the business. An employee commented:

> The job cuts created a level of anxiety never seen before in the St. Louis operation. The organization had always been growing, and this was the first time that we had ever moved in such a direct way to cut costs. CWH's general policy is that layoffs are a last resort, but DeltaAg management went directly to this solution—and they implemented the changes brutally. Moreover, we added another layer of management at a time when most companies were trying to reduce their management hierarchy.

In an effort to restore morale following the layoffs, a team of consultants was employed to involve employees in an exercise to identify the core values within the organization. One of the consultants explained:

> We tried to create a common culture in the business and to heal some of the wounds caused by the 1988 reorganization. We got everyone at St. Louis into groups and worked with them to identify the key success factors in the business and their role in delivering them. We thought that ideas would flow back and forth and people would talk about where they were and where they wanted to be as an organization. There was a lot of cynicism, however, and it became clear that the vice-presidents had not really bought into the exercise. The president, who was committed, was reluctant to push the others very hard because the groups said "this exercise is about trust—so trust us." The end result was that some people signed on, but a lot did not.

1991—ANOTHER LOOK AT THE ORGANIZATION

By early 1991, it was clear that the previous year had not been a financial success for DeltaAg. Virtually all measures of profitability had fallen from previous years, and as shown in Exhibit 2, all were far below budget. David Jans, the Vice-President of Finance for DeltaAg explained the situation:

> The 1988 strategy looked great on paper, but we never implemented it. Since then, we have built in even more fixed costs—probably hitting a billion in 1990. Last year we delivered to CWH only 50% of the cash that they were expecting! It does not take a genius to figure out that our absolute priority now has to be to cut costs. We cannot go before CWH management this summer without a cost cutting plan already being implemented.
>
> At the instigation of John Finlayson, we recently looked at cutting the number of active ingredients that we produce by 50% and selling through distributors in about half of the 45 or so countries in which we currently maintain company operations. At the outset this looked very attractive, because like most organizations we make 80% of our total gross margin with 20% of our products and in about 20% of our markets. However, the study was very disappointing. Our country managers indicated that they could not cut their number of employees very much if they dropped their worst selling products. And we would not be able to save much on the production side either. The net result was that eliminating the bottom half of our product line and markets served would actually reduce our return on capital.
>
> But we still need to do something. Corporate is not happy with us.

In early 1991, DeltaAg management instituted a 13% cost cut across-the-board. All departments were to comply. Also, John Finlayson was asked to begin a study of the organization to see how it could be streamlined. He believed that DeltaAg needed lower costs, fewer people doing more rewarding jobs, clearer accountabilities, and better coordination between the functional departments in St. Louis. He explained:

> We need to change this organization to get rid of the duplication and cross-functional boundaries. My approach is to begin by trying to determine exactly what transactions are necessary to the successful functioning of the organization. Once we know that, we will be in a position to decide how to organize, and we will know where we can cut, and where we cannot.
>
> To do this, I have set up two task forces. One is to examine the product supply chain within the company, the other is to study the new product introduction chain. These are both lateral processes that cut across the functional departments. Each task force is to identify the key interactions and figure out how they could be performed more efficiently—I am sure that there is room for great improvement. I may also set up a group to look at the role of head office here in St. Louis vis-à-vis the national organizations around the world. They say that we collect too much information from them, and do nothing with it. They also complain that we exercise too much control over their strategies. Are they right? We need to find out the minimum required to manage this company, not the 'nice to have.' Let's push decision-making down to the lowest possible level, stop the second guessing, and make decisions only once.
>
> We do not have the kind of performance measures you'd expect in a company this well established. Personal reward and gain have to be more direct.

An employee who had been working in the development department at St. Louis for two years (after spending four years in another part of CWH) applauded the organizational review. She commented:

> My job is to help get the technical resources in this company applied to real world projects where they are needed most—for the product areas that I cover. I am a coordinator—I have no direct power—and to be successful, I have to influence people in different parts of the organization to work together. Working up the hierarchy is not effective because I don't get a quick enough response, and often the information that does come back is not useful. It seems like there are eternal gripes between the people who make things and the people who sell things. There are endless circles going up and nothing going across. For the past 18 months, I have been trying to get $80 000 of formulation time devoted to a product that could give us an immediate $10 million return in the market. I can't get the time, and I can't figure out why not. Right now, the project is in limbo and I've run out of options to move it forward. It's unbelievably frustrating.

THE 1991 STRATEGY REVIEW

CWH's management system called for a comprehensive strategy review of each of its businesses every third year. DeltaAg's review was due in the summer of 1991, and in April, Alan Jemison called a management meeting to discuss the DeltaAg submission. After the meeting, he commented:

> This strategy review is a major event and I hope we can take advantage of it. There is no doubt that the business needs to be more profitable—even if that means making it smaller. We should probably cut the product line a little and step out of some markets. We also need to change our R&D strategy to concentrate on fewer, larger product developments. Our strategy of incrementalism has worked well, but with the rising cost of registration, it is getting too expensive to maintain. Finally, we need to devolve headquarter's functions to the national companies—we

must learn to stop doing things for them. The trouble is that a lot of our people here don't feel right unless they are out in the field selling something.

My challenge is to get people to buy into the strategy-making process—to take it seriously. I will be retiring in 24 months and no one knows whether my successor will be appointed from inside DeltaAg or from another part of CWH. There is a lot of speculation, and not enough emphasis on improving the business.

I do not believe that we need to change the organization. We have had a lot of organizational changes, and we now need stability. I hear people saying that we need to get rid of the vice-presidential layer—I don't think so. What we do need is to turn the managers at the top of this company into a team—a committed team with a common objective.

Other senior DeltaAg executives commented on the situation facing the business in 1991.

Senior Vice-President of Research and Development

This is a technically-driven business, and the success of any company in it depends on its ability to create new, high margin, active ingredients. In the short-term, we could cut our research spending and it would improve the bottom line—but we would be giving away our future. We need to preserve our research skills, and work toward developing more significant new products. At the moment, we have too many marginal products and too many marginal territories. What we need to do is identify the key product/territory combinations and focus on them.

Vice-President of Human Resources

I came from the chemicals subsidiary of an American oil company to join this business in 1990. I see my role as being a change agent. This business is too complex, and people seem to revel in its complexity. Managers make their careers here by winning arguments. A decision is the starting point for a debate rather than a move to action. I heard that Alan once gave a clear instruction that a product under development was to be cancelled. When this happened the researchers began to work on it secretly, and even introduced it to the market a few years later. It failed.

To take this organization forward we need to do two things:

1. We need to create horizontal business processes that will increase communication between the functional areas. As well, we need a flatter organization. The middle level and junior employees see this vice-presidential layer and it drives them crazy. Until senior management gets its act together, they say, why should we behave any differently?
2. We need to reduce the number of products that we produce and markets that we serve. We need to create the mix that will produce the most cash in the short term, and growth for the longer term.

Senior Vice-President of Marketing

I have discussed the situation with my vice-presidents and we agree that we should not cut back our product line or reduce our territorial coverage. Our customers need our full line, and every product that we sell makes money. There is no point in throwing away gross margin. Of course, we can improve our efficiency, and we are already doing this. We have moved from 18 operating units in Europe down to 8, and we're looking at a plan that would bring us down to only three formulation plants for the whole region.

To increase profitability, we need to reduce fixed manufacturing costs. We are using a lot of old manufacturing equipment that requires a lot of maintenance. We could get some of our formulation manufacturing done by outside companies— it certainly would be cheaper and we would not need these far flung plants all over the world.

Vice-President of Operations

In the mid-1980s, at the insistence of CWH senior management, we introduced MRP 2 into this business, and it has made a tremendous difference. Our manufacturing performance has increased dramatically over the past few years.

If our priority is to cut costs, we need to look first at cutting back our research. Research has two major laboratories, one in California and the other in the UK that came with one of the acquisitions. That British lab is costing in the neighbourhood of $75 million per year. I believe that we should shut it down and fold its operations into our U.S. operation. British researchers are difficult to control, and the British management team has a tendency to use the lab for their own pet projects; they're also duplicating some of the work that we are doing here.

We also need to reduce the complexity of the business. In spite of what the marketing people say, we do have too many marginal products and too many marginal territories.

JOHN FINLAYSON'S DECISION

At the end of May 1991, John Finlayson was reviewing his situation. He felt that he could not continue to manage Westec and spend so much time working on DeltaAg issues. It was time to make a decision.

I have to move one way or the other. I am concerned that without my full time presence in DeltaAg, some of the things that we are doing, like the task forces, will not have any impact. I am already worried that they are losing their way and are just going through the motions. Whether I join the company or not, I think that we should create a vice-president of planning position and give that person the job of managing the change that has to happen. Everyone else is just too busy to give it the time it needs.

The other thing that makes me think that I should move into DeltaAg is the impending strategy review. Alan sent me a draft of their first attempt at a strategy and I found it too conservative—too much business as usual. In the past week, I have put together something stronger—what I call a focused strategy. It clearly separates our winning territories and products, and specifies different levels of service for them than for our more marginal products and areas. I've shown it to a few people in DeltaAg and they seem to like it. Some say it is obvious and what we are already doing—but no one has said it does not make sense.

On a personal level, I don't think that Alan has strong feelings either way about the possibility of my moving over there. We have discussed it, and it's pretty clear that the decision is mine to make. I might be able to move into one of the senior vice-president spots, or perhaps we could create a new one.

EXHIBIT 1 **Partial Organization Chart**

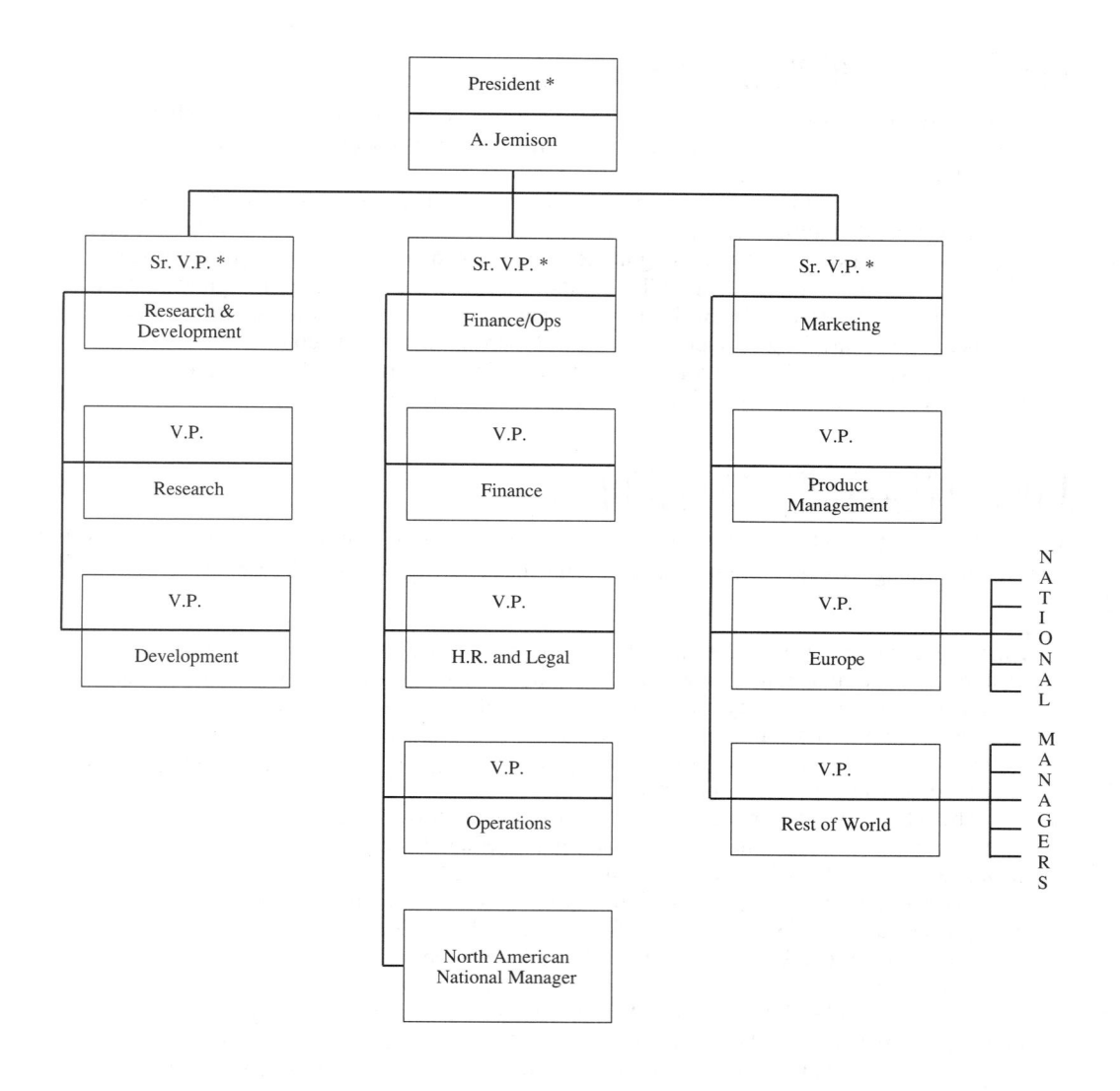

* These four executives plus John Finlayson comprised the Delta Agrochemicals, Inc. management board, responsible for overseeing the company's activities.

EXHIBIT 2   **Financial Performance** (millions of dollars)

	1986	1987	1988	1989	Actual 1990	Budget 1990
Sales	1 350	1 610	2 160	2 452	2 485	2 570
Gross Margin	665	815	1195	1360	1392	1445
% of Sales	49%	51%	55%	55%	56%	56%
R&D, Sales, Admin	548	564	830	942	1000	980
Depreciation	32	36	60	70	82	80
Other	4	20	26	24	40	28
Operating Profit	81	195	279	324	270	357
	—	—	—	—	—	—
Cash Flow						
Operating Profit	81	195	279	324	270	357
Depreciation	32	36	60	70	82	80
Capital Investment	(114)	(74)	(128)	(176)	(152)	(152)
Acquisition Reorganization			(30)			
Working Capital Changes	(48)	28	(22)	(145)	(42)	42
Cash to Consolidated Western Holdings	(49)	185	159	73	158	327

HIRAM WALKER-GOODERHAM & WORTS (A)

Joseph N. Fry

I n 1985, Hiram Walker-Gooderham & Worts (Hiram Walker) was one of the world's largest and most profitable producers of distilled spirits. Hiram Walker's five key brands—Canadian Club Canadian whisky, Ballantine's Scotch whisky, Courvoisier cognac, and Kahlua and Tia Maria coffee liqueurs—were sold internationally and held strong positions in their individual categories. Revenues were steady at about $1.5 billion, yielding consistent after tax returns of between 15% and 16% on invested capital. Hiram Walker's recently appointed President and Chief Executive Officer, H. Clifford Hatch Jr., was pleased with the company's performance and impatient to build on its prosperity: "We have done a great job with profitability ... but we want to grow, and we have yet to show results in this area ... we have to work this out, how are we going to grow?"

THE WORLD DISTILLED SPIRITS BUSINESS

Achieving growth would not be easy. World consumption of distilled spirits had peaked in recent years, and was now in slow decline. Shifting consumer tastes and aggressive competitive activity were threatening traditional product and brand positions. Market share had become a major source of growth and power, triggering a consolidation of producer and distributor structures. Observers expected these trends to continue, and to create unprecedented opportunities and risks for industry participants.

Demand

From a global perspective, the demand for spirit products and brands was highly fragmented. Product preferences varied widely by country market in relation to local traditions, tastes and pricing. And within markets these same factors often led to a broad distribution of brand preferences across local brands and global brands, which may or may not be locally produced (e.g., Smirnoff vodka, Baccardi rum), and global brands with unique national sources (e.g., Scotch whisky, cognac). Statistics for selected spirits product categories and country markets are presented in Exhibit 1.

In most country markets, domestic demand was served largely by local production. The reasons for this, which varied in importance by market, included unique national tastes, production and distribution economics, and government protection. The residual import volumes, which amounted to about 15% of world demand, were still significant, however, and crucial to the exporters of unique source products.

The United States was widely regarded as the most attractive of the world's spirits markets. The U.S. market accounted for about 22% of total world spirits demand and about 46% of world imports, and it was relatively open to competitive innovation. Thereafter the opportunities represented by specific markets dropped rapidly in magnitude, and became dependent on a wide variety of specific local conditions.

Competition

In spite of on-going consolidation, competitive concentration in the spirits industry was still quite low. In the U.S., for example, 30 brands sold over 1 000 000 cases per year, and the top 60 brands, sold by 24 different firms, held only 60% of the market. There were very large firms in the industry, of course. Table 1 lists the sales, profits and growth rates of the top 18 companies. In spite of their scale, however, these firms probably accounted for less than 40% of world spirit sales. The balance of business was done by virtually dozens of smaller competitors.

The emergence of intense competition had been an unsettling development for many participants in the spirits business. They were used to dealing in what was historically known as a gentlemans' trade. Now they were engaged in an all-out battle, in which the major weapons were aggressive new product and brand marketing, forward integration to control distribution, and acquisitions to balance and expand product portfolios.

Marketing

The great strength of the multinational firms was in their ability to build and support global brands. Their established premium brands provided very attractive returns and were protected from attack to some degree by traditional tastes and habits, and, in most countries, government regulations that limited advertising, sampling, price promotion and so on. Even when a tradi-

TABLE 1 Top 18 International Spirits Firms,[1] 1985 (US$000 000s)

	Sales	Operating Income	Sales Growth (%)	
Distillers Co. (UK)	$1 600	$293	5.2	(81–85)
Seagram (Canada, U.S.)	2 821	246	0.4	(81–85)
Hiram Walker (Canada)	1 102	213	0.9	(81–85)
Grand Metropolitan (UK)	1 319	181	18.7	(80–84)
Brown-Forman (U.S.)	905	167	4.1	(81–85)
Heublein (U.S.)	N/A	152	N/A	
Bacardi (Bahamas)	950	150	8.0	(80–84)
Moet-Hennessy (France)	597	120	25.2	(80–84)
Allied-Lyons (UK)	1 334[2]	85	7.1	(81–85)
Pernod-Ricard (France)	581	78	−2.1	(80–84)
Schenley (U.S.)	416	48	−11.7	(80–84)
Arthur Bell (UK)	305	48	5.0	(80–84)
Martell (France)	236	38	18.0	(80–84)
Whitbread (UK)	672	34	N/A	
National (U.S.)	648	28	−2.8	(81–83)
Wm. Grant (UK)	101	19	7.9	(81–83)
Remy Martin (France)	110	16	11.4	(80–84)
Suntory (Japan)	2 191	N/A	−7.4	(83–85)

[1] Estimates for spirits and wine divisions where possible.
[2] Includes wines, spirits and soft drinks.
SOURCE: Hiram Walker records.

tional brand was affected by new developments, its decline was more a matter of erosion than critical failure. There was another side to this, of course. It was very difficult to grow in these mature, competitive markets. New product launches were expensive, time-consuming and risky. Similarly, campaigns to capture market share by the further penetration of current markets or geographic expansion required long-term thinking and a willingness to make risky investments.

Competitive innovation in the industry was focused on three fronts. The first was the introduction, often by local producers or distributors, of low-priced brands into traditional categories. The second was the search and exploitation of niches as demand in the mature categories fragmented—such as in the promotion of single-malt Scotch whiskies. The third was in the pursuit of "new" categories, like those in the liqueurs business in the U.S., where there was a constant parade of new formulas and flavours—from peach, to kiwi, to root beer. Collectively these efforts created considerable turmoil in the industry, and chipped away at the traditional brand leaders.

Forward Integration

There were two basic channels of distribution for distilled spirits. In the monopoly markets, which included 18 American states, Canada and the northern European countries, spirits products were sold by a producer or import agency directly to government distribution organizations. In the open markets, which accounted for the majority of industry revenue, two- and three-tier channel structures were common—involving producer sales companies and/or import agencies, distributors, and retailers.

In the open markets the proportion of sales through retail chain organizations was increasing. This had stimulated the development of fewer and larger distributors. Producers were facing increasing demands for marketing support, price concessions and private brands, and were finding it more difficult to keep channel attention on marginal brands.

One of the producer responses to increasing channel power was forward integration through the purchase of channel units. There was by no means a consensus in the industry that this was a wise move. It was expensive, took distillers beyond their traditional expertise, and could result in channel conflict. Nevertheless, many of the major firms were moving in this direction.

Horizontal Diversificaiton

A number of major firms were pursuing acquisitions to diversify and to achieve greater market power. These included steps to diversify (1) outside the alcoholic beverage industry, such as with Seagram's purchase of a major position in DuPont; (2) across the major product classes within the alcoholic beverage industry, such as with Guinness' (a brewer) acquisition of Bell's (whisky) and takeover bid for Distillers (mainly spirits); and (3) across product categories within distilled spirits, such as with Hiram Walker's acquisition of Tia Maria. There was agreement throughout the industry that acquisition activity would accelerate in the coming years.

HIRAM WALKER'S BACKGROUND

In 1856, Hiram Walker crossed the Detroit river from Michigan, and built a distillery in the raw timberland on the Canadian side. The company grew, and a small community called Walkerville developed around the distillery. In the 1870s, Walker was the first to brand a Canadian whisky, calling his premium product Canadian Club.

Hiram Walker died in 1899, and his family managed the firm for the next quarter century. In 1926, Harry C. Hatch organized the purchase of Hiram Walker from the family, and merged its operations with those of the Toronto-based Gooderham & Worts distillery. The new company was in an ideal position to benefit from the prohibition laws in force at the time in the U.S. Spirits could not legally be produced or sold in America, but if products made and sold in Canada found their way south, well, so be it.

By the end of prohibition in 1934, Canadian whisky in the U.S. market had become a preferred drink beyond all previous measure. Canadian distillers such as Hiram Walker and Seagram moved quickly to consolidate their gains, and to establish new and now legal distribution and sales organizations.

Over time Hiram Walker added to its key brand portfolio, and broadened its geographic sales coverage. The major brand acquisitions were Ballantine's (1935), Tia Maria (49% in 1954, increased to 100% in 1984), Courvoisier (1964), and Kahlua (1964). Under Harry Hatch's son, H. Clifford Hatch, who became president in 1964, Hiram Walker developed the potential of these brands, grew profitably, and became a truly multinational operation.

Hiram Walker Resources

In response to the threat of a takeover, Hiram Walker was merged in 1980 with Consumers Gas and its subsidiary Home Oil to form what was ultimately known as Hiram Walker Resources (HWR). The new company encountered some early and serious difficulties with a major resource investment, but by 1985 it had recovered and was regarded as a healthy management company with holdings, as outlined in Table 2.

TABLE 2 Hiram Walker Resources Holdings, 1985 ($000 000s)

	Identifiable Assets	Revenue	Operating Earnings
Distilled spirits	$ 1 511	$ 1 516	$ 282
Natural resources	2 052	482	167
Gas utility	1 634	1 767	216
Other investment	551		
Total	$ 5 748	$ 3 765	$ 665

SOURCE: Hiram Walker Resources Ltd. annual report, 1985.

TABLE 3 Hiram Walker Five-Year Performance Summary (C$ 000 000s)

Fiscal Year Ending August 31	1985	1984	1983	1982	1981
Sales:					
Cases (000s)	20 780	20 616	20 575	21 899	22 975
Revenue	$ 1 504.8	$ 1 437.4	$ 1 394.5	$ 1 435.8	$ 1 435.9
Gross Margin	695.6	659.2	623.6	623.7	624.1
%	46.2	45.9	44.7	43.4	43.5
Operating income	291.2	294.5	290.3	320.8	294.0
Net (after tax) operating income	176.4	169.1	175.1	189.6	N/A
Invested capital*	1 171.5	1 089.1	1 059.4	1 199.2	N/A
Return on average invested capital (%)	15.6	15.7	15.5	15.6	N/A

* Invested capital was comprised of current, net fixed and other assets less non-bank current obligations and deferred income taxes. This is a different concept than "identifiable assets" as used in Table 2. Other smaller accounting differences explain the discrepancies in revenues and income numbers between Tables 2 and 3.
SOURCE: Company records.

Hiram Walker's Role in HWR

Hiram Walker was a significant contributor to HWR earnings. Hiram Walker's revenue and profit trends were essentially flat, however, as shown in Table 3. Up to very recently the company had not been encouraged to grow by acquisition. A new and provisional role statement had opened the acquisition avenue, although Cliff Hatch Jr. noted that there was no particular pressure from HWR's board to pursue it because "they are more interested in the energy business." HWR's position was that:

> Hiram Walker is responsible for all HWR's distilled spirits and wine business. Requiring only small capital expenditures, Hiram Walker provides HWR with high levels of cash flow that can be used for additional investment. Hiram Walker is expected to maintain its relative industry strength with high steady return on invested capital of 16–18% from its current brands and assets. In addition, Hiram Walker is expected to capitalize on industry rationalization and propose profitable beverage alcohol acquisitions of at least $250 million within the next five years.

HIRAM WALKER'S STRATEGIC POSITION

In 1985, Hiram Walker operations encompassed production plants, marketing units and investments throughout the world. The company's key brands accounted for over 60% of Hiram Walker's revenues, and over 70% of profit contribution after direct selling expenses. Geographically, the U.S. accounted for about 60% of corporate revenues. The strategic positions of the key brands are outlined below. A summary of sales trends is presented in Exhibit 2.

Canadian Club

Canadian Club was Hiram Walker's historic flagship brand. It was produced and bottled in Canada for domestic and international sale. The brand's primary market was in the U.S. There, for years, Canadian Club and its arch rival, Seagram's V.O., had dominated the Canadian whisky business. Of late, however, both brands had been losing ground to lower priced entries, such as Canadian Mist and Windsor Supreme, that were imported in bulk from Canada. The loss of nearly a million cases of volume each over the past five years had left Hiram Walker and Seagram with significant problems of balancing current production levels and maturing stock inventories. Seagram had to some extent buffered its V.O. sales decline by the successful promotion of its super premium Crown Royal brand. Until 1985, however, there was no Hiram Walker entry in this category.

The strength of Canadian Club was with older, traditional whisky drinkers who, unfortunately, represented a declining market base. To revitalize the brand, Hiram Walker was shifting its marketing focus toward younger, upscale adults. The total advertising approach was being changed, and spending levels were being increased somewhat. Furthermore, a super premium brand, Canadian Club Classic, was being introduced to support and extend the brand range.

Ballantine's

Ballantine's was the world's fourth largest selling brand of Scotch whisky, after Johnny Walker, J&B and Bell's. Ballantine's was strong in continental Europe and selected markets throughout the world. It was weak, however, in the UK and U.S., which together represented about 50% of the world's Scotch whisky consumption.

Hiram Walker expected Ballantine's to show volume increases of a little less than 2% per year through 1990. To this point Hiram Walker had not attacked the UK because of a very competitive and relatively low-profit market environment there. Further, in the U.S., Hiram Walker was unhappy with its current distribution arrangements. These were in the hands of an independent distributor who had been under contract since 1938. The company had yet to find a satisfactory resolution for this situation.

Courvoisier

Courvoisier's share of the cognac market had varied over time from a low of 12% in 1965 to a high of 21% in 1975, at which point it was the leading brand in the industry. Courvoisier's position had fallen more recently to 15.3%, placing it third behind Hennessy and Martell. Geographically, Courvoisier was strong in the UK and U.S., but relatively weak in continental Europe and the Far East.

The drop in Courvoisier's share was attributed to product development and marketing spending problems. Courvoisier had been late with new super premium qualities and package formats. This problem was now being addressed. There was a continuing issue, however, with respect to the unprecedentedly high marketing spending of Hennessy and Martell, which Courvoisier, to this point, had been reluctant to match. Striking a trade-off between profit and market share was a key strategic issue for the brand.

Kahlua

Kahlua was Hiram Walker's most profitable brand. It was a premium priced coffee liqueur produced in Mexico and sold primarily in the U.S. and Canada.

Hiram Walker's Los Angeles-based Maidstone Wine & Spirits organization had capitalized on Kahlua's versatility to build a strong position in the liqueur market. Kahlua was marketed variously as a traditional liqueur, as a spirit to be used in a mixed drink (e.g., with milk in the "Brown Cow" or vodka in the "Black Russian"), or as a flavouring in a host of cooking applications. Kahlua's position was now being challenged directly by low-price imitators, and indirectly by the emergence of rapidly changing taste fads for liqueurs and liqueur-based drinks.

In Hiram Walker's view, the major growth opportunities for Kahlua were outside the U.S. and Canada. Here there were two as yet unresolved positioning issues: whether Kahlua would be sold as a traditional liqueur or as a multiple-use product, and how the potential positioning and distribution overlap with Tia Maria should be handled.

Tia Maria

Tia Maria was a coffee-based liqueur produced in Jamaica. Tia Maria's traditional positioning was as an upscale, imported, classic liqueur product. Its prime market's were the U.S., Canada and the UK. The brand was faltering in all of these markets, however, as a result, it was thought, of inadequate focus and effort, shifts in liqueur market tastes, and the ambiguity (in the U.S. and Canada) of positioning and emphasis relative to Kahlua.

The strategic issues facing Tia Maria were those of revitalizing the brand in its key markets, and developing distribution in other markets, particularly in western Europe. The latter efforts would be particularly complicated since Tia Maria, by itself, was in a relatively weak bargaining position in seeking distribution. It needed to be allied with other brands, but such natural allies as Ballantine's might not be available if, for example, Ballantine's and Kahlua were combined together in another distribution portfolio.

HIRAM WALKER'S ORGANIZATION

Hiram Walker was run through a functional management structure of production, marketing, financial and administrative units (Exhibit 3). This structure reflected a long standing management philosophy of engaging top management in critical strategic and operating issues. Decisions involving brand strategy, price, image, packaging and labelling, distributor representation, trade practices production levels, quality assurance, and so on, were made at Walkerville.

The top management group at Hiram Walker's consisted of Cliff Hatch Jr., Jim Ferguson, Jim Ford, John Giffen, Steve McCann and Ian Wilson-Smith. Short biographies of each are given in Table 4. Ferguson, Giffen and Wilson-Smith each headed up functional units as outlined in Exhibit 3. At the time of the case there was no corporate level marketing head. This role was being covered by Cliff Hatch Jr. Ford and McCann, both company veterans, were responsible, respectively, for the Courvoisier and Ballantine's supplier companies.

TABLE 4   Hiram Walker's Senior Management

H. Clifford Hatch Jr., 44, was a native of Windsor, Ontario, and a graduate of McGill University and the Harvard Business School. He joined Hiram Walker in 1970, and in 1976 was appointed CEO of Corby Distilleries Ltd. (a Canadian firm in which Hiram Walker held a majority interest). In 1979, he became corporate vice-president for marketing of Hiram Walker, and became president and CEO in 1983.

James P. Ferguson, 49, was born in Landis, Saskatchewan, and earned a degree from McGill University. He worked for several years with the accountancy firm of Price Waterhouse, and joined Hiram Walker in 1974. He was currently corporate vice-president for finance and treasurer of the company.

James D.N. Ford, 49, was raised in Glasgow, Scotland, and was a graduate of the University of Glasgow and a chartered accountant. He joined Courvoisier in 1965, and moved to Canada in 1968 as controller of Hiram Walker and later vice-president. He returned to Courvoisier in 1980, and presently was head of French operations.

John A. Giffen, 47, came from Ingersoll, Ontario, and held B.Sc. (Engineering) and M.B.A. degrees from the University of Windsor. He became Hiram Walker's corporate vice-president for production in 1980.

TABLE 4   (continued)

W. Steve McCann, 64, was a native of Edinburgh, Scotland, where he received his education and became a chartered accountant. He joined Hiram Walker in the Ballantine's organization, and became managing director of the Scottish operations in 1971.

Ian M. Wilson-Smith, 52, was born in Middlesex, England, and was a graduate of Cambridge University. His early experience was in production with Harveys of Bristol England, and later in production and general management positions with other firms in the beverage alcohol business in England and Canada. He joined Hiram Walker in 1980, and was currently corporate vice-president for administration.

The Marketing Units

Hiram Walker International and the American and Canadian sales companies were the primary marketing units. They were responsible, within their territories and for assigned brands, for proposing marketing strategies and budgets, building distributor relationships and achieving sales targets. Special marketing services for legal, packaging, research and other needs were provided by Walkerville staff groups. Revenues and direct marketing expenses were directly attributable to each of the line marketing units, and further analysis of profitability was possible after allocating product and other costs.

The Supply Units

The supplier units, such as Courvoisier, were responsible for product availability, quality and cost and, depending on the situation, performed local accounting and administrative functions. The supply unit heads in North America, with the exception of wine operations, reported to John Giffen. Those in Europe reported directly to Cliff Hatch Jr., although the European units drew on technical assistance from John Giffen's groups. Wine operations, which were relatively small by Hiram Walker standards, reported to Ian Wilson-Smith, who had a special interest and expertise in this area. The supplier units were essentially cost centres, although profitability could be assessed by the attribution of revenues and marketing costs.

Formal Integration

The annual budgeting process was the primary vehicle for tying the marketing and supply units together. Budgets were initiated by the marketing units, reviewed and extended by the supplier units, and approved at the corporate level. In practice this was a complicated process. Hiram Walker International, for example, had to deal with forecasts and marketing budgets for a number of brands across a range of countries, distributors and currencies. Further, as the planning process progressed, Hiram Walker International had to strike agreements with the supplier units, whose interests—in brand progress, capacity utilization, operational stability, and so on—were not always consistent with the marketing view. Finally all of this had to be assembled by marketing units across suppliers, and by supplier units across sales entities for corporate review.

Over the years the budget process had become increasingly complicated and time-consuming. This was the result of more complex operations and the tendencies of senior managers to micro-manage the operating units. John Harcarufka, head of W.A. Taylor in the U.S., would note, for example, that he had more autonomy in pricing and promoting Drambuie, an agency brand, than he did for Courvoisier. With the latter, he had to negotiate detailed approvals two ways, as he put it, with both Courvoisier in France and corporate marketing in Walkerville. There was also a strong feeling within the operating units that "Walkerville's" requests for information were too frequent, too detailed, occasionally unrealistic, and often unnecessary.

At the corporate level, the primary formal groups for coordinating the functional units were the management and strategic planning committees. The management committee consisted of Hatch, Giffen, Ferguson and Wilson-Smith; it met formally on a regular basis to consider corporate issues, and to review the proposals and performance of the marketing and supply units.

Informal Integration

A great deal of the burden of coordinating Hiram Walker activities was accomplished informally, by old hands working together. Hiram Walker took pride in the long service of its people, and in their development and advancement. The company promoted from within whenever possible; most of the top and middle management positions were filled by individuals who had worked their way up from entry level positions.

The management committee members worked together very closely. Their working relationships were strengthened by their long experience in the industry, the traditions of the company, and even by the relatively small size and isolation of corporate headquarters. Formal systems and meetings aside, it was perhaps more important for the running of the company that these managers met casually and frequently in the course of the day, in their offices, at lunch in the executive dining room, and in business and social entertaining.

The members of the management committee comprised the first circle of internal influence on corporate affairs. The second level included Jim Ford and Steve McCann who, in spite of distance, maintained a fairly high level of interaction with the Walkerville group through membership on the strategic planning committee, phone, correspondence and travel. The second circle might also have included David Evans, head of Hiram Walker International, except that he had only recently (1981) joined the company from Nestlé, and had not had the same opportunity to work with the Walkerville executives. The third circle of influence consisted of perhaps eight to ten executives, most of whom were marketing unit heads in North America and Europe.

Strategic Planning

Formal strategic planning at Hiram Walker was coordinated by a strategic planning committee consisting of the members of the management committee plus Ford and McCann. This committee met annually for two or three days to consider issues of corporate direction and priority, and to review progress in specific project areas such as acquisitions. On an informal basis, it served as a sounding board for most corporate initiatives.

For years Hiram Walker had based its forward planning on five-year rolling forecasts submitted by the operating units. These were discussed with Walkerville, adjusted where necessary, and used as the based for corporate financial and production forecasts. This forecast system was still in use, although top management was concerned that it placed too much reliance on a projection of the status quo. The February 1985, corporate forecast submitted to HWR projected 1989 revenues from continuing operations of $1 925 million and operating income of $350 million.

To remedy the limitations of existing procedures, the strategic planning committee started in 1982 to introduce a new strategic planning process. The aim was to push strategic thinking as far down the organization as possible—corporate management would be responsible for developing strategic guidelines and conducting reviews, while the unit managers would be responsible for proposing and implementing strategy for their operations. The process was tied to the existing organizational units, but strategy reviews were separated from forecast/budget activities.

The new process was slow to take hold. In spite of adjustments to provide headquarters coordination for new products and "brand champions" to coordinate information on existing brands, the system was not generating clear-cut priorities, commitment and action. Many of the business possibilities that had been identified remained just that. The terminology that came into use was that "more bite" was needed in the planning process, meaning more definitive guidelines and choices, more resources to back approved programs, and more delegation of authority and responsibility to get ideas implemented.

THE BIG ISSUES

As fiscal 1985 closed, very profitably but still without tangible progress on growth, Cliff Hatch Jr. was growing increasingly concerned. He had recently asked Ian Wilson-Smith to survey 35 to 40 unit managers to seek their ideas about what the company could do to become more aggressive in the market. Virtually all of the managers polled had responded in writing, often after consulting their colleagues and subordinates, and cumulatively they had offered literally dozens of suggestions. There was a focus, however, on three broad issues: (1) acquisitions, (2) new product development and (3) organizational refinement. A summary of the views together with comments by members of the top management group follows.

Acquisitions

It was generally agreed that acquisitions were necessary to improve Hiram Walker's growth and competitive position. The sheer volume of suggestions from the management ranks on potential acquisitions and new ventures outnumbered the rest by a wide margin. The major themes were the need to think big rather than small, the desirability of acquiring a few significant "white goods" brands (vodka, gin, etc.), the need to increase Walker's involvement in the wine industry, and a strong interest in beer (especially high-image imports) soft drinks and mineral waters. The general opinion would have squared with John Giffen's remark that "the pluses and minuses of the existing brand areas add up to really slow growth ... our only avenue for real progress is through acquisition."

The problem in acquisitions, as expressed by several managers, was that Hiram Walker was simply not moving aggressively enough. Jim Ferguson put it bluntly: "Our strategic planning hasn't accomplished very much ... we haven't done anything yet!" While this was not strictly true—since the company had made three small acquisitions—it captured the prevailing view that significant action was needed.

Although the formal position of the strategic planning committee was to focus on acquisitions within the spirits industry, there was informal disagreement about this focus within the group. The arguments were classic. Several managers felt that acquisitions should be limited to the business Hiram Walker knew, and within this were concerned about availability, cost, synergy and returns. Other managers cast a wider net, suggesting the spirits industry was in decline, and that diversification was necessary, at least into allied fields of prestige products such as perfumes and cosmetics.

There was some feeling that the procedures for screening and pursuing acquisitions were delaying the acquisition process. Currently, various members of the strategic planning committee were asked to follow up on possibilities under the general coordination of Cliff Hatch Jr. and Ian Wilson-Smith. A count of the assigned projects indicated that most managers on the committee had upwards of five leads to pursue. The formation of a dedicated headquarters unit to screen and analyze acquisitions had been discussed by the committee, but no action had been taken on this matter.

New Product Development

There was an ongoing controversy in the company over what were perceived to be unnecessary delays in bringing new product initiatives—including types, flavours, packaging, labels, etc.—to market. On the one hand, some managers, primarily from marketing positions, argued that more resources and more discretion were necessary to speed up the pace of development. They saw a newly formed product development committee as a dubious solution, as just another corporate hurdle of which there were already too many. Gerry Gianni, who had joined Hiram Walker in 1981 from a large spirits import house and now ran Hiram Walker Incorporated in the U.S., commented on the four years that it had taken to bring Canadian Club Classic to market: "A disaster ... the project was mandated from the top, but after that nothing seemed to happen ... the very first thing you should not do is appoint a committee, nor set set up a coordinator that will not be around to see the project through ... politics and bureaucracy set in and the coordinator was forced into a referee's position deciding who should win instead of thinking about benefits for the consumer ... we are still trying to come to grips with packaging."

Other executives argued that checks and balances were necessary to avoid expensive product proliferation, to provide for the orderly development of production facilities, and to ensure that new initiatives were consistent with corporate policy. As one production executive pointed out, "Some of the marketing units seem to change their priorities with the weather ... one moment it's miniatures in plastic for the airlines, the next it's 1.75 litre bottles ... they don't seem to appreciate the supply, inventory and equipment complications." Furthermore, at the corporate level, the traditional position was reiterated: "We rely on just a few brands and we operate in markets where brand and corporate reputations are crucial factors ... we can't afford to have someone going off half-cocked and creating a quality or public relations problem."

The Organization

Organizational suggestions were abundant in the managers' responses. The recurring themes were the need to decentralize decision-making, adopt a profit centre approach, and set up separate and properly staffed units to handle acquisitions and new products. These comments were echoed by Jim Ford and Ian Wilson-Smith. Ford noted that "Hiram Walker's highly centralized functional management structure is inappropriate for an increasingly competitive environment ... it creates confusion and conflict between the functions and between field and geographical management...further, under the present structure, I cannot see us developing the well rounded businessmen we will need in the future ... we will always have to go outside in the crunch." Ian Wilson-Smith was of a similar mind: "We have no adequate framework for the integrated management of our key brands on a world-wide basis or, indeed, of our key markets on a geographical basis; we have succeeded in getting the worst of both worlds and the end result is a further reinforcement of the centralized decision-making process ... we need major structural changes to combine production and marketing activities into manageable business units, integrate the responsibility for our key brands on a world-wide basis and redefine the role of corporate headquarters."

Other top managers disagreed. They admitted that the organization was not working as well as it should but argued that the current structure was essentially sound. All that was needed were refinements in staffing, policy and procedures. Jim Ferguson's position was, as he put it, "You have to understand that our big problem is not in operations ... we have strong brands and we are doing well ... it is that we haven't gotten on with acquisitions ... (Insofar as current operations are concerned) ... what we need to do is get a marketing vice-president into place and get Cliff out of that role ... and then use our budgeting and accounting procedures to hold the sales companies more clearly responsible for results ... we haven't pushed hard enough." Steve McCann spoke of international operations, "I was involved (in 1965) in the initial conception of HWI and my position then was that the brand owning companies (e.g., Hiram Walker Scotland) should be complete entities entirely responsible for success and failure ... this view was not accepted and HWI was made responsible to Walkerville. While I continue to prefer my original position in principle, I cannot see how HWI can now be unscrambled (whether by returning its functions to the brandowner—in whole or part—or in in some other way) without great disruption. And the likely benefits are insufficient to compensate for the disruption ... HWI should be allowed to get on with its job without interference from Walkerville, which, in my view, should confine itself to decisions on ... (elements of brand, strategy, operating policy) ... the approval of the annual budget and rigorous ex post facto examination of HWI's performance." Another top manager put the point bluntly in an informal conversation: "There is *no* way that we are going to reorganize this company."

ACTION CONSIDERATIONS

Cliff Hatch Jr. was quite prepared to act, subject to two broad conditions. First, he ruled out major strategic or organizational gambles. As he noted: "I have no mandate to wreck this company." Change could and should proceed, but the steps would have to be carefully developed. He was particularly concerned that the disagreements among managers demonstrated that the obstacles to growth were not well understood. As a result, he had tried to this point to keep the options for change open, and to avoid the endorsement of specific "solutions." One of this reasons for postponing the appointment of a corporate vice-president of marketing, for example, was that this would tend to reinforce past structure and practices.

Second, change would have to respect the corporate values that had helped to build Hiram Walker. "As a company," Hatch said, "we have tried to take the long-term view, to build lasting relationships, and to respect individuals and individual contributions. We have tried to avoid short-term and temporary solutions. I believe these principles will serve us as well in the future as they have in the past."

EXHIBIT 1 Demand for Alcoholic Beverages in Selected Categories and Countries, 1984 (9 litre case equivalents, 000s)

	Canadian Whisky	Scotch Whisky	Bourbon	Cognac	Brandy	Gin	Vodka	Rum	Cordials	Other Popular Liqueurs	TOTAL Spirits	TOTAL Wine	TOTAL Beer
United States	23 800	19 200	36 700[1]	1 800	5 200	14 300	31 200	12 200	16 300		179 400	232 900	2 385 300
Growth rate (80/84)	-0.5	-5.7	-4.3	10.0	-1.0	-2.0	.0	1.9	4.7		-1.3	4.1	0.7
Canada	6 700	1 200	LV	300	700	1 600	2 500	3 100	2 000		18 800	25 200	212 000
Growth rate (80/84)	-6.2	-3.9		3.5	-1.4	-7.6	-1.0	-2.9	1.7		-3.8	4.0	-1.4
United Kingdom	LV	12 000	LV	1 000	1 000	3 400	3 700	2 100	1 700		25 500	68 700	691 200
Growth rate (79/84)	-3.8	-5.3	3.4	-3.0	1.5	-5.3	3.6	-2.9	4.6		-1.8	-2.4	2.9
West Germany	LV	1 900	500	900	10 600	400	900	5 800	4 000	9 500[4]	44 000	178 000	985 700
Growth rate (79/84)	LV	-3.7	-7.7	-1.8	-0.8	-2.0	1.8	-3.5	-7.5	.0	-3.7	0.7	-0.1
France	LV	5 300	200	800	1 000	300	300	2 100	N/A	12 700[2]	30 000	522 000	250 000
Growth rate (79/84)	LV	6.2	6.8	-8.0	-4.6	14.8	9.9	-7.4	N/A	-1.4	-0.6	-1.9	-1.6
Italy	LV	3 100	100	200	6 900	300	200	100	3 400		24 800	525 400	119 700
Growth rate (79/84)	LV	2.4	20.0	-1.7	-3.5	15.0	9.9	-7.4	-3.0		-3.6	-1.9	2.7
Spain	LV	2 000	LV	LV	11 200	6 700	500	2 400	5 200	1 600[3]	50 800	200 800	251 000
Growth rate (80/84)	LV	1.9	LV	LV	-3.9	1.0	-8.3	-13.0	-3.0	10.4	-1.2	-1.9	2.7
Japan	LV	2 200	LV	500	2 000	200	N/A	300	LV	31 700[6]	332 800[5]	10 300	516 200
Growth rate (79/84)	LV	-4.1	LV	10.7	10.6	1.0	N/A	0.4	-0.3	LV	4.0	2.9	2.9
Australia	LV	1 900	LV	LV	800	200	300	800	400		4 900	35 000	204 700
Growth rate (79/84)	LV	3.7	LV	LV	10.6	-2.7	-2.0	4.8	-0.5	-0.3	2.9	6.5	0.7
World consumption (1982)		65 000	8 900		43 000	59 400	51 800						
Growth rate (79/84)		3.7	1.5		1.5	-2.0	1.3	3.4	-0.5			5.9	-0.8

1 Includes straight bourbon and blends
2 Anis, ougo
3 Spanish whisky
4 Korn, aquavit
5 Totals include sake consumption of 186 million cases
6 Japanese whisky
Note: LV—Low volumes.

EXHIBIT 2   Sales of Selected Hiram Walker Brands in Selected Areas[1] (9 litre case equivalents, 000s)

	Canadian Club	Ballantine's	Kahlua	Courvoisier	Tia Maria
United States, 1984 case sales (000)	2 900	380	1 570	540	130
Market share, point change (84/80)	12.1, –4.9	2.0, 0.3	26.1, –7.4	29.8, –3.3	2.1, –2.7
Canada, 1984 case sales (000)	650	130	210	60	130
Market share, point change (84/80)	9.7, –2.3	10.5, –0.2	18.6, –1.6	21.6 ,–5.0	11.5, –10.4
United Kingdom, 1983 case sales	LV	90	LV	320	120
Market share, point change (83/79)			1.0, N/A	30.0, 2.2	6.8, –3.2
Selected European,[2] 1983 case sales	LV	1 401	LV	160	LV
Market share, point change (83/79)			13.5, –1.1	8.2, 1.0	
Japan and Hong Kong	LV	130	LV	100	LV
Market share		10.0, N/A			
Company shipments, 1985 fiscal year	3 300	3 500	2 200	1 350	683
% Change (85/84)	–5.6	–10.3	3.0	1.8	N/A

[1] Individual brand/market data based on commercial estimates of wholesalers depletions known to somewhat overstate actual volumes. Market share based on category totals, e.g., Canadian Club share of Canadian Whisky sales.

[2] France, Italy, West Germany. Excludes duty free sales.

Note: LV—Low volumes.

EXHIBIT 3 Hiram Walker-Gooderham & Worts (A) Simplified Organization Structure

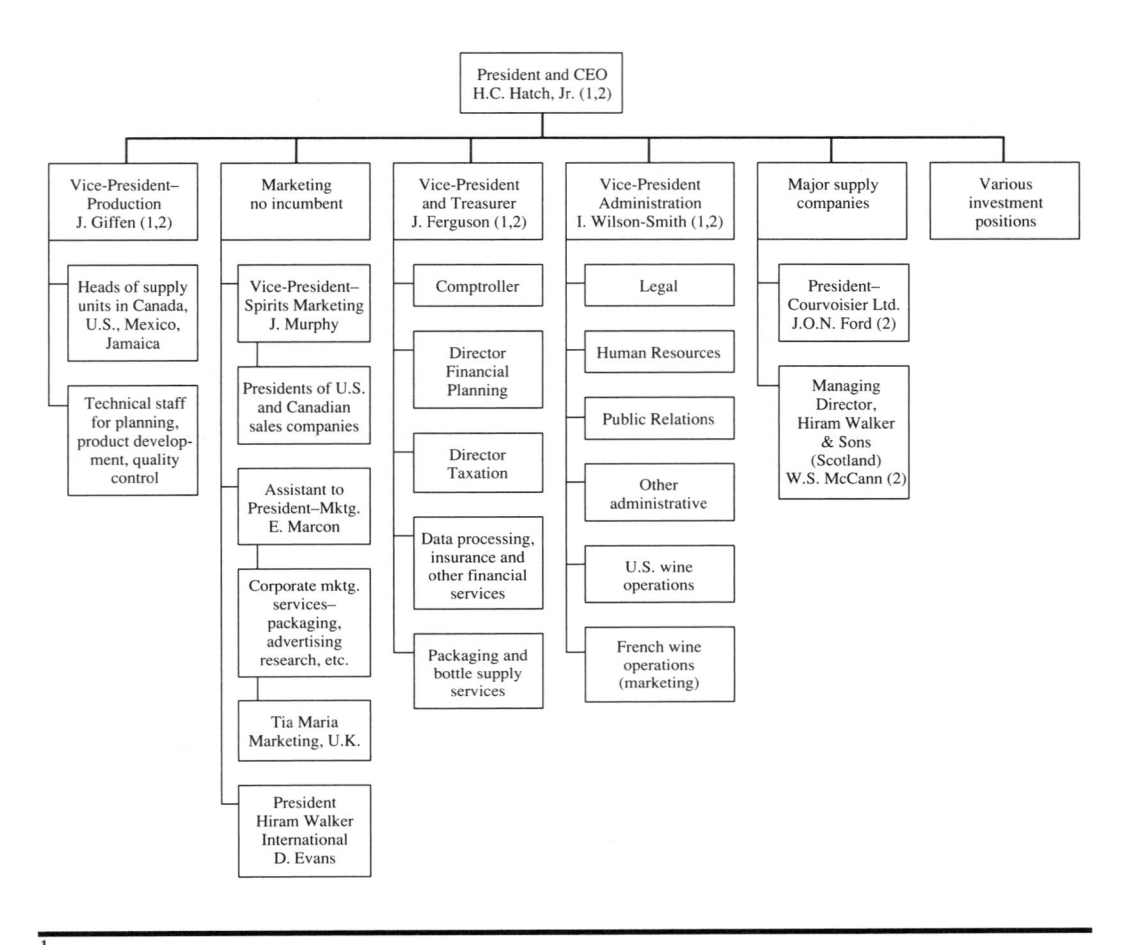

[1] Member, Management Committee.

[2] Member, Strategic Planning Committee.

SOURCE: Derived from company documents.

THE LONDON FREE PRESS (A): STRATEGIC CHANGE

Mary M. Crossan and Detlev Nitsch

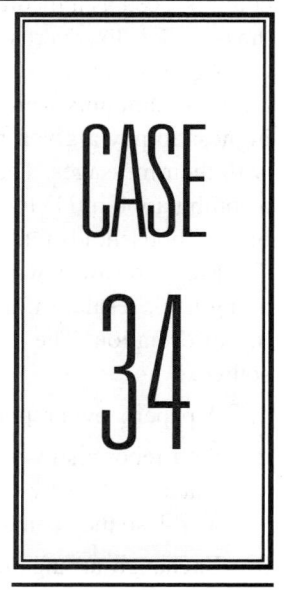

CASE 34

Phil McLeod had been appointed as the new editor of the *London Free Press* (LFP) in November 1987, with a mandate to make changes. Like most other North American daily newspapers, the LFP had been gradually losing readership, and its share of advertising revenues in the community was shrinking. Despite its ability to remain profitable, McLeod thought that it was not living up to its potential, especially since it was the only daily newspaper in London. He feared that there were ominous signs of a continuing decline in market share, which could only mean still lower profits in the future.

McLeod had been hired from the *Toronto Star* and put in charge of LFP's newsroom and editorial department to do whatever was necessary to reverse this trend. Now, in 1991, he wondered if it would be possible to stop the slow decline of the newspaper or if its shrinkage was an inevitable consequence of broader trends in the information industry and Canadian society.

THE NEWSPAPER INDUSTRY

Newspapers obtained revenues from two sources: from readers, who paid for papers through regular subscriptions or on a single-copy basis, and from advertising clients, who hoped to expose their messages to as many members of a community as possible. Conceptually newspapers could be seen as a medium that attracted readers with its editorial content, and in turn delivered those readers to advertisers as potential purchasers.

Advertising sales accounted for about three-quarters of a typical paper's total revenues, but these amounts were closely linked to the paid circulation of the paper. Advertisers' willingness to pay a given rate depended on the size of the audience they could expect to reach with their messages. The price advertisers paid for space in a newspaper was usually based on a combination of (1) total circulation and (2) penetration, expressed in terms of the percentage of total households reached.

McLeod saw newspapers as having two basic functions: gathering information, and packaging it for resale. Information came in two varieties: public "news;" and private, or advertising information. The news information-gathering function could be further broken down by source:

1. A paper's own reporters gathering local news.

2. Staff reporters responsible for news from distant locales. Many larger newspapers had "bureaux" staffed by their own people in important cities around Canada and the rest of the world, so they could have proprietary access to any information these reporters uncovered.

3. Exchange arrangements through the corporate umbrella—for example, LFP had a contractual link with Southam News that enabled it, for a fee, to tap into this large organization's worldwide network of news sources. This also allowed papers access to news developed initially for other media.

4. Wire services. Canadian Press (CP), American Press (AP) and Reuters were examples of news agencies that existed solely to provide news on a fee basis to anyone who was willing to pay for it. In some cases (CP for example), the agency was a cooperative owned by newspapers.

The LFP was fairly typical of daily newspapers in that approximately 60% of its space was allocated to advertising (paid messages), with the "newshole," or editorial content, occupying the rest. Of the 40% of the available space dedicated to the newshole, 60% was purchased from wire services or other sources. McLeod estimated that approximately 30% of his $10 million editorial budget was spent on purchased news; one-third of the balance was devoted to reworking or repackaging these stories for publication, and the rest was spent on maintaining the LFP's in-house news-gathering apparatus.

As advertisers became more sophisticated, they were no longer merely interested in a newspaper's raw circulation figures, but rather in its ability to reach those most likely to purchase their products. Electronic media in particular were often able to target very narrow market segments with a high degree of precision. Television programming was being geared to ever-smaller segments of the population, as cable and satellite proliferation expanded the choices available to consumers. With sophisticated demographic market research data, programmers could produce and schedule shows designed to appeal to specific groups, and have relatively high confidence that their target would be reached. This was attractive to advertisers because they could spend their advertising budgets more efficiently, avoiding messages sent to members of the community who were not potential customers. In contrast, daily newspapers were seen as a rather blunt instrument, with potentially broad mass-market coverage but little ability to ensure that a given message had reached its target segment.

Past Performance, Future Outlook

Newspaper companies had enjoyed a very profitable history in North America: at the beginning of the 1980s they boasted a median 9.6% profit margin, compared to a median of less than 5% for Fortune 500 Industrials. Even though, depending on commodity prices, newsprint accounted for anywhere from 20–25% of total costs, newspapers' return on sales ranged from 14–18%, while industrials averaged 6%. In 1992, U.S. newspaper companies enjoyed a resurgence in the stock market, outperforming index averages by a large margin (Exhibit 1). This followed several years of sluggish performance during which consolidation and downsizing were the norm in the industry.

Despite this evidence of good performance potential, there were several signs that indicated a long-run trend to declining circulation, reduced revenues and smaller profit margins. Exhibit 2 shows the decline in profitability of a typical North American newspaper company.

Newspapers' level of penetration, or market share as a percentage of households reached, was dropping for newspapers all across North America. In the U.S., 124 copies of daily newspapers were sold for every 100 households during the 1950s. By the 1970s, the comparable figure was 77, with the drop attributable in part to a decline in the number of two-newspaper households. The Canada-wide circulation growth rate, at 1.7%, was also well below the growth rates of the adult population (2.1%) and of households (3.0%) during the 1970s, even though it still outpaced the growth of total population (1.0%). Similar trends seemed to apply to London, where McLeod had noted that the LFP was losing about a percentage point per year in penetration, down to below 60% in the early 1990s.

While the total circulation of daily newpapers was still increasing, other indicators such as average daily circulation and penetration levels suggested that newspapers were losing readers, and were thus becoming less attractive as an advertising medium. As recently as 1973, daily newspapers had attracted 30.5 per cent of total Canadian advertising expenditures, compared to television in that year with 13.4 per cent. In fact, until 1977, daily newspapers held a larger share of ad revenues than radio, television, and weekly newspapers combined. But the long-run trend since 1972 showed a gradual decline in the newspapers' share, while television and other media continued to gather strength. Daily newspapers still had the largest share of total advertising revenues, but this share was gradually shrinking, (Table 1).

TABLE 1   Canadian Advertising Expenditures Percent Share of Total, by Medium

Medium	1973	1989 (Estimates)
Daily Newspapers	30.5	22.8
Catalogues, Direct Mail	20.6	21.9
Television	13.4	15.6
Radio	10.8	8.3
Weekly Newspapers	5.1	6.9
Magazines	2.4	3.1
Other	17.2	21.4

SOURCE: Maclean Hunter Research Bureau.

Breaking total advertising revenues down into national and local categories yielded further insights into the differing strengths of the competing media. For example, in 1973–1974 daily newspapers received 19.8% of their advertising revenues from national accounts. The corresponding figure for television was 73.9%, which shifted upward to 75.3% by 1980, while the dailies' proportion fell to 18.7%. This suggested that newspapers' heavy reliance on local retail and classified advertising was, if anything, increasing.

Demographics of Readership: Long-Run Implications

A 1986 study of newspaper readers showed that most readers were in the over-35 age category, and that 75% of people in their 20s did not regularly read the paper. In the past, there had been some support for the notion that newspaper reading habits grew as individuals aged. Cross-sectional studies had turned up much the same data decade after decade, as young non-readers in an early study evolved into 50-year-old newspaper aficionados 30 years later.

But McLeod feared that times had changed, and that these non-readers would be difficult to turn into loyal newspaper customers in the future. The current crop of young adults were the first who had been raised in an age in which television was accepted as a legitimate news source. Unlike previous generations, these people believed and trusted what they saw on the small screen, and did not feel the need to see it in print. The public's familiarity and comfort level with television had grown over time, aided by the medium's presence on the scene of historic events such as the 1963 assassination of U.S. President Kennedy, and the first moon landing in 1969. Also, McLeod admitted that television had proved competent in areas where newspapers were once thought to have a competitive advantage: background and analysis. Network news and news-only cable TV channels were increasingly supplying high-quality, in-depth coverage of important events, with a timeliness and sense of immediacy that newspapers could not match.

Television's new-found strengths might make it impossible for newspapers to attract the current group of younger people. This meant that the expected shift in preference, from television to newspapers as people aged, might not take place this time. Thus the old assumption that readership would stay more or less constant over time appeared to rely on a "no change" scenario which did not fit reality.

Some evidence suggested that, by 1991, newspaper readership was recovering from its precipitous decline. Gross circulation was actually up by 32% from 15 years before, while population had only risen 16%. Also, the proportion of Canadian adults reading newspapers had increased from 63% to 68.5%. However, McLeod thought that these numbers were misleading because they focused on overall total circulation instead of daily averages, and they ignored the fact that new newspaper formats had begun to penetrate the market. The gross circulation statistic compared present total readership with comparable figures before the "tabloid era" in many major Canadian centres. Tabloids were new and very different newspapers, adding 700 000 new readers who were, arguably, in a different category than traditional ones. Also, 14 new Sunday editions had been started in the past seven years, contributing another 1.5 million new readers to the circulation total, but not raising the daily average circulation. Thus, while total circulation was up, daily average circulation per newspaper was still in decline across the country (Table 2).

TABLE 2   Daily Circulation Averages (For 12 Months Ended March 1991, Change from Previous 12 Months)

Vancouver Sun	Down 5.5%
Montreal Gazette	Down 5.2%
Ottawa Citizen	Down 4.0%
Kitchener Record	Down 3.7%
Kingston Whig-Standard	Down 3.7%
London Free Press	Down 3.6%
Calgary Herald	Down 3.4%
Calgary Sun	Down 2.5%
Toronto Sun	Down 2.4%
Hamilton Spectator	Down 2.4%
Toronto Star	Down 2.2%
Edmonton Sun	Down 1.3%
Edmonton Journal	Down 0.6%
Windsor Star	Even
Vancouver Province	Up 2.6%

SOURCE: LFP internal documents.

On this basis, circulation was being outpaced by population growth in virtually every market in Canada. Among other things, this had also placed increasing pressure on the sales function. The *London Free Press* in 1990 had to sell 81 364 new subscription orders to maintain its average daily home delivery at 85 646 in the city of London. In the previous year, the home delivery average had been slightly higher but only 63 000 new orders had to be sold.

A recent study conducted in the United States and Canada had suggested three main reasons why readers were abandoning newspapers:

1. No time:
   * your paper is hard to read
   * I really don't have any time
   * you don't make it clear why I should make time

2. No news:
   * I saw it all on TV; you gave me nothing new
   * insufficient insight, understanding, depth

3. No interest:
   * nothing for me in the paper
   * I don't share your idea of what is new or important
   * you don't care about what I care about—in fact you often belittle the things my friends and I enjoy

The same study had reconfirmed that one of the causes of newspapers' decline in importance to readers was the fact that other media, principally television, had made news more easily consumable by the public. Comparing statistics over time exposed a trend away from newspapers on virtually every dimension (Table 3).

TABLE 3   Comparison of Television and Newspapers (percentage of respondents who responded positively to each question)

	1986	*1991*
Main source of international news:		
Television	63%	73%
Newspapers	21%	16%
Main source of national news:		
Television	69%	75%
Newspapers	19%	16%
Main source of local news:		
Television	41%	43%
Newspapers	34%	35%
Most believable:		
Television	no data	30%
Newspapers	no data	24%
Most accurate:		
Television	no data	33%
Newspapers	no data	19%
Most likely to be fair:		
Television	no data	33%
Newspapers	no data	19%

SOURCE: Environics, reproduced in LFP internal documents.

Industry Consolidation Trend

The competitive dynamic among newspapers in Canada had changed gradually over the years. In the past, newspapers had competed as a collection of geographically-dispersed individual markets. While there had been virtually no competition between cities, there had often been intense rivalry among papers within cities. But by the 1980s, cities with two or more dailies had become a rarity (Table 4). Even in the few locations that still had more than one daily, the papers tended to be positioned in fairly well-defined niches, such as Toronto's *Globe and Mail*, *Sun*, and *Star*. Through consolidation and attrition, the industry had evolved into a series of local newspaper monopolies.

Consolidation had also led to domination of the Canadian industry by a few national or regional chains. Advantages to group ownership were (1) shared resources, including pooled information services from abroad; and (2) the owner's deep pockets, which enabled a chain newspaper to weather temporary downturns in its financial performance, and gave it access to capital for major investments in technology.

The two largest chains, Southam and Thomson, together controlled 58% of the English-language circulation in Canada. Southam, with 17 of the total 95 Canadian English dailies, had 33.5% of overall circulation, while Thomson, with 36 papers, had 24.5%. These percentages did not, in themselves, suggest that the newspaper market had taken on the characteristics of a monopoly. But by avoiding head-to-head competition among papers in individual cities, the chains' newspapers had managed to enjoy local monopolies and high profits.

TABLE 4   **Major Newspapers with Circulations (1993)**

City	Newspaper	Daily Average Circulation
Calgary	*Herald*	125 000
	Sun	76 000
Winnipeg	*Free Press*	154 000
Regina	*Leader-Post*	68 000
Hamilton	*Spectator*	135 000
Edmonton	*Journal*	137 000
	Sun	69 000
Vancouver	*Province*	185 000
	Sun	221 000
Victoria	*Times-Colonist*	77 000
Winnipeg	*Free Press*	154 000
Halifax	*Chronicle Herald*	97 000
Waterloo	*K-W Record*	75 000
London	*Free Press*	115 000
Ottawa	*Citizen*	178 000
Toronto	*Star*	544 000
	Globe and Mail	311 000
	Sun	272 000
Windsor	*Star*	86 000
Montreal	*Gazette*	163 000
	Journal de Montreal	293 000
	La Presse	205 000
Quebec City	*Journal de Quebec*	102 000
	Le Soleil	99 000

SOURCE: Canadian Advertising Rates and Data, March 1994.

Threat to the Public Interest?

Critics of industry consolidation favoured some form of government intervention to help support financially troubled newspapers and to preserve competitive rivalry. Arguing out of concern for the public interest, they cautioned that in single-paper monopolies, readers' opinions would be manipulated by selective reporting and by opinion masquerading as objective journalism. Further, since advertisers would have no alternative outlets for their print messages, they would be at the mercy of greedy newspaper owners, and would become the victims of price-gouging and other undesirable tactics.

Those who saw no problem with the demise of direct competition maintained that newspapers in monopoly markets were able and willing to sustain a high level of journalistic quality, because their resources were not eroded through needless duplication and price competition with rivals. A section of the 1981 Royal Commission on Newspapers suggested that there was no evidence of declining quality or journalistic integrity as a result of industry consolidation. Publishers in single-newspaper towns were characterized as being able to "afford excellence," while still having to compete with other media for advertisers' dollars.

Neither was the trend to group ownership of newspapers seen, by these observers, as a threat to editorial independence. Publishers of chain newspapers frequently made mention of their freedom from interference by their corporate bosses. In support of this contention they cited the fact that some of Canada's most respected papers were being run at a loss by large chains (for example, Thomson's *Globe and Mail*), implying that high quality standards were not being eroded in pursuit of corporate profitability.

Even the Supreme Court of Canada had indirectly supported the position that the public interest was not threatened by industry consolidation. In ruling on a 1977 case brought under anti-combines legislation, the court held that "the Crown was unable to prove, as the law requires, that a single owner of the [only] five dailies in New Brunswick would be detrimental to the public." In reaching this conclusion, the Court noted the Irving chain's success in increasing the circulation of all five papers, the fact that capital investment had been made in them, and that money-losing papers had been subsidized to enable them to continue operating.

Social Role of Newspapers

In Western society, the press had long been viewed as an expression of the right of free speech, and as one of the pillars of democracy. Independence from government and other interference was held to be absolutely essential if editorial quality and integrity were to be preserved. The press was seen as the "watchdog" charged with informing the public about the activities of the state.

There was a sense that the press had a larger role in society than that of other commercial enterprises. Some observers and industry insiders had concluded that newspapers have higher ideals than just making money, and responsibilities beyond simply keeping shareholders happy. While admitting that, at some level at least, financial viability was important, many people nevertheless felt that newspapers had an altruistic mission to present the complete truth, and that the naked pursuit of larger profits would put their editorial objectivity at risk. Newspapers were thus seen to be driven by both a service ethic and a market ethic.

Partly as a result of this extra-commercial role, a mystique had arisen about journalism which led to the belief, among many reporters, that journalists alone were competent to judge what stories the public should see in print, and in what form they should be presented. Among many traditionalists, journalistic quality (as defined by them) should be emphasized over the pursuit of mere profit. Papers which "sold out" in order to target a larger audience were seen to be pandering to the whims of an unsophisticated public whose members often did not know what was good for them.

McLeod saw the notion of newspapers, "altruistic mission" as a self-serving rationalization. He felt it was invoked to support the idea that maintaining the existing editorial process was more important than the consumption of the product, thus providing a rationale for preservation of the status quo. The result, he thought, was that newspapers had lost touch with their communities. By refusing to respond to readers' needs, under the pretext of preserving journalistic integrity, papers were becoming increasingly irrelevant to many potential readers. Print journalism's insular mentality, bred of a grandiose view of its role in society, its professional arrogance, and its past success, had isolated it from those on whom it depended for its survival.

Evidence about the relative profitability of different editorial approaches was equivocal, in any event. Observers could point to successful and unsuccessful examples at both ends of the "quality" continuum. For example, the *Globe and Mail*, widely perceived as a high-quality paper, was operating at a loss, while other quality papers such as the *Washington Post* and the *New York Times* were earning money. At the tabloid end of the spectrum, the *Toronto Sun* was a financial success, while *USA Today* was still struggling to break even. It seemed that, for all the criticism levelled at papers which tried to boost circulation by appealing to a larger and, arguably, less discriminating mass market, this "sell-out" tactic was no guarantee of profits. There seemed to be profitable market niches for newspapers following either strategy.

THE LONDON FREE PRESS

The London Free Press was the only daily newspaper in London, Ontario, a southwestern Ontario city of approximately 300 000. It was part of the Blackburn Group Inc. (BGI), which was made up of businesses in the communication and information fields. Begun in 1849, *The London Free Press* had been owned and operated for five generations by the Blackburn family of London, and maintained a strong tradition of community service.

As communications technology evolved, so did the organization's activities in various media. An AM radio station was started in 1922, and in 1953 television was added to the Blackburn empire.[1] An FM radio station completed the growing conglomerate's coverage of the available "instant media."

In addition to these holdings, BGI had also launched Netmar Inc. in 1974, and purchased Compusearch in 1984. Netmar published and distributed weekly newspapers, shopping guides, and advertising flyers in Ontario and Alberta. Compusearch, based in Toronto, was a North American leader in market information and analysis.

In 1991, BGI established Blackburn Marketing Services Inc. (BMSI), an investment and management company formed to develop a portfolio of businesses in the direct marketing area. BMSI had made inroads into the U.S. market through acquisitions and mergers with American market research organizations.

BGI and its operating subsidiaries were private companies, and had been run under Blackburn family control since their founding. The LFP had the longest history, and was the most "legitimate" in terms of traditional journalistic values. Blackburn's senior management were proud that they had been able to maintain both the financial health of the paper and its high journalistic quality while creating a work environment that was described as caring and paternalistic.

The LFP had up-to-date production facilities, and its distribution system was described by McLeod as leading-edge, given the current state of technological development. Minimizing printing and distribution costs was an ongoing effort at the LFP, but any gains made in this area would be incremental. For true strategic impact, McLeod thought he had to focus on the revenue-generating side of the profit equation. This placed the onus for change on the editorial department.

---

[1] The TV Station was sold in 1993 because the Blackburn Group felt it no longer fit the news focus of its other holdings, and because it needed substantial new investment to stay competitive in the entertainment field.

Organization

The LFP, like most newspapers, was organized along functional lines. The principal departments were advertising, production, administrative and editorial. The editorial department of approximately 130 employees was headed by McLeod, and divided into sections that corresponded to the principal sections of the newspaper. Staff were assigned to sports, entertainment, business, political, or local/regional sections on a more or less permanent basis, under the leadership of a senior editor who was in charge of that part of the paper.

Exhibit 3 presents a chart showing the organization of editorial staff within sections of the paper. In operation, it worked as follows: For a typical local news event, a reporter was sent into the field by a senior editor to gather the facts, and to write the story. The piece was then turned over to a copy editor, who would check spelling and grammar, alter its length, or make other changes. After this step, the graphics people took over, adding pictures, diagrams, or maps as required, and physically reworking the story to fit into the page layout that was being planned for that edition. Again, the original story could be changed to meet space restrictions.

McLeod saw several weaknesses in this system. For example, a typical reporter might be assigned to cover local news, and be routinely sent to cover regular meetings of some special-interest group. This reporter might return with a story about a particularly colourful and lively meeting, at which members expressed various forms of outrage and stated their political positions for the record. The story would run in the newspaper, suitably headlined with attention-getting phrases, and the responsible section editor would feel that the job of covering local news had been accomplished. However, the only "outrage" felt might be on the part of the 20 people attending the meeting, and the significance of the event for the greater community could be nonexistent. Without probing more deeply into the reasons behind the meeting, and investigating the possible consequences on a level that went beyond the narrow interests of a particular group, the LFP might not be reporting anything meaningful to readers. Many reporters' roles had been created in response to a specific need in the past, but were maintained today, McLeod had decided, more out of habit than for the intrinsic "newsworthiness" of the material that was ultimately written. When making decisions about how to deploy limited reporting resources to the best possible effect, the test of community relevance was often not applied.

Another problem was that, throughout the traditional process, there was little or no communication between the various production stages. Because the printing schedule of the LFP dictated that the presses start rolling at midnight, the latter steps in the process were often not done until evening, while the original story may have been written that morning. By the time the editors and graphics people first saw the story, its original author could be home in bed, with no opportunity for input or influence over how it would finally appear in the paper.

The lack of a perceived connection with the community was symbolized by the LFP's physical premises as well. With only one access door, the building itself was not easy for the public to enter. Once inside, they faced a forbidding security checkpoint, a symbolic barrier between the public and the reporters who chronicled their lives. At the same time, McLeod remarked on the fact that none of the editorial staff had a view of the outside from their work area. The lack of a visual link to the city of London reinforced the inward-directed focus of those who purported to be writing about issues and events that were important to the community.

The organization structure also isolated departments within the newspaper from one another. Each section was conceptually and editorially an independent entity, and there was little communication or sharing of information among them. McLeod thought that this arrangement had led, on occasion, to stories falling through the cracks because they did not fit neatly into one of the pre-defined categories. An example of this occurred when a major World Wrestling Federation (WWF) event was scheduled to be held in London. The match was to be held at the London Gardens, which was the biggest arena in the city, and frequently the venue for major music concerts and sports events. *The London Free Press* often reported on these activities in the next day's edition, and it had been informed by the WWF's sophisticated publicity department about the major wrestling stars who would be making a rare appearance in London. The most popular and biggest money-making wrestlers were more accustomed to appearing in places such as New York's Madison Square Garden or the Fabulous Western Forum in Los Angeles than in a relative backwater such as the 8 000 seat London Gardens.

As it happened however, the sports section of the LFP declined to cover the WWF event because they felt that professional wrestling was not a true "sport," but more a form of staged entertainment. The entertainment editor meanwhile assumed that, since wrestling billed itself as a sport, and its participants were "athletes," the sports section would be reporting on it. The lack of communication between sections, and the fact that professional wrestling could not be neatly pigeonholed as either "sport" or "entertainment," led to neither section covering what was, for many London residents, a major news item.

Strategic Response

To halt further declines in readership, a major makeover of the LFP was undertaken in 1989, to give it a different look and make it more contemporary, "breezy," and attractive to readers. In what was seen in the trade as a major departure from tradition, the front page was redesigned. The number of stories it contained was reduced in favour of making it more of a road map for the contents of the inside pages. More colour was used, in conjunction with other cosmetic changes designed to make the paper look more user-friendly and less boring.

These changes, while hardly revolutionary to the eye of an average reader, were perceived by some members of the editorial staff as an abandonment of its tradition of editorial excellence. They interpreted the emphasis on readability and graphic attractiveness as an effort to lure readers with pretty pictures and colourful presentation. In the detractors' opinions, an emphasis on the quality of writing was being supplanted by less meaningful priorities.

The increased use of graphics meant that, for the first time, charts, maps and graphs were incorporated into stories right from the outset, as opposed to being added as an afterthought on a "space available" basis. One group which felt threatened as a result was the staff photographers, who saw their work competing for space with that of the graphics designers. Another unhappy group was the reporters. They felt their pre-eminent position in the LFP newsroom being eroded, since now much of what they wrote might be captured in a chart or graph. While this had always been the case to a certain extent, graphics and pictorial summaries of key story points were now intended to be an integral part of the creation of an article, to be included in the process right from the start. Reporters thought that their influence over how a story would be presented would now have to be shared with others, who often might have little training in journalism.

Results

Reader response to the changes was mixed. Evidence favouring and criticizing the changes was gathered from focus groups, and was revealed in letters to the editor. From these sources, it became clear that some readers were upset with the new look of the paper and found it disconcerting that items they were interested in were relocated to unfamiliar sections. On the other hand, some reported that they liked the new format, and saw it as a step toward making the paper more readable. While it was difficult to draw quantitative conclusions from this, McLeod estimated that the split "for" and "against" the redesign was about 50–50.

Circulation for 1990, the first full year of operation with the new format, was down 3% from the year before. However, London was just beginning to feel the effects of a recession at that time, and this made it difficult to disentangle the effect of the change from broader economic trends. The question of how much circulation would have dropped without a change remained impossible to answer.

At the same time as changes in the appearance of the LFP were being implemented, a drive to unionize the newsroom was successfully completed. Though professing considerable philosophical discomfort with their decision, supporters of the unionization effort had decided that this was the only way they could combat what they saw as unilateral and wrong-headed action by the paper's management. In what many saw as a result of the unhappiness of editorial staff about the new direction the LFP appeared to be taking, they voted to go on strike in early 1990. The strike was settled after a few weeks, during which the paper was put together by managerial staff, but unresolved ill feelings remained.

Package versus Content

McLeod had come to believe that, while a newspaper's packaging was closely linked to its content, the two "must become disentangled in our minds" in order for progress to be made. He had changed the package, following the tradition of consumer goods marketers. Now perhaps something a little more substantive was in order.

In order for readers to see the LFP as an important source of information, the content of the paper would need to reflect their wishes more closely. But changing the content would not be easy. As McLeod put it, a newspaper is like a sausage factory:

> You can put as many good ideas as you want into the front end of the machine, but unless that machine has been retooled to think and act in new ways, it will always turn out more or less the same thing. In other words, whatever goes in, sausages come out. Perhaps sausages with better texture or taste, less fat and fewer calories, but sausages nevertheless.

McLeod felt that the changes would require a substantial "rewiring of our heads," and would be risky because they conflicted with traditional attitudes about journalism. More stories needed to be written about topics that readers were actually interested in, and they needed to be covered in greater depth. At the same time, McLeod no longer believed that each piece in the paper had to be written, edited and laid out in the final few minutes before the press deadline. "While I wouldn't know the details of the stories, I can tell you two days in advance what 80% of our paper is going to look like," he said. "If we know, broadly, what the subject matter is going to be, why can't we do a better job of background and analysis on those stories we already know are going to be in the paper?"

Potential Resistance

Opposition to any proposed changes could be high. McLeod was risking criticism for tampering with the natural order of the way newspapers were run, because of the strong entrenched culture that existed in the profession. According to one view, he might be allowing the process of producing a newspaper to be unduly tainted by customer influence.

On a more personal level, the changes might shake many staffers' strongly-held beliefs about how newspapers should be produced, and about the role of journalism in a society. Some reporters thought that the atmosphere in the newsroom was already poisoned because of a strong polarization between those in favour of and those opposed to change. Some, who were suspicious of any attempts to solicit their opinion, were guarded about their comments regarding the organizational changes. While these individuals expressed deep concern over the future of the newspaper, they felt alienated, disenfranchised, and devalued because of the changes that had been implemented or proposed. Some had gone for stress counselling to help them deal with the effects.

Opponents also felt that a sacred trust established by the late Walter Blackburn was being violated. The LFP had, until recently, been regarded as a writer's paper because of the consistently high quality of its journalism, as judged by other journalists. There was a strong tradition of editorial freedom, and the reporters had become accustomed to being treated as highly trained and valued professionals. Some feared that, with change, their skills would be devalued in favour of *People* magazine-style writing, which could be executed by relatively unskilled individuals.

One reporter commented:

> Management should be trying to involve people, rather than alienating them. Many of us are deeply concerned about what's going on, but management isn't paying any attention. We've been left behind in this whole thing; nothing coming from us has been listened to. Many people feel disenfranchised, devalued. There's a high level of distrust here, and an adversarial climate. In fact, the environment is so poisoned, I'm worried that what I say to you [that is, the case writer] might be used against me.

There was also resistance to what some saw as the "scourge of MBAs." Market research reports which suggested declining profits and an unsustainable future for the newspaper had been shared with the staff, but they were dismissed by dissidents as mere spreadsheet manipulation. The report authors were characterized as pinstriped automatons bent on forcing higher short-term profits out of a venerable institution by squeezing out its lifeblood. Opponents of change pointed out that none of the blue-suit crowd's forecasts ever came true anyway, and saw the doom and gloom scenarios, with their accompanying recommendations, as a stratagem that allowed the MBAs to increase their own consulting revenue.

Scepticism and mistrust was further fuelled by the fact that McLeod's own managerial style was sometimes less than tactful, especially when he was challenging some of journalism's sacred cows. A typical comment about a proposed story might be: "Who cares?" which was intended to mean: "Do our readers feel strongly about this story, or does the way we've presented it give them a reason to care?" However, some reporters, not accustomed to thinking this way, might misinterpret the remark as a personal criticism or as a lack of confidence in their writing ability.

McLEOD'S POSITION

Although he felt strongly that change was needed, McLeod was in a quandary about what form it should take, the urgency with which it should be implemented, and what support or resistance the changes might encounter. BGI management had hired McLeod from the *Toronto Star* with the expectation that he would be a change agent. The culture of the *Star*, of which McLeod was a product, was perceived as much less family-like and paternalistic than the LFP. This was partly because it operated in a much more competitive market, but also because of the long tradition of Blackburn family influence on the way the London paper was run. The Blackburn legacy implied that employees would be cared for during difficult periods in their personal and professional lives, and would not be treated as interchangeable chattels or disposable factors of production. McLeod's arrival on the scene, with his outsider's background and perspective, was a signal to some that these traditions might be consigned to history, to be replaced by a much more impersonal bottom-line focus.

Previous editors had also tended to put high-quality journalism at the top of their agenda. As a result, the LFP was widely perceived, both internally and by outsiders, as a "writer's paper." Any change which threatened these priorities would meet with stiff opposition. BGI executives were willing to support any reasonable initiative—Phil McLeod's challenge lay in choosing the right one and avoiding the most serious pitfalls.

EXHIBIT 1   Year-End Newspaper Results, 1992 Stock Market Performance

	Gain(**)
A.H. Belo (NYSE - BLC)	30.4%
Dow Jones (NYSE - DJ)	23.7%
Gannett (NYSE - GCI)	11.4%
Knight Ridder (NYSE - KRI)	17.7%
McClatchy (NYSE - MNI)	21.9%
Media General (ASE - MEGA)	17.2%
Multimedia (NASDAQ - MMEDC)	9.8%
New York times (ASE - NYTA)	68.8%
Times Mirror (NYSE - TMC)	47.5%
Tribune (NYSE - TRB)	37.7%
Washington Post (NYSE - WPO)	23.5%
Average Gain	28.6%
Standard & Poors	
—400 Industrials	6.2%
—500 Composite	10.3%

SOURCE: Company Reports, Alex Brown & Sons estimates.

EXHIBIT 2   Thomson—North American Newspapers (millions of dollars)

	1988	*1989*	*1990*	*1991*	*1992*
Revenues	981	1 081	1 158	1 142	1 160
Operating Profit	306	317	282	228	205
Operating Margin	31.2%	29.3%	24.4%	20.0%	17.7%

SOURCE: Company Reports, Alex Brown & Sons estimates.

EXHIBIT 3   Partial Organization Chart circa 1987

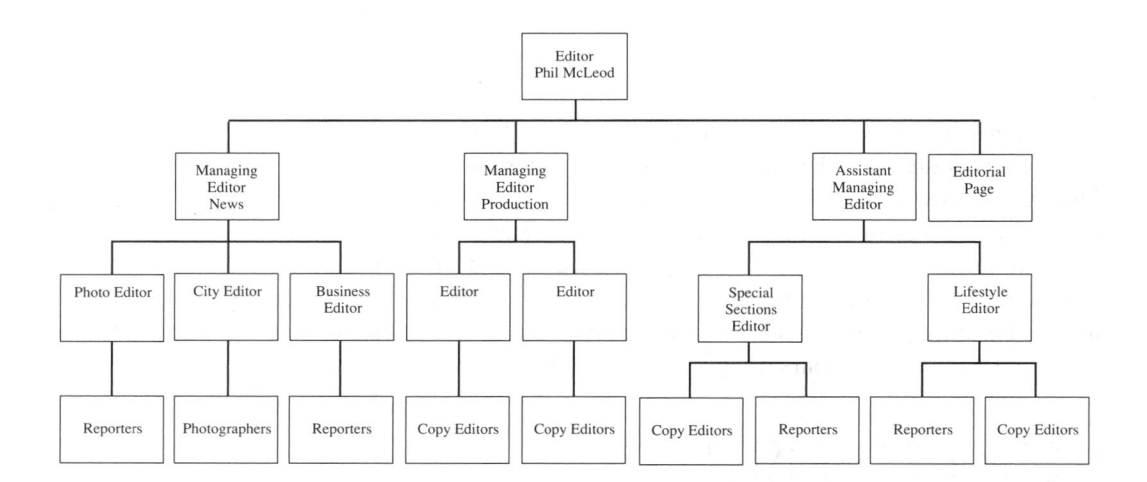

SOURCE: Philip McLeod interview.

ICI COLOURS: FIGHTING FOR THE CUSTOMER

Terry Deutscher and Joyce Miller

In January 1989, Patrick Kelly, ICI Colours and Fine Chemicals' (C&FC) UK Regional Manager, was urging Mike Parker, C&FC's Commercial Director, to formalize the Customer Charter initiative under the umbrella of "Fighting for the Customer." The intention of the Customer Charter was to hammer out a mutually agreeable service package with key customers and to monitor and report C&FC's performance against their requirements. The programme was based on the promise to trace back and forever eliminate service deficiencies at their source. Forming partnerships with customers was a powerful idea, but some concern had been expressed within the Colours organization about its ability to deliver.

THE COLOURS INDUSTRY

Colouring was one of the earliest recorded industries. Some 3 000 years ago, the Phoenicians used pigments from ores and minerals to colour fibres and leathers. Pigments were obtained by grinding these strongly coloured insoluble materials into a fine powder so that particles of colour would be dispersed throughout the material. Alternatively, an article could be dyed. In this case, colour was transferred to a piece of cloth, for instance, which was immersed in a liquid in which a soluble colouring agent had been dissolved. Discoveries in the 19th century enabled the manufacture of synthetic colorants. In 1988, 800 000 tonnes of synthetic dyestuffs and pigments were produced. As an example, 150 grams of dye were sufficient to colour six suits, while 50 grams of pigment were enough to paint a small car.

Six European companies dominated the world market for dyes and organic pigments and accounted for more than half of the industry's US$10 billion sales in 1988:

Ciba-Geigy	20%
Sandoz	8%
ICI C&FC (dyes and pigments)	7%
Hoechst	9%
Bayer	5%
BASF	9%

In recent years, "nontraditional" suppliers had begun producing increasing quantities of colorants. These suppliers were mostly agents located in Eastern Europe, Taiwan and China. The Soviet Union also occasionally exported dyestuffs to obtain hard currency when excess production was available. Product quality and delivery were inconsistent as was the case with most non-traditional sources. An industry analyst observed:

> Non-traditional suppliers are biting at the ankles of the six majors, but they mostly compete with each other. They have little overhead and no real structure to get a toehold into the developed markets. The Japanese are really the ones with the ability to make an impact as their chemical industry becomes more developed; their whole mindset is built around total quality and the philosophy is to have one supplier of key materials who never lets you down.

Dyestuffs were used primarily in the textile industry, whereas industrial colours (pigments) were used in the paper, ink, leather, paints and plastics industries. Overall, the market was fairly mature with 2% annual growth, although certain segments like plastics and printing inks were expanding at a faster rate. Demand in most customers' industries tended to follow the business cycle. Consequently, movements in the cycle had direct repercussions on demand levels, prices and margins for dyes and pigments.

On the textile side, the fashion-conscious developed countries of Europe and North America drove the demand for dyestuffs, particularly for colouring knitgoods, denim and polyester blends. The fashion industry experienced continuous change and producers succeeded by rightly anticipating shifts in demand for materials and colours. As a result, dyestuffs buyers were pressuring their suppliers for more information, better response time, and improved delivery reliability. While the turnaround time for industrial colours orders ranged from two days to a week, a textile customer typically wanted delivery within 24–48 hours.

Industrial colours tended to be more price-sensitive than dyes. This was especially the case in the ink industry where pigments represented about 20% of total materials costs. In addition to price, industrial colours buyers valued dependable delivery and consistency from batch to batch. Many were not wholly satisfied with their current suppliers. As one American ink manufacturer said:

> If one of the ingredients for mixing a batch of ink isn't right, we have to adjust the formula, at a high cost in terms of time and production capacity. Furthermore, delivery is critical. If you promise it to me in two weeks, on the 15th, I can schedule around it until then. But get it to me on the 15th, don't dribble it in at the end of the month.

Would I pay 10% more for a perfectly consistent product that was always delivered when promised? Hell, yes! But I'm sceptical that any supplier can actually do it.

ICI COLOURS & FINE CHEMICALS (C&FC)

Located in Blackley, near Manchester, C&FC was a leading global supplier of dyestuffs, industrial colours, and certain chemicals. In 1988, C&FC generated £400 million in revenues through the sale of some 2 000 products to over 14 000 customers worldwide. ICI had national selling organizations in 60 countries and serviced many more through agent or dealer arrangements. Geographically, sales were as follows: 17% in the UK, 33% in Western Europe, 21% in Asia/Pacific, 20% in the Americas, and 9% in Eastern Europe and Africa. An organization chart is contained in Exhibit 1.

The sale of industrial colours contributed about one quarter of C&FC revenues. Customers were generally major international groups who looked at prices globally and had rigorous standards for pigment consistency. In the case of automotive paint, ten organizations represented 65% of the market worldwide. On the other hand, the textile industry was extremely fragmented and customers ranged dramatically in size. Here, a supplier's success was rooted in quick response time and right-the-first-time product quality. Dyestuffs accounted for over 50% of C&FC sales. The remaining revenue was derived from products used to provide distinguishing effects in agrochemicals, pharmaceuticals and household products such as detergents.

The physical dye or pigment was generally a powder or liquid in a drum. Manufacturing was contracted through ICI's Fine Chemicals Manufacturing Organization (FCMO) which operated as a cost centre serving five ICI businesses. Tony Rodgers, the Principal Executive Officer (PEO) of C&FC, also served as Chairman of the FCMO. C&FC was the FCMO's largest customer and accounted for 73% of its direct expenses. Specialty Chemicals, Agrochemicals, Pharmaceuticals, and Polyurethanes represented the balance of the FCMO's activities. Manufacturing facilities were located primarily in the UK and France, although some production was also carried out in Australia, Brazil, India, Korea, Mexico, Pakistan and the United States.

The process to produce dyes and pigments was complex and could take several months to complete, although typically the product was "in the pot" (i.e., directly in process) for only a few weeks of that period. Batches often underwent 10–12 stages in four or five different plants. Equipment breakdowns and batch failures could extend production and distribution lead times. The FCMO's Operations Director, Hugh Donaldson, commented:

> The synthesis of organic chemicals involves multiple stages; it's toxic and sometimes difficult to do. Each reaction requires a minimum of two days which means that the chemistry alone can take three or four weeks. For some products, we needed 18 months' lead time, although the average has gone from nine months down to five through better planning and scheduling and improved plant reliability. The difficulty is that our organisation's ability to detect changes in demand falls short of our ability to change manufacturing direction. As a result, the plants are loaded up with stuff we don't want. We not only end up with slow-moving stock, we've also missed opportunities in the market.

Given the complexity of the production process and the inevitable variability in naturally occurring raw materials, it was a real manufacturing challenge to produce a perfectly consistent product. Moreover, because of the nature of the production process, workers were a long way from tangible end products, and they typically had a limited appreciation of customer applications and the range of C&FC's business. For a number of years, the major objective of FCMO had been to minimize the cost of production while maintaining rigid quality standards in the face of very difficult manufacturing conditions.

C&FC'S HISTORY

ICI had been in the business of producing colorants since its formation in 1926. For 50 years, it was a technological leader in expanding markets and had a strong record of growth. The oil shocks of the late 1970s caused a sharp downturn in demand worldwide, throwing the industry into overcapacity and frequent price wars. Like other British producers, C&FC was hit hard by the added effects of high inflation and overvalued currency. This was at a time when C&FC's technology was becoming less unique as competitors picked up products coming off patent.

In hindsight, the situation was exacerbated by the 1982 acquisition of Francolor, a large French textile dye and pigments supplier. This deal was done under a privatization program by the French government. At the time, C&FC was in an expansion phase and believed that Francolor would provide economies of scale as well as an enhanced product line to enlarge its market position. C&FC subsequently discovered, after a £100 million investment, that Francolor was a business "on its last legs." Significant operating costs could not be easily extracted, its products were in very mature market areas, and no new product development was underway. In the 1982–84 period, the attention of C&FC management was increasingly diverted toward managing internal issues and away from the marketplace.

In 1984, C&FC had an 80% working capital-to-sales ratio and experienced a £20 million trading loss and £50 million in extraordinary losses. On-time delivery averaged 57% and there was a chronic deficiency in customer satisfaction. Tony Rodgers was appointed to run the business with a mandate to restore profitability. Some dramatic steps were undertaken. Plants were rationalized and 1 200 people were laid off. The product line was trimmed from 5 000 to 2 000 products, which, in effect, moved C&FC's profile back to where it was prior to the Francolor purchase. This restructuring was keenly felt. An observer noted:

> The Colours business was in bad shape; people were arrogant and unconcerned about their connection to the rest of the company and to their customers, and this was in the middle of a financial downturn. People were used to paternalism and lifetime employment, but the truth finally dawned that, if the business didn't perform, it could get shut down. There's nothing like a wolf at the door to focus the mind. This was a time of great uncertainty and organizational change where everything seemed up for grabs. The challenge was how to get people to believe there even was a future after this.

FIGHTING FOR THE CUSTOMER

Under Rodgers' leadership, a programme of "Fighting for the Customer" (FFTC) was launched in 1985 to remotivate C&FC's 5 000 UK and 1 000 French staff across a dozen key works and sites. FFTC was to be a symbol that people could rally behind, a symbol of recovery. The FFTC campaign was intended to get people thinking outward, away from internal issues and toward the customer. This was the first major customer service initiative undertaken within ICI. It was distinguished not only by its scale but by its highly visible top leadership.

Moreover, it was not just about moving the business back to profitability. FFTC aimed to bring about a cultural change on a grand scale, a change from an internally-focused operation to one which was market-focused and customer-oriented. Rodgers explained:

> The intention was to create a new spirit and currency for the organization in which the *customer*—not the technicalities of chemical products and their manufacture - became the driving force in the culture and strategic approach of the business.

The thinking behind FFTC was that the product itself was no longer the competitive edge. The basic chemistry across competitors was essentially the same; in fact, the last new molecule had been invented in 1956. Although patentable innovations still occurred in the industry, they were not major scientific breakthroughs. Service was one of the few significant ways in which a company could differentiate itself. The critical underlying assumption was that a customer whose product and service expectations were consistently met would buy more and be willing to pay a premium.

Initially, the FFTC message was carried by Tony Rodgers and his executive team through numerous site visits and a video. A three-month "Hollywood Stars" competition, judged by customers, involved the whole work-force in submitting ideas for improving customer service. A booklet was distributed which described "how the world had changed" and used cartoon characters to explain what C&FC had to do to succeed in the "new world" (see Exhibit 2). These were unusual, even extraordinary, programs for ICI. Donaldson reflected:

> The 'boxing gloves' imagery was right for the time and the organization was ripe for a quality initiative. FFTC was a way to channel the Brits' natural aggression and it was an inspired way to get at quality. It gave the weekly staff something to feel good about.

During this period, the grounds around C&FC's headquarters in Blackley were landscaped to send a symbolic message that senior management was confident of success.

In early 1987, a Fighting for the Customer Steering Group was formed to direct several initiatives taken under the FFTC umbrella (see Exhibit 3). The Commercial Services Group was made responsible for introducing the Business Control Project (BCP), a materials requirement planning system to improve the scheduling and measurement of materials flows. At the same time, the FCMO undertook to register its plants according to British quality standards. Donaldson commented:

> My guys are terror-stricken about losing their registration. This can be a powerful instrument to drive a manufacturing system. We were used to having a high level of work-in-process which insulated us from seeing the problems. But we can't afford to run a fat ship any longer. Moreover, the quality standards audits will uncover any slipping back into the 'old ways' of operating. As for materials requirement planning, it was too long in coming. We weren't getting good quality information and we weren't measuring the right things. We had to be able to answer the question "Is the product available?" which means: "Can a customer book it and when can it be delivered?" BCP went quite a distance toward alleviating the rock-throwing mentality that was developing between the FCMO and the businesses. Ultimately, BCP and plant registration are more than just quality initiatives and software systems; they're attempts to put a different culture in place.

On the marketing side, the MARS programme (Managed Activities to Realize Strategy) aimed at changing the sales philosophy away from volume and towards profit. As part of this, sales managers throughout the Colours organization worldwide were asked to define key accounts in key segments. In the UK, 80 key textile customers were identified and 35 were selected on the Industrial Colours side. As a continuation of MARS, the Delta programme set out to identify the gaps in knowledge and skills at the sales rep level that would have to be addressed to effectively carry out FFTC initiatives. Exhibit 4 shows C&FC's financial position through to mid-1988.

THE OCTOBER 1988 CRISIS WITH STANDFAST

In the midst of ongoing activities to build the FFTC infrastructure, a crisis was developing in the Sales Office. In early October 1988, Mike Bradbury, C&FC's UK Textile Sales Manager, received a letter from Standfast Dyers & Printers which expressed extreme dissatisfaction with the standard of service from the Dyestuffs group and the intention to withdraw its entire business over the next three months and hand it over to a major competitor. Standfast was part of the Courtaulds Group, a British textile and chemicals organization which operated globally. Standfast was a longstanding customer for several C&FC dye specialties and accounted for £750 000 in annual purchases.

C&FC's performance on the Standfast account in terms of both delivery and quality had deteriorated markedly over the past three years. The situation was so severe in 1987 that it was virtually guaranteed that any product Standfast requested would be stocked out or off-quality. Faced with the prospect of losing a major UK customer, Bradbury held a meeting with representatives from manufacturing, sales, marketing, quality control, order processing, and scheduling. Bradbury recounted:

> The many meetings I'd already had to try and sort out this situation failed miserably. I could fire out the shots but the departmental walls were so high and so thick that they didn't even penetrate. The meeting I convened in early November 1988 started out on an acrimonious note as well. The Manufacturing people said it wasn't their fault—they manufacture based on forecast demand and they can only meet a request if the raw materials are on hand. The Quality Control people said it wasn't their fault—they need two weeks' lead time to test products. Marketing said it wasn't their fault—they give demand forecasts to the Works but the Works goes ahead and makes the products it can, then Marketing has to figure out how to sell them. The Sales people said it wasn't their fault—they're just selling products to customers and they can't sell them if they don't have them. No one would take responsibility.
>
> The Standfast ultimatum made these people realize what poor service they were giving the customer. They finally pulled together. Each department took away action plans. Sales would ask Standfast for offtake information on a rolling basis. Quality Control said they would do same-day testing for Standfast's products. In all this, we discovered a fault in the BCP system that never brought raw materials forward through the Works to produce certain specialty products. We were having stockouts because no one had planned for the next production run.

By January 1989, the Standfast situation was completely turned around. C&FC was able to meet Standfast's next-day delivery requirement with good quality products. Bradbury commented:

> Before, we weren't talking to Standfast about the things that really mattered—production levels, where the demand was. The salesmen talked about football and rugby; this was the way they related with customers. Once we asked, Standfast gave us information about their anticipated demand. All this required was the push of a button. Then it was a matter of scheduling manufacturing so that the right products were on hand when Standfast called. What we really did was look at an individual customer's needs and develop a service package to meet those requirements. The crisis with Standfast actually pushed our hand a bit. The idea of in some way forming partnerships with customers had been kicking around the Sales Department for some time.

Even after the Standfast problem was addressed, however, the question of long-term effects remained. Was this another case of ICI "swarming" a problem and fixing it without really making a fundamental change in the root cause, which related directly to the way the business was being run?

THE CUSTOMER CHARTER PROJECT

In the months preceding the crisis with Standfast, there had been a great deal of discussion over an idea put forward by Patrick Kelly, the UK Regional Manager in C&FC's sales organization. He envisioned giving customers something like a "bank statement" which would provide a regular account of transactions to inspire a feeling of confidence in ICI as a supplier. Kelly recounted:

> If we're really prepared to fight for our customers, we should be giving them a statement of service; we need to do better on service than we're doing now and we need to regularly report to customers that we are meeting the promises we make.

Based on the success with Standfast, Kelly saw the potential for adopting something more like a partnership with customers throughout the UK. He called this the Customer Charter. It would involve identifying problems, tracing them back through the organization, and telling the customer about it. Kelly had recently approached Mike Parker, C&FC's Commercial Director, with the idea of formalizing the initiative as the next logical step in the FFTC campaign.

The cornerstone of the Customer Charter was providing a differentiated level of service to a particular set of customers—key customers. By definition, this would mean comparatively lowering the level of service to some others. Kelly likened this to the way airlines arranged their seating:

> Everyone is on board, but the service package is different. Our key customers are treated like first class passengers. Key prospects are in club class while the cash generators sit in economy. Small customers fly standby. To put it simply, some customers are prepared to pay more for quality service.

Customers chosen for "chartering" would not be selected according to some mathematical formula based strictly on their size or purchasing history. The criteria would be a combination of volume, financial viability, and whether the customer was a leader in its field or operating in segments of interest in the future. Kelly imagined that the Charter document would be hand-delivered by a C&FC account team who would explain the Charter philosophy as well as the mechanics of the performance audit and corrective action plans.

C&FC's performance would be measured against "seven pillars of quality." These represented the most important influences on purchasing according to a UK market study which C&FC had commissioned in 1987. The seven dimensions could be weighted to reflect the supplier attributes a particular customer deemed important (see Exhibit 5). A zero defect performance resulted in an aggregate score of 200. In a bimonthly audit, C&FC's performance would be rated across the seven pillars. Action plans would be put in place to eliminate the defects that caused performance to fall short of the maximum score. These defects would then be traced back and eliminated at their source.

Kelly believed that the Charter would break down the walls between departments and create a robust, ongoing dialogue about customer needs. Furthermore, the information gained through the auditing process would significantly improve forecast accuracy. Early warning of potential supply problems would mean that corrective actions could be taken in advance of a crisis.

However, some of the people in the Colours organization shared a much different opinion of the Charter. Their sentiments are typified by the remark of a manager in the UK regional office in Bolton:

> My first reaction to the Charter was that we're asking for trouble; we're just exposing all our warts to the customer, showing mistakes that customers might have missed or didn't care about, and now they'll know. Some people are not convinced of the strategy; they say there aren't enough people to do it, it's not adding value, and we shouldn't be wasting time with Charter activities. At the end of the day, customers want the right products delivered on time and they won't give a monkey about some Charter document.

Russell Bond, the UK Sales Manager for Industrial Colours, added:

> One of the problems is that the Charter will have to compete with other quality initiatives. ICI has a lot of initiatives running concurrently: salary reviews, organizational changes, and then ICI France may have launched some programme we don't even know about. We've got too much change all at the same time. People at my level are caught up in resource issues. Then there's the whole question of whether we can even make the kind of changes the Charter requires. The organization is geared for the efficient running of plant and equipment. Customer awareness stops outside the Sales Department.

IMPLEMENTING THE CHARTER

Over the past three months, the UK textile sales team had collected performance data under "dummy charters" that had been set up for several major customers. One market officer in the Bolton sales office elaborated:

> Implementing live Charters seemed like a daunting task after this, and doing the first Charter would be a nightmare. It was taking us up to five days to prepare a single customer audit with the dummy charters. The information had to be manually collected from different files and different systems. The sales office didn't even have a picture of when an order came in and the process it went through. The only indication of how well we performed was if a customer rang up with a problem. And then the complaints were mostly technical: the product was too thick, too weak, the wrong shade. The way the sales office usually worked it out was to throw bricks at anything that got in the way of serving customers.

Clearly, the Charter would require a major systems effort to ensure that the necessary information was collected and available in a usable format. Alan Spall, C&FC's Finance Director, noted "this isn't exciting stuff but it's the stuff that will trip you up if you don't get it right." Exhibit 6 illustrates the range of data that would have to be matched against the Charter's seven pillars. One difficulty was that systems had been installed over the years without too much concern for compatibility in order to meet purely local needs like order processing. These systems simply could not capture the Charter's full dimensions. A package would have to be developed which imbedded local functions within the Charter framework. Ongoing support would be required to ensure that those in the field were not overburdened with the work of collating the Charter data. The first challenge was to agree on terminology, align product definitions, and so on. Mike Bradbury reflected:

C&FC has been trying for years to get customers in a pecking order, but the Centre and the national selling offices all have different definitions of what a key customer is. We're really not very good at picking key customers; we're good at picking big customers. If the customer has ancient computer systems and the Works are falling down, my guess is it won't be around in a the year 2000.

Implementing the Customer Charter would require some dramatic changes. Foremost, was a change in the role of the internal sales support staff. Rather than be troubleshooters interfacing with customers regarding their immediate problems, the sales coordinators would be asked to analyze, anticipate and prevent problems. Bradbury commented:

> At present, the 'inside people' correct invoices that are wrong, sort out price queries, get authorization to ship non-standard product, and so on. They also get into a lot of delivery issues because order processing sits within the sales office. These are bright, young people who know the sales organization and can fix anything in it. It's all based on personal contact. They're very successful getting things done in a reactive way, and they get a lot of satisfaction from this. Everyday, they can say 'I'm a hero, I've solved problems.'
>
> The Charter not only lessens their customer contact, it asks them to be more inward than outward looking, to be more proactive, to prevent problems from happening in the first place through data collection and analysis and lengthy audit preparation. A lot of these people will say 'you've killed the job.' There will be a lot of dissatisfaction coming from this group. The Charter asks them to solve problems within the bureaucracy, frequently outside the sales office. For some, this would be a deep psychological and cultural change.

Nichola Greening, a sales co-ordinator in the Bolton Office, continued:

> The way I understand it, we would identify non-conformances, trace the defects back through the organization to their source, and put together action plans to try and resolve the problems from our level. The action plans will likely cross functional boundaries, and I'll be interacting with people in Technical Service, Commercial Service, Administration, and so on.
>
> I can see where the Charter will help to identify quality and delivery problems. If we had the product in stock but failed to give it to the customer, I can put an action plan in place. But it gets harder when a product is off-quality or stocked out because these defects would be traced back to a department outside the sales office. These people may understand the Charter concept at an intellectual level, but what if they act the same way as they have in the past. These people have always had a defensive response.
>
> To give an example, we've always had a problem with a yellow vat dye that we have to buy in from Hoechst. The difficulties with delivery, shade, and strength have been highlighted many times, and the sales office has never been able to get a satisfactory response from the centre. With the Charter, I guess I would now raise this non-conformance with the purchasing department and somehow get them to take action.

Bradbury added:

> I have trouble seeing how we'll pull this Charter thing off. In the sales office, we're close to the customer every day and we can see the value of the Charter. But some departments might resist the ground forces telling them how they have to act differently, although we might manage to drag a few people along. Implementing the Charter will require a complete change in how we operate, and that's not just in the sales office, it's the whole organization.
>
> As it is, Bolton is only a 20 minute drive from the centre in Blackley, but we barely talk to each other. How are the sales coordinators going to get action on areas when we've never been able to do it before? And will we be able to get marketing on board? The marketing department talks about 20–30 key markets and the sales department talks about key customers. Under the Charter, meeting commitments to key customers ultimately means taking away from other markets within the current system. But there's no mechanism to ensure that product is avail-

able for key customers. The way it works now is that if Hong Kong puts in an order for an extra 10 tonnes of Product X, when the UK comes along and asks for its scheduled offtake for a key customer, only nonstandard product might be left. The sales co-ordinator will raise this problem with the marketing department, but the corrective action will be vague. Someone has to say it's our job to sell the right products to the right customers.

Patrick Kelly acknowledged that the Customer Charter was simple to articulate but it would be hard to deliver. It required a complete organization behind it and involved a major change in how C&FC did business. Kelly elaborated:

> C&FC has to differentiate itself in ways not easily duplicated by competitors. The Customer Charter creates a mindset that imbeds responsiveness into all of our activities. More importantly, the Charter provides clear evidence of the value of the relationship, and it will make customers think long and hard about what they want to tradeoff or take out of the relationship. The bottom line is that the Charter is a basis for securing price increases on key accounts. In this business, a 1% increase in price generates almost as much margin as a 2% increase in volume.
>
> Of course we have a long way to go; not all the salespeople are equipped with the skills and confidence to carry it off. There's also the danger that the Charter will be seen as a gimmick, just another 'flavour of the month,' another head office cost that will have to be met out in the field. There might also be cynicism in the works from those who see the Charter as strictly a sales initiative. The programme will have to appear ingrained, sustainable, and long term. We've got to demonstrate that 'fighting for the customer' is more than just wind. At the same time, we need to build in some slack and be careful to promise only what we can achieve.

Kelly was planning to approach Chilton Brothers in late January 1989 as the first step towards chartering 1 200 key customers worldwide. Privately owned by two brothers, Chiltons was a major British manufacturer of dyed and finished knitted goods and one of C&FC's most important customers.

Mike Parker appreciated Kelly's enthusiasm for the Customer Charter and knew that he was anxious to launch the initiative, but was it the right idea and was it too soon? Had they really thought out what implementation would mean for the organization? And how serious were the obstacles?

EXHIBIT 1   Colours & Fine Chemicals

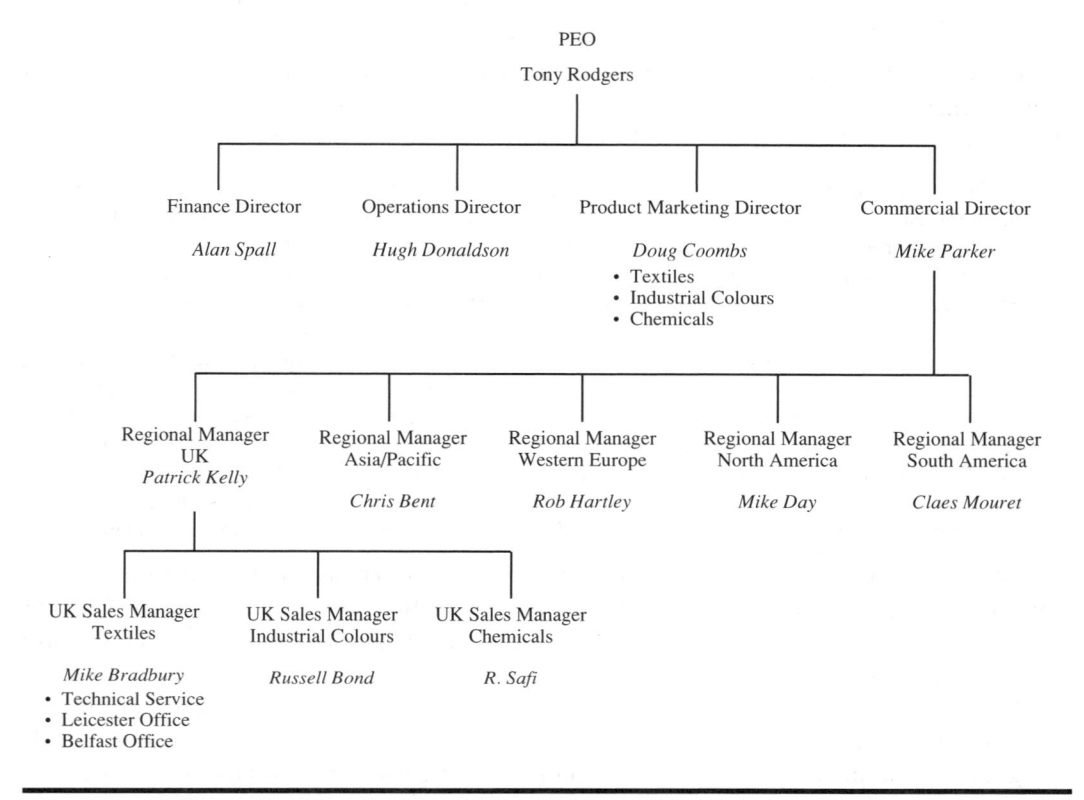

Note: Other staff in the sales offices include sales reps, sales coordinators, market officers, and order clerks.

EXHIBIT 2   **Excerpts**

FIGHTING FOR THE CUSTOMER

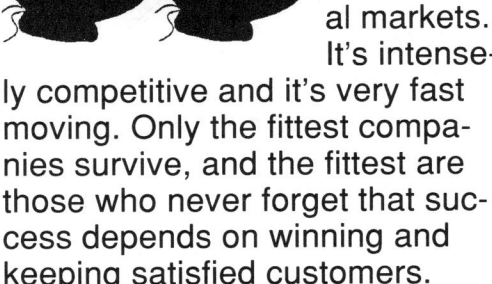

Life is tough in the battle for international markets. It's intensely competitive and it's very fast moving. Only the fittest companies survive, and the fittest are those who never forget that success depends on winning and keeping satisfied customers. This is what FIGHTING FOR THE CUSTOMER is all about.

We've already come a long way in adjusting to the painful changes in world markets over the last few years. We are a lot fitter. We have won new markets. We have the products, the know how and the people to compete internationally. But we could still be a lot smarter.

Fighting for the customer involves us all—in everything we do, everyday. By working together as a team, in FIGHTING for our customers, we can all win.

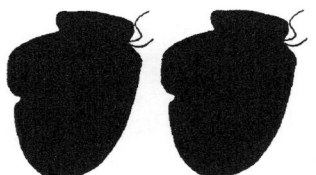

THE SUCCESS FORMULA TO GUIDE OUR ACTIONS—
FOCUS ON CUSTOMER NEEDS

• Focus on the right products and services—
Benefit-focused product innovation.
Quality on time production.
On time distribution.
Profit-focused sales.

• Focus on winning customers.
Grow with industry winners who need and can pay for the best.

• Deliver what we promise.
Good service earns repeat orders and good prices.
Good service can make all the difference.

• Look and act as champions—professional, committed, confident.

EXHIBIT 3 **Performance Improvement Initiatives**

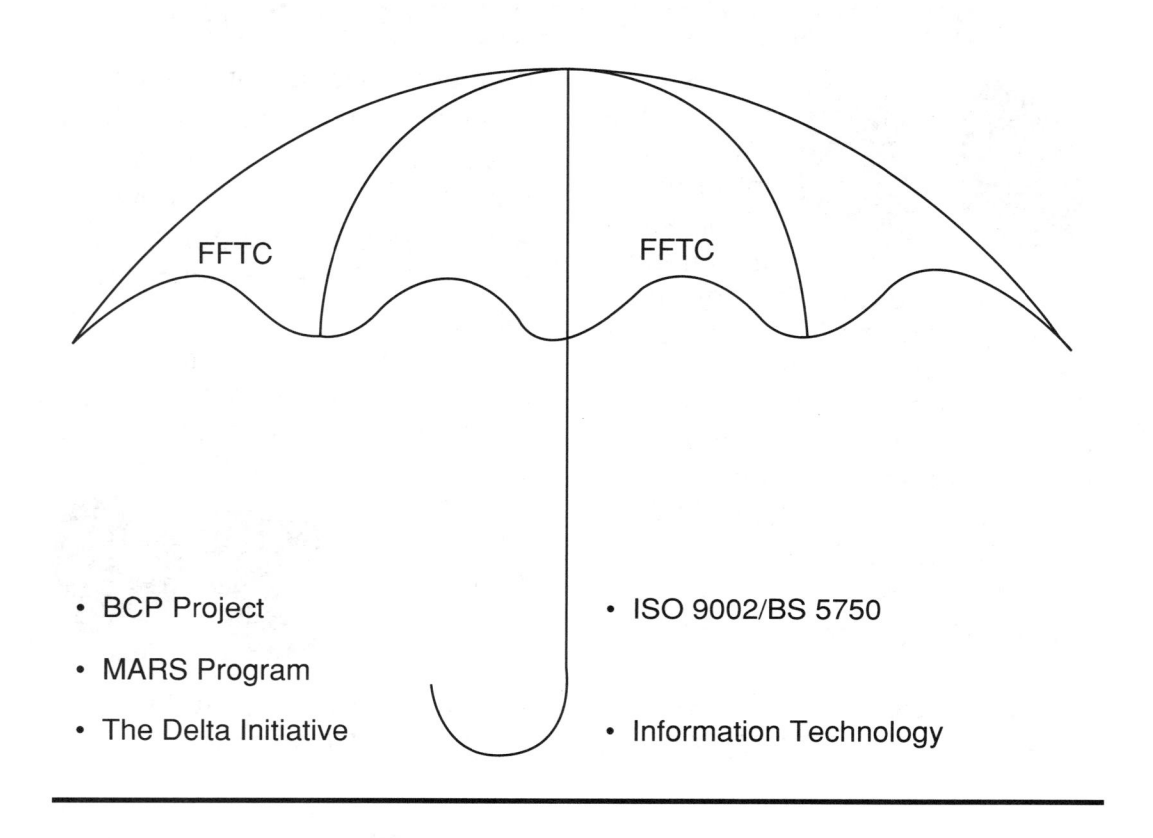

- BCP Project

- MARS Program

- The Delta Initiative

- ISO 9002/BS 5750

- Information Technology

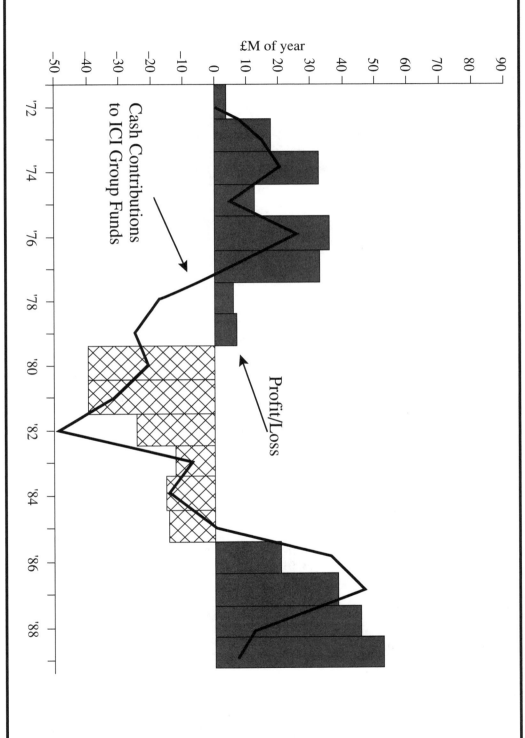

EXHIBIT 4   C&FC's Profit and Cash Position, 1972–Mid–1988

£M of year

Cash Contributions
to ICI Group Funds

Profit/Loss

EXHIBIT 5 Customer Charter's Scoring Mechanism

Some variations on weighting the seven pillars of quality. A zero defect performance across all dimensions aggregates to 200.

	Customer 1	*Customer 2*	*Customer 3*
Quality of Product	60	40	60
Delivery	40	40	40
Communication	10	20	40
Documentation	20	20	10
Complaint Handling	10	20	10
Visits	30	20	20
Technical Support	30	40	20
	200	200	200

EXHIBIT 6 **Data Capture**

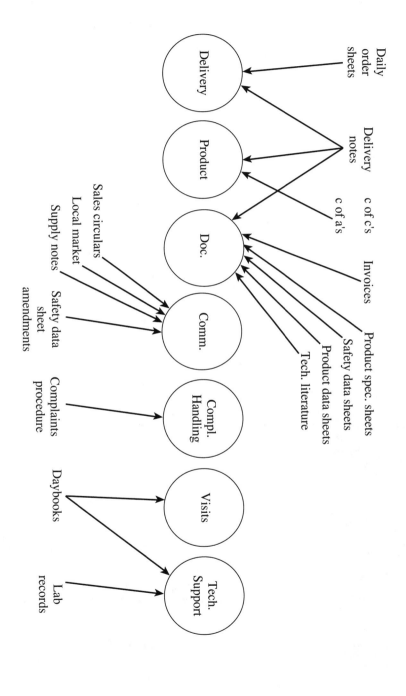

STRATEGIC ANALYSIS AND PERSONAL ACTION

PART

10

TACO BELL
BACKGROUND NOTE

Mary M. Crossan and
Catherine Paul-Chowdhury

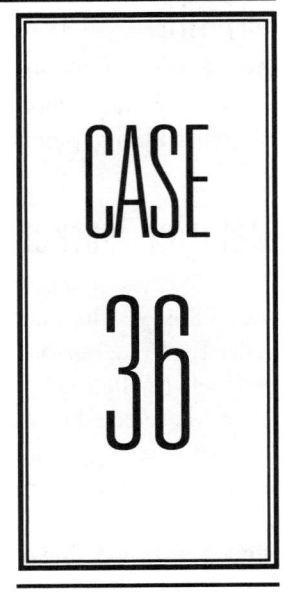

CASE
36

The $267 billion food service industry in the United States comprised independent establishments and restaurant chains. The market share of the restaurant chains had grown at the expense of independents' market share, accounting for 54% of all U.S. restaurants in 1993, up from 37% in 1986. Chain sales were estimated to grow at 8% in 1993, twice as fast as independent sales.

INDUSTRY OVERVIEW[1]

The fragmented, capital-intensive restaurant industry was characterized by low margins and vulnerability to shifts in consumer tastes and spending. For every consumer dollar spent in the typical fast-food restaurant, 30 cents covered the cost of food and packaging, while the remainder paid for advertising, marketing, capital and fixed costs, and labour. Exhibit 1 lists the major fast food chains, their market segments, sales and number of units.

[1] Articles from *Restaurants & Institutions; Restaurant Business; Business Week; The Wall Street Journal; Marketing News; Harvard Business School Case*; Interviews.

TRENDS

By the early 1990s, the following significant trends were changing the structure of the fast-food[2] restaurant industry: the maturing market, changing customer tastes and the introduction of nontraditional points of distribution.

Maturing Market

After decades of substantial growth, the market for quick service food began to mature during the 1980s. As the market became more saturated, the importance of market share grew. In order to attract customers, quick service restaurants increased the rate of introduction of new products (including low-fat versions of existing menu items as well as new types of food), cut prices on selected menu items and introduced play areas for children.

Although expanded menus resulted in incremental business, they also led to disruptions in the production flow and decreased kitchen efficiency as products were introduced which were incompatible with existing facilities. The rapid introduction of new products contributed to higher costs and slower service in an industry based upon low costs and fast service.

Changing Consumer Tastes

The changing tastes of health-conscious consumers was another factor driving the introduction of new menu items. This shift resulted in growth in chicken, pizza and Mexican food restaurant segments.

The increasing popularity of Mexican food, in particular, could be seen in the upscale restaurant and grocery sectors as well as in quick service. As traditional markets in the Southwestern United States became saturated, Mexican chains pushed eastward into relatively untapped markets.

Nontraditional Points of Distribution (PODs)

Perhaps the most important trend in the quick service restaurant industry was the introduction of nontraditional points of distribution (PODs). These included express stores, kiosks and mobile carts in shopping malls, schools, hospitals, stadiums and airports. With lower capital costs than traditional stores, they were an attractive investment alternative. Traditional quick service restaurants had been labour intensive, taking advantage of pools of inexpensive labour. However, changing demographics and increasing minimum wages dictated a need for the smaller PODs with fewer workers.

With many quick service restaurants currently experimenting with these alternative points of distribution, a fundamental change had taken place in their service objectives. Instead of locating "wherever customers want to purchase the food," they increasingly had to position themselves "wherever customers want to consume the food." Located in such places as schools and sports complexes, non-traditional PODs also allowed finer segmentation of customer markets.

---

[2] At Taco Bell, it was known as the "quick service restaurant" industry.

COMPANY BACKGROUND[3]

A Subsidiary of Pepsico

Taco Bell was a wholly-owned subsidiary of PepsiCo Inc. Originally known as a soft-drink company, the Purchase, N.Y.-based PepsiCo had evolved into a global food giant. PepsiCo's three flagship businesses were: soft drinks under the Pepsi name; restaurants including the Pizza Hut; Kentucky Fried Chicken (KFC) and Taco Bell chains; and snack foods under the Frito-Lay brand. As noted by Chairman and CEO Wayne Calloway, the soft drink division generated more revenue in 1991 than General Mills Inc., the restaurant group was bigger than Campbell Soup Co., and the snack food business was about the size of Kellogg Co. Taco Bell accounted for 30% of the Restaurant Division's 1992 sales and 30% of its operating profits. This represented 11% of PepsiCo's sales and 9% of operating profits.

With market leaders such as Coca-Cola and McDonald's Corp. as its major competitors, PepsiCo was under significant pressure to be cheaper, faster and tastier than the competition. To this end, PepsiCo was building an organization which was capable of supporting continuous change, innovation and risk. For several years, PepsiCo had been removing layers of management, and moving decision-makers closer to the customer. Marketing, operations and research and development were decentralized to push down decision-making and increase market responsiveness.

The company's culture was embedded in a common value system based on integrity and results. Calloway was known for his tough quarterly and annual performance goals. Acting as a check on the performance orientation, however, the concept of integrity went beyond honesty to include showing respect to others and trusting people to do their jobs. The other key element in PepsiCo's culture was the importance of continuous change. The company regularly revamped its marketing, operations and field management in anticipation of the competition rather than in response to it.

THE VALUE STRATEGY

John Martin joined Taco Bell as President and CEO in 1983, inheriting a fringe competitor in the fast food industry. He instituted a series of incremental changes designed to make the organization competitive with the major chains. He clearly defined the company's business and customer, and updated its image, facilities and menu. He also introduced new production techniques, including electronic point-of-sale systems and improved assembly lines. Martin increased training and development for Restaurant Managers (RMs) and Assistant Restaurant Managers (ARMs).

Reflecting on the company's position at the end of the 1980s, however, Martin knew that Taco Bell was a small competitor. He anticipated declining margins in the maturing quick ser-

---

[3] Articles from *Restaurant Business; The Wall Street Journal; Irvine World News; Financial World; Computer World; Harvard Business School Case;* PepsiCo's *Annual Report.*

vice industry. Instead of competing head-to-head with the major fast food chains, Martin decided to change the basis of competition.

He chose to focus on value. The two components of value were quality and price. Traditionally, the industry had viewed high quality and low price as contradictory goals, with one sacrificed in pursuit of the other. Martin realized, however, that delivering value meant providing both.

FACT

Studies commissioned in 1987 and 1989 revealed that customers wanted *FACT*: fast-food *Fast*; orders *Accurate*; a *Clean* restaurant; and food at the appropriate *Temperature*. FACT became the company's standard for customer service, and the non-monetary portion of the value strategy. The studies also showed that customers did not place any importance on the preparation of food on the premises.

By 1991, many Taco Bell menu items in the United States were priced at one of three low price points: $0.59, $0.79 and $0.99 (or $0.69, $0.89 and $1.09 in some markets). While the value strategy dramatically increased Taco Bell's sales, the lower prices squeezed already slim margins.

To reduce costs while providing higher levels of service and maintaining its high quality product, Martin redefined Taco Bell's business from "making food" to "feeding people." He knew from the studies that customers wanted value, which was defined as FACT at the lowest possible prices, and recognized that the front line service workers (crew, RMs and ARMs) were in the best position to provide FACT and keep costs down. He began to refocus the organization, eliminating everything that did not support the front line in the provision of value.

K-Minus

Having redefined its business from food manufacturer to food retailer, Taco Bell introduced the K-Minus (kitchen minus) program to invert the space configuration in the restaurants to 30% kitchen and 70% dining room. To achieve this, the preparation of food in the restaurant was minimized and simplified. Virtually all of the food was prepared elsewhere, and arrived at the restaurant ready to be heated or cooled, and used. The kitchen was limited to a heating and assembly space.

In addition to reducing the size of the kitchen, K-Minus allowed the front line workers to spend less time on chopping, cooking and washing up, and to focus more of their efforts on sales and quality of service. It also helped to improve the consistency of the food products. As well, K-Minus increased potential kitchen output, allowing more take-out, drive-through and other out-of-restaurant sales.

SOS

The Speed of Service (SOS) program, introduced in 1990, was designed to reduce the waiting time for customers. It involved reformulating certain recipes, and borrowing the McDonald's system of keeping food in a heated holding area for up to ten minutes. Taco Bell was able to inventory the majority of its most frequently ordered menu items in this way, increasing peak hour transaction capacity by 54% and decreasing customer waiting time by 71% to 30 seconds.

TACO

The Total Automation of Company Operations (TACO) featured the installation in every store of a computer networked to headquarters. TACO provided Restaurant Managers (RMs) with timely information support and communications functions unparalleled in the quick-service industry. Information included cash position, promotional sales, food cost, labour cost, inventory, perishable items and period-to-date costs, all with variances from budget. TACO helped the RMs with labour scheduling and product production planning, while the communications function allowed District and more senior managers to send messages to any combination of their restaurants. This technology let them spend less time in a given restaurant, and manage a larger number of restaurants.

RM paperwork was reduced by up to 16 hours per week. More importantly, TACO provided RMs with the tools necessary to identify and solve problems without involving people any higher in the organization. It supported the empowerment of front line service workers.

In the TACO program, Taco Bell had a comprehensive and evolving system of information and control. As management layers became thinner, however, and supervision less intense, other checks were required to ensure that standards were being maintained. Taco Bell used three mechanisms to monitor restaurant operations: a 1-800 number for customers to call with comments, mystery shoppers and marketing surveys.

Restaurant General Managers (RGMs)

The new organizational focus on value required new behaviours at the RM and Assistant Restaurant Manager (ARM) levels. Supported by TACO and new training, managers were expected to make decisions, manage their restaurants' profits and losses, motivate employees, and generally take ownership of the operations. With this greater responsibility came a significant increase in autonomy. To symbolize the new, self-sufficient role of the restaurant managers, Taco Bell renamed the positions Restaurant General Manager (RGM) and Assistant Restaurant General Manager (ARGM).

Compensation structures were redesigned (see Exhibit 2). Salary ranges and bonus opportunities were increased substantially. The new compensation system continued to reward sales performance and cost management, as well as placing additional emphasis on customer service and teamwork. The increased responsibility dictated that management style move toward management by exception, more coaching and broadening spans of control.

Market Managers (MMs)

The former District Managers (DMs) were renamed Market Managers (MMs) and given responsibility for an increasingly large number of restaurants. Spans of control increased from six to 12 to over 20 restaurants in the space of two years. With only 24 hours in the day, it became impossible to continue managing details, so MMs were forced to create organizations where they could manage by exception, and coach instead of police their RGMs. MMs nevertheless seemed to spend much of their time "fighting fires." Many could not make the transition from DM to MM, and either became RGMs or left the organization.

As with the RGMs, compensation structures were redesigned (see Exhibit 2). The maximum salary almost doubled, bonus targets increased over five-fold, and zone performance was included in the new bonus calculation. Bonuses were based on market and zone performance, and progress made toward achieving corporate strategic goals. In the new, flatter organization, creating adequate opportunities for MMs' career advancement was a challenge. Taco Bell had to redefine career success in terms of staying and growing with the job. To support this mindset, the salary range for MMs was very broad, and divided into thirds. MMs progressed through the range on the basis of performance, the complexity of their markets and tenure.

TACO BELL, 1993[4]—ORGANIZATION

With the successful introduction of its Value program, Taco Bell had become a distinctive and formidable competitor in the quick service restaurant industry. It was widely recognized in business and academic communities alike as a leading model for service industry innovation and organization. Worldwide system sales reached $3.9 billion in 1993, having averaged 17.1% annual growth over the preceding five years. Taco Bell had 4 153 restaurants worldwide at the end of 1992, of which 4 078 were located in the United States. It also enjoyed a 70% share of the U.S. Mexican-style restaurant market segment, and a 4% share of the total U.S. quick service restaurant market.

Taco Bell was organized into seven North American Zones, reduced from 13 a year before. Zones were subdivided into between five and 23 markets, reporting to zone vice-presidents (ZVPs). Exhibit 3 shows Taco Bell's organization chart.

EXPANSION OBJECTIVES AND STRATEGY

Although Taco Bell's growth had been rapid, its future expansion objectives were explosive. From a 1993 $3 billion in sales, the company planned to achieve sales of $20 billion and 200 000 points of distribution by the year 2000. It viewed its potential market in terms of "share of stomach," or share of calories consumed per day. By redefining its business as "feeding people," Taco Bell increased the size of its market by approximately ten times. Growth so far had been primarily in the U.S. market, with limited expansion into Canada, Mexico, Puerto Rico and the U.K.. Taco Bell saw tremendous opportunity for expansion overseas, but continued rapid growth at home consumed much of the available resources and management attention.

To disseminate its bold growth objectives and strategy for achieving them, Taco Bell developed a variety of internal communication materials. Some information was sent out in the form of posters or games. For example, "The New Strategic Intent Game: DOMINATE by becoming the Convenient Food leader and dominating all food occasions!" outlined Taco Bell's mission and strategies as follows:

> Taco Bell's mission is to become the dominant force in an entire new business that we'll create: Convenient Foods. As we did with 'value,' we're not just going to change a few rules, but instead create a whole new way to take our food to anywhere hungry people gather—not only in customary places, but in points of access like stadiums, malls, universities, vending machines, grocery stores—even our own refrigerators.

---

[4] Articles from *Restaurant Business*; Taco Bell Internal Documents; PepsiCo's *Annual Report*; Interviews.

DOMINATE went on to discuss Taco Bell's four strategies for reaching its goal:

- *Exploding distribution* meant expanding to "tens of thousands of new places ... wherever customers want us to be."
- *Leveraging innovation* was a call to "accelerate business transformation" through innovation at every level of the business.
- *Institutionalizing self-sufficiency* was in response to the realization that the only way to achieve such ambitious growth was to "continue giving people bigger, broader jobs and responsibilities ... (and) more freedom and empowerment to do their jobs."
- *Building superbrands* referred to the Disney tradition of developing product names which could stretch, in Taco Bell's case, "across many food occasions and points of access."

The Can-Am Zone[5]

Although two of the seven North American Zones encompassed parts of both Canada and the United States, only one MM straddled the two countries. The Can-Am Zone had been created during a restructuring in November 1992, which had increased it from 35 to 110 stores. It was comprised of five distinct markets: Eastern Ontario, Southwestern Ontario, Upstate New York, Boston and New England. Zone vice-president (ZVP) Martin Annese, was based in Mississauga, Ontario. In May 1993, Sanjiv Yajnik, MM for Southwestern Ontario was also given responsibility for Upstate New York. This increased responsibility was in recognition of the fact that Sanjiv had been very successful in achieving profitability in the previously troubled Southwestern Ontario market. Taco Bell believed that north–south integration facilitated consistency and marketing coordination in neighbouring geographic areas.

Sanjiv Yajink

Sanjiv had graduated from a leading Canadian MBA program in May 1992, and joined Taco Bell as MM for Southwestern Ontario in July of that year. Before starting his MBA, Sanjiv had completed a degree in marine engineering in India, then worked for over 12 years in positions of increasing responsibility as a chartered engineer and chief engineer with Mobil Shipping & Transportation Co. Ltd., in the U.S.

Sanjiv reflected on his management approach at the time he joined Taco Bell as a new MBA:

Coming out of the MBA program, I had a long-term, big picture focus. My big concerns were driving profit and customer choice. I was most concerned with long-term profitability. I was surprised by the tactical, day-to-day pressures of what seemed to be a simple business, but was really a business growing and changing at a furious pace.

Southwestern Ontario and Upstate New York

There were ten stores in the Southwestern Ontario market when Sanjiv Yajnik joined as MM. Typically, these restaurants were 12–15 years old, and widely spread throughout small towns

---

[5] Taco Bell Internal Documents; Interviews.

in the area. Since Taco Bell had traditionally been viewed as less important than Pizza Hut, some of its stores were placed so as to make better use of Pizza Hut land, not strategically located to attract customers. Sales were weak compared to sales in the Toronto area.

The markets and restaurants had been run by a succession of managers in recent years. They were what Zone Manager of Human Resources Christine Maxwell described as "traditional" restaurant managers.

> They were hired from the restaurant industry. They were predominantly low drive, maintenance people. And they were in small communities, so they didn't feel the need to grow. . . . Some of the RGMs needed to learn significantly new behaviours in order to contribute in the new organization, particularly those who were great followers, but not drivers. We've been concentrating on upgrading the talent at the RGM and ARGM levels, both in Southwestern Ontario and Upstate New York.

Sanjiv discussed the markets he inherited in terms of people, operations, facilities, marketing and growth:

> Many of the facilities in Ontario were old, but were in reasonable condition. Some people were not used to being held accountable, and were lax in their jobs. Others were willing, but lacked the skills required to meet their new tasks and responsibilities. All employees had been told that they had to be self-sufficient, that they had to work in teams, etc., but there was no understanding of how to get there. The deficient skills and lack of direction impacted negatively on store operations in the market.
>
> The situation in New York was similar to that in Southwestern Ontario, but the lack of skills and direction was even more pronounced. Overall, the employees were not ready for change: they did not see the need to change, and they did not have the necessary skills. Not surprisingly, the operations were substandard. Some of the facilities were new, but were improperly maintained, and had already fallen into disrepair.
>
> There is minimal market penetration in Southwestern Ontario. As a rule of thumb, we like to have one store for approximately 20 000 people. In London, for example, we have one per 100 000 people. Sales are growing at 15–20% annually.
>
> Sales growth in the New York market has been relatively flat. I see this as a function of market penetration, value perception and competition, the quality of operations and the location of the units.

Higher ingredient and labour costs in Canada resulted in a fundamental difference in focus between the Ontario and New York restaurants. All food purchasing was done in New York. Canadian restaurants needed to add duty, the Goods and Services Tax, transportation, and currency translation costs to the price of ingredients. In addition, higher labour costs meant that the number of employees used in Canadian restaurants had to be much lower than in their U.S. counterparts if they were to meet the same target of approximately 28% of sales. Because combined ingredient and labour costs represented a higher portion of the price of a menu item, a smaller portion remained available to cover other costs for any given price point. Therefore, while a 100% productivity level was required to meet target in the U.S. restaurants, the required level in Canadian restaurants was 105%. As a result, the greater focus of the Canadian restaurants was on lowering costs and increasing productivity, while the focus of the U.S. restaurants was on generating sales.

RESTAURANT OPERATIONS[6]

Taco Bell's Highbury Avenue restaurant in London, Ontario, provides an example of restaurant operations. It employed 60 people, including two ARGMs and two shift facilitators. Full-time workers represented most of the day and overnight crew, while part-time employees tended to work afternoons, evenings and weekends. Full-time employees were typically homemakers who had returned to the work force, and high-school graduates, some of whom were working for a few years before going back to school. Although full-time employees were up to 35 years of age, the majority were in the 19–20 year range. Part-time employees were typically high-school or sometimes college students.

The Highbury Avenue store did not have an RGM. Sanjiv explained this phenomenon:

> I need extremely competent people for these positions. But it can be difficult to interest university graduates in managing fast-food restaurants. We call it a 'job snob' attitude. Many people don't want to work in this type of service industry, especially in a demanding hands-on job. They are unaware of the opportunities for professional growth and the financial rewards. I refuse to hire someone who is not up to the standard we need. In 18 months or so, I think the ARGMs will have the experience to take on the RGM positions. But I hope we don't have to go that long. Not having RGMs puts additional strain on me and on the ARGMs.

It was the responsibility of the ARGMs to ensure that everything ran smoothly. ARGM Eleni Katsoulas described her position:

> I am responsible for sales, labour costs, overtime, food costs, other controllable costs, speed of service and customer feedback. I am measured on these things and held accountable. Our target for labour costs is around 28% of sales. On sales of $1.5 million annually, even running labour at 32% of sales adds up fast. I check how we are doing every few hours. If we are over 28%, I suggest that someone take a break (for every five hours staff members work, they are required to be given a half-hour unpaid break), or ask if anyone would like to go home.
>
> Food costs should be approximately 42% of sales. Even a percent or two more puts us well over budget. Overfilling products by an ounce each creates a significant problem over the hundreds of tacos we sell every day. So if it's not prohibitively busy, we weigh every third item. And we try to keep waste at 0.5%. But cooked ground beef only keeps for three hours and chicken and steak for two. And the meat takes half an hour to cook. So planning ahead for peak times is very important.
>
> There are also challenges associated with such a young crew. Remember that they're at a stage in life when everyone is nagging at them and they become very good at blocking it out! So I can't just say, 'Don't overfill.' I can't just say, 'The customer is always right.' I have to explain that the average household spends $10 000 on fast food in a lifetime. And if one dissatisfied customer tells nine friends what's wrong with Taco Bell then that's $100 000 we lose for every dissatisfied customer. So if we want to keep our jobs ... .
>
> I get frustrated sometimes. I have so many ideas that I want to implement. But I'm always so busy doing what's necessary that I rarely get time to implement them! And the business is changing so fast that often by the time I can get to something, it's no longer as useful as I thought it would be! In any case, we are innovating all the time. And Sanjiv is trying to move toward four shift facilitators and four crew trainers in the store, so that will give me time to focus on more external things.

---

[6] Taco Bell Internal Documents; Interviews.

The Market Manager Position[7]

RESPONSIBILITIES In 1993, the average MM managed approximately 30 restaurants, compared to an average of six or seven restaurants for a DM five years earlier. The number of restaurants an MM managed was determined on the basis of quantitative and qualitative performance. Key financial numbers included sales, food costs, labour costs, overhead and profits. Nonfinancial considerations included customer satisfaction and progress in areas such as self-directed work teams. The reward for strong results in existing restaurants was more stores to manage. When Sanjiv had joined Taco Bell in 1992, he had been responsible for ten restaurants, compared to his current portfolio of 27 stores. He described this portfolio as the same size as that of a comparable manager at McDonald's.

The MM was responsible for the development of his or her market through additional points of distribution, as well as for restaurant performance. A job description is shown in Exhibit 4.

John Martin's ideal Taco Bell consisted of the CEO and many restaurants, with nobody in the middle. While the organization was still a long way from that ideal, middle managers at the ZVP and MM levels understood that their ultimate goal was to "coach themselves out of a job." The uncertainty inherent in such a goal was partially offset by the potential for movement within the PepsiCo organization, particularly at the vice-president level.

Ultimately, however, "the only job security was performance," a view echoed by Sanjiv, Eastern Ontario MM Barry Telford, and Zone Human Resources Manager Christine Maxwell. Managers were expected to be forward-looking and to take risks, but were driven primarily by aggressive sales and profit targets.

Barry described the paradigm for evolution in the PepsiCo organization:

> Certain people with certain skills are necessary to bring the organization to a higher level, then new people or new skills are needed to pull the organization to the next level. Not everyone has the same capacity to stretch by themselves. ... We try to focus on the bottom third performers every year and either develop them, or promote other people, or hire externally.

Throughout the organization, Taco Bell fostered a self-sufficient, "can do" attitude. An internal communication described the seven shared values promoted in daily business practice: focus on the customer, integrity, teamwork, diversity, balance, accountability and commitment to growth. Employees described a feeling of camaraderie, born of teamwork, common values and lofty goals. At every level, they were encouraged to share ideas and innovations with their counterparts elsewhere in the organization.

Performance Measurement

Some markets were much more developed than others. Because of this disparity, performance was measured primarily in relation to that of other MMs in the same zone.

Performance was measured according to ambitious quarterly and annual sales and profit targets, as well as specific customer service objectives. In the U.S., zones were held responsible for a certain level of projected sales through existing and new units. A standard formula

---

[7] Articles from *Restaurants & Institutions*; Taco Bell Internal Documents; Interviews.

was applied to projected sales to arrive at optimum cost and profit levels. The zone's sales and profit commitment was then allocated among markets based on current performance and the MM's growth and cost projections. When Sanjiv assumed responsibility for the Upstate New York market, he inherited a budget developed with the input of his predecessor. A series of storms earlier in the year had resulted in significantly lower sales volumes than projected.

The budgeting process in Canada was somewhat different. The Taco Bell head office, through the Senior V.P. International, told the zones what their profit levels would have to be. MMs then worked with their ZVPs to develop plans to meet the required profit level. Despite apparent differences in the level of input MMs had in the U.S. and international budgeting processes, Sanjiv emphasized the fundamental similarity:

> Sales budgets are based to a large extent on our market projections. The cost targets are aggressive, but achievable and fairly standardized throughout the company. Cost targets can vary a bit depending on the market. For example, food costs are higher in Canada than in the U.S. But budgets are really not the result of negotiation at the market manager level. The targets are given to us, based on our input. We have control over all the factors necessary to meet them. My task is always the same: to squeeze costs and inefficiencies out of the system, and to increase profits.
>
> If my sales are above plan, approximately 40% of each additional sales dollar has to flow through to profit, or I am not managing my costs. On higher levels of sales, having profit above plan in absolute terms is not enough!

Targets for individual restaurants were set by the RGM and MM. MM bonuses, with a target of $1 200 per unit supervised, were based on market sales and profit, zone performance, customer service, and specific individual criteria. The unique criteria against which Sanjiv was evaluated included: successfully (defined in terms of sales, costs and customer satisfaction) opening new units; fulfilling responsibilities as the zone's link with the marketing and finance support departments at headquarters; and raising customer satisfaction ratings by a specified amount. Fifty percent of the bonus was based on market performance, and was only awarded to those MMs who were within 90% of their sales commitment and 95% of optimum profit targets.

It was not enough, however, to focus on short-term objectives. The Taco Bell organization was changing continuously, pushing toward a new product concept, and a much broader, flatter structure with self-directed work teams. While ZVPs assessed restaurant performance quarterly and annually, it was monitored continuously, sometimes in great detail. Sanjiv described the process:

> We have 13 four-week periods when the ZVPs look at performance and follow up. But the TACO system gives them minute-by-minute information every day, and they can call us for an explanation at any time. A lot can happen in a few days. A couple of weeks ago I took four days off to move. When I came back, I had 24 pages of e-mail. That's 200 messages! ... Some managers will push you harder for details than others.

However, in a high volume, low margin business such as Taco Bell, the details were of critical importance. Sanjiv explained:

> A $100 mistake each day for 30 days, over 4 000 units becomes a lot of money.

Personal Strategy

MMs had considerable leeway in how they ran their restaurant portfolios. They made the hiring, firing and training decisions. They were free to recommend the closing and relocation of poorly performing restaurants, but needed to work with senior corporate people as well as the real estate department. Sanjiv was reluctant to close a poorly performing store and simply fire everybody without a thorough evaluation of the alternatives. According to him, the key to successfully managing a market was the development of an effective personal strategy:

> I started by thinking, 'Where are we now and where do we want to be?' I want this to be the most competitive market both within Taco Bell and compared to outside competitors. What will success look like and how will it come? We need to focus on revenues, costs, competition and shareholder returns. We can't afford to just do a few things well; we need to do everything well!
>
> Do I hire stars, or develop strong middle-of-the-road people? Which is more sustainable? We will need some good talent and extremely strong leadership. I would prefer to develop people than to replace them. But people are limited by their skill sets and, in a high-growth business such as this one, we need people who already have a strong skill base. Not everyone has the same capacity to develop in ways required by this organization's culture and time frames.
>
> I am convinced that 95% of an organization's problems are due to inadequate management direction. It's like that at any level: 95% of this market's problems are because I haven't provided sufficient direction. I haven't given clear guidelines, or properly thought through the actions necessary to achieve goals. Ninety-five percent of a restaurant's problems are because the RGM hasn't done those things. It's easy to set goals and hold people accountable. What's *not* easy is coaching people to reach those goals and making sure that the goals are attainable and supported by organizational processes.
>
> One of the things I need to do is take the company's broad strategic goals and translate them into specific actions. Let's take self-sufficiency. When one of my RGMs phones me with a question, I say: 'Did you really need to call me? How did I add value in this situation? Would it have been more efficient if you had made this decision yourself or gone directly to corporate office? Remember that I trust you to make good decisions, and I support the decisions you make.' At 10 minutes per call and 27 restaurants, that's $4^1/_2$ hours per day of making RGM decisions, which is a big waste of my time. Overlapping responsibilities and supervision are value lost. In a flat organization, there can be no duplication of effort.
>
> I am committed to two things: fairness and performance. These are the principles underlying every decision I make.

Self-Directed Work Teams

John Martin was ever alert to new developments in management practice which might increase efficiency at Taco Bell. He believed that self-directed work teams (SWTs) would be necessary for achieving the flat management structure he envisioned within the company. Although much had been written about the benefits of SWTs, relatively little was known about how best to implement and manage them. Recognizing how difficult it would be to develop a company-wide training program given the high level of uncertainty, Martin pushed the responsibility for learning about these work teams to the front line. Market and restaurant managers were expected to experiment with and eventually implement SWTs in their stores, and were evaluated on their progress in this endeavour.

The development of SWTs was reflected in the MM's performance appraisal under the broader sections on Managing the Business and Leading People. Performance appraisals were then used in the calculation of salary adjustments. They were also used as the primary input into annual meetings between ZVPs and Human Resources to rank MMs, and determine their professional potential and ultimate career paths. Sanjiv explained that not having SWTs would have little effect on his career or compensation in the short term, but that a strategy including

SWTs was important in determining an MM's performance and resulting job security in the longer term, relative to his or her peers.

Sanjiv commented on the move toward SWTs:

There's no shared definition of what constitutes a self-directed work team or how an MM should implement one. We each need to find the time to create our own versions. I do know that the first steps toward self-directed work teams must be vision alignment and technical training. This is not really urgent, but it's very important. Maybe later, when we see which models are working, the company will develop a more comprehensive program.

I see some major issues associated with these work teams. The most important one is who's in control? Who is ultimately assuring the safety of the food, the security of the physical premises and customer service? We cannot let these slip, even for a moment. How can we add fail-safe mechanisms to support the teams and avoid major mishaps? And we must remember that this system means a great deal more responsibility for front-line crew. What factors make one person better able to cope with a situation than another?

Another critical issue is how to implement the work teams without either customer service or financial performance being negatively impacted in the short term. If the uncertainty associated with the change causes inattention to some detail, then we could lose a customer. We don't have the luxury of a trial period. In an industry as competitive as this one, an unsatisfied customer simply switches to a competitor.

Because of the low margins in this industry, we *must* meet profit targets. Every dollar in this organization is accounted for. This is especially important in Canada, because, since Canada is considered to be part of the International Division, our profits are used to fund international growth. So if I want to implement SWTs, then I need to find the money to fund them in my controllable costs and labour costs while still meeting my targets. I estimate that it would cost approximately $200 000 to start moving all my units toward SWTs, and only 50–60% would actually be able to make the conversion. Of the $200 000, approximately $130 000 would be used to train employees. That training would be technical in nature, improving employees' levels of competence in product assembly, customer service and working in groups. That number is as low as I can get it. It provides for a consultant to train the RGMs and ARGMs, and we would do the rest in-house. The remaining $70 000 would be for process re-engineering. And then there are any operational inefficiencies resulting from the change process. I see the gain from SWTs being in the area of competitive advantage, not lower costs.

Introducing SWTs to one unit at a time is not a viable option. It could take eight to 12 months to convert one store, so doing them individually would take a lifetime! Ideally, I would want to introduce SWTs throughout the market over the period of a year. There are efficiencies in training and experience to be gained from making the changes in several units simultaneously. Also, experience in the U.S. has shown that inconsistencies in culture within a market make people feel that they are being treated unfairly.

EXHIBIT 1   **Major Fast Food (FF) Chains**

Rank '93 ('92)	Company	Segment	'92 Sales in $ millions (% Change)[*]	'92 Units (% Change)[*]
1 (1)	McDonald's	FF hamburgers	21 855 (9.8)	13 093 (5.4)
2 (3)	KFC [**]	FF chicken	6 700 (8.1)	8 729 (2.9)
3 (2)	Burger King	FF hamburgers	6 400 (3.2)	6 648 (4.1)
4 (4)	Pizza Hut [**]	FF pizza	5 700 (7.5)	9 450 (5.0)
5 (6)	Wendy's	FF hamburgers	3 613 (12.1)	3 962 (4.2)
6 (5)	Hardee's	FF hamburgers	3 400 (9.7)	3 365 (5.2)
7 (8)	**Taco Bell** [**]	**FF Mexican**	**3 300 (17.9)**	**4 000 (9.0)**
8 (7)	ARA Services	Contract mgt.	2 900 (2.5)	2 767 (1.7)
9 (9)	Marriott Mgt. Services	Contract mgt.	2 620 (4.8)	2 519 (5.0)
10 (12)	Gardner Merchant Food Services	Contract mgt.	2 500 (15.8)	4 600 N/A

[*]   Percent change from 1991 level
[**] Owned by PepsiCo
SOURCE: *Restaurants & Institutions*, July 1993.

EXHIBIT 2   **Compensation Structures** (US$)

Position	1993	Position	1988
RGM	Salary range: $27 100 – 40 700	RM	Salary range: $22 000 – 33 100
	Bonus target: $10 000		Bonus target: $4 320
	Bonus based on: store sales, store profit, store customer service, team sales "kicker"*		Bonus based on: sales, food costs, direct labor costs, controllable costs
MM	Salary range: $50 000 – 90 000	DM	Salary range: $30 600 – 45 800
	Bonus target: $36 000		Bonus target: $6 240
	Bonus based on: market sales, market profit, zone financial performance, individual objectives, customer service "kicker"*		Bonus based on: district sales, district profit, turnover, individual objectives, customer service "kicker"*

* A "kicker" refers to an amount over and above the bonus target.
SOURCE: Taco Bell Internal Documents.

EXHIBIT 3   **Partial Taco Bell Organization Chart—Company Operations**

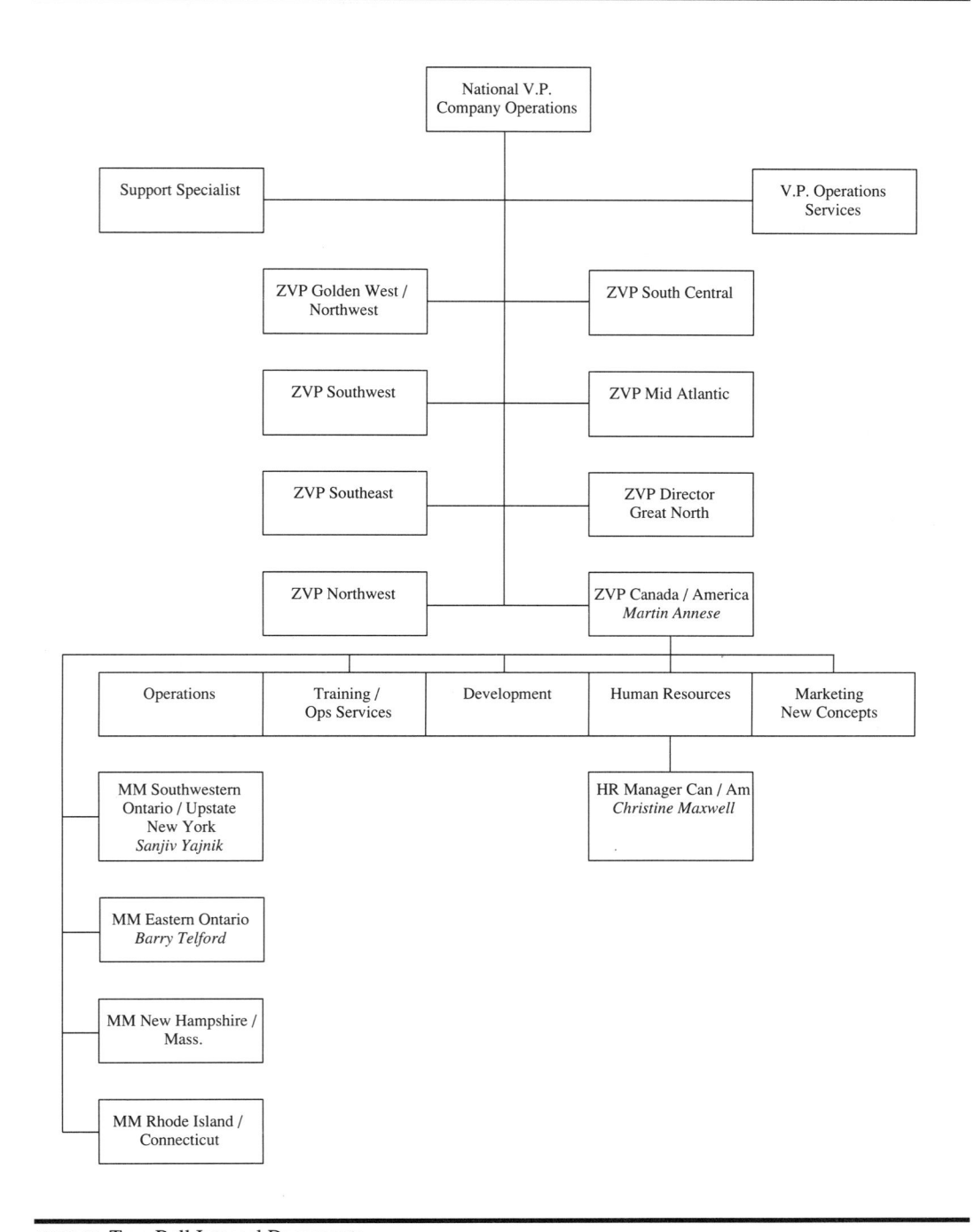

SOURCE: Taco Bell Internal Documents.

EXHIBIT 4   Market Mananger Job Description

Purpose / Objective of the Position

The Market Manager serves as a leader and an expert operations resource to hire, coach, develop and assist 20 to 30 Restaurant General Managers and Team Managed Units Managers in achieving sales and profit plans. These restaurants are typically geographically isolated, requiring the incumbent to demonstrate independence and autonomy in supervision.

Dimensions / Scope

Number of restaurants = 20 to 30
Total sales = $20 to $40 million
Employees = 600 to 1200

Knowledge / Skills

College degree or equivalent experience required, with a Master's preferred
4–8 years of multi-unit success in Fortune 500 retail, sales, hospitality or customer operations
People leadership / supervision a must
Proven fast track record
Diverse experience a plus
Direct P&L responsibility
Knowledge of restaurants / hospitality not required

Detailed Performance Accountabilities

1. Leading Your People

Proactively builds market toward 100% Restaurant General Manager self-sufficiency.
Promotes teamwork and communications across the market.
Creates alignment between market and company value strategy.
Has an effective staffing plan which recognizes RGM opportunities within the market and addresses them.
Sets a strong personal example of integrity and commitment to employee development.

2. Serving the Customer

Follows up on customer complaints to ensure action.
Analyzes and acts on customer intercept data to spot trends and corrects them.
Maintains accuracy, hospitality, quality, service and cleanliness (AHQSC) scores at or above the area of dominant influence (ADI) or peer group average.
Demonstrates strong personal commitment to customer satisfaction.
Identifies and removes barriers to maximizing customer value.

3. Representing the Company

Participates in events and public service organizations which enhance the image of the company.
Knows business influences within the market and works to impact them.
Maintains solid, professional relations with the vendors.

Nature of the Job

Challenge

Maintaining strong HQSC, sales and profits through consultative management and management by request and exception only.
Significant upgrading of manager quality and skill level.
Manage positive interpersonal relationships and motivate with infrequent personal contact.

SOURCE: Taco Bell Internal Documents.

SABENA BELGIAN WORLD AIRLINES (A)

Mary M. Crossan and Barbara Pierce

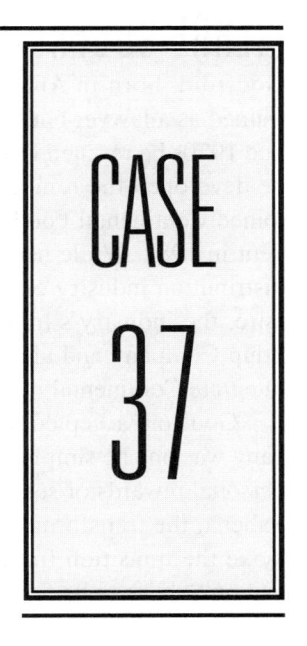

CASE

37

On July 3, 1990, Carlos Van Rafelghem, Chairman of Sabena Belgian World Airlines suffered a massive stroke and never recovered consciousness. For months he lay in a coma. When it became obvious that Van Rafelghem would not return to his position, the Belgian government began to search for a suitable replacement. Jean Luc Dehaene, the Belgian Deputy Prime Minister and Minister of Communications knew that finding a suitable replacement would be a difficult assignment. He described his task as seeking out a "rare bird." Given the unfavourable condition of the global airline industry and the difficulties Sabena was experiencing due to months of interim leadership, it seemed obvious that the person hired to replace Van Rafelghem should already have proven himself in the airline industry.

Rumours of potential candidates had been rampant; the Belgian press speculated for months as to possible successors. The much anticipated announcement of the new Chairman for Sabena Belgian World Airlines caught the entire nation by surprise. On November 9, 1990, the government announced that Pierre Godfroid, Vice-President of European Operations for the U.S. based Campbell Soup Company, would be the new head of the Belgian national air carrier. Dehaene, in making the announcement, explained that the government felt Godfroid's skills in industrial restructuring would more than outweigh his lack of direct involvement in the airline business. It would fall to Godfroid, a man with no experience in managing an airline, but with skills in restructuring, to find a way to ensure the continued survival of Sabena; a clearly troubled airline, in clearly troubled times.

PIERRE GODFROID

Godfroid, born in Antwerp, was a 56-year-old Belgian of Flemish descent. He had been trained as a lawyer but in his early career he worked primarily as an investment banker. In the late 1970s he rescued France's leading catalogue sales company from bankruptcy. By doing so he developed the reputation as a highly competent turnaround manager. In 1981 Godfroid joined Continental Foods, a major European food distribution company and became its President in 1982. While head of Continental, he assumed a leadership role in the European food distribution industry eventually becoming president of the Fédération de l'Industrie Alimentaire, the industry's trade association. In 1984, Continental was acquired by the Campbell Soup Company and after the takeover, Godfroid remained with the company to successfully integrate Continental into Campbell's worldwide operations.

Godfroid accepted the job at Sabena because he felt that the challenge of saving the company was one he simply could not turn down. He knew that the risk of failure was great but the personal rewards of success would be equally significant. If things could be turned around for Sabena, the transformation would establish a model for other state run businesses trying to make the transition from public to private enterprise. There was potential for the impact he had on Sabena to be felt well beyond the borders of one struggling company.

Godfroid strongly believed that business success was the result of competent leadership and "good people." Leadership set the direction and tone for individual employees to follow but it was their competence, applied within a framework established by the leader, which produced positive results. "I only believe in people—they make the difference." He felt that the right kind of people were those with a simple approach; people who were not pretentious, who saw what needed to be done and went ahead and did it. He stated that, "Success comes to those who are willing to take the greatest risks." He was willing to tolerate mistakes in the belief that the problems they caused would be more than offset by the learning that accompanied failure. Godfroid had little tolerance for bureaucratic ritual or unnecessary paperwork; direct, hands-on control, was not of primary importance.

SABENA'S HISTORY

Founded in 1923, Belgium's Sabena Airlines was one of the oldest air carriers in the world. The Belgian people were very proud of the fact that their country had a national airline whose roots could be traced back to the early days of aviation. They believed that a national airline was necessary to ensure Belgium remained connected to the rest of the world. Over the years Sabena had developed air connections throughout Europe and to a lesser extent to North America, but the airline played its most crucial role in the development of Belgium's colonial ties to Africa. The routes which carried wealthy colonists between Africa and Europe linked Belgium to its colonies and at the same time allowed the airline to prosper in spite of Belgium's relatively small domestic market. What was good for the development of the country was good for the development of Sabena.

On a number of occasions, Sabena aircraft had been directed to African trouble spots to air lift Belgian nationals in emergency situations. The airline was seen as a lifeline to the home country and its ability to respond in a crisis increased the perception among Belgians that the airline was an important component of their national sovereignty.

The airline's dependence on African routes, eventually, resulted in long run problems when the ties between Belgium and its African colonies were broken. In 1963, after the colonies achieved independence, the government of Zaire, the former Belgian Congo, ended Sabena's monopoly on routes to Europe. It later expelled the company from domestic air services altogether. The loss of these routes, together with the fact that the company had neglected development of more lucrative routes to North America and Asia while its competition had not, almost resulted in the company's collapse. However, the Belgian government, cognizant of the air line's historical position and its importance as a source of employment (over 12 000 Belgians worked for the airline), continued to support Sabena during the tough times. As long as the company did not lose too much money, there were strong political forces keeping it afloat.

INDUSTRY ENVIRONMENT

In 1990, the European airline industry consisted of over 20 national and private carriers of varying size and profitability. Most of these carriers were wholly owned or significantly supported by their home governments and they enjoyed a strong hold on their national markets (Exhibit 1). Smaller independent regional and charter airlines had emerged and were positioning themselves for smaller niche or under-serviced markets. However these start-up airlines were not perceived to represent significant competition because of their size and the limited nature of their services.

According to the International Civil Aviation Organization, the world's airlines transported over 1.1 billion passengers in 1989; however there was growing concern that some markets were beginning to mature and growth would slow (Exhibit 2) in future years. In addition, industry profits were extremely variable. While some major airlines were doing extremely well, (Singapore, Delta and AMR) others were on the brink of bankruptcy (Texas Air, Pan Am and TWA). As noted in Exhibit 3, Sabena was the 34th largest airline in the world on the basis of revenues and the 44th on the basis of passenger miles in 1989.

FIXED COSTS

The basic operating economics of an airline hinged upon high fixed costs. Once the airline set its routes, established flight frequencies, and decided on the type of aircraft, most of its costs were in place. Every passenger represented contribution and the airline was under great pressure to fill the planes. Exhibit 4 provides the cost structure for a typical commercial airline. Since fuel costs were about the same for a full plane as an empty one, and the number of flight crew depended on the type of aircraft rather than the number of passengers, the only true variable expenses were services like ticketing and customers' meals. Most airlines used some form of product differentiation to attract customers, preferably high yield customers such as business travellers and first-class passengers.

A UNIFIED EUROPE

In the fall of 1990, a number of changes and potential changes were facing the European airline industry and uncertainty was the most accurate way to describe the state of affairs. A key unknown was the impact of a unified Europe, planned for 1992. No one was sure what impact this new political alignment would have on the airline industry, but companies were beginning to position themselves to take advantage of the anticipated freer borders and the reduced regulatory environment. The European Commission, the regulatory body for European aviation, was seeking greater powers to ensure a competitive environment for post 1992. It was particularly concerned about a potential rise in predatory practices on the part of dominant carriers. For example, such airlines could flood the market with capacity or frequencies, charge fares below a carrier's fully allocated costs, or grant override commissions and other benefits to travel agents and frequent flier programs which locked in customers to one airline. The Commission was exploring ways in which it could encourage open competition so the consumer would benefit from increased services and lower costs. At the same time it was trying to determine the best way to intervene so that the industry would avoid the pitfalls evident in the post deregulation environment of the United States. European airlines, having had the advantage of watching the U.S. experience realized that deregulation would inevitably lead to fierce competition and likely result in industry consolidation. There was developing concern among industry officials that, in a deregulated environment, many of the smaller airlines could not survive in their current configuration. There was also uncertainty as to whether the European Commission would be given the appropriate power to intervene to protect the more vulnerable airlines.

ALLIANCES

The potential for industry consolidation seemed even more certain given the emerging trend to privatize national airlines. Many governments were no longer willing, and in many cases, no longer able, to prop up unprofitable operations. With reduced fiscal support and regulatory protection from home governments, airlines were beginning to realize that they could not continue to depend on their governments for preferential treatment. Governments had little to offer in support of their flag carriers. Many of the smaller airlines, seeing the handwriting on the wall, were not waiting to be taken over but were investigating the possibility of joining with competitors in some form of operational alliance. For example, in the spring of 1990, Austrian Airlines joined Finnair, Swissair and SAS in a European alliance created to serve an expanded market in Eastern and Southern Europe, North Africa, the Middle East and India. Sabena had been holding talks with a number of airlines and had recently received a firm proposal to join with British Airways and KLM to develop a European hub in Brussels. However these alliance relationships were new and untested and industry analysts wondered about the long term stability of such arrangements.

The independent competitors were fighting such alliances preferring to see the collapse of the smaller carriers. Alliances captured landing rights within existing operations and did not free up slots for expansions or new entrants. The start up operations were dependent upon access to existing slots because the current European airport infrastructure did not allow for the creation of new and expanded airline operations. Most governments did not have the money to build new airports or even to improve existing facilities. A special report for the International Air Transport Association found that capacity at ten major European airports would be seriously restricted between 1995 and 2000 without major improvements and a total of 27 major Western European airports would be unable to accommodate traffic demand by the year 2000 without significant enhancements. This meant that airlines with existing slots had a valuable commodity to bargain with, in alliance negotiations.

THE GULF CRISIS

Another major uncertainty facing the airline industry concerned the impact of the Persian Gulf Crisis on airline operations. Since tensions began to mount in the summer of 1990, oil prices had increased significantly resulting in increased airline fuel costs. At the same time, passenger travel declined as people concerned about the unstable conditions delayed or cancelled travel plans. How long would the crisis last and how would it be resolved? How long would the tensions last and would there be any lasting repercussions? Would the oil prices decline when the situation stabilized? The little profitability that remained in the industry was being squeezed out by this unforseen event.

SABENA BELGIAN WORLD AIRLINES

Sabena had always operated as an instrument of the Belgian government and reflected many of the hallmarks of a government run bureaucracy. The organization functioned more like a public authority staffed by civil servants than a competitive airline. Under these conditions, the priority was not necessarily what was best for Sabena as a competitive business but rather what was seen as best for the people of Belgium. For example, it was not unusual for purchasing decisions to be made, not on the basis of the least cost alternative, but on the basis of other more politically important criteria.

The government saw the airline as a source of employment and did what it could to maximize the number of people working at Sabena. If this meant that the company lost money, then the government encouraged the airline to protect employment and covered losses until profitability improved. Systems to improve efficiency were given lower priority especially if their implementation resulted in job losses. As a result, the airline was seriously overstaffed and operated with probably the worst efficiency of any airline in Europe. Internal studies had shown that the airline did not have a good image among consumers and was not known for the quality or consistency of its service.

The company had 16 directors, many of whom were appointed because of the need to accommodate Belgium's various political parties, labour unions and linguistic factions. Staffing selections as well were influenced by the need to ensure balanced representation among Belgium's linguistic factions.

The airline operated out of Zaventem Airport, 30 km outside of Brussels and controlled most of the landing rights and runway slots. Access to Zaventem was one of Sabena's most valuable assets since the airport was strategically located near the centre of Western Europe (see Exhibit 5 for map). Many felt that Zaventem would make an ideal hub location if the European airlines decided to replicate the American approach to airline operations.

Management at Sabena

When Godfroid took over many of those in management positions had been appointed to their posts for political reasons and did not necessarily have appropriate work experience or managerial competence. It was not unusual for managers to act in the interests of the people who appointed them rather than the interests of the corporation which employed them. Skilled individuals who rose through the ranks to attain leadership positions in the company found it difficult to function among less motivated or competent colleagues. Some left in frustration because of the amount of political interference and their inability to function in a true management role. Most of the current senior managers had either an aeronautics or engineering background and saw technical concerns as the focus of their efforts. The planes and equipment were of excellent quality and well maintained, but management had much less appreciation for marketing and customer service requirements.

The management structure at Sabena was multi-layered and hierarchical with management clearly separate from workers. There were no accurate organizational charts or job descriptions. This meant that the organizational units within Sabena developed as separate fifedoms reflecting the unique relationships developed among managers and workers within the unit. There was little coordination at the management level except in crisis situations and it was not uncommon for open hostility to break out as one set of managers blamed another if problems arose.

There was a similar lack of competence at the supervisory level. Because of rigid compensation rules it was difficult to reward individual performance or to provide increased wages to employees who exceeded maximum levels in specified wage categories. It was common practice, therefore, to create special supervisory positions or to promote individuals to existing supervisory positions to justify a pay raise. This meant that a large number of supervisors were in these positions for administrative reasons rather for their ability to manage people. Such supervisors did not see themselves as management's representatives in their relations with hourly workers. It was not uncommon for them to provide weak leadership on the floor and to provide poor implementation of management direction.

Management did as little as possible to communicate directly with the workers, preferring instead to instruct through written communications and memos. There were those who suggested that management was afraid of the work force and avoided face to face confrontations whenever possible. Management treated the workers as machines which were not expected, or encouraged, to think for themselves. When an employee had a work related problem, it was presented to a supervisor for a solution. Employees took no initiative beyond their limited responsibilities. Each worker performed his or her specific job unconcerned about the functioning of the whole. They took little or no pride in the outcome of their work. This attitude, coupled with ineffective supervision, meant that a significant amount of pilfering, work avoidance and shirking took place. Absenteeism was running at 9% per day.

Employer/Union Relations

The unions in Belgium were extremely powerful and dominated every aspect of Belgian life. They were established, not on the basis of job function or industry designation but rather on political affiliation. There were three unions, all of which were represented at Sabena: Socialist

(30% of Sabena workers), Christian Democrats (30%) and Liberals (10%). In the past, unions had dominated management at Sabena. Industrial relations were strained and when the unions disagreed with management actions, strikes were a common occurrence. Human Resource (HR) managers at Sabena had not kept up with trends in HR management. They preferred to continue to manage according to the existing status quo, which was unquestionably adversarial. Under this approach both management and unions had clearly defined "roles" and ongoing relations followed well established rules of the "game." The workers held a trump card, however, in that if they didn't like what they were told by management, their unions would complain to the politicians, who in turn would direct the Chairman to comply with the union demands.

Management was tightly bound by the terms and conditions of collective agreements. Workers were hired and trained to carry out very specific and limited functions. If there was no work available, workers would wait until appropriate work was found. Workers at Sabena were paid well, earning significantly more and working significantly less than workers in private industry. In addition to high wages, the level of employee benefits provided workers in Belgium approached 31% of their salary, significantly more than was required in the countries of competitor firms.

The workers at Sabena knew that they had well paid and secure employment. Wage increases were based on length of service. Pay hikes were automatically awarded for each year of continuous service, for a period of up to 33 years. As long as the worker continued on the payroll, he or she was guaranteed an increase in wages regardless of productivity or performance. It was almost impossible to fire anyone and there was virtually a no lay-off policy. If attempts were made to lay off workers, the union would intervene with the government and the Chairman would be directed to back down.

Corporate Restructuring

Van Rafelghem felt that the lack of management accountability had been a major source of reduced profitability. To resolve this problem he divided the company up into semi-autonomous subsidiaries or divisions. His plan was to hold each division accountable for the management of the assets under its control and to establish clear profit centres to monitor results. There were 12 of these subsidiaries established (airlines, flight school, catering, techniques [airline maintenance and repair], real estate, tourism, finance) each reporting to a holding company referred to as Sabena S.A. Among these subsidiaries, Sabena World Airlines (SWA) was the largest and most important. The Chairman and Vice-Chairman of Sabena S.A. held the same positions in each of the 12 subsidiaries but after that, there was much duplication of administrative functions. This was not perceived as a problem because employment, not efficiency, was the government's key priority. In fact, the restructuring had a positive effect in that it resulted in the creation of a number of new managerial positions.

Although the intent to decentralize and introduce divisional accountability had merit, problems arose because of the lack of complementary integrating mechanisms to focus the subsidiaries on common purposes or goals. Immediately upon establishing the subsidiaries, boundaries were drawn between divisions and coordination became an almost impossible task. Although the change was intended to increase accountability, every time a problem occurred, individual divisions would pass the buck claiming the trouble was the fault of another division. Instead of solving problems, more problems were created. The fragmentation of management effort directed at internal problems diverted the company's attention from the truly important environmental challenges facing it.

Splitting Sabena up into smaller subsidiaries had, unfortunately, taken place before the completion of information systems to track corporate results in line with the new divisions. Although a great deal of effort had been directed at developing information and accounting systems, the company was not capable of sorting out data in meaningful ways to assist in identifying responsibility and the MIS systems were of no help in resolving jurisdictional disputes.

Financial Position

The Belgian state owned 53% of Sabena's shares with the remainder belonging to regional governments or state run investment funds. In the past, the Belgian government had only asked that the company be marginally profitable. It was willing to absorb small losses from time to time, as long as Sabena provided a maximum number of jobs for the Belgian economy. By 1990, however, the state was beginning to grow concerned about the company's steady stream of losses. Like many countries, Belgium was beginning to feel the effects of deficit financing and the country was experiencing a worsening debt problem. Political pressure was beginning to build to bring the national debt under control. The government was not sure how much longer it could tolerate the continuing drain of Sabena's poor financial results. Sabena expected to post a loss of BFr 3 billion (US$98 million) to BFr 4 billion in 1990, its worst performance in 15 years. In addition it was facing a capital expenditure over the next ten years of BFr 100 billion to pay for new planes on order. It was clear that the poor financial results were showing no signs of reversal. In fact, the losses were escalating at such an alarming rate that the company's equity had all but disappeared (Exhibit 6).

Van Rafelghem had been working on establishing a joint venture with British Airways (BA) and KLM . He was hoping to interest the two carriers into buying into SWA. Both would purchase a 20% equity share leaving Sabena (the Belgian government) with 60% ownership. The intent of the venture would be to establish a European hub at Brussel's Zaventem airport. This would allow these airlines to use the underutilized Zaventem airport to link secondary destinations throughout Europe. Interest in this alliance had cooled, however, because of anti-trust concerns among other competitors and Sabena's fears about its loss of autonomy under this arrangement. However, the hub idea had merit in and of itself and there were some who felt that Sabena should consider going it alone or consider interesting other more appropriate airlines in a Brussel's hub arrangement.

After Van Rafelghem's stroke, Sabena's Deputy Chairman Pahault stepped in to take over, but he was in no position to effectively replace Van Rafelghem. The Deputy Chairman position had been established as one of convention to appease Belgium's main linguistic factions. The tradition had been that if the Chairman was of Flemish descent, the Vice Chairman would be French and vice versa. In this case, since Van Rafelghem was Flemish, so Pahault, of French descent, had been appointed as Vice Chairman. Much of the knowledge about the company and how it functioned however, resided only with Van Rafelghem and it was inaccessible as long as he lay in a coma. Some even speculated that establishment of Sabena S.A. had been a masterful feat of financial engineering intended to increase equity through the creation of goodwill. Regardless of Van Rafelghem's intent, it was clear that the situation Pahault inherited was a company very near bankruptcy; immediate action was critical. Recognizing the financial crisis the company faced, Pahault brought in a group of McKinsey consultants to try and straighten out its financial position and to identify cost saving measures to get Sabena's costs under control. In their report, McKinsey suggested that to ensure its survival Sabena either drastically downsize its operations to become a low cost regional carrier or it find the funds to invest in the development of a European hub (estimated to be in the neighbourhood of US$250 million).

GODFROID'S TASK

In offering him the position Dehaene had asked Godfroid to help with the transformation of Sabena from public to private enterprise. The government requested that he prepare a business plan by February 1, 1991, outlining his program for raising new capital and reorganizing the airline. The government was willing to release its control of the company reducing its level of ownership from 53% to 25%, allowing for a much needed infusion of new equity from private sources. To avert bankruptcy, Sabena would need to improve its profitability dramatically and to attract new partners from the private sector. Godfroid had just under two months to come up with a plan to achieve these objectives. What direction should he take the airline and how should he manage this mammoth undertaking? Was Sabena worth saving or would it inevitably be swallowed up by a larger and stronger competitor? Godfroid knew he had to set his direction soon since there was little time to waste.

EXHIBIT 1 European Airlines

Airline	Country
Aer Lingus	Ireland
Air France	France
Air Malta	Malta
Alitalia	Italy
Austrian Airlines	Austria
British Airways	Great Britain
CSA Czechoslovakian Airlines	Czechoslovakia
Finnair	Finland
Iberia	Spain
Iceland air	Iceland
JAT Yugoslavian Airlines	Yugoslavia
KLM	Netherlands
Lufthansa	West Germany
Luxair	Luxembourg
Malev Hungarian Airlines	Hungary
Olympic Airlines	Greece
Sabena	Belgium
SAS	Sweden
Swissair	Switzerland
TAP - Air Portugal	Portugal
Turkish Air	Turkey

EXHIBIT 2 Selected RPK Forecasts (billions)

Domestic Market				1989 RPK		Forecast Average Annual Growth Rate 1990–2000
U.S.				505.1		5.1
WESTERN EUROPE				52.2		6.3
ASIA-PACIFIC				70.5		6.3
TOTAL DOMESTIC				627.8 out of total Domestic Market: 981.5		

Between Europe and	1989	1990	1991	1993	1995	2000
Intra-Europe	67.8	72.6	77.7	88.9	100.4	125.7
North America	168.2	178.9	190.0	213.1	237.2	303.3
South America	19.8	21.2	22.7	25.7	28.9	37.8
Africa	34.9	37.0	39.2	43.8	48.8	62.9
Middle East	35.9	37.3	38.8	42.0	45.4	55.2
Asia[1]	33.2	39.4	45.9	58.9	70.9	101.6

[1] Does not include the Indian subcontinent.
SOURCE: Boeing Commercial Airplane Group.

EXHIBIT 3 Top 50 Airline Companies: Rank by Revenues

Rank by Revenues			Country	1989 Revenues		Profit		Traffic	
1989	1988	Airline Company		US $ Millions	% Change from 1988 (U.S.)	$ Millions	Rank	Billions of Passenger Kms.	Rank
1	2	AMR	U.S.	10 589.5	20.0	454.8	3	118.5	1
2	1	UAL	U.S.	9 914.5	10.0	324.2	6	112.3	2
3	4	Japan Airlines[1]	Japan	8 509.0	17.4	157.3	10	54.4	8
4	5	Delta	U.S.	8 0889.5	17.0	460.9	2	55.9	3
5	7	British Airways[1]	Britain	7 529.1	12.5	309.5	7	90.2	6
6	6	Lufthansa	W. Germany	6 941.2	3.0	56.8	22	57.9	12
7	3	Texas Air	U.S.	6 768.7	(21.0)	(885.6)	47	81.3	4
8	10	NWA	U.S.	6 553.8	16.0	355.2	5	73.7	5
9	9	USAIR Group	U.S.	6 257.3	9.6	(63.2)	41	54.4	9
10	8	Air France	France	6 216.9	4.4	132.0	12	37.0	11
11	11	All Nippon[1]	Japan	4 858.4	9.7	60.2	19	26.0	16
12	12	Scandinavian Airlines	Sweden	4 567.3	3.5	N.A.	—	15.3	26
13	13	Trans World	U.S.	4 507.3	3.4	(298.5)	45	56.4	7
14	15	Hanjin Group	South Korea	4 243.6	13.7	69.6	18	17.9	23
15	14	Pan Am	U.S.	3 794.4	(8.9)	(336.6)	46	46.6	10
16	16	Alitalia	Italy	3 734.2	14.6	(168.1)	44	20.8	21
17	17	Swissair	Switzerland	3 174.5	1.7	103.3	16	15.8	25
18	20	Air Canada	Canada	3 104.3	11.8	125.8	13	26.3	15
19	18	Iberia	Spain	3 015.5	4.9	52.5	25	21.1	20
20	19	KLM[1]	Netherlands	2 938.9	4.1	184.2	8	24.0	17
21	21	Qantas[2]	Australia	2 655.1	18.1	144.3	11	26.6	14
22	22	Singapore[1]	Singapore	2 295.8	15.9	494.7	1	28.9	13

EXHIBIT 3 (contiued

23	24	PWA	Canada	2 252.9	27.7	(47.3)	40	23.7	18
24	23	Cathay Pacific	Hong Kong	2 212.6	14.4	425.2	4	22.1	19
25	25	Saudia	Saudi Arabia	1 910.1	12.5	(140.0)	43	16.3	24
26	26	Varig	Brazil	1 862.1	21.6	10.4	39	13.9	28
27	28	Ansett Transport[2]	Australia	1 743.9	32.7	108.0	15	7.7	42
28	27	Thai International[3]	Thailand	1 683.8	17.9	182.1	9	18.7	22
29	29	Japan Air System[1]	Japan	1 418.3	12.7	12.2	36	7.3	43
30	30	Air Inter	France	1 356.5	9.5	18.3	32	8.5	39
31	34	China	Taiwan	1 246.4	20.3	115.6	14	10.5	33
32	31	Garuda	Indonesia[1]	1 232.6	11.6	N.A.	—	12.9	29
33	33	Hudson Investments[4]	Britain	1,211.6	11.6	11.7	37	6.9	45
34	36	Finnair[1]	Finland	1 160.9	13.5	18.3	33	9.2	35
35	32	Sabena	Belgium	1 146.9	4.9	18.0	34	6.8	46
36	37	Air New Zealand[1]	New Zealand	1 108.7	9.0	46.6	26	10.6	31
37	38	LTU	West Germany	1 094.4	13.6	N.A.	—	9.8	34
38	35	UTA	France	1 058.1	3.2	38.1	28	5.6	48
39	39	Southwest	U.S.	1 031.7	22.6	71.6	17	15	27
40	43	Australian[2]	Australia	1 013.8	27.9	57.4	21	6.1	47
41	45	America West	U.S.	1 004.2	29.5	20.0	31	12.7	30
42	40	Alaska Air Group	U.S.	929.2	14.1	42.9	27	7.1	44
43	49	S. African Airways[1]	S. Africa	912.2	(9.3)	55.9	24	9.0	37
44	44	Aer Lingus	Ireland	899.5	14.5	56.2	23	3.4	49
45	•	Austrian	Austria	850.5	9.7	11.6	38	2.4	50
46	42	Olympic Airways	Greece	*785.0	*(2.2)	*(123.1)	42	8.1	40
47	47	Mexicana	Mexico	764.3	2.0	13.7	35	10.5	32
48	48	Air India[1]	India	745.4	1.2	28.1	29	9.0	36
49	•	El Al	Israel	713.6	7.3	24.2	30	7.7	41
50	•	Malaysian[1]	Malaysia	712.8	14.0	59.0	20	9.0	38

* Estimate.
[1] Figures are for fiscal year ended March 31, 1989.
[2] Figures are for fiscal year ended June 30, 1989.
[3] Figures are for fiscal year ended September 33, 1989.
[4] Figures are for fiscal year ended October 31, 1989.
Note: All figures converted to U.S. dollars using the average official exchange rate during each company's fiscal year.
SOURCE: Kenneth Labich, "America Takes on the World," *Fortune*, September 24, 1990, p. 52.

EXHIBIT 4 Airline Operating Cost Distribution
International Civil Aviation Organization Airlines—1988

Direct Costs		*Indirect Costs*	
Fuel	14.5%	Ticketing and Sales	17.6%
Maintenance	11.6%	User fees, Station expense	14.1%
Flight Operations	11.4%	Passenger Service	10.4%
Depreciation	7.8%	General/Admin.	8.9%
		Landing Fees	3.7%
Total	45.3%	Total	54.7%

SOURCE: Boeing Commercial Airplane Group, *Current Market Outlook*, February 1990.

EXHIBIT 5 **British Airways Plan for a Brussels Hub**

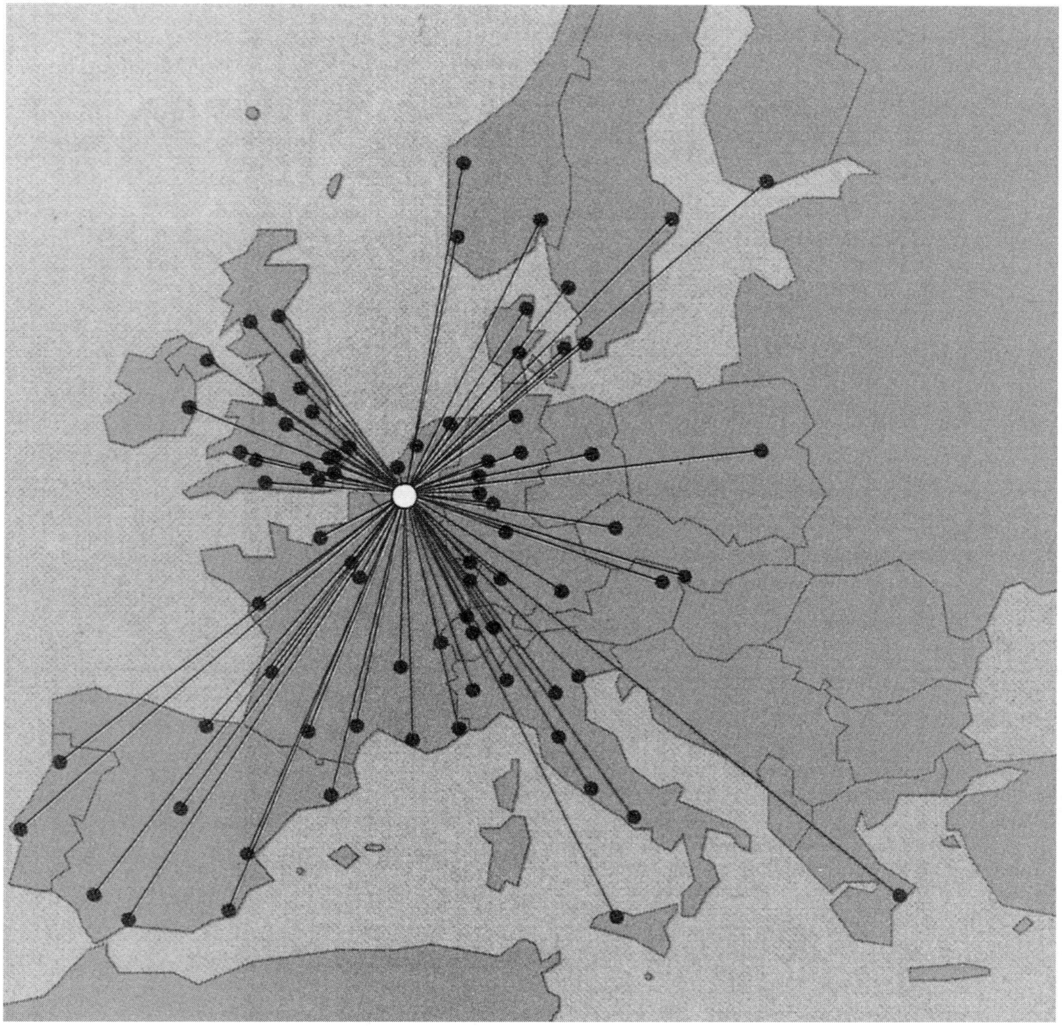

British Airways told the British MMC it plans to link 75 cities in Euroope by 1995 through a hub-and-spoke network at Brussels if its proposed 20% stake in Sabena World Airlines is approved.
SOURCE: *Aviation Week & Space Technology,* May 14, 1990.

EXHIBIT 6 **Financial History of Sabena 1984–90** (billion BFr)

	Debit [*]	*Equity*
1984	17.0	2.4
1985	19.3	4.8
1986	23.5	10.5
1987	25.4	10.7
1988	25.9	9.0
1989	31.2	7.5
1990	43.4	.1

[*] Does not include debt owed to the Belgian Government.

COMPREHENSIVE

PART

11

NESTLÉ–ROWNTREE (A)

James C. Ellert, J. Peter Killing and Dana G. Hyde

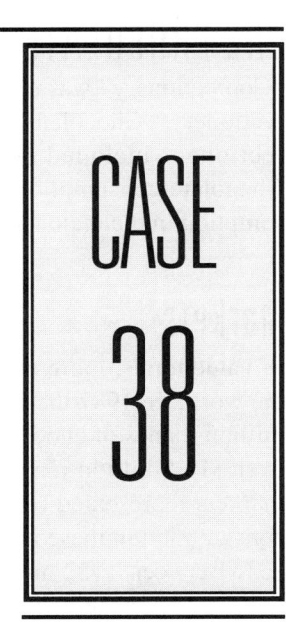

CASE 38

Wednesday, April 13, 1988, 10.30 A.M.

"Our offer to help remains open, Mr. Dixon, and I urge you to reconsider our proposals. Please keep in touch." Mr. Helmut Maucher, Managing Director of Nestlé S.A., replaced the receiver and shook his head regretfully as he looked out from his office over Lake Geneva. On receiving the news of Jacobs Suchard's dawn raid on Rowntree plc, Mr. Maucher had called Mr. Kenneth Dixon, Rowntree's Chairman, to offer Nestlé's help and renew Nestlé's earlier proposal to purchase a stake in Rowntree.

Rowntree had been an attractive takeover target for some time, and Mr. Maucher and his colleagues had often discussed the possibility of making a bid. However, it was clear that Rowntree would aggressively contest any takeover attempt and, as Nestlé had never engaged in a hostile takeover, Mr. Maucher had done nothing more than initiate talks with the British-based confectioner. But as he prepared for the meeting with his Comité du Conseil that afternoon, Mr. Maucher worried about Rowntree falling into the hands of one of Nestlé's major competitors.

THE CHOCOLATE INDUSTRY

"Confectionery" was conventionally divided into "chocolate" confectionery and "sugar" confectionery. "Chocolate" confectionery included products made with chocolate; "sugar" confectionery included boiled sweets, toffees, chewing gum, and other gums and jellies. Chocolate consumption represented a stable 54% of the total volume of confectionery consumption in the major world markets between 1982 and 1987.

Markets

In value terms, more chocolate was consumed than any other manufactured food product in the world. In 1987 the population of the world's eight major markets consumed more than 2.7 million tonnes of chocolate (the equivalent of over 100 billion Kit Kats), with a retail value of over $19.5 billion (Exhibit 1). In volume terms, chocolate consumption in the eight major markets represented 61% of total world chocolate consumption in 1987. Average per capita consumption in these markets was 4.3 kg per annum, with an annual per capita expenditure of $31. Between 1982 and 1987, volume growth averaged 2.8% per annum in the eight major markets. Future growth was estimated at 2.2% per annum for the next five years, with some variations across individual markets (Exhibit 2).

Product Types

Within chocolate confectionery there were three major product types:[1]

Blocks: generally molded blocks of chocolate, with or without additional ingredients (Hershey's Chocolate Bar, Nestlé Cailler, Suchard's Toblerone);

Countlines: generally chocolate-covered products, sold by count rather than weight (Mars' Mars Bar and Snickers, Rowntree's Kit Kat and Smarties);

Boxed chocolates: included assortments (Cadbury's Milk Tray, Rowntree's Black Magic) and also products such as Rowntree's After Eights.

A few manufacturers had succeeded in branding *block chocolate*, but in many markets block chocolate was considered a commodity product. Each manufacturer's range included a standard variety of block chocolate (milk, dark, white, etc.), and additional ingredients (nuts, fruit, etc.) sold in standard sizes (usually 100g and 200g). Block chocolate was sold mainly through grocery outlets, where it was displayed by manufacturer's range; all of the Nestlé block chocolate products would be grouped on one section of the store shelf, with the other manufacturers' ranges displayed in adjacent sections.

In contrast to block chocolate, *countlines* comprised a wide range of branded products, which were physically distinct from each other in size, shape, weight, and composition. Countlines had wider distribution than the other two product types, with a higher proportion sold through non-grocery outlets including confectioneries, news agents, and kiosks.

---

[1] Product definitions varied widely by country. For the purposes of this case, British product definitions have been used.

Boxed chocolates comprised a wide range of individually branded products, although in some markets boxed chocolates were marketed under the manufacturer's name, and displayed by manufacturer's range. Because boxed chocolates were regarded as a "gift/occasion" purchase, sales were very seasonal. Approximately 80% of sales took place at Christmas and Easter, a high proportion through grocery outlets; steady sales through the remainder of the year were made through non-grocery outlets.

The popularity of the three product types varied by market. In 1987, for example, Europe consumed approximately twice as much block chocolate and four times as many boxed chocolates as North America. The British and French together accounted for about 70% of European boxed chocolate consumption; North Americans consumed 44% of the world's countline consumption, followed by the British at 20%.

At 7% average annual growth between 1982 and 1987, countlines was the fastest growing segment of the world chocolate market. Block chocolate sales showed an average annual volume increase of 1% over the same period, while sales of boxed chocolates had declined by an average of 1% per year. By 1987 countlines represented 46% of the world chocolate market by volume, up from 38% in 1982; block chocolate had declined to 30% from 33%, and boxed chocolates to 24% from 29%. In addition to growing demand for countline products, future growth was expected from "indulgence" products such as chocolate truffles, and from specialist branded chocolate retailing.

Industry Structure and Performance

In 1987, there were six major producers in the world chocolate industry: Mars, Hershey, Cadbury-Schweppes, Jacobs Suchard, Rowntree and Nestlé. With individual world market shares ranging from 18% (Mars) to 4% (Nestlé), these six companies accounted for 50% of the total world volume of chocolate confectionery. With the exception of Jacobs Suchard and Nestlé, countline production represented the largest proportion of the chocolate confectionery portfolios of the major confectionery producers (Exhibit 3; additional detail on the product segment and geographic positioning of each company is outlined in Exhibits 4, 5 and 6).

The next tier of competitors included Ferrero, George Weston Ltd., Nabisco, and United Biscuits, each of which sold 2% or less of the total world volume of chocolate confectionery. The remainder of the market was supplied by a large number of smaller (largely national) companies.

The major industry competitors had healthy rates of profitability. Because Mars was a privately held U.S. company, it did not publish sales and profit figures. For the other major competitors, trading profit on sales averaged 9.3% over the five-year period ending in 1987; trading profit on assets averaged 16.1%, and the rate of return on stockholders' equity averaged 16.1% (Exhibit 7; Exhibits 8–12 provide additional financial information for these companies).

Over the past five years, several major producers had acquired a number of smaller, national chocolate companies. Between 1986 and 1988 Jacobs Suchard acquired six confectioners, including E.J. Brach (the third largest confectioner in the U.S., behind Mars and Hersey), Van Houten (Holland), and Cote d'Or (a famous Belgian chocolatier which Nestlé had also considered acquiring). In 1987 Hersey purchased the Canadian confectionery assets of RJR Nabisco. In early 1988 Cadbury acquired Chocolats Poulain, a famous French chocolatier, and

Nestlé was negotiating the purchase of Buitoni, an Italian food group which included the leading chocolatier Perugina.

Business System

Chocolate was made from kernels of fermented and roasted cocoa beans. The kernels were roasted and ground to form a paste, which was hardened in molds to make bitter (baking) chocolate, pressed to reduce the cocoa butter content, and then pulverized to make cocoa powder, or mixed with sugar and additional cocoa butter to make sweet (eating) chocolate. Sweet chocolate was the basic semi-finished product used in the manufacture of block, countline, and boxed chocolate products.

Average costs for a representative portfolio of all three product types of sweet chocolate could be broken down as follows:

Raw material	35%
Packaging	10
Production	20
Distribution	5
Marketing/sales	20
Trading profit	10
Total	100% (of manufacturer's selling price)

For countline products, raw material costs were proportionately lower because a smaller amount of cocoa was used. For boxed chocolates, packaging costs were proportionately higher.

RESEARCH AND DEVELOPMENT

Research and development (R&D) generally focused on making a better chocolate, and on developing new products, although one executive related, "there is never really anything brand new in the confectionery market, just different ways of presenting combinations of the same ingredients." There were minor differences in R&D across the product types, although R&D in the countline segment tended to emphasize applied technology.

RAW MATERIALS

The major ingredient in chocolate confectionery was cocoa, followed by sugar and milk. Although Jacobs Suchard claimed to benefit from large purchase hedging, some manufacturers purchased cocoa supplies as needed at the spot price quoted on the major cocoa exchanges, while others purchased cocoa a year or two in advance to obtain the "best price" and to ensure long-term supplies. Between 1977 and 1988, the international cartel of cocoa producers had fallen into disarray; the price of cocoa had fallen by 50% ($US terms), and surplus cocoa stocks continued to accumulate.

Industry practice was for manufacturers to absorb raw material price changes internally to smooth extreme changes in consumer prices. However, Mars had made an unprecedented move in taking advantage of the falling cocoa price to stimulate volume demand. The company held the price of its Mars Bar and increased the product weight in the late 1970s by 10%, and then by another 15% in the early 1980s, enabling Mars to gain market share.

PRODUCTION In general, it was difficult to sustain a competitive advantage based on manufacturing process, or on product features due to the lack of proprietary technology. However, some manufacturers had developed countline products which were difficult to duplicate (e.g., Rowntree's After Eights and Kit Kat). The major manufacturers tried to be low-cost producers through increased scale economies. Scale economies were more easily achieved in the production of block chocolate and countlines (both relatively capital intensive), and less easily in the production of boxed chocolates (which was more labour intensive). While minimum efficient scale varied by product, most major producers were moving toward fewer and more concentrated production plants, some dedicated to one or two products.

DISTRIBUTION Confectionery had the widest distribution of any consumer product. In the UK, for example, wholesalers serving thousands of small "Confectionery-Tobacco-Newsagent" (CTN) outlets accounted for 50% of total confectionery sales, with multiple grocery stores accounting for 30%, and department stores and multiple confectionery stores the remainder. While distribution patterns and the balance of power between manufacturers and distributors varied across markets, retail concentration was on the increase. Canada and Western Europe (in particular the UK, France, and West Germany) were noted for high levels of retail concentration. Manufacturers' trading margins in these countries averaged 8–12%, compared to U.S. averages of 14–16%.

In general, European multiple retailers tended to stock narrower ranges of competing products than their U.S. counterparts. As one industry executive commented, "In Europe you pay more of a premium to get shelf space in a store. In addition, many of the (multiple) retailers stock only the leading brand and the Number Two. If you are third, you lose visibility, and this damages brand reputation."

MARKETING Consumers displayed considerable brand loyalty. As one industry executive explained, "Most people have a 'menu' of products they like and know. They will buy a new product perhaps once or twice, but the tendency is to go back to the 'old familiars,' the popular established brands." The most popular brands of chocolate were over 50 years old; Mars Bar, for example, was introduced in 1932, and Kit Kat in 1935.

In 1987 the six largest producers spent over $750 million per year on chocolate advertising. In recent years, manufacturers had dramatically increased their overall level of marketing spending, particularly with respect to launching new products. By 1988 one manufacturer estimated that new products, which generally had a much shorter life span than established brands, would have to generate at least $25 million in sales over the first two years to cover product development and marketing costs. Manufacturers therefore tended to focus on brand extensions into new product segments and particularly into new geographic markets.

MAJOR COMPETITORS

Mars

With the world's best selling chocolate bar, and other famous global brands such as Snickers, M&Ms, Twix and Milky Way, Mars was the world leader in chocolate confectionery. In 1987 confectionery was estimated to account for $4 billion of Mars' $7 billion total turnover of confectionery, pet food and electronics products.

With 38% market share, Mars dominated the world countline sector, with particular strength in North America and Europe (Exhibit 4). In 1987, Mars held the largest share of the European chocolate market, and was a close third to Cadbury Rowntree in the UK (Exhibit 5). Like Rowntree and Cadbury, Mars spent approximately £25 million annually on advertising in the UK. In 1987 Mars was one of the top 30 U.S. advertisers ($300 million), and had five of the top ten best-selling chocolate bars in the U.S.

The 1986 introduction of Kudos, a chocolate-covered granola bar, was Mars' first new product in over ten years. Since 1986, however, Mars had mounted a major effort to acquire and develop new products, particularly those which would capitalize on the Mars brand name. Recent product launches included a Mars milk drink and Mars ice cream.

Mars' strategy was consistent across all brands: produce high quality, technologically simple products at very high volumes on automated equipment dedicated to the production of either "layered" (Mars, Snickers) or "planned" (M&Ms, Maltesers) products; and support the brands with heavy marketing spending and aggressive sales organizations and retailing policies. The company's future strategy focused on building and strengthening Mars' global brands. In 1987, for example, Mars had dropped Treets, a £15 million UK brand, and repositioned Minstrels under the Galaxy label, both in order to strengthen the 1988 launch of M&Ms into the UK market.

Hershey Foods

Founded as chocolate company in 1893, by 1987 Hershey was a diversified food group with total turnover of $2.4 billion. More than 90% of that turnover was in the U.S. (Exhibit 6); confectionery accounted for 66% of total turnover and 80% of trading profit. Although Hershey was a quoted company, it could not be taken over easily because 77% of the company's voting stock was owned by a charitable trust.

Hershey's strength was in block chocolate in North America, where it held a 62% market share. With Hershey's Chocolate Bar, Reese's Peanut Butter Cup and Hershey's Kisses all in the 1987 U.S. "top ten," Hershey was second only to Mars in the U.S. chocolate market. Hershey also produced major Rowntree brands under licence in the U.S.

Between 1981 and 1987, Hershey had increased its advertising and promotion spending from 8.5% to 11.5% of total turnover to "consolidate market share." Hershey's chocolate production was concentrated in Hershey, Pennsylvania, which supplied export markets in Japan, South Korea and Australia. The company also licenced some production in the Far East, Sweden and Mexico, normally under joint venture agreements.

Hershey's corporate strategy was to reduce exposure to cocoa price volatility by diversifying within the confectionery and snack businesses. The company had expanded into branded sugar confectionery, pasta products and ice cream restaurants, largely through acquisitions. By 1987, only 45% of Hershey's sales came from products composed of at least 70% chocolate, down from 80% in 1963.

Cadbury Schweppes

Cadbury Schweppes plc was founded in 1969 with the merger of the Cadbury Group plc and Schweppes Ltd. In 1987, confectionery represented 43% of Cadbury's total turnover of £2,031 million.

With 7% of the world chocolate market and brands such as Dairy Milk, Creme Eggs, Crunchie, Flake and Milk Tray, Cadbury was a major world name in chocolate. Cadbury was the market leader in Australia, and three Cadbury brands (Mounds, Almond Joy and Peppermint Patties) were in the U.S. "Top 20." However, Cadbury's main business was in the UK, where it held 30% of the market, and had five of the top ten best-selling chocolate products. In 1986 and 1987, Cadbury had launched nine new UK brands.

During the late 1970s, Cadbury expanded overseas, and diversified within and beyond the food sector. However, with the appointment of Mr. Dominic Cadbury as Chief Executive in 1983, Cadbury Schweppes embarked on a more focused product and market strategy. Mr. Cadbury announced a restructuring of the Group "to concentrate resources behind (our) leading beverage and confectionery brands in those markets which offer the best opportunities for their development."

Major divestments were made, involving secondary activities in the food and nonfood sectors, and the assets of some under-performing core businesses. Acquisitions were made to strengthen the mainstream branded product lines, and to gain access to new geographic markets. The acquisition of Chocolats Poulain, for example, provided Cadbury's first manufacturing facility in Europe. In January 1987, General Cinema Corporation (which controlled the largest U.S. Pepsi bottling operation) announced the acquisition of an 8.5% shareholding in Cadbury Schweppes and, in November 1987, increased that holding to 18.2%. While General Cinema was less than half the size of Cadbury in market capitalization, industry observers speculated that the company was planning a leveraged buyout of Cadbury Schweppes.

Jacobs Suchard

Controlled by the Jacobs family and based in Zurich, the Jacobs Suchard Group was formed in 1982 in a reverse takeover by Jacobs (a West German coffee company) of Interfood, the parent company of the Suchard and Tobler chocolate firms. In 1987, Suchard's principal businesses were still coffee and confectionery, which accounted for 57% and 43% respectively of Suchard's 1987 turnover of SF6.1 billion.

Europe was Suchard's largest market, accounting for 83% of 1987 turnover. However, Jacobs Suchard operated in more than 20 countries, represented by subsidiaries and licensees, and exported its products to over 100 countries. The Group also had substantial operations in the trading of raw materials for coffee and chocolate production.

Jacobs Suchard held 23% of the European block chocolate market. Leading brands included Toblerone, Suchard, Milka and Cote d'Or. Developing and expanding its portfolio of global brands was of primary importance to the Group; as Mr. Klaus Jacobs, the entrepreneurial Chairman of the Board, stated, "We firmly believe that global brands are the wave of the future." An increasing number of Jacobs Suchard's brands were marketed globally, under the sponsorship of global brand managers.

Since 1984 Suchard had been concentrating production of individual brands in fewer and larger plants in an effort to gain absolute cost leadership. In 1987, European production of chocolate and confectionery took place in 17 plants; Suchard planned to reduce this number to 7 by 1991, as improvements were made in its cross-border distribution system.

Rowntree

Rowntree was founded in York in 1725 by a cocoa and chocolate vendor who sold the business to the Rowntree family in 1862. In 1970, Rowntree merged with John Mackintosh & Sons, Ltd., a British confectioner nearly half the size of Rowntree. In 1988, Rowntree's headquarters were still in York and, with 5 500 workers, the company was by far York's largest employer. Many of the traditions of the Rowntree family, including a strong concern for employee and community welfare, had been preserved; many of the current employees' parents and grandparents had also worked for Rowntree.

In 1987, Rowntree was primarily a confectionery company (Exhibit 13), with major strengths in the countline and boxed chocolate segments. Rowntree's major market was the UK where, with a 26% market share, it was second only to Cadbury. Rowntree's Kit Kat was the best-selling confectionery brand in the UK (where 40 Kit Kats were consumed per second), and number five in both the U.S. and Japan. Kit Kat was part of a portfolio of leading global brands; many of these brands—Kit Kat, Quality Street, Smarties, Rolo, Aero, Black Magic—were launched in the 1930s; After Eights in 1962; and Yorkie and Lion in 1976. Since 1981 Rowntree had launched seven new brands in the UK, including Novo, a chocolate cereal bar.

In 1987 Rowntree operated 25 factories in nine countries and employed 33 000 people around the world, including close to 16 000 in its eight UK operations. Group turnover was £1.4 billion, with the UK and Ireland accounting for 40% of total turnover (Exhibit 14).

Rowntree was headed by Mr. Kenneth Dixon, age 58, who had been with Rowntree for 32 years, and was appointed as Chairman and Chief Executive in 1981. In the words of a long-time senior Rowntree executive, "Mr. Dixon fostered a real sense of positive change in the company."

During the late 1970s, Rowntree's operating performance had shown significant deterioration (Exhibit 15). To reverse this trend, Mr. Dixon initiated a long-term program to improve the efficiency of the UK core business, and led diversifications into related businesses, principally through the acquisition and development of brand names. Mr. Dixon also delegated more responsibility to the operating levels of the company, while maintaining a central brand and product strategy.

Branding was the essence of Rowntree's strategy. According to Mr. Dixon, "The fundamental idea which drives Rowntree is branding, the creation of distinct, differentiated, positively identifiable and market-positioned goods. Rowntree seeks to build brands by marketing products and services at competitive prices, positioning them accurately in the markets they serve, and giving them clear identity and character."

In the 1960s, Rowntree granted Hershey a long-term license to manufacture and sell Rowntree products in the U.S. With its expansion into continental Europe underway at the time, Rowntree believed that it lacked the resources to develop an effective marketing presence in both continental Europe and the U.S. In 1978 the agreement with Hershey was renegotiated, giving Hershey rights in perpetuity to the Kit Kat and Rolo brand names in the U.S., which would be retained by Hershey in the event of a change in Rowntree ownership. Rowntree was still free to enter the U.S. market with its other brand names. In 1987 royalties from this agreement contributed about £2 million toward Rowntree Group profits.

Between 1982 and 1987, Rowntree invested nearly £400 million to upgrade manufacturing facilities, and develop high-volume, product-dedicated equipment for several of the company's leading global brands, including Kit Kat, After Eights, and Smarties. Products produced on this equipment had a consistent formulation, and were sold all over the world; the Hamburg After Eights plant, for example, shipped to 16 countries. By 1987 Rowntree's investment program for rationalizing capacity was well underway. The associated productivity gains were expected to continue to accumulate over the next few years.

In 1987 Rowntree's £100 million investment in continental Europe was still showing modest financial returns. Rowntree had entered the continental European market in the 1960s, establishing production facilities at Hamburg, Dijon, Elst (Holland) and Noisiel (France). Although advertising and promotion spending (as a percentage of sales) was double that of the UK, volume growth had not met Rowntree's expectations; as one manager explained, "Kit Kats go well with a cup of tea, but not with wine and beer!"

The trading margin on the Continental European business had inched up very slowly, from 1.0% in 1985 to 3.7% in 1987. However, in early 1988 Rowntree believed that the long-term brand building strategy was finally beginning to pay off, with Lion Bar the second-best selling chocolate bar in France and with more After Eights sold in West Germany than in the UK. Between 1983 and 1987, Rowntree spent nearly £400 million on acquisitions (Exhibit 16). The acquired companies expanded the company's presence in some traditional businesses, and also provided new activities, particularly in the area of branded retailing of specialist confectionery products. The retail shops acquired by Rowntree were viewed not as outlets for Rowntree brands, but rather as acquisitions of brands in their own right. Because of these acquisitions, a significant stream of Rowntree's profits were being earned in North America. While Rowntree had hedged its foreign exchange risk exposure on the balance sheet, it took a long-term view with respect to foreign exchange risk exposure on the income statement. The resulting transactions exposure concerned some financial analysts.

By 1987 Rowntree's capital investments were beginning to pay off. Over the past five years, the number of UK personnel had been reduced from 19 700 to 15 600, and productivity improvements were running at 9% per annum. Trading margins had nearly recovered to the high level previously achieved in 1977, and Rowntree executives were confident that 1988 trading margins would continue to show improvement.

In a highly competitive U.S. market, Rowntree's snack food acquisitions were not generating trading margins consistent with other company activities (Exhibit 13). In January of 1988, Rowntree announced its intention to divest its major snack food businesses to concentrate on confectionery, retailing, and UK grocery activities where the potential to develop distinct consumer brands was considered more promising.

Although Rowntree's overall operating performance continued to improve, the company's common share price performance between 1986 and early 1988 was weaker than that achieved by the *Financial Times* "All Share" and Food Manufacturing Indexes on the London Stock Exchange (Exhibit 17). In early 1988, London's financial analysts published mixed opinions regarding Rowntree's immediate prospects (Exhibit 18). Mr. Nightingale, Rowntree's Company

Secretary, recalled, "For years we have been trying to get the value of our brands reflected in our share price, but without much success. As a consequence, there have always been takeover rumours."

Nestlé

The Nestlé Group grew from the 1905 merger of the Anglo-Swiss condensed Milk Co., a milk processing firm founded in 1866, and Henri Nestlé, a Swiss infant food company founded in 1867 in Vevey. In 1988 the Nestlé headquarters were still in Vevey, and the Group operated 383 factories in 59 countries. In 1988 Nestlé employed 163 000 people, 10 000 in the UK.

Nestlé was the world's largest food company, and the world's largest producer of coffee, powdered milk, and frozen dinners. In 1987, drinks, dairy products, culinary products, frozen foods, and confectionery products accounted for 79% of Nestlé turnover of SF35.2 billion; other food products accounted for 18%, and non-food products 3%. Only 2% of the Group's turnover came from sales within Switzerland. The 20 companies acquired between 1983 and 1985 (at a total purchase price of $5 billion) added new brands of coffee, chocolates and fruit juice to Nestlé's lineup of strong world brands such as Nescafé, Stouffer's, Maggi and Findus. In 1985 Nestlé increased its U.S. presence through the $2.9 billion purchase of Carnation and, in early April 1988, was finalizing the $1.3 billion purchase of Buitoni-Perugina.

This series of acquisitions had been spurred by Mr. Helmut Maucher, age 60, who joined Nestlé as an apprentice in 1948, and who was appointed Managing Director of Nestlé S.A. in 1981. Under Mr. Maucher's direction, Nestlé had cut costs and divested less profitable operations, including the $180 million Libby's U.S. canned food business.

Mr. Maucher explained Nestlés approach to acquisitions. "At Nestlé we are not portfolio managers. Acquisitions must fit into our corporate and marketing policy. In other words, they must strengthen our position in individual countries or product groups, or enable us to enter new fields where we have not so far been represented. Acquisitions are part of an overall development strategy. That's why we cannot leave acquisition decisions purely to financial considerations. Of course, you must have some figures to evaluate an acquisition, but more important is the feel you have about why you can do with the brands."

Mr. Maucher was a strong believer in the importance of a long-term outlook. On his appointment as Managing Director, he had banned monthly 25-page reports and quarterly profit and loss statements in favour of a monthly one-page report which highlighted key numbers such as turnover, working capital, and inventories. As Mr. Maucher explained, "With quarterly reports all managers care about is the next three months, and they manage for the next quarter instead of for the next five years." For this reason, Mr. Maucher was reluctant to list Nestlé's shares on any stock exchange which required the disclosure of quarterly reports.

Nestlé entered the chocolate market in 1929 with the purchase of Peter-Cailler-Kohler, a Swiss chocolate group originally founded in 1819. Since 1981, confectionery sales had represented approximately 8% of annual turnover, and in 1987 confectionery was Nestlé's fifth largest business. Nestlé's main product strength was in block chocolate, where it held 15% and 14% respectively of the European and American markets (Exhibit 4). Nestlé's leading brands included Milkybar in the U.S. and Crunch in the UK. Recent research into the new generation of chocolate and confectionery products had produced "Yes," a pastry snack product, and "Sundy," a cereal bar.

As a result of Nestlé's market-oriented organization structure, Nestlé's block chocolate products were generally produced and positioned according to the tastes of local markets. For example, Nestlé's white block chocolate products, often produced in the same plants as coffee and other food products, were made from several recipes and marketed under several brand names. In the UK, Nestlé's white chocolate brand, "Milkybar," was positioned as a children's chocolate, whereas in the U.S., it was called "Alpine White" and was oriented toward the "female indulgence" market. "Block chocolate is a traditional product with traditional tastes," Mr. Maucher explained. "A local market orientation is particularly important, because this kind of chocolate must taste the way you got it as a child from your grandmother, whether you are French or Italian or German, and so on. This is true for the traditional chocolate products, not so much for the new generation of products such as countlines."

During the 1970s, Nestlé's confectionery operations had been among the smaller and often relatively less profitable businesses in the company. However, Mr. Maucher saw opportunities in the confectionery business: "The key success factors in confectionery are technology, quality, creativity, and marketing skills, and Nestlé has all of those. If Nestlé cannot be successful at this business, then there is something wrong with Nestlé!"

NESTLÉ–ROWNTREE

In the early 1980s, Mr. Maucher made confectionery a strategic priority. Nestlé increased investment in research and development, and acquired two small U.S. confectionery companies. Nestlé then began to analyze the possibilities for significant expansion in the world confectionery market. "It will take 25 years to develop a major stake in this industry," Mr. Maucher said, "so we are looking at acquisitions to accelerate that development." According to Mr. Ramon Masip, Executive Vice-President in charge of the European market, "For some time we have discussed making a 'big move' into the confectionery business, and Rowntree has always been the number one choice."

"We have always seen Rowntree as a 'perfect fit,'" Mr. Masip continued, "because its strengths would complement Nestlé's." Rowntree's strong position in the growing countlines segment would complement Nestlé's strength in block chocolate. In addition, Rowntree's strong position in the non-grocery outlets such as CTNs would complement Nestlé's strong contacts with the multiple grocery retailers. Rowntree also held a stronger position in the UK and in some markets in continental Europe.

Although Nestlé was interested in Rowntree's recent success in launching new products such as the Lion bar. "We are much more concerned with the brands that Rowntree already has in the market!" Mr. Masip exclaimed. Rowntree's strong, well-established world brands were the key reason for Nestlé's interest. "There are very, very few companies in the world with their brands and with their skills in this particular business," Mr. Masip concluded.

Nestlé believed that, should the opportunity to acquire Rowntree arise, additional operating synergies could be achieved in research and development, administration, and the sales force. With the potential acquisition, it was estimated that substantial savings—perhaps 5–15% of Rowntree's fixed overhead expenses—could be realized from combining the two companies' operations.

November 1987

In November of 1987, Mr. Maucher and Mr. Masip met in Paris with Mr. Dixon and Mr. Masip's counterpart in Rowntree, Mr. Guerin. The proposal for this meeting had stemmed from quiet discussions between Messrs. Masip and Guerin regarding possible Nestlé-Rowntree cooperation in continental Europe. For over a year, Mr. Maucher had wanted to arrange a meeting with Mr. Dixon to discuss possible forms of cooperation between Nestlé and Rowntree. In fact, some of Mr. Maucher's external financial advisors had advised him to take a position in Rowntree stock, but Mr. Maucher had always replied, "That is not our policy. We do not do anything behind any company's back and, as I have told Mr. Dixon, we will not do anything that would be perceived as unfriendly to Rowntree."

The Paris meeting in November 1987 began with Mr. Dixon advising Mr. Maucher, "Nestlé does not appear to be interested in confectionery, and Rowntree is prepared to buy Nestlé's confectionery business on a worldwide basis." Mr. Maucher exclaimed, "We propose just the opposite!" The ensuing discussion explored possibilities for cooperation in production, marketing, distribution, or in various geographic markets, in order to optimize the situation for both companies. To facilitate development of long-term commitment and cooperation, Mr. Maucher suggested purchasing a 10–25% stake in Rowntree.

After a lengthy and amicable discussion, Mr. Dixon promised to examine Nestlé's suggestions and take them to the Rowntree Board for consideration. According to Mr. Dixon, Rowntree had already considered cooperation with several parties as a basis for market development, particularly in Europe, but "we felt at Rowntree that we could proceed on our own and would prefer to do so." After making this reply to Mr. Maucher in February 1988, he added, "Unfortunately, any sort of association with a company of your size can only have one ending, and at this time we don't feel we need to make that kind of commitment to anyone." Mr. Dixon, responding to Mr. Maucher's grave concerns regarding the persistent takeover rumours, admitted, "This does not mean that we do not recognize there is a risk."

April 13, 1988

At 8:30 on the morning of Wednesday, April 13, 1988, Rowntree was advised that there was significant activity in the trading of Rowntree shares. By 9:15 a.m., Jacobs Suchard held 14.9% of Rowntree plc. While the firm had made no contact with Rowntree, Suchard had begun acquiring Rowntree stock in mid-March, and by April 12th held just under 5% of Rowntree shares. At the start of trading on the London Stock Exchange on April 13th, Suchard's intermediary telephoned major institutional holders of Rowntree shares, offering a 30% premium on the opening share price of 477p[2] if they sold immediately. The shareholders did not know to whom they were selling their shares, but in less than 45 minutes Suchard increased its holding to 14.9%, the maximum allowable under the City Code[3] for such a transac-

---

[2] 1£ = 100 pence (p).
[3] Refer to Exhibit 19 for a description of the City Code rules which regulated takeover activity in the UK.

tion. When the news of Suchard's raid reached the markets, Rowntree's share price jumped to over 700p.

In what was later described as a "tactical error" by some City observers, on the morning of April 13th, S.G. Warburg issued the following press release on behalf on its client, Jacob Suchard:

> We have acquired a 14.9% investment stake in Rowntree. The stake is a strategic investment in that Rowntree is a company with a great potential based on its excellent global brands. We intend to acquire not more than 25%, at a maximum price of 630p. As you know, we are only permitted to take our holding to 15% today. We hope to buy the remaining 10%, but at no more than the price we are currently offering. This is not a prelude to a full bid and there is no intention of increasing the holding beyond this 25%-figure for at least a year although we reserve the right to do so if there is a full bid from a third party in the meantime.

Exercising its interpretive responsibility, the City Takeover Panel swiftly ruled that Warburg's statement prevented Suchard from purchasing any further Rowntree shares for the next 12 months, provided that the Rowntree share price stayed above 630p, unless a full bid for control came in from another party during that time period.

Reaction from the City of London Financial Community

After years of persistent rumours of a Rowntree takeover, Suchard's move ignited speculation on potential counter-bidders. Hershey was identified by City analysts as a leading candidate; purchasing Rowntree would make it second only to Mars in world confectionery. Other rumoured candidates included RJR Nabisco, Philip Morris, Unilever and United Biscuits.

As external financial advisor to Rowntree, Mr. David Challen, a Director of J. Henry Schroder Wagg, was encouraged by the Takeover Panel's ruling. As he explained, "The ruling puts Jacobs in a box. Provided that Rowntree's share price stays above 630p, he cannot purchase additional shares for at least a year. This gives Rowntree the necessary time to prepare an effective takeover defence." Mr. Challen argued that it would be "madness" for another bidder to enter the battle now, as the new bidder would be restricted to accumulating shares (beyond 15%) at the price of its initial offer. However, the entry of another bidder would free Suchard to bid above this price to accumulate more shares. In the scenario predicted by Mr. Challen, Suchard would ultimately emerge with 30% of the shares and be poised to make an offer for the remaining shares. The second bidder would be restricted by the City Code to accumulating 15% of the shares and would always be behind Suchard in share accumulation terms. Thus the second bidder would face a "mega disadvantage" in gaining effective control. Mr. Challen concluded that the situation facing Rowntree was not urgent: "The real challenge for Rowntree is to keep the stock price above 630p so that Suchard cannot accumulate more shares."

Mr. Peter St. George, a Director of County Natwest (Nestlé's financial advisor), recalled discussions with Nestlé in the summer of 1987 regarding a possible takeover bid for Rowntree: "We were in a raging bull market then; paper, not cash, was king; and the takeover bid premium required to purchase Rowntree could not be justified on the fundamentals. Besides, any takeover attempt would have been viewed as hostile by Rowntree."

County NatWest had approached Nestlé in early 1988, advising a raid on Rowntree. "Since the October 1987 crash, the world had changed," Mr. St. George explained. "Share prices had fallen to reasonable levels where one could justify paying takeover premiums. The market no longer wanted paper; cash was king now, and Nestlé had cash. However, Mr. Maucher demurred, stating that hostile raids were not in Nestlé's style."

"Suchard's raid put Rowntree 'in play,'" Mr. St. George concluded. "We contacted Nestlé as soon as we heard the news and encouraged them to make a counter bid for Rowntree. We advised them to act quickly and go into the market with a credible price to test (the fundraising capability of) Jacobs Suchard. We cautioned Nestlé, however, that a successful bid would require a substantial premium on the current Rowntree share price." (See Exhibit 19 for a description of the size of recent takeover bid premiums; Exhibit 20 contains financial market reference data.)

Rowntree's Reaction

The dawn raid came as a complete surprise to Rowntree, and reaction was swift. Mr. Dixon stated in a press release that morning:

> Rowntree does not need Jacobs. We regard the acquisition of a stake by Jacobs as wholly unwelcome and believe that the price at which Jacobs acquired its shares is wholly inadequate for obtaining a major stake in the Group. Rowntree has one of the best portfolios of brand names of any confectionery company in the world, far better known than Jacobs' own. We do not believe that it is in the interests of Rowntree, its shareholders, or its employees that a Swiss company with nothing like the breadth of Rowntree's brands should have a shareholding in the Group. Jacobs may need Rowntree, but Rowntree does not need Jacobs.

Nestlé's Reaction

Suchard's dawn raid also came as a surprise to Nestlé. Mr. Maucher's first reaction was to contact Mr. Dixon; in his telephone phone call that morning Mr. Maucher said, "I am sorry that what I warned you about has happened. I repeat our offer to help." He urged Mr. Dixon to reconsider Nestlé's earlier proposal to acquire a stake in Rowntree.

Mr. Dixon thanked Mr. Maucher for his offer of help, but replied that he did not expect Suchard to make any further moves in the short term. "According to the Takeover Panel, Jacobs cannot move for 12 months," he told Mr. Maucher, "and while I know that Suchard will try to become more involved with Rowntree, we have no intention of having any form of co-operation with Suchard. We fully intend to remain independent. It is our hope and belief that the situation will calm down and that nothing more will come of it." However, Mr. Dixon promised that he and his Board would nonetheless consider Mr. Maucher's proposal.

Mr. Maucher concluded the discussion by saying, "Our offer stands, and I hope you will reconsider and keep in touch. However, I fear that because of Suchard's move your independence is now an illusion. I must now feel free to act in Nestlé best interests."

Average Currency Equivalents, 1983–88
(SF = Swiss Franc; $ = U.S. Dollar; £ = British Pound)

	1 Swiss Franc equals		*1 British Pound equals*		*US$1 equals*	
1983	$0.48	£0.31	SF 3.23	$1.55	SF2.08	£0.65
1984	0.43	0.32	3.13	1.34	2.33	0.75
1985	0.41	0.32	3.13	1.28	2.44	0.78
1986	0.56	0.38	2.63	1.47	1.79	0.68
1987	0.67	0.41	2.44	1.63	1.49	0.61
1988*	0.71	0.39	2.57	1.83	1.41	0.55

* As of April 1, 1988.
SOURCE: Schweizerische Nationalbank.

EXHIBIT 1   Major Chocolate Confectionery Markets Consumption and Expenditure Per Capita, 1987

	*Chocolate Consumption (000 tonnes)**	*Chocolate Expenditure (US$ millions)*	*Population Mid-1987 (millions)*	*per Capita (kg/annum)*	*Expenditure Consumption per Capita ($/annum)*
U.S.	1 189	5 202	243.8	4.9	21
UK	455	3 480	56.9	8.0	61
W.Germany	409	3 387	61.2	6.7	55
France	233	2 750	55.6	4.2	49
Japan	157	1 867	122.1	1.3	15
Canada	101	464	25.9	3.9	18
Italy	106	1 813	57.4	1.8	32
Australia	80	576	16.2	4.9	36
Total	2 730	19 539	639.1	4.3	31

* One metric tonne = 1000 kilograms.
SOURCES: *United Nations Industrial Statistics Yearbook*; World Bank; National Trade Associations; Trade Estimates.

EXHIBIT 2 Actual and Forecasted Chocolate Consumption in Major Markets

	Consumption (000 tonnes)			Compound Average Annual Growth Rate (%)	
	1982 Actual	*1987 Actual*	*1992 Forecast*	*1982–87*	*1987–92*
U.S.	1 003	1 189	1 364	3.5%	2.8%
UK	411	455	469	2.0	0.6
W. Germany	401	409	412	0.4	0.1
France	192	233	251	3.9	1.5
Japan	148	157	166	1.2	1.1
Italy	83	106	127	5.0	3.7
Canada	99	101	106	0.4	1.0
Australia	63	80	95	4.9	3.5
Above 8 Markets	2 400	2 730	2 990	2.6	1.8
Rest of World	1 495	1 740	1 990	3.1	2.7
Total	3 895	4 470	4 980	2.8%	2.2%

SOURCES: Joint International Statistics Committee of IOCCC; *Euromonitor; United Nations Industrial Statistics Yearbook*; IMEDE.

EXHIBIT 3 Chocolate Product Portfolios of Major Confectionery Companies, 1987

	Mars	*Hershey*	*Cadbury*	*Rowntree*	*Suchard*	*Nestlé*	*Others*
Tonnes (000s)	800	400	320	300	220	190	2 240
World Market Share	18%	9%	7%	7%	5%	4%	50%
Companies' Turnover by Product Type:[*]							
Block	1%	46%	46%	11%	81%	73%	29%
Countline	99	54	36	55	8	17	32
Boxed	—	—	18	34	11	10	39
Total	100%	100%	100%	100%	100%	100%	100%

[*] For example, countline sales represented 99% of Mars' total chocolate confectionery turnover in 1987; block chocolate sales represented 1% of Mars' total chocolate turnover.

SOURCES: International Chocolate Workshop, *Vevey*, 1988; Trade Estimates; IMEDE.

EXHIBIT 4   **Market Shares of Major Competitors by Product Type and Region, 1987**

	Total Market*	Percentage Market Shares						
		Mars	*Hershey*	*Cadbury*	*Rowntree*	*Suchard*	*Nestlé*	*Others*
North America:								
Block	280	—	62%	16%	2%	3%	14%	3%
Countline	898	53%	23	5	2	—	1	16
Boxed	112	—	—	11	17	1	5	66
Total	1 290	53%	29%	8%	2%	—	4%	18%
EEC:								
Block	541	1%	—	9%	4%	23%	14%	49%
Countline	611	49	—	8	19	2	1	21
Boxed	437	—	—	7	14	4	2	73
Total	1 589	19%	—	8%	12%	10%	6%	45%
Rest of World:								
Block	521	—	2%	10%	1%	9%	4%	74%
Countline	544	4%	1	4	6	1	3	80
Boxed	526	—	—	3	4	1	1	91
Total	1 591	1%	1%	6%	4%	4%	3%	81%
World:								
Block	1 342	1%	14%	11%	2%	13%	10%	49%
Countline	2 053	39	10	6	8	1	2	34
Boxed	1 075	—	—	6	9	2	2	81
Total	4 470	18%	9%	7%	7%	5%	4%	50%

* In tonnes (000s).

SOURCES: International Chocolate Workshop, *Vevey*, 1988; Trade Estimates; IMEDE.

EXHIBIT 5   **European Chocolate Market Shares by Major Competitor, 1988**

	Mars	*Suchard*	*Rowntree*	*Ferrero*	*Cadbury*	*Nestlé*	*Others*
UK	24%	2%	26%	2%	30%	3%	13%
Austria	4	73	—	—	—	5	18
Belgium	6	82	2	5	—	3	2
France	11	13	17	6	8	10	35
Italy	1	—	—	4	—	5	60
Netherlands	23	—	13	—	—	—	64
Switzerland	9	17	—	—	—	17	57
W. Germany	22	15	3	6	—	8	36
Total	17%	13%	11%	10%	8%	9%	32%

SOURCE: Henderson Crossthwaite.

EXHIBIT 6 **Percentage Breakdown of Total Turnover by Region for Major Confectionery Competitors, 1987**

	Nestlé	Rowntree	Jacobs Suchard	Cadbury Schweppes	Hershey
Europe	43%	61%[1]	83%[2]	63%[3]	
N. America	29	29	17	18	> 90%
Asia	13				
Oceana	2	4		19	<10
Others	3	6	1		
Total	100%	100%	101%[4]	100%	100%

[1] UK and Ireland = 40% of total turnover.
[2] West Germany and France = 58% of total turnover.
[3] UK = 47% of total turnover.
[4] Does not add up to 100% due to rounding errors.
SOURCE: Company accounts.

EXHIBIT 7 **Operating Financial Performance of Major Competitors, 1983–87**

	Confectionery Turnover as % of Total Turnover[1]	Total Trading Profit[2] as % of Total Turnover	Total Trading Profit[2] as % of Average[3] Assets	Net Income as % of Average[3] Shareholders' Equity
	1987	Average 1983–87		
Hershey Foods	76%	14.7%	15.8%	17.2%
Cadbury-Schweppes	43	7.5	20.5	17.1
Rowntree	76	8.3	25.5	16.8
Jacobs Suchard	57	5.9	12.3	16.3
Nestlé	8	10.2	14.3	13.1

Note: As a measure of relative risk, the "beta" values for the common stocks of publicly traded confectionery companies generally clustered around a value of 1.0.
[1] Turnover = Net sales.
[2] Trading profit = Operating profit before interest and taxes.
[3] Average of beginning and end of year.
SOURCE: Company accounts.

EXHIBIT 8   Hershey Foods Corp.—Selected Financial Data, 1984–87

A. Financial Statement Data ($ millions)		1984	1985	1986	1987
1	Turnover (Sales)	1 848.5	1 996.2	2 169.6	2 433.8
2	Gross Profit	578.7	640.4	716.2	821.7
3	Trading Profit	222.8	244.8	270.6	294.1
4	Net Income	108.7	120.7	132.8	148.2
5	Depreciation	45.2	52.4	59.0	70.6
6	Liquid Assets	87.9	110.6	27.6	15.0
7	Current Assets	385.3	412.3	393.4	484.9
8	Fixed Assets	727.3	785.1	962.9	1 160.3
9	Total Assets	1 122.6	1 197.4	1 356.3	1 645.2
10	Current Liabilities	203.0	195.3	222.2	299.8
11	Long-term Liabilities	258.7	274.2	406.2	513.0
12	Stockholders' Equity	660.9	727.9	727.9	832.4

B. Per Share Data ($)					
13	Earnings	1.16	1.19	1.42	1.64
14	Dividends	0.41	0.48	0.52	0.58
15	Stock Price (Average)	11.60	15.00	22.80	29.30
16	Price-Earnings (Average)	10.00	9.70	16.10	17.90
17	Equity Book Value	7.00	7.70	8.10	9.20

SOURCE: Company accounts.

EXHIBIT 9 Cadbury Schweppes PLC—Selected Financial Data, 1984–87

A. Financial Statement Data (£ millions)		1984	1985	1986	1987
1	Turnover (Sales)	2 016.2	1 873.8	1 839.9	2 031.0
2	Gross Profit	746.8	683.0	739.9	853.8
3	Trading Profit	154.4	113.0	140.4	180.6
4a	Net Income[1]	72.5	47.8	76.1	112.1
4b	Net Income[2]	65.1	41.9	102.0	110.7
5	Depreciation	55.9	54.7	60.4	63.3
6	Liquid Assets	36.6	47.1	177.4	139.9
7	Current Assets	710.7	618.9	723.4	795.5
8	Fixed Assets	627.5	594.0	555.4	603.5
9	Total Assets	1 338.2	1 212.9	1 278.8	1 399.0
10	Current Liabilities	531.2	479.3	536.7	688.7
11	Long-term Liabilities	288.3	262.6	278.9	233.6
12	Share Capital & Reserves	518.7	417.0	463.2	476.7
B. Per Share Data (pence)					
13	Earnings[1]	15.7	9.3	14.3	19.1
14	Dividends	5.9	5.9	6.7	8.0
15	Stock Price (Average)	137.0	153.0	170.0	238.0
16	Price-Earnings (Average)	8.7	16.5	11.9	12.5
17	Equity Book Value	112.0	92.0	87.0	83.0
18	Employees (000s)	35.5	33.8	27.7	27.5

[1] Earnings before Extraordinary Items.
[2] Earnings after Extraordinary Items.
SOURCE: Company accounts.

EXHIBIT 10   Jacobs Suchard Group—Selected Financial Data, 1984–87

A. Financial Statement Data (SF millions)		1984	1985	1986	1987
1	Turnover (Sales)	5 111	5 382	5 236	6 104
2	Gross Profit	1 104	1 156	1 304	1 955
3	Trading Profit	244	265	338	471
4	Net Income		120	150	191265
5	Depreciation	84	092	103	128
6	Liquid Assets	230	788	1470	705
7	Current Assets	1 390	2 008	2 920	2 206
8	Fixed Assets	666	674	832	886
9	Total Assets	2 056	2 682	3 752	3 092
10	Current Liabilities	796	843	1 417	1 120
11	Long-term Liabilities	483	487	885	829
12	Shareholders' Equity	777	1 352	1 450	1 143[*]

B. Per Share Data (SF per bearer share)					
13	Earnings	351.0	353.0	414.0	19.1
14	Dividends	150.0	155.0	160.0	8.0
15	Stock Price (Average)	5 028.0	6 101.0	7 324.0	238.0
16	Price-Earnings (Average)	14.3	17.3	17.7	12.5
18	Employees (000s)	10.6	9.3	10.0	27.5

[*] It is normal accounting practice for Swiss companies to write off "goodwill" when acquiring businesses. Nestlé wrote off SF3.2 million of shareholders' equity on its purchase of Carnation in 1985. Jacobs Suchard reduced equity by SF1.1 million in 1987 due to depreciation of goodwill.

SOURCE: Company accounts.

EXHIBIT 11 Nestlé S.A.—Selected Financial Data, 1984–87

A. Financial Statement Data (SF millions)		1984	1985	1986	1987
1	Turnover (Sales)	31 141	42 225	38 050	35 241
2	Gross Profit	11 301	14 926	13 603	13 616
3	Trading Profit	3 206	4 315	3 671	3 651
4	Net Income	1 487	1 750	1 789	1 827
5	Depreciation	1 004	1 331	1 157	1 184
6	Liquid Assets	6 168	3 853	5 619	6 961
7	Current Assets	16 407	15 236	15 820	16 241
8	Fixed Assets	8 067	9 952	9 275	8 902
9	Total Assets	24 474	25 188	25 095	25 143
10	Current Liabilities	7 651	8 858	8 119	7 547
11	Long-term Liabilities	3 834	5 092	4 775	4 939
12	Shareholders' Equity	12 989	11 238*	12 201	12 657

B. Per Share Data (SF per bearer share)					
13	Earnings	480.0	515.0	526.0	537.0
14	Dividends	136.0	145.0	145.0	150.0
15	Stock Price (Average)	5 062.0	7 400.0	8 600.0	9 325.0
16	Price-Earnings (Average)	10.5	14.4	16.4	17.4
18	Employees (000s)	138.0	154.8	162.1	163.0

* It is normal accounting practice for Swiss companies to write off "goodwill" when acquiring businesses. Nestlé wrote off SF3.2 million of shareholders' equity on its purchase of Carnation in 1985. Jacobs Suchard reduced equity by SF1.1 million in 1987 due to depreciation of goodwill.

SOURCE: Company accounts.

EXHIBIT 12 Rowntree plc—Selected Financial Data, 1983–87

A. Income Statement Data (£ millions)		1983	1984	1985	1986	1987
1	Turnover (Sales)	951.9	1 156.5	1 205.2	1 290.4	1 427.6
1a	Cost Of Sales	617.9	739.0	759.4	790.2	837.1
2	Gross Profit (1-1a)	334.0	417.5	445.8	500.2	590.5
2a	Fixed Overhead Expenses	265.6	328.3	350	400.5	465.8
2b	Other Operating Income	4.2	4.6	6.0	6.0	5.4
3	Trading Profit (2-2a+2b)	72.6	93.8	101.3	105.7	130.1
3a	Interest	12.2	19.3	22.0	21.7	18.0
4a	Profit After Tax	46.3	58.0	60.7	66.2	87.9
4b	Extraordinary Items	13.5	11.5	16.5	11.3	0.0
4c	Net Profit After Tax	32.8	46.5	44.2	54.9	87.9
5	Depreciation (£m)	28.6	36.2	39.1	43.7	51.0

B. Balance Sheet Data (£ millions)						
6	Liquid Assets	25.1	55.7	41.8	69.2	96.7
6a	Debtors (Receivables)	145.9	171.1	178.7	208.5	214.9
6b	Stocks (Inventories)	159.1	172.9	170.2	176.9	163.2
7	Current Assets	330.1	399.7	390.7	454.6	475.1
8	Fixed Assets	359.7	408.5	403.1	475.1	463.2
9	Total Assets	689.8	808.2	793.8	929.7	938.3
10	Current Liabilities	217.8	229.3	242.4	310.2	270.1
11	Long-term Liabilities	123.0	186.3	177.0	228.1	259.6
12a	Preferred Stock	2.7	2.7	2.7	2.7	2.7
12b	Share Capital & Reserves	346.3	389.9	371.7	388.7	405.9

C. Per Share Data (pence)						
13	Earnings*	31.0	36.0	34.8	35.0	40.8
14	Dividends	9.8	11.0	12.2	13.6	15.5
15a	Common Stock Price (High)	258.0	392.0	450.0	545.0	590.0
15b	Common Stock Price (Low)	200.0	212.0	337.0	363.0	367.0
16	Average Price-Earnings*	7.4	8.4	11.3	13.0	11.7
17	Equity Book Value (12b/19)	233.0	243.0	214.0	206.0	189.0

D. Other Data						
18a	Employees, UK (000s)	19.7	18.9	17.7	16.4	15.6
18b	Employees, World (000s)	31.2	32.4	32.0	32.5	33.1
19	Ordinary Shares (000 000s)	149.5	160.6	173.9	188.7	215.0
20	Cash Flow (4a + 5)	74.9	94.2	99.8	109.9	138.9
21	Capital Expenditures (£m)	59.9	59.9	71.5	76.2	82.5
22	Business Acquisitions (£m)	159.6	3.3	34.2	189.9	14.2
23	Asset Divestitures (£m)	4.0	3.1	4.5	4.2	5.2

* Earnings based on line 4a (net profit after tax but before extra-ordinatry items) minus preferred dividends.
  Average of high and low stock prices.

SOURCE: Company accounts.

EXHIBIT 13 **Rowntree plc—Breakdown by Activity, 1987** (£ millions)

Activity	Turnover	% of Total Turnover	Trading Profit	% of Total Trading Profit	Trading Margin
Confectionery	1 088.5	76.2%	101.0	77.6%	9.3%
Snack Foods	191.8	13.4	14.5	11.1	7.6
Retailing	97.3	6.8	8.1	6.2	8.3
Grocery (UK)	50.0	3.5	6.5	5.0	13.0
Total	1 427.6	100.0%	130.1	100.0%	9.1%

SOURCE: Company accounts.

EXHIBIT 14 **Rowntree plc—Breakdown by Region, 1987**

Region	Turnover	% of Total Turnover	Trading Profit	% of Total Trading Profit	Trading Margin
UK & Ireland	566.4	40%	61.7	47%	10.9%
Cont'l Europe	300.4	21	11.0	8	3.7
North America	416.1	29	41.0	31	9.8
Australasia	57.1	4	4.7	4	8.2
Rest of World	87.6	6	11.7	9	13.4
Total	1 427.6	100%	130.1	100%	9.1%

SOURCE: Company accounts.

EXHIBIT 15 **Rowntree plc—Operating and Financial Performance, 1976–81** (£ millions)

	1976	1977	1978	1979	1980	1981
Turnover	340.90	469.20	562.70	601.30	629.80	688.00
Trading Profit	36.80	46.90	51.70	46.60	44.80	48.00
Net Profit[1]	16.90	30.40	34.40	27.20	17.50	29.10
Average[2]	194.90	246.80	332.50	396.60	412.50	448.60
Average Owner's[2] Equity	77.30	120.60	182.30	218.40	231.80	278.90
Trading Margin %	9.60	10.00	9.20	7.80	7.10	7.20
Trading Profit/Assets %	18.90	19.00	15.60	11.80	10.90	10.70
Turnover/Assets	1.83	1.66	1.47	1.46	1.52	1.38
Net Profit/Equity %	21.80	25.20	18.90	12.50	7.60	10.30

[1] Net after-tax profit attributable to ordinary common shares.
[2] Average of beginning and end of year.
SOURCE: Company accounts.

EXHIBIT 16 Rowntree plc—Major Business Acquisitions, 1983–87

Company	Location	Primary Area of Business Activity	Year of Purchase	Purchase Price (£m)
Tom's Foods	U.S.	Snack foods	1983	£138
Laura Secord	Canada	Branded retailing	1983	19
Original Cookie Co.	U.S.	Branded retailing	1985	32
Hot Sam	U.S.	Branded retailing	1986	14
Sunmark	U.S.	Branded confectionery	1986	154
Gales	U.S.	Honey products	1986	1
Smaller Acquisitions	U.S., UK, France, Australia	Snack foods, Confectionery, Branded retailing	1983–87	29
				£399

SOURCE: Company Accounts.

EXHIBIT 17 Rowntree plc—Share Price Performance, 1980–87

Rowntree Share Price Performance compared to the *Financial Times'* Market and Food Manufacturer's Price Indexes on the London Stock Exchange (01/01/80 to 31/21/87, weekly).

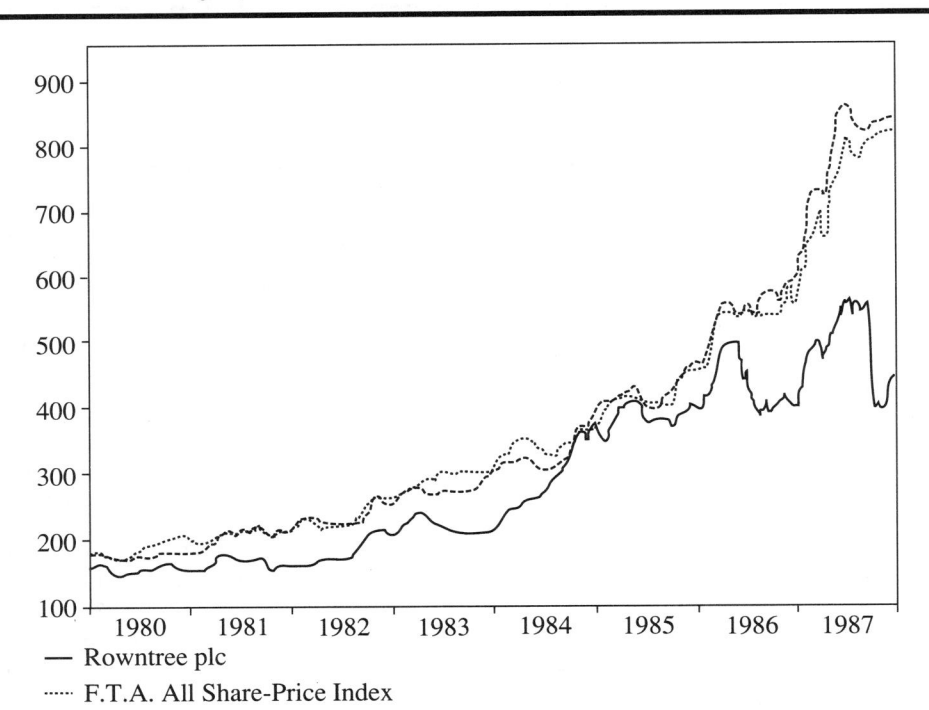

— Rowntree plc
····· F.T.A. All Share-Price Index
---- F.T.A. Food Manufacturers - Price Index (Marked)

SOURCE: *Financial Times.*

EXHIBIT 18 Stockbroker's Comments on Rowntree

Name of Broker	Date of Report	Forecast of 1988	Summary of Major Comments and Recommendations
County Natwest	01/21/88	125	Sell — Dollar weakness limits prospects for 1988.
BZW	01/25/88	127	Decision to sell snack food business correct but unable to give final verdict until consideration is known.
County Natwest	01/26/88	125	Surprise disposals, but good move.
BZW	02/24/88	127	Buy — Current rating of shares is not expensive with absence of bid premium.
Warburg Securities	03/17/88	128	Hold — Core business performed well but reversal in snacks and slowdown in retailing leaves strategy looking threadbare.
Hoare Govett	03/17/88	127	Over-valued in short term. Longer term outlook remaining clouded by current divestment/ acquisition plans.
BZW	03/17/88	129	Hold — Lower consideration for disposals than expected would lead to downgrading of forecast. Share price will be susceptible to strengthening of sterling.
County Natwest	03/18/88	125	Good results. Disposal of snack business an excellent move.
Kleinwart Grievson	03/18/88	129	Hold — Fully valued.

SOURCE: Stock brokerage reports.

EXHIBIT 19 The City Code and the UK Takeover Climate

Takeover bids for public companies in the UK were conducted according to a complex set of formal rules contained in the City Code on Takeovers and Mergers. The City Code was designed to ensure fair and similar treatment for all shareholders of the same class, mainly through responsible, detailed disclosure and the absence of stock price manipulation. The City Code was administered by the Takeover Panel, a self-regulatory body whose members included Bank of England appointees and representatives of participants in the UK securities markets. The Panel was authorized to make rulings and interpretations on novel points arising during the course of a takeover attempt.

The City Code identified consequences associated with the acquisition of certain benchmark percentages of the equity of a takeover target. For example, within 5 days of acquiring 5% of more of the capital of a company, the purchaser was required to inform the target company of its interest; the target company was then required to make an immediate announcement of this fact to the London Stock Exchange.

A purchaser could not acquire 10% or more of the capital of the target within any period of 7 days if these purchases would bring its total interest above 15% of the voting rights in the target company. Between 15% and 30% interest, the purchaser could accumulate shares by tender offer or by a series of share purchases; however, each series of share purchases could not result in the acquisition of more than 10% of the total equity of the target during any 7-day period. Once acquiring an interest totalling 30%, the bidder was obliged to make a general offer for the remaining 70% of the voting capital (at the highest price previously paid by the bidder). After a bidder had obtained 90% ownership of a class of shares, it could compulsorily acquire the outstanding shares from the minority shareholders; similarly, any remaining

EXHIBIT 19   (continued)

minority shareholders could require the bidder to purchase their shares at the highest price previously paid by the bidder.

Proposed acquisitions could also be reviewed by the Office of Fair Trading (OFT), a subsection of the Department of Trade and Industry. The OFT had responsibility for deciding whether the competitive implications of the merger warranted investigation. The OFT could refer merger cases to the Mergers and Monopolies Commission (MMC), an independent tribunal which ruled on whether the merger should be blocked in the interests of national competition policy. Referral to the MMC was often prized by managements of takeover targets. Aside from allowing the possibility of a referral decision favouring the target, the referral process gave the takeover target additional time (3–7 months) to mount a more effective takeover defence.

Takeovers of UK public companies were either recommended by the Board of the target company or contested. Action by the Board of a target to frustrate an offer for the target company was prohibited without the approval, in a General Meeting, of the shareholders. Recommended offers in the UK were generally restricted to smaller companies; they were relatively rare for companies with market capitalization in excess of £200 million.

Between 1985 and 1987, takeover bids were initiated for 14 large UK companies, each with individual market capitalizations in excess of £1 billion. Only one of these bids was recommended; the rest were contested. Ultimately, four of these bids were successful while ten failed. For the three successful cash bids, the average share price premium paid was 60%; the individual premiums paid ranged from 40% to 80%.[*]

More recent acquisition activity in France and the UK provided reference points for the value of brand names. During 1987 and 1988, Seagrams (a Canadian drinks group) and Grand Metropolitan (a UK drinks and hotel group) waged a fierce takeover battle to acquire Martell (the second largest French cognac house). In February 1988, Seagrams emerged the victor, but only after bidding an estimated 40x the 1987 earnings of Martell. In March 1988, United Biscuits paid a price-earnings multiple of 25x to purchase the frozen and chilled foods division of Hanson Trust. At that time, the average price-earnings ratio for five comparable UK food companies was 11.9x.

[*] Share price premiums were calculated by comparing final bid offer prices against the share prices of the target companies two months prior to the date of the final offer.

EXHIBIT 20   Selected Financial Market Rates, 1984–87

	1984	1985	1986	1987	1988 (1st quart. annualized)
Inflation[*](%):					
Switzerland	3.0	1.0	0.8	1.4	3.5
UK	5.0	6.0	3.4	4.3	1.8
U.S.	4.3	3.5	2.0	3.6	2.6
Long-Term Government Bond Yield (%):					
Switzerland	4.7	4.8	4.3	4.1	4.1
UK	10.7	10.6	9.9	9.5	9.4
U.S.	12.5	10.6	7.7	8.4	8.4

[*] Based on the Consumer Price Index.
SOURCE: International Monetary Fund.